Labor in the New Economy

Studies in Income and Wealth
Volume 71

National Bureau of Economic Research
Conference on Research in Income and Wealth

Labor in the New Economy

Edited by **Katharine G. Abraham,
James R. Spletzer, and
Michael J. Harper**

The University of Chicago Press

Chicago and London

KATHARINE G. ABRAHAM is professor in the Joint Program in Survey Methodology, adjunct professor of economics, and faculty associate of the Maryland Population Research Center, University of Maryland, and a research associate of the National Bureau of Economic Research. JAMES R. SPLETZER is a senior research economist at the U.S. Bureau of Labor Statistics. MICHAEL J. HARPER is associate commissioner for productivity and technology at the U.S. Bureau of Labor Statistics.

The University of Chicago Press, Chicago 60637
The University of Chicago Press, Ltd., London
© 2010 by the National Bureau of Economic Research
All rights reserved. Published 2010
Printed in the United States of America

19 18 17 16 15 14 13 12 11 10   1 2 3 4 5
ISBN-13: 978-0-226-00143-2   (cloth)
ISBN-10: 0-226-00143-1   (cloth)

Library of Congress Cataloging-in-Publication Data

Conference on Research in Income and Wealth (2007: Bethesda, MD)
    Labor in the new economy / edited by Katharine G. Abraham, James R. Spletzer, and Michael J. Harper.
        p. cm. — (Studies in income and wealth ; v. 71)
    Includes revised versions of the papers and discussions presented at the Conference on Research in Income and Wealth, held in Bethesda, Maryland, Nov. 16–17, 2007.
    Includes bibliographical references and index.
    ISBN-13: 978-0-226-00143-2 (alk. paper)
    ISBN-10: 0-226-00143-1 (alk. paper)
    1. Labor market—United States—Congresses. 2. Wage differentials—United States—Congresses. 3. Job security—United States—Congresses. I. Abraham, Katharine G. II. Spletzer, James. III. Harper, Michael J. IV. National Bureau of Economic Research. V. Title. VI. Series: Studies in income and wealth ; v. 71.
    HD5724.C683 2007
    331.120973—dc22
                                                                    2010012103

♾ The paper used in this publication meets the minimum requirements of the American National Standard for Information Sciences— Permanence of Paper for Printed Library Materials, ANSI Z39.48-1992.

Relation of the Directors to the
Work and Publications of the
National Bureau of Economic Research

1. The object of the NBER is to ascertain and present to the economics profession, and to the public more generally, important economic facts and their interpretation in a scientific manner without policy recommendations. The Board of Directors is charged with the responsibility of ensuring that the work of the NBER is carried on in strict conformity with this object.

2. The President shall establish an internal review process to ensure that book manuscripts proposed for publication DO NOT contain policy recommendations. This shall apply both to the proceedings of conferences and to manuscripts by a single author or by one or more co-authors but shall not apply to authors of comments at NBER conferences who are not NBER affiliates.

3. No book manuscript reporting research shall be published by the NBER until the President has sent to each member of the Board a notice that a manuscript is recommended for publication and that in the President's opinion it is suitable for publication in accordance with the above principles of the NBER. Such notification will include a table of contents and an abstract or summary of the manuscript's content, a list of contributors if applicable, and a response form for use by Directors who desire a copy of the manuscript for review. Each manuscript shall contain a summary drawing attention to the nature and treatment of the problem studied and the main conclusions reached.

4. No volume shall be published until forty-five days have elapsed from the above notification of intention to publish it. During this period a copy shall be sent to any Director requesting it, and if any Director objects to publication on the grounds that the manuscript contains policy recommendations, the objection will be presented to the author(s) or editor(s). In case of dispute, all members of the Board shall be notified, and the President shall appoint an ad hoc committee of the Board to decide the matter; thirty days additional shall be granted for this purpose.

5. The President shall present annually to the Board a report describing the internal manuscript review process, any objections made by Directors before publication or by anyone after publication, any disputes about such matters, and how they were handled.

6. Publications of the NBER issued for informational purposes concerning the work of the Bureau, or issued to inform the public of the activities at the Bureau, including but not limited to the NBER Digest and Reporter, shall be consistent with the object stated in paragraph 1. They shall contain a specific disclaimer noting that they have not passed through the review procedures required in this resolution. The Executive Committee of the Board is charged with the review of all such publications from time to time.

7. NBER working papers and manuscripts distributed on the Bureau's web site are not deemed to be publications for the purpose of this resolution, but they shall be consistent with the object stated in paragraph 1. Working papers shall contain a specific disclaimer noting that they have not passed through the review procedures required in this resolution. The NBER's web site shall contain a similar disclaimer. The President shall establish an internal review process to ensure that the working papers and the web site do not contain policy recommendations, and shall report annually to the Board on this process and any concerns raised in connection with it.

8. Unless otherwise determined by the Board or exempted by the terms of paragraphs 6 and 7, a copy of this resolution shall be printed in each NBER publication as described in paragraph 2 above.

Contents

Prefatory Note

This volume contains revised versions of most of the papers and discussions presented at the Conference on Research in Income and Wealth entitled "Labor in the New Economy," held in Bethesda, Maryland, on November 16–17, 2007.

Funds for the Conference on Research in Income and Wealth are supplied by the Bureau of Economic Analysis, the Bureau of Labor Statistics, the Census Bureau, the Federal Reserve Board, the Internal Revenue Service, and Statistics Canada. We are indebted to these organizations for their support.

We thank Katharine G. Abraham, James R. Spletzer, and Michael J. Harper, who served as conference organizers and editors of the volume.

Executive Committee, November 2007

Introduction

Katharine G. Abraham, James R. Spletzer, and
Michael J. Harper

The structure of the economy has changed a great deal in recent decades. Both researchers and policymakers have been concerned with how workers are faring in today's new economy. Themes explored in popular press accounts on this subject include the changing demographics of the labor force, the increased prevalence of flexible and alternative employment arrangements, declining job stability, increased wage inequality, and, more generally, the fear that good jobs are disappearing. This volume contains twelve chapters, prepared by leading economists in both academia and government and presented at a conference held in Bethesda, Maryland on November 16 and 17, 2007, that examine the evidence on these topics.

One motivation for the conference was simply to review what we know and don't know about the labor market trends that matter to American families—trends in the inequality of earnings and other forms of labor compensation, trends in job security and the dynamics of employment more generally, trends in employer reliance on temporary and contract workers, trends in hours of work, and trends in workplace safety and health—and to update and extend findings about these trends reported in previous studies.

A second objective of the conference was to bring together and foster discussions among a set of scholars concerned with the *measurement* of labor market activity. The authors of the volume's chapters tackle a host of measurement issues—from the treatment of outliers, imputation methods and

Katharine G. Abraham is a professor in the Joint Program in Survey Methodology, adjunct professor of economics, and faculty associate of the Maryland Population Research Center, University of Maryland, and a research associate of the National Bureau of Economic Research. James R. Spletzer is a senior research economist at the U.S. Bureau of Labor Statistics. Michael J. Harper is associate commissioner for productivity and technology at the U.S. Bureau of Labor Statistics.

weighting in the context of specific surveys to evaluating the strengths and weaknesses of data from different sources. Especially in the case of surveys that researchers have not used extensively, the documentation provided by the statistical agencies often provides a somewhat limited treatment of these topics. The chapters' discussion of important measurement issues should be helpful to other researchers working with the same data, as well as helping to frame the proper interpretation of findings based on these different sources.

Since the date of the conference, the U.S. economy has experienced a severe recession from which, as of this writing, it is showing only the first signs of recovery. Though the recent period has without question been a highly significant economic event, it is still too early to say how its effects will play out in the labor market. Many of the trends the volume documents and discusses—for example, the long-term growth in contract employment arrangements and the changing demographics of the U.S. labor force—seem unlikely to be much affected by recent developments. In any case, rather than attempt to speculate about the labor market effects of these developments, we simply acknowledge the fact that the recent period has been tumultuous and leave the evaluation of this period and its labor market implications for the future.

New Evidence on Recent Labor Market Trends

One of the most important labor market developments of recent decades has been the long-term growth in earnings inequality, a subject that is the topic of Thomas Lemieux's chapter, "What Do We Really Know about Changes in Wage Inequality?" Among other findings based on a careful analysis of data from the Current Population Survey (CPS), Lemieux reports that, despite a slowdown in the growth of male wage inequality overall, the gap between the 90th percentile and the 50th percentile of the male wage distribution grew faster between 1989 and 2005 than it had between 1974 and 1989. In contrast, after having risen during the late 1970s and 1980s, the gap between the 50th percentile and the 10th percentile of the male wage distribution actually fell between 1989 and 2005. The very different recent trends in dispersion in the different parts of the wage distribution seem difficult to square with simple explanations based solely on supply and demand. Lemieux's findings lead him to the conclusion that any plausible explanation for the behavior of wage inequality over time must combine the effects of multiple influences, including not only supply and demand forces but also institutional factors such as changes in the level of the minimum wage.

Additional evidence about changes in labor market inequality is offered by Brooks Pierce in his chapter, "Recent Trends in Compensation Inequality," which looks at the value of employment-related benefits such as health insurance, pensions, and paid vacation leave, in addition to the wages and salaries that employers pay. It is not obvious ex ante whether accounting for the value of nonwage compensation should attenuate or amplify observed trends in wage inequality. On the one hand, because health insurance is so important and most plans offer similar coverage, one might expect growing health insurance costs to flatten proportional differences in compensation across workers. On the other hand, high-wage workers are more likely to receive employer-provided health insurance, and the value of benefits such as paid leave and employee pensions clearly rises with employee wages. Pierce's results establish that, taking everything into account, the growth in compensation inequality actually exceeded the growth in wage inequality over the twenty years from 1987 to 2007.

Henry Farber's chapter, "Job Loss and the Decline in Job Security in the United States," includes a careful examination of trends in job tenure. Looking at the most recent CPS data, Farber finds clear evidence that older men have experienced a marked decline in job tenure. For men aged fifty, for example, he shows that mean tenure has fallen by more than two years, from an average of 13.5 years in the 1973 to 1983 period to 11.4 years in the 1996 to 2006 period, and the declines for men aged sixty are even larger. Interestingly, the declines in male job tenure have been restricted to the private sector, and no similar decline in average job tenure is observed for women.

The chapter by Matthew Dey, Susan Houseman, and Anne Polivka, "What Do We Know about Contracting Out in the United States? Evidence from Household and Establishment Surveys," offers a systematic review of evidence on contracting out and the use of temporary help service workers. One of this paper's innovations is to generate new information on the types of work performed by contract workers based on data from the Occupational Employment Statistics (OES) survey. The OES is a large employer survey that provides detailed data on employment by occupation within industries. Dey, Houseman, and Polivka identify selected occupations with significant employment in which there is reason to think that contract firms may account for a sizeable share of employment—for example, janitors and school bus drivers—and examine data on the industries in which these workers are employed. They are able to document the growing share of employment in several of these large occupations that is accounted for by contract firms. Their chapter provides concrete evidence of the growth in contracting out that is only hinted at by more anecdotal sources of information.

Measurement Themes

While the substantive insights to be gleaned from the chapters are valuable—and the examples cited in the preceding paragraphs of the interesting findings the chapters report are intended only to be illustrative—the volume also seeks to shed light on the *measurement* of labor market activity. In addition to the discussion of measurement issues specific to each chapter's topic, three recurring measurement themes cut broadly across the chapters.

First, several of the chapters highlight the value of using data from multiple sources to learn about a phenomenon or trend. Among other considerations, whether the estimates from multiple surveys are consistent with one another can be enormously helpful both for deciding how much confidence to place in the estimates obtained and for diagnosing the source of possible problems with the data. A second and overlapping theme concerns the strengths and limitations of employer-reported as compared to household-reported data. The preponderance of U.S. labor market research has rested on data from the CPS and other household surveys, but this volume's chapters make clear the value of data collected from employers for answering many questions about the labor market. Finally, several of the chapters address the ways in which changing workforce demographics may affect key measures of labor market activity and the conclusions to be drawn from those statistics.

Value of Data from Multiple Sources

The first of the recurring measurement themes threaded through the volume is the value of having data from multiple sources for learning about a trend or phenomenon. Especially in the survey methodology literature, evaluations of the quality of survey estimates often focus on indicators such as the size of the survey sample, unit response rates, the findings from response analysis studies that examine how well respondents understand the survey questions, and so on. In addition to looking at information that is internal to the survey in question, however, it can be informative to look at the consistency of the survey estimates with related estimates from other sources. There may be reasons for two seemingly similar measurements to diverge, but such divergences also may indicate that there are problems with one or more of the measurements. In a world of ever-tightening budgets, statistical agencies are under continuing pressure to streamline and consolidate the collection of information. Although the reasons for this pressure are entirely understandable, an unintended consequence of going down this path could well be to undermine our ability to evaluate the quality of the data collected and, thus, ultimately users' confidence in our data system.

To take one example of the value of having related data from multiple sources, consider the chapter by Steven Davis, Jason Faberman, John Haltiwanger, and Ian Rucker, "Adjusted Estimates of Worker Flows and Job Openings in JOLTS," which examines estimates based on the Job Openings and Labor Turnover survey (JOLTS). On their face, the JOLTS estimates seem reasonable enough, but a more careful comparison of these estimates to those from other sources suggests there is a serious problem: the difference between the JOLTS job accession and job separation rates should yield a net employment growth rate that is comparable to that in the monthly Current Employment Statistics (CES) survey, but, in fact, it is consistently higher. Comparison of the cross-sectional distribution of month-to-month employment changes in the JOLTS sample to that in the Business Employment

Dynamics (BED) database reveals that JOLTS respondents include too few establishments that have experienced sharp employment declines, with the result that employment separations are understated. This, in turn, suggests a method, described in greater detail in the chapter, for producing more accurate JOLTS estimates by reweighting the responses received to reproduce the cross-sectional employment growth rate distribution. Neither the diagnosis of the problem with the JOLTS estimates nor the development of the suggested remedy would have been possible absent multiple sources of information on business employment dynamics.

The chapter by Harley Frazis and Jay Stewart, "Why Do BLS Hours Series Tell Different Stories about Trends in Hours Worked?," examines estimates of weekly work hours from several different sources. The chapter seeks to understand why estimates of work hours based on the CPS are so much higher than work hours estimates based on the CES survey, the monthly Bureau of Labor Statistics (BLS) survey of employer payrolls, and why CPS hours have not shown the steady decline that is so apparent in the CES hours data. One common speculation is that household survey respondents systematically exaggerate the number of hours they work (Robinson and Bostrom 1994; Abraham, Spletzer, and Stewart, 1998, 1999), leading to an overstatement in reported CPS hours. To learn whether this is so, Frazis and Stewart compare CPS hours estimates to estimates from the American Time Use Survey (ATUS). Because they are based on contemporaneous reports of how people spent their time on a specific day, time diary data often are presumed to provide highly reliable measures of how individuals allocate their time. The fact that CPS estimates of hours of work exceed the ATUS estimates seems at first blush to lend credence to the idea that the CPS hours estimates are too high. When attention is restricted to ATUS data collected during CPS reference weeks, however, so that the ATUS and the CPS respondents are reporting for the same time periods, the estimates of hours from the two sources are very similar. The difference between the published CPS and ATUS estimates appears instead to reflect the fact that, by design, the CPS reference weeks avoid major holidays and hours of work tend to be lower, on average, during the excluded weeks. Again, having data from multiple sources proves to be of value, this time for an improved understanding of the CPS average weekly hours data.

The chapter by Kevin Hallock and Craig Olson, "New Data for Answering Old Questions Regarding Employee Stock Options," carries out a different sort of exercise. As its title suggests, this chapter focuses on employee stock options, which have become a more important component of employee compensation in recent decades. Unlike benefits such as health insurance and pensions, however, government surveys collect little information about employee stock options, largely because there is no consensus about how they should be valued. How to value employee stock options is the central question that motivates the empirical analysis reported in the Hallock and

Olson chapter. Their results make clear that the standard Black-Scholes valuation theorem frequently applied to market-traded options is not applicable to nonmarketable employee stock options. In addition to reporting new empirical evidence, the Hallock and Olson chapter also reviews the various sources of existing data on stock options and their utility for addressing different sorts of research questions. Compared to some of the other topic areas addressed by chapters in the volume, the literature on stock options is less well developed. In this case, exploratory analyses using a variety of data sources not only should add to our understanding of stock options and their effects but also should inform how any eventual data collection activity that is undertaken by the federal statistical system might most usefully be structured.

Strengths of Household-Based versus Employer-Based Estimates

A second measurement theme addressed by several of the chapters in the volume is the distinctive contributions of household-based versus employer-based data. Household surveys are the best source of many sorts of information about both individuals and their families. On the other hand, certain types of information may be difficult to collect from household survey respondents—for example, information about the characteristics of employer-provided benefit plans or other details of individuals' employment arrangements. Further, household survey respondents' reports may be susceptible to bias resulting from the desire to put themselves or other household members in a favorable light (Tourangeau, Rips, and Rasinski 2000). Employers are more likely than workers to possess accurate information on many workplace-related topics. Moreover, there is less reason to fear that employer reports will be subject to social desirability bias of the sort that is a concern with household surveys. At the same time, there is a great deal of information about workers and their families that an employer simply does not possess. To give a simple illustration of the practical implications of these considerations, household surveys are needed to learn about the personal characteristics of those with and without health insurance coverage or whether those who lack health insurance coverage through their job have coverage through another source. On the other hand, detailed information about health plan provisions generally must be collected from employers or plan providers.

As already noted, labor economists have devoted considerable attention to the growth in the inequality of labor market earnings since the 1970s. Most of this research, including the Lemieux chapter in the present volume, has been based on data from the CPS. The CPS data have many advantages for studying this topic—they provide annual information on earnings for a large sample of individuals together with a considerable amount of demographic information for the same individuals, allowing comparisons to be made across population subgroups and permitting researchers to quantify the contributions of potential experience, education, and other factors to overall inequality trends. An important limitation of the CPS data, however, is the lack of information about employee benefits. This is not a trivial omission—as of June 2008, employer data from the National Compensation Survey (NCS) carried out by the BLS show that benefits accounted for about 30 percent of the value of total compensation. Unfortunately, reliable information about the value of employer-provided benefits would be difficult to collect from CPS respondents, most of whom would be hard pressed to report accurately about their own work-related benefits much less about those of other employed persons in their households. It is only by examining employer-reported data on benefit costs, collected through the NCS, that Pierce is able to say how trends in compensation inequality have compared to trends in wage inequality and, further, to document the contributions of different components of the compensation package to the overall growth in inequality.

Differences between household-reported and employer-reported data are the explicit focus of the chapter by Katharine Abraham and James Spletzer, "Are the New Jobs Good Jobs?," which compares estimates of employment in higher-paying and lower-paying industry/occupation cells from the CPS to similar estimates based on the OES survey, a large employer survey. Even after every effort has been made to put the two sets of estimates on the same footing—restricting attention in both cases to wage and salary positions in the nonagricultural private sector and modifying the CPS data so that they count number of jobs rather than number of employed people—there are far more management jobs in the CPS than in the OES. Abraham and Spletzer hypothesize that the discrepancy between the two data sources reflects a tendency on the part of household informants to describe their work to the CPS interviewer in ways that exaggerate its significance. If this is correct, analysts would be well advised to rely where possible on employer reports rather than household reports of occupational information.

In their chapter on the measurement of contracting activity, Dey, Houseman and Polivka present evidence that points toward a similar conclusion regarding the best source of information on the arrangements under which individuals are employed. In every year the authors examine, employment in the employment services industry, which consists primarily of temporary help firms and professional employer organizations (PEOs), is more than twice as large in data from the BLS payroll survey (employer reported) than in data from the CPS (household reported). Further, the large increase in employment in the employment services industry that is apparent in payroll survey data between 1995 and 2001 does not register in the CPS data available for the same period. Even when more explicit questions are asked in periodic CPS supplements to determine whether an individual worked for a temporary help firm rather than being paid directly by the firm on whose premises their job duties are performed, the number of temporary help workers in the CPS falls far short of the number in the CES. These discrepancies suggest that, for whatever reason, individuals find it difficult to report accurately the arrangements under which they or other members of their households are employed. To the extent they are available, employer-provided data thus may be a better source of information about trends in temporary help employment and, more broadly, employment under other alternative work arrangements.

A related measurement theme concerns the use of information on job tasks rather than worker qualifications to characterize the labor market. Existing research has paid much more attention to worker characteristics than to the characteristics of the jobs that workers perform, but there are a range of questions that can best be addressed using the latter type of information. One such question is addressed by Bradford Jensen and Lori Kletzer in their chapter, "Measuring Tradable Services and the Task Content of Offshorable Services Jobs." Because both skilled and unskilled jobs may be outsourced, information on workers' qualifications is of little direct relevance to determining whether a job is vulnerable to outsourcing. The nature of the work performed, however, may be highly relevant. In their chapter, Jensen and Kletzer use data on the tasks associated with different services jobs from the Occupation Information Network (O*Net) database to infer whether incumbents in these jobs need to be located in physical proximity to the service recipients. O*Net was developed by the U.S. Department of Labor as a replacement for the Dictionary of Occupation Titles. The extensive information on the responsibilities and other characteristics of more than 1,000 distinct occupations included in the O*Net database derives primarily from surveys of incumbents in these jobs. Though it has been used widely by researchers in other fields, few economists are familiar with the O*Net database, and one of the contributions of the Jensen and Kletzer chapter is to raise the visibility of O*Net within the economics profession.

Effects of Changing Demographics on Labor Market Statistics

A third and final measurement theme that is manifest in a number of the chapters concerns the effects of changing demographics on labor market statistics. As is well known, the U.S. workforce is aging—the oldest baby boomers, those born in 1946, will turn sixty-five in 2011, and by 2029, the last of the baby boomers will have reached that age. Workers aged fifty-five and older accounted for 12.9 percent of the labor force in 2000, and that share is projected to rise to 20.3 percent by 2020 before beginning to fall. Female labor force participation grew rapidly during the 1960s and 1970s and has remained high, raising the share of the workforce that is female from 33.4 percent in 1960 to 42.5 percent in 1980 and 46.3 percent in 2006. And the workforce has become more ethnically and racially diverse—in 1980, 81.9 percent of the labor force were non-Hispanic whites, but by 2006, that share had fallen to 69.7 percent and continued declines are forecast (Toossi 2002, 2007).

The policy implications of these demographic changes—for Social Security and Medicare, for private pensions, for K-12 and higher education, and for a range of other matters—have been widely discussed, but it has been less recognized that they also have important implications for the measurement of labor market activity. Economists long have recognized, for example, that changes in the age structure of the labor force may have an effect on measured unemployment that is independent of underlying labor market conditions (see, for example, Perry [1970] and, more recently, Shimer [1999]). Young people are more likely to enter and exit the labor force and also to change from one job to another. Despite the fact that they tend to have unemployment spells that are relatively short, because of their higher turnover rates, young workers have unemployment rates that are very high compared to the rates for older workers. It is important, therefore, to take the age structure of the workforce into account in interpreting the unemployment rate—if unemployment is lower because the share of young workers in the labor force has fallen, as has occurred since the mid-1970s, for example, one should not necessarily conclude that labor market performance has improved.

In their chapter titled "The Effect of Population Aging on the Aggregate Labor Market," Bruce Fallick, Charles Fleischman, and Jonathan Pingle extend this line of argument, arguing that other measures of labor market activity, including the labor force participation rate and measures of labor market flows and earnings, also are likely to be affected by the changing age structure of the population. Consider, for example, the effects of recent shifts in the age distribution of the workforce on average hourly earnings. Fallick, Fleischman, and Pingle report that average hourly earnings rose from $16.19 per hour (in 2005 dollars) in 1979 to $18.17 per hour in 2005. In part, however, this growth reflects the fact that the workforce has gotten older and thus, on average, more experienced. By comparing actual hourly wages with an alternative fixed-weight measure that uses the 2005 age-by-sex workforce shares to reweight the data for other years, Fallick, Fleischman, and Pingle conclude that about half of the observed increase in average real wages is a direct result of the aging of the workforce. These results suggest that the hourly earnings trend is less favorable than might on the surface appear to be the case.

Lemieux's chapter on trends in earnings inequality also makes the case for a focus on measures that have been adjusted for changes in the composition of the labor force so that underlying trends in inequality are not confounded by the effects of changing demographics on the dispersion of workers' earnings. Lemieux looks separately at men and women and considers measures that are adjusted both for changes in potential experience (age minus estimated age at completion of schooling) and for changes in educational attainment. Lemieux's adjustment for composition effects has a noticeable dampening effect on the long-run trend growth in the variance of wages both for men and for women. While there was some disagreement among participants in the conference at which the volume's chapters were presented about whether it is appropriate to adjust for changes in educational attainment in studying trends in wage inequality, there was strong agreement that some age-related adjustment is desirable to produce more meaningful trend estimates.

Farber also is sensitive to the potential impact of changing demographics and, especially, the changing age distribution of the labor force, on labor market statistics. The first section of his chapter, "Job Loss and the Decline in Job Security in the United States," seeks to document changes in job tenure and the incidence of long-term employment. Because job tenure tends to rise with age, simple statistics on average job tenure may give a misleading picture of changes in job attachment. For these reasons, Farber focuses on measures of job attachment at particular ages, analyzing men's and women's experiences separately, rather than looking at measures for the labor force as a whole. Previous studies commonly have treated age as a control variable, regressing measures of job tenure on year and age dummies, and then examining the behavior of the year dummy coefficients. While for many purposes this may be a reasonable representation of the data, Farber's careful examination of age-specific trends illuminates important changes in the pattern of job attachment that have been less apparent in previous analyses.

Nicole Nestoriak and John Ruser, authors of "Emerging Labor Market Trends and Workplace Safety and Health," study the effects of changes in the composition of the workforce on measures of workplace safety and health. As with other measures of labor market outcomes, there is value in knowing the extent to which observed increases or decreases in injury and illness rates are the result of demographic factors as opposed to other factors. The incidence and severity of workplace-related injuries and illnesses show clear differences by age and sex. Looking forward, however, Nestoriak and Ruser's modeling efforts show that expected changes in the demographic composition of the workforce are likely to have relatively small effects on the aggregate number of injuries and illnesses. As noted by discussant Jeff Biddle, most of the dramatic decline in injury and illness rates since 1992 appears to reflect changes in "how work is done within particular industries and firms," a development Biddle suspects is related to the incentives created for employers by rising medical costs and the resulting growth in the cost of workers' compensation claims, rather than to demographic changes. On a related note, Nestoriak and Ruser speculate that changes in how employment is structured—for example, the growing use of leased employees who may not be integrated into the workplace in the same way as regular employees—may have important implications for future trends in safety and health. This is something that, unfortunately, existing data systems are not well designed to capture and to which greater thought ideally should be given.

In her chapter titled "Measuring Labor Composition: A Comparison of Alternate Methodologies," Cindy Zoghi focuses on the measures of labor input that are used in productivity calculations. If labor productivity—output per hour worked—is rising, a natural next question is whether this is because the quality of labor has improved, because each unit of labor has more capital to work with, or for other reasons. As Zoghi explains, those attempting to account for changes in labor quality typically treat workers' relative wages as indicative of their relative quality. Between 1984 and 2004, data from the Survey of Income and Program Participation (SIPP) show that the share of hours worked by individuals with twenty-five or more years of experience increased by nearly 20 percentage points. In addition, the share of hours worked by persons with at least some education beyond high school rose by about 15 percentage points. Zoghi experiments with a variety of approaches to accounting for the effects of these and other changes in labor composition on labor productivity. Although there is some variation across the different specifications, the basic conclusion that changes in experience and education added roughly 10 percent to output per hour over the 1984 to 2004 period is robust to the different specifications Zoghi examines. In a comment on this chapter, Stephanie Aaronson urges the BLS to retain a measure of experience, rather than using age as a proxy for experience, in their labor composition model. Aaronson points out that experience is the correct concept from the standpoint of the human capital model and that women's experience, relative to age, has changed substantially over recent decades.

Improving the Data Infrastructure for Labor Economics Research

As noted, until quite recently, most empirical labor economics research has relied on data from large household surveys conducted either by the federal government or with federal government support. Several of the chapters analyze data from large *employer* surveys that to this point have been little exploited by researchers. The surveys analyzed include the National Compensation Survey (Pierce), the Occupational Employment Statistics survey (Abraham and Spletzer; Dey, Houseman, and Polivka), the Job Openings and Labor Turnover Survey (Davis, Faberman, Haltiwanger, and Rucker) and the Survey of Occupational Injuries and Illnesses (Nestoriak and Ruser). Although these employer survey data have great research potential, unlocking that potential is not a trivial task. It is to be hoped that a final contribution of the volume will be to encourage further work that makes use of these interesting data.

One logistical challenge to working with employer survey data collected by the federal government is that the need to protect the confidentiality of individual employer records generally precludes the release of public use data files of the sort that are common for household surveys. Though still not fully worked out, mechanisms for providing researcher access to these data are evolving (see Abraham [2005] for a discussion). More fundamental challenges arise as a consequence of the fact that none of the employer surveys used in the chapters we are discussing was designed with research uses in mind. Rather, each exists for the purpose of producing a particular set of published estimates. The design of the survey sample, the way in which the survey data are processed once they have been collected, the structure of the databases in which the survey responses are stored, and other aspects of the survey operations all are designed to support the survey's publication goals. In addition, written documentation of the sort that would enable an outside researcher to understand exactly how the survey data are collected and processed may be absent or difficult to obtain. In the same way that the community of scholars working with household survey data over a period of many years has produced a better understanding of these data and how they should be analyzed, it is to be hoped that the development of a community of scholars working with data from the various employer surveys will help to create the same sort of understanding about these data over time.

The chapters that follow are organized according to the substance of the topics with which they are concerned. The volume begins with four chapters that are focused on trends in compensation and job quality—Lemieux's chapter on wage inequality, Pierce's chapter on compensation inequality, Abraham and Spletzer's chapter on trends in job quality, and Hallock and Olson's chapter on the valuation of stock options. These are followed by four chapters that, in different ways, are concerned with labor market dynamics, job security and job attachment—the Davis, Faberman, Haltiwanger, and Rucker chapter on accessions and separations; the Farber chapter on job tenure and job loss; the Dey, Houseman, and Polivka chapter on contracting out; and the Jensen and Kletzer chapter on the potential susceptibility of different jobs to offshoring. Frazis and Stewart's chapter examines trends in hours of work. And the remaining three chapters have in common an interest in the effects of changing demographics on the labor market—Fallick, Fleischman, and Pingle's chapter looking at how demographic changes affect various labor market statistics; the Nestoriak and Ruser chapter focused on occupational injury and illness measures; and the Zoghi chapter concerned with productivity measurement. In addition to its twelve chapters, the volume includes written comments from a distinguished set of discussants who provide valuable perspectives on the research that is reported.

References

Abraham, Katharine G. 2005. Microdata access and labor market research: The U.S. experience. *Allgemeines Statistisches Archiv* 89 (12): 121–39.

Abraham, Katharine G., James R. Spletzer, and Jay C. Stewart. 1998. Divergent trends in alternative wage series. In *Labor statistics measurement issues,* ed. John C. Haltiwanger, Marilyn E. Manser, and Robert Topel, 292–324. Chicago: University of Chicago Press.

————. 1999. Why do different wage series tell different stories? *American Economic Review* 89 (2): 34–39.

Perry, George. 1970. Changing labor markets and inflation. *Brookings Papers on Economic Activity,* Issue no. 3:411–41. Washington, DC: Brookings Institution.

Robinson, John, and Ann Bostrom. 1994. The overestimated workweek? What time-diary measures suggest. *Monthly Labor Review* 117 (8): 11–23.

Shimer, Robert. 1999. Why is the U.S. unemployment rate so much lower? In *NBER macroeconomics annual 1998,* ed. Ben S. Bernanke and Julio J. Rotemberg, 11–61. Cambridge, MA: MIT Press.

Toossi, Mitra. 2002. A century of change: The U.S. labor force, 1950–2050. *Monthly Labor Review* 125 (May): 15–28.

————. 2007. Labor force projections to 2016: More workers in their golden years. *Monthly Labor Review* 130 (November): 33–52.

Tourangeau, Roger, Lance J. Rips, and Kenneth Rasinski. 2000. *The psychology of survey response.* Cambridge, England: Cambridge University Press.

I

Trends in Compensation
and Job Quality

1

What Do We Really Know about Changes in Wage Inequality?

Thomas Lemieux

1.1   Introduction

It is very well known that wage and earnings inequality has grown substantially over the last thirty years. The initial burst of inequality growth in the 1980s attracted a lot attention among labor economists. This resulted in a set of influential papers published in the early 1990s, in particular Katz and Murphy (1992); Bound and Johnson (1992); Levy and Murnane (1992); and Juhn, Murphy, and Pierce (1993). These papers laid down the main facts and possible explanations for the dramatic increase in wage inequality of the 1980s. At the time, the leading explanation that emerged was based on a pervasive increase in the demand for all dimensions of skills that was mitigated, in part, by swings in relative supply linked to the baby boom cohort. A number of papers later argued that the leading source of increase in the relative demand for skills was skill-biased technological change (SBTC) linked, in large part, to the computer and information technology revolution.[1]

Over the last fifteen years, however, further research has cast some doubt on the basic view that inequality growth is driven by a combination of demand changes linked to SBTC and the computer revolution. This "revisionist" view, to borrow the term suggested by Autor, Katz, and Kearney (2008), is mostly based on the observation that the bulk of broad-based inequality growth was concentrated in the 1980s. In particular, Card and DiNardo (2002) argue that this "episodic" aspect of inequality growth is

Thomas Lemieux is professor of economics at the University of British Columbia, and a research associate of the National Bureau of Economic Research.
1. See, in particular, Krueger (1993); Berman, Bound, and Griliches (1994); Autor, Katz, and Krueger (1998); Autor, Levy, and Murnane (2003).

inconsistent with a simple supply and demand explanation that should instead predict an unabated growth in inequality throughout the 1990s. The episodic view of inequality changes is corroborated in recent work by Lemieux (2006a), who argues that the growth in within-group inequality is also concentrated in the 1980s. This somehow contradicts the earlier work of Juhn, Murphy, and Pierce (1993), who document a continuing growth in this dimension of inequality throughout the 1970s and 1980s.[2] Lemieux (2006a) argues that various measurement issues and composition effects account for these different views about the timing of the growth in within-group inequality.

In response to these recent findings, Autor, Katz, and Kearney (2008) point out that inequality in the upper end of the distribution (top-end inequality) has kept growing steadily throughout the 1990s and early 2000s, a trend that they attribute to relative demand shifts induced by technological change of the type proposed by Autor, Levy, and Murnane (2003). The steady and continuing growth in top-end inequality has also been well documented by Piketty and Saez (2003) using tax data which, unlike data from the Current Population Survey (CPS) or the Census, are not topcoded.

In light of these seemingly diverging views, the main goal of this chapter is to identify in the clearest possible way, using CPS data, what have been the main changes in inequality and the wage structure since the early 1970s. The purpose of this exercise is to establish the basic facts that are robust to the variety of measurement problems frequently encountered in the litera-ture, that is, identify what it is that we really know about changes in wage inequality. These measurement problems include topcoding, the growing nonresponse to earnings item in the CPS, and differences in wage measures in the March and outgoing rotation group (ORG) supplements of the CPS. A first substantive conclusion of the chapter is that, with the exception of the growth in within-group inequality for men in the 1970s, all the main trends appear to be highly robust to these measurement issues. More generally, the results confirm the view of both the "revisionists," who find that changes in broad-based measures of inequality are concentrated in the 1980s, and of Autor, Katz, and Kearney (2006, 2008), who find smooth growth in top-end inequality.

The related goal of the chapter is to assess what these trends tell us about the underlying sources of changes in inequality. I discuss what challenges these findings pose for existing explanations and propose alternative expla-nations linked to broadly defined wage setting institutions (minimum wage, unions, and performance pay) to help reconcile these often contradictory sets for facts.

2. Katz and Autor (1999) and Acemoglu (2002) also find that within-group inequality kept increasing in the 1990s.

One difference between this chapter and most of the existing literature is that the majority of basic trends in inequality reported here have been adjusted for changes in the skill (experience and education) composition of the workforce. A more standard approach is to report basis trends without these adjustments for composition effects and then perform decompositions where composition effects are one of the sources of overall change in inequality (see, for example, Juhn, Murphy, and Pierce 1993). One drawback of these approaches is that what is often presented as the basic inequality trends end up mixing up composition effects and true underlying changes in the wage structure. Lemieux (2006a) shows this has important consequences in the case of within-group, or residual, inequality where composition effects are large. Because my goal here is to document the main trends in the wage structure, and in summary measures of inequality induced by changes in the wage structure, I focus on an approach where composition effects are systematically adjusted for.

The wage measure used throughout the chapter is the hourly wage rate that purely reflects the "price" of different types of labor, as opposed to earnings that mix up the hourly wage rate with hours decisions. The primary source of data used to do so is the 1979 to 2006 ORG supplements of the CPS, supplemented with similar wage data from the 1973 to 1978 May CPS. All inequality trends are also presented separately for men and women. Using hourly wage rates, as opposed to weekly earnings for full-time workers (or other earnings measures), is particularly important for women, who are less likely to work full-time and generally exhibit more variation in hours of work than men.

Section 1.2 briefly discusses the data and presents the measurement framework used to compute the various measures of inequality adjusted for composition effects. The basic trends are presented in section 1.3, and the robustness of these trends to a number of measurement issues is discussed in section 1.4. The main findings are summarized in section 1.5, while section 1.6 concludes by discussing the implications of these findings for different explanations about the sources of change in wage inequality.

1.2   Data and Measurement Framework

1.2.1   Data Issues

Data issues are discussed in detail in the data appendix, which explains the construction of wage measures for the May-ORG and March CPS Supplements. I only briefly discuss how the May and ORG supplements of the CPS are processed here. As mentioned in the preceding, the wage measure used is the hourly wage rate. The main advantage of this measure is that theories of wage determination typically pertain to the hourly wage rate.

For example, the interplay of demand and supply considerations has direct implications for the hourly price of labor. By contrast, the impact of these factors on weekly or annual earnings also depends on the responsiveness of labor supply to changes in the hourly wage rate.

The Dual Jobs Supplement of the May CPS for 1973 to 1978 asks questions about wages on the main job held during the survey week to all wage and salary workers. For workers paid by the hour, the May CPS asks workers directly about their hourly rate of pay. This is the hourly wage measure that I use for this group of workers (about 60 percent of the workforce). For the other workers, I compute an hourly wage rate by dividing usual weekly earnings by usual weekly hours of work. I use the same procedure for the 1979 to 1993 ORG supplements that ask the same wage questions as the May CPS. The wage questions in the 1994 to 2006 ORG supplements are similar except that workers not paid by the hour can choose the periodicity at which they report earnings. I compute their hourly wage rate by dividing earnings by hours over the corresponding time period. The merged outgoing rotation group (MORG) files combine this information for all twelve months of the year.

One important advantage of the MORG supplement is that it is roughly three times as large as the May or March supplements of the CPS.[3] Another advantage over the March CPS is that we know the union status of workers in the May-ORG CPS, but not in the March CPS. A potential disadvantage is that wage data in the May-ORG CPS only goes back to 1973, while it is possible to go back to the 1960s using the March CPS. This is of little consequence here, however, because most of the relevant movements in wage inequality and the wage structure only started in the 1970s.

Unlike in the ORG and March supplements of the CPS, in the 1973 to 1978 May CPS, wages were not allocated for workers who refused to answer the wage questions. To be consistent, I only keep workers with nonallocated wages in the 1979 to 2006 ORG supplements in most of the analysis. As a consequence, observations are for 1994 and the first eight months of 1995, in which the workers with missing wages are dropped from the sample when only nonallocated observations are used. Following most of the literature, I trim extreme values of wages (less than $1 and more than $100 in 1979$) and keep workers aged sixteen to sixty-four with positive potential experience.

In the main results presented in the chapter, I adjust for topcoding by

3. The May 1973 to 1978 and March supplements are administered to all (eight) rotation groups of the CPS during these months. By contrast, only one-quarter of respondents (in rotation groups four and eight) are asked the questions from the ORG supplement each month. Combining the twelve months of data into a single MORG file yields wage data for twenty-four rotation groups compared to eight in the May or March supplements (plus the hispanic and Medicare [post-2000] oversamples in the March CPS).

multiplying topcoded earnings by a factor of 1.4. In the case of the March CPS, I also compare this rudimentary adjustment to a more sophisticated stochastic imputation procedure based on the assumption that top earnings follow a Pareto distribution with a parameter estimated separately for each year in the tax data of Piketty and Saez (2003).

Finally, I weight all wage observations by hours of work (in addition to the usual CPS weights). In the case of the May-ORG CPS, weekly hours of work are used, while annual hours are used for the March CPS. Doing so has two main advantages. First, it effectively provides a distribution over all hours worked in the economy that do not put excessive focus on workers who only supply very few hours to the labor market. For instance, DiNardo, Fortin, and Lemieux (1996) argue that failing to do so would put excessive weight on the bottom end of the distribution where many workers around the minimum wage provide relatively fewer hours to the labor market than most other workers. Another advantage is that weighting by hours of work makes the March and May-ORG wage distributions more directly comparable (Lemieux 2006a).[4]

1.2.2   Measurement Model

As discussed earlier, unadjusted trends in wage inequality may either reflect underlying changes in the wage structure or composition effects that confound the changes in the wage structure. A simple way of adjusting for composition effects is to reweight the data so that the distribution of education and potential experience remains constant over time (e.g., DiNardo, Fortin, and Lemieux 1996). Doing so is straightforward in cases where the data can be divided up in a finite number of cells. In such cases, the weight attached to each cell can be held constant by multiplying the sample fraction in year t by the average fraction of observations in this cell for all years combined or for an arbitrary base year. Because results can be sensitive to the choice of base year, I follow Juhn, Murphy, and Pierce (1993) and hold the sample composition constant at the average fraction for all years combined. One additional reason for using this average weight over all years combined is that it yields results similar to those obtained using a more sophisticated chain-weighted approach.[5]

After various experimentations, I divided the data into 130 cells defined on the basis of six education groups (elementary, high school dropouts, high

---

4. Abraham, Speltzer, and Steward (1998) also weight by hours for the same reason (i.e., make different data sources comparable) in their study comparing the evolution of average real wages rates from different data sources, including the March and May-ORG CPS.

5. I thank Lawrence Katz for this suggestion. In the case of the within-group variance discussed in the following, the change in variance between year t and $t-1$ holding the workforce composition at its year $t-1$ level is $\Delta W_{t,c} = \Sigma_{jk}\, \theta_{jkt-1}(v_{jkt} - v_{jkt-1})$. The chain-weighted composition adjusted variance in year t, $W_{t,c}$, is equal to the base period variance, W_0, plus the sum of year-to-year changes defined in the preceding: $W_{t,c} = W_0 + \Sigma_{s=1\,to\,t}\, \Delta W_{s,c}$.

school graduates, college graduates, and college postgraduates) and twenty-two two-year experience groups.[6] The R-square of a wage regression using this set of cell dummies is very close to the R-square for an unrestricted model, and using these broader cells limits the problem of very small cells that can generate excessive variability in the reweighting procedure.[7]

In the first set of results presented in the chapter, the measure of wage dispersion used is the variance of log wages (between and within components) as well as standard wage differentials based on differences across education and experience groups. All these measures can be directly computed as functions of the mean and variance of wages in each cell. Let y_{jkt} denote the average wage of workers with education j and experience k in year t. The variance within this group is v_{jkt}, the share of workers in this group in year t is θ_{jkt}, and the average share over all years is θ_{jk}. The composition unadjusted within- ($W_{t,u}$) and between-group ($B_{t,u}$) variance in year t are

$$B_{t,u} = \Sigma_{jk} \, \theta_{jkt}(y_{jkt} - y_{t,u})^2, \text{ and}$$

$$W_{t,u} = \Sigma_{jk} \, \theta_{jkt} v_{jkt},$$

where $y_{t,u} = \Sigma_{jk} \, \theta_{jkt} \, y_{jkt}$ is the unadjusted mean (grand mean) over all groups. The corresponding expressions adjusted for composition effects are obtained by simply replacing the year t weights, θ_{jkt}, with the average weights θ_{jk}:

$$B_t = \Sigma_{jk} \, \theta_{jk}(y_{jkt} - y_t)^2, \text{ and}$$

$$W_t = \Sigma_{jk} \, \theta_{jk} v_{jkt},$$

where $y_t = \Sigma_{jk} \, \theta_{jk} \, y_{jkt}$ is the composition adjusted mean over all groups.

A standard approach for estimating experience and education wage differentials is to run ordinary least squares (OLS) regressions. I use a slightly different approach by computing separate measures of education differentials for each experience category and vice versa. The experience-group-specific education wage differentials are then aggregated up into a single differential by averaging up the experience-group-specific education differentials using the average sample fraction in each experience group over all years combined.

6. Note that the twenty-second experience category includes workers with forty-two years and more of potential experience because some of the two-year experience cells with very high level of experience (forty-three to forty-four or forty-five to forty-six) were too small. Note also that there are no observations in (a) the cell with the lowest level of education (eight years or less) and the lowest level of experience (zero to one years of experience), and (b) the cell with the highest level of education (eighteen year or more) and the highest level of experience (forty-two years or more of experience) because observations in these cells do not fall into the age range (sixteen to sixty-four) used in this paper. This explains why 130, as opposed to 132 (twenty-two experience times six education groups) cells are used in the empirical analysis.

7. In the case of men, the average R-square in 1973, 1979, 1989, 1999, and 2006 in the model with 120 cells is .3466, compared to .3511 in models with an unrestricted set of experience-education dummies based on single years of experience and education. The corresponding average R-square for women are .3110 and .3135, respectively.

Let θ_j represent the fraction of workers (of all experience groups) with education j in all years combined, and θ_k represent the fraction of workers (of all education groups) with experience k in all years combined. The composition-adjusted wage differential between education group j' and j in year t is defined as

$$D_{j',jt} = \Sigma_k \, \theta_k \, (y_{j'kt} - y_{jkt}).$$

Similarly, the composition-adjusted wage differential between experience group k' and k in year t is

$$D_{k',kt} = \Sigma_j \, \theta_j \, (y_{jk't} - y_{jkt}).$$

One important advantage of the variance as a measure of wage inequality is that it can be exactly decomposed as the sum of the between- and within-group components W and B. The decomposition can be directly linked to various "price effects" once composition effects have been adjusted for using the preceding procedure. Using the terminology of Juhn, Murphy, and Pierce (1993), the between-group component solely reflects "observable price effects," that is, differences in mean wages among experience and education groups. By contrast, the within-group component solely captures "unobservable price effects" under the assumption that the distribution of unobservables (ability, school quality, etc.) within a fixed experience-education group does not change over time.

One important disadvantage of the variance, however, is that it is only a summary measure of inequality that does not indicate what happens where in the distribution. This is a major problem in light of recent evidence that inequality is changing very differently at different points of the wage distribution. A simple and popular way of showing what happens at different points of the distribution is to look separately at each wage percentile and compute summary measures such as the 90-50 gap (the difference between the 90th percentile and the median of log wages) and the 50-10 gap (the difference between the median and the 10th percentile of log wages). One important drawback of this approach is that these alternative inequality measures can no longer be decomposed as the sum of a within- and between-group component that add up to the overall inequality measure. For example, the 90-50 gap is not equal to the sum of the 90-50 gap in group means and the 90-50 gap in residuals. As a result, it is not completely clear how to compute the contribution of observable and unobservable prices to changes in the 90-50 or related gaps.

Following Juhn, Murphy, and Pierce (1993); Lemieux (2002); and Autor, Katz, and Kearney (2005), a number of approaches can nonetheless be used to get some indications on the contribution of the various price components to changes in inequality at different points of the distribution. One approach is to look at the distribution of residuals. Consider an individual wage observation y_{ijkt}. The residual u_{ijkt} can be readily computed as the difference between the individual wage observation and the cell mean y_{jkt} so that $u_{ijkt} = y_{ijkt} - y_{jkt}$.[8] Looking at changes in the distribution of residuals provides some information on changes in unobservable prices.

Another possible approach is to perform a decomposition in spirit of Juhn, Murphy, and Pierce (1993). First remember that the focus here is to first control for composition effects to then see what is explained by changes in the wage structure. Adjusting unconditional quantiles for composition effects is straightforward in the cell-by-cell case considered here. Observation i with education j and experience k in year t can simply be reweighted by the factor θ_{jk}/θ_{jkt} so that the distribution of education and experience remains constant over time (DiNardo, Fortin, and Lemieux 1996; Lemieux 2002). Changes in observable prices can then be controlled for by replacing the actual conditional mean of wages, y_{jkt}, with the average conditional mean for the cell over all years combined, y_{jk}. This yields a counterfactual wage $y'_{ijkt} = y_{ijkt} + (y_{jk} - y_{jkt})$. Remaining changes in the counterfactual wage y'_{ijkt} should then only depend on changes in unobservable prices.

1.3 Basic Results from the May-ORG Data

In this section, I present the basic descriptive facts as well as the decomposition results using the 1973 to 2006 May-ORG data. In this first set of results, I only keep observations with unallocated wages and fix for topcoding using the 1.4 correction factor. I later discuss in section 1.4 what happens when (a) the March CPS is used instead of the May-ORG CPS, (b) allocated wage observations are included (for 1979 on), and (c) other assumptions are used to deal with topcoding. The results are presented using a set of figures and are also summarized in table 1.1. The table shows various measures of wage dispersion at five points of time. At each of these points, three years of data are pooled together (1973 to 1975, 1978 to 1980, 1988 to 1990, 1998 to 2000, and 2004 to 2006) to increase the precision of the results.

1.3.1 Variance over All Experience and Education Groups

The evolution of the overall variance of wages (sum of the between and within component) is first reported in Figure 1.1 for men and women, respectively. A couple of clear patterns emerge from these figures. First, the bulk of the growth in the variance is concentrated in the 1980s. Second, adjusting for composition effects noticeably reduces the long-term growth in the variance. In the case of men, the variance is very stable in the 1970s and 1990s but starts increasing again after 1999. The same pattern can roughly

---

8. It is not clear whether the residual should be defined relative to the conditional mean or median. Juhn, Murphy, and Pierce (1993) and Lemieux (2002) use the conditional mean, while Autor, Katz, and Kearney (2005) use the conditional median. A few experimentations suggested that this choice had little impact on the results.

Table 1.1   **Summary measures of wage inequality for men and women, May-outgoing rotation group Current Population Survey**

	Inequality level					Inequality change		
	1974	1979	1989	1999	2005	1974–1989	1989–2005	1974–2005
A. Men								
Unadjusted variance								
Total	0.251	0.250	0.324	0.340	0.359	0.073	0.035	0.108
Within	0.175	0.173	0.205	0.209	0.218	0.030	0.013	0.044
Between	0.076	0.077	0.119	0.131	0.141	0.043	0.022	0.065
Adjusted variance								
Total	0.262	0.256	0.328	0.330	0.344	0.066	0.016	0.082
Within	0.183	0.179	0.206	0.198	0.202	0.024	−0.005	0.019
Between	0.080	0.076	0.122	0.133	0.143	0.042	0.021	0.063
Other (adjusted) inequality measures								
90-10 gap	1.309	1.285	1.447	1.463	1.498	0.139	0.051	0.190
50-10 gap	0.700	0.696	0.732	0.668	0.660	0.032	−0.072	−0.039
90-50 gap	0.609	0.590	0.715	0.795	0.838	0.106	0.123	0.229
Education wage gaps								
High school-dropout	0.171	0.172	0.218	0.222	0.220	0.047	0.002	0.049
College-high school	0.367	0.320	0.461	0.526	0.548	0.093	0.087	0.181
Post graduate-college	−0.007	0.040	0.098	0.193	0.220	0.105	0.122	0.227
Experience wage gap								
20–29 years-0–9 years	0.390	0.404	0.474	0.399	0.421	0.083	−0.052	0.031
B. Women								
Unadjusted variance								
Total	0.189	0.173	0.261	0.285	0.307	0.072	0.046	0.118
Within	0.137	0.130	0.177	0.180	0.193	0.041	0.016	0.057
Between	0.052	0.043	0.084	0.105	0.114	0.032	0.030	0.062
Adjusted variance								
Total	0.202	0.183	0.262	0.271	0.287	0.061	0.025	0.086
Within	0.143	0.137	0.177	0.166	0.172	0.034	−0.004	0.030
Between	0.059	0.046	0.085	0.105	0.115	0.027	0.030	0.056
Other (adjusted) inequality measures								
90-10 gap	1.069	1.054	1.310	1.315	1.338	0.241	0.028	0.269
50-10 gap	0.503	0.465	0.627	0.550	0.559	0.124	−0.068	0.056
90-50 gap	0.567	0.589	0.683	0.765	0.779	0.117	0.096	0.213
Education wage gaps								
High school-dropout	0.193	0.172	0.244	0.232	0.245	0.051	0.001	0.052
College-high school	0.370	0.320	0.458	0.539	0.560	0.088	0.101	0.189
Post graduate-college	0.189	0.181	0.166	0.230	0.233	−0.023	0.067	0.044
Experience wage gap								
20–29 years-0–9 years	0.130	0.155	0.264	0.275	0.302	0.134	0.038	0.171

Notes: Inequality measures computed by pooling groups of three years centered on the year listed in the table. For example, "1974" corresponds to year 1973 to 1975, and so on. The "adjusted" variance (and other inequality measures) are adjusted for composition effects using the procedure described in the text.

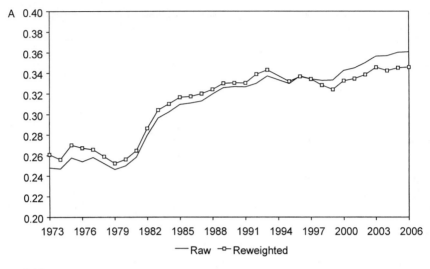

A

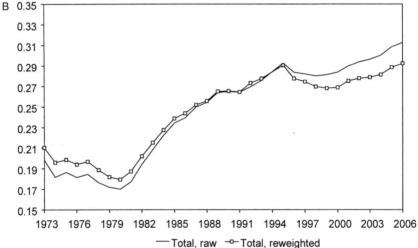

B

Fig. 1.1 Total variance: *A*, Men; *B*, Women

be observed for women, with the notable difference that the variance clearly declines in the 1970s.

Figure 1.2 presents a first decomposition by showing separately the evolution of the between- and within-group components of the variance. Three interesting patterns emerge from these figures. First, the pattern of change in the between- and within-group components is remarkably similar over time. For both men and women, both the within- and between-group components grow sharply in the 1980s, grow less in the 2000s, and remain stable or decline (for women in the 1970s) in the 1970s and 1990s. For men, both components

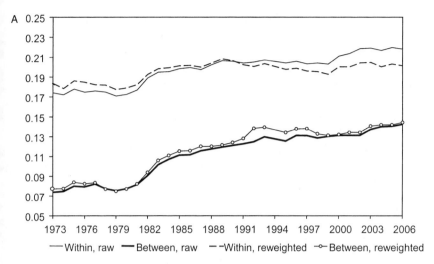

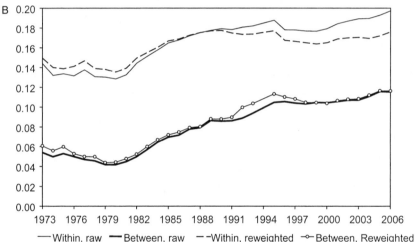

Fig. 1.2   **Within- and between-group variances: *A*, Men; *B*, Women**

decline slightly in the 1990s once composition effects are adjusted for. For women, the 1990s is the only period where the between- and within-group components move in opposite directions. I argue in the following, however, that part of the growth in the between-group variance for women likely captures a different type of composition effect linked to the growth in actual labor market experience given potential experience. So, on balance, the pattern of change in the within- and between-group components is very similar.

A second important finding is that, consistent with Lemieux (2006a), composition effects account for a very substantial part of the growth in the within-group variance. By contrast, composition effects play little role in long-run changes in the between-group component. This result holds for both for men and women. The third finding is that the between-group component accounts for most of the growth in the overall variance, especially once composition effects are adjusted for. This particular result is sensitive to the data used (March versus May-ORG CPS) and will be further discussed in section 1.4.

I also show in figure 1B.3 (for men) that using a chain-weighted procedure (see footnote 5) instead of the fixed-weighted approach used in figures 1.1 and 1.2 has very little impact on the results. This suggests that using the fixed-weighted procedure with average weights computed over the whole sample period provides a simple and accurate way of controlling for composition effects and is not as arbitrary as using either base-period or end-period weights.[9]

1.3.2   Relative Wages and Variances by Education and Experience Groups

Because the groups (cells) used from the decomposition are solely based on education and experience, the source of the growth in the (composition-adjusted) between-group component must either come from a growth in education or experience wage differentials. Figure 1.3 shows the evolution of education wage differentials over time, while figure 1.4 shows the evolution of the returns to experience. As is well known, education wage differentials increased for both men and women in the 1980s. Relative to high school graduates, panel A of figure 1.3 shows that the wage advantage of men with some college or more increased, while the wage disadvantage of high school dropouts or those with eight years of education or less (elementary category in the figure) also expanded, albeit more modestly. By contrast, in the 1990s and 2000s, most education wage differentials remained stable except for college graduates and postgraduates, who kept gaining relative to high school graduates.

Looking at the whole 1973 to 2006 period, the striking fact is that most of the expansion in wage differentials has been happening at the top of the education distribution. In particular, the gap between college postgraduates and high school graduates more than doubled over time. College graduates and people with some college also experienced substantial gains, while relative wages among workers with a high school diploma or less remained very stable over time. This mirrors the finding by Lemieux (2006b) of a growing convexification in the relationship between wages and education. In other words, wage differentials at the top end of the education distribution have increased steadily over time, while wage differentials at the bottom end remained more or less stable. As I will show in the following, this fits with

9. The adjustment for composition effects in the within-group variance are substantially larger when base-period are used instead of end-period weights (Lemieux 2006a).

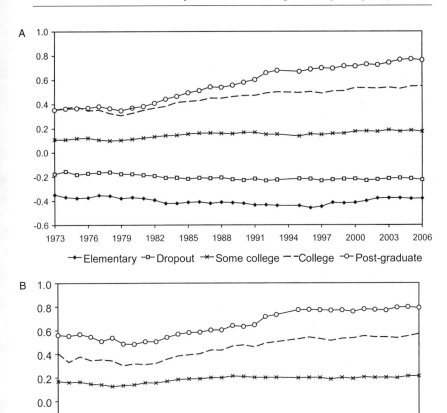

Fig. 1.3   Education wage differentials (relative to high school graduates): *A,* **Men;** *B,* **Women**

the general pattern that inequality has kept growing at the top end but not at the low end of the distribution (Autor, Katz, and Kearney 2005). Note also that the results for women in panel B of figure 1.3 are qualitatively similar to those for men.

The evolution of experience wage differentials is shown in figure 1.4. Because it would not be very informative to present the differentials for each of the twenty-one experience groups, I have regrouped the two-year experience groups into in four major experience groups (zero to nine, ten to nineteen, twenty to twenty-nine, and thirty to thirty-nine years of experience) by computing a weighted mean of the wages differentials for the

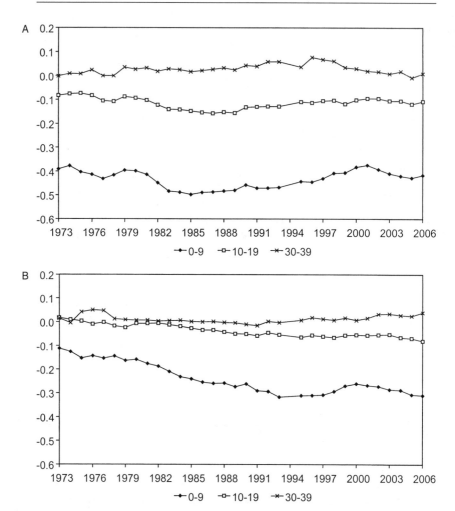

Fig. 1.4   Experience wages differentials (relative to 20–29 years of experience):
A, Men; *B*, Women

smaller groups. The differentials reported in the figure show the gap relative to workers with twenty to twenty-nine years of experience. Consistent with earlier studies such as Katz and Murphy (1992), there is a clear
expansion in experience wage differentials in the 1980s. The differentials
start contracting again, however, in the late 1980s, and by the end of the
sample period, the differentials are more or less back to their initial 1973
levels. The situation is quite different for women (panel B of figure 1.4).
Differentials keep expanding over time except in the late 1990s when inexperienced (zero to nine years of experience) women gain ground again, probably because of the very strong labor market at that time. By 2006, the gap

between experienced (twenty to twenty-nine years of experience) and inexperienced (zero to nine years of experience) women is three times as large as back in 1973 and has almost caught up with the level of the corresponding gap for men.

The most plausible explanation for growing experience gaps for women is that the large increases in female employment rates have lead to a corresponding increase in the level of actual labor market experience conditional on potential experience.[10] For instance, women with twenty years of potential experience now have much more actual experience than they used to. As a result, their wage advantage over inexperienced women should have increased substantially even if the return to actual experience did not grow over time. If actual experience was measured in the CPS, changes in actual experience could be corrected for by holding the distribution of education and actual (as opposed to potential) experience constant over time. Because only potential experience is available in the CPS, the change in experience wage differentials documented in panel B of figure 1.4 should be interpreted with caution. Trends in experience differentials for men are more reliable and suggest that "real" returns to experience played little role in the growth in wage dispersion.

Taken together, the results in figures 1.2 to 1.4 suggest that, at least for men, changes in the between-group variance induced by growing top-end education wage differentials account for most of the growth in the variance of wages, a results also found in more formal decompositions by Lemieux (2006b); Firpo, Fortin, and Lemieux (2007); and Goldin and Katz (2007).

Turning to the within-group component, figures 1.5 and 1.6 show the evolution of the within-group variance by education and experience groups. Like the wage differentials, the within-group variance by education groups are computed as fixed-weighted averages across experience groups and vice versa. The within-group variance for education group j at time t is

$$V_{jt} = \Sigma_k \, \theta_k \, v_{jkt},$$

while the within-group variance for experience group k at time t is

$$V_{kt} = \Sigma_j \, \theta_j \, v_{jkt}.$$

As before, the different experience groups are combined into four broader groups for the ease of exposition.

Figure 1.5 shows that the within-group variance moves quite differently over time for different education groups. Dispersion increases among all education groups in the 1980s, keeps growing for the more-educated groups (college graduates and postgraduates) after 1990, but remains stable or even

10. Using Panel Study of Income Dynamics (PSID) data, Blau and Kahn (1996) show that actual experience has indeed increased a lot over time for given levels of potential experience.

A
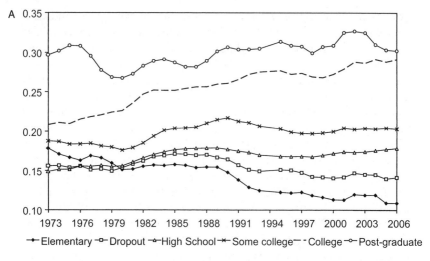

B
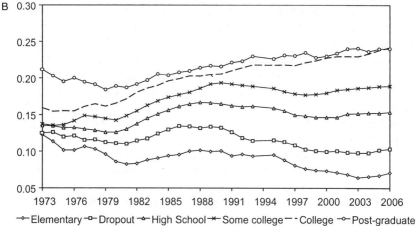

Fig. 1.5   Within-group variance by education groups: *A*, Men; *B*, Women

declines for less-educated groups. Interestingly, the evolution in within-group dispersion closely mirrors the evolution of relative wages by education groups, which reinforces the earlier conclusion that inequality growth in concentrated at the top end of the distribution.

By contrast, changes in within-group wage dispersion by experience groups are more homogenous across groups. Roughly speaking, the within-group variance increases for all experience groups during the 1980s but remains more or less constant after 1990. The only exception is inexperienced women for whom the within-group variance declines after reaching a peak in the late 1980s.

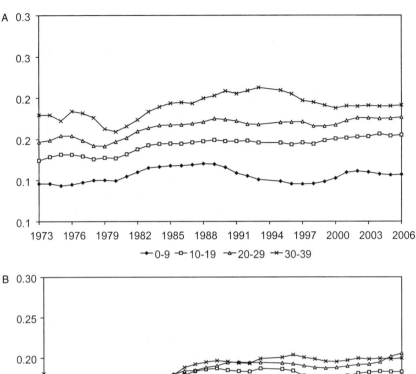

Fig. 1.6   Variance by experience groups: *A*, Men; *B*, Women

Note also that education has a much larger effect on the within-group variance than experience. In figures 1.5 and 1.6, the range of variation in within-group variances (in a single year) is about twice as large between the lowest and the highest variance groups for education as it is for experience. This suggests that secular changes in the distribution of education potentially account for more of the composition effects than changes in the distribution of experience. Panels A and B of figure 1B.4 indicate that this is indeed the case and that about two-thirds of the composition effects can be linked to changes in the distribution of education.[11]

Taken together, the results in figures 1.2 to 1.6 suggest that changes in the relative wages and variances of highly educated workers is a key element in the growth of wage inequality since the late 1970s. There is indeed a very intriguing parallel between what is happening to the between- and within-group components of wage dispersion. For both components, changes are concentrated in the 1980s, and long-run growth is concentrated among college graduates and postgraduates. This suggests that both components may be reflecting the same underlying changes in the labor market, an issue to which I return in section 1.6. This also suggests, consistent with Autor, Katz, and Kearney (2005), that changes in the top end of the distribution are very different from changes at the low end. I now explore this issue in more detail by looking at what happened at different percentiles of the wage distribution.

1.3.3   Changes at Different Percentiles

Figure 1.7 plots the changes in real wages at each percentile over the 1974 to 1989, 1989 to 2004, and the whole 1974 to 2004 period. I use fifteen-year changes for both periods for the sake of comparability and also pool three years of data around 1974 (1973 to 1975), 1989 (1988 to 1990), and 2004 (2003 to 2005) to increase the precision of estimates at each percentile. Similar results for wages residuals are presented in figure 1.8. The results essentially reproduce the findings of Autor, Katz, and Kearney (2005). The main point is that, consistent with Juhn, Murphy, and Pierce (1993), wage changes are more or less a linear and positively sloped function of percentiles during the 1974 to 1989 period, suggesting similar changes in wage dispersion at all points of the wage distribution. The situation is radically different for the 1989 to 2004 period, however. While wage dispersion keeps growing above the median, wages become more compressed below the median as real wage gains at the bottom end exceed those around the median, a phenomena Autor, Katz, and Kearney (2006) refer to as the polarization of the labor market. Note that this phenomenon can be observed both for wages and wage residuals (figure 1.8).

Figure 1.9 then performs a Juhn, Murphy, and Pierce (1993) decomposition on the 90-50 and 50-10 gap using the procedure described in section 1.2. The results are, once again, very similar to those of Autor, Katz, and Kearney (2005). Basically, the figures show that at the top end, composition effects explain little of the growth in the 90-50 gap, while prices of observables account for more than half of the growth in the gap. As shown in the preceding, the relevant observable prices that likely account for most of the

---

11. The lines labeled "education fixed" in panels A and B of figure 1B.4 show what happens when the distribution of education is fixed to its average value over the whole sample period while the distribution of experience conditional on education remains as observed in the data.

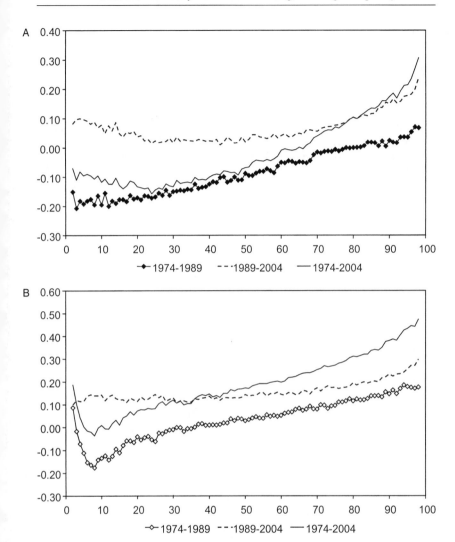

Fig. 1.7   Change in real wages by percentile: *A*, Men; *B*, Women

growth in the 90-50 gap are the wage differentials between college graduates and postgraduates relative to high school graduates. The remaining change in the 90-50 gap is due to changes in unobservable prices that are also likely driven by changes (growing within-group variance) happening among highly educated workers.[12]

12. Using a more sophisticated quantile decomposition, Firpo, Fortin, and Lemieux (2007) indeed find that education accounts for the bulk of the growth in the 90-50 gap. Their education "effects" include both the between- and within-group components.

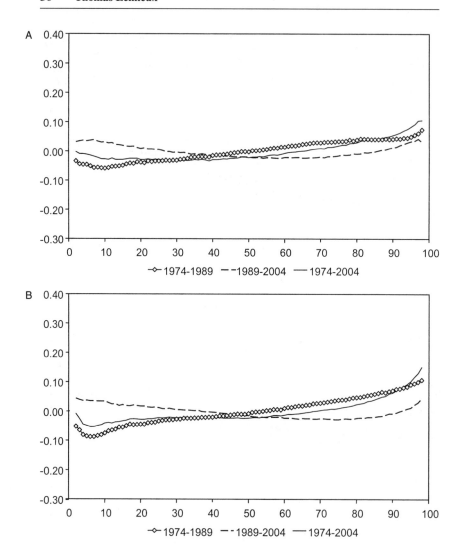

Fig. 1.8   Change in wages residuals by percentile: *A,* **Men;** *B,* **Women**

The situation is very different at the lower end of the distribution (50-10 gap). Unlike the case of the 90-50 gap, there are also substantial differences between men and women. I thus discuss these two cases separately. For men, the unadjusted 50-10 gap reported in panel B of figure 1.9 grows in the 1980s but more or less returns to its 1970s level by the late 1990s or early 2000s. After controlling for composition effects, however, the 50-10 declines substantially and is lower in the early 2000s than in the 1970s. While observable prices explain a substantial part of the growth in the 1980s and decline in the 1990s, they have little impact on long-run changes between 1973 and 2006.

A
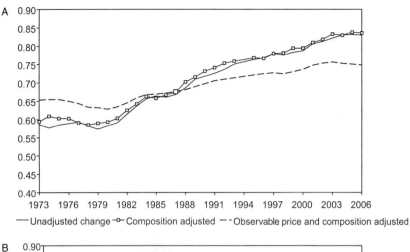
— Unadjusted change -□- Composition adjusted — - Observable price and composition adjusted

B
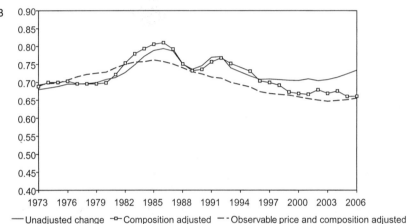
— Unadjusted change -□- Composition adjusted — - Observable price and composition adjusted

Fig. 1.9   Decomposition of changes in 90-50 and 50-10 gaps: *A*, Decomposition of changes in 90-50 gap, men; *B*, Decomposition of changes in the 50-10 gap, men; *C*, Decomposition of changes in 90-50 gap, women; *D*, Decomposition of changes in 50-10 gap, women

The pattern of changes suggests that movements in the return to experience plays an important role here. The fact that the relative wages of young workers fell in the 1980s and went back up in the 1990s likely accounts for the swings in the 50-10 gap because young workers are overrepresented at the bottom of the wage distribution. Furthermore, the stability of education differentials at the low end of the education distribution is consistent with the lack of observable price effects in the change in the 50-10 gap. Finally, the "residual" explanation for the decline in the 50-10 after adjusting for composition and observable price effects likely has to do with the decline in the within-group variance among less-educated workers.

C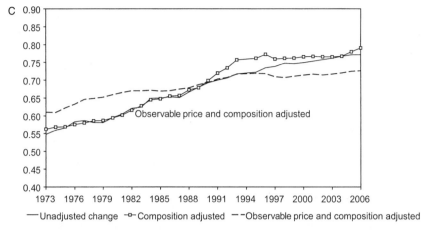

—Unadjusted change -□-Composition adjusted - -Observable price and composition adjusted

D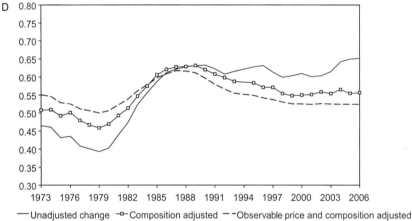

—Unadjusted change -□-Composition adjusted - -Observable price and composition adjusted

Fig. 1.9   (cont.)

In the case of women, there is a much steeper growth in the 50-10 gap in the 1980s, a phenomena likely linked to the large decline in the real value of the minimum wages over this period (DiNardo, Fortin, and Lemieux 1996).[13] As a result, the 50-10 gap in the early 2000s remains substantially higher than in the 1970s. As in the case of men, composition effects account for a substantial part of the growth in the 50-10 gap. Unlike men, however, changes in observable prices also account for a significant part of the growth in the 50-10 gap, which is consistent with the continuing growth in experience wage differentials documented in panel B of figure 1.4. Remember, however,

13. DiNardo, Fortin, and Lemieux (1996) find that over 60 percent of the increase in the 50-10 gap between 1979 and 1998 can be accounted for by the decline in the real value of the minimum wage.

that composition effects linked to the mismeasurement of actual experience likely accounts for much of these changes. By 2006, the 50-10 gap is a little smaller than back in 1973, suggesting that, as in the case of men, changes in unobservable prices lead to a small reduction in the 50-10 gap over time.

1.4   Measurement Issues: What Are the Robust Facts?

All the findings reported up to now are based on unallocated wage observations from the May-ORG CPS where topcoding is adjusted for using a 1.4 imputation factor. I now look at how robust the main results are to these data processing assumptions, focusing on trends in the (composition-adjusted) within- and between-group variance.

1.4.1   Wage Allocation

As mentioned in section 1.2, wages were not allocated (imputed) for individuals who failed to report their wages and earnings in the 1973 to 1978 CPS. In 1979, the Census Bureau started allocating wages for these individuals using the well-known hot deck matching procedure. Back in 1979, 17.9 percent of male and 14.8 percent of female workers did not report their wages. By 2006, the nonresponse rate had grown to a staggering 35.6 percent for male workers and 34.1 percent for female workers. Unless nonresponse is completely random, excluding workers with allocated wages could bias the trends in wage inequality measures. Of course, correcting for nonresponse is not perfect either, as assumptions have to be made about the determinants of nonresponse. The standard approach used by the Census Bureau to correct for nonresponse is to use a matching procedure where the missing wage is replaced with the wage of a "donor" with similar observed characteristics (location, education, age, race, etc). Note that this matching or hot decking procedure can be thought of as a stochastic imputation procedure. Instead of imputing a wage based on a regression model (e.g., Lillard, Smith, and Welch 1986), such a matching procedure preserves the wage dispersion conditional on characteristics, which is important when looking at wage dispersion, in general, and at within-group wage dispersion, in particular.

Figure 1.10 shows the difference in the between- and within-group variances computed with and without allocated wage observations. The series with allocated wage observations only starts in 1979 because, as mentioned earlier, the Census Bureau did not provide allocated wage observations in the 1973 to 1978 May CPS (Hirsch and Schumacher 2004). The main message from figure 1.10 is that, fortunately, the trends in wage inequality are fairly robust to the treatment of allocated wage observations. For both men and women, adding back the allocated wage observations reduces the between-group variance and increases the within-group variances. In terms of trends, however, the only noticeable difference is that the between-group component grows a little slower over time when allocated wage observations

A

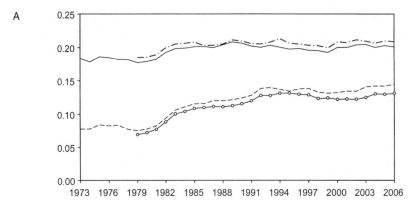

—Within, allocated out ‒‒Between, allocated out‒··Within, allocated in ‒○‒Between, allocated in

A

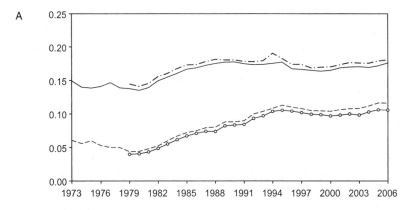

—Within, allocated out ‒‒Between, allocated out‒··Within, allocated in‒○‒Between, allocated in

Fig. 1.10   Variance with and without allocated wages controlling for composition effects: *A*, Men; *B*, Women

are included. Another noticeable difference is the "blip" in the within-group variance in 1994, the year the redesigned and computer-based CPS was introduced. Because allocation flags were not included in the 1994 (and part of 1995; see section 1.2) CPS, I computed the 1994 data points in the series without allocators as a simple interpolation based on the 1993 and 1995 numbers. As such, the two series are not comparable for 1994. Because 1994 seems to be just a one time blip, I did not perform any systematic adjustments to take account of the CPS redesign in 1994.[14]

---

14. If anything, the sharp increase in the within-group variance between 1993 and 1994 would suggest that the redesign lead to a spurious increase in the within-group variance, which reinforces the conclusion that the within-group variance did not increase after 1990.

1.4.2   Topcoding in the May-ORG CPS

Figure 1.11 compares the variance with and without the 1.4 topcoding adjustment. First notice that, in the case of women (panel B of figure 1.11), adjusting for topcoding has essentially no effect on either the between- or the within-group variance. This is hardly a surprise because only a small fraction of women have earnings at or above the topcode.

The adjustment for topcoding has a more noticeable impact in the case of men (panel B of figure 1.11). The impact of the increase in the topcode in 1986 and 1998 is clearly visible in the case of the within-group variance, where the unadjusted series experience unusual jumps in those two years. The impact of the increases in the topcode is also visible in the case of the between-group variance. Generally speaking, the impact of the correction for topcoding is larger for the within- than for the between-group component. Overall, adjusting for topcoding tends to modestly increase the growth in inequality over time. This pattern is consistent with the finding of Piketty and Saez (2003) that inequality at the very top end of the distribution has increased rapidly since the 1970s. Because an important part of these changes are missed because of the topcoding in the CPS, it is natural to expect the topcoding adjustment to result in more inequality growth. What is not clear, however, is whether a simple and time-invariant adjustment like the 1.4 imputation factor adequately captures all of the inequality growth at the very top end. I will return to this issue in more detail in the case of the March CPS where additional information from the tax data can be used to devise a better imputation procedure.

1.4.3   March versus May-ORG CPS

Differences in inequality trends in the May-ORG and March supplements of the CPS have been well documented by Lemieux (2006a) and Autor, Katz, and Kearney (2008). The most striking discrepancy between the series shown in figure 1.12 is that the within-group variance is substantially higher in the March than in the May-ORG supplement of the CPS. Lemieux (2006a) shows that this gap mostly reflect the fact that wages of workers paid by the hour are less precisely measured in the March CPS relative to the May-ORG CPS. This particular finding is reproduced in panels A (men) and B (women) of figure 1B.1. The problem with the March CPS is that all workers are only asked about their annual earnings and hours. An hourly wage is then obtained by dividing annual earnings by hours. In the May-ORG CPS, however, workers paid by the hour are asked directly about their hourly wage rates, which yields a more precise measure of hourly wages than in the March CPS (Lemieux 2006a).

Because (classical) measurement error cancels out when wages are averaged out at the cell level, mismeasurement of hourly wages in the March CPS should not affect much the between-group variance. This yields the simple

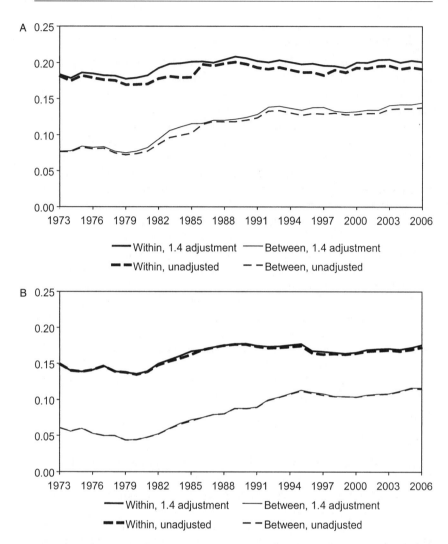

Fig. 1.11   Effect of topcoding adjustment, controlling for composition effects:
A, **Men;** *B,* **Women**

prediction, strongly supported by the data in figure 1.12, that the between-group variance should be about the same in the March and May-ORG CPS, and that the within-group variance should be larger in the March than in the May-ORG CPS.

A more challenging pattern to explain on the basis of these measurement issues is the fact that the trend growth in the within-group variance is higher in the March than in the May-ORG CPS. One possible explanation suggested by Lemieux (2006a) is that the fraction of workers paid by the

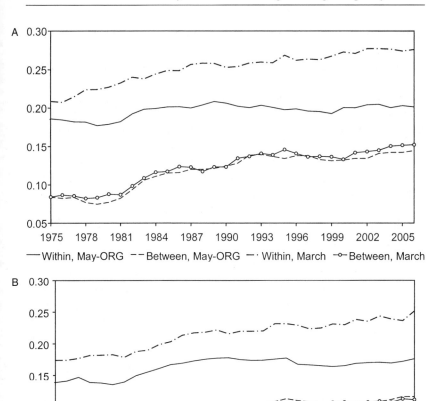

Fig. 1.12 Variance in May-ORG versus March CPS, controlling for composition effects: *A*, Men; *B*, Women

hour has increased over time (Hamermesh 2002), thereby magnifying the mismeasurement problems in the March CPS. As pointed out by Autor, Katz, and Kearney (2005), however, this could also bias down the trend in the within-group variance if there is less measurement error in wages of hourly than nonhourly paid workers in the May ORG CPS. In any case, Lemieux (2006a) also shows, using an error-components analysis, that changes in the fraction of hourly rated workers cannot account for most of the discrepancy between the two series. The evidence rather points out to measurement error (conditional on the hourly pay status) increasing over time in the March CPS, though no explicit story is provided for why this may be the case.

More important, however, both data sources show that the within-group variance grew much faster before than after the late 1980s, once composition effect are controlled for (as they are in figure 1.12). The only difference is that the within-group variance completely stops growing in the May-ORG CPS, while it grows at a much slower rate in the March CPS. So while the two series yield slightly different patterns of growth, in both cases the secular trends in the within-group variance closely mirror those observed for the between-group variance, which also grows much more slowly after than before the late 1980s. The only case where the two data series clearly differ is men in the 1970s. Consistent with Juhn, Murphy, and Pierce (1993), the within-group variance for men in the March CPS increases in the 1970s, while the between-group component remains more or less stable during this period. This particular series stands out as the only exception where inequality grows in the 1970s. By contrast, the within-group variance for women, the within-group variance for men in the May-ORG CPS, and the between-group variance all remain stable in the 1970s. This suggests that, at a minimum, the growth in the within-group variance for men in the March CPS should be interpreted with caution as it is not a very robust finding.

Leaving the 1970s aside, an important point is that, for men, most of the growth in the variance of wages between 1980 and 2006 comes from the between- as opposed to the within-group component. This is similar to what was documented earlier using the May-ORG CPS data. This highlights, once again, the importance of the growing education premia for college educated workers in the overall growth in wage inequality. For women, the growth in the overall variance during this period is, more or less, evenly split between the within- and between-group components. On balance, the earlier results that most of the growth in inequality is due to the between-group component are thus reasonably robust to the choice of data set.

1.4.4   Topcoding in the March CPS

Figure 1.13 shows what happens to the within-and between-group variances when (a) topcoding is not corrected for (as was done for the May-ORG data), and (b) a more sophisticated imputation procedure is used to allocate earnings for topcoded observations. Unlike the May-ORG CPS, other data sources can be used to make reasonable assumptions about the distribution of annual earnings above the topcode. In particular, because tax data are not topcoded, they provide direct information on the distribution of earnings above the topcode. The usual assumption made is that the upper tail of the earnings distribution follows a Pareto distribution. Piketty and Saez (2003) use the Pareto distribution to smooth their data on top incomes from

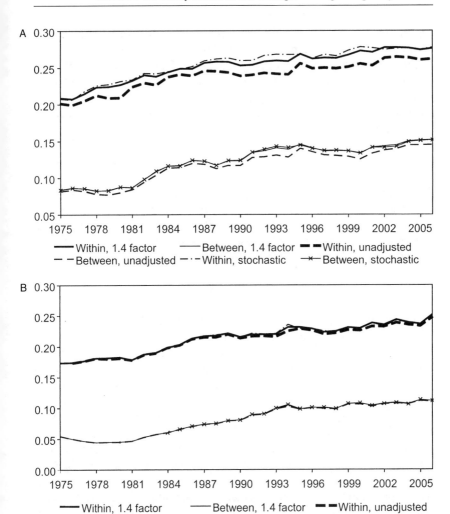

Fig. 1.13   **Topcoding adjustments in March CPS, controlling for composition effects:** *A*, **Men;** *B*, **Women**

tax data, and I use their implied Pareto parameter for each year to impute earnings above the March CPS topcode.[15]

Another limitation of the standard "fixed" imputation procedure based on a factor of 1.4 or 1.5 is that it does not preserve the distribution of earnings in the upper tail of the distribution. Intuitively, using a fixed as opposed to a stochastic imputation procedure likely has little impact for the between-

15. I use the updated series available at http://elsa.berkeley.edu/~saez/TabFig2005s.xls to compute the Pareto parameter up to 2005 and then use for 2006 the same parameter as in 2005.

group variance, but it could bias down the within-group variance by understating wage dispersion among topcoded workers.

Figure 1B.2 shows the topcoding adjustment factors obtained from Piketty and Saez's (2003) tax data. One very convenient feature of the Pareto distribution is that the Pareto parameter, α, can be estimated using only the value of a topcode y_{TC}, and the mean value for observations above the topcode, μ_{TC}, using the formula

$$\frac{\mu_{TC}}{y_{TC}} = \frac{\alpha}{(\alpha-1)}.$$

Because we typically work with log wages, it is also convenient to compute the mean log value from a Pareto distribution. Another convenient property is that when y follows a Pareto distribution with a parameter α, then $\log(y/y_{TC})$ follows an exponential distribution with a parameter α. The mean of $\log(y/y_{TC})$ is thus $1/\alpha$, which implies that

$$E[\log(y)] = \log(y_{TC}) + \frac{1}{\alpha}.$$

With the standard 1.4 imputation factor, it follows that $y = 1.4y_{TC}$. This corresponds to the case of a Pareto distribution with $1/\alpha = \log(1.4) = 0.336$, where the mean value of $\log(y)$ from this distribution is imputed to all observations. Figure 1B.2 shows that the actual value of $1/\alpha$ has been growing over time as top-end inequality expanded, though it decreased a bit following the end of the high-tech bubble around 2000. The figure also shows another adjustment factor from the March CPS. Since 1995, topcoded observations in the March CPS have their earnings replaced by the average earnings for their relevant (broadly defined) demographic group. This is now doable because earnings are no longer topcoded in the CPS (computerized) questionnaire, though they are topcoded in public use files. The implied Pareto parameter is remarkably similar to the one from the tax data, which gives a lot of confidence in the imputation procedure based on the tax data.[16]

In practice, I implement the stochastic imputation procedure by randomly drawing value z from an exponential distribution (with mean 1) and transforming them into draws from a Pareto distribution by exploiting the link between the Pareto and the exponential distribution discussed in the preceding:[17]

$$\log(y) = \log(y_{TC}) + \frac{z}{\alpha}.$$

16. I use the number of married white males, by far the largest group of topcoded workers, to compute the Pareto parameter in the CPS.

17. I use a three-year moving average for the adjustment factor from the tax data to smooth for some of the erratic behavior shown in figure 1B.2.

The results reported in panel A of figure 1.13 for men show that using either the 1.4 fixed imputation factor or the stochastic imputation procedure yield very similar estimates of the between-group variance. As in the case of the May-ORG, failing to adjust for topcoding slightly biases down the secular growth in the between-group variance, but the overall impact is very small.

Turning to the within-group variance, the fixed and stochastic imputation procedures yield, perhaps surprisingly, fairly similar results. In fact, the change in the within-group variance between 1973 and 2006 is essential identical under the two imputation procedures. One small difference is that the stochastic imputation procedure tends to produce a larger variance from the mid-1980s to the late 1990s, which slightly accentuates the slowdown in the growth in the within-group variance after the late 1980s. Another difference is that the within-group variance obtained using the stochastic imputation procedure does not change when the topcode is raised in 1995 and 2002. By contrast, the within-group variance computed with the fixed 1.4 correction jumps almost as much as the uncorrected series in these two years. This suggests that the stochastic imputation procedure does generally a better job at correcting for topcoding and that year-to-year changes are better measured using this procedure instead of the fixed imputation procedure. In terms of general inequality trends, however, panel A of figure 1.13 suggests that the two topcoding adjustments produce very similar results. Because the topcode has been gradually increased over time, even the unadjusted series more or less capture the correct long-run trends, though year-to-year variations are highly sensitive to changes in the value of the topcode.

1.5   Changes in Wage Inequality: A Summary

The last two sections have shown that there are a number of clear patterns of changes in wage inequality and in the wage structure that are highly robust to measurement issues. The only notable exception has to do with changes in within-group wage inequality for men in the 1970s, where the March and May-ORG supplements of the CPS yield substantially different answers. I will underplay this particular aspect of inequality changes in this section but discuss its implication for the interpretation of inequality changes in the next section.

The main results about "what we really know" about changes in wage inequality can be summarized as follows. Unless otherwise indicated, the results are based on inequality measures adjusted for composition effects:

1. Changes in broad-based measures of inequality, such as the variance, are concentrated in the 1980s. This holds for both the between- and within-group components of wage dispersion.

2. Trends in broad-based measures of inequality hide important

differences at different points of the distribution. At the top end of the distribution, inequality has grown steadily throughout the 1980s, 1990s, and 2000s. At the low end of the distribution, inequality only grew in the 1980s and remained constant or declined during the 1970s, 1990s, and 2000s.

3. The pattern of change in inequality across education groups is highly consistent with the broader changes at the top end and low end of the distribution. Mean wages of college graduates and postgraduates increased steadily relative to high school graduates, though the growth in more marked in the 1980s. Similarly, the within-group variance of these two highly educated groups has grown steadily over time. By contrast, the wage disadvantage of workers without a high school degree relative to those with a high school degree only increased (by a small amount) in the 1980s. The within-group variance for workers with a high school degree or less increased a bit in the 1980s but then remained stable or declined in the 1990s and 2000s.

4. Experience wage differentials go up and down over time but contribute little to long-run changes in wage inequality. These differentials increase more for women, but this likely reflects spurious changes linked to the changing relationship between actual and potential experience.

These main changes are also summarized in table 1.1, which shows the evolution in the different measures of wage inequality over the 1973 to 2006 period. While all the findings reported in the table can also be seen in the various figures, it is clear from the table that the growth in inequality is concentrated in the upper end of the distribution and in the 1980s.

1.6   Possible Explanations: Some Concluding Comments

Looking back at explanations for inequality growth suggested fifteen years ago, the new developments documented in the preceding pose a major challenge to the view based on a general increase in the demand for all dimensions of skill. A first puzzle is that if relative demand for skilled workers kept going up over the last fifteen years, how can one explain the decline in the returns to experience over this period or the stability of the skill premium between high school graduates and less-educated workers?

In the case of the return to experience, a possible answer is that relative supply, as opposed to relative demand, is the key factor behind secular changes in this wage differential. Just like the entry of baby boomers first depressed the wages of young workers in the 1970s and early 1980s (Welch 1979), as this cohort ages, the negative pressure of supply on wages is increasingly moving to the upper end of the experience distribution, which reduces the experience premium. While this hypothesis should be probed in more detail, it is also reasonable to expect that relative demand pressures are less important in the case of experience than education. Indeed, while it is sensible to think that the computer and information technology revolution is "education-biased," it is far from clear that it is also "experience-biased." This suggests that the growth in both education and experience differentials in the early 1980s may simply be a coincidence linked to demand factors driving the growth in the education premium and supply considerations driving the growth in the experience premium.

This view that the 1980s was a "perfect storm" where different factors resulted in an expansion in inequality at different points of the distribution, as opposed to a ubiquitous increase in the demand for skill, can also help shed light on some other puzzles. For instance, the large decline in the real value of the minimum wage during the 1980s helps explain why low-end inequality increased sharply during this period but not in other periods. DiNardo, Fortin, and Lemieux (1996) and Lee (1999) find that most of the growth in the 50-10 gap in the 1980s was due to the minimum wage (all of the change in Lee 1999). After adjusting for this factor, the remaining changes in 1980s were, thus, concentrated at the top end of the distribution.

Once several explanations are allowed to affect inequality at different points of the wage distribution, it becomes simpler to think of possible explanations for the secular growth in top-end inequality, without requiring these explanations to also account for swings in inequality growth at the bottom end. Because the growth in inequality at the top end of the distribution has attracted a lot of attention in recent years, a number of candidate explanations are available in the literature. For instance, Autor, Katz, and Kearney (2006) use Autor, Levy, and Murnane's (2003) model of technological change to explain why the labor market became polarized in the 1990s and 2000s. The model is based on a distinction between skilled and routine tasks where computers are substitutes for the latter. In this model, the introduction of computer technologies depresses the middle of the distribution where workers perform skilled but routine tasks, which results in increasing inequality at the top end but decreasing inequality at the low end. Firpo, Fortin, and Lemieux (2007) show that continuing deunionization yields similar predictions. Another possible explanation for the growing inequality at the top end includes the growth in pay for performance (Lemieux, MacLeod, and Parent 2007). None of these three explanations can account very well, however, for why inequality at the low end increased in the 1980s and decreased later, which highlights the value of combining these explanations with changes in the minimum wage.

Another important finding presented here that does not sit well with explanations suggested fifteen years ago is the fact that within-group inequality does not play as an important role in inequality changes as was thought back then. Note, however, that the basic insight of Juhn, Murphy, and Pierce (1993) that changes in the between- and within-group components are driven by similar factors remains consistent with more recent developments. For example, the fact that both the relative wages and the within-group dispersion of highly educated workers grew over time suggests that these developments are closely linked. Lemieux (2006b) shows that this follows naturally in a model with heterogenous returns to skill where the demand for college education increases. The fact that trends in the overall within- and between-group inequality are similar over time also points out to similar factors explaining both phenomena.

The one finding of Juhn, Murphy, and Pierce (1993) that is much less clear now than fifteen years ago is related to changes in within-group inequality in the 1970s. Using March CPS data, Juhn, Murphy, and Pierce (1993) argue that the growth in the within-group inequality in the 1970s provides evidence that relative demand was already increasing in the 1970s. As shown earlier, this last conclusion did not turn out to be very robust. This being said, whether within-group inequality increased in the 1970s does not play a crucial role in understanding why inequality has been changing over time. For both theoretical and empirical reasons, it is more appropriate to try to understand what drives changes in returns to education instead of within-group inequality over time. On the empirical side, the evidence presented in this paper shows that the basic facts about returns to education are very robust to measurement issues, which is not the case for within-group inequality. On the theoretical side, the basic idea of a race between relative supply and demand can be tested in the case of education, while the relative supply of unobserved skills underlying within-group dispersion is a fairly nebulous concept.

In terms of potential for future research, arguably the most important fact documented in this chapter and in related work (Lemieux 2006b; Goldin and Katz 2007) is the dramatic importance of education in changes in wage inequality. Fifteen years ago, most observers would probably not have thought that education could play such an important role in inequality growth. After all, the R-square of wage equations in the CPS are typically in the .3 to .4 range, with only part of the explanation coming from education. Furthermore, Juhn, Murphy, and Pierce (1993) had shown that most of the growth in wage inequality in the March CPS was coming from the within-group component, which was not surprising given the low R-square of wage regressions.

As I have shown in this chapter, however, the dominant source of long-run growth in the between-group component is the growth in relative wages of college-educated workers, while the dominant source of growth in the within-group component is the increase in within-group inequality among the same workers. These two related facts also help explain why inequality has mostly increased in the top end of the distribution where these workers are concentrated, as opposed to the low end of the distribution. In retrospect, this is a fairly unexpected development that deserves further investigation.

Data Appendix A

May-ORG and March CPS Data
This appendix explains in more detail how the March and May-ORG CPS are processed to make the wage samples as comparable as possible. It closely follows the data appendix in Lemieux (2006a). Both the May-ORG and the March CPS can be used to compute hourly wage rates. The March Supplement of the CPS asks about total earnings during the previous year. An hourly wage rate can then be computed by dividing last year's earnings by total hours worked last year. The latter variable is computed by multiplying two other variables available in the March CPS, usual weekly hours of work last year and weeks worked last year.

I limit the analysis of wages in the March CPS to the period starting with the earnings year 1975 (March 1976 survey) because an hourly wage rate cannot be computed in earlier years. Another reason for starting with the wage data for 1975 is that the other wage measure available in the May-ORG CPS is only available from May 1973 on. Because one contribution of the chapter is to compare the two data sources, the gain of using a more precise and comparable measure of hourly wages from the March CPS clearly outweighs the cost of losing two years of data for 1973 and 1974.

There are important differences between the way wages are measured in the March and May-ORG CPS. First, while the March CPS asks about retrospective measures of wages and earnings (last year), the May-ORG supplement asks about wages at the time of the survey. Second, the May-ORG wage questions are only asked to wage and salary workers. To get comparable wage samples, I limit my analysis of the March data to wage and salary earnings. One problem is that when workers have both wage and salary and self-employment earnings, we do not know how many hours of work pertain to wage and salary jobs versus self-employment. To minimize the impact of these considerations, I limit my analysis to wage and salary workers with very limited self-employment earnings (less than 10 percent of wage and salary earnings).

Another difference is that the ORG supplement only asks questions about the worker's main job (at a point in time), while the March CPS includes earnings from all jobs, including second jobs for dual job holders. Fortunately, only a small fraction of workers (around 5 percent typically) hold more than one job at the same time. Furthermore, these secondary jobs represent an even smaller fraction of hours worked.

Finally, because the May-ORG CPS is a "point-in-time" survey, the probability that an individual's wage is collected depends on the number of weeks worked during a year. By contrast, a wage rate can be constructed from the March wage information irrespective of how many weeks (provided that it is not zero) are worked during the year. This means that the May-ORG wage observations are implicitly weighted by the number of weeks worked, while the March wage observations are not.

One related issue is that several papers like DiNardo, Fortin, and Lemieux (1996) also weight the observations by weekly hours of work to get a wage distribution representative over the total number of hours worked in the economy. Weighting by weekly hours can also be viewed as a reasonable compromise between looking at full-time workers only (weight of one for full-time workers, zero for part-time workers) and looking at all workers as "equal" observations irrespective of the number of hours worked. Throughout the chapter, I thus weight the March CPS observations by annual hours of work and weight the May-ORG observations by weekly hours of work.

In both the March and ORG supplements of the CPS, the Census Bureau allocates a wage or earnings item for these workers using an "hot deck" procedure. The CPS also provides flags and related sources of information that can be used to identify workers with allocated wages in all years except in the January 1994 to August 1995 ORG supplements.[18] By contrast, in the May 1973 to 1978 CPS, wages were *not* allocated for workers who failed to answer wage and earnings questions. For the sake of consistency across data sources, all results presented in the chapter only rely on observations with nonallocated wages, unless otherwise indicated.

Wages and earnings measures are topcoded in both the March and May-ORG CPS. Topcoding is not much of an issue for workers paid by the hour in the May-ORG CPS. Throughout the sample period, the topcode remains constant at $99.99, and only a handful of workers have their wage censored at this value. By contrast, a substantial number of workers in the March CPS, and nonhourly workers in the May-ORG CPS, have topcoded wages. When translated on a weekly basis for full-year workers, the value of the topcode for annual wages in the March CPS tends to be comparable to the value of the topcode for weekly wages in the May-ORG CPS. For instance, in the first sample years (1975 to 1980), the weekly topcode in the May-ORG CPS is $999 compared to $962 for full-year workers in the March CPS (annual topcode of $50,000). Toward the end of the sample period (1998 to 2002), the weekly topcode in the ORG CPS is $2,884, which is identical to the implied weekly topcode for full-year workers in the March CPS (annual topcode of $150,000 divided by 52). As discussed in the chapter, I adjust for topcoding in both the May-ORG and the March CPS by multiplying topcoded wages by a factor 1.4.

Several further data adjustments are also performed before applying the 1.4 factor to topcoded wages. In the May-ORG CPS, the topcode on the edited weekly earnings variable for workers not paid by the hour goes from

18. Allocation flags are incorrect in the 1989 to 1993 ORG CPS and fail to identify most workers with missing wages. Fortunately, the Bureau of Labor Statistics (BLS) files report both edited (allocated) and unedited (unallocated) measures of wages and earnings. I use this alternative source of information to identify workers with allocated wages in these samples.

$999 in 1973 to 1988, to $1,923 in 1989 to 1997, and to $2,884 in 1998 to 2006. Between 1986 and 1988, however, it is possible to use the unedited weekly earnings variable that is topcoded at $1,999 instead of $999. Though the unedited variable is not computed for workers who fail to respond to the earnings question, this does not matter here because I focus on workers with unallocated wages and earnings. I thus use the unedited earnings variable for the 1986 to 1988 period.

Several adjustments also have to be performed before applying the 1.4 factor to the March CPS data. Until March 1989, wages and salaries were collected in a single variable pertaining to all jobs, with a topcode at $50,000 until 1981 (survey year), $75,000 from 1982 to 1984, and $99,999 from 1985 to 1988. Beginning in 1989, the March CPS started collecting wage and salary information separately for main jobs and other jobs, with topcodes at $99,999 for each of these two variables. The topcodes were later revised to $150,000 for the main job and $25,000 for other jobs in March 1996, and to $200,000 for the main job and $35,000 for other jobs in March 2003.

Prior to March 1996, the earnings variable of workers who are topcoded simply takes the value of the actual topcode. Starting in March 1996, however, the value of earnings for topcoded workers is replaced by the mean earnings among all topcoded workers. Mean earnings are separately computed for different demographic groups. To maintain consistency over time, I first construct a topcoded variable for total wage and salary earnings from March 1989 on. For 1989 to 1995, I simply keep the pre-1989 $99,999 topcode. Because both main job and other job earnings are separately topcoded at $99,999, I simply add these two earnings variables and topcode the sum at $99,999. After various experiments, I decided to use a topcode of $150,000 for total wage and salary earnings from 1996 on. Unfortunately, it is not possible to topcode total wage and salary earnings in a way that is completely consistent with the pre-1996 situation. The problem is with workers who earn less that $125,000 on their main job but have earnings from other jobs topcoded at $25,000. It is not possible to know whether total earnings of these workers are above or below $150,000. After some experiments, I decided to compute total earnings as the sum of main job earnings (censored at $150,000) and earnings on other jobs where I use the actual earnings provided in the CPS (where topcoded observations are imputed the actual mean earnings among topcoded workers).

These adjustments likely have little impact because, in the March 1996 to 2007 CPS, less than 1 percent of workers have main job earnings below $125,000 and are topcoded on their other jobs earnings. Finally, once total wage and salary earnings have been censored in a consistent fashion, I multiply the earnings of workers at this consistent topcode by the standard 1.4 factor. I also follow the existing literature by trimming very small and very large value of wages to remove potential outliers (less than $1 or more than

$100 in 1979 dollars) and limit the analysis to workers aged sixteen to sixty-four with positive potential experience (age-education-6).

One last point about the ORG CPS is that, starting in 1994, workers are first asked what is the earnings periodicity (hourly, weekly, biweekly, annual, etc.) that they prefer to use in reporting their earnings on their current job. But as before, all workers paid by the hour are asked for their hourly wage rate. Hourly rated workers are asked this question even if "hourly" is not their preferred periodicity in the first question. Workers not paid by the hour are then asked to report their earnings for the periodicity of their choice. An hourly wage rate can again be computed by dividing earnings by usual hours of work over the relevant period. In 1994, the CPS also introduced "variables hours" as a possible answer for usual hours of work. I impute hours of work for these workers using a procedure suggested by Anne Polivka of the BLS.

Appendix B

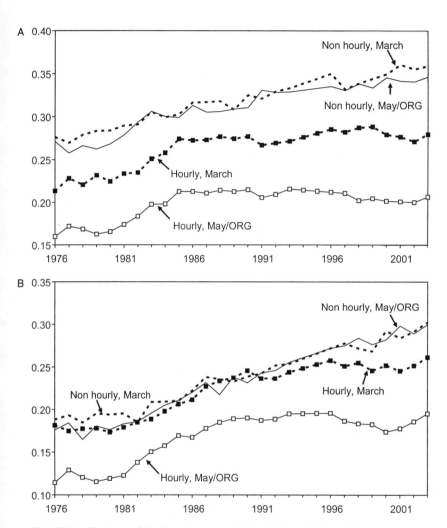

Fig. 1B.1   Variance of log hourly wages with both May-ORG and March wages (matched sample): *A,* Men; *B,* Women

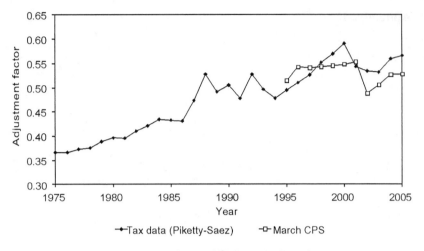

Fig. 1B.2   Topcoding adjustment factor (1/α) log annual earnings

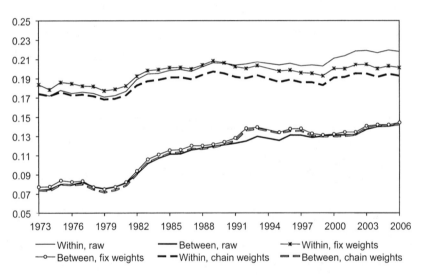

Fig. 1B.3   Comparing chain-weighted and fix-weighted composition-adjusted variances, Men

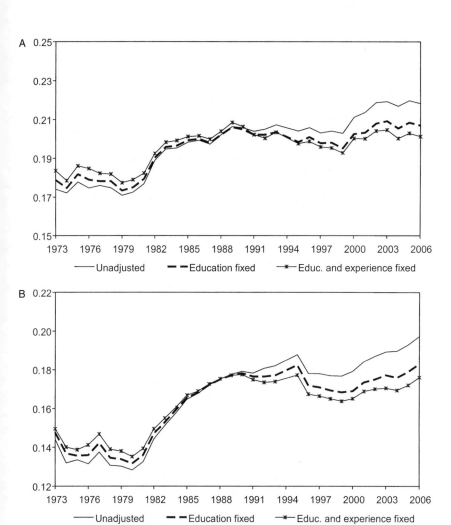

Fig. 1B.4   Role of education and experience in composition effects in the within-group variance: *A,* **Men;** *B,* **Women**

References

Abraham, K. G., J. R. Speltzer, and J. C. Steward. 1998. Divergent trends in alternative wage series. In *Labor statistics measurement issues,* ed. J. Haltiwanger, M. E. Manser, and R. Topel, 293–324. Studies in Income and Wealth, vol. 60. Chicago: University of Chicago Press.

Acemoglu, D. 2002. Technical change, inequality, and the labor market. *Journal of Economic Literature* 40 (1): 7–72.

Autor, D. H., L. F. Katz, and M. S. Kearney. 2005. Rising wage inequality: The role of composition and prices. NBER Working Paper no. 11628. Cambridge, MA: National Bureau of Economic Research.

———. 2006. The polarization of the U.S. labor market. *American Economic Review: Papers and Proceedings* 96 (2): 189–94.

———. 2008. Trends in U.S. wage inequality: Re-assessing the revisionists. *Review of Economics and Statistics* 90 (2): 300–323.

Autor, D. H., L. F. Katz, and A. B. Krueger. 1998. Computing inequality: Have computers changed the labor market? *Quarterly Journal of Economics* 113 (4): 1169–1213.

Autor, D. H., F. Levy, and R. J. Murnane. 2003. The skill content of recent technological change: An empirical investigation. *Quarterly Journal of Economics* 118 (4): 1279–1333.

Berman, E., J. Bound, and Z. Griliches. 1994. Changes in the demand for skilled labor within U.S. manufacturing: Evidence from the Annual Survey of Manufactures. *Quarterly Journal of Economics* 109 (2): 367–97.

Blau, F. D., and L. M. Kahn. 1996. Swimming upstream: Trends in the gender wage differential in the 1980s. *Journal of Labor Economics* 14 (4): 1–42.

Bound, J., and G. Johnson. 1992. Changes in the structure of wages in the 1980s: An evaluation of alternative explanations. *American Economic Review* 82 (3): 371–92.

Card, D., and J. DiNardo. 2002. Skill biased technological change and rising wage inequality: Some problems and puzzles. *Journal of Labor Economics* 20 (4): 733–83.

DiNardo, J., N. M. Fortin, and T. Lemieux. 1996. Labor market institutions and the distribution of wages, 1973–1992: A semiparametric approach. *Econometrica* 64 (5): 1001–46.

Firpo, S., N. M. Fortin, and T. Lemieux. 2007. Decomposing wage distributions using influence function regressions. University of British Columbia. Mimeograph.

Goldin, C., and L. F. Katz. 2007. Long-run changes in the U.S. wage structure: Narrowing, widening, polarizing. *Brookings Papers on Economic Activity,* Issue no. 2: 135–65. Washington, DC: Brookings Institution.

Hamermesh, D. S. 2002. 12 million salaried workers are missing. *Industrial and Labor Relations Review* 55 (4): 649–66.

Hirsch, B. T., and E. Schumacher. 2004. Match bias in wage gap estimates due to earnings imputation. *Journal of Labor Economics* 22 (4): 689–722.

Juhn, C., K. M. Murphy, and B. Pierce. 1993. Wage inequality and the rise in returns to skill. *Journal of Political Economy* 101 (3): 410–42.

Katz, L. F., and D. H. Autor. 1999. Changes in the wage structure and earnings inequality. In *Handbook of labor economics.* Vol. 3A, ed. O. Ashenfelter and D. Card, 1463–1555. Amsterdam: Elsevier Science.

Katz, L. F., and K. M. Murphy. 1992. Changes in relative wages, 1963–1987: Supply and demand factors. *Quarterly Journal of Economics* 107 (1): 35–78.

Krueger, A. B. 1993. How computers have changed the wage structure: Evidence from microdata, 1984–1989. *Quarterly Journal of Economics* 108 (1): 33–60.

Lee, D. S. 1999. Wage inequality in the United States during the 1980s: Rising dispersion or falling minimum wage. *Quarterly Journal of Economics* 114 (3): 977–1023.

Lemieux, T. 2002. Decomposing wage distributions: A unified approach. *Canadian Journal of Economics* 35 (4): 646–88.

———. 2006a. Increasing residual wage inequality: Composition effects, noisy data, or rising demand for skill? *American Economic Review* 96 (3): 461–98.

———. 2006b. Post-secondary education and increasing wage inequality. *American Economic Review: Papers and Proceedings* 96 (2): 195–99.

Lemieux, T., W. B. MacLeod, and D. Parent. 2007. Performance pay and wage inequality. *Quarterly Journal of Economics* 124 (1): 1–49.

Levy, F., and R. J. Murnane. 1992. U.S. earnings levels and earnings inequality: A review of recent trends and proposed explanations. *Journal of Economic Literature* 30 (3): 1333–81.

Lillard, L., J. P. Smith, and F. Welch. 1986. What do we really know about wages? The importance of nonreporting and census imputation. *Journal of Political Economy* 94 (3, Part 1): 489–506.

Piketty, T., and E. Saez. 2003. Income inequality in the United States, 1913–98. *Quarterly Journal of Economics* 118 (1): 1–39.

Welch, F. 1979. Effects of cohort size on earnings: The baby boom babies' financial bust. *Journal of Political Economy* 87 (5): S65–S98.

Comment   Lawrence F. Katz

Thomas Lemieux has produced a terrific chapter documenting the basic facts about changes in the U.S. hourly wage structure over the past three decades using the May-outgoing rotation group (ORG) and March Current Population Survey (CPS) data. He also does a very nice job of examining how conclusions about wage inequality trends are affected by different choices for handling crucial measurement issues related to the topcoding of high earnings, the treatment of imputed (allocated) earnings observations, adjustments for changes in the education and experience composition of the workforce, and whether to use direct point-in-time wage measures from the May-ORG CPS versus wage measures based on past year annual earnings, weeks worked, and usual hours worked from the March CPS.

Lemieux carefully documents large increases in overall hourly wage inequality (as measured by the variance or 90-10 log wage gap) for both men and women since 1980. He shows that overall wage inequality grew most rapidly in the 1980s when both upper-end (90-50) and lower-end (50-10) wage inequality increased. But lower-end wage inequality stopped increasing (and even decreased after adjusting for education-experience composition

Lawrence F. Katz is the Elisabeth Allison Professor of Economics at Harvard University, and a research associate of the National Bureau of Economic Research.

changes) after the late 1980s, while upper-end wage inequality continued rapidly rising from 1989 to 2006.

Educational wage differentials have increased rapidly and "convexified" since 1980 with particularly large increases in the returns to college and especially postcollege graduate education. Rising educational wage differentials are the largest single contributor to increases in U.S. wage inequality since 1980 and probably account for the majority of increased wage inequality. Furthermore, within-group wage inequality has increased much more for the college and postcollege educated than for less-educated workers. Thus, rising U.S. wage inequality is concentrated in the upper half of the wage distribution and substantially driven by rising educational wage differentials and increased within-group inequality for the college educated.

Lemieux shows these patterns of changes in the wage structure are not sensitive to reasonable measurement choices using the May-ORG CPS related to the handling of allocated earnings and to topcoding issues. The size and importance of within-group inequality increases since the late 1980s is somewhat sensitive to whether one adjusts the data for changes in education-experience composition and to whether one uses the May-ORG CPS or the March CPS. But that rising education returns are a major source of increased inequality and that most of the increase in wage inequality since the late 1980s is happening in the upper half of the distribution are robust findings to all sensible measurement decisions using May-ORG and March CPSs. Lemieux's main findings are quite consistent with other recent studies of U.S. wage inequality trends such as Autor, Katz, and Kearney (2006, 2008) and with the emphasis on the role of the race between education and technology in rising educational wage differentials of Goldin and Katz (2007, 2008).

I do have some minor qualms related to some of Lemieux's preferred measurement choices and interpretation of wage structure trends. The first relates to the appropriateness and interpretation of wage inequality measures that have been "adjusted" for changes in the education-experience composition of the workforce. I believe the composition adjustments for experience (or age structure) make a lot of sense as a reasonable demographic adjustment because age structure changes are pretty exogenous, and there are clear life-cycle patterns of wage dispersion related to job shopping, on-the-job training, and labor market learning factors that vary with age or experience.

In contrast, I am less comfortable with the adjustments for changes in the education composition of the workforce, especially given that education is a choice variable. There are two cases to consider. In the first case, education has a causal impact on wage dispersion just like we believe it has on earnings levels. Education could increase opportunities for jobs with more upside on wages as well a greater wage variability, education returns are likely to be quite heterogeneous, and some individuals may take their "returns" to education in nonpecuniary aspects of jobs (like becoming academics). If educational investments have a causal impact on wage dispersion among individuals (beyond their between-group impacts on educational wage differentials), then it is not clear why one wants to "adjust" away this source of changes in wage inequality and calls it an ignorable demographic compositional factor. The causal impact of educational investments on wage dispersion should be an interesting component of wage inequality to consider in its own right.

In the second extreme case, cross-section differences in wage variance by education groups (such as those documented by Lemieux in figure 1.5) are spurious and simply reflect differences in the heterogeneity of individuals in high- versus low-education groups. In this case, changes in educational composition have no "real" compositional effects on wage dispersion, and there is no need to adjust for education composition in wage inequality measures. Thus, in the first case of causal education impacts on wage dispersion, one might want to look at education composition adjustments but to consider them a factor of interest rather than a nuisance. And, in the second case of no causal education impacts on wage dispersion, it is inappropriate to adjust wage inequality for educational composition. The logic here is that some of the growth in within-group wage inequality that Lemieux adjusts away with his educational composition adjustments may reflect real growth in wage inequality that should be included in analytical studies rather than removed before thinking about alternative economic and institutional sources of wage structure changes.

Several other wage inequality measurement issues could use further analysis beyond what is contained in Lemieux's excellent study. The first is that the larger increase in within-group hourly wage inequality in the March CPS than in the May-ORG CPS since the late 1980s does remain a mystery. It is unclear why measurement error should be rising in the March CPS but not in the ORG CPS samples in recent years. The second is that hourly wage measures depend not just on the measurement of earnings but on measurement of hours worked for nonhourly workers in the May-ORG samples and for all workers in the March CPS. There appears to have been an increase in the share of high earning and highly educated workers who report very high usual weekly hours. It is unclear how to interpret this trend. Weekly wage inequality even among full-time workers has increased by more than hourly wage inequality in both the May-ORG and March CPS as measured hourly wages and weekly hours show an increased positive covariance. If the meaning of hours worked is becoming more ambiguous in many salaried (nonhourly) jobs, it may be preferable to focus on weekly earnings inequality (at least for full-time workers) to get at what is going on, especially in the upper-part of the distribution. The third is it would be nice to also have some comparisons of earnings inequality trends in the March and May-ORG CPSs with other data sources such as the Internal Revenue Service (IRS) tax data, social security earnings data, the Survey of Income and Program

Participation, the Panel Study of Income Dynamics (PSID), the National Longitudinal Survey (NLS) samples, and the American Community Surveys and decennial censuses.

In conclusion, Tom Lemieux has performed a valuable service in his comprehensive and careful work documenting the evolution of the U.S. hourly wage structure in CPS data and showing the sensitivity of one's conclusions to measurement issues and compositional adjustments. I echo Lemieux's conclusion that understanding rising educational wage differentials and increased within-group wage inequality among the highly educated are the key issues for understanding recent U.S. wage inequality trends. But one needs to look at quantities of workers by skill group and not just wages (prices) to draw conclusions about the role of market forces versus institutions.

The slowdown in the growth of U.S. skill supplies since 1980 from a slowing of the growth of the educational attainment of post-1950 U.S. birth cohorts combined with rapid secular growth in the demand for more-educated workers for skill-biased technological change goes a substantial distance to understanding the post-1980 rise in the college wage premium (Goldin and Katz 2007, 2008). And a "polarization" of labor demand favoring the top-end of the skill distribution and disadvantaging the middle of the distribution from computerization (and possibly from international offshoring as well) can help explain the recent "convexification" of returns to education and growing top-end wage inequality. The strong positive covariation of changes in prices (wage) and quantities employed along the whole wage distribution since the late 1980s strongly suggests demand shifts rather than purely institutional factors (declining unions and minimum wage) play a key role in rapidly rising upper-half wage inequality combined with stagnant or declining lower-half wage inequality (Autor, Katz, and Kearney 2008).

References

Autor, David H., Lawrence F. Katz, and Melissa S. Kearney. 2006. The polarization of the U.S. labor market. *American Economic Review* 96 (May): 189–94.
———. 2008. Trends in U.S. wage inequality: Revising the revisionists. *Review of Economics and Statistics* 90 (May), 300–323.
Goldin, Claudia, and Lawrence F. Katz. 2007. Long-run changes in the wage structure: Narrowing, widening, polarizing. *Brookings Papers on Economic Activity,* Issue no. 2: 135–65. Washington, DC: Brookings Institution.
———. 2008. *The race between education and technology.* Cambridge, MA: Harvard University Press.

2

Recent Trends in Compensation Inequality

Brooks Pierce

2.1 Introduction

While changing wage inequality in the United States is the subject of a large and vibrant literature, relatively little is known about changing inequality of compensation more broadly defined. Workers choose jobs partly on the basis of the job's wage-benefits mix, and higher-wage workers are likely to choose different mixes than lower-wage workers for a number of reasons. Furthermore, employers' provision of benefits such as health insurance and pensions, and the costs associated with those benefits, have changed substantially over the recent past. Such changes impact high- and low-wage workers differently, and one might expect compensation and wage inequality to differ in systematic and changing ways.

This chapter documents changing compensation costs for labor, and changing compensation inequality, using employer survey microdata on wages and benefit costs. These data are rather unique in that they capture employer cost information for wages as well as a broad array of benefits including health insurance, defined benefit pensions and defined contribution retirement savings plans, and paid leave. These data allow one to compare the wage distribution to the distribution of employer costs, as defined to include these forms of compensation. The data also allow one to isolate changes in particular benefits by position in the wage distribution. Did the run-up in health insurance costs over the past decade impact high- or low-

Brooks Pierce is a research economist in the Compensation Research and Program Development group at the Bureau of Labor Statistics.

Views expressed are my own and do not reflect the views or policies of the Bureau of Labor Statistics (BLS) or any other agency of the U.S. Department of Labor.

wage workers more? Have increased bonuses been isolated in the highest-wage jobs?

The employer survey data on fringe benefits and wage costs show changing wage inequality broadly consistent with tabulations from household survey data sources (Autor, Katz, and Kierney 2008; Lemieux, chapter 1 in this volume). Wage inequality grew over the two-decade period from 1987 to 2007. Wage compression occurred in the bottom half of the wage distribution, especially over the 1987 to 1997 decade. Higher-end wages grew more than median or lower-end wages throughout these two decades.

The employer cost data also indicate that benefits' costs to employers rose more in high-wage than low-wage jobs. This differential growth was great enough so that inequality in compensation more broadly defined grew at least as much as did inequality in wages. In terms of particular fringe benefits, health insurance costs rose substantially, especially over the 1997 to 2007 period. Health insurance costs as a fraction of wages rose especially in jobs with wages near the median. Rising pension costs in the last decade added to compensation growth in above-median wage jobs. There is also some evidence that variable pay such as sales commissions and bonuses played a role in compensation growth in high-wage jobs.

I augment these data on employer-provided fringe benefits with data on another important job-related amenity, workplace safety. The substantial decline in the risk of workplace injuries over the recent past is underappreciated in the labor economics literature (Nestoriak and Ruser, chapter 11 in this volume). This secular trend toward lower risk is evident in the risk of both fatal and nonfatal injury. Although it is difficult to cost-out workplace safety as a fringe benefit, the data do allow one to compare changing job-related risks of injury or fatality in high- and low-wage sectors of the economy. The improvement in workplace safety was wide ranging in that it occurred for a wide variety of occupations and, therefore, presumably for workers throughout the wage spectrum.

2.2 The Employment Cost Index (ECI) Data

The data on fringe benefits costs used in this chapter are from the employer survey microdata used to produce the Employment Cost Index (ECI). The ECI is a quarterly index measuring changes over time in the cost of wages and various nonwage compensation costs. The ECI survey scope is the civilian workforce, excluding agricultural, federal government, self-employed, and private household workers. The ECI survey is an establishment-based survey, meaning that establishments rather than firms are selected for inclusion in the sample. Within a sampled establishment, one to eight jobs are selected, depending on establishment employment. The unit of observation in the microdata is, therefore, a "job," as determined primarily by the employer-assigned job title. Information is collected on the wages, other compensation costs, and work schedules of the individual incumbents in the sampled jobs. Various categories of nonwage compensation are collected, including health and life insurance, several forms of leave, pension and savings plans, bonuses, and legally required expenditures on Social Security, workers' compensation, and unemployment insurance. This data is converted to a cost per hour worked and averaged over the incumbents within a job. Data are collected quarterly; quarterly samples over the 1987 to 2007 period average about 30,000 job observations from 7,000 establishments.

Several caveats are in order. The cost data refer to employer costs, which will differ from employee valuations due to tax and other considerations (Famulari and Manser 1989). The data are subject to nontrivial measurement error. The survey attempts to collect data at the level of the job, but respondents may only be able to report data relevant for a broader group of workers than the job incumbents. For instance, a respondent might report an establishment-wide average for white collar workers' health insurance premiums, or an establishment average employer contribution rate to a defined contribution plan. Also, the data miss variation in wages and benefit costs across workers in the same job and establishment.[1] The data do not contain information on job incumbents, such as gender or schooling levels. Much wage inequality research, by contrast, separately describes the experiences of men and women and investigates changing returns to schooling as a contributory factor to inequality changes. Nonetheless, these data are some of the best available for this particular application as they span a substantial time period, include cost measures for several important fringe benefits, and are derived from employer and administrative records.

Table 2.1 gives sample means for various periods. The table gives costs per hour worked, benefits' share of total compensation, and an incidence rate for some key benefit categories. Because cost data are averaged over job incumbents, the fraction of jobs with positive employer costs exceed true coverage rates that would be derived from individual data. The hourly wage rate is a straight-time hourly earnings figure adjusted to include overtime premium pay and shift differentials. Cost figures are deflated to 2007 dollars using the Consumer Price Index for All Urban Consumers (CPI-U). The data are hours-weighted for all statistics presented in this chapter. However, published tabulations by the Bureau of Labor Statistics (BLS) using these data do not weight by hours worked. Hours-weighting facilitates a comparison with most recent published studies on wage inequality using other data such as the Current Population Survey (CPS).

---

1. Certain job characteristics (full-time status, union status, and presence of piece rates or commissions) that correlate with pay and benefits provision also enter into the definition of the "job." For example, full-time and part-time workers in the same establishment and with the same job title are separately subject to being sampled. Hence, differences in wages and benefits attributable to full-time status are captured in the survey and are not averaged away in computing a job-level statistic.

Table 2.1   **Sample means**

	1987	1997	2007	Whole period average
Employer costs per hour ($)				
Wage	19.66	18.91	20.55	19.57
Compensation	26.66	26.12	29.15	27.11
Health insurance	1.31	1.57	2.30	1.77
Retirement and savings	1.20	1.05	1.25	1.08
Paid leave	2.01	1.84	2.16	1.97
Benefit's share in compensation				
Health insurance	.048	.058	.078	.063
Retirement and savings	.035	.030	.032	.030
Paid leave	.067	.061	.062	.063
Other nonlegally required	.012	.014	.013	.013
Legally required	.088	.094	.089	.092
Fraction of jobs reporting positive costs				
Health insurance	.851	.789	.789	.808
Retirement and savings	.663	.665	.700	.671
Paid leave	.930	.904	.905	.917

Notes: Cost figures are in CPI-U deflated 2007 dollars. "Retirement and savings" category includes defined benefit pensions and defined contribution plans. "Paid leave" includes vacations, holidays, sick leave, and other paid leave. "Other nonlegally required" benefits include nonproduction bonuses, severance pay, life insurance, sickness and accident insurance, and supplemental unemployment insurance. "Legally required" category includes Social Security, Medicare, Worker's Compensation, and state and federal unemployment insurance.

For the period as a whole, about 74 percent of ECI compensation takes the form of wages, and about 26 percent of compensation is in the form of benefits. The costliest single benefit is health insurance, with average expenditures of $1.77 per hour worked. Retirement and savings benefits costs are fairly substantial at $1.08 per hour worked. Retirement benefits include defined benefit pensions as well as defined contribution vehicles, such as 401(k) and deferred profit sharing plans. The ECI data reflect current pension costs, which in the case of defined benefit plans, can vary with pension asset returns and firms' chosen liability accounting methods. Therefore, these costs can only approximate the long-run actuarial obligation associated with a pension plan. Paid leave of various sorts accounts for costs of $1.97 an hour, on average. Leave is an aggregate of paid vacation time, holidays, sick leave, and an "other" category. Of these, the vacation and holidays components are the most important. Vacation and holiday benefits are each typically collected in time units at some accrual rate (four hours per biweekly pay period, eight days per year, etc.), converted to an hours accrued per hour worked basis and then valued at the job's hourly wage. Leave may simply represent one margin of labor supply, or leave plans may reflect firms' attempts to monitor and coordinate work time. I interpret leave to also represent some flexibility to the worker in scheduling hours or coordinating time for nonwork purposes.

Paid leave benefits are probably not captured as part of the calculated wage in household survey data such as the CPS, as those calculations include earnings while on leave but probably do not adjust the hours worked to reflect leave time. Leave is treated here as a "benefit" in an attempt to parallel CPS measures. The chapter later gives results for separate benefit components so that this treatment of leave does not obscure results for health insurance or retirement plans.

Table 2.1 also reports summary statistics on benefit shares in compensation and the fraction of the data with positive employer costs for the various benefit categories. About 9.2 percent of compensation costs come in the form of legally required compensation, the bulk of which is attributable to Social Security, Medicare, and Worker's Compensation. Leave and health insurance shares are each 6.3 percent. The retirement savings category accounts for 3 percent of hourly employer costs, and miscellaneous other nonlegally required benefits (mainly nonproduction bonuses) account for a little more than 1 percent of compensation, on average. Almost 92 percent of the sample has some positive leave costs, about 81 percent have some positive health insurance costs, and about 67 percent have some positive retirement vehicle costs.

Table 2.1 gives beginning- and end-of-period statistics as well. Real hourly wage rates in this sample grew 4.5 percent, and real hourly compensation grew about 8.7 percent over this period. These growth rates were larger in the second half of this period. Among the benefit categories, health insurance and retirement plan costs rose the most. Note that the whole-period average health insurance costs are similar to the 1997 level. Health insurance premiums have grown at a faster rate than benefit costs in general, except for a brief period in the mid- to late-1990s.[2] There was a slight decrease in the fraction of jobs reporting positive health insurance costs. Not apparent from table 2.1 is the shift toward defined contribution plans, which tend to have lower reported employer costs. That shift has been accompanied by an increase in the overall fraction of jobs reporting positive retirement plan costs.

2.3   Wage Inequality in the ECI and CPS

One useful exercise is to compare wage dispersion in the ECI to similar statistics derived from CPS data. It would be convenient if the two data sets showed substantially similar trends in dispersion. In that case, one could more confidently imagine measured ECI effects on inequality due to health insurance and so forth as applying in a straightforward manner to the better-documented CPS trends. However, the two data sets do give noticeably different results for some inequality growth measures. The largest difference

---

2. See the ECI indexes for health insurance, tabulated at www.bls.gov/ncs/ect/sp/echealth.pdf.

between the data sources appears to be the fact that measured wage growth in the last decade is larger in CPS than ECI data in the upper quintile of the wage distribution. This may reflect different samples or different wage measures, but, in any case, it suggests that readers should exercise proper caution in generalizing ECI trends to other data sources.

Although the ECI and CPS data are collected and processed in quite different ways, the CPS can be restricted to a sample with scope ostensibly similar to the ECI scope. As a practical matter, this mainly involves using CPS self-reports on employment status in the "class of worker" fields to eliminate federal government and self-employed workers. This is a crude proxy for the restrictions in the ECI survey scope that operate implicitly through the BLS sampling frame for establishment surveys, which is constructed mainly from required unemployment insurance (UI) reports.

To construct a CPS data sample, I take outgoing rotation group (CPS ORG) data on earnings for the period 1989 to 2007. The sample excludes agricultural industries, federal government and postal workers, the self-employed, and private household workers. Federal workers are identified separately from state and local government workers beginning in 1989. Hourly earnings are hourly wage rates for those reporting earnings on an hourly basis and are usual weekly earnings divided by usual hours worked per week for those reporting earnings with other than hourly periodicity.

The resulting CPS samples have lower wages than the ECI data; the 1989 to 2007 whole period average is $19.56 in the ECI versus $18.53 in the CPS. This is consistent with a view, for example, that the ECI sample panel data reflects the experience of somewhat longer-lived establishments. Both the CPS and ECI data exhibit slight decreases in real wages in 1989 to 1995, increases over the 1996 to 2002 period, and little change post-2002.

Possibly a more relevant consideration relates to how the ECI and CPS wage inequality trends compare. To facilitate comparison to more standard CPS data results, this chapter focuses primarily on wage percentiles although some statistics do refer to compensation percentiles. I define percentiles to include the 1 percent of the (weighted) data centered on the relevant percentile value. Statistics of interest are averaged within percentile so defined. This averaging abstracts from the within-percentile variation in benefit costs and other data elements. Smoothing away variation in benefit costs or benefit shares within percentile helps extract most of the information in the data in a nonparametric fashion.[3]

Figures 2.1 and 2.2 give wage growth by percentile for the CPS and ECI data for the 1989 to 1997 and 1997 to 2007 periods. During the 1989 to 1997

---

3. I compute whole-distribution dispersion measures such as the Gini coefficient on microdata rather than percentile-averaged data.

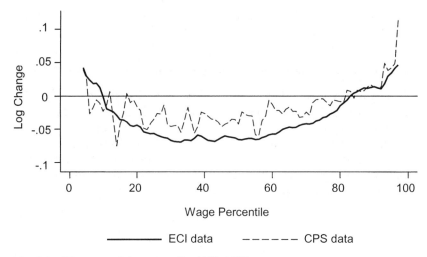

Fig. 2.1   Wage growth by percentile, 1989–1997

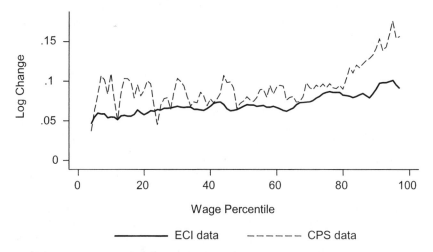

Fig. 2.2   Wage growth by percentile, 1997–2007

period, ECI wages compressed in the bottom of the wage distribution, while wage inequality grew in the top half of the wage distribution. These patterns are evident in this CPS sample and are shown elsewhere in greater detail, for example, see Lemieux (chapter 1 in this volume). During the last decade, wage growth has been more pronounced in the CPS than the ECI, especially at the top end of the wage distribution. The largest difference between the data sources is that wage growth in the upper decile is about 5 log points more in the CPS than ECI data.[4] But in coarse terms, the ECI and CPS tell similar stories about wage dispersion changes.

2.4   The Cross-Sectional Relationship between Benefits Costs and Wages

The cross-sectional relationships between benefits costs and wages are well-established (Woodbury 1983). Nevertheless, it is useful to document them here as a prelude to understanding benefit inequality growth.

Looking at benefit costs as a share of total compensation is a useful device to understand how the wage differential between two jobs compares to the analogous compensation differential. Define total compensation per hour, c, as wages per hour, w, plus various benefits per hour, b_j,

$$c = w + \sum_j b_j = w + \sum_j s_j c$$
$$= w + sc$$
$$= \frac{w}{1 - s},$$

where $s_j = b_j/c$ is benefit j's share in total compensation, and s is the sum of these shares over the benefit components indexed by j. Then, for example, the log compensation differential between jobs at the 90th percentile wage and the median wage can be written as

$$(1) \qquad \ln(c^{90}) - \ln(c^{50}) = \ln(w^{90}) - \ln(w^{50}) - [\ln(1 - s^{90}) - \ln(1 - s^{50})]$$
$$\approx \ln(w^{90}) - \ln(w^{50}) + \frac{(s^{90} - s^{50})}{1 - \bar{s}},$$

where superscripts refer to location in the wage distribution and where $\bar{s}$ is the average of the 90th percentile and median benefit shares. Note that the benefit cost share at any percentile can further be split into component (s_j) parts.

This accounting framework helps in describing contributions of separate benefits to inequality or inequality changes. It, in essence, treats benefit costs as a fractional add-on to wages and asks how much the add-on differs across the wage distribution and how the add-on difference changes through time.[5]

---

4. One possible cause for such differences lies in the fact that the ECI data tend to incorporate more averaging (across quarters and, especially, across individuals within a single sampled job). For example, the greater percentile-to-percentile variation in the CPS data evident in these figures, especially below the median, partially reflects a greater bunching of observations at round nominal dollar figures.

5. Relationships like equation (1) are more simply derived using a benefit add-on (b/w) rather than a cost share. Specifying equation (1) in terms of cost shares is attractive mainly in that data are often tabulated and analyzed in this form. Note also that equation (1) uses the same data ordering for both the compensation and wage differentials. Moving from wage to compensation dispersion requires an additional term that quantifies the effects of resorting when moving from a wage to a compensation distribution.

Figure 2.3 graphs the share of compensation costs taken in the form of benefits against the percentile of the compensation distribution, for the whole 1987 to 2007 period. Voluntary (not legally required) nonwage compensation is shown, along with all nonwage compensation. The benefit shares are relatively smooth increasing functions of the percentile. The immediate implication is that wage differentials tend to understate compensation differentials, especially in the lower half of the wage or compensation distribution. The difference between the two plotted series is attributable to legally required compensation costs. This difference is somewhat larger at lower percentiles, reflecting the fact that some of these costs have fixed cost attributes. For example, unemployment insurance costs are often a percentage of earnings up to some relatively low earnings cutoff.

Figure 2.4 graphs the benefit share in compensation for leave, pensions and savings plans, and health insurance against compensation percentile. The health insurance share is quite low at the 10th percentile, increases rapidly through about the 40th percentile, stays roughly constant in the middle of the distribution, and tails off noticeably above the 60th percentile. Health benefit costs per hour are rising over the entire range but not proportionately with total compensation beyond the 60th percentile. The share falls by about 2 percentage points on a base of about 8 percentage points from the 50th to 90th percentiles.

The pattern that holds for health insurance is somewhat different from those for leave and pensions. Although retirement compensation represents on average only about 2 to 3 percent of compensation, it can substantially

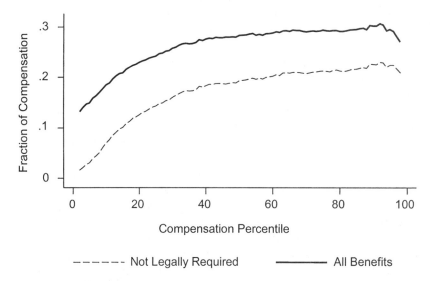

Fig. 2.3   Benefit share of compensation, 1987–2007 average, by compensation percentile

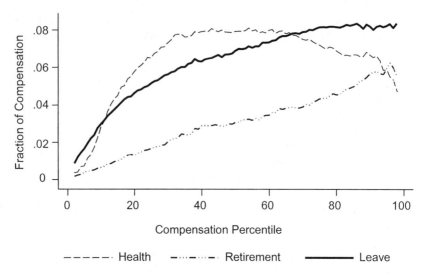

Fig. 2.4   Component benefit shares, 1987–2007 average, by compensation percentile

affect inequality calculations. Jobs in the bottom quartile of the compensation distribution have very little in the way of retirement benefits, while jobs in the top decile have over 5 percent of compensation in this form. Retirement compensation tends to increase compensation inequality in the upper as well as the lower tail of the distribution. The share of compensation taken as leave increases with compensation but somewhat more rapidly in the lower half of the distribution.

Table 2.2 brings together the results from these figures. The table gives wage and compensation dispersion across various points of the distribution and indicates each group of benefits' contribution to compensation inequality using the approximation in equation (1). For example, the first row indicates that the log wage differential between the 90th and 10th percentile of the wage distribution is 1.468. The log compensation differential between these two points (again, in the wage distribution) is 1.573. Therefore, about 0.105 log points in compensation dispersion can be attributed to various benefits. Table 2.2 breaks out benefits by type, including "other voluntary" and "legally required" benefits categories. The wage dispersion column and the first four benefits columns add up to the "voluntary dispersion" column; adding in the last benefit component ("legally required") gives the wage-sorted compensation dispersion. The final column of table 2.2 gives compensation dispersion based on the compensation-sorted distribution of the data. Reordering the data by compensation per hour rather than by the wage rate must increase overall compensation dispersion measures.

Consider the broadest range, the 90th to 10th differential. The leave and

Table 2.2   Benefits' contribution to compensation dispersion

		Benefit's contribution					Compensation dispersion		
Distributional range	Wage dispersion	Leave	Retirement	Health insurance	Other voluntary	Legally required	Voluntary compensation	Compensation (wage sort)	Compensation
90–10	1.468	.059	.056	.023	.016	−.050	1.623	1.573	1.601
90–50	.778	.011	.028	−.023	.008	−.021	.802	.794	.797
50–10	.690	.048	.028	.047	.008	−.028	.821	.793	.804

Notes: ECI quarterly data from the first quarter 1987 to the fourth quarter 2007 are pooled and equally weighted to obtain these statistics. The "distributional range" column indicates the percentile range over which comparisons are made. Statistics are based on averages over the five percentiles of the data centered on the relevant point; for example, the row "90–10" refers to differences between the 88th–92nd and the 8th–12th percentile ranges. In all columns except the last, the percentiles reference place in the wage distribution; for the last column, percentiles reference place in the compensation distribution. Wage and compensation dispersion columns are log wage and log compensation differentials.

pensions components each add .05 to .06 in log points to measured compensation dispersion. Health insurance adds less, about .023. At least over the whole distribution, leave and pension benefits are more important in determining compensation dispersion than are health insurance benefits. The "other voluntary" category adds about .016 log points. The sum of these nonlegally required benefits gives 0.154 in log points. Legally required compensation costs tend to equalize the compensation distribution substantially.

There are also interesting differences among benefits components across the various parts of the 90th to 10th percentile range. These differences are apparent in previously referenced figures: leave effects occur mostly in the bottom half of the wage distribution, pension effects operate throughout the distribution, and health insurance is important in adding to dispersion in the lower half of the distribution but is equalizing in the upper half.

2.5   Changing Wage and Compensation Inequality

Wage inequality grew over this period in the upper half of the distribution and shrank in the lower half of the distribution. Further, the results in table 2.1 show some benefit cost growth over this period. That growth did not occur uniformly across the wage spectrum. To see the effects on compensation inequality, figure 2.5 overlays plots of real compensation growth by compensation percentile with plots of real wage growth by wage percentile. The top panel gives the whole 1987 to 2007 period, while the bottom panels give two ten-year subperiods. Wage and compensation growth rates were

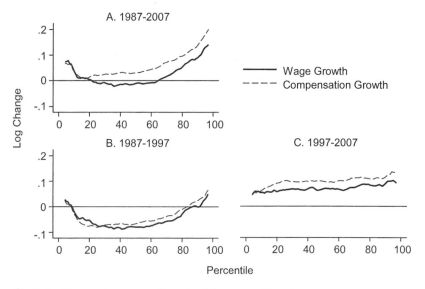

Fig. 2.5   Wage and compensation growth by percentile

highest above median values, meaning that wage and compensation inequality increased above the median. This was true for the period as a whole as well as for each subperiod taken separately. The greater growth rates below the median than at the median imply reduced inequality among medium- and low-wage jobs. In ECI data, that effect operated in the early but not the later subperiod. Compensation grew slightly faster than wages, on average, with the differences more noticeable in the middle and upper part of the respective distributions. This suggests that below-median compression is slightly more apparent for wages than for overall compensation.

Table 2.3 gives wage and compensation differentials across various parts of the distribution. Overall inequality, as measured by the standard deviation or Gini coefficient, increased slightly for both log wage and log compensation rates in the ECI data. This is true for each subperiod. Of course, the experience above and below median differs. The measured 90-50 differentials indicate increased inequality of .103 log points for wages and .110 log points for compensation over the whole period. The analogous 50-10 differential indicate compression of .049 for wages and .007 for compensation. Table 2.3 also shows statistics derived from the CPS ORG data for 1989 to 2007. Although the statistics generally agree with the ECI wage data, the CPS data show greater inequality growth over the 1997 to 2007 subperiod, especially above the median.

To sum up, in the 1987 to 1997 period, there was wage compression below

Table 2.3 **Wage and compensation dispersion**

		Percentile differentials			
	Standard deviation	90–10	90–50	50–10	Gini coefficient
I. Employment Cost Index data					
A. Log wage					
1987	.564	1.456	.723	.733	.317
1997	.578	1.474	.804	.671	.329
2007	.592	1.510	.828	.684	.340
Change 1987–2007	.029	.054	.103	−.049	.023
B. Log compensation					
1987	.597	1.563	.738	.825	.326
1997	.620	1.612	.829	.783	.346
2007	.639	1.666	.848	.818	.354
Change 1987–2007	.042	.103	.110	−.007	.028
II. Current Population Survey outgoing rotation group data					
A. Log wage					
1989	.566	1.452	.733	.719	.318
1997	.585	1.475	.780	.695	.331
2007	.608	1.530	.845	.685	.343
Change 1989–2007	.042	.078	.112	−.034	.035

Note: See text for sample details.

median and wage expansion above median, and compensation growth modestly exceeded wage growth above the median(s). In the 1997 to 2007 period, compensation growth was greater than wage growth everywhere but at low percentile values. As a result, it appears that compensation growth totalled over the twenty-year period was greater than wage growth and slightly more so in the upper half of the respective distributions.

2.6   Benefits' Contribution to Inequality Growth

As discussed previously, changing benefit cost shares give some sense for how compensation and wage growth differ. This section documents individual benefits' contributions to inequality growth by in essence describing how the benefit share-percentile relationships shown in figure 2.4 changed through time.

2.6.1   Health Insurance

Health insurance differs from the other main benefit components in that changing relative prices in the form of rising insurance premiums are behind many of the observed changes. Higher health insurance costs have likely induced firm and worker adjustments such as higher plan costs directly borne by the worker, greater firm reliance on part-time workers, and possibly adjustments to wage rates paid. The employer cost data as used here reflect such adjustments as well as the underlying relative price shifts.[6]

Figure 2.6 shows how the benefit share for health insurance has changed, by percentile in the wage distribution. In this figure, the benefit shares for 1987, 1997, and 2007 are smoothed (over wage percentile) and overlaid. Table 2.1 shows that health insurance costs rose at a faster rate than wages over this period. Figure 2.6 also shows greater share growth in the 1997 to 2007 subperiod. This makes some sense in light of health management organization (HMO)-related premium growth slowdown of the mid-1990s, which gave way to more usual rates of medical price inflation by the end of the 1990s.

Health insurance premium growth without other changes would cause proportionate increases (not a parallel shift) in the cost share, but figure 2.6 shows more-than-proportionate increases among jobs with wages in the middle half of the wage distribution. Jobs in the highest quartile experienced substantial benefit cost growth but also experienced rapid wage growth. That accounts for the relatively moderate health insurance share growth in high-wage jobs. Jobs in the lower quartile experienced greater wage growth than did jobs in, say, percentiles 30 to 60. Below-median wage jobs may be ones where worker and firm adjustments occur most. One suspects that part-time

---

6. For some evidence on the effects of increased health insurance premiums, see Baicker and Chandra (2006).

Fig. 2.6   Health insurance share by wage percentile

and full-time jobs are more substitutable from the employer's perspective for jobs with below-median wage rates. It is also possible that lower-wage workers are more price sensitive to health insurance premium growth and that changing health insurance participation plays a role for them as well.

An open question at this point is whether changing offer or take-up rates have affected employers' costs. Because the ECI unit of observation is a job within an establishment, one cannot readily calculate a health insurance coverage rate analogous to what one might calculate from household survey data. The closest construct involves calculating the fraction of the sample with positive employer costs for health plans. Such a calculated fraction is conceptually closer to an employer offer rate than a health insurance coverage rate. If employers continue to offer health plans but fewer workers within a job take up the offer, then the ECI data will tend to reflect that change not as a lower incidence rate but, instead, as lower employer costs for given incidence.

The March CPS is a good source for health insurance coverage rate data (see Levy [2006] and Farber and Levy [2000] for studies using various CPS supplements). The March CPS identifies those with health insurance coverage and determines whether that coverage is through the individual's employer (although we do not know if an uninsured worker's employer offered health insurance). The March CPS supplement data is retrospective in that it asks about earnings and hours worked in jobs in the prior year. The wage measure for the March sample is derived as annual wage and salary earnings, divided by the product of weeks worked and usual hours worked per week in the prior year. I impose several exclusions in the CPS data so that it more closely resembles the ECI sample. This primarily involves excluding self-employed workers and workers in the federal sector. I also restrict the CPS sample to full-time, year-round workers. I restrict attention to the 1992 to 2007 period, which is the time frame available at this writing from the Census Bureau's automated download Web site.

Table 2.4 shows the trends in CPS and ECI incidence rates, as well as the trend in ECI health insurance costs, measured here relative to compensation in the form of a share. Note that the compensation share fell substantially over the early 1994 to 2000 period. The ECI for health insurance benefits did, in fact, become negative (or effectively zero) for some isolated quarters over this time period. Over the later 2000 to 2007 period, the health insurance share in compensation rose by more than enough to offset the early period decline.

Figure 2.7 juxtaposes March CPS and ECI incidence measures by position in the wage distribution. Here wage position is summarized by quintiles; I use coarser wage distributions because March CPS data has fewer observations and, perhaps, different wage measures than the CPS ORG data referenced earlier. As expected, the ECI positive cost incidence measure exceeds

Table 2.4   Health insurance plan trends

| | ECI Data | | |
Year	Fraction positive costs	Share of compensation	March CPS coverage fraction, FTYR workers
1992	.820	.065	.707
1993	.816	.066	.710
1994	.808	.065	.701
1995	.796	.062	.682
1996	.797	.060	.688
1997	.786	.057	.681
1998	.784	.056	.683
1999	.785	.057	.689
2000	.787	.059	.682
2001	.803	.062	.674
2002	.804	.066	.668
2003	.800	.070	.658
2004	.793	.072	.653
2005	.793	.075	.647
2006	.795	.076	.640
2007	.788	.077	

Notes: March Current Population Survey (CPS) coverage rates refer to a sample of full-time, year-round (FTYR) workers (who usually work thirty-five or more hours per week, for fifty or more weeks in the year prior to the survey). The CPS sample is chosen to roughly correspond to the Employment Cost Index (ECI) scope and so excludes federal government and unincorporated self-employed workers, private household workers, and workers in agricultural industries.

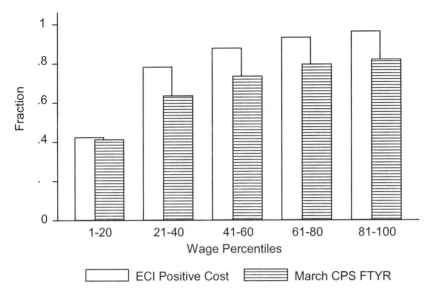

Fig. 2.7   Health insurance incidence by wage percentiles, 1992–2006 average

the CPS individual-based coverage rate. The difference between measures is fairly small in the bottom quintile but otherwise does not vary greatly with position in the wage distribution.

Figure 2.8 compares the CPS coverage rate over time at different points in the wage distribution. The coverage rate fell over time for each quintile group. The decrease was not particularly greater at lower than higher wage quintiles. Figure 2.9 shows the comparable figure using the ECI incidence measure. The ECI measure fell, but only modestly, over this period. One hypothesis is that the health insurance coverage rate declines found in the CPS data are more due to declining rates of take-up than to declining rates of employer offer. Of course, health insurance offers typically come conditional on worker contributions to costs, and employers may have changed the terms of offer over this period (Blostin and Pfuntner 1998). One implication is that the cost data in the ECI will reflect not only general health insurance premium inflation, but also any declining propensity for workers to enroll in employer-based health plans. However, the CPS data appears to imply that changing take-up rates were not a substantial cause for the differences by percentile in the health insurance share growth exhibited in figure 2.6 during the later 1997 to 2007 decade. The ECI coverage rates did fall, and disproportionately so, in lower wage jobs in the 1987 to 1992 period. Other CPS data (Farber and Levy (2000)) suggest falling coverage rates during that period as well, so it is likely that changing coverage or take-up patterns can explain some of the distributional patterns in the 1987 to 1997 period displayed in figure 2.6.

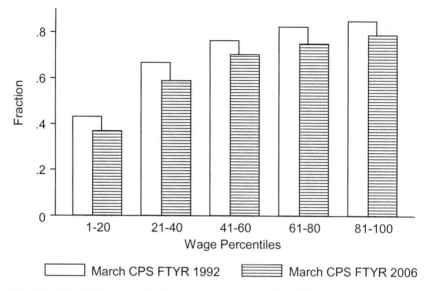

Fig. 2.8 Health insurance incidence by wage percentiles, 1992 and 2006

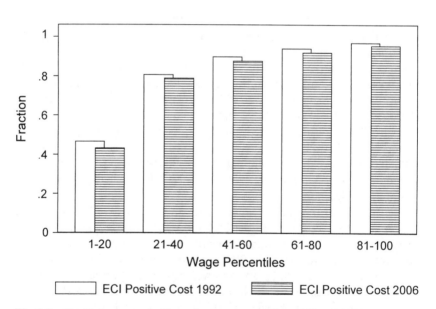

Fig. 2.9 Health insurance incidence by wage percentiles, 1992 and 2006

2.6.2   Retirement and Savings Plans

Figure 2.10 gives benefit cost share series for the retirement and savings category. For the whole period change, the series are noisy, and no large change is apparent. It is safe to say that the percentile range chosen for analysis matters. Over the 1997 to 2007 subperiod, there is some evidence that retirement benefits have contributed to increased dispersion in compensation in above-median wage jobs.

In describing the trends in retirement and savings plan costs, it is useful to distinguish between defined benefit (DB) and defined contribution (DC) plan costs. The ECI began separately publishing statistics for these categories in 1996. The DB and DC plans tend to look different in terms of the distributional accounting. Figure 2.11 shows the fraction of the sample, as averaged across the years 1996 to 2007, with positive employer costs at given wage percentile for each of the two categories. The DC plan costs tend to be more prevalent than the DB plan costs, especially at and below the 80th percentile wage. Figure 2.12 gives benefit shares for DB and DC plans separately. The DB plan costs exceed the DC plan costs, on average, over this period. This is entirely an above-median phenomenon.

The whole period averages in figures 2.11 and 2.12 obscure some important trend changes. Table 2.5 shows these trends. Of course, DC plans have become increasingly prevalent, while no new DB plans (other than cash balance plan conversions) have been started for (literally) years. But table 2.5 also shows some important changes in the employer costs associated with the two types of plans. The DC plan cost shares increased slightly

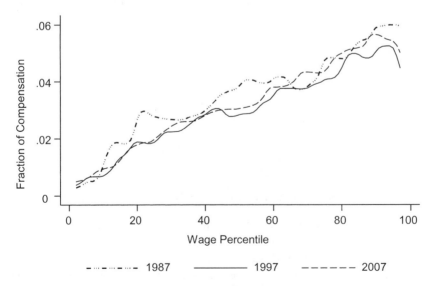

Fig. 2.10   Retirement share by wage percentile

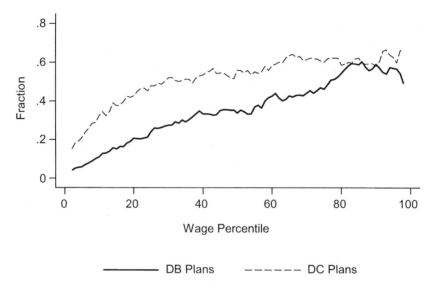

Fig. 2.11   Fraction with positive retirement plan costs, 1996–2007 average, by wage percentile

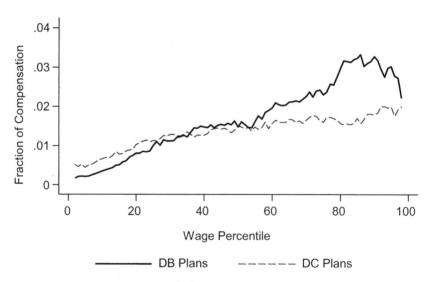

Fig. 2.12   Retirement plan benefit shares, 1996–2007 average, by wage percentile

over this period. However, the DB plan costs fell substantially from 1996 to 2002, then rose tremendously over the following short period of time. From 2002 to 2007, the DB plan costs per hour rose about 50 percent. The rapid change after 2002 is widespread in the ECI data and is not due to sample turnover. This rapid increase is likely a response to falling pension

Table 2.5   **Retirement and savings plan trends**

	Defined benefit plans		Defined contribution plans	
Year	Fraction positive costs	Share of compensation	Fraction positive costs	Share of compensation
1996	.413	.019	.436	.011
1997	.384	.018	.451	.012
1998	.370	.017	.465	.012
1999	.354	.016	.490	.013
2000	.337	.014	.508	.014
2001	.335	.014	.539	.015
2002	.336	.013	.541	.014
2003	.338	.014	.545	.014
2004	.338	.018	.544	.014
2005	.338	.019	.547	.014
2006	.326	.019	.559	.014
2007	.312	.018	.561	.014

Note: The Bureau of Labor Statistics began publishing separate statistics for defined benefit and defined contribution plans with 1996 data.

funding levels brought on by declines in the market value of stocks. Pension fund assets include company stock, and falling stock values eventually require further dedication of assets to maintain fund solvency. The observed time lag accords with accounting rules allowing averaging or smoothing responses to plan underfunding over multiple years.[7]

Because DB plans have a larger effect on above-median wage jobs, this surge in DB plan contributions had a noticeable impact on compensation growth above the median and on compensation dispersion measures. It is likely that DB compensation cost growth above the median understated true values of added actuarial pension obligations early in this period (when stock values were rising) and overstated true values in the more recent past. The DB plan cost growth, at least as measured in the ECI data, slowed in 2007 to 2008, but a recent large stock market downturn may reverse this trend. Whether DB plan costs are a near-term driver for compensation dispersion increases will likely depend on what happens to DB pension funding levels going forward.

2.6.3   Variable Pay: Nonproduction Bonuses and Incentive Pay

Lemieux, MacLeod, and Parent (2007) suggest that performance-pay jobs were important vehicles for changing wage inequality during the 1980s, especially at the top end of the male wage distribution. The ECI data do have

---

7. Pension Benefit Guarantee Corporation (PBGC) premium revenues rose substantially after 2002, reflecting deteriorating plan funding (PBGC 2006, available at www.pbgc .gov/docs/2006databook.pdf).

some information relevant to the general question of whether variable pay is an important conduit for wage growth.[8]

The ECI data distinguish between variable pay directly tied to individual worker product and other bonuses. Variable pay directly tied to worker product includes piece rates and sales commissions. Those payments are reported as part of worker earnings and are not broken out separately. However, in more recent ECI data, jobs subject to such production bonuses are identified separately. Those jobs are referred to here as "incentive-pay" jobs.

Bonuses not tied directly to individual worker product are reported separately from earnings. Examples of such bonuses might include end-of-year payments tied to revenues generated by a broader employee group or business line. Those payments are referred to here and in BLS tabulations using these microdata as "nonproduction bonuses." These payments are the main component of the "other voluntary" or "other nonlegally required" benefits categories shown in table 2.2.[9]

Over the 1994 to 2007 period, on average, about 5.8 percent of the jobs in the ECI are incentive-pay jobs. As is well-known, these jobs are often sales-related or managerial jobs, but incentive-pay jobs also appear in service and blue-collar occupations as well. Figure 2.13 gives the 1994 to 2007 average incentive-pay incidence fraction by wage percentile. The figure shows that these jobs are observed broadly throughout the wage distribution. Jobs with above-median wages are somewhat more likely to have an incentive-pay component. However, jobs with wages in the very upper tail are much more likely to have an incentive-pay component. For instance, over the 1994 to 2007 period, 14.6 percent of jobs in the upper 3.5 percent of wages have an incentive pay component.[10] Incentive-pay jobs in the very upper tail of the wage distribution are often in financial services industries.

Over the 1994 to 2007 period, the ECI samples show a slight decrease in the fraction of jobs with incentive-pay components. The 1994 figure is 6.2 percent versus a 5.2 percent figure for 2007. The profile with respect to the wage distribution does not appear to exhibit any pronounced trend. That is, incentive-pay jobs do not appear to have become increasingly concentrated in higher-wage jobs over this period.

About 38.4 percent of the ECI data over the 1987 to 2007 period have positive nonproduction bonuses. Figure 2.14 shows this fraction by wage percentile for the 1987 to 2007 pooled period. Note that the fraction with

8. I thank Anthony Barkume for helpful discussions on variable pay.

9. The ECI survey scope excludes workers who set their own pay, including owners and directors who might be paid substantially via nonproduction bonuses. The intent is to restrict the data to arms-length transactions. Tips are not part of any compensation in the ECI.

10. Incentive-pay jobs tend to pay more than observationally similar jobs without incentive-pay mechanisms (Barkume 2004). The wage premium might reflect induced effort, risk premiums, unobserved positive selection on ability, or other factors. Other BLS establishment survey data also show, at least in recent data, that incentive-pay jobs tend to have greater within-job wage dispersion. As discussed earlier, ECI data do not capture that variability.

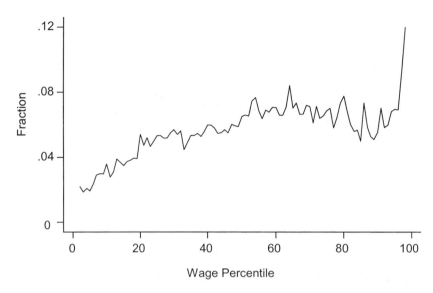

Fig. 2.13   Fraction with incentive pay, 1994–2007 average, by wage percentile

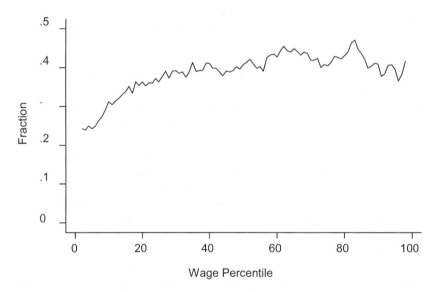

Fig. 2.14   Fraction with nonproduction bonus, 1987–2007 average, by wage percentile

positive nonproduction bonus payments is higher in above-than below-median wage jobs. However, there is not an apparent uptick in incidence at the highest wage levels.

Figure 2.15 shows the fraction of compensation attributable to nonproduction bonuses, conditional on receiving such a bonus, by wage percentile for the pooled 1987 to 2007 period. The figure shows the raw averages plotted

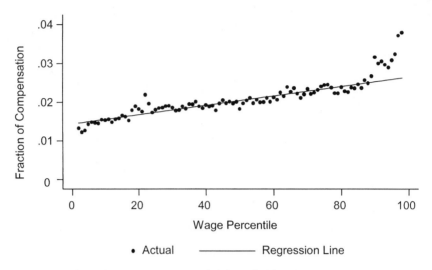

Fig. 2.15   **Bonus share conditional on receipt, 1987–2007 average, by wage percentile**

alongside a regression prediction based on the lower 90 percentiles. Clearly the upper decile has nonproduction bonus payments exceeding what one might expect based on patterns in the lower 9 deciles. Taken together, figures 2.14 and 2.15 indicate that nonproduction bonuses tend to increase dispersion in the cross section; this is why the statistics in the "other voluntary" column of table 2.2 are consistently positive. Figures 2.14 and 2.15 further indicate that dispersion may be more sensitive to nonproduction bonus payments in jobs in the upper wage decile than elsewhere in the distribution, a result not apparent from table 2.2.

Figure 2.16 shows the fraction of compensation attributable to nonproduction bonuses by wage percentile, in 1987, 1997, and 2007. Although the scale of change is small relative to the wage growth shown in figure 2.5, figure 2.16 shows that increased nonproduction bonuses in jobs in the upper half of the wage distribution did contribute to increased compensation dispersion over this period. This contribution is most evident in the upper decile of the wage distribution.

To sum up, very-high-wage jobs tend to have a higher incidence of sales commissions and piece rate pay. Because we do not know sales commissions and other variable-pay components separately from other earnings, we cannot tabulate them as a source of wage growth. It is possible that fluctuations in those forms of variable pay could disproportionately affect compensation dispersion at the very top of the ECI distribution. The ECI does separately identify nonproduction bonuses. Such bonuses are not direct commissions or piece rates but are better thought of as discretionary annual payments from a bonus pool. Bonuses have acted (in an accounting sense)

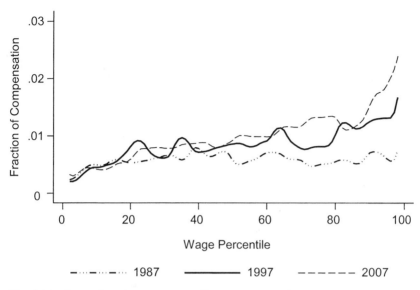

Fig. 2.16   Bonus share by wage percentile

to increase compensation dispersion above the median over the 1987 to 2007 period.

2.6.4   Point Estimates

Table 2.6 provides point estimates and standard errors for some of the trends described in the preceding. The first column gives the change in wage dispersion over the 1987 to 2007 period for the relevant percentile range. The next four columns give the contribution of benefit categories to compensation inequality, as operationalized by equation (1). The last column in the table gives changing dispersion in total compensation, where the distributional range continues to be defined based on points in the wage distribution. The point estimates for the benefit contribution columns are often small and not statistically different from zero. However, a case can be made that some health insurance cost changes contributed toward equalizing compensation differentials at or above the median wage, and contributed toward increased compensation differentials when comparing low-wage and median-wage jobs. Retirement and savings plan costs contributed only modestly to greater compensation dispersion in the upper half of the distribution. Leave costs growth tended to increase compensation dispersion over this period. For example, incorporating leave to obtain a better per-hour-worked wage measure would result in somewhat larger observed inequality growth in the ECI over this period.

As a general statement, it appears that including benefits costs in compensation measures would result in inequality growth at least as great as that

Table 2.6   Changing wage and compensation dispersion, 1987–2007

				Change in:		
			Benefit's contribution			
Distributional range	Wage dispersion	Leave	Retirement	Health insurance	All voluntary	Compensation dispersion (wage sort)
90–10	.054	.016	.003	.015	.041	.089
	(.004)	(.004)	(.004)	(.005)	(.010)	(.011)
90–50	.103	.018	.011	−.019	.015	.110
	(.003)	(.004)	(.005)	(.004)	(.008)	(.009)
50–10	−.049	−.003	−.008	.034	.026	−.021
	(.003)	(.004)	(.004)	(.005)	(.010)	(.011)

Notes: The "distributional range" column indicates the wage percentile range over which comparisons are made. Statistics are based on averages over the five percentiles of the data centered on the relevant point; for example, the row "90–10" refers to differences between the 88th–92nd and the 8th–12th percentile ranges. "Wage dispersion" and "compensation dispersion" columns show changes through time in the log wage and log compensation differentials between different points in the wage distribution. Standard errors are in parentheses.

observed in wage rates alone. The reader will, of course, have noted that this result depends on time period and the particular inequality measures chosen. That, at least, is one advantage to looking at the nonparametric graphs presented earlier.

2.7 Workplace Safety

The discussion thus far has centered on costing out various forms of compensation that are not part of earnings. Of course, some job attributes are implicit and not so amenable to costing out in this fashion. Hamermesh (1999a,b) relates increased wage inequality and changing incidence of other such job attributes. This section discusses results for one attribute, workplace safety.

The BLS conducts the Survey of Occupational Injuries and Illnesses (SOII), an annual survey of employers used to estimate the number of non-fatal work-related injuries. As part of that effort, the BLS collects information on injured workers and the characteristics of the injuries for the subset of injuries that require days away from work (see Nestoriak and Ruser, chapter 11 in this volume). In addition, the BLS conducts an annual census of fatal work-related injuries (the Census of Fatal Occupational Injuries, or CFOI program). While these data do not include direct wage measures, they do include factors that correlate with wages, such as age and gender of the affected worker, the occupation held by the worker, and the industry of the employer.

In order to create graphs analogous to those in the preceding for health or pension benefits, I construct injury and fatality rates and plot them against wages. Wage positionals are calculated using CPS ORG wage data, and cell means of on-the-job injury and fatality risk are assigned to individuals and their associated wage positional. Individual risk is proxied with cell average risk.

To be more specific, I construct injury and fatality rates for cells given by year, gender, age group, coarse industry group (goods producing versus other), and occupation. The denominator for the rate statistics are cell totals for hours worked as constructed using CPS Basic Monthly survey data. These cell-specific injury rates are merged to CPS ORG individual level data. Individual wage rates form the basis for a wage positional, and the injury rate estimate for the individual's gender-age-industry-occupation cell is, in effect, an imputed work-related injury risk. Because occupation is an important correlate of wages and injury risk, I construct cells so that much of the variation in the data comes from the occupational dimension (there are five age groups, two genders, two industries, and approximately forty occupational categories).[11] Because of changing occupational codes,

---

11. Hamermesh's (1999a) study on workplace safety used industry variation, for an earlier period.

the time frame is limited to 1994 to 2002 data. The SOII data at the national level are available for private-sector workers.

Figure 2.17 shows the cross-sectional relationship between wage position and imputed work-related injury risk. Unlike earlier graphs, better work environments display as lower values in the graph (risk is a negative amenity). The relative injury risk for a cell during any year is the particular cell's injury rate for that year, divided by the year's injury rate aggregated over cells. Because the risk measure is relative, the measure averages to 1 within year. Figure 2.17 shows data for the entire pooled period. The obvious point is that higher wage workers are in cells with lower work-related injury risk. This appears to be especially true at the highest wage positions. Because much of the constructed variation is along occupational lines, this is a statement mainly about the occupations that high-wage workers occupy.

There were quite large declines in injury rates over this period. The rate of injuries and illnesses requiring days away from work fell from 2.8 per 100 full-time equivalent (FTE) workers in 1994 to 1.6 per 100 FTE in 2002. This raises a question of what sorts of occupations, industries, and workers disproportionately experienced those declines. Figure 2.18 tries to get at that question by graphing the begin- and end-of-period cross-sectional relationships analogous to the whole-period average shown in figure 2.17. Here the relative risk measure incorporates changes through time. That is, a cell's injury risk is now measured not relative to the year's average injury rate, but relative to the whole 1994 to 2002 average. To help eliminate noise,

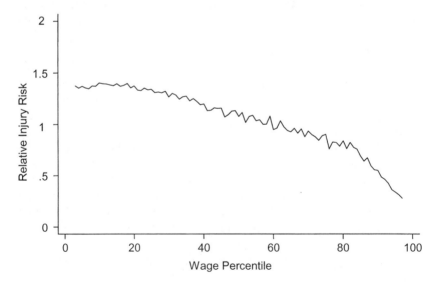

Fig. 2.17   Work-related injury risk, 1994–2002 average, by wage percentile

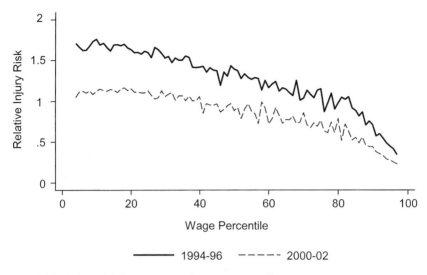

Fig. 2.18   Injury risk improvements by wage percentile

I average three years of data at the beginning and end of this time window, so the change is approximately a six-year change.

The risk measure shown here fell more for lower-wage workers. Because much of the variation here is along an occupational dimension, and because there is not much change over time in which cells are high-wage and which are low-wage, figure 2.18 implies the declining injury risk apparent in the total trend in injury rates is broad-based occupationally. In fact, injury rates are declining by similar proportions (but different percentage amounts) in almost all of the occupational categories used here. That is, the risk decline was proportionate to the initial probability of injury.

Figures 2.19 and 2.20 give analogous results for fatality rates. Fatalities are documented in the CFOI, an annual accounting of all work-related fatal injuries in the United States. To make results here comparable in scope to the earlier injury results, I restrict the analysis to private-sector employees. Fatality rates are constructed using employment and hours worked data from the CPS basic monthly files. Cells are the same as in the injury rate analysis, meaning that cells are defined by occupation, gender, age group, and coarse industry. As in the injury rate analysis, wage positionals are defined for CPS ORG data, and each individual is assigned a probability of fatality equal to the cell average fatality rate.

Figure 2.19 gives whole-period average relative risk. The plot actually slopes up in the lowest wage quintile and is roughly flat between, say, the 25th and 75th wage percentile. This is partly due to the very large gender differences in fatality propensity: women tend to have lower wages, and

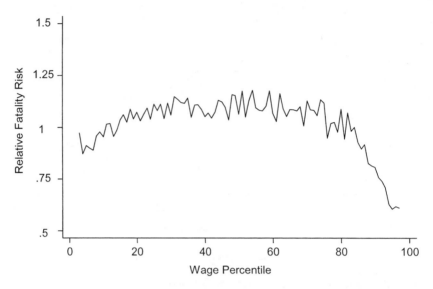

Fig. 2.19   Work-related fatality risk, 1994–2002 average, by wage percentile

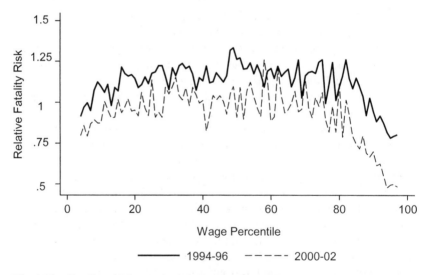

1994-96   ----- 2000-02

Fig. 2.20   Fatality risk improvements by wage percentile

women have a much lower propensity of suffering a work-related fatality.[12] Beyond the 75th percentile, the risk of fatality declines sharply as one moves

12. Were figure 2.19 restricted to male workers, the graph would show a downward sloping curve beyond approximately the 25th percentile (where percentile still refers to place in the pooled distribution, not to the gender-specific distribution). The upward sloping and flat portions of figure 2.19 are due to gender composition shifts. However, the results shown in figure 2.20 are not at all sensitive to pooling men and women.

up the wage distribution. The reader will note that the range of relative risk shown in figure 2.19 is smaller than that shown in figure 2.17 for fatalities. Note also that the plot for fatalities is noisier than that for injuries because fatalities are relatively rare events.

Figure 2.20 shows trend changes. As in figure 2.18, three-year averages are taken at the beginning and end of the period. For fatalities, there has been a fairly substantial reduction in risk over this period although the change is not of the same magnitude as the reduction in nonfatal injury risk. The reduction in fatality propensity was modestly larger in the upper quintile of the wage distribution. This is a somewhat different picture than the change in injury risk.

However, these are qualitative results, in the sense that risk is not priced-out, as the employer-provided benefits discussed earlier can be to some degree. Of course, this risk is notoriously difficult to price-out, and, in fact, these graphs serve as a reminder that compensating differentials for risk are often estimated to be negative. The most reasonable summary of these findings is that the safety improvements in figures 2.18 and 2.20 are widespread with respect to wage.

2.8   Conclusion

The intent of this chapter is to present facts on the level and distribution of fringe benefits, on the relationship between wages and fringe benefits, and on how these relationships have changed over the past two decades. It seems clear that health insurance premium increases acted to raise measured compensation more for workers in jobs in the broad middle of the wage distribution. There is some further evidence that other employer-provided benefits' costs rose most in those portions of the wage distribution experiencing the greatest wage growth. In total, inequality in compensation more broadly defined increased at least as much as wage inequality. It further appears that work-related safety risk improvement was broad-based and not concentrated in particular occupations over this period.

The changes documented here point to several interesting open questions. One set of questions relates to how wages and compensation adjust in response to the recessionary environment of 2008 to 2009. For example, there may be a recessionary impact on wages and bonuses in high-wage, incentive-pay jobs, which are frequently in sectors such as finance, which were particularly impacted by the recession. As another example, declining pension plan funding levels could eventually lead to greater employer pension contributions, especially for high-wage workers.

A second set of open questions relates to the labor market adjustments to more expensive health insurance. Because it has certain fixed cost attributes, rising premiums are especially likely to impact low- to moderate-wage workers with employer-provided health insurance coverage. To what extent will employers adjust by shifting employment to part-time or high-skill, long-hours jobs? Or pass on costs through required employee contributions or lowered wages?

A third open question is whether observed patterns in fringe benefit cost growth are partly attributable to income effects. If wages are rising faster for some workers than others, and if benefits or workplace amenities are income elastic, then wage inequality changes will cause predictable changes in benefits provisions. This is explicitly the view of Hammermesh (1999a,b) and Pierce (2001). Determining the extent of the income effects is challenging because conflating factors, including substitution effects, may differentially operate across the wage distribution. For example, it is not clear that technical innovations in workplace safety provision were neutral with respect to the wage. To the extent that fringe benefits are income elastic, benefits growth will tend to reinforce wage growth and broader-based compensation measures will give similar or slightly amplified patterns when calculating changing inequality.

Appendix

ECI Microdata

For background on the ECI, see also U.S. Department of Labor (1997).

Panel Aspects and Weighting

The ECI measures changing wages and compensation costs over a sample of fixed jobs. To do so, it follows panels of sampled establishments and jobs over multiple quarters. Sample replenishment takes the form of replacing a small fraction of establishments every quarter. The new subsample, except for subsequent attriters, remains in the ECI sample for approximately four and a half years. Sample weights are constructed at the time of initiation into the sample and reflect aggregate employment in the industry.

The panel aspect of the data raises some issues relevant to treating the data as annual cross sections. To correct for attrition, sample weights are adjusted quarter by quarter so that the cross section maintains a proper industry distribution. This reweighting does not correct for nonrandom attrition within industry or the fact that the distribution of sampled jobs is static within panel. This treatment is similar to what the BLS undertakes in producing its annual Employer Costs for Employee Compensation (ECEC) release. Also, cross sections are not independent at high frequencies. Finally, the data are hours-weighted. Published ECEC statistics are not hours-weighted.

Leave Costs and Scheduled Hours versus Hours Worked

The ECI calculates leave costs as the hourly wage times the ratio of leave hours to hours worked (which is scheduled hours minus leave hours). A perfectly logical treatment would be to add leave costs so defined to the wage rate to obtain a better estimate of wages per hour worked. However, it is unlikely that CPS wage rates net-out leave time in this manner, and I, therefore, do not, in hopes of making wage measures across the two data sets more comparable.

Within-Job Compensation Variation

One way in which ECI-based inequality statistics differ from those based on household survey data is that the ECI microdata unit of observation is the job rather than the individual. The inequality statistics presented in the chapter are, therefore, interpretable as what one would observe using individual microdata, except that individuals' wages and benefit costs are proxied by their job averages. That is, one misses within-job wage and benefit cost dispersion. From a firm's perspective, this may not be very relevant—the within-job dispersion in, say, health insurance take-up rates may reflect ex post outcomes rather than ex ante expected costs—but it would be relevant from the perspective of the individual workers.

For wage rates, evidence from other establishment survey data suggests that relatively little of the total log wage variation is within-job (Groshen 1991). More recent evidence from another establishment survey, the National Compensation Survey, indicates that within-job log wage variance is on the order of 3 to 4 percent of total log wage variance (calculations by author). The sampling design and data collection for these surveys are similar, suggesting that wage dispersion measures as presented in the paper are quite like what would obtain were individual wage rates observed.

I have little evidence on within-job differences in benefit costs. Within-job dispersion in legally required benefit costs should approximately equal the within-job wage dispersion because those costs tend to be direct functions of earnings. And obviously there is no within-job variance where costs are zero, which is a substantial portion of the data for some benefits. For observations with positive voluntary benefits costs, one can conceptually attribute within-job cost differences to differences in employer offers or in employees' take-up. One would expect within-job differences in employer benefit offers to be small because of nondiscrimination rules and the desire to be perceived as treating similar workers in a similar fashion. Note in this regard that ECI sampling treats full-time and part-time workers as occupying different jobs, even if they have the same job title (the same treatment holds for differences in union status and incentive-pay status). Therefore, any dispersion due to full-time or part-time differentials in health insurance (etc.) offers will be reflected in the ECI data as dispersion across jobs and so will be incorporated in the paper's inequality calculations. The data will, however, miss within-job differences in take-up or intensity of use for benefits, such as defined contribution plans and health insurance, which one suspects can be substantial.

CPS Data

Outgoing Rotation Group (ORG) Data

Outgoing panels from the CPS are asked supplemental questions on earnings, hours worked, and various aspects of their current job. These are fairly well-known data, and so I refer readers elsewhere for details (see, for example, Lemieux, chapter 1 in this volume). To construct data similar in scope to the ECI, I exclude agricultural industries, federal government and postal workers, the self-employed, and private household workers. The ECI survey scope explicitly excludes workers who set their own pay, so I exclude the self-employed, whether they are incorporated or unincorporated. Federal workers are identified separately from state and local government workers beginning in 1989.

Hourly earnings are hourly wage rates for those reporting earnings on an hourly basis and are usual weekly earnings divided by usual hours worked per week for those reporting earnings with other than hourly periodicity. Topcoded earnings are multiplied by 1.5 prior to calculating hourly wages, which is a typical treatment in the literature. Very-low-wage rate observations ($< \$1$ nominal) are discarded. For the remaining distribution, wages are bottom-coded at one-half the minimum wage, topcoded at $200 per hour, and deflated using the CPI-U. This is a similar treatment to the ECI microdata, except for the topcoding. In ECI data, very-high-wage rates arise from valid but large earnings responses; in CPS data, very-high wages often arise from suspiciously low reported hours. This topcoding treatment does not qualitatively alter the chapter's findings. Statistics are hours-weighted.

March CPS Data

Sections of this paper describing health insurance coverage use data from the March CPS supplements. March CPS data are retrospective, referring to individuals' prior year employment. The wage measure for the March sample is derived as annual wage and salary earnings, divided by the product of weeks worked and usual hours worked per week in the prior year. To construct data similar in scope to the ECI, I exclude agricultural industries, federal government and postal workers, the self-employed, and private household workers. I also restrict the CPS sample to full-time, year-round workers. At the time of this writing, March CPS data are available for years

1992 to 2007 via the Ferret download system at http://dataferrett.census.gov/index.html.

Injury and Fatality Data

For background on these data, see also U.S. Department of Labor (1997) and Nestoriak and Ruser (chapter 11 in this volume).

The SOII is a large annual establishment survey that collects information on number and rate of nonfatal work-related injuries and illnesses. For the subset of injuries that result in days away from work, the SOII collects information about the affected workers and their cases. These data include age and gender, the occupation held by the worker, and the industry of the employer; they do not include earnings or hours worked by individuals. For national data the SOII scope is private employers, excluding small farms.

The CFOI is an annual census of all work-related fatalities in the United States. It is based on compiled information from multiple sources, including death certificates, Occupational Safety and Health Administration (OSHA) reports, police records, and media reports. The CFOI and SOII data have similar data fields. The scope of the fatality census is much broader than the SOII survey as it includes for example government employees and the self-employed. The BLS time series tabulations of fatalities typically exclude workers who died in the attacks of September 11, and I follow that convention here. In this chapter, I also restrict the fatality data to roughly correspond to the scope of the SOII data, primarily by excluding self-employed and government workers.

References

Autor, David H., Lawrence F. Katz, and Melissa S. Kearney. 2008. Trends in U.S. wage inequality: Revising the revisionists. *Review of Economics and Statistics* 90 (2): 300–323.

Baicker, Katharine, and Amitabh Chandra. 2006. The labor market effects of rising health insurance premiums. *Journal of Labor Economics* 24 (3): 609–34.

Barkume, Anthony J. 2004. Using incentive pay and providing pay supplements in U.S. job markets. *Industrial Relations* 43 (3): 618–33.

Bloom, David E., and Richard B. Freeman. 1992. The fall in private pension coverage in the United States. *American Economic Review* 82 (2): 539–45.

Blostin, Allan P., and Jordan N. Pfuntner. 1998. Employee medical care contributions on the rise. *Compensation and Working Conditions* 3 (Spring):46–51.

Famulari, Melissa, and Marilyn E. Manser. 1989. Employer-provided benefits: Employer cost vs. employee value. *Monthly Labor Review* 112 (12): 24–32.

Farber, Henry S., and Helen Levy. 2000. Recent trends in employer-sponsored health insurance coverage: Are bad jobs getting worse? *Journal of Health Economics* 19 (January): 93–119.

Groshen, Erica. 1991. Sources of intra-industry wage dispersion: How much do employers matter? *Quarterly Journal of Economics* 106 (3): 869–84.

Hamermesh, Daniel S. 1999a. Changing inequality in markets for workplace amenities. *Quarterly Journal of Economics* 114:1085–1123.

———. 1999b. The timing of work time over time. *Economic Journal* 109:37–66.

Lemieux, Thomas, W. Bentley MacLeod, and Danial Parent. 2007. Performance pay and wage inequality. NBER Working Paper no. 13128. Cambridge, MA: National Bureau of Economic Research, May.

Levy, Helen. 2006. Health insurance and the wage gap. NBER Working Paper no. 11975. Cambridge, MA: National Bureau of Economic Research, January.

Pension Benefit Guarantee Corporation (PBGC). 2006. *Pension insurance data book, 2006.* Alexandria, VA: PBGC.

Pierce, Brooks. 2001. Compensation inequality. *Quarterly Journal of Economics* 116 (4): 1493–1525.

U.S. Department of Labor. 1997. *Handbook of labor statistics.* Bureau of Labor Statistics Bulletin no. 2490. Washington, DC: U.S. Department of Labor.

Woodbury, Stephen A. 1988. Substitution between wage and nonwage benefits. *American Economic Review* 73 (1): 166–82.

Comment   Daniel S. Hamermesh

In his massive and comprehensive effort, Brooks Pierce has demonstrated a large body of new facts about the development of the American labor market in the last quarter century. The ones that seem most important are the following:

1. Except for the very highest centiles, the Current Population Survey (CPS) (worker-based) evidence that most of the rise in wage inequality has occurred entirely in the upper half of the wage distribution is confirmed and strengthened by employer-based evidence from the Employment Cost Index (ECI).

2. The growth in compensation inequality has been even sharper than that of earnings inequality, providing very strong evidence for a high income elasticity of demand for nonwage compensation.

3. The well-documented huge decline in workplace injury rates that occurred through the mid-1990s continued steadily through the early 2000s and, most interestingly, was matched by nearly as sharp declines in workplace fatalities. These decreases are observed at all points of the wage distribution.

I have no difficulties at all with most of Pierce's calculations and, indeed, admire both their breadth and depth. I am somewhat bothered by the treat-

Daniel S. Hamermesh is the Sue Killam Professor in the Foundations of Economics at the University of Texas at Austin, professor of labor economics at Maastricht University in the Netherlands, a research fellow of the Institute for the Study of Labor (IZA), and a research associate of the National Bureau of Economic Research.

ment of paid hours reductions (e.g., vacation and paid sick leave) as benefits to be priced like monetary benefits. I would prefer to have seen them included in the denominator—they should be treated as hours reductions and the hourly (or forty-hour-week) earnings recalculated accordingly. While no individual benefit accounts for huge increases in compensation inequality (see Pierce's table 2.2), widening inequality of leave time is an important contributor in his calculations of rising inequality. It would loom still more important if it were treated as a reduction in hours.

Several of the figures in the chapter provide suggestions about wage and compensation inequality *within* the upper decile. This is useful, both as it indicates the sharp growth in inequality there and suggests substantial differences between estimates based on the CPS and the ECI. These suggestions are rare to nonexistent in the literature—economists have blindly followed the initial work on inequality (Juhn, Murphy, and Pierce 1993) and concentrated almost exclusively on 90-50, 50-10, and 90-50 differences, with these now enshrined in official Census calculations. Pierce's hints at the importance of changes within the upper decile of earnings deserve much more notice, both in this chapter and in the widespread professional and popular discussions about changing inequality. So, too, his evidence on the disagreement between results from the CPS and ECI in the upper tail of the wage distribution merits much more scholarly attention.

To examine just one aspect of this issue, I take the CPS-merged outgoing rotation groups (MORG) for 1994 and 2006 (essentially matching Pierce's later period) and examine wage inequality among nonfederal employees whose usual weekly hours of work were thirty-five or more. To account for weekly hours being higher among higher-wage workers (see Kuhn and Lozano 2008), I adjust the logarithm of weekly earnings by a cubic in weekly hours and calculate weekly earnings as if weekly hours were forty for all respondents. The crucial difference here compared to Pierce's table (and all those in the literature, including the frequently cited Autor, Katz, and Kearney [2008] study) is the examination of differentials based on earnings above the 90th percentile.

Table 2C.1 presents the changes between 1994 and 2006 in the average logarithm of these adjusted weekly earnings measures at various centiles of the earnings distribution, along with changes in differentials between certain centiles. The results for the bottom 90 percent of the earnings distribution duplicate Pierce's work. Because of topcoding of earnings in the CPS, we can only go up to the 98th percentile. Nonetheless, the calculations demonstrate that the biggest issue by far in earnings inequality in the past fifteen years seems to have been the tremendous growth in earnings differences between the top few and the comfortably well-off. The growth in earnings differences between the 98th and 90th percentiles in these data far exceeds that between the 90th and the 50th (or the 90th and the 10th) percentiles.

My quibbles with Brooks Pierce's work should not detract from the attention that it deserves and, I hope, will receive. His evidence that, by looking

Table 2C.1   Adjusted log weekly earnings, full-time employees, Current Population Survey-merged outgoing rotation groups, 1994, 2006

	Change in log points
Percentile	
5	0.379
10	0.375
25	0.376
50	0.365
75	0.442
90	0.583
95	0.807
98	1.047
Differentials	
90-10	0.208
90-50	0.218
50-10	−0.010
95-50	0.442
95-90	0.224
98-50	0.683
98-90	0.464
98-95	0.240
Percent topcoded	
1994	1.5
2006	1.7

only at earnings inequality, we understate the growth in inequality that has arisen from the concentration of gains in the upper half of the distribution of earnings, is crucial. The central point is that the economic gains of the past fifteen years have been even more tilted toward the better-off than we had previously thought.

References

Autor, David H., Lawrence F. Katz, and Melissa S. Kearney. 2008. Trends in U.S. wage inequality: Revising the revisionists. *Review of Economics and Statistics* 90 (2): 300–323.
Juhn, Chinhui, Kevin M. Murphy, and Brooks Pierce. 1993. Wage inequality and the rise in returns to skill. *Journal of Political Economy* 101 (3): 410–42.
Kuhn, Peter, and Fernando Lozano. 2008. The expanding workweek? Understanding trends in long work hours among U.S. men, 1979–2006. *Journal of Labor Economics* 26 (2): 311–43.

3

Are the New Jobs Good Jobs?

Katharine G. Abraham and James R. Spletzer

3.1 Introduction

Interest in whether the jobs generated in the U.S. economy are "good jobs" or "bad jobs" is a hardy perennial in both the academic and policy worlds. Jobs have multiple attributes—including wages, benefits, hours of work, working conditions, opportunities for advancement, and other characteristics—and changes along any of these dimensions could affect a job's perceived quality (see, for example, Farber and Levy 2000; Clark 1998, 2001, 2005; Kalleberg, Reskin, and Hudson 2000). Interest in job quality, however, most commonly has focused on wages, with jobs that pay higher wages considered to be better jobs. In addition to research that has looked directly at changes in the wage structure, an important strand of the literature on job quality has focused instead on the industry or occupation composition of net additions to employment. The basic strategy in these latter studies is to categorize jobs in different industries, occupations, or industry/occupation

Katharine G. Abraham is professor in the Joint Program in Survey Methodology, adjunct professor of economics, and faculty associate of the Maryland Population Research Center, University of Maryland; and a research associate of the National Bureau of Economic Research. James R. Spletzer is a senior research economist at the U.S. Bureau of Labor Statistics.

We are grateful to Matt Dey, Carrie Jones, Laurie Salmon, and George Stamas for help with the Occupational Employment Statistics (OES) data; Mary Bowler, Peter Horner, Randy Ilg, Tom Nardone, Anne Polivka, and Jay Stewart for help with the Current Population Survey (CPS) data; and Laura Kelter for help with the Current Employment Statistics (CES) data. Comments from Erica Groshen and participants at the Conference on Research in Income and Wealth (CRIW) Labor in the New Economy conference held November 16–17, 2007, and from participants in a seminar held at the Brookings Institution on April 1, 2008, have improved the paper. The views expressed in this paper are solely those of the authors and do not necessarily reflect the official positions or policies of the U.S. Bureau of Labor Statistics (BLS) or the views of other staff members.

employment cells according to the average wage paid and then to examine the growth in the number of jobs in higher- versus lower-wage cells. This focus on industry and occupation is appealing for two reasons. Industry and occupation account for a substantial fraction of the overall variation in earnings. Moreover, thinking about jobs in terms of their industry and occupation is a step toward being able to characterize the structural changes that underlie changes in the distribution of earnings.

Previous studies of growth in employment in industry/occupation cells at different positions in the wage distribution have been based on household data from the Current Population Survey (CPS). A concern about these studies is that we know the occupations reported by household survey respondents do not always agree with the occupations recorded by the employers of the same individuals (Mellow and Sider 1983; Mathiowetz 1992). The Occupational Employment Statistics (OES) survey is a very large employer survey designed to produce point-in-time estimates of occupational employment and wages at fine levels of industry, occupation, and geography. Published data from the CPS and the OES are not strictly comparable, but the differences in the occupational distribution of employment in the two surveys nonetheless are striking. In CPS data for 2004, 10.5 percent of employed persons hold management jobs; in contrast, in OES data for the same year, just 4.8 percent of jobs are management positions. In the CPS, 30.3 percent of employed persons hold either administrative or service jobs; in the OES, the share of jobs falling in those categories is 20 percent larger (36.6 percent).[1]

A major goal of the present study is to assess the feasibility of using the OES data to examine year-over-year changes in the composition of employment. The OES program documentation states clearly that the survey is not designed to support such comparisons. Challenges to using the OES data for time series analysis include the design of the survey sample to support estimates based on a rolling three-year sample rather than estimates based on data for a single year, changes in the classification of occupation and industry over time, and other changes in OES survey procedures. The chapter discusses how we have addressed each of these challenges.

Our analysis reexamines trends in the industry and occupational composition of employment over the period from 1996 through 2004, a period that includes the last several years of the economic boom of the 1990s, the 2001 recession, and the labor market's stagnation and eventual recovery following the 2001 recession. The OES data confirm the slow growth of jobs in the middle of the wage distribution found in earlier studies using CPS data but suggest that the CPS exaggerates the growth in high-wage employment while understating the growth in low-wage jobs. An important reason for

---

1. The CPS figures are reported in table 9 of Employment and Earnings and the OES figures in http://www.bls.gov/oes/2004/may/table1.pdf.

this difference is the faster growth of management employment in the CPS as compared to the OES.

We begin in section 3.2 with a brief review of the relevant literature. Section 3.3 describes the OES and CPS data used in our analysis, explaining in particular how we used the OES data to construct annual estimates of employment by industry and occupation. Empirical results are presented in section 3.4. Section 3.5 offers some concluding thoughts and outlines plans for extending the analysis.

3.2   Literature Review

The most striking fact about recent trends in the U.S. wage structure is the substantial growth in the inequality of earnings since about 1980 (see Lemieux, chapter 1 in this volume). Since the late 1980s, the continued growth in overall earnings inequality in the United States has been the result of a widening gap between the top and the middle of the earnings distribution together with a stable or shrinking gap between the middle and the bottom of the distribution. Autor, Katz, and Kearney (2006) explain these findings with a model in which information technology has increased the demand for the most highly skilled workers, but reduced the demand for middle-skill workers and had little effect on the demand for low-skill workers, a pattern they refer to as polarization in the demand for labor.

Empirical evidence for assessing this hypothesis—and changes in the quality of jobs more generally—has been generated by looking at rates of growth in the number of jobs at different points in the wage distribution. The early literature used information about the industries or the occupations in which net employment growth occurred to draw conclusions about job quality. Both industry and occupation have a strong association with wages but considered independently provide different perspectives on whether the economy has been adding bad jobs or good jobs. As noted by Levine and Labonte (2004) in their review of this literature, 50 percent of the 20 million payroll jobs added between 1993 and 1999 were in the services industry, and 17 percent were in retail trade. These are the two lowest paying of the nine major industries, and figures on job growth by industry have been cited in support of the view that "bad jobs" were being created over this period. Looking at CPS data on employment by occupation for the same seven years, however, management occupations accounted for 33 percent of net job growth and professional occupations for another 31 percent. These are the two highest paying of the eight major occupations, and figures on job growth by occupation have been cited as support for the view that "good jobs" were being created.

In the mid-1990s, the Bureau of Labor Statistics (BLS) began regular publication of employment and wage information from the CPS for industry by occupation cells. Using data cross-classified by ten industries and nine occupations, Ilg (1996) shows that, during the first half of the 1990s, employ-ment grew more rapidly in industry/occupation cells in the top and the bot-tom thirds of the earnings distribution than in cells in the middle third of the earnings distribution. In a later article, Ilg and Haugen (2000) show that nearly all of employment growth over the decade from 1989 to 1999 was concentrated among relatively high- and relatively low-paid workers, with the strongest job growth occurring in the highest earnings group and scant employment growth among workers with mid-level wages. Ilg and Haugen use the term "polarization" to describe this pattern of employment growth.

In the academic literature, also using data on CPS employment in industry/occupation cells, Acemoglu (1999) finds that over the decade from 1983 to 1993, employment in job categories that typically pay close to the median of the wage distribution were being replaced by employment in higher- and lower-paying jobs. Autor, Katz, and Kearney (2006) com-pare the 1980s and the 1990s and show sharp differences between these two decades, with the 1990s being characterized by more rapid growth of employment in occupations at the bottom and top of the wage distribution relative to the middle of the skill distribution. Analyzing household survey data for Britain, Goos and Manning (2007) find similar evidence of polar-ization in employment growth rates in occupation and industry/occupation cells. Goos, Manning, and Salomons (2009) extend these findings in their analysis of data for sixteen European countries over the 1993 to 2006 time period.

In the U.S. context, it is more difficult to use CPS data from 2000 onward to examine job growth by position in the earnings distribution. First, the CPS industry and occupation classification systems changed in 2003, com-plicating comparisons that span the break in series. Second, in the updated versions of the published tables used in earlier work by Ilg (1996) and Ilg and Haugen (2000), there are several very large industry/occupation cells that lie near the earnings boundaries that separate the thirds of the earnings distribution, and the assignment of cells to wage categories is sensitive to which year's wage distribution is used to make the assignment.

3.3   Data

In this chapter, we analyze changes in job structure using annual estimates of employment in industry/occupation cells based on the OES and the CPS. Because of changes in the industry and occupation classification structures used in these surveys, much of the work we have done for this chapter has been focused on the creation of consistent industry and occupation employ-ment time series. Working with the microdata records allows us to break large cells that lie near the boundary between wage categories into smaller pieces, thereby avoiding some of the problems encountered by previous analysts working with CPS data for the 2000s. Because the OES data have been less widely used and are, therefore, less familiar than the CPS data, we describe the OES survey in some detail as well as explain the steps taken to produce estimates that are suitable for our purposes.[2]

3.3.1   The OES Data

The OES survey is an annual mail survey conducted by the BLS in collaboration with its state partners. The survey collects information on occupational employment from approximately 400,000 establishments each year. Self-employed workers, unpaid family workers, agriculture workers, and household employees are excluded from the survey sample.

Since 1996, the OES program has collected information on occupational wages in addition to occupational employment. The first portion of a typical OES survey form is displayed in appendix A. Establishments selected for the OES are asked to report employment in each cell of a matrix in which the rows refer to different occupations and the columns to wage intervals. Generally, for firms with twenty or more employees, the survey forms contain between 50 and 225 occupations, depending on the industry of the establishment completing the form. Prior to 2000, employers receiving these forms were asked to list numerically significant or new occupations that could not be reported in a detailed occupation and, therefore, were reported in an "all other" residual category. This information was used in revising the survey forms for later years. Beginning in 2000, employers have been asked to provide detailed occupational information for workers who cannot be placed in one of the listed occupations.

Since 1999, employers with fewer than ten employees have received a shorter unstructured form that contains no list of likely occupation titles; rather, the employer is asked to provide a brief description of each occupation represented in the establishment's workforce. The information on these forms is coded into occupational categories by survey staff in the state agencies.[3] The OES program also collects data from some large firms electronically. Multiestablishment firms may request that their data be collected through the firm's corporate headquarters rather than directly from individual establishments. These reporters provide the OES program with electronic records containing job title and wage information for their employees. The OES staff then builds crosswalks for coding these firms' data into Standard Occupational Classification (SOC) occupations and OES wage intervals.

The OES program converted from its own occupation coding system to the SOC system in 1999 and from the Standard Industrial Classifica-

---

2. The OES confidential microdata are available to eligible researchers via procedures described on the BLS Web site (http://www.bls.gov/bls/blsresda.htm).

3. Prior to 1999, several states developed their own unstructured short forms that were used to collect data from some small employers, but this was not a part of the formal survey protocol. Beginning in 2004, states were given the discretion to send unstructured forms to establishments with up to forty-nine employees.

tion (SIC) system to the North American Industry Classification System (NAICS) in 2002. These conversions created numerous breaks in series at the detailed occupation and industry level. Of the 769 detailed occupations included in the SOC when it was introduced in 1999, fewer than half could be cross-walked directly to occupations that previously existed in the old OES classification structure (Bureau of Labor Statistics, 2001, 24 and 175). During the transition to NAICS at the Bureau of Labor Statistics, only about half of establishments could be assigned NAICS codes based on their SIC classification (Mikkelson, Morisi, and Stamas 2000). In this chapter, we have relied upon concordances developed by Matthew Dey of the Bureau of Labor Statistics to construct more aggregated series for nineteen occupations and thirteen industries, listed in table 3B.1, that can be defined with reasonable consistency across the breaks in series.[4] In preliminary analyses using the 247 cells defined using these more aggregated occupations and industries, we noticed a few that were very large, including five with employment in 1996 in excess of 3 million. We further disaggregated these five large cells by splitting the included industries or occupations, as detailed in table 3B.2. These further breakouts add twenty-four cells, for a total of 271 industry/occupation cells.

In working with the data, it became apparent that, over our study period, the OES survey process had changed in other, less well-documented ways. The most important of these changes appear to have been new editing rules and new training for staff that were introduced over several years as part of the process of implementing the SOC. Our efforts to quantify and adjust for the effects of these changes in coding practices are discussed at a later point in the paper.

The wage information provided by establishments in the OES survey is recorded in intervals corresponding to different ranges of hourly and annual rates of pay, as shown in appendix A. Occupational wage data collected by the BLS Office of Compensation and Working Conditions for the National Compensation Survey (NCS) are used to determine the mean hourly wage for each interval. The interval mean for the bottom interval may vary across states depending on the level of the state minimum wage.[5]

The OES survey sample is designed to support detailed point-in-time estimates of staffing patterns and wages developed from a sample pooled over three years rather than estimates based on data collected in a single year. Samples of approximately 1,200,000 establishments are selected for the OES survey on a three-year cycle. Each selected establishment is assigned to an annual or semiannual panel. Prior to 2002, the survey sample was divided into three annual panels, each consisting of approximately 400,000

---

4. Details of the concordances are available upon request.
5. Kasturirangan, Butani, and Zimmerman (2007) provide further details on how mean hourly wages are calculated in the OES program.

establishments; within each panel, establishments were assigned an October, November, or December reference date. In 2002, the survey transitioned to a design with six semiannual panels. Under this new design, each panel consists of approximately 200,000 establishments; panel samples are drawn for each May and November reference date in each of the three years covered by the survey sample.[6] Survey responses from three annual or six semiannual panels are combined to produce estimates that are benchmarked to employment totals for the most recent reference period. The May 2006 published estimates, for example, rest on data collected for November 2003, May 2004, November 2004, May 2005, November 2005, and May 2006. In our work, we use only the data pertaining to a particular year to produce the estimates for that year. From 2002 onward, because we wanted the data for later years to be as comparable as possible to those for the earlier years, we use only the data from the November panel. Government is excluded from all of our tabulations.

Approximately 80 percent of establishments sampled for the OES provide usable responses; on an employment-weighted basis, the survey response rate is approximately 75 percent. Nearest neighbor hot-deck procedures that take data from another similar establishment are used to impute missing employment information for establishments that do not respond. Missing wage distributions also are imputed using distributions for similar establishments.

The weights used to produce official OES estimates are constructed at the level of cells defined on the basis of industry, establishment size, and geography. As noted in the preceding, the sample units used to produce each set of estimates are divided into panels spread across three years of data collection. Each sampled establishment is assigned a current weight that reflects its probability of selection into the panel to which it belongs.[7] If every cell in a panel contained at least one establishment, the weighted sum of employment calculated for an industry using the current weights would be approximately equal to total national employment in the industry as of the panel reference date(s). There are, however, a very large number of OES sampling cells—as of 2004, the survey was stratified by 343 industries, seven establishment size classes and 686 metropolitan or balance-of-state geographic areas—and individual panels contain a significant number of empty cells. Because employment in the empty cells is not represented, using the current weights to estimate national employment in an industry based

---

6. Prior to 1996, the three-year sample was divided by industry, with industries accounting for about a third of total employment surveyed in each year. Beginning in 1996, the sample design was changed so that each panel represents all industries. This feature was carried over to the six-panel design introduced in 2002.

7. The current weights also incorporate adjustments for differences between the way a unit was sampled and the way it was reported (e.g., one establishment at a company sampled but data reported for several establishments together).

on the responses to any single panel yields an estimate that lies significantly below the industry's true employment level.

To correct this problem with using the OES current weights for estimation purposes, we adjusted the current weights to ensure that weighted national employment totals would match the national November Current Employment Statistics (CES) estimates for each industry in each year. The adjustment factor for industry j in year t is

$$(1) \qquad \text{ADJFACTOR1}_{jt} = \frac{E_{jt}^{\text{CES}}}{\sum_i \text{CURRWT}_{ijt}^{\text{OES}} E_{ijt}^{\text{OES}}},$$

where ADJFACTOR1 is the industry weight adjustment factor, E is employment, CURRWT is the current weight from the OES data file, i indexes individual establishments, j indexes detailed industries, and t indexes years. These weight adjustment factors were calculated at the most detailed industry level possible.[8]

A further concern with the OES data is that, although the true distribution of employment by size of establishment within each of our thirteen industries appears to have been very stable over the period we study, the distributions in the data vary considerably from year to year. Reasons for this include the uneven distribution of the largest (certainty) units across panels; the effects of a 1999 experiment carried out in selected states to determine the feasibility of collecting data from all certainty establishments every year; and the introduction of establishments with one to four employees, previously represented by establishments with five to nine employees, into the survey sample in 1998. To correct this problem, we introduce a second weight adjustment factor that sets the share of employment in each of the thirteen industries that is accounted for by each of nine establishment size classes equal to the average share in the industry for that size class across the OES benchmark data files for 1998, 2001, and 2004:[9]

$$(2) \qquad \text{ADJFACTOR2}_{kst} = \frac{\text{AVESHARE}_{ks}^{\text{BMK}}}{\text{SHARE}_{kst}^{\text{OES}}},$$

where ADJFACTOR2 is the size class weight adjustment factor, AVESHARE is the average share of employment accounted for by the designated size class in the benchmark data, SHARE is the current year share in the OES data, k indexes broad industry, s indexes establishment size class,

---

8. The SIC classification structure used from 1996 to 2001 contained 934 detailed industries. The weight adjustment factors we applied to the 1996 data were calculated at the four-digit level for 310 of these industries, at the three-digit level for 383 industries, at the two-digit level for 225 industries, and at the one-digit level for 16 industries. For 2004, among the 1,171 detailed NAICS industries, weight adjustment factors were calculated at the five-digit level for 424 industries, at the four-digit level for 520 industries, at the three-digit level for 172 industries, and at the two-digit level for 55 industries.

9. The size class distributions observed across these three years are very similar.

and t indexes year. Applying both the industry and the size class adjustment factors yields

$$(3) \qquad \text{FINALWT}_{ijkst} = \text{ADJFACTOR1}_{jt} \times \text{ADJFACTOR2}_{kst}$$
$$\times \text{CURRWT}^{\text{OES}}_{ijkst}.$$

These final weights are used to produce all of the OES estimates we report.

3.3.2   The CPS Data

The more familiar CPS is a monthly household survey that collects information about the labor force status of persons aged sixteen and older. The survey is conducted in person or by telephone. Approximately 60,000 households are interviewed each month, with a single respondent generally reporting for all members of the household. Households selected for the CPS sample are interviewed eight times, with each selected household present in the sample for four months (month in sample (MIS); MIS-1 through MIS-4), out for eight months, and then in for another four months (MIS-5 through MIS-8). The survey sample in each month represents the civilian noninstitutionalized population.

The CPS collects occupation and industry on the main job every month for all employed persons. Occupation and industry on the second job are collected only in MIS-4 and MIS-8, the so-called outgoing rotation groups. Data on earnings on the main job also are collected only for the outgoing rotation groups; earnings on jobs other than the main job are not collected.

In contrast to the OES data, which pertain to *jobs,* the unit of observation in the CPS is the *person.* We use the information on both the main job and any second job collected in the CPS outgoing rotation groups to construct a CPS-based measure of the number of *jobs* in different industry/occupation cells. This measure misses some jobs reported by those who hold three or more jobs, but there are a very small number of such positions.[10] For comparability with the OES data, we exclude unincorporated self-employment jobs, agriculture jobs, and jobs in private households. Government jobs have been dropped from both surveys.

Industry/occupation cells were defined in the CPS jobs data using the same nineteen occupations and thirteen industries as in the OES data. Since 2003, the CPS has employed the 2000 Census occupational classification system, essentially equivalent to the SOC, and the 2000 Census industry

10. In annual estimates for the period since 1994, between 5.2 percent and 6.2 percent of workers in the CPS report that they hold multiple jobs. Unpublished tabulations for 2006 show that just 8.0 percent of these multiple job holders had more than two jobs, almost exactly the same as the 7.8 percent share observed in tests conducted as part of the process of redesigning the CPS questionnaire in the early 1990s (Polivka and Rothgeb 1993). Taken together, these figures imply that less than 1/2 of 1 percent of all workers are multiple job holders holding three or more jobs, and the share holding three or more private-sector wage and salary jobs almost certainly is lower.

classification system, essentially equivalent to NAICS. Prior to 2003, the CPS used the 1990 Census occupation and industry classification systems.

In the transition from the 1990 to the 2000 Census occupation codes in 2003, a number of detailed 1990 Census occupations were split across 2000 Census occupations belonging to different broad occupational categories. In most cases, the numbers of jobs affected were small, but a large number of jobs belonging to three management occupations—Managers, medicine and health; Managers, food serving and lodging establishments; and Management, not elsewhere classified—were reassigned to nonmanagement occupational categories under the 2000 coding structure. Had we followed the usual procedure of bridging all employment in each detailed 1990 occupation to a particular detailed 2000 occupation, management employment would have fallen by 1.5 million on a base of 12.6 million between 2002 and 2003, at the time when the 2000 Census coding was introduced. To avoid this problem, we divided the employment reported in the three occupations across 2000 occupations on a probabilistic basis reflecting the percentage distributions observed in dual-coded CPS data (see www.bls.gov/cps/cpsoccind.htm).[11]

The 1990 Census industry classification system is essentially equivalent to the SIC, and we used the same mapping to our thirteen broader industries for the pre-2003 CPS data as was applied to the pre-2002 OES data. As in the OES, we broke the five largest industry/occupation cells into the smaller pieces shown in table 3B.2. In the CPS, 5 of the resulting 271 industry by occupation cells were empty in one or more years between 1996 and 2004. We collapsed these cells with other cells in the same industry. For consistency, the OES cells also were collapsed in the same way, leaving us with 266 industry/occupation cells for use in our analysis.[12]

For workers paid by the hour, we use the hourly wage on the main CPS job as the measure of hourly earnings. For other workers, hourly earnings are calculated as weekly earnings on the main job divided by usual hours per week on the main job. Hourly wages were averaged across main jobs in an industry/occupation cell and cells assigned a position in the distribution

11. Among Managers, medicine and health, 33.6 percent of pre-2003 jobs were reassigned to the broad category of "Office and administrative support"; 14.4 percent of Managers, food serving and lodging establishments were assigned to the broad category of "All other services"; and among Management, not elsewhere classified (n.e.c.), 11.0 percent were assigned to "Office and administrative support," and 6.6 percent were assigned to "Sales and related." In each case, the employees reassigned to nonmanagement occupations were selected randomly from among a pool of twice the needed size consisting of those in the donor occupation who had the lowest reported hourly wages. In an earlier version of this chapter, we performed a similar adjustment based on data from a sample of approximately 100,000 wage and salary workers who completed the 1990 Census long form and whose occupations were dual-coded using both the 1990 and the 2000 Census occupation systems (Scopp 2003). The effects on our data series were very similar.

12. The five empty cells were Health care practitioners and technical occupations in the Mining, Construction and Information industries and Food preparation and serving occupations in the Mining and Construction industries. Health care practitioners and technical occupations were collapsed into Other professional and technical occupations and Food preparation and serving occupations into All other services, in each case within the same industry.

of average wages by industry and occupation.[13] Wages are imputed for a quarter to a third of CPS respondents, using a hot-deck imputation process that includes major occupation and a set of demographic variables as classifier variables.

For convenience in carrying out our calculations, we make use of the Unicon CPS outgoing rotation group data file. The fact that the composite weights used in CPS estimation are not publicly available for 1996 and 1997 creates minor discrepancies between weighted counts based on the Unicon file and published estimates. More important, the weights for 2000, 2001, and 2002 on the Unicon file that we are using do not incorporate adjustments associated with benchmarking to the 2000 Census. We created adjustment factors for the Unicon weights in these three years based on the ratio of published to constructed employment in each of fifty-three age by race by sex cells.[14] Because the Census Bureau has introduced new population controls several times during our study period, even the published CPS employment counts are not consistent from one year to the next. The most notable inconsistency occurs between 1999 and 2000—estimates from 2000 forward are benchmarked to 2000 Census totals, but the 1999 estimates are not—but there are also smaller inconsistencies attributable to the introduction of new population controls in January 2003 and January 2004. Using a method developed by BLS staff (see DiNatale n.d.; Bureau of Labor Statistics 2008), we constructed a second set of weight adjustment factors that smooth out the spurious fluctuations in estimated employment that result from changes in the population controls. Our estimation weights equal the product of the two weight adjustment factors times the original CPS weights.

3.3.3   Comparability of the OES and CPS Series with Each Other and Over Time

As already noted, we have tried to make the samples from the OES and CPS microdata as similar as possible. The OES data refer to jobs rather than people, and we have used information on second jobs to create a CPS data set that is "jobs-based" rather than "person-based." To the extent possible, consistent industry and occupation definitions have been applied to both data sets. Because the OES does not include them, we have excluded the unincorporated self-employed, agriculture jobs, and private household jobs in the CPS data. In addition, government jobs are excluded from both samples.

One remaining difference is that the two surveys have different reference periods. The OES survey is collected with an October, November, or Decem-

---

13. Earnings are not recorded for the self-employed incorporated or for second jobs. In addition, we have not calculated a wage rate for persons who reported variable hours of work.

14. We are grateful to Peter Horner of the Bureau of Labor Statistics for guidance regarding the adjustments made to the original CPS weights to incorporate the 2000 Census benchmark and for providing us with the data needed to construct similar adjustment factors ourselves.

ber reference period between 1996 and 2001, and we use the panels with November reference periods from 2002 through 2004. The CPS outgoing rotation group microdata represent all months in the calendar year.

Another difference is that, consistent with the benchmarking of the OES data to CES control totals by industry, the two sets of estimates display somewhat different patterns of aggregate employment growth. As can be seen in figure 3.1, the cumulative growth in CPS employment lags that in OES employment through 2000, but the gap between the two series closes in 2001. These time series patterns broadly reproduce the well-known discrepancy between the behavior of the CES and CPS employment series during this time period (see Bowler and Morisi 2006). The cumulative growth in CPS employment was 9.8 percent between 1996 and 2004; over the same period, OES employment grew 9.3 percent.

As discussed in the preceding sections, the OES switched occupational classification systems in 1999 and industry classification systems in 2002; the CPS switched both occupational and industry classification systems in 2003. Breaks in series associated with these classification system changes are a potential concern. Occupation and industry employment series that reflect all of the adjustments we have made are displayed in appendix C and appendix D. We find it reassuring that the aggregate series seem to move smoothly rather than exhibiting obvious discontinuities at the points of change in the industry and occupation classification structures.

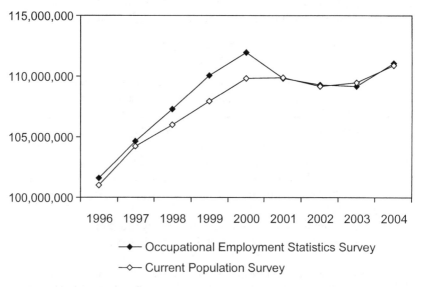

Fig. 3.1   Trend in total employment, Current Population Survey and Occupational Employment Statistics Survey, 1996–2004

Source: Authors' calculations using survey microdata.

3.4   Results

To characterize trends in job growth by position in the wage distribution, we categorized the jobs in each industry/occupation cell as high-wage, middle-wage, or low-wage. These assignments were made based on whether the cell falls in the top third, the middle third, or the bottom third of employment when all of the cells are sorted by mean hourly earnings. Cells that span the 1/3 and 2/3 points in the employment distributions were assigned to either the lower- or the higher-wage category on either side of the boundary to make the total base period employment assigned to each category as equal as possible. We then calculated growth in employment in the cells assigned to each of the three wage categories over the following eight years.

3.4.1   Basic Results

Our basic calculations assign each of the 266 industry/occupation cells defined for each survey an average wage calculated using 2004 data for the same survey. Using the ranking of cells implied by these average wages, the industry/occupation cells accounting for roughly the lowest, middle, and top thirds of 1996 employment were then identified.[15] The cumulative percent growth in employment over the 1996 to 2004 period for the three wage-level categories in the CPS and in the OES is shown in the top panel of table 3.1. Over the nine-year period, the CPS data show substantially more growth in high-paying industry/occupation cells (17.5 percent versus 9.7 percent cumulative growth), and the OES data show somewhat more growth in low-paying industry/occupation cells (12.6 percent versus 9.9 percent cumulative growth). Consistent with there having been a "hollowing out" of the job structure, both data sources show the lowest rate of job growth for the middle wage category.

Graphing the employment series we have constructed allows us to look at the year-to-year patterns of growth by wage level category. Figure 3.2 displays indexes of the number of jobs in each cell wage category over time (1996 = 100). In the CPS, high-wage jobs show more consistent growth than either middle- or low-wage jobs. In the OES, employment growth rates for all three wage categories were very similar between 1996 and 2001, but employment in the middle-wage category then fell sharply and did not regain its relative position.

We can also look at how the *share* of employment in each of the three categories has changed over time. Looking at the data in this way highlights *relative* growth and comparisons are not muddied by differences in overall employment growth between the two data sources. As can be seen

15. In the CPS data, there were 33.5 million jobs in the low-wage category, 34.3 million in the middle-wage category, and 33.2 million in the high-wage category in 1996. In the OES, the three categories included 34.0 million, 33.3 million, and 34.3 million jobs, respectively.

Table 3.1   Employment growth in industry/occupation cells by wage category, 1996–2004 (cumulative percent change)

	Industry/occupation cells		
Source of growth estimates	Low-wage	Middle-wage	High-wage
Base calculations: Cells assigned to categories based on 2004 wage rankings			
CPS	9.9	2.3	17.5
OES	12.6	5.6	9.7
Sensitivity analysis: Employment in borderline cells based on 2004 wage rankings split across wage categories			
CPS	9.9	2.4	17.2
OES	12.5	5.7	9.8
Sensitivity analysis: Wage rankings from different years used to assign CPS cells to wage categories			
1996	10.0	3.4	16.2
1997	9.7	3.9	15.9
1998	10.1	2.5	16.9
1999	9.7	2.5	17.3
2000	10.4	1.6	17.6
2001	9.7	3.9	15.9
2002	10.3	2.0	17.4
2003	9.5	2.2	17.9
2004	9.9	2.3	17.5
Sensitivity analysis: Wage rankings from different years used to assign OES cells to wage categories			
1996	13.5	3.9	10.4
1997	13.5	4.4	10.3
1998	13.4	5.0	9.5
1999	13.9	4.0	9.9
2000	12.5	5.3	10.3
2001	12.9	5.2	9.8
2002	12.1	6.6	9.2
2003	11.7	6.2	10.0
2004	12.6	5.6	9.7
2004 CPS wage rankings used to assign cells to wage categories, OES growth applied			
1996 CPS base employment	13.2	3.6	11.5
2004 OES wage rankings used to assign cells to wage categories, CPS growth applied			
1996 OES base employment	8.3	3.2	17.7

Note: CPS = Current Population Survey; OES = Occupational Employment Statistics survey.

in the top panel of table 3.2, in the CPS data, only the share of employment in high-wage industry/occupation cells has risen. In contrast, in the OES data, only low-wage industry/occupation cells have gained significant employment share. The observed share increases in both data sources have come at the expense of a decline in the share of employment in middle-wage industry/occupation cells. This pattern is even more apparent in figure 3.3,

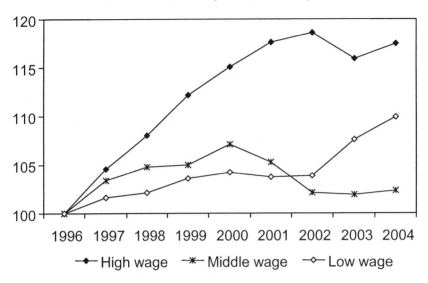

Current Population Survey

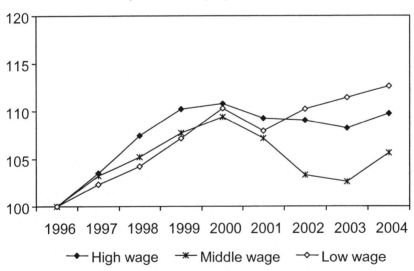

Occupational Employment Statistics Survey

Fig. 3.2   Trends in the number of jobs by wage-level category, Current Population Survey and Occupational Employment Statistics Survey, 1996–2004 (1996 = 100)
Source: Authors' calculations using survey microdata.

Table 3.2   **Change in employment shares in industry/occupation cells by wage category, 1996–2004 (cumulative percent point change)**

	Industry/occupation cells		
Source of share change estimates	Low-wage	Middle-wage	High-wage
Base calculations: Cells assigned to categories based on 2004 wage rankings			
CPS	0.03	–2.33	2.30
OES	0.99	–1.11	0.12
Sensitivity analysis: Employment in borderline cells based on 2004 wage rankings split across wage categories			
CPS	0.03	–2.26	2.23
OES	0.96	–1.10	0.14
Sensitivity analysis: Wage rankings from different years used to assign CPS cells to wage categories			
1996	0.06	–1.98	1.92
1997	–0.03	–1.82	1.85
1998	0.09	–2.23	2.14
1999	–0.05	–2.23	2.28
2000	0.18	–2.50	2.32
2001	–0.05	–1.82	1.87
2002	0.15	–2.42	2.27
2003	–0.10	–2.36	2.47
2004	0.03	–2.33	2.30
Sensitivity analysis: Wage rankings from different years used to assign OES cells to wage categories			
1996	1.26	–1.61	0.35
1997	1.25	–1.55	0.29
1998	1.23	–1.29	0.05
1999	1.42	–1.60	0.18
2000	0.97	–1.26	0.29
2001	1.09	–1.23	0.14
2002	0.89	–0.86	–0.03
2003	0.73	–0.93	0.20
2004	0.99	–1.11	0.12
2004 CPS wage rankings used to assign cells to wage categories, OES growth applied			
1996 CPS base employment	1.17	–1.80	0.63
2004 OES wage rankings used to assign cells to wage categories, CPS growth applied			
1996 OES base employment	–0.46	–1.97	2.43

Note: CPS = Current Population Survey; OES = Occupational Employment Statistics survey.

which graphs the cumulative change in the employment share of jobs in high-, middle-, and low-wage industry/occupation cells.

3.4.2   Sensitivity Analysis

In our basic results, industry/occupation cells that are on the borderline between wage categories are assigned to one or the other so as to make the base period level of employment across the three categories as equal as

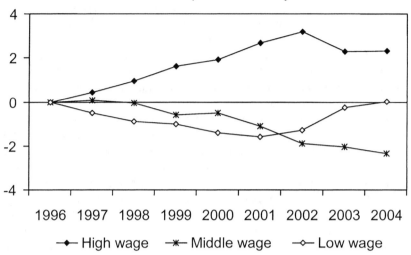

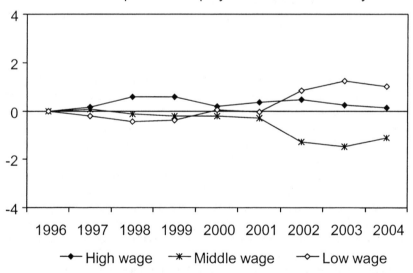

Fig. 3.3 Change in employment share by wage-level category, Current Population Survey and Occupational Employment Statistics Survey, 1996–2004 (cumulative change relative to 1996 share)

Source: Authors' calculations using survey microdata.

possible. An alternative would have been to split employment in these cells across categories to make employment in each of the three categories exactly equal and then carry out the same calculations assuming the same employment growth rate for both pieces of the split cell. As can be seen in the second panel of table 3.1 (for employment growth rates by wage category) and table 3.2 (for changes in employment shares by wage category), this alternative calculation produces results that are virtually identical to those obtained using our original approach.

Other analysts have found that the choice of years used to rank industry/occupation cells by wage level can affect the results obtained. The third panel of table 3.1 shows the rates of growth in high-, middle-, and low-wage CPS employment cells calculated using wage category assignments based on wage rankings for each of the years 1996 through 2004. In all cases, these rankings are applied to the 1996 employment data to form wage categories of approximately equal size. The fourth panel of table 3.1 shows the results of similar calculations using the OES data. The growth rates of employment by wage category in both the CPS and the OES are relatively insensitive to the choice of which year's wage ranking is used to make the assignment of industry/occupation employment cells to the high-, middle-, or low-wage categories. The changes in employment share by wage-level category using wage rankings from different years, shown in the third and fourth panels of table 3.2, are similarly robust to the choice of year used to determine the wage rankings.[16]

3.4.3   Accounting for the Differences between the CPS and OES Results

The CPS and OES data tell somewhat different stories about the pattern of job growth over the 1996 to 2004 period. While both show middle-wage employment growing most slowly and the share of jobs that are middle wage declining, CPS data show substantially faster growth in high-wage jobs, whereas the OES data show more rapid growth in low-wage jobs. We would like to know what accounts for these differences.

One explanation for these differences across the two data sources could be that they reflect differences in the ranking of industry/occupation job cells by wage level. In fact, however, the two surveys are in substantial agreement about relative wage rates across industry/occupation cells. The unweighted correlation between the rank order of the 266 OES industry/occupation cells, sorted by the 2004 OES wage, and the rank order of the 266 CPS industry/occupation cells, sorted by the 2004 CPS wage, is 0.8887.

To further explore the differences between the CPS and OES results, we ask hypothetically what the rate of growth in high-, middle-, and low-wage jobs would have been had we retained the original assignment of

16. The choice of year would have mattered more had we not broken the five industry/ occupation cells with employment in 1996 in excess of 3 million into smaller pieces.

industry/occupation cells to wage categories but assumed the growth in each detailed cell's employment from the other survey. The results of those hypothetical calculations are shown in the bottom panel of table 3.1. They make clear that the differences in growth rates by wage category between the two surveys reflect differences in the amount of job growth recorded within comparably defined industry/occupation cells, rather than differences in the ranking of cells by wage level. For example, had the industry/occupation cells in the CPS high-wage category experienced the same growth in employment as the corresponding cells in the OES, the growth in CPS high-wage employment would have been 11.5 percent rather than 17.5 percent, much closer to the 9.7 percent growth in high-wage employment in the OES. Similarly, had the industry/occupation cells in the OES high-wage category experienced the same growth in employment as the corresponding cells in the CPS, the growth in OES high-wage employment would have been 17.7 percent rather than 9.7 percent, very close to the 17.5 percent growth in high-wage employment in the CPS.

Changes in the shares of employment accounted for by high-, middle-, and low-wage jobs under the same hypothetical scenario are shown in the bottom panel of table 3.2. Here, too, it is clear that the differences between the two surveys reflect primarily differences in the amount of growth within industry/occupation cells rather than differences in the ranking of cells by wage level. For example, had employment in each of the CPS industry/occupation cells grown by the same amount as employment in the corresponding OES industry/occupation cell, the share of high-wage jobs in the CPS would have grown by just 0.63 percent rather than 2.30 percent between 1996 and 2004, much closer to the 0.12 percent in the OES data. Similarly, had employment in the OES industry/occupation cells grown by the same amount as employment in the corresponding CPS industry/occupation cells, the share of high-wage jobs in the OES would have grown by 2.43 percent rather than 0.12 percent, very close to the 2.30 percent in CPS data.[17]

3.4.4   Measuring the Number of Management Jobs

Earlier in the chapter, we referred to published data on employment by

17. We experimented with other counterfactuals for helping us to understand the differences between the CPS and OES results, but the counterfactual discussed in the text seems most informative. One alternative was to use the CPS category assignment with the OES data (or vice versa) and look at whether the same differences between the two surveys remain. Because management employment is so much higher in the CPS than in the OES, however, using the CPS (OES) category assignments with the OES (CPS) data produced a high-wage category that was much too small (much too large). A second alternative was to apply the CPS cell growth rates to the OES data, or vice versa, and look at whether the two surveys then tell a more similar story. A troubling feature of this counterfactual is that, because individual cells may be of rather different sizes in the two surveys, large proportional change in a small cell in one survey can have an exaggerated effect in the other survey. Both for the CPS and for the OES, the implied total 2004 employment level obtained using this method significantly exceeds the actual level.

occupation from the CPS and the OES, noting the substantially larger share of management employment in the CPS. These published data differ across the two surveys both in the unit of observation (people versus jobs) and in scope (most important the inclusion of all self-employed persons in the CPS). In table 3.3, we report the distribution of employment in each survey across the occupations that appear in published CPS data, but based on the numbers of wage and salary jobs in the private sector exclusive of agriculture and private households. Defined on a comparable basis, the share of employment in managerial occupations remains markedly higher in the CPS than in the OES, and the shares of employment in service occupations and office and administrative support occupations correspondingly lower.

As has been remarked by others (e.g., Baily and Lawrence 2004), the CPS and OES data also show substantially different *trends* in management employment. Between 1996 and 2004, the number of management jobs across all industries grew by 1.7 million in the CPS (an 18.6 percent increase) but fell by 2.6 million in the OES (a 35.3 percent decrease). The top panel of figure 3.4 shows the number of management jobs, and the bottom panel shows the share of employment accounted for by management jobs. In the CPS, both the number and share of management jobs drifted rather steadily upward through 2002 and then leveled off in 2003 and 2004. In the OES, management employment trended downward, falling especially sharply between 1999 and 2001. The different trends in management employment are the primary reason for the faster growth of employment in the high-wage category in the CPS as compared to the OES.

Our first thought was that business restructuring might explain the different trends in management employment in the two surveys. All else the same, changes in firms' job classification structures to eliminate layers of management would reduce the number of management jobs in the OES. But to the extent that individuals whose jobs were reclassified from, say, "manager" to "team leader" or "lead analyst" continue to describe themselves as managers, this would not be reflected in the CPS, leading to a widening discrepancy between the estimates of management employment in the two surveys. This explanation would lead us to expect the divergence in management employment in the two surveys to be concentrated in the larger establishments that typically have more formal job classification systems. In fact, however, the largest decline in management employment in the OES occurred in the very smallest establishments, suggesting that this cannot be the whole story. We also speculated that job restructuring might have reduced the number of management jobs in the OES while increasing the number of first-line supervisor jobs, without having a corresponding effect in the CPS. As shown in figure 3.5, however, estimated employment of first-line supervisors is higher in the CPS than in the OES and, more important for our purposes, that discrepancy has been very stable over the period covered by our study.

Table 3.3   Occupational distributions of 2004 employment calculated on a comparable basis using Current Population Survey (CPS) and Occupational Employment Statistics (OES) survey microdata

Occupational category	Number and percent of jobs from the CPS		Number and percent of jobs from the OES survey	
Management	11,080	10.0%	4,837	4.4%
Business and financial	4,484	4.0%	4,612	4.2%
Professional and related	18,996	17.1%	17,988	16.2%
Service	17,707	16.0%	21,044	18.9%
Sales and related	15,066	13.6%	13,762	12.4%
Office and administrative support	16,187	14.6%	19,550	17.6%
Construction and extraction	5,956	5.4%	5,357	4.8%
Installation and maintenance	4,035	3.6%	4,515	4.1%
Production	12,708	11.5%	14,795	13.3%
Transportation	4,683	4.2%	4,600	4.1%
Total	111,191	100.0%	111,064	100.0%

Notes: The figures for both surveys are in thousands and refer to jobs rather than people. They exclude the self-employed, agriculture jobs, private household jobs, and government jobs. Details of the calculations are provided in the text.

3.4.5   Changes in Coding Procedures in the OES

Although the two series would have diverged even without the sharp drop in management employment in the OES between 1999 and 2001, the decline over those two years was so marked that we were forced to wonder whether it could be a measurement artifact. In contrast to the classification structure it replaced, the SOC includes explicit principles intended to guide the assignment of jobs to occupations. In essence, this guidance states that only individuals who devote at least 80 percent of their time to management activities should be classified as managers. While there was no obvious break in the management employment series between 1998 and 1999 when the SOC was introduced, changes in coding practices associated with the implementation of the SOC that were phased in more gradually could have had an effect.

As part of the implementation of the SOC, the BLS introduced a series of data edits designed to identify questionable occupational assignments. One new set of edits flagged establishments in which employment was reported in a management occupation (e.g., financial manager) without the reporting of employment in any of the expected subordinate occupations (e.g., financial specialists or clerks) for further checking. These edit checks were applied in a limited fashion in 1999 and phased in more fully over the following years.[18]

18. Similar edit checks were introduced for other occupations that should not be expected to appear in isolation, but it is the management edits that are most relevant to our analysis.

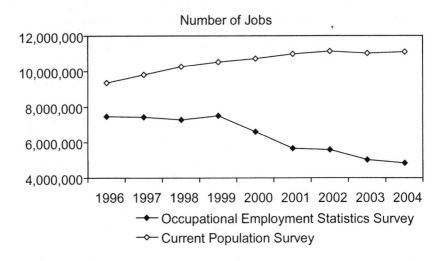

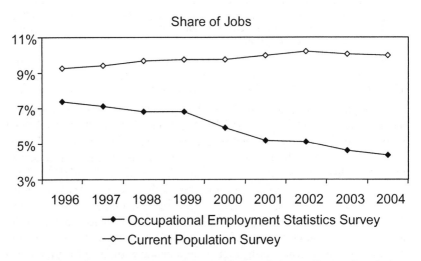

Fig. 3.4   Trend in management employment, levels and shares, Current Population Survey and Occupational Employment Statistics Survey, 1996–2004

Source: Authors' calculations using survey microdata.

To gauge how much the introduction of the dependent-occupation edits on their own might have affected the trend in management employment, we created the counterfactual management employment series shown in the top panel of figure 3.6. The counterfactual series shows how management employment would have trended had the dependent occupation edits been fully implemented in the OES data starting in 1999.[19] For this purpose,

19. Because the occupational classification structure changed in 1999, the dependent occupation edits cannot be applied to data for earlier years.

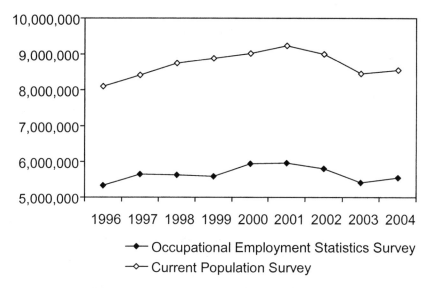

Fig. 3.5   Trend in employment of first-line supervisors, Current Population Survey and Occupational Employment Statistics Survey, 1996–2004
Source: Authors' calculations using survey microdata.

any management employment that is flagged by the dependent occupation test is treated as having been incorrectly classified and subtracted from the management total, though in actuality in some cases it might have been determined that the initial coding was correct. This adjustment has very little effect on the management employment series. In 1999, the actual series was 5.5 percent larger than the counterfactual series; in 2004, it was 2.3 percent larger, the smaller gap a result of the phasing in of the edits in the actual data. These numbers imply that the dependent occupation edit reduced measured management employment by a cumulative total of about 150,000 jobs from 1999 through 2004, a small fraction of the 2.6 million overall decline actually observed between 1996 and 2004.

A second set of edits also first introduced in 1999 was designed to flag establishments with an excessive number of managers. In establishments with fewer than ten employees, the editing system's default parameters flagged the data for establishments in which more than 50 percent of employees were classified as managers as suspect; the threshold percentages fell to 40 percent for establishments with eleven to twenty employees, 30 percent for establishments with twenty-one to thirty employees, and 20 percent for those with thirty or more employees.

To gauge the potential effects of these management share edits, we carried out an exercise similar to that performed for the dependent occupation edits. Specifically, we created a counterfactual management employment series, shown in the bottom panel of figure 3.6, by subtracting the weighted sum of management jobs in excess of the threshold number for sampled

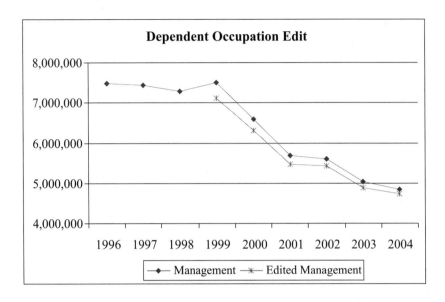

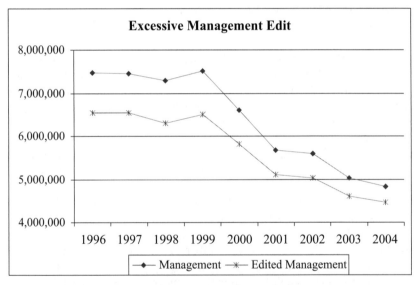

Fig. 3.6   Number of management jobs in the Occupational Employment Statistics survey, with and without corrections for changes in editing rules, 1996 to 2004
Source: Authors' calculations using survey microdata.

establishments in each year from 1996 through 2004. Both the original and the counterfactual management employment series decline sharply between 1999 and 2001. In 1998, the actual series was 15.6 percent larger than the counterfactual series; by 2004, the gap between the two series had fallen to 8.2 percent, reflecting the growing effects of the management share edits on the actual data. These numbers imply that the management share edits reduced management employment by about 330,000 jobs between 1998 and 2004, still leaving the large majority of the observed decline over our study period unexplained.

Beyond the explicit dependent occupation and management share edits just described, implementation of the SOC also included training designed to explain the new classification structure and coding principles to program staff. This training reinforced the message that jobs previously classified as management positions might be categorized differently under the SOC. Staff who attended SOC training courses in 1999 and later years were instructed that management jobs reported on establishment schedules that did not include an intervening layer of supervision generally should be recoded. It is possible, of course, that someone might legitimately be performing management duties without there being an intervening layer of supervision between them and their subordinates. New SOC training introduced in 2007 attempts to make this clear but occurred after the end of our study period.

The introduction of the unstructured survey form for small establishments in 1999 may have amplified the effects of the SOC training on the OES management employment series. Whereas employers typically are responsible for coding the jobs they report and only a fraction of these schedules can be reviewed, survey staff code all of the occupations reported on the unstructured forms. The "rule" that no job should be coded as a management position unless the schedule also includes a first-level supervisor position is easy to apply and seems to have been embraced as a guide to coding the unstructured schedules. To the extent that changes in coding practices are responsible for the decline in OES management employment, we would expect the decline to have been concentrated in the smallest establishments.

As shown in figure 3.7, the decline in both the number of managers and the share of employment accounted for by managers are indeed most pronounced in the smallest establishment size classes. Interestingly, to the extent that we are able to isolate growth in management employment by unit size in the March CPS Annual Demographic supplement, no similar decline is observed.[20] The overall decline in OES management employment largely reflects a growing share of establishments with no managers—exactly what one would have expected if the cause of the decline were application of the "rule" that jobs should not be coded as management jobs without an intervening layer of supervision.

Under the assumption that, absent the application of the new editing

---

20. The March CPS asks respondents about the size of the firm (not establishment) for which they worked on the longest job held in the prior year. In those data, management employment increased between 1996 and 2002 in firms with 100 or more employees and was flat in firms with one to nine, ten to forty-nine and fifty to ninety-nine employees. Because the March CPS data differ in several respects from the OES data, the comparison we are making between the two data sources should be considered no more than suggestive. We thank Jay Stewart for providing us with the March CPS microdata.

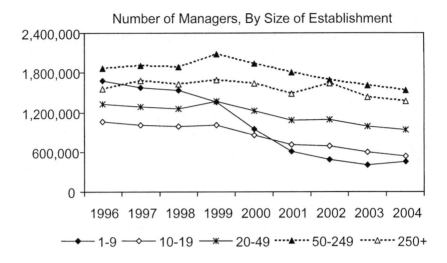

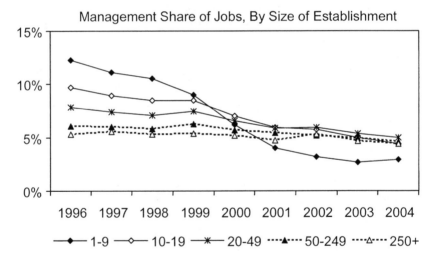

Fig. 3.7   Trend in management employment in the Occupational Employment Statistics Survey, levels and shares, by size of establishment, 1996–2004

Source: Authors' calculations using survey microdata.

rules and the other changes in coding practices, the share of establishments in each establishment size class reporting zero managers, one manager and two or more managers would have held steady between 1998 and 2001, we have devised a method for reversing the effects of these SOC-related changes. To illustrate, between 1998 and 1999, the share of establishments in the one to nine employee size class with no managers increased from 64.9 percent to 69.6 percent. We randomly select 4.7 percent of all establishments in the size category from among those with no managers and reassign one employee to the management category, selecting that employee from the highest occupational wage interval represented in the establishment's data. After making this adjustment, the data show an increase in the share of establishments in the size class with exactly one manager from 24.2 percent in 1998 to 25.3 percent in 1999. Accordingly, we randomly select 1.1 percent of all establishments in the one to nine employee size class from among those now recorded as having one manager and move all of the employees in the highest nonmanagement-occupation wage interval in each of those establishments into the management category. This adjustment ensures that the shares of establishments in the one to nine employee size class with no manager, one manager, and two or more managers remain constant between 1998 and 1999. Similar adjustments were made to the data for each of five employment size classes (1 to 9, 10 to 19, 20 to 49, 50 to 249, and 500 plus) for 1999, 2000, and 2001. In 2002 and later years, similar adjustments remove from the data the effects of changes in the number-of-managers distribution that occurred between 1998 and 2001 but permit changes that occur in later years to be registered in the data.[21]

The effects of the adjustments just described can be seen in figure 3.8, which plots the number of managers and the management share of employment by establishment size class in our adjusted data. The adjustment removes the sharp declines in management employment between 1999 and 2001 that were apparent in the unadjusted data, especially for the smallest size class. Figure 3.9 displays the aggregate trend in management employment, both in levels and as a share of total employment, in the CPS, the original OES, and the adjusted OES data. In the original OES data, management employment as a share of total employment fell from 6.8 percent in 1998 to 5.2 percent in 2001. Our adjustments do not affect the management share of employment in 1998 (6.8 percent) but raise the management share of employment in 2001 to 6.6 percent. To the extent that the effects of the changes in coding practices that followed the introduction of the SOC in the 1999 round of data collection were fully realized by the completion of the 2001 data collection round, our adjustments should largely have corrected for those effects.

3.4.6   Revised Estimates

Having reverse-engineered the OES data for 1999 through 2004 as best we can to restore the management jobs eliminated by the introduction of the new coding practices associated with the adoption of the SOC, we return to the question of what the data imply about recent changes in the composi-

---

21. The approach described in the text attempts to make the new OES data consistent with the old OES data. This is because it seemed more feasible to reassign nonmanagement jobs identified as having high wages to the management category (several to one) than to assign management jobs to nonmanagement categories (one to several).

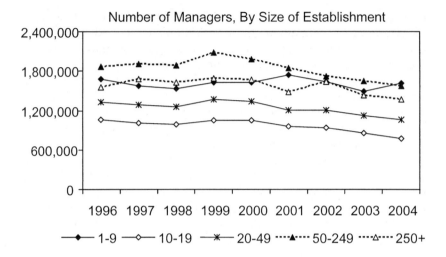

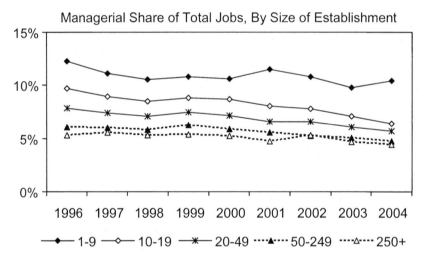

Fig. 3.8   Trend in management employment in the Occupational Employment Statistics Survey, levels and shares, by size of establishment, 1996–2004, after adjustment for comparability of estimates over time

Source: Authors' calculations using survey microdata.

tion of employment. The top panel of table 3.4 shows the percent growth in employment by wage-level category over the 1996 to 2004 period in the CPS, original OES, and adjusted OES data. The adjustments we have made close about a third of the gap in the rate of growth for high-wage jobs between the two data sources, but the CPS growth rate still exceeds the OES growth rate by a substantial margin. The original OES data show employment in

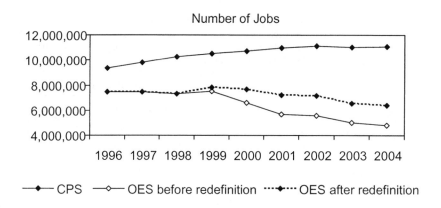

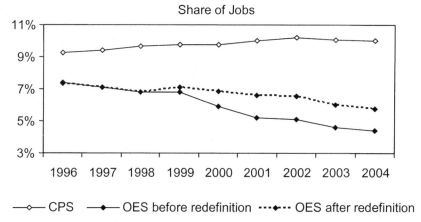

Fig. 3.9   Trend in managerial employment, levels and shares, Current Population Survey and Occupational Employment Statistics Survey, 1996–2004, after adjustment for comparability of OES estimates over time

Source: Authors' calculations using survey microdata.

low-wage jobs to be growing more rapidly than employment in high-wage jobs; in the adjusted data, these growth rates are fairly similar. It remains the case, however, that the OES shows more growth in the number of low-wage jobs than does the CPS. The year-by-year pattern of job growth by wage level category in the adjusted OES data can be seen in figure 3.10; for comparison purposes, the corresponding CPS figures are also displayed.

The bottom panel of table 3.4 shows the change in the employment shares of low-, middle-, and high-wage jobs in the CPS, original OES, and adjusted OES data. As shown previously, in the CPS data, employment share gains are concentrated in the high-wage category, whereas the gains in OES employment share occur predominantly among low-wage jobs. In the

Table 3.4   Employment growth and employment share changes in industry/occupation cells by wage category, Current Population Survey (CPS), Occupational Employment Statistics survey (OES), and adjusted OES data, 1996–2004 (cumulative percent change)

	Industry/occupation cells		
Estimate and source	Low-wage	Middle-wage	High-wage
Employment growth rates			
CPS	9.9	2.3	17.5
OES	12.6	5.6	9.7
Adjusted OES	11.6	4.0	12.3
Employment share changes			
CPS	0.03	−2.33	2.30
OES	0.99	−1.11	0.12
Adjusted OES	0.68	−1.60	0.92

adjusted OES data, the share gains at the top and the bottom of the wage distribution are more balanced, with the high-wage share gain slightly larger than the low-wage share gain. As before, however, that the CPS shows larger growth in the high-wage employment share than does the OES, and the reverse is true for growth in the low-wage employment share. Both surveys show declines in the share of middle-wage jobs. For completeness, figure 3.11 displays the year-by-year changes in employment share by wage level category for the CPS and adjusted OES data, leading to the same basic conclusions.

3.5   Conclusion

As will by this point be apparent, working with the OES data to analyze trends in employment by industry and occupation is more complex than we had anticipated. Changes in industry and occupational classification systems are a familiar problem and, while implementation can be difficult, there are familiar strategies for dealing with these problems. Survey changes that are phased in over time and whose effects are not well documented, such as the changes in occupational coding practices in the OES following the adoption of the SOC, are considerably more challenging to address. The OES data have great potential value for studying the evolution of the job structure. Indeed, the BLS occupational projections program already uses these data as a primary source of information about changes in occupational structure over time. Going forward, we would urge that the maintenance of continuity in coding practices and other aspects of survey operations be given a higher priority than has been the case in the past.

Substantively, the CPS data show job growth to be concentrated in the highest-wage jobs, whereas the OES data show substantial relative growth

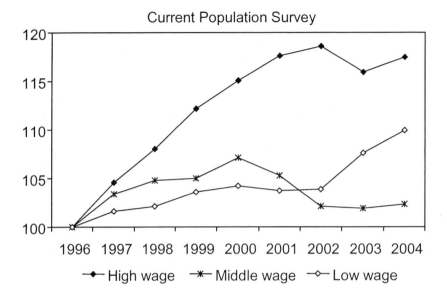

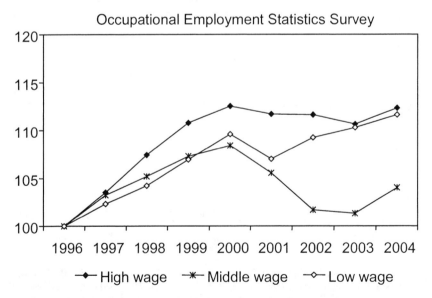

Fig. 3.10   Trends in the number of jobs by wage-level category, Current Population Survey and Occupational Employment Statistics Survey, 1996–2004, after adjustment for comparability of OES estimates over time (1996 = 100)

Source: Authors' calculations using survey microdata.

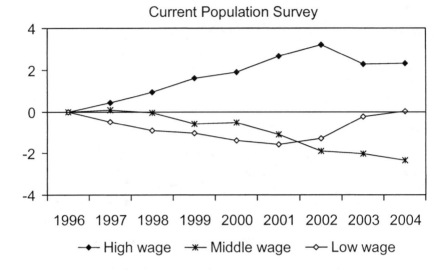

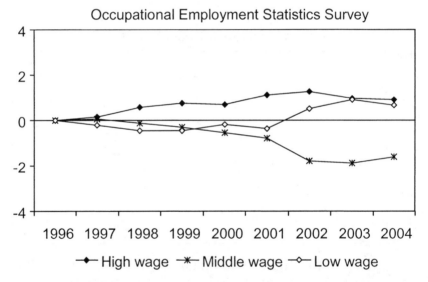

Fig. 3.11   Change in employment share by wage-level category, Current Population Survey and Occupational Employment Statistics Survey, 1996–2004, after adjustment for comparability of OES estimates over time (cumulative change relative to 1996 share)

Source: Authors' calculations using survey microdata.

in low-wage employment. Both in the CPS and in the OES, relative employment gains in jobs at the top or bottom of the wage scale have come at the expense of middle-wage jobs. The greater growth in high-wage jobs in the CPS as compared to the OES is accounted for by growth in management employment. Management employment has trended steadily upward in the CPS, but declined markedly in the OES, and this general characterization is robust to our best efforts to adjust for the effects of changes in coding practices associated with the introduction of the SOC on the number of OES management jobs.

Should we believe that management employment has been stable or growing, as shown in the CPS, or that management employment has been falling, as the OES data seem to be saying? There is ample evidence in other contexts of social desirability bias in reporting in situations in which answers may reflect either positively or negatively on individual survey respondents (see Tourangeau, Rips, and Rasinski [2000, 255–88] for a review of the relevant literature). It seems plausible that individuals responding to household surveys will have a tendency to exaggerate the occupational status of household members and, in an economy that is increasingly white collar, also plausible that the number of people reported to hold management jobs when, in fact, their tasks are more menial might have grown. Further, the business press is replete with reports of corporate restructuring and management downsizing that seem consistent with the decline in management employment that we observe for larger establishments even in the adjusted OES data.

Whatever the explanation for the discrepancy, conclusions about the changing role of managers in today's labor market could be affected by the use of OES information in place of data from the CPS. Osterman (2006), for example, remarks on the fact that, despite years of restructuring and downsizing, the management share of employment has been stable or growing. At least over the period we have studied, however, the OES data tell a different story. The conclusions of sector-specific studies also could be affected by the use of employer-reported rather than individual-reported occupational information. Dietz and Orr (2006), for example, use CPS data to analyze the skill mix of occupations within manufacturing. They conclude that the manufacturing workforce has become substantially more skilled since the early 1980s and that much of the increase in skill level can be accounted for by growth in employment in managerial and professional specialty occupations. Our numbers show that, in the CPS, the management share of jobs in manufacturing grew from 9.1 percent in 1996 to 11.7 percent in 2004. In the OES, in contrast, the management share of manufacturing employment fell from 6.1 percent in 1996 to 4.8 percent in 2004, without adjustments to the OES data, or to 5.2 percent, after the adjustments described earlier in the text. Our findings suggest that it would be worthwhile to reexamine the trends in the occupational composition of manufacturing employment using data from the OES.

The analysis reported in this chapter can be extended in several ways. First, while changes in the industry and occupation classification structures used in the OES have caused numerous breaks in series, it should be possible to exploit more fully the enormous amount of detail in the OES to look at where in the wage distribution job growth has occurred. Further, by attaching job characteristic information to our data files, it should be possible to say something not only about growth in employment at different points of the wage distribution but also about the *characteristics* of the jobs in which growth has occurred and the changing labor market rewards for different job characteristics.[22]

It also should be possible to extend the analysis backward in time. Although OES microdata like those we have analyzed for the 1996 to 2004 period are not available for earlier years, the Occupational Employment Projections (OEP) program at BLS has produced an annual employment matrix based primarily on OES data that tracks the number of jobs in fairly detailed industry/occupation cells defined on a consistent basis over the 1983 to 1998 time period. Because industries were surveyed for the OES only once every three years prior to 1996, industry staffing patterns had to be interpolated in the years between surveys. In addition, occupational wage data were not collected in the OES prior to 1996. Nonetheless, the OEP employment matrix contains information that it should be possible to exploit to examine trends in employment by industry and occupation over a longer period of time.

22. Using data for 2003 and 2004, Abraham and Spletzer (2009) find larger returns to cognitive skills in the OES data than in the CPS, a finding they attribute to more accurate coding of occupations in the OES.

Appendix A

OCCUPATIONAL TITLE AND DESCRIPTION OF DUTIES	NUMBER OF EMPLOYEES IN SELECTED WAGE RANGES (Report Part-time Workers According to an Hourly Rate)												
Hourly (part-time or full time)	A under $6.75	B $6.75-8.49	C $8.50-10.74	D $10.75-13.49	E $13.50-16.99	F $17.00-21.49	G $21.50-27.24	H $27.25-34.49	I $34.50-43.74	J $43.75-55.49	K $55.50-69.99	L $70.00 and over	T Total Employment
Annual (full-time only)	under $14,040	$14,040-17,679	$17,680-22,359	$22,360-28,079	$28,080-35,359	$35,360-44,719	$44,720-56,679	$56,680-71,759	$71,760-90,999	$91,000-115,439	$115,440-145,599	$145,600 and over	

Management Occupations
(Managers in this section have other managers/supervisors reporting to them.)

	A	B	C	D	E	F	G	H	I	J	K	L	T
Chief Executives- Determine and formulate policies and provide the overall direction of companies or private and public sector organizations within the guidelines set up by a board of directors or similar governing body. 11-1011	A	B	C	D	E	F	G	H	I	J	K	L	T
General and Operations Managers- Plan, direct, or coordinate the operations of companies or public and private sector organizations. Duties include formulating policies, managing daily operations, and planning the use of materials and human resources, but are too diverse in nature to be classified in any one functional area of management or administration 11-1021	A	B	C	D	E	F	G	H	I	J	K	L	T
Marketing Managers- Determine the demand for products and services offered by a firm and its competitors and identify potential customers. Develop pricing strategies with the goal of maximizing the firm's profits or share of the market. 11-2021	A	B	C	D	E	F	G	H	I	J	K	L	T
Computer and Information Systems Managers- Plan, direct, or coordinate activities in such fields as electronic data processing, information systems, systems analysis, and computer programming. 11-3021	A	B	C	D	E	F	G	H	I	J	K	L	T

Figure 3A.1 Sample page from Occupational Employment Statistics survey form

Appendix B

Table 3B.1   **19 occupation and 13 industry categories**

Occupations	Industries
Management	Mining
Business and financial operations	Construction
Engineering	Manufacturing
Life, physical, and social science	Wholesale trade, transportation, and utilities
Computer and mathematical	Retail trade
Health care practitioners and technical	Information
Other professional and technical	Finance, insurance, and real estate
Sales and related	Professional and business services
Office and administrative support	Educational services
Protective service	Health care and social assistance
Food preparation and serving related	Arts, entertainment, and recreation
Building/grounds cleaning and maintenance	Accommodation and food services
All other services	Other services
Production supervisors	
Installation, maintenance, and repair	
Construction and extraction	
Production	
Transportation and material moving	
Production helpers	

Table 3B.2   **Industry and/or occupation breakouts applied to five largest industry/ occupation cells**

Industry/occupation cell	Industry and/or occupation breakouts
Retail trade industry	General merchandise stores; grocery stores; and other retail.
Sales and related occupations	First line supervisors; cashiers; and other sales and related.
Construction industry	No breakouts.
Construction and extraction occupations	Carpenters; electricians; painters; plumbers; and other construction and extraction occupations.
Manufacturing industry	Food, tobacco, textiles and apparel (nondurables); paper, chemicals, petroleum, and plastics (nondurables); lumber, furniture, stone, and fabricated metal (durables); primary metal and transportation (durables); industrial machinery, electrical equipment, instruments (durables); and miscellaneous.
Production occupations	No breakouts.
Health care and social assistance industry	Hospitals; and other health care and social assistance.
Health care practitioners and technical occupations	Physicians; registered nurses; and other healthcare and technical occupations.
Accommodation and food services industry	No breakouts.
Food preparation and serving related occupations	Waiters and waitresses; cooks; and other food preparation and serving related occupations.

Appendix C

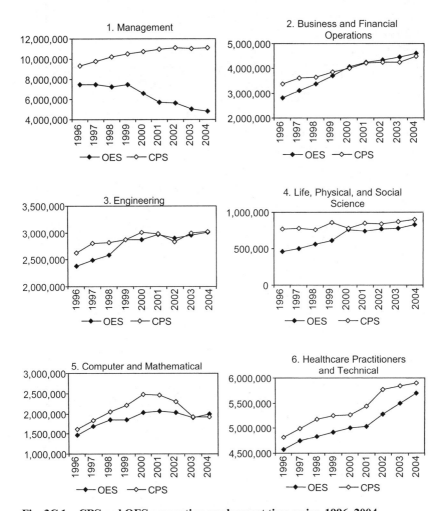

Fig. 3C.1   CPS and OES occupation employment time series, 1996–2004

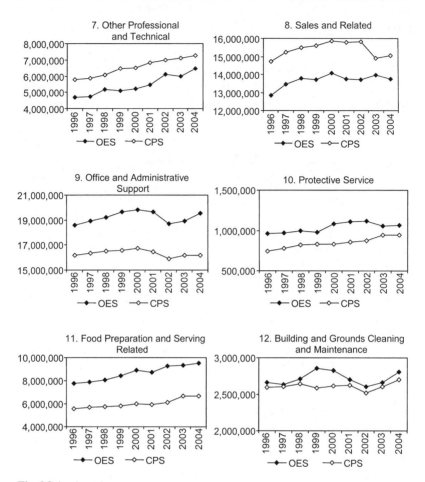

Fig. 3C.1   (cont.)

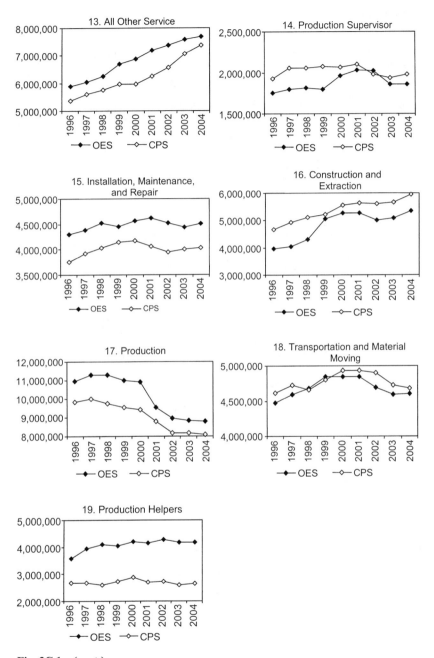

Fig. 3C.1   (cont.)

Appendix D

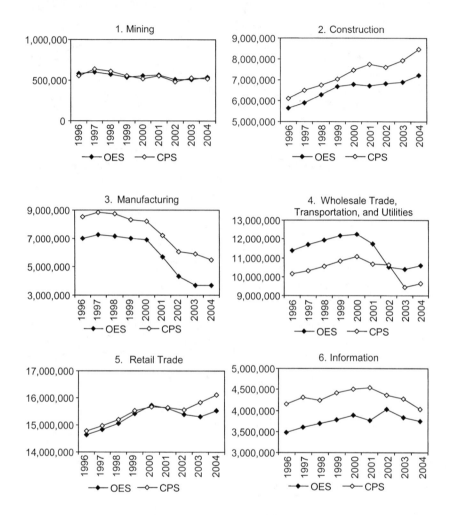

Fig. 3D.1   CPS and OES industry employment time series, 1996–2004

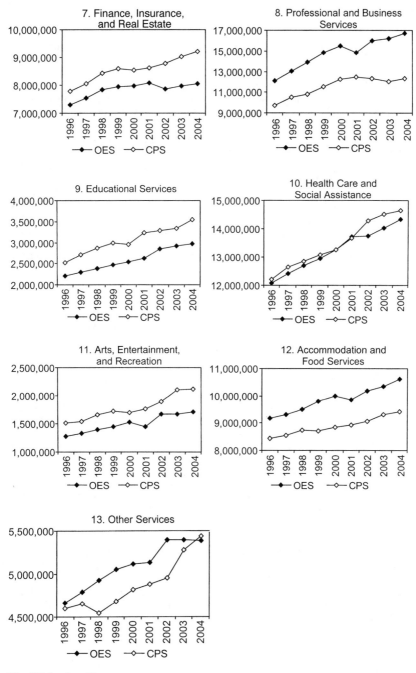

Fig. 3D.1   (cont.)

References

Abraham, Katharine G., and James R. Spletzer. 2009. New evidence on the returns to job skills. *American Economic Review* 99 (2): 52–57.

Acemoglu, Daron. 1999. Changes in unemployment and wage inequality: An alternative theory and some evidence. *American Economic Review* 89 (5): 1259–78.

Autor, David H., Lawrence F. Katz, and Melissa S. Kearney. 2006. The polarization of the U.S. labor market. *American Economic Review* 96 (2): 189–94.

Baily, Martin Neil, and Robert Z. Lawrence. 2004. What happened to the great U.S. job machine? The role of trade and electronic offshoring. *Brookings Papers on Economic Activity,* Issue no. 2:211–84. Washington, DC: Brookings Institution.

Bowler, Mary and Teresa L. Morisi. 2006. Understanding the employment measures from the CPS and CES survey. *Monthly Labor Review* 129 (2): 23–38.

Bureau of Labor Statistics. 2001. *Occupational employment and wages, 1999.* Bulletin no. 2545. Washington, DC: Government Printing Office. http://www.bls .gov/oes/1999/oes_pub99.htm.

———. 2008. Labor force and employment estimates smoothed for population adjustments, 1990–2007. http://www.bls.gov/cps/cpspopsm.pdf.

Clark, Andrew E. 1998. What makes a good job? Evidence from OECD countries. Paper presented at CSLS conference, the State of Living Standards and the Quality of Life in Canada, Ottawa, Canada.

———. 2001. What really matters in a job? Hedonic measurement using quit data. *Labour Economics* 8 (2): 223–42.

———. 2005. Your money or your life: Changing job quality in OECD countries. *British Journal of Industrial Relations* 43 (3): 377–400.

Dietz, Richard, and James Orr. 2006. A leaner, more skilled U.S. manufacturing workforce. *Current Issues in Economics and Finance* 12 (2): 1–7.

DiNatale, Marisa L. n.d. Creating comparability in CPS employment series. http://www.bls.gov/cps/cpscomp.pdf.

Farber, Henry S., and Helen Levy. 2000. Recent trends in employer-sponsored health insurance coverage: Are bad jobs getting worse? *Journal of Health Economics* 19:93–119.

Goos, Maarten, and Alan Manning. 2007. Lousy and lovely jobs: The rising polarization of work in Britain. *Review of Economics and Statistics* 89 (1): 118–33.

Goos, Maarten, Alan Manning, and Anna Salomons. 2009. Job polarization in Europe. *American Economic Review* 99 (2): 58–63.

Ilg, Randy E. 1996. The nature of employment growth, 1989–95. *Monthly Labor Review* 119 (6): 29–36.

Ilg, Randy E., and Steven E. Haugen. 2000. Earnings and employment trends in the 1990s. *Monthly Labor Review* 123 (3): 21–33.

Kalleberg, Arne L., Barbara F. Reskin, and Ken Hudson. 2000. Bad jobs in America: Standard and nonstandard employment relations and job quality in the United States. *American Sociological Review* 65 (April): 256–78.

Kasturirangan, Mallika, Shail Butani, and Tamara Sue Zimmerman. 2007. Methodologies for estimating mean wages for Occupational Employment Statistics (OES) data. BLS Statistical Survey Paper. http://www.bls.gov/ore/pdf/st070010 .pdf.

Levine, Linda, and Marc Labonte. 2004. *The quality of new jobs from the 1990s through June 2004.* CRS Report for Congress no. FL32576. Washington, DC: Congressional Research Service.

Mathiowetz, Nancy. 1992. Errors in reports of occupation. *Public Opinion Quarterly* 56:352–55.

Mellow, Wesley, and Hal Sider. 1983. Accuracy of response in labor market surveys: Evidence and implications. *Journal of Labor Economics* 1 (4): 331–44.

Mikkelson, Gordon, Teresa L. Morisi, and George Stamas. 2000. Implementing the NAICS for business surveys at BLS. Paper presented at the Second International Conference on Establishment Surveys, Buffalo, New York.

Osterman, Paul. 2006. The changing employment circumstances of managers. In *America at work: Choices and challenges,* ed. E. Lawler and J. O'Toole, 193–209. New York: Palgrave Macmillan.

Polivka, Anne E., and Jennifer M. Rothgeb. 1993. Overhauling the Current Population Survey: Redesigning the CPS questionnaire. *Monthly Labor Review* 116 (9): 10–28.

Scopp, Thomas S. 2003. *The relationship between the 1990 Census and Census 2000 Industry and Occupation classification systems.* Technical Paper no. 65. Washington, DC: U.S. Census Bureau.

Tourangeau, Roger, Lance J. Rips, and Kenneth Rasinski. 2000. *The psychology of survey response.* Cambridge, England: Cambridge University Press.

Comment   Erica L. Groshen

What's actually happened to the distribution of U.S. jobs recently? This chapter bolsters the evidence that the share of jobs in the middle-income ranges continues to decline but cannot yet answer the question of what is happening at the upper and lower ends: is the hollowing out caused by disproportionate expansion of low-wage jobs, high-wage jobs, or both? We still don't know. Nevertheless, Abraham and Spletzer make several important methodological contributions that could only be accomplished by careful, even tedious work with normally inaccessible data and supporting information. And extensions of their work on these data holds promise for further progress.

In these comments, I offer my views on the importance of the chapter, consider the challenge of the title, suggest some extensions, and close with my take-aways from the chapter.

Importance of the Paper

The goal of the chapter is to describe, on a granular level, how the distribution of jobs in the United States has changed since the mid-1990s. The answer and further work built on it can provide insight into the causes, consequences, and policy implications of the U.S. labor market's profound transformation. From the causal perspective, this description could help estimate, project, and contrast the impacts of the recent evolution in trade, technology, human resource practices, or corporate structures. In terms of

Erica L. Groshen is vice president and director of regional affairs in the Communications Group of The Federal Reserve Bank of New York.

consequences, the exercise could answer key questions about the path of wage inequality, particularly, what sort of society are we headed for if current trends continue? Finally, knowing likely trends in the distribution of jobs should be useful in guiding key policy decisions, including regional economic development plans, workforce training allocations, public finance budgeting that rely on tax revenues, and so on. Thus, the question is important.

The authors put forth a strong case that the Current Population Survey (CPS) is unlikely to provide adequate granularity and accuracy for these purposes because of its small sample size and potential for error arising from reliance on household members and self-reports. Indeed, efforts to date using the CPS yield markedly different results for exercises based on occupational versus industrial classifications.

Thus, they analyze a new source, the Occupational Employment Statistics (OES) from 1996 to 2004. The OES features large samples of employer-reported wages and employee counts for detailed occupation and industry codes. To verify their results and shed light on any differences, they also perform a very careful, comparable exercise on the CPS. Preparing a new data set for analysis is never easy, but this case stands out as remarkably complex, with a full set of bridging, timing, coding, and comparability issues. One can almost feel the pain each time another issue surfaced.

Yet the authors persisted and have produced some convincing results, some intriguing puzzles and a data set that can potentially reveal a lot more than could be covered in this chapter.

What Makes a "Good Job"?

While this chapter falls well within the literature on good jobs versus bad jobs, the authors never actually try to answer the question in their title. Most likely, they skirt the issue because the concept of a "good job" is so poorly defined.

Fundamentally, this study and much of the literature begs the question: what makes a "good job"? Is it a high wage? Or is a good job one that pays well for the skill level of the worker, particularly, one that pays middle-class wages to lower-skill workers, such as many manufacturing jobs once did? If so, does that mean that middle-wage jobs for higher-skill workers are not "good jobs"? Reaching further, does job security matter, too? What about a good career path?

The chapter never takes a stand on these questions, which keeps the results too general for most policy purposes. Of course, the appropriate definition depends strongly on the policy context in which the term "good job" is being asked and could affect measure trends in the number of good jobs. Thus, the authors leave these distinctions to the reader and the policy community. They stick to carefully reporting the facts they uncover, not defining a good job—except implicitly as one that paid a wage in the upper third in 1996. By contrast, readers with particular policy interests will need to take a stand to define, apply, and defend a particular set of criteria. They are likely to find the results reported here not very useful yet.

The authors clarify that their focus on jobs is a quantity-side, or compositional complement, to studies of changing wage structure (and relationship to demographics) found in the inequality literature. The advantage of this approach is that is offers a lens to look at the "within" variance, that is, wage variation unexplained by demographics. This approach is thus more complete and has a policy resonance because it is tied to the tangible attributes of occupation and industry.

The challenge posed by the approach is that these attributes (occupation and industry) are not neatly tied to human capital theory. Thus, it is conceptually difficult to move between the heterogeneity of occupations and industries and a conceptual story for patterns described in the paper. This challenge is neither new nor insurmountable, but it bears mentioning as a limitation of the approach taken here.

Thus, the chapter is essentially descriptive and has an implicit demand-side focus. That is, the trends observed are most easily described as the result of changes in the demand for labor. However, the authors are very careful not to overemphasize the demand-side perspective. Researchers who follow in their footsteps should bear in mind that labor supply could also have a role to play in the outcomes described here. For example, the bimodal distribution of skill level of recent immigrants to the United States would push in the direction seen here. And so could the impact of the simultaneous increase in college enrollment and the stagnation of the high school graduation rate.

Managers Puzzle

Abraham and Spletzer spent a lot to time working on the large (CPS vs. OES) discrepancy for employment shares (and trends) for managers between the CPS and OES. This is an intriguing discrepancy between data sets that are comparable in so many other respects. It was worth their attention and bears further effort as it remains largely unresolved, despite their best efforts.

One possible explanation centers on the adjustment path for industries with rapid declines in production workers. Such declines could be due to technological change or outsourcing. When the production staff falls, firms may not cut managerial proportionally because need for these higher-skilled workers may depend more on production volume than number of workers supervised or because of some fixed or transition costs. With such reductions in span of control, firms might accurately reclassify the senior workers' jobs into nonmanagerial occupations, while the incumbents might reasonably continue to define themselves as part of management. The companies may not be eager to report themselves to investors and others as suddenly management-heavy. Thus, on the books, these downsizing firms have reasons to "downgrade" some positions and report it accordingly in the OES.

However, the employees may still consider themselves to have managerial jobs (and report it to the CPS) because they are doing much of the same work but supervising fewer employees to get the job done.

This story is eminently testable by investigating whether the discrepancy in levels and trends is wider in industries with fast declines in production jobs. Note that this may not be limited to manufacturing. Nonmanufacturing industries that come to mind include software and accounting firms.

A Grid Approach

In follow-up work, it may be useful to consider a grid (two-dimensional) approach to exploit occupational and industrial heterogeneity more fully. In particular, it could shed light on the comparisons between the CPS and OES and to link results to explanations of the shrinking middle.

Right now, the authors use occupation and industry information only to identify comparable cells over time and across data sources. This is a minimal use of the rich information provided by occupation and industry codes and their characteristics.

As a start, identifying high- and low-wage occupations as well as high- and low-wage industries and tracing their wage and job count trends could provide a link to some explanations for the evolutions of the wage structure. That is, occupation wage differentials can be linked to skills and compensating differentials. By contrast, industry wage differentials are more likely driven by skill sorting, efficiency wages, and rent-sharing. This approach would lead naturally to questions about how the skill mix has changed within and between industries and how wage differentials have evolved.

Operationally, this approach would entail estimation of occupation and industry wage differentials above a set wage threshold, set to W, for bad jobs. Then if β = premium for high-wage occupations, and α = premium for high-wage industries, we can classify jobs into three categories:

- Good jobs: Wage = $W + \alpha + \beta$ (High-wage occupation in a high-wage industry)
- Middle jobs: Wage = $W + \alpha$ or $W + \beta$ (High-wage occupation or high-wage industry)
- Bad jobs: Wage = W

Tracing the development of these categories could compare the importance of hypotheses such as the following:

- Loss of high-wage industry jobs ($W + \alpha$)—from less rent-sharing and firm-specific human capital? versus
- Gains in high-wage occupation jobs ($W + \beta$)—from skill-biased technical change and trade?

This approach could also lead to a comparison of the impact on inequality of changing wage differentials versus changes in the numbers of workers per occupation/industry cell. And, has growth in β for some occupations transformed some occupations into good jobs? Similarly, have some formerly high-industry jobs transitioned from good jobs to middle or bad jobs?

A Few More Suggested Extensions

To look further into the discrepancies between the OES, future work could look at wage dispersion within occupation/industry cells. For example, high mean wage or rank-order discrepancies (OES vs. CPS) for cells with high within-cell dispersion suggests troublesome industry or occupation definition conversions. Or high within-cell dispersion in cells with a high concentration of second jobs in the CPS suggests that the wages of full-time jobs may not be comparable. Sampling or sample size issues might also be more evident.

Finally, I offer two unanswered questions to consider:

- What role, if any, do regional variations play? If permitted by the sample sizes—this could also be very interesting.
- What about the excluded jobs in government, agriculture, self-employment and private households? What do we know about their size and trends, and how they would change the overall story?

Conclusion: What I Learned

Methodologically, the paper makes a convincing case for the value of the OES as a resource for understanding the recent evolution of wages that is superior to the CPS. It also demonstrates the challenges in preparing such a rich data set for analysis. In particular, while we knew that occupations were hard for households to report consistently, now we see that coding them is difficult for statistical agencies also.

Substantively, here are my three personal take-aways:

- Middle-wage jobs lost shares during 1996 to 2004, although not quite as dramatically as seen in CPS results.
- CPS-based findings of almost exclusive growth in high-wage jobs is not confirmed in the OES data.
- There's an intriguing puzzle in the trend in management jobs that bears future work. Did management jobs grow by 1.7 million jobs (CPS) or decline by 2.6 million jobs (OES) from 1996 to 2004? And why do the CPS and OES differ by so much on this one point?

I look forward to seeing more results from further analysis of the OES data.

4

New Data for Answering Old Questions Regarding Employee Stock Options

Kevin F. Hallock and Craig A. Olson

4.1 Background

An employee stock option is the right an employee has to buy a share of stock at a set price at some time in the future, subject to vesting and other provisions. The dramatic growth in the use of stock options in the past decade (Hall and Murphy 2003), new Financial Accounting Standards Board (FASB 2004) standards on how to account for stock options in firm balance sheets, new disclosure requirements for highly paid executives in U.S. firms, and a growing debate over how to handle stock options in national accounts (in the United States and elsewhere) have sparked considerable interest in the study of stock options in recent years.

In keeping with the tradition of the National Bureau of Economic Research (NBER) Conference on Research in Income and Wealth (CRIW), this chapter aims to provide a review and update on some important questions in stock options research and practice, explore a variety of new and interesting data sets for the careful and credible study of employee stock options, discuss implications of options in the national accounts, and pro-

Kevin F. Hallock is professor of labor economics and human resources (HR) studies at Cornell University, and a research associate of the National Bureau of Economic Research. Craig A. Olson is LER Alumni Professor of Labor and Employment Relations and professor of economics at the University of Illinois at Urbana-Champaign.

We thank the Center for Advanced HR Studies (CAHRS) at Cornell and the Center for Human Resource Management (CHRM) at Illinois for support. We are grateful to Katharine Abraham, Hank Farber, Mike Harper, S. K. Kothari, Thomas Lemieux, Rosemary Marcuss, Chris Riddell, Jeffrey Schildkraut, Jim Spletzer, and participants at the National Bureau of Economic Research (NBER) Conference on Research in Income and Wealth (CRIW) preconference at the University of Maryland in Spring 2007 and the main conference in Fall 2007 in Bethesda, Maryland for helpful suggestions.

vide some new empirical evidence on the value of options to employees using a decade of data from a large U.S. firm.

There are a host of reasons why learning more about stock options is important for firms, employees, and public policymakers. First, over the past twenty years, there has been dramatic growth in the use of stock options for senior-level executives and, beginning in the mid-1990s, substantial growth in the use of options for nonexecutive employees that was only partially dampened by the market adjustment in 2001. For example, among publicly traded firms, Hall and Murphy (2003) report that option grants to managers and employees who are not among the top five highest paid in the firm has grown from less than 85 percent of the total options granted to employees in the mid-1990s to over 90 percent by 2002. While there is some evidence that options to nonexecutives have become less common in recent years, they clearly remain an important dimension of compensation in many firms. Research on options may both help researchers understand why firms grant options and inform firms about how they should evaluate their employee stock option policies and practices. Whenever a firm decides to grant options, it must decide whether it is better off granting the options or some alternative form of compensation. In order to do this appropriately a firm must know (a) how employees value the options relative to other forms of compensation, (b) the costs of the options to the firm, and (c) the relative incentive effects of the options (e.g., do they influence the employees to work harder)? Even if the options "cost" the firm more than other forms of pay, the firm may still want to provide them if incentive effects or other benefits are sufficiently large.

A second reason research on options is important is that it may provide insight into the widespread debate about the appropriate method of estimating the cost and value of options to firms. Although there are many strongly held opinions and new FASB regulations on how firms should expense options, there is no consensus on a theoretical model and empirical method for estimating employee stock option costs to the firm. Black and Scholes (1973) and Merton (1973) developed a widely accepted model used for pricing market traded options for risk-neutral, diversified investors that has been used (with modifications) successfully for more than three decades. While the same techniques have been extended to consider the value of options to employees and their cost to the firm, many have pointed out that the value of an option to an employee, and its cost to the firm may be considerably different than the value to an outside investor (e.g., Lambert, Larcker, and Verecchia 1991). Using this idea, Hall and Murphy (2002) have run simulations of option values to risk averse senior managers that show employees value options at a level that is substantially less than the Black-Scholes value and the cost of the option to the firm.

Understanding the cost of options to the firm may also provide insight into how employee stock options should be treated in national accounts and estimates of employee compensation. Proper measurement of stock options is important for the valid measurement of the national accounts since, as of March 2003, "8 percent of private industry workers had access to stock options" (Schildkraut 2004,1). Current work on this topic by the Bureau of Economic Analysis (BEA) is investigating major data collection, conceptual and practical measurement, and timing issues (Moylan 2007).

Stock option data are not carefully collected in many common data sources in the United States. For example, the National Compensation Survey (NCS) considered the incidence and provisions of stock option plans in a 1999 pilot survey, perhaps with intent to further collect the information (Bureau of Labor Statistics [BLS] 2000; Crimmel and Schildkraut 1999; Crimmel and Schildkraut 2001). But the BLS has not further pursued this path, in part given that there is not a standard costing method that would allow employers to report costs at an occupational level. The NCS does collect information on access to stock options (BLS 2007).

The first section of this chapter briefly describes a typical stock option grant and the famous Black-Scholes option pricing formula for valuing publicly traded stock options. We then discuss why the value of *employee* (nonmarket tradable) options may differ from the valuation of market tradable options. We will also discuss how these alternative valuations relate to the controversy regarding the treatment of stock options in the national accounts. The second section details a set of data sources on stock options within the United States and internationally. We also consider how newer data could improve what we know in the national accounts. The chapter concludes with a case study of employee valuation of stock options in a large nonmanufacturing firm. We examine the value employees place on stock options using data from multiple large grants of stock options to a large set of managerial and professional employees in a multibillion dollar U.S. non-manufacturing firm. We show that employee exercise decisions are broadly consistent with employee risk aversion and inconsistent with the risk neutral valuation of market-traded options that is predicted by the Black-Scholes model for market-traded options. Our hope is that our work is a useful guide to researchers, policymakers, and practitioners interested in stock options.

4.2   Theoretical Perspective

This section has four main goals. First, we define an employee stock option grant and provide some context. Second, we describe the Black-Scholes method for valuing publicly traded options. Third, we describe why the value employees place on stock options may differ from the well-known Black-Scholes value. Fundamental to this discussion are the differences between market tradable options, for which the Black-Scholes option pricing formula was created, and employee stock options. Finally we discuss implications of alternative valuations for the national accounts.

4.2.1   Defining Stock Options

An option to buy a share of stock at a set price (the strike or exercise price) can be executed by an employee after the option is held for a period of time known as the vesting period. Employee stock options typically vest within one to three years, are forfeited if the employee leaves the firm, and expire (typically) ten years after the grant date. Shorter vesting periods and option terms are common among high-technology firms, and, on some occasions, they gradually vest (e.g., one-third of the options vest at the end of year one, one-third vest at the end of year two, and one-third vest at the end of year three). Finally, employees cannot sell their options to a third party. This limitation ensures that until the options are exercised, the options continue to tie worker compensation to firm outcomes.

4.2.2   Black-Scholes Method of Valuing Publicly Traded Options

A discussion about the value of options to employees begins with the pioneering work of Black and Scholes (1973) and Merton (1973), who describe the value to diversified investors of market traded stock options. The famous diagram shown in figure 4.1 summarizes the basic relationship between the Black-Scholes value (BSV) of an option to buy a share of stock at a fixed price in the future (a call option), the firm's stock price, and the option's exercise price. The kinked *intrinsic value* line equals max($[SP_t - EP]$, 0), where SP_t is the price of the firm's stock in period t, and EP is the strike or exercise price of the stock option and corresponds to the payoff that could be made by immediately exercising the option and then selling the acquired share at the firm's stock price. The curved line in the figure is the BSV and is the predicted price that an unexercised option could be bought or sold for based on the Black-Scholes theory. The BSV is a function of six variables—the risk-free interest rate, the expiration date of the option, the variance in the firm's stock returns, the firm's dividend rate, the option exercise price, and the current stock price. Figure 4.2 shows the BSV values for an option with an exercise price of $10 that expires in 10, 5, and 0.5 years for a "typical" firm.[1] When the stock price is $10 and the option expires in ten years, the BSV estimate of the market value of the option is $5.57. Thus, even though a profit cannot be made by immediately exercising the option on the grant date, it has significant value because of the expectations of investors that at the end of the ten-year period a significant profit is expected (but not guaranteed) because of the expected positive per-period returns over the option's term. The market value of the option on the option grant increases as the duration of the option increases because the distribution of returns on the expiration date have a larger mean and variance as the

1. The standard deviation of the firm's returns over a year is .3, no dividends are paid by the firm, and the risk-free interest rate is 6 percent.

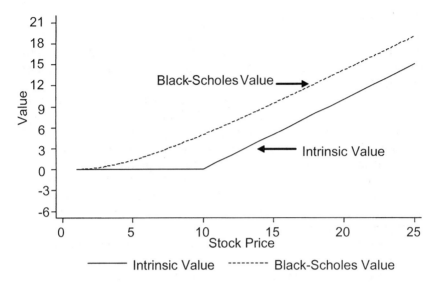

Fig. 4.1   **Black-Scholes value and the intrinsic value of an option**

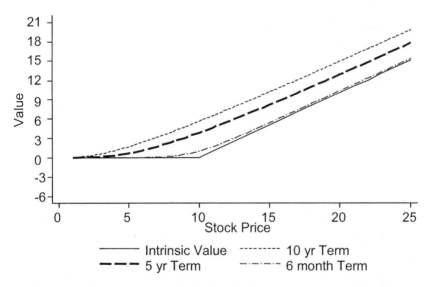

Fig. 4.2   **Black-Scholes value and the intrinsic value of an option and the value of options with different terms**

option's duration increases.[2] If the option shown in figure 4.2 expires in five years, its value at a $10 stock price is $3.80, and, if the option expires in six months, its market value is $.99 at a $10 stock price. The relationship between the stock price and BSV for options with these terms is shown in figure 4.2.

An important result shown by Black, Scholes, and Merton is that the market value of an option depends on the riskless rate of return and does not depend on the firm's expected return, which includes a firm-specific risk premium. The prediction that owners of market traded options can only expect to earn the riskless rate of return by holding the option is because investors can eliminate the risk that the option will be worthless when it expires because the stock price is less than the exercise price with a hedging strategy. For example, an investor could buy a "put" option that gives the owner the right to *sell* a share of stock at $10 per share in period T. This put option will pay a profit to its owner if the call option is "underwater" (SP_T < EP). Owning this put ensures the investor will make a profit at time T no matter what the stock price happens to be on the expiration day. While firms discourage employees from owning put options because these options are a "bet against the company" and earn money only if the firm's stock price falls, for outside investors this example illustrates a simple way of eliminating the risk associated from owning a call option. The ability of investors to hedge risk means competitive market pressures cause options prices to converge to a price that earns only a riskless rate of return.

More formally, the Black-Scholes option pricing formula is

$$BSV = (SP)\Phi\left[\frac{\ln(SP/EP) + (r_f + \sigma^2/2)t}{\sigma\sqrt{t}}\right]$$
$$- (EP)e^{(-r_f t)}\Phi\left[\frac{\ln(SP/EP) + (r_f + \sigma^2/2)t - 1}{\sigma\sqrt{t}}\right],$$

where r_f is the risk-free rate of interest, σ is the standard deviation of returns for the underlying stock, t is time in years until the option expires, and Φ is the cumulative standard normal distribution function. The model assumes the firm's stock returns are normally distributed and uncorrelated from one period to the next. The assumption that returns are normally distributed means the price of a riskless asset in T periods is drawn from a log-normal price distribution. As the option expiration date approaches, the Black-Scholes line shifts toward the intrinsic value line because the chance of drawing a "large" positive return from the return distribution on the expiration date declines.

2. Because the terminal stock price distribution is log-normally distributed, the expected price at the expiration date is a function of both the mean and variance of the per-period return. As we explain shortly, the per-period return investors of market traded options expect to earn equals the risk-free interest rate.

4.2.3   Why the Value of Employee Options May
          Diverge from the Black-Scholes Value

An important prediction of the Black-Scholes model is that a diversified investor will never exercise the right to buy a share of stock until the moment before it expires because, as figure 4.2 shows, at any earlier date the expected gain from holding the option until the expiration date is greater than the profit that can be made by immediately exercising it. The expectation of a positive return between now and the expiration date means the Black-Scholes value is greater than the profit that could be made by immediately exercising the option and receiving the option's intrinsic value, $(SP_t - EP)$. Therefore, the Black-Scholes model predicts that prior to the expiration date, an investor will sell an option rather than exercise it if they wish to convert an option to cash because the BSV, the sale price, is greater than $(SP_t - EP)$.

The Black-Scholes model predicts that market traded options held by diversified investors will rarely be exercised early because options can almost always be sold for more than the option's intrinsic value (stock price – exercise price).[3] The Black-Scholes model makes no prediction at all about how long the owner of a market traded option will own an option; it only predicts an option will be sold rather than exercised if its owner wants to liquidate his or her position prior to the expiration date. "Early" exercise behavior by employees occurs because they cannot sell their options, and their only choice during the term of the option is between exercising the option or holding the option for another period.

For some time, researchers have noted that the value employees place on employee stock options is likely to be different from the value diversified investors place on market tradable options. The major piece of empirical evidence cited to support this conclusion is the observation that employees frequently exercise employee stock options "early" or well before the option's expiration date (Huddart and Lang 1996; Carpenter 1998). In the firm we study in section 4.4, 86 percent of employees exercised their options prior to the month before the options expired, and half of the sample exercised some of their options at least twenty-seven months prior to the option's expiration date.[4] Lambert, Larcker, and Verecchia (1991) who, among others, argue that because employees are not risk neutral, are heavily invested in their firm (firm-specific human capital and deferred compensation), and may face liquidity constraints, they are likely to value employee options in their firm at a level lower than the Black-Scholes value and may also exercise their options earlier than predicted by Black-Scholes. Simulation work by

---

3. If firm dividends are sufficiently high, there may be a date prior to the option's expiration date when it is optimal to exercise an option early. This explanation cannot account for widespread exercise behavior over the term of the option and after the vesting date.

4. These data are for the first large employee stock option grant awards made to the middle-level managers included in this study.

Hall and Murphy (2002) shows that, conditional on a set of assumptions about risk aversion and the wealth they hold in firm stock, executives valued options at a level significantly less than the Black-Scholes value for market tradable options and exercised "early" to lock in gains from large stock price increases and diversify their portfolio. Contrary to Black-Scholes, Heath, Huddart, and Lang (1999) find that employees tend to exercise options when the firm's stock price exceeds a target or referent price based on recent stock price highs.[5]

It must certainly be true that for those employees who exercise their options prior to the expiration date, the value they place on holding the option is less than the option's BSV. Because the BSV of an option is greater than the option's intrinsic value and an employee will exercise an option when the profit from exercising early (the option's intrinsic value) is greater than the value of holding the option, then the value of holding the option must be less than BSV when employees exercise their options. This result, however, does not say anything about the value of the options held by employees who have not yet exercised their options. While the differences between market traded options and employee stock options discussed earlier predicts the value of options held by employees is less than BSV, evidence of early exercise behavior by employees only shows employees who do not exercise their options value the options at an amount greater than the option's intrinsic value. The decision by an employee to continue to hold their options does not say anything about the value of the options relative to their BSV. Because employees cannot sell their options or use the options as collateral to borrow money, they have no market signals that could inform them of the value outside investors would place on their options.

The observation that employees frequently exercise employee stock options "early" compared to the Black-Scholes prediction for market traded options reflects the fact that employees cannot sell the options they receive from their employer and must exercise the options if they wish to liquidate their position to diversify their portfolio or meet a household demand for cash. This feature of employee stock options implies information about an option's value to an employee is revealed each period by observing whether a vested option is exercised. If an option is not exercised in a period, then the value to the employee of holding the option and reserving the right to exercise it in a later period is greater than the value from immediately exercising the option and receiving the option's intrinsic value. On the other hand, when an employee exercises an option, we know the value of holding the option another period is less than what is gained by exercising the option and receiving a payment equal to the stock price minus the exercise price. Thus, the decision to exercise immediately or hold an option for at least another

5. Because an employee must typically forfeit her options if she leaves the firm, early exercise decisions may also be caused by voluntary or involuntary employee turnover (Carpenter 1998).

period is an indicator of the current value to an employee of holding the option relative to the option's intrinsic value.

One important implication of the preceding prediction is that variation in the length of time until employees exercise their options reflects heterogeneity in the value employees place on holding their options for another period. This heterogeneity in the value of an employee stock option could reflect differences in turnover intentions because employees must typically forfeit their employee stock options when they leave the firm. It may also reflect differences in household risk aversion, the effects of binding liquidity constraints, or different predictions about the future stock price of the firm. More risk-averse employees may exercise early to "lock in" profits (Hall and Murphy 2002), and the inability of employees to borrow against their employee stock options may cause some employees to exercise options to meet family financial commitments (buying a house, college tuition, or unanticipated health care expenditures). While these same sources of heterogeneity also characterize owners of market traded options, because Black-Scholes predicts owners of market traded options can sell and hedge their options, market traded options are identically valued (conditional on the six variables identified in the preceding), regardless of the risk preferences and liquidity constraints of their owners. Thus, heterogeneity in exercise times is strong evidence that Black-Scholes does not measure the value of employee stock options to employees.

4.2.4   Stock Options, National Accounts, and How Valuation Matters

Accounting for stock options in the United States, National Economic Accounts poses a variety of difficult issues.[6] One problem is that there are, in fact, two types of employee stock options; incentive stock options (ISO) and nonqualified stock options (NSO). Incentive stock options are not deductible for the employer or to the employee. However, when the stock is sold, the difference between the exercise price and the stock price is taxed as a capital gain for the individual (Moylan 2007). The NSOs are much more common and have different tax implications for employees and firms. When an employee exercises an NSO, he or she must pay income tax on the difference between the stock price and the exercise price just as if that compensation had been paid in cash. The firm can count a tax deduction of the same magnitude at the same time.

Collecting options data for the national accounts is very difficult.[7] Given recent advances in the disclosure of employee equity awards, including stock and employee stock options, through the Securities and Exchange Commission Web site, we could imagine that collecting timely data is now easier than

---

6. As pointed out in Lequiller (n.d.), this is also a problem is many other countries.
7. The Employment Cost Index, another important government statistic, does not include compensation in the form of stock options (Ruser 2001).

at any time in the past. However, there are a series of barriers in considering the valuation of options in the national accounts, even with access to better data. Carol Moylan carefully outlines many of the important issues with the treatment of employee stock options in the U.S. national accounts (Moylan 2007).

One of the issues is that of timing. Cynthia Glassman, undersecretary for economic affairs in the economic and statistics administration of the commerce department, noted (in a paper from the 2008 Allied Social Sciences Association [ASSA] meetings), "proceeds from the exercise of stock options are included in compensation estimates for the quarter in which exercise occurs, and the proceeds are excluded from corporate profits for the same quarter. This means that stock option compensation is not recognized for some time—possibly years after employees actually receive the option grants . . . It also means that any divergence between accounting and tax profits creates a headache for BEA . . ." (Glassmam 2008, 65). Note also that the BEA does not produce a single quarterly Gross Domestic Income (GDI) estimate but many "vintages" of GDI estimates for each quarter. This "reflects a compromise between providing timely estimates based on less-than-complete data and providing increasingly accurate estimates with lags that reflect the availability of better and more complete data" (Glassman 2008). Another issue discussed by Moylan (2007) is that it is unclear when to count the compensation as earnings—at the time of the grant or the time of the exercise of the option.

Moylan (2007) carefully describes that stock options do have value and should be treated as a form of compensation. One problem is *when* to count the compensation. Some argue that options should be counted as compensation at the time of the *grant* and not at the time of *exercise* as they are currently counted in the national accounts.[8] A difficulty with this view as pointed out by many is that employee options are subject to vesting, and, in a sense, the compensation is not earned until after vesting has occurred. So, therefore, perhaps the options should count as compensation at the time of vesting or some time between the grant date and vesting. After vesting, the gains from options could be thought of as a type of capital gain and, therefore, may no longer be considered compensation but as investment income. (Eurostat n.d.; Australian Bureau of Statistics 2002). Therefore, there is difficulty, from a theoretical point of view, about whether stock options are a form of pay, an investment, or a combination of the two.

Moylan (2008) notes that "under most UI laws, wages and salaries include bonuses, tips, the cash value of meals and lodging provided by the employer,

---

8. The discussion in the text is focused on options in the national accounts. This should not be confused with recent Financial Accounting Standards Board changes that now require firms to expense (and disclose in financial statements) options at the time they are granted. This differs from the tax treatment of options and from the national accounts practice of recognizing options as compensation when they are exercised.

the gain on the employee exercise of certain stock options, and employee contributions to certain deferred compensation plans" (9). She and others (e.g., McIntosh n.d.) note that in calculating compensation for the national accounts, the BEA assumes that compensation includes the exercise of NSOs but not ISOs. One problem, however, is that "there is evidence that some states are inconsistent in their coverage" (Moylan 2007, 2). Also, and as noted by Glassman (2008), the BLS quarterly census of employment and wages (QCEW) are reported with a lag of five months.

One reason properly accounting for options in the National Accounts is extremely difficult is the difference in accounting and tax treatment of stock options in the United States. For many years, there was a "disconnect" between the valuation of options for tax purposes and for purposes of reporting profits in company financial reports. Given the recent FASB change and the requirement for firms to "expense" options in their balance sheet, one would think that it may be easier to account for options in the national accounts.

4.3   Sources of Data on Stock Options

Along with the explosion in the past few decades in the use of stock options by firms in the United States, there has been a dramatic increase in research on employee stock options. In this section, we provide a general review of data sources on stock options and how these data can be useful for answering different questions about their incentive effects, their value to firms and employees, and data that could potentially be useful in the treatment of stock options in the national accounts. We will also try to address whether there are gaps in the set of data sources.

4.3.1   General Review of Sources of Data and How They Can Help Answer Questions

We have categorized the types of data on stock options into seven types: (a) commercial executive-level and firm-level sources, (b) individual firm financial records at the firm level, (c) individual firm financial records at the person level, (d) consulting firm data, (e) employee perception data from surveys, (f) government and nonprofit sources, and (g) international sources. Table 4.1 outlines the data and lists a set of sources that have used each. The set of sources listed in table 4.1 is by no means exhaustive. In each section, we briefly describe the types of data and mention ways that the data have been or could be used.

4.3.2   Commercial Executive-Level and Firm-Level Data Sources

There are at least three available commercial data sources on executive pay at the person level and firm level that are now relatively widely used. The first, ExecuComp (Executive Compensation data base) is produced by

Table 4.1   Types of data sources (and examples of each) on employee stock options

Type	Authors	Comments
Commercial sources		
Execucomp	Bergman and Jenter (2007)	1,500 firms, details on options of top 5 execs from 1992–2003
	Chidambaran and Nagpurnanand (2003)	Focus on repricing
	Mehran and Tracy (2001)	Review
Equilar, salary.com		
Individual firm financial records (firm-level)	Aboody (1996)	National Automation Accounting Research System (NAARS) library of financial statement footnotes
	Carpenter (1998)	Average exercise times by firm
	Core and Guay (2001)	Nonexec option holdings, grants, and exercises from 756 firms from 1994–1997
Individual firm detailed case study (person-level)	Armstrong, Jagolinzer, and Larcker (2006)	10 publicly traded firms
	Bajaj et al. (2006)	Two firms, enormous number of option grants
	Hallock and Olson (2007b)	Large firm outside of manufacturing, 13 grants to 2000 middle managers over a decade
	Hallock and Olson (2007a)	Data from a different firm on pay mix, including options
	Heath, Huddart, and Lang (1999) and Huddart and Lang (1996)	Individual grant and exercise data from seven firms
Consulting firm data	Farrell, Krische, and Sedatole (2006)	Training data from equity compensation planning firm
	Heron and Lie (2007)	7.2 million stock and options transactions
	Landsman et al. (2006)	1,354 firm-year observations from S&P500 from 1997–2001
Perception data from surveys	Farrell, Krische, and Sedatole (2006)	Training data from equity compensation planning firm
	Hodge, Rajgopal, and Shevlin (2006)	Executives in class
Government and nonprofit sources	Kroumova and Sesil (2006) and Oyer and Schaefer (2006)	National Center for Employee Ownership (NCEO) survey sent to plan administrators with plans in place—firm-level data for 600 firms
	Oyer and Schaefer (2006)	Bureau of Labor Statistics establishment-level data from 1,437 establishments
International data	Ikäheimo, Kuosa, and Puttonen (2006)	14 plans, 6 firms, 27,808 transactions in Finland
	Jones, Kalmi, and Makinen (2006)	Option plans in all firms in Finland from 1900–2002
	Kato et al. (2005) and Pendleton (2006)	644 stock option plan adoptions in Japan following 1997 rule change

Standard and Poor's Corporation and is likely the most widely used source of data for research on executive pay, including stock options. This source has available data from 1992—present on the compensation of the top-five highest paid employees of U.S. publicly traded firms who have managerial control in roughly 1,500 firms per year. These firms include those listed in the Standard and Poor's (S&P) 500, the S&P SmallCap 600, and the S&P MidCap 400. The data source starts in 1992, which was (until four years ago) the last major change in executive pay disclosure rules. A wide variety of questions can be answered with these data including issues of pay for performance for corporate managers, studies of corporate ownership, and research on the composition (salary, bonus, options, stock, etc.) of executive pay. This data set is perhaps the most popular among academic researchers. Examples of work using these data that are mentioned in table 4.1 include Bergman and Jenter (2007), who examine employee optimism; Chidambaran and Nagpurnanand (2003), who study repricings; and Mehran and Tracy (2001), who provide a summary of some executive pay research using data from ExecuComp.

Two other commercial executive pay sources are Equilar and salary.com. Each also provides comprehensive data sets of executive compensation but have a larger focus on marketing to the for-profit firm and compensation consulting market. These sources are frequently used by compensation design practitioners and consultants to help design executive pay plans (and to set comparison groups), including detailed equity and employee stock option plans.

One problem with all three of these sources is that they only focus on the most senior executives with managerial control over the firm. If one is interested in the compensation of any employee who is not in the top-five highest paid, these data sources are not particularly useful. They do, however, reveal the fraction of options given to the sum of the top-five highest-paid officers so that one can calculate the fraction granted to the rest of the employees in the firm. Another drawback of these data is that they only cover publicly traded firms. Finally, ExecuComp is for a limited set of firms. Data from Equilar and salary.com are more expensive but include information from a wider variety of firms.

4.3.3   Individual Firm Financial Records (Firm Level)

A host of scholars have also considered firm financial records at the firm level but have not used the well-known ExecuComp and related sources; rather, they have dug deeper for more unique sources of information. We will discuss a selection of these examples here. Examples of this include Aboody (1996), who used the National Automation Accounting Research System (NAARS) library on Lexis/Nexis in 1988 in a study of the relationship between outstanding options and stock; Core and Guay (2001), who study the determinants of nonexecutive employee stock option holdings, grants, and exercises; and Carpenter (1998), who collected information on average time to exercise, stock prices at the time of exercise, and vesting periods using data from 10-Ks, proxies, and S-8 forms (the option plan prospectus).

The latter is an example of a study that required the use of significant "digging" beyond what was easily available in machine-readable form. This kind of work is expensive and time consuming but can open doors to many interesting findings.

4.3.4   Individual Firm Detailed Case Study Data (Person-Level)

There have been an increasing number of individual firm case studies over the past decade that have greatly enriched our understanding of employee stock options. Although these kinds of studies have the obvious drawback that the results may apply to one (or a small number of) firm(s), they are often extraordinarily rich in detail about the firm and individual. Too often, economic and financial scholars are interested in discovering things such as the "incentive effects" of a particular pay policy. In fact, the viability of a particular pay plan may depend quite a bit on the type of workers the firm employs and the strategy and objectives of the firm. That is to say, a particular pay practice may work more effectively in one firm than another, even when firms are in similar industries and employ observably similar workers.

Armstrong, Jagolinzer, and Larcker (2006) study "option-exercise-timing-adjusted" employee option valuation models using detailed data from ten publicly traded U.S. firms including information on strike price, maximum term, and vesting schedule for each option grant to each employee. Their sample includes several tens of thousands of options. In some of our own work (Hallock and Olson 2007a,b), we examine data from two separate firms to consider the value of options to employees and employees' choice of mix of pay. Two very important and early papers that use unique data from firms are Heath, Huddart, and Lang (1999) and Huddart and Lang (1996). The authors use individual-by-individual option grant and exercise data from 50,000 individuals at seven corporations. Bajaj et al. (2006) use data from two firms to consider the valuation of employee stock options and find that employee stock option valuation methods suggested by Financial Accounting Standard (FAS) 123R, such as adjusting the expected life of the employee stock options and making adjustments to the Black-Scholes value, lead to substantial biases in option valuation.

Again, each of these papers makes a unique contribution and shows the details that can be learned from extraordinarily specific data. However, each study also suffers from the drawback that they are studying a very small nonrandom sample of firms.

4.3.5   Consulting Firm Data

An increasing number of scholars have made connections with consulting firms to use data from a variety of firms at once in one study. These have the obvious advantage that more firms are included. In some cases, there are fewer details than in some of the case studies previously discussed. Heron and Lie (2007) investigated whether stock option backdating explained price patterns around executive stock option grants. The authors use data on stock options grants from Thomson Financial, which collects information from insider transactions of stock and derivative grants and exercises from Securities and Exchange Commission (SEC) forms 3, 4, 5, and 144. Landsman et al. (2006) consider which approach to accounting for stock options best reflects market pricing. They use 1,354 firm-year observations drawn from the S&P 500 from 1997 to 2001. Relationships with data providers are very hard to establish but the payoff from such data collection can be great.

4.3.6 Employee Perception Data from Surveys

One way to estimate the value employees place on stock options is to ask employees. Farrell, Krische, and Sedatole (2006) use "confidential training data files" of New Worth Strategies, Inc. (NWSI), a national leader in equity compensation planning services to investigate this issue. They examine how a training program may help employees understand their employee stock options better. Hodge, Rajgopal, and Shevlin (2006) investigate individual perceptions of the value of stock options and restricted stock. This is an alternative to observing actual exercise behavior and is complementary to the work of others (including that described in section 4.4). A benefit of this method is that the data are easily collected. A disadvantage is that respondents may not take the questions as seriously as they would if they were faced with an actual financial decision. The obvious problems with perception data still exist. It may be possible to try to elicit employee perception or utility by actually offering them choice and observing their behavior. A recent example of this is Hallock and Olson (2007a).

4.3.7 Government and Nonprofit Sources

There are also a set of government and nonprofit data sources that contain different types of information on employee stock options. Kroumova and Sesil (2006) consider the predictors of the use of employee stock option plans using data from the National Center for Employee Ownership (NCEO) in 1998 on 600 public and private firms sponsoring some form of broad-based stock option plan merged with information from Compustat. Oyer and Schaefer (2005a, 2006) have two papers that use these types of sources. Other government sources on stock options include the data from Unemployment Insurance (UI) records that are used in calculating the national accounts and the 1999 special survey conducted by the NCS.

4.3.8 International Data

Although the focus of this chapter is on employee stock options in the United States (and rules on grant, exercise, and taxation of options vary widely) international data on employee options are also available. Ikäheimo, Kuosa, and Puttonen (2006) examine the "most actively traded employee stock option companies (14 plans of 6 companies), which represents 98.7 percent of total value of employee stock option trades on the Helsinki Stock Exchange (HEX)" (353). In another study using Finnish data, Jones, Kalmi, and Makinen (2006) use firm-level data on option plans from all Finnish firms from 1990 to 2002. Kato et al. (2005) investigate 644 adoptions of stock option plans announced by Japanese firms following the amendment of the Japanese commercial code in May 1997. Pendleton (2006) investigated the behavior of participants in the United Kingdom's Save as You Earn (SAYE) stock option programs.

Data from different countries certainly add to the richness of what we know about employee stock options. At the same time, we need to be careful in interpreting results across countries due to the quite different reporting and tax rules on stock and employee stock options across country boundaries. These differences, of course, provide a potential source of exogenous variation that can be used to understand the adoption of employee stock option plans and the behavior of firms and individuals covered by these plans. There is also substantial international interest in the national accounts measurement and timing issues we discussed previously, including as described in Lequiller (2002).

4.3.9   Gaps in the Set of Option Data and What to Do

Although there are many excellent data sources on stock options, there are significant gaps. These include the difficulties with trying to gain access to firm financial records, difficulty in collecting publicly available data, problems in reporting and understanding by individuals, and the issues of timing and measurement with the national accounts.

Many significant advances in the literature on stock options have been made because of researcher access to data from individual firms or data from consulting companies. The obvious problem is that the firms may have little to "gain" by providing their data to researchers. In one of our recent experiences (Hallock and Olson 2007b), we were turned down by as many as five companies (it could have been much worse) before we got access to the kinds of data we needed. In another (Hallock and Olson 2007a), we had a personal connection and an executive with a keen intellectual interest that helped us out. These types of data collection are very time consuming. In the end, we hope that firms will continue to share their data with researchers so more can be learned about options.

A second problem is that there are many publicly available data sources but the data are not yet "machine readable." This is a substantial barrier to researchers. However, there have been considerable improvements in the kinds of data being collected. For example, all "Form 4" data on stock and option transactions by senior executives in publicly traded firms are posted on the SEC Web site, and commercial sources (such as Thomson Financial) are publishing these data as well.

All is not bad news, however. An example is new requirements for firm reporting of executive pay packages. The changes in the recent proxy seasons (relative to the years before) are extraordinary. Included among these changes is amazing detail on each individual option grant given to each individual executive. These kinds of changes and easy to use machine-readable sources will hopefully contribute to our further understanding of employee stock options.

4.4 Case Study of Employee Exercise Decisions

In this section, we investigate the value of options to employees using a case study of option exercise decisions by over 2,000 middle-level managers and professionals in a large nonmanufacturing firm. The data we have include the entire ten-year exercise history for a sample of employees in the firm holding options that were granted on a common set of exercise dates. All the options from a single grant had the same strike price, expired ten years from the grant date, and vested after two years.[9] These common features mean that on each day in the ninety-six month exercise window the same profit could be earned by exercising an option from a common grant date, but the profit varies from grant to grant because of different exercise prices. Regardless of the option grant date, all option holders faced the same public information about the firm and the same exogenous macroeconomic environment on each calendar day in the exercise window. We also focused only on the exercise behavior of the 1,735 option holders who remained with the firm for the entire ten-year term of the option. This largely eliminates heterogeneity in option valuation because of anticipated turnover.

Daily data on employee exercise decisions for one large option grant were aggregated into calendar months, and figure 4.3 shows the distribution of first exercise times over the ninety-six-month exercise window. Evidence from this grant provides the strongest and simplest evidence of substantial heterogeneity in the value of stock options to employees unrelated to turnover intentions. This figure shows options were exercised over almost the entire ninety-six months with about 1 percent of the sample exercising options each month after about two years except for the final months when exercise activity increased.

Is the variation in exercise time in figure 4.3 substantial? As noted earlier, if employees valued options based on Black-Scholes and they could sell their options, the distribution of exercise times would have a single mass point equal to 1.0 in month ninety-six; all the options would be exercised in month ninety-six. Or, if employees identically valued options at another value, all

---

9. Two-year vesting means the options could not be exercised until twenty-four months after the grant date.

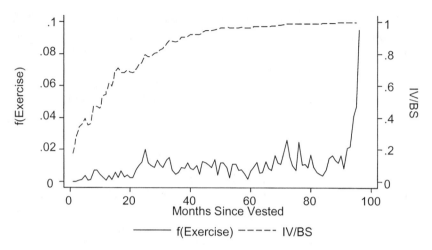

Fig. 4.3   Distribution of exercise times and intrinsic value/Black-Scholes value

of the exercise activity would have occurred in another month. The data clearly reject the prediction of a single exercise date.

The variation in exercise times implies substantial heterogeneity in the value employees place on holding their options. What more can be said? First, the upward sloping dotted line and the right vertical scale in figure 4.3 shows the profit an employee could have made by exercising an option divided by the option's BSV (i.e., $[SP_k - EP]/BSV_{t=k}^T$, $k = 1, 2 \ldots 96$). This ratio approximates the portion of the option's market value that is captured by exercising in any particular month rather than holding the option until the expiration date. One minus this ratio also indexes the penalty employees incur because they cannot sell their options. For example, for this option grant in month twenty, an employee lost about 30 percent of the option's value by immediately exercising the option. The variation in the potential value of the option sacrificed by "early" decisions indexes the substantial variation in the value of options to employees.

While much of the exercise activity summarized in figure 4.3 is "early" relative to what would be expected if employee stock options could be sold, the exercise pattern may be optimal for risk-averse employees who cannot sell their options and who also have their careers, human capital, and retirement income tied to the company. The different value employees place on options with identical terms may reflect differences in employee risk aversion with the least risk-averse employees holding options until the end of the exercise window. This hypothesis can be investigated by focusing on the 18.3 percent of the sample in figure 4.3 that held their options until close to the end of the exercise window and exercised their options in months ninety-four, ninety-five, or ninety-six. For this option grant, the intrinsic value of the option at the start of month ninety-four was about $240 per option, and the average option holder owned about 200 options. Thus, almost 20 percent of the sample were willing to forego the $240 profit per option at the start of month ninety-four for the opportunity to capture the expected gain from holding the option for, at most, an additional three months. What could employees expect to gain over this three-month period, and what does their behavior imply about their risk aversion?

Assuming the stock price at the beginning of month ninety-four equals $280, and the exercise price equals $40,[10] the Black-Scholes value of an option expiring in three months is $240.70 using reasonable values for the other Black-Scholes parameters.[11] Thus, a diversified, risk-neutral investor would be willing to hold their option for the remaining three months to collect the expected gain of about $.70 per option or a return of 0.29 percent above what could be earned by immediately exercising the option.

The Black-Scholes value of the option at the end of month ninety-four can also be compared with the value from holding the option until month ninety-six for a risk-averse employee who predicts the firm's stock price at the end of month ninety-six using the firm's expected risk adjusted return and the variance in these returns. Following the Hall and Murphy (2002) methodology, the dollar value to a risk-averse employee from holding the option until the end of month ninety-six is the certainty-equivalent dollar value of the uncertain payoffs from holding the options another three months. In these calculations, we follow Hall and Murphy (2002) and define the utility of w dollars to a risk-averse employee to be $(w^{(1-RA)})/(1 - RA)$, where RA is a risk aversion parameter.[12] At the start of month ninety-four, we assume the stock price at the end of month ninety-six is defined by a stock return drawn from a normal distribution of annual returns ($\sigma = .30$) centered on the risk-free return (6 percent) plus the risk premium investors expect to earn by holding this firm's stock (14 percent).[13] The utility function and the ending stock price distribution is used to calculate the certain cash payment employees would be willing to receive at the end of month ninety-three that would make these employees indifferent between exercising the option and holding the option until the expiration day. Because the average number of options or grants that employees received in our sample is about 200, the certainty-equivalent values were calculated by assuming an employee

10. Again, we do not report the precise values because we are unable to disclose the name of the firm. The stock and exercise prices are the prices unadjusted for stock splits that occurred after the option grant date. Therefore, these calculations show the payoff from exercising one of the original options that were granted to the employee and not an option that reflects the effects of the stock splits.

11. This assumes the short-term risk-free interest rate equals 6 percent per year and the standard deviation of yearly firm returns equals .30. These numbers are roughly representative of the firm and time period for this option grant.

12. If RA = 1, then $U(w) = \ln(w)$.

13. The certainty-equivalent values are computed by approximating the log-normal price distribution at the end of month ninety-six using a binomial price tree with 121 terminal prices.

was deciding when to exercise 200 options in the final three months of the option's term.

Table 4.2 shows the results from this exercise for different levels of risk aversion. The first row of numbers are based on the Black-Scholes model and report the expected value of the options at the end of month ninety-six assuming risk-free returns are earned on the options. These calculations give a value of $244.23 per option or $48,846 for 200 options. Discounting this value back to the end of month ninety-three gives the BSV of $48,140 in column two. The remaining rows of the table give the certainty equivalent values for different levels of risk aversion where the final stock price is based on a draw from an annual return distribution centered on the firm's expected risk-adjusted return ($N[.20, .3^2]$). The second row reports the risk-neutral evaluation of the options. This value is greater than the BSV in row one because the BSV assumes market traded options earn an expected rate of return equal to the risk-free interest rate (6 percent), while an employee owning an option that cannot be sold predicts the firm's stock price will increase at an expected rate that includes the firm's risk premium (.06 + .14). For the risk-neutral employee, this difference produces an expected gain larger than the BSV. For a risk-neutral employee, the dollar value at the end of month ninety-three of holding the option until the expiration date is $50,136. This risk-neutral employee would hold their options because this value is greater than the $48,000 profit that could be earned by exercising the options at the end of month ninety-three. The value at the end of month ninety-three of holding the options until the expiration date is also almost $2,000 greater than the BSV of $48,140 for market traded options. This example illustrates the point that risk-neutral employees could value employee

Table 4.2   **Certainty equivalent dollar values of 200 three-month options with an exercise price of $40 and a current stock price of $280**

	Assuming no discounting ($)	Discounted at risk-free interest rate ($)
Black-Scholes value	48,846.40	48,140.00
Certainty-equivalent values		
Risk aversion parameter[a]		
Risk-neutral	50,871.20	50,135.60
1.0	50,107.60	49,383.00
1.5	49,727.60	49,008.60
2.0	49,348.80	48,635.20
2.5	48,971.20	48,263.00
3.0	48,594.80	47,892.00
3.5	48,219.60	47,522.20

Note: The risk-neutral interest rate is 6 percent, the firm's risk premium is 14 percent, and the standard deviation of firm returns is .30.

[a] $U(x) = W^{(1-RA)}/(1-RA)$ for RA $\neq$ 1 and $U(x) = \ln(x)$ for RA = 1.

stock options at more than their BSV even when they are prohibited from selling their options.

Economists generally believe that individuals are risk averse, and there is no reason to believe the midlevel managers and professionals in this sample have different preferences. Therefore, the remaining rows in table 4.2 report more plausible certainty equivalent values for different levels of risk aversion. Hall and Murphy's evaluation of past research leads them to conclude that a risk-aversion parameter between two and three is a reasonable range for senior executives who are substantially wealthier than the sample of employees included in this analysis. The third row of table 4.2 shows that for a risk aversion parameter of 1.0, the certainty-equivalent value at the end of month ninety-three for the 200 options is $49,383, or $1,383 more than the $48,000 profit that could be earned by immediately exercising the options. The remaining rows show the certainty equivalents for other levels of risk aversion. At RA equal to 2.0, the value at the end of month ninety-three of holding these options to the end of month ninety-six is $635 more than the profit earned by immediately exercising them. When RA equals 3.0, the certainty equivalent value is $47,892, or $108 less than the value from immediately exercising the options. Rational option holders who have a value of risk aversion of 3.0 would be expected to exercise their 200 options at the end of month ninety-three. A risk-aversion parameter of 2.85 gives a certainty-equivalent value exactly equal to $48,000. Thus, individuals less risk averse than this value are predicted to hold their options, and those more risk averse are predicted to exercise their options. Because almost 20 percent of the sample held their options into month ninety-four, these calculations suggest a substantial minority of individuals owning options from this grant had a risk aversion parameter less than 2.85.

The calculations in table 4.2 show that moderately risk averse employees could form rational expectations about the firm's future stock price, decide to hold their options past the 93rd month, and place a value on the options greater than the options' BSV. Employee valuation of options that exceed the option's BSV and could not be sustained if employees could sell their options. If employees holding options at the end of month ninety-three with a risk-aversion parameter < 2.8 were allowed to sell their options, they would discover they had overvalued their options because the market would pay no more than the BSV. This leads to the prediction that the heterogeneity in valuations implied by the dispersed exercise times in figure 4.3 would disappear if options were tradable because employee valuations would converge to the BSV. When employees cannot sell their options, their valuations can exceed BSV because they cannot observe market prices for options with comparably long terms (ten years), and they can't borrow money from a bank using the options as collateral. Market information on options with terms comparable to employee stock options or borrowing terms from lenders might cause employees to value options closer to BSV.

Because employees lack these market signals, these calculations and their exercise behavior suggest they overvalue employee stock options compared to the BSV because they forecast the firm's future stock price distribution using the observed, risk-adjusted return earned by the firm's shareholders and not the risk-free return earned by owners of market traded options. Firms, of course, don't allow employees to sell their options or use them as collateral because they want employees to hold the options to encourage worker commitment to the firm and its objectives.

4.4.1 Inferring the Value of Options to Employees from Their Exercise Decisions

The basic ideas used to construct table 4.2 can be used in a statistical analysis of the exercise behavior for the entire sample of employees. This analysis can provide an estimate of employee risk aversion and the value of stock options to employees. We define the Employee Value Function ($EVF_{k,j,t}$) to be equal the value or utility (in dollars) to person j in month t from holding an option from grant k another time period t measures the months since the option vested and ranges from one to ninety-six because we study ten-year option grants with a two-year vesting period. In each month after vesting, we assume the employee decides between holding the option another period or exercising the option by comparing the profit from exercising the option (the intrinsic value) with the value of holding the option at least another period. Because the stock price minus the exercise price equals the certain cash payment the employee receives from exercising the option, the option will be exercised if this cash payment is greater than the monetary value to the employee of holding the option. In other words, the option is exercised in month t if

$$(1) \qquad (SP_t - EP_{k,j}) > EVF_{k,j,t}$$

and the option is held another period if

$$(1') \qquad (SP_t - EP_{k,j}) \le EVF_{k,j,t}.$$

The left side of equation (1) is observed and equals the intrinsic value of the option or the profit that is made by exercising the option in month t. The key parameter we wish to estimate is the risk-aversion parameter employees use to discount the uncertain future payoffs from holding the option. Thus, the variable we focus on is the certainty equivalent value from holding the option implied by different levels of risk aversion. The model underlying the calculations in table 4.2 imply an option is held another period if

$$(1'') \qquad (SP_t - EP_{k,j}) \le CE[RA, f(SP_{96} - EP_{k,j}), rf_t, rm_t, \sigma^2]_{k,j,t},$$

where CE(.) is the certainty-equivalent value of holding the option until it expires. This depends on risk aversion (RA), the distribution of the option's intrinsic value on the option's expiration date, the risk-free interest rate (rf_t), the firm's risk premium (rm_t), and the variance in the firm's returns

(σ_t^2). Equation (1″) could form the basis for estimating a probit model of employee exercise decisions. However, experimentation with different empirical specifications showed that this model fits the data poorly compared to specifications that included other covariates. Therefore, the estimates we report are based on a model where the probability an option is exercised in period t equals

(2) $\Pr(\text{Exercised in } t) = \Pr(\text{SP}_t - \text{EP}_{k,j}) > \beta_0$

$$+ \beta_1 \text{CE}[\text{RA}, f(\text{SP}_{96} - \text{EP}_{k,j}), rf_t, rm_t, \sigma^2]_{k,j,t}$$

$$+ XC + v_{k,j,t}, \text{ where } v_{k,j,t} \sim N(0,\sigma_v^2).$$

The variables included in the X matrix included a set of dummy variables indicating whether period t was within two months of a stock split, a dummy variable indicating whether the stock price surpassed the high price in the past twelve months, the differential between the stock price in month t and the high price in the previous twelve months, and average firm returns in the previous three months and the next six months. Using data from all the option grants in the data set and not just the one grant used in table 4.2 permits us to estimate a random effects probit model because most individuals in the sample held options from grants made on different dates in the early to mid 1990s.

One other problem had to be addressed before the exercise decision model described by equation (2) could be estimated using standard statistical software. The certainty-equivalent value of holding the option until expiration is a nonlinear combination of the parameter RA and the variables $f(\text{SP}_{96,i} - \text{EP}_{k,j})$, rf_t, rm_t and σ_t^2. Using the utility function described in the preceding, the certainty-equivalent value of holding the option until it expires equals $\exp[1/(1 - \text{RA}) \times \ln(E(\text{utility of holding option until expiration}) \times (1 - \text{RA}))]$ discounted to the current period (t) at the risk-free interest rate. The E(utility of holding option until expiration) $\sim \Sigma f(\text{SP}_{96,i} - \text{EP}_{k,j}) U(\text{SP}_{96,i} - \text{EP}_{k,j})$, where $f(\text{SP}_{96,i} - \text{EP}_{k,j})$ is calculated from a discrete estimate of the log-normal stock price distribution at the end of month ninety-six using a twenty-step binomial price tree and $U(\text{SP}_{96,i} - \text{EP}_{k,j}) = (\text{SP}_{96,i} - \text{EP}_{k,j})^{(1-\text{RA})}/(1 - \text{RA})$. These steps mean RA cannot be directly estimated in a standard linear-in-the-parameters probit or linear probability model of exercise decisions because CE(.) is a highly nonlinear function of the risk aversion parameter we wish to estimate. Therefore, we estimate the risk-aversion parameter indirectly by selecting different values of RA and then calculate the certainty-equivalent values implied by each risk aversion value for each observation in the data. A random effects probit model was then fit for each risk aversion value and the log-likelihood values for models computed using different values of RA were compared. The risk-aversion value that best fits the exercise decisions comes from the model with the maximum log-likelihood value.

Before describing the results, we briefly describe the sample and data. We have data for a sample of 2,180 middle managers and professionals who received multiple option grants at different exercise prices and at different points in calendar time from the studied firm. The firm is a large, long-established firm outside of manufacturing that has many tens of thousands of employees, billions of dollars in sales, and locations throughout the United States.[14] The employees in the sample received options at thirteen different exercise prices on thirteen different days in the 1990s with the majority of the grants occurring on two calendar dates where one exercise price was almost twice the magnitude of the other exercise price.[15] The research summarized here uses data on the exercise decisions made by employees for options received in the first two grants an employee participated in during the 1990s, where the options from the grants had vested before the fall of 2003.

Table 4.3 contains descriptive statistics on the sample of option grants. A total of 3,712 options grants were received by the 2,180 employees, and all but 1,127 of these grants were exercised during the study period (e.g., were not right-censored). Twenty-five percent of the grants are exercised by the 34th month following vesting, the median exercise time is sixty-nine months and the 75th percentile of the exercise distribution is ninety months. The exercise hazard rate is relatively low and stable during the first seventy-two months and then increases sharply in the final year as unexercised options are exercised before they expire. Consistent with the results for the one grant shown in figure 4.3, over the first seventy-two months of the exercise window, an average of 1.11 percent of unexercised option grants were exercised for the first time in each month.

An interesting feature of the experience in this firm is that not all options from a grant were exercised in the same month. In about 42 percent of the option grants where we observe the first exercise date (e.g., the exercise time is not right-censored), the employee did not exercise all of the options in the grant. On the other hand, overall 77 percent of the total options from the grants were exercised by employees on their first exercise date for a grant. For this reason only, the time until the first option from a grant is exercised is analyzed.

A final important feature of the sample is that it excludes managers who joined the firm during the 1990s or managers who received options during the 1990s but left the firm before the fall of 2003. Thus, these results describe the exercise decisions of long-tenured, stable employees who did not exercise options in anticipation of leaving the firm. Excluding option recipients who left the firm during the study period simplifies the analysis because

14. A condition for obtaining data from the firm included a promise that we would not reveal the identity of the firm. Therefore, we cannot provide a more detailed description of the firm or make the data available to other researchers.

15. In all cases, the options were granted "at the money." That is, the exercise price was equal to the firm's stock price on the day of the grant.

Table 4.3   **Summary statistics on exercise decisions**

No. of employees receiving options	2,180
No. of option grants	3,712
No. of option grants where time to first exercise date is censored	1,127
Mean options/grant	1,302
Mean hazard rate/month	0.0128
25th percentile of time to first exercise date (months)	34
Median time to first exercise date (months)	69
75th percentile of time to first exercise date (months)	90
Options exercised on first exercise date as fraction of options in the grant	0.765
Fraction of first exercise decisions where 100% of options in grant were exercised	0.576

we don't have to jointly model employee turnover and option exercise decisions.[16]

4.4.2   Estimates of Employee Risk Aversion

Table 4.4 reports the log-likelihood values for models that include the certainty-equivalent values of holding an option calculated from different risk-aversion values. For each RA value, the log-likelihood values are shown for two models; one model that includes only CE(.) and the option's intrinsic value and a second model that also includes the other covariates.[17] Across all the values of RA, a comparison of the likelihood values for the two specifications show the model that includes CE(.) and the other covariates does a much better job of predicting exercise decisions than a model with just CE(.) and the option's intrinsic value. Therefore, the discussion focuses on the results in the second column of table 4.4.

The results in column (2) show a clear pattern. For the values shown in the table, the log-likelihood value is maximized at $-12,409.44$ in the model where RA equals 2.20 and deviations from 2.20 in either direction produce results with smaller log-likelihood values. Additional models were estimated for RA values around 2.20, and a RA value of 2.21 produced a maximum log-likelihood value of $-12,409.437$. This method of inferring RA does not produce an estimated standard error. Note, however, the risk-neutral specification implies $RA = 0$, and for this model the log likelihood value is $-12,455.24$. A likelihood ratio test comparing $RA = 0$ and $RA = 2.21$ clearly rejects the hypothesis that these employees were risk neutral in their option

16. Firms often report that they provide options to improve employee retention. Modeling option exercise decisions and turnover is difficult. While options might reduce turnover, employees that are planning to leave the firm can be expected to exercise vested options before their departure. This creates a positive correlation between exercise decisions and the probability of turnover in the "near term." Modeling exercise decisions and turnover behavior jointly would require a more elaborate competing risk framework and data on employees who did not receive options.

17. The log-likelihood value for the model that includes the option's intrinsic value and the X variables but not CE(.) is $-12,475.29$.

Table 4.4   **Log-likelihood values for models that include certainty-equivalent values of holding an option for different levels of risk aversion**

	Model includes:	
Risk aversion	Intrinsic value, CE(.)	Intrinsic value, CE(.), X
Risk-neutral	−12,488.67	−12,455.240
0.50	−12,484.42	−12,452.822
1.00	−12,473.70	−12,443.847
1.50	−12,461.13	−12,433.029
1.75	−12,451.98	−12,424.170
2.00	−12,442.12	−12,413.851
2.20	−12,437.94	−12,409.443
2.25	−12,438.13	−12,409.661
2.30	−12,438.95	−12,410.499
2.50	−12,447.87	−12,419.073
3.00	−12,487.56	−12,453.232
3.50	−12,520.71	−12,475.175

Notes: A model with just the option Intrinsic Value (IV) and the X variables has a log-likelihood value of −12,475.29. The six variables in the **X** matrix include the differential between the stock price in the month and the twelve-month stock price high, the average firm stock return over the previous three months, the average stock return over the next six months, and separate dummy variables indicating whether the stock price in the month exceeds the twelve-month price high, and indicators for two months prior to a stock split and two months after a stock split. The log-likelihood value is maximized (−12,409.437) for a model where RA = 2.21.

evaluations. In addition, the results are consistent with the model described by equation (2) because any of the specifications that include CE(.) fit the data better than a model without CE(.) ($\log L = −12,475.3$).

The estimates summarized in the preceding imply all employees in the sample have identical risk preferences. This is unlikely to be true. Indeed, heterogeneity in risk aversion may be an important variable explaining the variability in exercise times observed in the data. One variable we have that may be negatively correlated with risk aversion is an employee's earnings in the firm. Although this sample is a fairly homogeneous sample along earnings relative to the earnings distribution for the entire firm or for the U.S. labor force, the variation in wages in the sample may be sufficient to identify variation in risk aversion.

The sample of employees was divided into wage quartiles based on real earnings in the first month an option held by an individual vested. The empirical method used in the preceding for the entire sample was then replicated for each subsample to identify the value of RA that maximized the log-likelihood value for each subsample. The results are consistent with the hypothesis that lower-wage workers are more risk averse than higher-wage workers. For workers in the first quartile, the best fitting model had an RA value of 2.34; the value for the second quartile was 2.18; 2.15 for the third quartile; and 2.09 for the highest wage quartile. Although we cannot statistically test whether these values are different from one another, the point estimates suggest variation in risk aversion in the predicted direction.

The values of RA for models that best predict exercise decisions for the entire sample and each wage quartile can be used to calculate the certainty-equivalent value to an employee of holding an option until the expiration date. These option values to employees can be compared to the value the market would place on the same options using Black-Scholes. Figure 4.4 shows these values for thirty-six to eighty-four months after the option vests for a ten-year option with an exercise price of $15 and a current stock price of $50. The figure shows BSV and the certainty-equivalent values of the option for RA = 2.34, 2.21, and 2.09. As expected, the uncertain payoff from holding the option means the option's value declines as risk aversion increases. For example, at sixty months after vesting or seven years since the option was received, the value of holding the option is $38.61 when RA = 2.34, $41.14 when RA = 2.21, and $43.41 when RA = 2.09.

The other key point shown in this figure is that for these three risk-aversion parameters, an employee places a higher value on holding the option than what Black-Scholes predicts the option could be sold for in the market. As discussed earlier, this finding supports the point made from table 4.2 that the exercise behavior of these employees implies they value their options at values in excess of the option's BSV because of fundamental differences

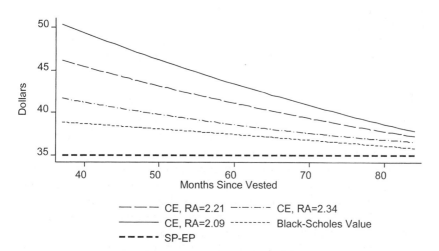

Fig. 4.4   Certainty equivalent and Black-Scholes values 36–84 months after vesting for a 10-year option where SP = 50, EP = 15

Notes: Expected firm return = .2, risk free return = .06, SD returns = .3. Each period the certainty equivalent (CE) values are computed from a terminal stock price distribution estimated from a forty-step binomial price tree. See text for description of the utility function. The CE lines are smoothed estimates through the CE values. SP = stock price. EP = exercise price.

between employee stock options and market traded options. Because employees cannot sell their options or use them as collateral to borrow money, they have no market signals to evaluate their worth to outside investors. The estimates suggest that employees value their options based on the firm's expected returns rather than the risk-free return the market uses to value options. The constraints that prohibit employees from selling their options or using them as collateral are imposed by the firm to further the firm's objectives. For senior managers who have substantial impact on the success of the firm, these features encourage executives to hold onto their options and make decisions that are beneficial to shareholders. In the firm studied here, the employees are not at a sufficiently high level in the firm to individually have a large impact on profitability. However, the firm may gain a more committed management workforce by providing options and encouraging employees to hold on to them.

This section focuses on how employee exercise decisions can be used to infer the risk aversion of employees and the value employees place on employee stock options. These results have implications for many of the research and policy questions summarized in earlier sections of the chapter. For example, the cost of options to the firm depend on when employees exercise their options and the sensitivity of their exercise decisions to changes in the firm's stock price. Using Black-Scholes to cost options assumes options are held until the expiration date and the stock price at expiration is drawn from a log-normal distribution. Because these assumptions do not describe the option grants studied here, the BSV provides a poor estimate of the cost of these options to the firm. However, the empirical model of exercise decisions estimated here can be used to predict when employees exercise their options and the sensitivity of their exercise decisions to the firm's stock price.

4.5 Open Questions and Conclusion

In the past few years, there have been dramatic shifts in public perceptions of and government regulations over how executives and other employees are paid in the United States. Until just recently, firms in the United States were not required to "expense" stock options in their balance sheets. Now that U.S. firms have to report options as an expense in the balance sheet and not just in footnotes to financial statements, decisions to grant options to employees are likely to be subject to greater scrutiny. While much has been learned about employee stock options over the past ten to fifteen years, numerous issues important to firms, policymakers, and employees remain unresolved. In this chapter, we highlight some of these issues, discuss recent policy shifts affecting options, and summarize the data sources on options available in the United States and elsewhere. In the last section, we present some of our own work on options that explore the value employees place on options that, in turn, has implications for the cost of options to the firm.

There are several new and continuing regulatory issues on the horizon that deal with compensation and stock options. One that is interesting is the way that firms have been required to report on executive compensation. Even though there has been considerable reform, there is still confusion about the way firms report options in the "summary compensation table." Firms are given wide leeway in the assumptions they can make about certain forms of compensation and how they report. We anticipate more reforms and changes along these lines in the future.

Another is how to explicitly deal with employee stock options in the national accounts. As is it today, ISOs are not counted at all and the much more prevalent NSOs are, but as discussed previously, there are considerable problems with how and when these data are reported. Recent attempts by the BEA to examine this have been fruitful, but there are still unresolved conceptual and data issues to be addressed.

There is a series of other interesting questions on options where some progress has been made but more is to be done. Some of these questions have been answered, but many have solutions that are not yet known. The questions include why do firms grant options (Hall and Murphy 2003), do options retain employees (Hall and Murphy 2003), do they motivate employees (Hall and Murphy 2003), do they attract employees (Oyer and Schafer 2005b), why are they granted (in some cases) throughout the firm (Oyer and Schafer 2005b), will the recent FASB changes alter the way employees are paid (Bodie, Kalpan, and Merton 2003), how well do options work, why don't more firms use indexed options (e.g., relative performance evaluation work by Antle and Smith 1986; and Gibbons and Murphy 1990), are options efficient, what is the value employees place on options (Hall and Murphy 2003; Hallock and Olson 2007b), what is the cost of options to the firm (Hallock and Olson 2007b), and what are issues surrounding options backdating (Lie 2005, 2007; Yermack 1997)?

New work on stock options has the potential to have a practical impact on firms and the national accounts. If firms do not have a credible estimate of how employees value stock options or other forms of compensation and firms alter the mix of pay, there could be consequences related to employee attraction, retention, and turnover and problems reconciling the national accounts. We hope that our work is a useful step in the right direction of understanding more about compensation and employee stock options.

References

Aboody, David. 1996. Market valuation of employee stock options. *Journal of Accounting and Economics* 22:357–91.
Antle, Rick, and Abbie Smith. 1986. An empirical investigation of the relative per-

formance evaluation of corporate executives. *Journal of Accounting Research* 24:1–39.

Armstrong, Christopher S., Alan D. Jagolinzer, and David David F. Larcker. 2006. Timing of employee stock option exercises and the valuation of stock option expense. Stanford, Working Paper.

Australian Bureau of Statistics. 2002. Treatment of stock options in the national accounts: Summary of views expressed by the EDG. Paper presented for the OECD Meeting of National Accounts Experts, Chateau de la Muette, Paris.

Bajaj, Mukesh, Sumon C. Mazumdar, Rahul Surana, and Sanjay Unmi. 2006. A matrix-based lattice model to value employee stock options. *Journal of Derivatives* 14 (1): 9–26.

Bergman, Nittai K., and Dirk Jenter. 2007. Employee sentiment and stock options compensation. *Journal of Financial Economics* 84 (3): 667–712.

Black, Fischer, and Myron Scholes. 1973. The pricing of options and corporate liabilities. *Journal of Political Economy* 81 (3): 637–54.

Bodie, Zvi, Robert Kaplan, and Robert C. Merton. 2003. For the last time: Stock options are an expense. *Harvard Business Review* (March): 63–71.

Brealey, Richard A., Stewart C. Myers, and Alan J. Marcus. 1995. *Fundamentals of corporate finance.* Inc. New York: McGraw-Hill.

Bureau of Labor Statistics (BLS). 2000. Pilot survey on the incidence of stock options in private industry in 1999. USDL no. 00-290. Washington, DC: Bureau of Labor Statistics.

———. 2007. National Compensation Survey: Employee benefits in private industry in the United States, March 2007. Summary no. 0705. Washington, DC: Bureau of Labor Statistics.

Carpenter, Jennifer, N. 1998. The exercise and valuation of executive stock options. *Journal of Financial Economics* 48:127–58.

Chidambaran, N. K., and R. P. Nagpurnanand. 2003. Executive stock option repricing, internal governance mechanisms, and management turnover. *Journal of Financial Economics* 69: 153–89.

Core, John E., and Wayne R. Guay. 2001. Stock option plans for non-executive employees. *Journal of Financial Economics* 61:253–87.

Crimmel, Beth Levin, and Jeffrey L. Schildkraut. 1999. National Compensation Survey collects test data on stock option plans. *Compensation and Working Conditions* (Winter):17–20.

———. 2001. Stock option plans surveyed by NCS. *Compensation and Working Conditions* (Spring):3–21.

Eurostat. n.d. Employee stock options. Paper prepared for the Advisory Expert Group on National Accounts. Unpublished Manuscript.

Farrell, Anne M., Susan D. Krische, and Karen L. Sedatole. 2006. Employees' perceived value of their stock option holdings: How training affects the cost-value gap. University of Illinois and Michigan State University, Working Paper.

Financial Accounting Standards Board (FASB). 1995. Accounting for stock-based compensation. FASB Standard no. 123. Norwalk, CT: FASB. www.fasb.org or 72.3.243.42/pdf/fas123.pdf.

———. 2004. Accounting for stock-based compensation. FASB Standard no. 123 (Revised 2004). Norwalk, CT: FASP. http://www.fasb.org/summary/stsum123r.shtml.

Gibbons, Robert, and Kevin J. Murphy. 1990. Relative performance evaluations for chief executive officers. *Industrial and Labor Relations Review* 43 (February): 30S–51S.

Glassman, Cynthia. 2008. Regulatory rules and estimating economic growth: Two perspectives on expensing stock options. Notes from a speech presented at the 2008 ASSA meeting, New Orleans, LA.

Hall, Brian J., and Kevin J. Murphy. 2002. Stock options for undiversified executives. *Journal of Accounting and Economics* 33:3–42.

———. 2003. The trouble with stock options. *Journal of Economic Perspectives* 17 (3): 49–70.

Hallock, Kevin F., and Craig A. Olson. 2007a. Employees' choice of method of pay. Cornell University and University of Illinois, Working Paper.

———. 2007b. The value of stock options to non-executive employees. Cornell University and University of Illinois, Working Paper.

Heath, Chip, Steven Huddart, and Mark Lang. 1999. Psychological factors and stock option exercise. *Quarterly Journal of Economics* 114 (2): 601–27.

Heron, Randall A., and Erik Lie. 2007. Does backdating explain the stock price pattern around executive stock option grants? *Journal of Financial Economics* 83:271–95.

Hodge, Frank D., Shivaram Rajgopal, and Terry J. Shevlin. 2006. How do managers value stock options and restricted stock. University of Washington, Working Paper.

Huddart, Steven, and Mark Lang. 1996. Employee stock option exercises: An empirical analysis. *Journal of Accounting and Economics* 21:5–43.

Ikäheimo, S., N. Kuosa, and V. Puttonen. 2006. The true and fair view of executive stock option valuation. *European Accounting Review* 15 (3): 351–66.

Jones, Derek C., Panu Kalmi, and Mikko Makinen. 2006. The determinants of stock options compensation: Evidence from Finland. *Industrial Relations* 45 (3): 437–68.

Kato, Hideaki Kiyoski, Michael Lemmon, Mi Luo, and James Schallheim. 2005. An empirical examination of the costs and benefits of executive stock options: Evidence from Japan. *Journal of Financial Economics* 78:435–61.

Kroumova, Maya K., and James C. Sesil. 2006. Intellectual capital, monitoring, and risk: What predicts the adoption of employee stock options? *Industrial Relations* 45 (4): 734–52.

Lambert, R. A., D. F. Larcker, and R. E. Verecchia. 1991. Portfolio considerations in valuing executive compensation. *Journal of Accounting Research* 29:129–49.

Landsman, Wayne P., Ken V. Peasnell, Peter F. Pope, and Shu Yeh. 2006. Which approach to accounting for employee stock options best reflects market pricing? *Review of Accounting Studies* 11:203–45.

Lequiller, F. 2002. Treatment of stock options in national accounts of non-European OECD member countries. Working Paper. Organization for Economic Cooperation and Development.

Lie, Erik. 2005. On the timing of CEO stock option awards. *Management Science* 51 (5): 802–12.

———. 2007. Web page. University of Iowa. http://www.biz.uiowa.edu/faculty/elie/backdating.htm.

McIntosh, Susan Hume. n.d. Accounting for stock options in the United States. Board of Governors of the Federal Reserve System. Unpublished Manuscript.

Mehran, Hamid, and Joseph Tracy. 2001. The effect of employee stock options on the evolution of compensation in the 1990s. *Economic Policy Review* 7 (December): 17–34.

Merton, Robert C. 1973. The theory of rational option pricing. *Bell Journal of Economics and Management Science* 4 (Spring): 141–83.

Moylan, Carol E. 2007. Treatment of employee stock options in the U.S. national economic accounts. Bureau of Economic Analysis. Unpublished Manuscript.

————. 2008. Employee stock options and the national accounts. Bureau of Economic Affairs (BEA) Briefing, February.
Oyer, Paul, and Scott Schaefer. 2005a. Accounting, governance, and broad-based stock options grants. Stanford University and Northwestern University, Working Paper.
————. 2005b. Why do some firms give stock options to all employees? An empirical examination of alternative theories. *Journal of Financial Economics* 76:99–133.
————. 2006. Costs of broad-based stock option plans. *Journal of Financial Intermediation* 15 (4): 511–34.
Pendleton, Andrew. 2006. Incentives, monitoring, and employee stock ownership plans: New evidence and interpretations. *Industrial Relations* 45 (4): 753–77.
Ruser, John W. 2001. The Employment Cost Index: What is it? *Monthly Labor Review* 124 (September): 3–16.
Schildkraut, Jeffrey L. 2004. Stock options: National Compensation Survey update. BLS Compensation and Working Conditions Online. Washington, DC: Bureau of Labor Statistics.
Yermack, David. 1997. Good timing: CEO stock option awards and company news announcements. *Journal of Finance* 52:449–76.

Comment   Chris Riddell

Stock options and, in particular, equity awards broadly defined, remain an area with many unanswered questions. Why do companies use stock options (or other equity awards)? do they motivate employees; lead to greater retention? What value do employees place on equity awards? We still know relatively little about these fundamental questions. Further, in light of recent changes in accounting practices for stock options where firms are now required to recognize compensation expense at the time of the grant, as well as international generally accepted accounting principles (GAAP) standards likely coming to the United States, there are many policy issues still to be addressed such as what types of option pricing models may or should be mandated in the future.

A key reason why our knowledge is so limited in the area of equity compensation is data availability: to think deeply about issues such as those in the preceding, we require detailed information on the contractual parameters of a stock grant coupled with personnel records for a reasonable time period (e.g., long enough to examine such behavior as turnover or exercising and so forth). Locating such data is, unfortunately, far from straightforward! Hallock and Olson have done an admirable job in finding several sources of such data resulting in a series of exciting papers (also see Hallock and Olson 2007a,b).

In this chapter, the authors focus primarily on how employees value stock

Chris Riddell is an assistant professor in the School of Policy Studies at Queen's University.

options. In a separate section, they also provide a useful discussion on the wide variety of data sources that have been used for analyzing equity compensation, including the pros and cons of each. The latter will be a nice resource for researchers interested in the field. In my comment, I focus on the following: using data on employee exercising to learn about stock option valuation.

The main part of the chapter uses ten years of data from several stock grants made by a company to its middle managers as part of a stock purchase plan. This data contains the complete exercising history from this set of grants and all key contractual parameters. This is the exact sort of data that, while difficult, risky (because these attempts often do not pan out), and time consuming to compile, can lead to important insights into the role of compensation policy within the firm. The authors describe the Black-Scholes-Merton (BSM) method for option pricing, which has traditionally been the main method for computing fair value for tradeable options and show how basic exercising behavior—in particular, early or suboptimal exercising (i.e., exercising before the expiration date)—is inconsistent with BSM. Moreover, this finding comes from a sample of managers who remain with the company for the entire term of the grants. The authors then develop a framework for estimating the value of these options to employees. The key finding is that this group of middle managers valued their options at much less than the BSM value.

In keeping with the theme of the conference, and given that I only have a small set of comments on the empirical work, the main purpose of my comment is to bring some of the institutional framework up to speed with current practices in option pricing and, in particular, draw attention to how this type of data can be used to test other approaches to the valuation of stock options and other equity awards. On the latter point, it is useful to stress that (in addition to compensatory stock options) many other equity awards, including stock appreciation rights (SARs), performance-vesting awards, and phantom stock have had to be expensed since 1993.[1] The recent changes to the accounting of stock options, therefore, creates a level playing field for equity awards. Many practitioners are predicting that this will lead to a decline in the use of stock options and an increase in the use of other equity-related vehicles, where often the firm can be much more creative, and incentive-oriented, in the contractual parameters.

How employees value stock options is very important because for accounting purposes—including budget planning for firms because they have to issue (or buy back) new shares—we want to know what amount they have been compensated (just as with cash compensation). If, as most studies including this one have found, employees value stock options at substantially less than BSM, then stock options may be a rather expensive way

---

1. Specifically, since the first FAS 123 standard.

to compensate employees. Moreover, understanding how employees value stock options will surely help understand their effectiveness from a compensation policy standpoint. However, the analysis in the chapter should be framed within a more up-to-date institutional framework. Specifically, the chapter is framed solely within the context of BSM for computing fair value for equity awards. The BSM method is a simple, static, six-variable formula that is literally calculated by a single cell-Excel formula (in practice). It is referred to as closed-form given that the input variables are fixed assumptions and, therefore, cannot change over time or interact with other variables (such as exercising behavior). Most other papers in this literature, from the ones I am familiar with, do this as well because BSM has been, by far, the main method for the valuation of tradeable stock options.

While it may be true that BSM is still regarded as the workhorse valuation method, this appears to be changing. The 2004 revised Financial Accounting Standards Board (FASB) exposure draft Share-based Payments (FAS 123R), which led to the new requirement that noncompensatory stock options are expensed to the income statement at the time of the grant using a fair-value method, says a great deal more about models for valuing stock options.[2] To be brief, FAS 123R notes: "a lattice model is more fully able to capture and better reflects the characteristics of a particular ESO . . . is preferable and should be used if it is practical to do so." Lattice models (i.e., binomials, trinomials) are, thus, now considered the preferred technique. Most practitioners believe lattice models (or other preferred numerical methods, such as Monte Carlo simulation) were denoted as preferred rather than mandated because the latter methodologies were—at that time—not readily available commercially and because companies may not have had the necessary data on input variables not required under BSM such as exercising behavior. I will say more on this in the following. But even a crude look through the major consulting firms that work in this area, as well as the many software packages that have emerged in the last few years, reveals that the BSM approach is quite likely on the way out.[3] Also, in practice, the "preferred" designation means that once firms switch, they will be essentially unable to go back. Given the current state of the practice on equity compensation valuation, it would have been a useful addition for the authors to show how their total cost calculations differ when the preferred valuation models are applied to the data. Moreover, this would distinguish the chapter from the others in the literature where multiple authors have

2. Compensatory stock options actually had to be expensed before FAS 123R, but—based on what practitioners have written in many articles in the practitioner journals—most firms avoided expensing options by making them noncompensatory with a strike price equal to the current market price (despite it being quite clear, even in job ads, that they were a form of compensation).

3. The more advanced methodologies are now very approachable with several plug-and-play Excel-based options on the market.

developed a new framework and found that employees value options at less than BSM.[4]

Hallock and Olson provide a very nice summary of the assumptions inherent to BSM, but a couple of additional points can be made, although it should be stressed that not all of the following issues necessarily hold to the specific case examined in the chapter. There are several reasons why employees may have undiversified portfolios that make employee stock options valuation inconsistent with standard financial theory. Clearly a key feature is that a stock option cannot be sold, but other possibilities are contractual requirements that the individual must have large holdings of the company's stock (more common for executives, however) or that such holdings are encouraged. As well, other contractual parameters such as vesting conditions (both time-based and performance-based), forfeiture of unvested or out-of-the-money options when an employee leaves, and blackout periods can also make stock option valuation more complex than standard option valuation. FAS 123R solidifies the use of more advanced methods in its recommendation on using lattice (and several other) models by noting that such approaches: (a) allows for changes in the traditional six variables over the contractual term, and (b) allows for estimates of early exercising patterns and postvesting termination over the term (thereby providing a more accurate adjustment for nontransferability). Overall, exercising behavior, in particular, is likely to be key in advancing this literature.

Hallock and Olson note that rigorously modeling turnover and exercising is a difficult step. Indeed, the expectation for employers appears to be that data on previous grants is used to simply calculate some average values for these variables. But, with this data, the authors can test not only BSM, as they have currently done, but also the preferred methods and, in particular, draw a more transparent link between their approach (which, of course, builds off of exercising behavior) and other available methods including those in the academic literature. We know, as far I can tell, very little about the interactions between market conditions, exercising behavior, and exiting the firm, but such decisions made by employees are going to be important for future option-pricing models. Moreover, a rigorous analysis of exercising and exit rates from the firm will have stronger implications for compensation policy as a behavioral lever, particularly given the prediction that FAS 123R may lead to an increased use of other equity vehicles, such as SARs and performance-vesting awards, where firms can be more creative in the terms of the contract.

There are two empirical issues in the chapter worth considering, particularly given the important policy and practitioner implications of the chapter.

---

4. Other related papers not discussed that interested readers can look at include Bettis, Bizjak, and Lemmon (2003), Detemple and Sundaresan (1999), and Ingersoll (2006). Interestingly, Hodder and Jackwerth (2005) find that managers who have control over the risk level in the firm value options at considerably more than the BSM amount.

First, it is unclear that restricting the sample to individuals who stayed with the firm for the duration of the contractual term is reasonable. This certainly simplifies the analysis and yields a strong test of heterogeneity in exercising behavior (because we know everyone stayed until the expiration date). But, if the model is to be taken seriously as a way employees value options, we need to, among other things, account for employees exercising "early" as a joint decision with leaving the firm.[5] Further, even if the model is not meant to be an option-pricing methodology itself but rather an approach for testing key assumptions of valuation methods, we simply lose too much information about employee behavior that is common in practice and often noted as central to the limitations of BSM valuation. Second, and related to the preceding point, the empirical strategy relies on there being multiple grants so that we have multiple exercising decisions (across grants) for a given employee. This is a clever approach from an econometric standpoint but is problematic from an option-pricing standpoint because firms have to calculate fair value for a single grant.

Hallock and Olson have provided a nice review piece on current issues in stock options, including a thorough review of the various data sources available to researchers; a detailed summary of the Black-Scholes-Merton method for valuing options; and, most important, a summary of some of their evidence on exercising behavior using a detailed case study of a firm and the implications of these results for how we value stock options. The latter is exactly the kind of rigorous empirical work with detailed data and contractual information from a firm that we need to move the compensation literature forward.

References

Bettis, J. C., John Bizjak, and Michael Lemmon. 2003. The cost of employee stock options. Arizona State University. Unpublished Manuscript.

Detemple, Jerome, and Suresh Sundaresan. 1999. Nontraded asset valuation with portfolio constraints: A binomial approach. *Review of Financial Studies* 12 (4): 835–72.

Hallock, Kevin, and Craig Olson. 2007a. Employees' choice over method of pay. Cornell University and University of Illinois, Working Paper.

———. 2007b. The value of stock options to non-executive employees. Cornell University and University of Illinois, Working Paper.

Hodder, James, and Jens Jackwerth. 2005. Employee stock options: Much more valuable than you thought. University of Wisconsin-Madison. Unpublished Manuscript.

Ingersoll, Jonathon. 2006. The subjective and objective evaluation of incentive stock options. *Journal of Business* 79 (2): 453–87.

5. As noted in the preceding, even practitioners will likely need to start building in simple assumptions on exercising and turnover into their valuation models. Indeed, Monte Carlo models of option valuation—now also readily available in Excel-based option-pricing software—explicitly allow for users to include such assumptions.

II

Labor Market Dynamics, Job Security, and Job Attachment

5

Adjusted Estimates of Worker Flows and Job Openings in JOLTS

Steven J. Davis, R. Jason Faberman, John C. Haltiwanger, and Ian Rucker

5.1 Introduction

The Job Openings and Labor Turnover Survey (JOLTS) is an innovative data program that delivers national, regional, and industry estimates for the monthly flow of hires and separations and for the stock of unfilled job openings. Analysts have seized on JOLTS data as a valuable source of insights about U.S. labor markets and an important new research tool for evaluating theories of labor market behavior. Recent studies draw on JOLTS data to investigate the cyclical behavior of hires and separations (Hall 2005); the Beveridge curve relation between unemployment and job vacancies (Valetta 2005; Fujita and Ramey 2007; Shimer 2007a); the connection between quits and employer recruiting behavior (Faberman and Nagypál 2007); and the relationship among vacancies, hires and employment growth at the establishment level (Davis, Faberman, and Haltiwanger 2006, 2009). Given the key roles played by job vacancies and worker flows in prominent search-based

Steven J. Davis is the William H. Abbott Professor of International Business and Economics at the Booth School of Business, University of Chicago, and a research associate of the National Bureau of Economic Research. R. Jason Faberman is an economist at the Federal Reserve Bank of Philadelphia. John C. Haltiwanger is professor of economics at the University of Maryland, and a research associate of the National Bureau of Economic Research.

Ian Rucker was a bright young graduate student at the University of Maryland with a promising future. He died in May 2009 after he completed his work on this paper while working at the Bureau of Labor Statistics. He was a wonderful partner in research, and we will miss him. We thank Nathan Brownback for excellent research assistance and staff at the Bureau of Labor Statistics for much help with this project. We are also grateful to Robert Hall, Charlotte Mueller, John Wohlford, and the editors for helpful comments on an earlier draft. The views expressed in this paper are our own and do not reflect the opinions of the Bureau of Labor Statistics, the Federal Reserve Bank of Philadelphia, the Federal Reserve System, or their staffs.

theories of unemployment along the lines of Mortensen and Pissarides (1994), JOLTS will continue to attract keen interest from researchers.

In addition to notable virtues, the JOLTS program presents measurement issues that are imperfectly understood and not widely appreciated. Reasons for concern can be seen in three simple comparisons to other data sources. First, the aggregate employment growth implied by the flow of hires and separations in JOLTS consistently exceeds the growth observed in its national benchmark, the Current Establishment Statistics (CES) survey.[1] Cumulating the difference between hires and separations from 2001 to 2006 yields a discrepancy of 6.6 million nonfarm jobs. Second, JOLTS hires and separations are surprisingly small compared to similar measures in other data sources.[2] Third, the cross-sectional density of establishment growth rates shows much less dispersion in JOLTS than in data sources with comprehensive establishment coverage.[3]

These discrepancies arise, at least in part, from two aspects of JOLTS methodology. First, the JOLTS sample excludes establishment openings and very young establishments. Similar sample restrictions apply to many establishment surveys, but the consequences are more significant for the key statistics derived from JOLTS. To see this point, start with the observation that employees at new establishments have very short job tenures, which, in turn, are associated with very high separation rates.[4] Thus, the JOLTS sample systematically excludes a set of establishments with unusually high employee turnover. The volatility of employment growth rates is also extremely high at very young establishments, even after conditioning on size.[5] Greater volatility at the establishment level involves larger worker flows, as we show. In addition to these effects of JOLTS sample design on worker flows, new establishments surely account for a disproportionate share of job openings. Hence, the exclusion of new and very young establishments imparts a downward bias to both job openings and worker flows. It potentially affects cyclical patterns as well.

The second issue with JOLTS methodology involves adjustments for nonrespondents. Survey nonresponse rates are likely higher for establishments that exit or contract sharply. Compared to a randomly selected establishment, these establishments have high separation and layoff rates and low rates of hires and job openings. However, the JOLTS practice effectively imputes to nonrespondents the average rate among respondents in the same region-industry-size category. If the response rate is lower for exits and sharply contracting establishments, this imputation practice understates separations and overstates hires and job openings. It also imparts an upward

---

1. See Wohlford et al. (2003), Nagypál (2006), and Faberman (2005a).
2. See Faberman (2005a) and Davis, Faberman, and Haltiwanger (2006).
3. See Faberman (2005a).
4. See, for example, Mincer and Jovanovic (1981), Topel and Ward (1992), and Farber (1994).
5. See Davis and Haltiwanger (1999) and Davis et al. (2007).

bias to the employment change implied by the flow of hires and separations. Again, there are potentially important effects on cyclical patterns as well.[6]

In light of these measurement issues, we develop and implement a method for adjusting the published JOLTS estimates to more accurately reflect worker flows and job openings in the U.S. economy. Our method involves reweighting the cross-sectional density of employment *growth rates* in JOLTS to match the corresponding density in the Business Employment Dynamics (BED) data. The BED, which derives from administrative records in the unemployment insurance system, covers essentially all private-sector employers—including entrants, exits, and very young establishments. We apply the reweighted density of employment growth rates to calculate adjusted estimates for worker flows and unfilled job openings (i.e., vacancies). In doing so, we exploit the close cross-sectional relationship of worker flows and vacancy rates to the establishment-level growth rate of employment.[7]

To preview the main results, our adjusted measures of hires and separations exceed the published JOLTS estimates by about one-third. The adjusted layoff rate exceeds the published rate by more than 60 percent. Time series properties are also affected. For example, hires show more volatility than separations in the published statistics, but the reverse holds in the adjusted statistics. The impact of our adjustment methodology on estimated job openings is more modest, raising the average vacancy rate by about 8 percent. Our adjustments virtually eliminate the discrepancy between nonfarm private-sector employment growth in the CES or BED and the cumulative difference of hires and separations in JOLTS.

In terms of mechanics, our adjustments to the published JOLTS statistics can be understood by reference to two basic observations. First, the cross-sectional density of establishment growth rates in JOLTS data deviates systematically from the density in the underlying universe of establishment-level observations, as measured in the BED. Second, rates of worker flows and job vacancies vary greatly with establishment growth rates in the cross section. The cross-sectional relations are also highly asymmetric about zero. The underweighting of establishments with sharp negative growth rates in JOLTS yields an undercount of layoffs and an overstatement of the quit-layoff ratio. Correcting for this aspect of the JOLTS data substantially raises the average layoff rate and amplifies its variation over time.

---

6. In early 2009, following the conclusion of this research project, the BLS made substantial revisions to the published JOLTS statistics. The revisions reflected several of our suggestions and, consequently, resolve some of the issues noted in the following. For example, the revised JOLTS statistics now have net growth rates that are generally consistent with those derived from the CES. Revised worker flow rates are also higher, on average, though still below the magnitudes of the adjusted estimates in this chapter. The full details of the BLS revisions can be found at http://www.bls.gov/jlt/methodologyimprovement.htm. This study uses published data and microdata prior to the revisions.

7. For evidence, see Davis, Faberman, and Haltiwanger (2006, 2007) and section 5.3.

The more modest nature of our adjustments to the job openings rate reflects two opposing effects. The underweighting of establishments with sharp negative growth rates, which have low vacancy rates, imparts an upward bias to the published vacancy rate. The omission of births and very young fast-growing establishments imparts a downward bias. Our results indicate that the second effect dominates, on average, so that the adjusted vacancy rate exceeds the published rate.

The next section reviews certain aspects of the JOLTS sample design, JOLTS imputation and benchmarking methods, the BED data, and various measurement issues. Section 5.3 compares JOLTS data to other sources. Section 5.4 presents several striking patterns in the cross-sectional relationships of worker flows and job openings to employment growth. These cross-sectional relations play a major role in our adjustment method. They also shed new light on the cyclical behavior of labor market flows and unemployment, as stressed by Davis, Faberman, and Haltiwanger (2006). Section 5.5 sets forth our adjustment method and explains how we handle certain issues that arise in the implementation. Section 5.6 presents adjusted estimates for worker flows and job openings and compares them to the published JOLTS estimates. We conclude in section 5.7 with remarks about some broader implications of our results and several suggestions for improving JOLTS statistics.

5.2   Data Sources and Analysis Samples

Our study exploits BLS microdata from the Job Openings and Labor Turnover Survey (JOLTS) and the Business Employment Dynamics (BED) program.[8] This section reviews some important features of these two data sources, describes our analysis sample, and discusses a few measurement issues.

5.2.1   The Job Openings and Labor Turnover Survey

The published JOLTS statistics on worker flows and job openings derive from a sample of about 16,000 establishments per month. The JOLTS questionnaire elicits data on employment for the pay period covering the 12th of the month, the flow of hires and separations during the month, and the number of open job positions (vacancies) on the last business day of the month.[9] The JOLTS sample is stratified by major industry groups, four Census regions, and several establishment-size classes. JOLTS sample

---

8. See Clark and Hyson (2001) and Faberman (2005b) for information about the JOLTS program and Spletzer et al. (2004) for more information about the BED. Statistics derived from the JOLTS program are available at http://www.bls.gov/jlt/home.htm.

9. The JOLTS survey form instructs the respondent to report a job opening when "A specific position exists, work could start within 30 days, and [the establishment is] actively seeking workers from outside this location to fill the position." Further instructions define "active recruiting"

observations are weighted so that the employment level for each industry-region-size cell matches employment for the corresponding cell in the much larger Current Employment Statistics (CES) survey. The sample frame for both JOLTS and CES derives from the Quarterly Census of Employment and Wages (QCEW), which essentially covers the universe of establishments with paid employees.[10]

Simplifying somewhat, let E_i denote total employment in cell i of the JOLTS sample frame, and let e_{ik} be employment at establishment k for the same cell.[11] The JOLTS sample weight for establishments in cell i is given by

$$\omega_{ik} = \frac{E_i}{\sum_{k \in \text{all}} e_{ik}},$$

where "all" refers to all sampled establishments that are in scope for the JOLTS survey. Here, we index ω by the establishment identifier k, even though all sampled establishments in cell i have the same sample weight. To construct the ω sample weights, the Bureau of Labor Statistics (BLS) relies on establishment-level employment data from the comprehensive QCEW. These data are available with a lag to the BLS and the JOLTS program.

The ω sample weights do not account for unit nonresponse, that is, the failure of a sampled establishment to respond to the JOLTS survey. Hence, the BLS applies a "nonresponse adjustment factor": an employment-based ratio adjustment that scales up the sample weights so that the resulting cell-level employment figure again matches the sample frame employment for that cell. Specifically, the nonresponse adjustment factor for cell i in month m is

$$\text{NRAF}_{m,ik} = \sum_{k \in \text{all}} \omega_{ik} e_{ik} \Big/ \sum_{k \in \text{used}(m)} \omega_{ik} e_{ik},$$

where "used(m)" refers to the set of establishments that respond to the survey in month m. Aside from the index set used(m), all quantities on the right side of this expression reflect past employment values in the QCEW, that is, prior to month m.

---

as "taking steps to fill a position . . . [that] may include advertising in newspapers, on television, or on radio; posting Internet notices; posting 'help wanted' signs; networking or making 'word of mouth' announcements; accepting applications; interviewing candidates; contacting employment agencies; or soliciting employees at job fairs, state or local employment offices, or similar sources." Job openings are not to include positions open only to internal transfers, promotions, recalls from temporary layoffs, or positions to be filled by temporary help agencies, outside contractors, or consultants.

10. Independent contractors and unincorporated self-employed persons are out of scope for the QCEW, making them out of scope for the JOLTS, CES, and BED as well.

11. Our discussion in the text ignores outlier adjustments, sample rotation, and item nonresponse (as distinct from unit nonresponse). For more on the JOLTS estimation methodology, see Crankshaw and Stamas (2000).

The JOLTS sample weights are also adjusted over time to account for changes in CES employment estimates. These changes come in two forms. The first occurs each month because of regular BLS updates to the initial, preliminary CES estimates. The second occurs because of the annual "benchmarking" of CES estimates to the most recent data from the QCEW, which serves as the underlying population universe for both the CES and JOLTS. The benchmarking adjustment ensures that the final CES (and JOLTS) employment estimates are consistent with the administrative data in the QCEW.

The JOLTS program accounts for each of these benchmark adjustments in a similar manner. Each month, a "benchmark factor" is calculated for each establishment in the sample. This factor involves another employment-based ratio adjustment, one that constrains the JOLTS employment estimate to match the CES employment estimate for each sample cell. To construct the benchmark adjustment factor, let $\hat{E}_{m,i} \equiv \Sigma_k \mathrm{NRAF}_{m,ik}\omega_{ik}e^J_{m,ik}$ be the initial (prebenchmark) JOLTS employment estimate for cell i, where $e^J_{m,ik}$ is the month m employment level for employment establishment k in cell i according to JOLTS. Also, let $E^C_{m,i}$ be the month m CES employment estimate for sample cell i. The benchmark adjustment factor for sample cell i in month m is

$$\mathrm{BMF}_{m,ik} = \frac{E^C_{m,i}}{\hat{E}_{m,i}}.$$

Putting all this together, the final JOLTS sample weight for cell i in month m is

$$\theta_{m,ik} = \omega_{ik} \times \mathrm{NRAF}_{m,ik} \times \mathrm{BMF}_{m,ik}.$$

All survey response data in the JOLTS program are multiplied by these final sample weights to produce the published statistics on worker flows and job openings. Hereafter, references to the "weight" or "adjusted weight" refer to the JOLTS final sample weight.

At this point, it is essential to recognize that the nonresponse and benchmark adjustments do not address the sources of bias identified in the introduction. These adjustments ensure that sample-weighted JOLTS employment totals match CES employment totals at the cell level, but they do *not* ensure unbiased estimates for worker flows and job openings. In fact, the omission of establishment openings and very young establishments means that the JOLTS sample is unrepresentative in key respects that relate to worker flows and job openings. The administrative data that feed into the JOLTS sample frame are compiled with a lag of eight months or more, mostly due to the time it takes to transfer data from the states to the BLS. Once an establishment is captured by the QCEW, it takes at least one more month before it can be selected for the JOLTS sample. In sum, it takes at least nine months in the best-case scenario before a new establishment becomes available for inclusion in the JOLTS sample.

We have also suggested that JOLTS nonresponse rates are higher among establishments that exit or contract sharply. This nonresponse pattern, coupled with the current JOLTS procedure for handling unit nonresponse, also causes the JOLTS sample to be unrepresentative in key respects that relate to worker flows and job openings. We do not offer direct evidence that unit nonresponse rates are higher for establishments that exit or contract sharply, but sections 5.3 and 5.4 show that the JOLTS sample substantially underweights rapidly contracting establishments. Regardless of exactly why this type of underweighting occurs, it leads to a systematic bias in JOLTS-based estimates of worker flows and job openings.[12]

5.2.2   The Business Employment Dynamics Data

The BED data are essentially a longitudinal version of the QCEW. Hence, like the QCEW, the BED is a universe data set with comprehensive establishment coverage. In particular, it captures exits, entrants, and continuing establishments, including very young ones. The BLS relies on the BED to produce quarterly statistics on gross job gains and losses.[13] We use the BED to obtain the cross-sectional density of employment growth rates for the universe of private-sector establishments. We then adjust the cross-sectional density of employment growth rates in JOLTS to conform to the corresponding BED density. The main complication that arises in practice involves a difference in sampling frequency. The BED uses employment data for the third month of each calendar quarter, whereas JOLTS contains monthly observations.

5.2.3   Analysis Sample and Measurement Concepts

We consider a sample of JOLTS data from January 2001 to December 2006. We limit attention to private-sector establishments because the BED is restricted to the private sector. We rely on JOLTS data to estimate how worker flows and job openings vary with employment growth in the cross section of establishments. We calculate rates for employment growth, worker flows, and job openings using the average of current and previous period employment in the denominator. Measuring rates in this manner yields an employment growth rate measure that is symmetric about zero and bounded

---

12. In general, a sample that is representative with respect to levels, such as employment, need not be representative with respect to changes, such as employment growth rates. Worker flows and job openings are much more closely related to employment changes than employment levels. Hence, the benchmarking and nonresponse adjustments that constrain JOLTS employment totals to match sample frame employment do not ensure unbiased estimates of worker flows and job openings. See the recent National Academy of Sciences report by Haltiwanger, Lynch, and Mackie (2007) for additional discussion of the distinction between samples optimized for levels and samples optimized for changes.

13. These statistics are available at http://www.bls.gov/bdm/.

between –2 and 2. It also affords an integrated treatment of entering, exiting, and continuing establishments.[14]

As we remarked earlier, the JOLTS employment measure pertains to the payroll period covering the 12th of the month, whereas JOLTS hires and separations are flows during the month. This timing difference and the month-to-month changes in establishment-level sample weights complicate our adjustment methods. To deal with these complications, it is useful to compute lagged employment values that are consistent with current-month JOLTS values for employment, hires, and separations. We calculate this internally consistent measure of lagged employment as

$$(1) \qquad e_{m-1}^{IC} = e_m^J - h_m + s_m,$$

where h_m and s_m denote hires and separations during month m, and we have suppressed cell and establishment identifiers.

We use e_{m-1}^{IC} when calculating growth rates from $m-1$ to m. This approach ensures that an establishment's employment change equals the difference between its hires and separations and does so in a way that preserves reported hires and separations, a key focus of our study. It also allows us to calculate flow rates entirely from current month data, eliminating the need to restrict the sample to observations with consecutive months of reporting. We use the same approach for e_{m-3}^{IC} when calculating quarterly growth rates. See the appendix for an explanation of how we treat sample weight changes within the quarter when computing quarterly growth rates.

5.3 JOLTS Data Compared to Other Sources

Figure 5.1 compares the growth of nonfarm employment in JOLTS and CES data. For JOLTS, we measure the growth rate as the hires rate minus the separations rate. For the CES, we use the percent change in employment from one period to the next. We show quarterly growth rates because they are less noisy than monthly data. As seen in figure 5.1, the JOLTS-based measure of employment growth exceeds the CES measure in twenty-one of twenty-four quarters.

Figure 5.2 compares the evolution of CES employment to the cumulative change implied by hires minus separations in JOLTS. The thin line shows the cumulated difference between hires and separations from December 2000, and the bold lines show the cumulated difference from December of each year. Figure 5.2 demonstrates that the employment path implied by JOLTS data diverges upward relative to the CES path in each year except 2001. The divergence is large in four out of six years, and the cumulative discrepancy of 6.6 million jobs amounts to 4.8 percent of the December 2006 CES employment figure. The cumulative discrepancy is smaller but still sizable

---

14. See Davis, Haltiwanger, and Schuh (1996) for more on this growth measure. The BED program uses this growth rate measure in its published statistics for gross job gains and losses.

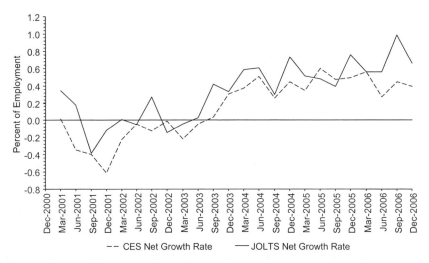

Fig. 5.1 CES and JOLTS employment growth rates compared

Notes: Figure depicts the quarterly net employment growth rates calculated from the JOLTS and CES data. The JOLTS growth rate is measured from the difference in total hires and total separations for each quarter. The CES growth rate is measured from the net change in employment levels between the third month of each quarter. Both rates are calculated using the average of the current and previous quarter's employment in the denominator.

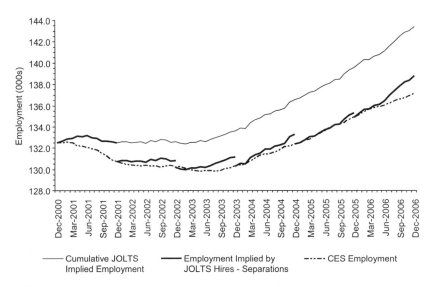

Fig. 5.2 CES employment path compared to cumulated differences between hires and separations in JOLTS

Notes: Figure depicts the employment levels implied from the JOLTS hires and separations data and reported in the CES data. The JOLTS level is reported two ways: as an accumulation of the difference between hires and separations each month (added to the December 2000 total) and as the accumulation over each year of the survey, added to the beginning-of-year employment level.

in the private sector at 3.0 million jobs, or 2.6 percent of December 2006 CES employment.[15]

Figure 5.2 also confirms that the sample weight adjustments that constrain JOLTS employment levels to match CES levels do not ensure consistency of employment changes, as calculated from hires and separations.

Turning to another issue, JOLTS statistics for worker flows are much smaller than comparable statistics produced from other sources. The published JOLTS statistics for hires and separations average about 3.3 percent of employment per month. Monthly hires and separations computed from Current Population Survey (CPS) data on gross worker flows are nearly twice as large, as reported in table 5.1. In addition, monthly analogs to quarterly accessions and separations computed from administrative wage records are at least twice as large as monthly hires and separations in JOLTS (Davis, Faberman, and Haltiwanger 2006). Current Population Survey gross flows and administrative wage records present their own measurement issues, and there are reasons to suspect that both sources overstate worker flows, but the much smaller magnitude of JOLTS worker flows warrants a closer inspection of the underlying data.

Delving into the microdata reveals that the JOLTS sample overweights stable establishments with small employment changes. To develop this point, table 5.2 compares cross-sectional distributions of employment growth rates in JOLTS and BED data. For the BED, table 5.2 summarizes the distribution of quarterly growth rates in the full universe and in a subset restricted to continuous units. A "continuous unit" in, say, the second quarter of 2003 is one with paid employees in both March and June. For JOLTS, the table summarizes three related objects: the distribution of monthly growth rates for all private-sector establishments, the distribution of monthly growth rates for a sample restricted to establishments with employees in all three months of the quarter, and the distribution of quarterly growth rates for the same restricted sample. This restriction yields a JOLTS sample that is directly comparable to the BED subset with continuous units.[16] Note that the full and restricted JOLTS samples yield similar monthly growth rate distributions.

Table 5.2 reports large differences between the BED and JOLTS cross-

15. Wohlford et al. (2003) point to education (mostly in State and Local Government) and temporary help (part of Professional and Business Services) as the main sources of the JOLTS-CES divergence. Using published JOLTS data, we confirm that the employment path implied by JOLTS hires and separations exhibits an especially large divergence from the CES employment path in Professional and Business Services. The cumulative discrepancy for this industry group is 3.6 million jobs, or 20.5 percent of the industry's December 2006 CES employment value. Education, Health, and Leisure and Hospitality also exhibit large cumulative discrepancies in the same direction. There are large cumulative discrepancies in the opposite direction in Construction (1.1 million jobs, 14.8 percent of employment) and Manufacturing (1.1 million jobs, 7.5 percent of employment). In short, several major industry groups show big cumulative discrepancies over the 2001 to 2006 period.

16. Recall that we construct internally consistent measures of lagged employment using current-quarter JOLTS data for hires, separations, and employment. In particular, if an estab-

Table 5.1   Average monthly worker flows as a percent of employment, 2001–2006

	Hires rate	Separations rate
JOLTS, published statistics	3.4	3.3
CPS gross flows, Fallick-Fleischman	6.4	6.4

Source: The statistics on Current Population Survey (CPS) gross flows are from Fallick and Fleischman (2004), as updated at http://www.federalreserve.gov/pubs/feds/2004/200434/200434abs.html.

Notes: Table entries report mean monthly rates for hires and separations from January 2001 to December 2006. CPS hires and separations include employment-to-employment flows. JOLTS = Job Openings and Labor Turnover Survey.

Table 5.2   Cross-sectional growth rate distributions, 2001–2006

	JOLTS			BED	
	Monthly		Quarterly	Quarterly	
Growth rate interval	Full sample	Restricted sample	Restricted sample	All observations	Continuous observations
–2.0 (exits)				0.7	
(–2.0, –0.20]	1.6	1.5	4.3	7.5	7.6
(–0.20, –0.05]	7.1	7.0	13.2	16.5	16.7
(–0.05, –0.02]	7.9	7.8	9.5	9.6	9.7
(–0.02, 0.0)	14.7	14.6	11.6	7.6	7.8
0.0	33.6	34.1	17.1	15.4	15.7
(0.0, 0.02)	16.5	16.6	13.1	7.9	8.0
[0.02, 0.05)	9.2	9.1	11.7	9.9	10.0
[0.05, 0.20)	7.9	7.8	15.1	16.7	16.9
[0.20, 2.0)	1.6	1.5	4.5	7.5	7.6
2.0 (entrants)				0.7	

Notes: Table entries report employment shares for the indicated establishment growth rate intervals in Job Openings and Labor Turnover Survey (JOLTS) and Business Employment Dynamics (BED) microdata from 2001 to 2006. Calculations on JOLTS data make use of the JOLTS final sample weights described in section 5.2.1. Each column in the table reports results for a different data set or sample. See the text for a detailed explanation of how the data sets and samples differ.

sectional growth rate distributions. For example, 24.8 percent of the mass in the JOLTS restricted sample falls in the open interval from 0 to 5 percent, compared to only 18.0 percent for the BED subset with continuous units. Similarly, 21.1 percent of the mass in the JOLTS restricted sample lies in the

---

lishment has employees in all three months of the current quarter, we calculate its growth rate using reported employment for the current quarter and the internally consistent measure of previous quarter employment. Thus, the restricted JOLTS sample captures establishments that operate continuously from the last month of the previous quarter to the last month of the current quarter. The JOLTS sample restriction removes 11.2 percent of the observations on a sample-weighted basis and a much smaller percentage when we further weight by size.

open interval from 0 to negative 5 percent, compared to only 17.5 percent for BED continuous units. The excess mass in the interval (–5.0, 5.0) for the restricted JOLTS sample amounts to 11.8 percent of employment relative to the BED subset with continuous units and 12.6 percent relative to the full BED. These results establish two important points: first, the JOLTS sample substantially overweights relatively stable establishments. Second, the overweighting of stable establishments does not arise mainly from the fact that births are out of scope for the JOLTS sample frame. That is, the JOLTS sample substantially overweights stable establishments relative to the BED even when we restrict attention to continuous units.

Figure 5.3 illustrates the first point graphically by comparing smoothed histograms of quarterly growth rate distributions in JOLTS and the BED. It is apparent to the naked eye that the JOLTS sample substantially over-weights stable establishments.[17] Stable establishments are likely to have smaller worker flows, a conjecture that we verify in the next section.

5.4 Cross-Sectional Patterns in Worker Flows and Job Openings

Figures 5.4 and 5.5 show how worker flows and job openings vary with employment growth rates in the cross section of establishments. To construct these figures, we pool monthly JOLTS data from 2001 to 2006 for private-sector establishments. We group the roughly 572,000 observations into growth rate bins, calculate employment-weighted mean outcomes in each bin, and plot the resulting relationships. We use narrow bins close to zero (width of 0.001, or 0.1 percent) and progressively wider bins as we move away from zero into thinner parts of the distribution. We also allow for a mass point at 0. Figure 5.4 shows the relationships over the full range of growth rate outcomes, and figure 5.5 zooms in to monthly growth rates from –25 to 25 percent. Figure 5.5 also shows cross-sectional relations for the twelve months with the highest or lowest growth rates of aggregate employ-ment.[18] The pattern for separations, not shown, is closely approximated by the sum of quits and layoffs.[19]

---

17. The overweighting of stable establishments in figure 5.3 and table 5.2 is not caused by our use of hires and separations to measure previous-period employment when calculating JOLTS-based measures of the employment growth rate. This point can be seen by inspecting figure 5 in Faberman (2005a), which shows that the employment-weighted growth rate distribution in the JOLTS sample is extremely similar whether we compute growth rates using the reported value of lagged employment or the imputed value based on the identity linking employment changes to hires and separations. Figure 5 in Faberman also shows that the JOLTS sample substantially overweights stable establishments relative to the BED for both approaches to the calculation of employment growth rates in the JOLTS sample.

18. When ranking the months by aggregate growth rates, we do not seasonally adjust the data. The unadjusted data have much larger variations in growth over time so are better suited for this exercise.

19. The other separations rate (not shown) rises with the contraction rate from about 0.3 percent of employment per month for mild contractions to 7.4 percent for the largest contractions.

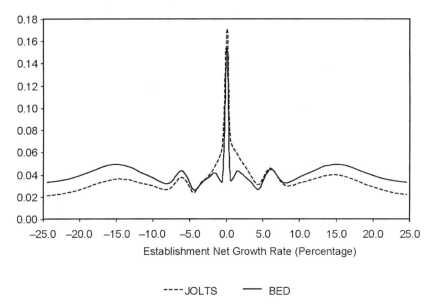

Fig. 5.3   Cross-sectional densities for establishment growth rates, 2001–2006

Notes: The densities are constructed as smoothed histograms of quarterly employment growth rates using establishment-level observations in JOLTS (restricted sample) and BED (all observations) from 2001Q1 to 2006Q4. Histograms are constructed over the full growth rate distribution, but the figure zooms in on growth rates from –25 to 25 percent per quarter. Histogram bins are narrower for smaller growth rates and allow for mass points at growth rates of –2.0 (exit), 0 (no change), and 2.0 (entry).

Figures 5.4 and 5.5 document several key results:

1. Hires dominate the employment adjustment margin for expanding establishments. The hires rate is lowest for establishments with little or no growth, essentially unrelated to growth for contracting establishments, and rises almost linearly with the growth rate for expanding establishments.

2. Separations dominate the adjustment margin for contracting establishments. Quit, layoff, and separation rates are also lowest for establishments with little or no growth, and they rise sharply with the contraction rate.

3. Layoffs dominate the adjustment margin for rapidly contracting establishments.

4. The job openings rate is lowest for stable establishments. It rises in both directions moving away from zero, more so for expanding establishments.

5. The cross-sectional relations are remarkably stable with respect to aggregate employment growth, especially for hires and layoffs. Conditional on establishment growth, quits occur more frequently when aggregate employment grows more rapidly. This cyclical aspect of quit behavior shows up mainly at contracting establishments.

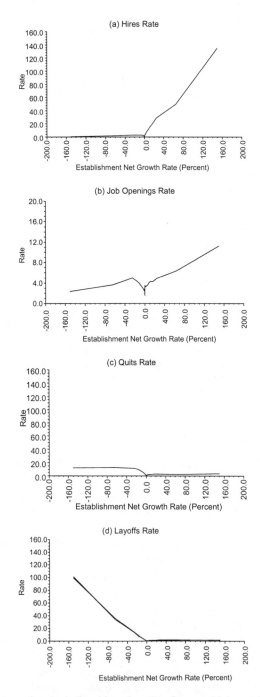

Fig. 5.4   Cross-sectional relationships of worker flows and job openings to establishment growth rates, monthly JOLTS data from 2001 to 2006, full range of growth rates

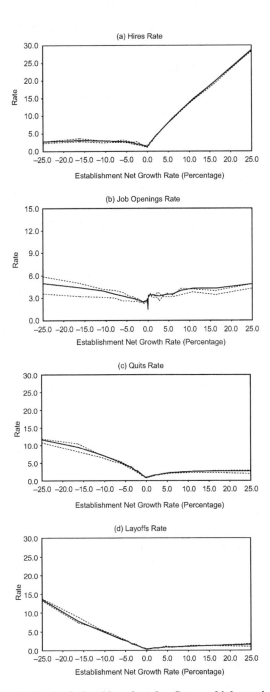

Fig. 5.5   Cross-sectional relationships of worker flows and job openings to establishment growth rates, monthly JOLTS data from 2001 to 2006, zoomed in on growth rates from –25 and 25 percent

Notes: Thick lines are constructed from the full 2001 to 2006 sample. Thin lines are constructed from samples restricted to the twelve months with the highest or lowest growth rate of aggregate employment. The upper thin lines typically correspond to the high-growth sample.

These results have important implications for JOLTS-based estimates of worker flows and job openings.[20] It is evident from figures 5.4 and 5.5 that the overweighting of stable establishments in the JOLTS sample imparts a downward bias in estimated hires, separations, quits, layoffs, and job openings. Less obviously, the bias is likely to vary systematically with aggregate employment growth. To see this point, consider the layoff rate and recall our earlier discussion of nonresponse adjustments in the JOLTS program. Suppose that nonresponse rates are higher among rapidly contracting establishments. Because rapidly contracting establishments are more prevalent in downturns, higher nonresponse rates among these establishments also has a greater effect on the estimated aggregate layoff rate in downturns. In other words, the published JOLTS statistics understate the amplitude of cyclical fluctuations in the layoff rate.

Figure 5.6 confirms a key element of this cyclical bias story. As in figure 5.3, figure 5.6 shows smoothed histograms of quarterly establishment growth rates using JOLTS and BED data. However, we now plot separate histograms for quarters with high and low growth in aggregate employment. Figure 5.6 shows that the overweighting of stable establishments in the JOLTS sample is more serious in downturns, that is, quarters with low aggregate growth. The BED-JOLTS difference in the 90-10 growth rate differential is 18.0 percentage points in high-growth quarters as compared to 20.3 percentage points in low-growth quarters. Moreover, the cyclical variation in the BED-JOLTS discrepancy is concentrated among contracting establishments: the BED-JOLTS difference in the 50-10 growth rate differential rises from 10.5 percentage points in high-growth quarters to 15.0 percentage points in low-growth quarters. This cyclical pattern in the BED-JOLTS discrepancy, coupled with the cross-sectional layoff relation shown in figures 5.4 and 5.5, implies that JOLTS understates the amplitude of aggregate layoff fluctuations.

Figures 5.4 and 5.5 also suggest a constructive approach to adjusting JOLTS-based estimates of worker flows and job openings. In particular, if we use the universe data in the BED to obtain the distribution of establishment growth rates, we can apply the cross-sectional relationships in figures 5.4 and 5.5 to obtain more accurate estimates for worker flows and job openings. The next section of the chapter formalizes this idea and sets forth the details.

5.5   A Method for Adjusting the Published JOLTS Estimates

Partition the range of establishment growth rates into bins indexed by b, allowing for mass points at -2 (exits), 0 (no change), and 2 (entry). Let

---

20. In related work (Davis, Faberman, and Haltiwanger 2006), we argue that the cross-sectional relations in figures 5.4 and 5.5 also have important implications for the cyclical behavior of unemployment.

(a) BED Distributions

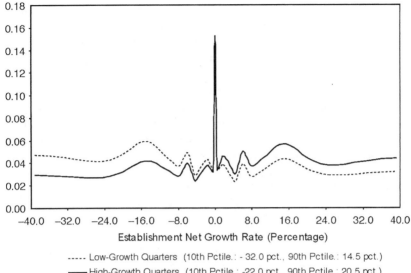

----- Low-Growth Quarters (10th Pctile.: - 32.0 pct., 90th Pctile.: 14.5 pct.)
——— High-Growth Quarters (10th Pctile.: -22.0 pct., 90th Pctile.: 20.5 pct.)

(b) JOLTS Distributions

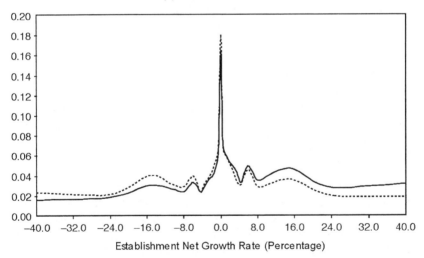

----- Low-Growth Quarters (10th Pctile.: - 17.0 pct., 90th Pctile.: 9.3 pct.)
——— High-Growth Quarters (10th Pctile.: - 11.5 pct., 90th Pctile.: 13.0 pct.)

Fig. 5.6   Quarterly growth rate distributions in high- and low-growth quarters, JOLTS and BED data

Notes: Figures depict employment densities at establishments with quarterly growth rates within a given interval in the BED (top panel) and a restricted panel of JOLTS data (bottom panel; see text for details of restriction) for 2001Q1 to 2006Q4. The distributions are split into the six quarters of highest growth and six quarters of lowest growth, based on their seasonally unadjusted aggregate growth rates in the BED. Vertical lines represent the growth rates at the 10th (shaded lines) and 90th (dashed lines) percentiles of the distribution, with the leftmost of each pair associated with each low-growth distribution.

$f_m(b)$ be the month m share of employment for establishments with growth rates in bin b, and let $x_m(b)$ denote the employment-weighted mean rate of hires, separations, layoffs, quits, or job openings for the bin. Express the corresponding month m aggregate rate as

(2) $$X_m = \sum_b x_m(b)f_m(b).$$

Sections 5.3 and 5.4 show that the JOLTS sample is not representative with respect to the $f_m(b)$ values. As a result, the current JOLTS program yields biased estimates for the estimated X_m values, that is, for published statistics on worker flows and job openings. We address this problem by relying on the BED to adjust the JOLTS $f_m(b)$ values. We then combine the adjusted $f_m(b)$ weights with JOLTS estimates for the $x_m(b)$ values, that is, the bin-specific rates of worker flows and job openings. We rely on other information for the x_m (exit) and x_m (entry) values, which the JOLTS sample does not provide.

In principle, this approach to adjusting JOLTS-based statistics on worker flows and job openings is easy to implement. The main complication in practice arises from the need to use *quarterly* BED data to adjust the *monthly* growth rate distributions in the JOLTS data. Readers who are uninterested in the details of this mapping between BED and JOLTS data can safely skip section 5.5.1 and resume the text in section 5.5.2.

5.5.1   Adjusting the JOLTS Monthly Growth Rate Distributions

Some additional notation will be helpful. It will also be useful in this section to distinguish between quarters, indexed by t, and months, indexed by m. Let $f_t^B(b)$ be the employment density of continuous BED establishments with quarter-t growth rates in bin b. Let $f_t^J(b)$ be the employment density of establishments with a quarter-t growth rate in bin b, using the restricted JOLTS sample with three monthly observations in quarter t. Finally, let $f_{m,t}^J(b)$ be the employment density of establishments with a monthly growth rate in bin b during month m of quarter t in the restricted JOLTS sample. We use narrow growth rate bins near zero (width of 0.25 percent), progressively wider bins as we move away from zero to thinner parts of the distribution, and allow for mass points at –2, 0, and 2. The resulting partition involves thirty-seven bins, although the JOLTS restricted sample and the continuous BED data contain no observations in the entry and exit bins.

After allocating the data to growth rate bins, the next step is to map the quarterly growth rate densities for BED data to consistent monthly growth rate densities. We use JOLTS data to model the mapping from quarterly to monthly densities, and we then apply the fitted mapping to obtain estimated monthly BED growth rate densities. After some experimentation with parametric and nonparametric methods, we settled on a simple regression model. Specifically, for each bin b, we fit a regression of the form

$$(3) \qquad f^J_{m,t}(b) = \alpha(b) + \sum_{n \in \text{Top}N(b)} \beta_n(b) f^J_t(b) + \varepsilon_{m,t}(b)$$

to seventy-two monthly observations from 2001 to 2006, where $\alpha(b)$ is a bin-specific constant, the $f^J_t(b)$ are quarterly densities, $\beta_n(b)$ is a regression coefficient that varies across five groupings of growth rate bins (two to the left of zero, two to the right of zero, and one that includes only zero), $\varepsilon_{m,t}(b)$ is an error term, and $\text{Top}N(b)$ is a set of N quarterly growth rate bins that varies with b.[21]

To select the bins in $\text{Top}N(b)$, we compute the mapping from quarterly growth rate bins to monthly growth rate bins in JOLTS data pooled over the entire sample from 2001 to 2006. For each monthly bin b in the pooled sample, this mapping gives the fraction of mass derived from the quarterly bins. We then identify the N quarterly bins that contribute the most mass to monthly bin b to form the set $\text{Top}N(b)$ for that b. We use $N = 5$ in our reported results but obtained similar results for values up to $N = 10$.[22]

Next, we construct three monthly counterparts for each quarterly BED density by substituting the BED density values into the right side of equation (3) along with estimated parameters in the ordinary least squares (OLS) regressions (3) fit to JOLTS data. These substitutions yield

$$(4) \qquad \tilde{f}_{m,t}(b) = \hat{\alpha}(b) + \sum_{n \in \text{Top}N(b)} \hat{\beta}_n(b) f^B_t(b),$$

which, after rescaling to ensure that the adjusted densities sum to 1, is our mapping from quarterly BED densities for continuous units to the corresponding monthly densities.

As a final step, we append entry and exit mass points to the estimated monthly distributions. We take a simple approach and set the monthly entry and exit rates to one-third of their values in the full BED distribution for the quarter. This approach involves two assumptions: first, that entry and exit rates are constant during the quarter and, second, that establishments do not enter and exit in the same quarter. One could relax these assumptions and improve upon this approach, but they are adequate for present purposes.

In a slight abuse of notation given our previous definition of $f^B_t(b)$, let $f^B_t(\text{entry})$ and $f^B_t(\text{exit})$ denote the entry and exit mass point values in the full BED for quarter t. Then we can write the estimated monthly growth rate densities as follows:

---

21. Allowing the β coefficients to vary by individual growth rate bin yields noisy estimates because of sparsely populated bins, particularly at the tails of the growth rate distribution. After some experimentation, we set the boundary for the two bins to the left and to the right of zero at ± 9 percent.

22. The choice of N has little effect on the magnitude or time series volatility of our adjusted worker flow rates and vacancy rates. However, alternative choices of N imply different paths for cumulative employment growth over the six-year sample period. The choice of $N = 5$ minimizes the absolute difference of cumulative employment growth between the adjusted JOLTS figures and the BED.

(5) $\hat{f}_{m,t}(\text{entry}) = \dfrac{f_t^B(\text{entry})}{3}$ and $\hat{f}_{m,t}(\text{exit}) = \dfrac{f_t^B(\text{exit})}{3}$;   and

$$\hat{f}_{m,t}(b) = \left[1 - \frac{f_t^B(\text{entry})}{3} - \frac{f_t^B(\text{exit})}{3} \right] \tilde{f}_{m,t}(b), \text{ otherwise.}$$

These equations describe our mapping from the BED growth rate distribution for quarter t to the corresponding monthly distributions.

Our method for obtaining equation (5) does not capture time variation in the monthly densities within a quarter. To address this shortcoming, one could estimate a richer regression specification (3) with covariates that capture within-quarter movements in the shape and location of the aggregate employment growth rate density. This approach could be implemented with any data source that provides monthly observations on the distribution of employment growth rates. We leave such refinements for future work.

5.5.2   Calculating the Adjusted Estimates

Henceforth, we suppress the quarterly index t except when needed for clarity. To calculate adjusted rates for worker flows and job openings, we apply equation (2) by combining the $\hat{f}_m(b)$ values in equation (5) with JOLTS-based estimates for the $x_m(b)$. For continuous units, we estimate the $x_m(b)$ values using the bin-specific employment-weighted mean rates for worker flows and job openings in month m, which we denote by $\hat{x}_m(b)$.

The JOLTS data do not provide estimates for worker flows and job openings in the entry and exit bins. For these bins, we use the values in table 5.3.

We obtain these values as follows. For exits, we assume no job openings or hires in the exit month, and we set quits and other separations to their average rates in the bin with the most rapidly contracting continuous establishments. These assumptions yield the values reported in the second row. For entrants, we assume no separations in the entry month, which implies a hires rate of 2. This assumption is conservative in the sense that it understates the level of worker flows at entrants. There are two sources of job openings not captured by the JOLTS sample design. First, some entrants have job openings at the end of their first month in operation. Second, new employers seek workers before they begin operations. For the first source, we use the end-of-month vacancy rate in the bin with the most rapidly growing continuous establishments, scaled to match the hires-to-vacancies ratio and the amount of hiring in excess of growth in the bin. This source yields a vacancy rate equal to 17.4 percent. For the second source, we set (beginning-of-month) vacancies to the lagged vacancy rate in the bin with the fastest-growing continuing establishments, again scaling for the hires-vacancy ratio and hiring in excess of growth. This source yields a vacancy rate of 20.8

Table 5.3   Rates for entry and exit bins

Bin	Hires	Quits	Layoffs	Other separations	Job openings
b = entry	2	0	0	0	0.382
b = exit	0	0.124	1.802	0.074	0

percent. Summing these two sources yields the figure for job openings in the top row.[23]

As a final step, we make an adjustment for sampling variability in our bin-specific estimates. Sampling variability is a significant concern in the tails of the growth rate distribution over continuous establishments. For example, the (–2.0, –1.0) and (1.0, 2.0) bins are quite wide, yet very few establishments in the JOLTS sample fall into these bins in a given month. In such cases, the bin-specific estimates can vary widely within a wide interval based on realized outcomes at very few establishments. To address this issue, we adjust the within-bin means for all but the zero bin (which is a mass point and, thus, immune to this form of variability) so that the implied difference between hires and separations equals the mean growth rate for the same bin in the BED. The appendix provides details.

Putting the pieces together, our adjusted estimates for worker flows and job openings in month m are given

$$(6) \qquad \hat{X}_m = \sum_b a_m(b) \hat{x}_m(b) \hat{f}_m(b),$$

where the $\hat{f}_m(b)$ are the mass values in the reweighted monthly growth rate density given by equation (5), the $\hat{x}_m(b)$ are the JOLTS-based bin-specific means for worker flows and job openings, and the $a_m(b)$ are the adjustments for sampling variability. We seasonally adjust the estimated $\hat{X}_m(b)$ using Census X-12 technique.

5.6   Adjusted Statistics for Hires, Layoffs, Quits, and Job Openings

Table 5.4 reports adjusted estimates for worker flows and job openings in the U.S. private sector and compares them to published JOLTS statistics. The adjusted worker flows are much larger than the published estimates. Hires and separations are about 5 percent of employment per month according to the adjusted estimates, as compared to 3.7 or 3.8 percent in the published statistics. The adjusted layoff rate, at 2.3 percent of employment per month,

---

23. This discussion suggests that the JOLTS program would benefit from retrospective questions about preentry job openings for new establishments. A similar point applies to other establishment surveys that seek to capture activities that are correlated with entry. For example, it would be helpful to add retrospective questions about initial investments for entrants in the Annual Capital Expenditures Survey.

Table 5.4   JOLTS summary statistics, published and adjusted statistics

	Published statistics	Adjusted statistics
Monthly means (monthly and quarterly standard deviations)		
Hires rate (H)	3.78	4.99
	(0.25, 0.23)	(0.17, 0.16)
Separations rate (S)	3.70	4.96
	(0.18, 0.16)	(0.21, 0.20)
Quits rate (Q)	2.06	2.36
	(0.17, 0.17)	(0.17, 0.15)
Layoffs and discharges rate (L)	1.40	2.29
	(0.09, 0.07)	(0.16, 0.15)
Other separations rate (R)	0.24	0.31
	(0.03, 0.02)	(0.07, 0.05)
Job openings rate (V)	2.71	2.94
	(0.39, 0.38)	(0.36, 0.34)
Unemployment rate (U)	5.29	
	(0.57, 0.58)	
Quarterly relative volatilities		
$\sigma(H)/\sigma(S)$	1.47	0.80
$\sigma(Q)/\sigma(L)$	2.35	1.00
$\sigma(H)/\sigma(V)$	0.61	0.47
$\sigma(V)/\sigma(U)$	0.66	0.59

Notes: Table lists the noted monthly statistics from the publicly available Job Openings and Labor Turnover Survey (JOLTS) estimates and the adjusted estimates (see text for details). Standard deviations of the monthly data, followed by the quarterly means of the monthly data (or third-month values in the case of the vacancy and unemployment rate), are in parentheses below each mean. Relative volatilities are the ratios of the quarterly standard deviations of the listed estimates. The period covers January 2001 to December 2006. The unemployment rate comes from the Current Population Survey.

is nearly two-thirds greater than the published layoff rate.[24] Our adjustments also lead to a higher quit rate. The adjusted job openings rate is 2.9 percent of employment per month compared to 2.7 percent for the published rate. Clearly, reweighting the cross-sectional growth rate density to conform to the BED, and capturing the role of entry and exit has a major impact on the estimated levels of worker flows and job openings.

Table 5.4 also shows that the adjustments substantially alter the time series properties of JOLTS statistics.[25] Focusing on quarterly data, the adjustments lower the variability of hires by about one-third, roughly double the

24. To understand the large upward adjustment in the layoff rate, recall that layoffs are disproportionately concentrated in establishments that exit or contract sharply (figures 5.4 and 5.5). These establishments are heavily underweighted in the JOLTS sample, as documented in table 5.2.

25. Given the limitations of our data and methods, we think our adjustments produce more reliable evidence for quarterly than for monthly fluctuations. For this reason, table 5.3 reports standard deviations of monthly and quarterly values, and the lower panel focuses on volatility statistics in quarterly data. However, the upper panel suggests that the choice between quarterly and monthly data matters little in this regard.

variability of layoffs and modestly reduce the variability of job openings. The quarterly standard deviation of hires is 47 percent greater than that of separations in the published data but 20 percent smaller in the adjusted data. Quits are more than twice as variable as layoffs in the published data but equally variable in the adjusted data.[26] The relative volatility of hires to job openings declines by about one-quarter. The relative volatility of job openings to unemployment, a statistic that receives much attention in the search and matching literature, declines by about 10 percent.[27]

Figure 5.7 shows that sizable level differences between published and adjusted estimates persist throughout the 2001 to 2006 period. The decline in the layoff rate after the middle of 2003 is noticeably larger in the adjusted data. Figure 5.8 shows that adjusted quits exceed layoffs in the relatively strong labor market of 2005 and 2006 but are otherwise very similar in magnitude.

As we remarked in the preceding, the cumulative employment growth implied by the flow of hires and separations in JOLTS exceeds employment growth in the CES and the BED. Our adjustments largely eliminate this discrepancy. The published JOLTS statistics imply an average monthly growth rate of 0.08 percent for private-sector employment. The corresponding growth rate in the CES is about 0.04 percent and the monthly analog of the BED growth rate is 0.03 percent. Our adjusted estimates imply a mean growth rate of 0.03 percent. This is in line with the monthly BED growth rate, the appropriate comparison because it is the rate our adjustment is constructed to reproduce. It is also quite close to the CES growth rate.

5.7   Concluding Remarks

JOLTS data are a valuable resource for understanding labor market dynamics and for evaluating theories of unemployment and worker turnover. They also present measurement issues that are not well understood or fully appreciated. A key point is that the JOLTS sample overweights relatively stable establishments with low rates of hires and separations and underweights establishments with rapid growth or contraction. The unrepresentative nature of the JOLTS sample with respect to the cross-sectional density of employment growth rates matters because hires, quits, layoffs, and job openings vary greatly with establishment growth rates in the cross section. As a result, the current JOLTS program produces downwardly biased estimates for worker flows and job openings. The extent of bias varies systematically with the growth rate of aggregate employment.

26. A careful inspection of figure 5.5 suggests that the impact of our adjustments on the relative volatility of hires and separations, or quits and layoffs, would be somewhat smaller if we extended the regression specification (3) to capture time variation in the cross-sectional relations.

27. For example, see Shimer (2005), Gertler and Trigari (2005), and Hagedorn and Manovskii (2007).

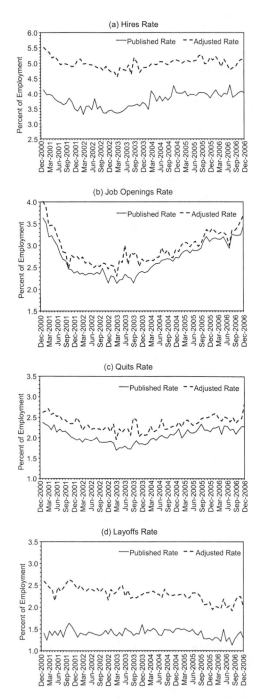

Fig. 5.7 Adjusted and published estimates of JOLTS worker flows and job openings

Notes: Each panel illustrates a worker flow or job openings rate, seasonally adjusted, from the published JOLTS statistics (dashed line) and our adjusted estimates (solid line). See text for details of the adjustment.

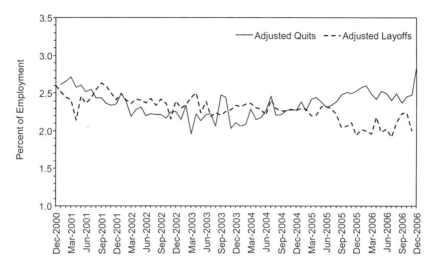

Fig. 5.8   Adjusted quit and layoff rates, JOLTS data

Notes: The figure illustrates the quit rate and layoff rate, seasonally adjusted, from our adjusted estimates. See text for details of the adjustment.

We develop and implement an adjustment method to address these issues. Our method reweights the cross-sectional density of employment *growth rates* in JOLTS to match the corresponding density in comprehensive BED data. In addition, our method supplements JOLTS data on worker flows and job openings at continuing establishments with estimates for worker flows and job openings at entering and exiting establishments. Our adjustments have a large effect on JOLTS-based estimates. Adjusted hires and separations exceed the published statistics by about one-third. Layoffs are much larger and much more variable in the adjusted statistics, and they account for a bigger share of separations.

There are several steps that the BLS can undertake to improve the JOLTS sample and JOLTS-based statistics. First, as part of a regular program to monitor the JOLTS sample, the BLS should compare the cross-sectional densities of employment growth rates in JOLTS data to the corresponding densities in the BED or other comprehensive source. Because of lags in the availability of administrative records that feed into the BED, it is not feasible to reweight the JOLTS density to conform to the BED as part of a real-time monthly production process. It is feasible to reweight the JOLTS density to conform to the growth rate distribution in the monthly CES, as adjusted for systematic differences between the CES and comprehensive sources in historical data.

Second, the BLS should explicitly incorporate adjustments for worker flows and job openings at establishments that are outside the JOLTS sample frame. The BLS already models the effects of entry and exit in its CES employment estimates. Adapting and extending BLS models to capture the effects of entry and exit on hires, separations, and job openings is entirely feasible using information available from JOLTS, BED, and CES data. It would also be useful to conduct special surveys with retrospective questions about worker flows and job openings at new establishments, including questions about the number of job openings before an entrant began operations. Information obtained from this type of survey would provide a strong basis for imputing worker flows and job openings to new establishments as part of a monthly production process.

Third, the BLS should investigate the potential payoff from sample stratification on establishment age and from corrections for the exclusion of very young establishments from the JOLTS sample frame. As discussed in the introduction, young establishments have unusually high worker flows, even after conditioning on establishment size. Our adjustment method does not directly address this source of downward bias in JOLTS-based estimates for hires and separations.[28] We suspect that very limited sample stratification on establishment age and simple corrections for the exclusion of very young establishments would go a long way to address this source of bias because hires and separations decline very rapidly with establishment age initially but then flatten out. Here as well, special surveys could provide a reliable basis for imputing worker flows and job openings to young establishments that are underweighted or excluded from the JOLTS sample frame.

Fourth, the BLS should carefully investigate how the unit nonresponse rate varies with the establishment growth rate in the JOLTS sample. In this regard, it is essential to evaluate the nonresponse rate throughout the entire distribution of growth rates. Suppose, for example, that the response rate is very high, on average, but is smaller in certain parts of the growth rate distribution. This type of nonresponse pattern leads to biased estimates for aggregate worker flows and job openings because these measures vary greatly with establishment growth rates in the cross section. Determining whether, and how, the unit nonresponse rate varies with the establishment growth rate is a straightforward exercise. It can be carried out by matching JOLTS micro data to data from the BED or other comprehensive source and then directly computing nonresponse rates as a function of the establishment growth rate. Having obtained this function, it would be a simple matter to adjust JOLTS-based estimates of worker flows and job openings for unit nonresponse rates that vary with the establishment growth rate.

Another potential issue in JOLTS data is respondent error—the propensity of establishments to misreport their true number of hires, separations, or job openings to the BLS. Wohlford et al. (2003) and Faberman (2005a)

---

28. Our adjustment method relies on JOLTS data to provide unbiased estimates for $\hat{x}(b)$ in equation (6). However, the underweighting of younger establishments in JOLTS data imparts a downward bias to the $\hat{x}(b)$ estimates.

express concerns about respondent error as a source of bias in JOLTS-based statistics. The methods we develop in this paper do not address respondent error. Thus, this chapter should be viewed as part of a broader effort to better understand and improve JOLTS-based statistics.

While measurement issues are our main focus in this chapter, our findings have implications for the broader study of labor market dynamics. In this regard, some authors have interpreted data on the relative volatility of separations and hires as favoring a hires-driven view of recession (Hall 2005; Shimer 2007b). We find that using a representative growth rate distribution to estimate worker flows substantially increases the variability of separations relative to hires—so much so that separations are more variable than hires according to our adjusted estimates.

The adjustment method we introduce in this chapter is potentially useful in other settings as well, and these settings are relatively easy to identify. In particular, when the outcome measure of interest varies with micro growth rates in the cross section, it is important to evaluate whether the sample produces a representative cross-sectional growth rate distribution. If the sample is not representative in this respect, and if the outcome variable varies systematically with growth rates in the cross section, then sample means of the outcome variable are biased. That is the essence of the problem in the JOLTS sample that we consider in this chapter. Analogous problems potentially arise in surveys of capital investment and disinvestment because investment outcomes differ systematically between declining and growing businesses.

Finally, we note that our adjustment method can be applied to "backcast" worker flows and job openings before the period covered by the JOLTS sample. In particular, one could combine historical data on the cross-sectional distribution of establishment growth rates from the CES, BED, or other source with JOLTS-based data on the cross-sectional relations displayed in figures 5.4 and 5.5 to construct historical time series for worker flows and job openings. Such an endeavor would greatly expand the time series dimension of data available for the study of labor market dynamics.

Appendix

Calculating Quarterly Flows and Growth Rates

In comparing JOLTS and BED data in table 5.2 and figures 5.3 and 5.6, we need a consistent measure of quarterly growth rates. There is an issue of how to measure quarterly growth rates in the JOLTS data because JOLTS sample weights change from month to month. To deal with this issue, we measure quarterly flows as the sum of weighted monthly values divided by the weight for the last month in the quarter:

$$x_t = \frac{\theta_{m,t} x_{m,t} + \theta_{m-1,t} x_{m-1,t} + \theta_{m-2,t} x_{m-2,t}}{\theta_{m,t}},$$

where x_t is the quarterly rate for quarter t, $x_{m,t}$ is the monthly rate for month m in quarter t, $\theta_{m,t}$ is the weight for month m in quarter t, and we have suppressed the index for establishments. When computing the internally consistent measure of lagged quarterly employment analogous to equation (1) in the main text, we use the level of employment in the last month of the quarter together with the quarterly measures of hires and separations defined in the preceding.

Adjusting the Bin-Specific Estimates for Sampling Variability

The sampling-variability adjustment factor for the estimate $\hat{x}_{m,t}(b)$ is given by

$$a_{m,t}(b) = \frac{n_t^B(b)}{[h_{m,t}(b) - s_{m,t}(b)]},$$

where $n_t^B(b)$ is the mean net growth rate for bin b in quarter t in the BED data, and h and s denote rates of hires and separations, respectively, in the JOLTS data. This adjustment factor constrains the resulting mean net growth rate in bin b in the adjusted JOLTS data to equal the mean net growth rate in the corresponding bin in the BED data. It would be better to impose this constraint using CES rather than BED data; however, the CES micro data were not available to us for this project.

References

Clark, Kelly A., and Rosemary Hyson. 2001. New tools for labor market analysis: JOLTS. *Monthly Labor Review* 124 (12): 32–37.

Crankshaw, Mark, and George Stamas. 2000. Sample design in the Job Openings and Labor Turnover Survey. *2000 proceedings of the Annual Statistical Association.* Alexandria, VA: American Statistical Association. CD-ROM.

Davis, Steven J., R. Jason Faberman, and John C. Haltiwanger. 2006. The flow approach to labor markets: New evidence and micro-macro links. *Journal of Economic Perspectives* 20 (3): 3–24.

———. 2009. The establishment-level behavior of vacancies and hiring. FRB of Philadelphia Working Paper no. 09-14.

Davis, Steven J., and John Haltiwanger. 1999. Gross job flows. In *Handbook of labor economics.* Vol. 3B, ed. Orley Ashenfelter and David Card, 2711–98. Amsterdam: North-Holland.

Davis, Steven, John Haltiwanger, Ron Jarmin, C. J. Krizan, Javier Miranda, Alfred

Nucci, and Kristin Sandusky. 2007. NBER Working Paper no. 13226. Cambridge, MA: National Bureau of Economic Research.

Davis, Steven J., John C. Haltiwanger, and Scott Schuh. 1996. *Job creation and destruction.* Cambridge, MA: MIT Press.

Faberman, R. Jason. 2005a. Analyzing the JOLTS hires and separations data. *2005 proceedings of the Annual Statistical Association.* Alexandria, VA: American Statistical Association. CD-ROM.

———. 2005b. Studying the labor market with the Job Openings and Labor Turnover Survey. BLS Working Paper no. 388. Washington, DC: Bureau of Labor Statistics.

Faberman, R. Jason, and Éva Nagypál. 2007. The effect of quits on worker recruitment: Theory and evidence. FRB of Philadelphia Working Paper no. 08-13.

Fallick, Bruce, and Charles A. Fleischman. 2004. Employer-to-employer flows in the U.S. labor market: The complete picture of gross worker flows. Federal Reserve Board of Governors, Finance and Economics Discussion Series Paper no. 2004-34.

Farber, Henry S. 1994. The analysis of interfirm worker mobility. *Journal of Labor Economics* 12 (4): 554–93.

Fujita, Shigeru, and Gary Ramey. 2007. Job matching and propagation. *Journal of Economic Dynamics and Control* 31 (11): 3671–98.

Gertler, Mark, and Antonella Trigari. 2005. Unemployment fluctuations with staggered Nash bargaining. New York University. Mimeograph.

Hagedorn, Marcus, and Iourii Manovskii. 2007. The cyclical behavior of equilibrium unemployment and vacancies revisited. University of Pennsylvania. Mimeograph.

Hall, Robert E. 2005. Job loss, job finding, and unemployment in the U.S. economy over the past fifty years. *2005 NBER macroeconomics annual:* 101–37.

Haltiwanger, John, Lisa Lynch, and Chris Mackie, eds. 2007. *Understanding business dynamics: An integrated data system for America's future.* Washington, DC: National Academies Press.

Mincer, Jacob, and Boyan Jovanovic. 1981. Labor mobility and wages. In *Studies in labor markets,* ed. Sherwin Rosen, 21–64. Chicago: University of Chicago Press.

Mortensen, Dale T., and Christopher A. Pissarides. 1994. Job creation and job destruction and the theory of unemployment. *Review of Economic Studies* 61 (3): 397–415.

Nagypál, Éva. 2006. What can we learn about firm recruitment from the Job Openings and Labor Turnover Survey? *Producer dynamics: New evidence from micro data,* ed. Timothy Dunne, J. Bradford Jensen, and Mark J. Roberts, 109–24. Chicago: University of Chicago Press.

Shimer, Robert. 2005. The cyclical behavior of equilibrium unemployment and vacancies. *American Economic Review* 95 (1): 25–49.

———. 2007a. Mismatch. *American Economic Review* 97 (4): 1074–1101.

———. 2007b. Reassessing the ins and outs of unemployment. University of Chicago. Mimeograph.

Spletzer, James R., R. Jason Faberman, Akbar Sadeghi, David M. Talan, and Richard L. Clayton. 2004. Business employment dynamics: New data on gross job gains and losses. *Monthly Labor Review* 127 (4): 29–42.

Topel, Robert H., and Michael P. Ward. 1992. Job mobility and the careers of young men. *Quarterly Journal of Economics* 107 (2): 439–79.

Valetta, Robert. 2005. Why has the U.S. Beveridge curve shifted back? New evidence using regional data. Federal Reserve Bank of San Francisco, Working Paper no. 2005-25.

Wohlford, John, Mary Anne Phillips, Richard L. Clayton, and George Werking.

2003. Reconciling labor turnover and employment statistics. *2003 proceedings of the Annual Statistical Association.* Alexandria, VA: American Statistical Association. CD-ROM.

Comment   Robert E. Hall

Though this chapter presents itself as a technical treatise on correcting some serious biases in the Job Openings and Labor Turnover Survey (JOLTS), it actually has important lessons for labor mobility and aggregate labor-market fluctuations. I've learned a lot over the years from the Davis-Haltiwanger team and appreciate the relentless pressure that they, especially Steve, have applied to me to correct my ways.

In this literature, there is something called the "hiring-driven view." According to this view, firms adjust employment mainly by varying their hiring rates. Separation rates are constant. Research on JOLTS has voided this view, which never had any factual support and is not an intrinsic part of the Hall-Shimer position on aggregate fluctuations. The hiring-driven view is an incorrect extrapolation from the correct proposition that separations, in the aggregate, are close to a constant fraction of employment.

The team's work with JOLTS demonstrates a simple proposition: firms raise employment by increasing hiring and cut employment by increasing layoffs or other separations. The micro relation between employment growth and hires has a beautiful kink right at zero—see panel A of figure 5.4 in the chapter. The layoff rate has a similar kink (panel D of figure 5.4). Interestingly, the quit rate also has a kink (panel C of figure 5.4). Workers figure out that it is time to quit when firms downsize or their employers take actions that make them decide to quit.

I have a particular interest in aggregate fluctuations. Now that I'm fully indoctrinated by the Davis-Haltiwanger team, my view is that aggregate fluctuations have little effect on the separation rate and large effects on the job-finding rate. This view is validated by this chapter and the body of Davis-Haltiwanger research.

Panel D of figure 5.7 shows the layoff rate in the corrected JOLTS. It shows no particular bulge during the large decline in employment in the recession that began in early 2001. There is a small spike associated with 9/11. The explanation for the large role of layoffs in contractions at the firm level and the complete unimportance of layoffs in aggregate contractions is simple: aggregate employment contractions are tiny, in the range of

Robert E. Hall is the Robert and Carole McNeil Hoover Senior Fellow and professor of economics at Stanford University, and director of the program on Economic Fluctuations and Growth at the National Bureau of Economic Research.

0.1 percent per month, while the layoff rate is above 2 percent per month at all times.

My worst error, which I now confess, has been to downplay the significance of the Davis-Haltiwanger measures of job destruction and job creation. Earlier I had said unfortunate things like "job destruction is just the negative part of employment growth and we don't know if it occurs because of layoffs or reduced hiring, so we can't relate it to worker flows." The work on micro-JOLTs data makes it clear that job destruction and job creation are useful measures. When establishment-level employment rises, it is almost entirely the result of hires; when employment falls, it is almost entirely the result of separations. Thus, adding up all of the establishment-level employment increases tells us gross hiring and adding up all decreases tells us gross separations. JOLTS has informed us that we don't really need a survey for gross flows because we can infer them quite accurately from establishment-level employment changes, following the idea that Davis and Haltiwanger pioneered.

One of the many benefits of the Davis-Haltiwanger research program has been the Business Employment Dynamics (BED) program at the Bureau of Labor Statistics (BLS). Now that I have realized that job destruction is a reasonable proxy for separations and job creation for hires, I can study them for aggregate movements, as in figures 5C.1 and 5C.2. The job-destruction rate has a little bump upward during the recession of 2001, shaded, and job

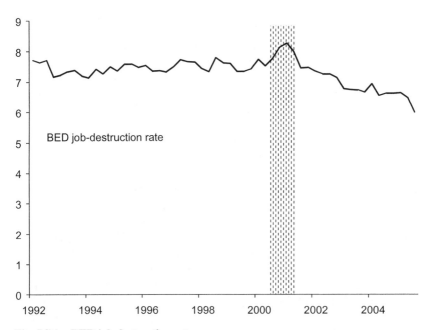

Fig. 5C.1   BED job-destruction rate

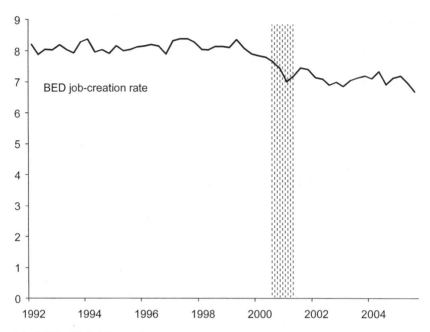

Fig. 5C.2   BED job-creation rate

creation a similar bump downward, but the view of general cyclical stability is confirmed.

The Davis, Faberman, Haltiwanger, and Rucker chapter is a big step toward reconciling worker flow rates and employer flow rates. Figure 5C.3 shows the separation rate in the Current Population Survey (CPS) since the 1994 improvements. It confirms the rise in separations in 2001, though the bump is not nearly as pronounced. The adjusted JOLTS separation rate in this chapter, the BED job-destruction rate, and the CPS rate are now within a reasonable range of each other.

As the chapter makes clear, the measurement of separations is tricky because they are concentrated among certain categories of firms and certain occupations. The median duration of a job in the United States is one day. Lots of separations occur in areas involving day work and highly transitory jobs, despite the low share of employment of those areas. Table 5C.1 shows the wide range of quarterly separation rates from different sources with different conceptual bases (this is from my 1995 Brookings paper, "Lost Jobs," so the CPS number does not include job-to-job separations).

Let me now turn to the theory of separations. One attractive hypothesis—to a follower of Ronald Coase—is that separations occur if and only if they are bilaterally efficient. Let J_t be the joint value achieved from the employment relationship by employer and worker, and let U_t be the value if they separate. I use U for unemployment on the supposition that the employer's

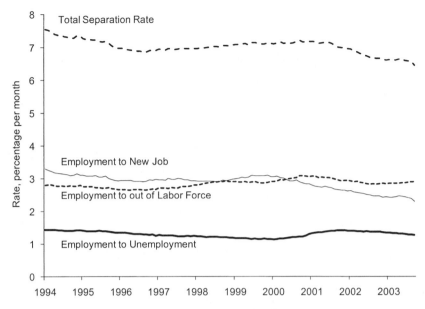

Fig. 5C.3   Separation rate in the Current Population Survey

breakup value is zero, a standard assumption in the matching literature. The Bellman equation for the employer-worker pair is

$$J_t = \max\left(a_t + \varepsilon_t + \frac{1}{1 + r}J_{t+1}, U_t\right).$$

Here a_t is an aggregate influence on the worker's productivity, and ε_t is the large idiosyncratic component, r is the discount rate. Let F be the cumulative distribution function of ε_t. Then the separation rate is

$$s = F\left(U_t - a_t - \frac{1}{1 + r}J_{t+1}\right),$$

and its response to an aggregate disturbance x is

$$\frac{ds}{dx} = f\left(U_t - a_t - \frac{1}{1 + r}J_{t+1}\right)\left(\frac{dU_t}{dx} - \frac{da_t}{dx} - \frac{1}{1 + r}\frac{dJ_{t+1}}{dx}\right).$$

This equation identifies two factors that could make the effect of x on separations fairly small, as we find in the data. One is that the density f could be small. This would imply that fairly few workers are close to the margin of separation. A low value of f would naturally occur if the dispersion of the idiosyncratic component is high. Davis, Faberman, Haltiwanger, and Rucker have demonstrated exactly that proposition in their work on microdata.

The other factor is that the aggregate influence on the unemployment

Table 5C.1   Measures of separation rates

Measures	Rate of job loss
Permanent separations, UI system data[a]	17.23
Current Population Survey (CPS) tenure survey, 1981[b]	10.04
All separations, CPS[c]	8.29
Gross employment reductions[d]	5.66
Permanent layoffs, PSID, 1985[e]	1.81
Displaced Workers Survey, all workers, 1991–1993[f]	0.61
Displaced Workers Survey, workers on the job for at least 3 years, 1991–1993[g]	0.59

[a]Anderson and Meyer (1994, table 2). Measured directly from unemployment insurance records.

[b]U.S. Bureau of Labor Statistics (1983, table 1, 1). Fraction of workers on the job for six months or less, stated at quarterly rate (unadjusted rate is 18.2 percent per six months).

[c]Blanchard and Diamond (1990, figure 1). Average monthly flows out of employment, 1968 to 1986, divided by civilian labor force for 1977 (Economic Report of the President, 1995, table B-33), stated at quarterly rate (unadjusted rate is 2.7 percent per month).

[d]Davis, Haltiwanger, and Schuh (1995, table 2.1) using the Longitudinal Research Database (LRD). Quarterly flow of "job destruction" in manufacturing, with adjustment for compounding (unadjusted rate is 5.5 percent per quarter).

[e]Topel (1990, figure 1). Annual frequency of job loss from employer going out of business, layoff or firing, and completion of job reported in Panel Study of Income Dynamics (PSID), stated at quarterly rate (unadjusted rate is 7.0 percent per year).

[f]U.S. Bureau of Labor Statistics (1994, table 8). Total number of workers displaced between January 1991 and December 1993, divided by the civilian labor force for 1992 (Economic Report of the President, 1995, table B-33), stated at quarterly rate (unadjusted rate is 7.1 percent per three years).

[g]U.S. Bureau of Labor Statistics (1994, table 1). Number of workers with tenure of at least three years displaced between January 1991 and December 1993, divided by the civilian labor force for 1992 (Economic Report of the President, 1995, table B-33), divided by the fraction of the labor force with tenure of at least three years (51.5 percent), (U.S. Bureau of Labor Statistics 1983, table 1, 1), stated at quarterly rate (unadjusted rate is 6.8 percent per three years).

value U and on the continuation value may be about the same. For example, if x is productivity, an increase in x will raise a and J, and on that account discourage separation. But it will also tighten the labor market, lower unemployment, and increase U because the next job is found faster. Or, if wages respond to productivity, U will rise on that account. The effect of aggregate shocks on separations is ambiguous and should be small.

Notice that this view makes no assumption about how employment changes are implemented—it is a true theory of separations. Robert Shimer and I have promoted the view that fluctuations in separations are not an important factor in the aggregate. This derivation shows that the view is completely consistent with the micro facts about labor market dynamics, where separations are highly volatile and important at the establishment level.

Ever since I first read the Davis, Faberman, Haltiwanger, and Rucker chapter, I've been urging everybody in labor macro, especially those interested in search and turnover issues, to read it carefully. The chapter has already changed the standard figure for the basic turnover rate, from the unadjusted figure in JOLTS of around 3.7 percent per month to 5 percent.

I've also come up with a two-sentence summary of the basic points of the chapter: (a) the person responsible for filling out the JOLTS questionnaire is the first person to be laid off when a company cuts back; (b) the BLS doesn't ask anyone to fill out a JOLTS questionnaire for new establishments.

References

Anderson, Patricia M., and Bruce D. Meyer. 1994. The extent and consequences of job turnover. *Brookings Papers on Economic Activity, Microeconomics:* 177–236.

Blanchard, Olivier Jean, and Peter Diamond. 1990. The cyclical behavior of the gross flows of U.S. workers. *Brookings Papers on Economic Activity,* Issue no. 2:85–155.

Davis, Steven J., John C. Haltiwanger, and Scott Schuh. 1995. *Job creation and destruction.* Washington, DC: Department of Commerce, Bureau of the Census, Center for Economic Studies.

Hall, Robert E. 1995. Lost jobs. *Brookings Papers on Economic Activity* 1:221–73.

Topel, Robert. 1990. Specific capital and unemployment: Measuring the costs and consequences of job loss. *Carnegie-Rochester Conference Series on Public Policy* 33:181–214.

U.S. Bureau of Labor Statistics. 1983. *Job tenure and occupational change, 1981.* Special Labor Force Report Bulletin no. 2162. Washington, DC: Department of Labor.

———. 1994. Worker displacement during the early 1990s. USDL no. 94-434. Washington, DC: Department of Labor.

6

Job Loss and the Decline in Job Security in the United States

Henry S. Farber

6.1 Introduction

There is ample evidence that long-term employment is on the decline in the United States. The common understanding that, after some turnover early in careers, most workers find a job (relationship with an employer) that lasts for a long period of time (a "lifetime" job), has been challenged in the last fifteen to twenty years, both in academic research and in the media, as large corporations have engaged in highly publicized layoffs and the industrial structure of the U.S. economy has shifted in the face of global competitive pressures. However, there is little evidence that rates of job loss have increased. This leaves a puzzle regarding the mechanism through which long-term employment relationships are becoming less common.

One possible explanation is that there as been an increase in the rate of job change by workers that is not captured by the Displaced Workers Survey (DWS). This could be in the form of voluntary job change, which accounts for the decline in job durations. The interpretation of what is a "job loss" and what is a "voluntary" job change is left to the respondent in the DWS. The result may be an underestimate of employer-initiated separations. For example, a firm may offer workers "buyouts." Workers who take these buyouts in lieu of a layoff may not report a job loss in the DWS. Unfortunately, there are no large-scale surveys that measure job change and reasons for job change generally.

Another possible explanation is that, while the overall rate of job loss has not increased, higher-tenure workers have become more susceptible to job loss. I begin my analysis by examining the decline in job tenure and long-

Henry S. Farber is the Hughes-Rogers Professor of Economics at Princeton University, and a research associate of the National Bureau of Economic Research.

term employment separately in the private and public sectors using data from various supplements to the Current Population Survey (CPS). From 1973 to 2008, I find that the decline in measures of job security is confined to the private sector and that these measures of job security show an increase in the public sector. I then document the lack of secular change in rates of job loss in either sector using data from the DWS from 1984 to 2008. Finally, I explore the extent to which the observed declines in job tenure and long-term employment in the private sector result from a relative increase in rates of job loss among high-tenure workers in the private sector. I find that there has been no such relative change and that reconciliation of the trends in the tenure and displacement data must lie with a failure to identify all relevant displacement in the DWS.

6.2   Background and Earlier Literature

The evolution of the job durations in the United States has played out in the context of dramatic growth in employment over the last forty years. Civilian employment was 85.1 million in 1973 and rose to 145.4 million in 2008.[1] Thus, 60 million jobs have been created on net in the past thirty-three years, for an average rate of employment growth of 1.5 percent per year over this period. Despite this record of sustained growth in employment in the United States, there is longstanding concern that the quality of the stock of jobs in the economy more generally is deteriorating. The concern about job quality is based in part on the fact that the share of employment that is in manufacturing has been declining over a long period of time.[2] This has led to the view that, as high-quality manufacturing jobs are lost, perhaps to import competition, they are being replaced by low-quality service-sector jobs (so-called hamburger-flipping jobs). The high-quality jobs are characterized by relatively high wages, full-time employment, substantial fringe benefits, and, perhaps most important, substantial job security (low rates of turnover). The low-quality jobs are characterized disproportionately by relatively low wages, part-time employment, an absence of fringe benefits, and low job security (high rates of turnover).

The perceived low quality of many newly created jobs fuels the concern that the nature of the employment relationship in the United States is changing from one based on long-term, full-time employment to one based on more short-term and casual employment. There has been concern that employers are moving toward greater reliance on temporary work-

1. These statistics are taken from U.S. Bureau of Labor Statistics Series ID LNU02000000. This is the civilian employment level derived from the CPS for workers aged sixteen and older.
2. The manufacturing share of nonfarm employment has been falling for over fifty years. Manufacturing's share was 30.9 percent in 1950 and fell to 9.8 percent in 2008. These statistics are taken from U.S. Bureau of Labor Statistics Series ID CEU00000001 and CEU30000001 derived from the Current Employment Statistics payroll data.

ers, on subcontractors, and on part-time workers. Potential motivation for employers to implement such changes range from a need for added flexibility in the face of greater uncertainty regarding product demand to avoidance of increasingly expensive fringe benefits and long-term obligations to workers. The public's concern arises from of the belief that these changes result in lower-quality (lower-paying and less-secure) jobs for the average worker.

6.2.1 Literature on Job Stability

There have been a series of analyses of job stability that have relied on mobility supplements to various January CPSs. An influential early analysis was carried out by Hall (1982). He used published tabulations from some of the early January mobility supplements to compute contemporaneous job retention rates. Hall found that, while any particular new job is unlikely to last a long time, a job that has already lasted five years has a substantial probability of lasting twenty years. He also finds that a substantial fraction of workers will be on a lifetime job (defined as lasting at least twenty years) at some point in their life. Ureta (1992) used the January 1978, 1981, and 1983 mobility supplements to recompute retention rates using artificial cohorts rather than contemporaneous retention rates.

Several more recent papers have used CPS data on job tenure to examine changes in employment stability. Swinnerton and Wial (1995), using data from 1979 through 1991, analyzed job retention rates computed from artificial cohorts and conclude that there has been a secular decline in job stability in the 1980s. In contrast, Diebold, Neumark, and Polsky (1997), using CPS data on tenure from 1973 through 1991 to compute retention rates for artificial cohorts, found that aggregate retention rates were fairly stable over the 1980s but that retention rates declined for high school dropouts and for high school graduates relative to college graduates over this period. I interpret a direct exchange between Diebold, Polsky, and Neumark (1996) and Swinnerton and Wial (1996) as supporting the view that the period from 1979 to 1991 is not a period of generally decreasing job stability. In Farber (1998a), I used CPS data on job tenure from 1973 through 1993 and found that the prevalence of long-term employment has not declined over time but that the distribution of long jobs has shifted. I further found that less-educated men were less likely to hold long jobs than they were previously but that this is offset by a substantial increase in the rate at which women hold long jobs. More recently (Farber 2000), I examined CPS data on job tenure from 1979 through 1996, and I found that the prevalence of long-term employment relationships among men declined by 1996 to its lowest level since 1979. In contrast, long-term employment relationships became somewhat more common among women.

Rose (1995) used data from the Panel Study of Income Dynamics (PSID) to measure job stability by examining the fraction of male workers who do not report any job changes in a given time period, typically ten years. Rose found that the fraction of workers who reported no job changes in given length of time was higher in the 1970s than in the 1980s. He argued that this is evidence of increasing instability of employment.

The Russell Sage Foundation sponsored a conference organized by David Neumark on "Changes in Job Stability and Job Security" in 1998.[3] The evidence presented here is mixed regarding whether job tenure was declining. Jaeger and Stevens (1999) used data from the PSID and the CPS mobility and benefit supplements on (roughly) annual rates of job change to try to reconcile evidence from the CPS and PSID on job stability. They found no change in the share of males in short jobs and some decline between the late 1980s and mid-1990s in the share of males with at least ten years of tenure.[4] Neumark, Polsky, and Hansen (1999) found a similar decline in long-term employment but concluded that this does not reflect a secular trend. Gottschalk and Moffitt (1999) use monthly data from the Survey of Income and Program Participation (SIPP), along with annual data from the SIPP and the PSID, and they found no evidence of an upward trend in job insecurity in the 1980s and 1990s. Valletta (1999) used data from the PSID from 1976 to 1993 and found some decline in long-term employment relationships.

In more recent work, Stewart (2002) used data from the March CPS to investigate two aspects of job security. The first, the likelihood of leaving a job, showed no particular trend from 1975 through 2000 based on these data. The second, the likelihood of making an employment-to-employment transition, increased over this period, while the likelihood of making an employment-to-unemployment transition decreased. Stewart concluded that the cost of changing jobs has decreased.

Stevens (2008) examined data from several longitudinal histories of older male workers (late 1950s and early 1960s) with regard to changes over time in the length of longest job held during careers. She found that there has been no change between the late 1960s and late early 2000s and concluded that there has not been a decline in the incidence of "lifetime jobs." A careful reading of her results show an increase in average longest tenure from about twenty-two years among older workers in 1969 to twenty-four years in 1980 followed by a decline to 21.4 years in 2002. A reasonable interpretation of this pattern is that the earliest cohorts had jobs interrupted by service in World War II, resulting in lower average longest tenure than subsequent cohorts. The decline since 1980 may then reflect a real decline in job durations. Additionally, the most recent cohort examined by Stevens was born

3. The proceedings of this conference are published in Neumark (2000), and a number of these papers are published in *The Journal of Labor Economics,* volume 17, number 4, part 2, October 1999.
4. Unfortunately, due to the design of the PSID, neither of these studies examined the mobility experience of women.

in the 1940s, so her analysis cannot shed light on the experience of more recent birth cohorts.

In Farber (2007), I used data from twenty-one supplements to the CPS over the 1973 to 2008 period that contain information on how long workers have been employed by their current firm. I found that, by virtually any measure, more recent cohorts of male workers have been with their current employers for less time at specific ages. I did not find a corresponding decline in age-specific tenure for women. This contrast reflects the increased commitment of women to the labor force tempered by the fact that many working women, when they have young children, either exit the labor force for a period of time or change jobs to one with different or more flexible hours.

Taken as a whole, I conclude from this earlier literature that there has been a decline in job tenure and in the incidence of long-term employment relationships.

6.2.2   Literature on Job Loss

In an earlier paper (Farber 1993), I used the five DWSs from 1984 to 1992 to examine changes in the incidence and costs of job loss over the period from 1982 to 1991. I found that there were slightly elevated rates of job loss for older and more-educated workers in the slack labor market in the latter part of the period compared with the slack labor market of the earlier part of the period. But I found that job loss rates for younger and less-educated workers were substantially higher than those for older and more-educated workers throughout the period. These findings are consistent with the longstanding view that younger and less-educated workers bear the brunt of recessions. I also confirmed the conventional view that the probability of job loss declines substantially with tenure.

Gardner (1995) carried out the first analysis of which I am aware that incorporated the 1994 DWS. She examined the incidence of job loss from 1981 to 1992. While she found roughly comparable overall rates of job loss in the 1981 to 1982 and 1991 to 1992 periods, she found that the industrial and occupational mix of job loss changed over this period. There was an decreased incidence of job loss among blue-collar workers and workers in manufacturing industries and an increase in job loss among white-collar workers and workers in nonmanufacturing industries.

In another paper (Farber 1997), I used the seven DWSs from 1984 to 1996 to revisit the issue of changes in the incidence and costs of job loss. I found that the overall rate of job loss increased in the first half of the 1990s despite the sustained economic expansion. Hipple (1999) carried out the first analysis of the 1998 DWS, and he found that the displacement rate among workers who had held their jobs for at least three years fell only slightly between the 1993 to 1994 period and the 1995 to 1996 period despite the sustained economic expansion.

There is a substantial literature using the DWS to study the postdisplacement employment and earnings experience of displaced workers.[5] This work demonstrates that displaced workers suffer substantial periods of unemployment and that earnings on jobs held after displacement are substantially lower than predisplacement earnings. In my earlier work (Farber 1993), I found that there was no difference on average in the consequences of job loss between the 1982 to 1983 recession and the 1990 to 1991 recession.

The earnings loss suffered by displaced workers is positively related to tenure on the predisplacement job. On the other hand, Kletzer (1989) found further that the postdisplacement earnings *level* is positively related to predisplacement tenure, suggesting that workers displaced from long jobs are more able, on average, than those displaced from shorter jobs. In more recent work, Neal (1995), using the DWS, and Parent (2000) using the National Longitudinal Survey of Youth (NLSY), found that workers who find new employment in the same industry from which they were displaced earn more than do industry switchers. This work suggests that Kletzer's finding that postdisplacement earnings are positively related to predisplacement tenure may be a result of the transferability of industry-specific capital. Workers who are reemployed in the same industry "earn a return" on their previous tenure, while those reemployed in a different industry do not.

In Farber (2004), I examined changes in the incidence and consequences of job loss between 1981 and 2001 using data from the DWS from 1984 to 2002. I found that the overall rate of job loss has a strong counter-cyclical component but that the job loss rate was higher than might have been expected during the mid-1990s given the strong labor market during that period. I found substantial earnings declines for displaced workers relative to what they earned before displacement. Additionally, foregone earnings growth (the growth in earnings that would have occurred had the workers not been displaced) is an important part of the cost of job loss for reemployed full-time job losers. There is no evidence of a decline during the tight labor market of the 1990s in the earnings loss of displaced workers who were reemployed full time. In fact, earnings losses of displaced workers have been increasing since the mid 1990s. In Farber (2005), I update my earlier work to include data on job loss through 2003. Not surprisingly, there were higher job loss rates and lower postdisplacement reemployment probabilities during the recession of the early 2000s.

With regard to overall rates of job loss, this literature suggests that job loss rates have a strong cyclical component. However, aside from several years with unusually high job loss rates in the mid-1990s, there has been no secular increase in rates of job loss.

5. See, for example, Podgursky and Swaim (1987), Kletzer (1989), Topel (1990), Farber (1993), Farber (1997).

6.3 The Decline in Long-Term Employment

In this section, I present evidence on job durations from a sample consisting of not-self-employed workers aged twenty to sixty-four from the twenty-one CPS supplements covering the period from 1973 to 2008. The sample contains 924,423 workers.[6] Because the factors highlighted as potentially causing a decline in job security are directly relevant to the private sector and less relevant to the public sector, I present separate analyses of job tenure in the two sectors.

6.3.1 Measuring the Change in Tenure over Time

I organize my analysis of changes over time in the distribution of job durations by examining age-specific values of various distributional measures of job tenure for each sampled year. No one statistic can completely characterize a distribution, and I focus on several measures here:

- Mean job tenure (years with the current employer): Note that this is not mean completed job duration since the jobs sampled are still in progress.
- The age-specific probability that a worker reports being in his or her job at least ten years: Because younger workers cannot have accumulated substantial job tenure, I restrict this analysis to workers at least thirty-five years of age, and I examine how these probabilities have changed over time.
- The age-specific probability that a worker reports being in his or her job at least twenty years: Because younger workers cannot have accumulated substantial job tenure, I restrict this analysis to workers forty-five years of age and older
- The age-specific probability that a worker reports being in his or her job for less than one year: This provides information on changes over time in the transition from the early job-shopping phase of a career to more stable longer-term employment relationships.

An important measurement issue is related to cyclical changes in the composition of the sample. It is clear that workers with little seniority are more likely than high-tenure workers to lose their jobs in downturns (Abraham and Medoff 1984). Thus, we would expect that the incidence of long-term employment, as measured by the fraction of workers with tenure exceeding some threshold, to be counter-cyclical. Tight labor markets will lead the distribution of job durations to lie to the left of the distribution in slack labor markets, and these cyclical influences need to be kept in mind when interpreting the results.

6. These data are described in more detail in the appendix.

6.3.2   Mean Tenure

Figure 6.1 contains separate plots by sex of mean tenure by age for three time periods covered by the data (1973–83, 1984–95, 1996–2008).[7] These figures show clearly that (a) mean tenure is rising with age, and (b) women have lower mean tenure than men after about age thirty. With regard to shifts over time in the tenure distribution, age-specific mean tenure for males has declined substantially, particularly for older workers. For example, mean tenure for males at age fifty declined from 13.6 years in the 1970s to 11.8 years in the early 2000s. In contrast, age-specific mean tenure for older women has increased. Mean tenure for females at age fifty increased from 8.9 years in the 1970s to 9.7 years in the early 2000s. This reflects the increased attachment to the labor force of more recent cohorts of women.

Interestingly, the decline in mean tenure is restricted to the private sector, and mean tenure has increased in the public sector. Figure 6.2 contains separate plots by sector of mean tenure for males by age for the three time periods. These figures show clearly that (a) mean tenure is rising with age in both the public and private sectors. With regard to shifts over time in the tenure distribution, age-specific mean tenure for males employed in the private sector has declined substantially, particularly for older workers. For example, mean tenure for private sector males at age fifty declined from 13.5 years in the 1973 to 1983 period to 11.3 years in the 1996 to 2008 period. The pattern in the public sector is the opposite. For example, mean tenure for public sector males at age fifty *increased* from 13.6 years in the 1973 to 1983 period to 15.8 years in the 1996 to 2008 period.

Figure 6.3 contains the same plots for females, and the pattern in the private sector is quite different than that for males. While mean tenure for females in increasing with age, tenure levels are substantially lower than those for males in the private sector. Importantly, there appears to have been no change in age-specific job tenure for females employed in the private sector. This is despite the well-documented increase in female attachment to the labor force. In contrast, females in the public sector have seen a substantial increase in mean job tenure. For example, mean tenure for public-sector females at age fifty increased from 9.3 years in the 1973 to 1983 period to 12.8 years in the 1996 to 2008 period. One explanation for this pattern may be that the increase in female labor force attachment in the last thirty years has been offset in the private sector by the same forces that have led to the decline in male tenure in the private sector.

Another approach to summarizing the data is to estimate a linear model of the natural logarithm of tenure of the form

(1) $$\ln(T_{ijt}) = Y_t + A_j + \varepsilon_{ijt},$$

---

7. Means are calculated weighted by CPS final sample weights.

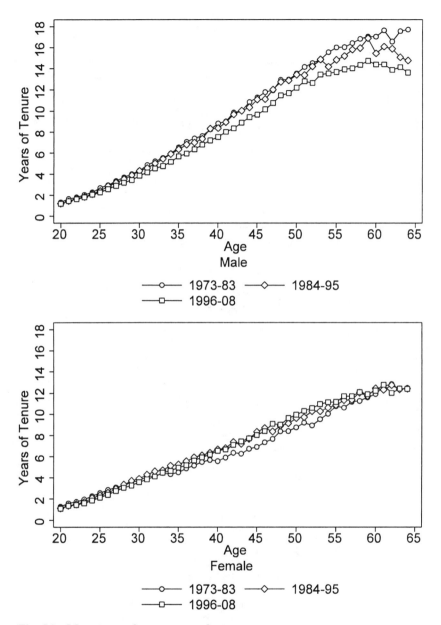

Fig. 6.1   **Mean tenure, by sex, age, and year**

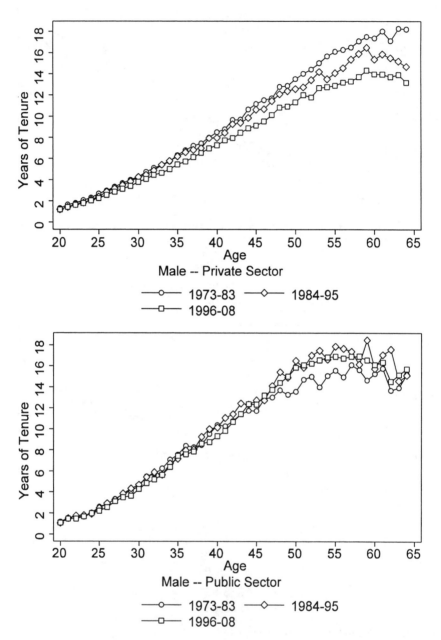

Fig. 6.2   Mean tenure for males, by sex, age, and year

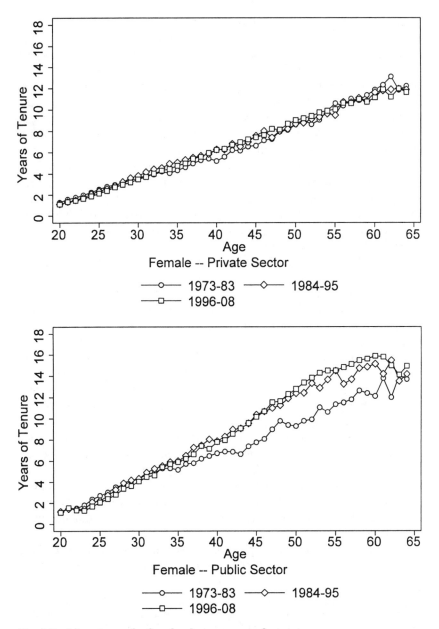

Fig. 6.3   Mean tenure for females, by sex, age, and year

where T_{ijt} is tenure in years for individual i at age j in year t, Y_t is a calendar year indicator, and A_j is a years-of-age indicator. This logarithmic specification embodies the plausible implicit assumption that proportional year effects on mean tenure are constant across ages and, equivalently, that the proportional age effects on mean tenure are constant across years.[8] A more detailed investigation would allow for year effects that vary by age because changes in job security could express themselves differentially at various ages. However, the model in equation (1) fits the data quite well, and it serves as a good summary of the data.[9]

I estimate the model in equation (1) separately for men and women in the private and public sectors using ordinary least squares (OLS), weighted by the CPS final sample weights. The estimated year effects on mean tenure, normalized at zero in 1973, are converted to proportional differences in mean tenure relative to 1973 as $\exp(\hat{Y}_t - \hat{Y}_{1973}) - 1$. These proportional differences are plotted in figure 6.4.

The patterns are quite different for the four groups of workers. There is a sharp decline of about 25 percent in age-specific mean tenure for male private-sector workers between the 1973 and 2008. In contrast, there is no systematic change over time in age-specific mean tenure for female private-sector workers. The public sector shows a dramatic increase in age-specific mean tenure both for men and for women over the sample period. Tenure for males in the public sector increased by about 18 percent between 1973 and 1983 before declining somewhat by 2008 to approximately the 1973 level. Age-specific mean tenure for females in the public sector was 30 percent higher in the early 1990s than in 1973 and remained about 20 percent higher in 2008 than it was in 1973.

These patterns are consistent with those found in figures 6.2 and 6.3. They suggest a decline in long-term employment opportunities in the private sector that is most evident for males and is offset to some extent for females by their increased attachment to the labor force. The increase in mean tenure in the public sector could reflect an increase in the security offered by public-sector jobs that is reinforced for females by their increased attachment to the labor force.

In addition to the increased presence of women in the labor force, there are other important changes that could be related to the decline in tenure.

---

8. I do not estimate this model using absolute tenure because the implicit assumption in that case would be that absolute year effects on mean tenure are constant across ages and, equivalently, that absolute age effects on mean tenure are constant across years. This is clearly not plausible on inspection of figure 6.1, given the fact that younger workers have very low levels of tenure.

9. I computed (separately for each of the four groups defined by sex and sector of employment) weighted mean tenure for each age or year combination and regressed these measures on a complete set of age- and year-fixed effects. This is essentially the main effects model in equation (1) aggregated to the cell level. The R-squareds from these regressions are all in excess of 0.95.

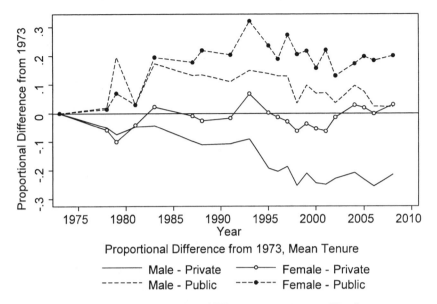

Fig. 6.4   Proportional difference from 1973, mean tenure, controlling for age

First is the well-known large increase in average educational attainment during the twentieth century. While there is not a clear relationship between educational attainment and tenure, I investigate how the decline in mean job tenure is related to the general increase in educational attainment.[10]

In order to provide a summary across educational categories of the proportional change in mean tenure over time accounting for changes in the educational distribution over time, I estimate, separately by sex and sector, an augmented version of the regression model for mean tenure in equation (1) as

$$(2) \qquad \ln(T_{ijt}) = \mathbf{ED}_i \gamma + Y_t + A_j + \varepsilon_{ijt},$$

where $\mathbf{ED}_i$ is a vector of dummy variables indicating educational attainment, and γ is a vector of associated coefficients. The estimated proportional change in mean tenure relative to 1973 ($\exp([\hat{Y}_t - \hat{Y}_{1973}]) - 1$) are plotted in figure 6.5, and they are very similar in shape to those derived without controlling for education (figure 6.4).

A second and potentially more important factor that could account for the decline in tenure is the increased presence of immigrants in the U.S. labor force. By definition, newly arrived immigrants cannot have substantial tenure. Data on immigration are not available in any CPS with tenure data

---

10. Mean tenure in my analysis sample for each of the four educational categories are $\mathbf{ED} <$ 12: 7.2 years, $\mathbf{ED} = 12$: 7.3 years, $\mathbf{ED}$ 13–15: 6.5 years, and $\mathbf{ED} \geq 16$: 7.4 years.

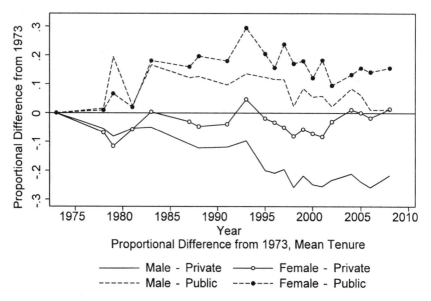

Fig. 6.5   Proportional difference from 1973, mean tenure, controlling for age and education

prior to 1995. Analysis of the data since 1995 illustrates both the sharp increase in immigrant share in the labor force and the fact that immigrants have lower job tenure than natives. The weighted immigrant fraction of the labor force in my sample increased steadily from 9.45 percent in 1995 to 15.1 percent in 2008. On average, between 1995 and 2008, immigrants had 2.08 years lower tenure than natives (s.e. = 0.032). Immigrants were only slightly younger than natives over the same period (average difference = 0.927 years [s.e. = 0.048]).[11]

An important question is how much of the decline in observed tenure since 1973 is due to the increased immigrant presence in the labor force. While not directly observable prior to 1995, immigrant status is strongly correlated with race and Hispanic ethnicity, which is observed in all years. Table 6.1 contains the immigrant proportion by race and Hispanic ethnicity for the 1995 to 2008 CPS data. The overall immigrant proportion of workers rose from 9.5 percent in 1995 to 15.1 percent in 2008. These immigrants are highly concentrated among nonwhites and Hispanics. Only 3.6 percent of white non-Hispanics are immigrants, while over 50 percent of Hispanics (white and nonwhite) are immigrants.[12] Additionally, a growing fraction of nonwhite non-Hispanics are immigrants, rising from 18.7 percent in 1995 to

11. See Farber (2007) for a detailed analysis of the change in job tenure since 1995 that controls directly for immigrant status.
12. The rather sharp drop in the immigrant proportion among nonwhite Hispanics is due to the change in the race identification coding in the CPS in 2004.

Table 6.1   Proportion immigrants by race and Hispanic ethnicity, 1995–2008

Year	All	White non-Hispanic	Nonwhite non-Hispanic	All Hispanic	White Hispanic	Nonwhite Hispanic
1995	0.095	0.030	0.187	0.506	0.509	0.492
1996	0.100	0.032	0.226	0.494	0.493	0.510
1997	0.109	0.032	0.232	0.516	0.518	0.484
1998	0.117	0.035	0.240	0.517	0.516	0.526
1999	0.111	0.033	0.222	0.495	0.498	0.448
2000	0.121	0.038	0.239	0.517	0.514	0.585
2001	0.129	0.039	0.261	0.522	0.520	0.557
2002	0.130	0.040	0.270	0.528	0.527	0.543
2004	0.142	0.042	0.280	0.531	0.538	0.439
2005	0.141	0.037	0.275	0.538	0.545	0.439
2006	0.147	0.039	0.282	0.550	0.556	0.469
2008	0.151	0.041	0.302	0.533	0.541	0.438
All	0.125	0.037	0.254	0.523	0.526	0.484

Notes: Based on data for not self-employed workers twenty–sixty-four years of age from eleven Current Population Surveys (CPS) covering the period from 1995 to 2008. Weighted by CPS final sample weights. $N = 515,759$.

30.2 percent in 2008. The rising overall immigrant share over this period is reflected in the growing share of Hispanics and nonwhites in the labor force. The Hispanic share of employment in my sample increased from 9.0 percent in 1995 to 13.5 percent in 2008, and the nonwhite share of employment increased from 15.2 percent to 17.7 percent over the same period.

Consistent with the upward trend in immigration and the decline in job tenure in the private sector is the fact that immigrants are disproportionately employed in the private sector. Fully 91.3 percent of immigrants are employed in the private sector between 1995 and 2008. In contrast, over the same period, only 81.9 percent of natives are employed in the private sector. These distributions are fairly constant over the period, implying that the increase in immigrant share of the total labor force could account for at least part of the private or public difference in the trends in job tenure.

In order to account, at least partly, for the role of increased immigration in the decline in tenure, I estimate age-specific proportional differences in mean tenure relative to 1973 controlling for race, Hispanic ethnicity and their interaction, as well as age and education. I derive the year effects by estimating

$$(3) \quad \ln(T_{ijt}) = \alpha_1 NW_i + \alpha_2 H_i + \alpha_3 H_i NW_i + \mathbf{ED}_i \gamma + Y_t + A_j + \varepsilon_{ijt},$$

where NW_i is an indicator for nonwhite, H_i is an indicator for Hispanic ethnicity, and $\mathbf{ED}_i$ is a vector of indicators for four educational categories.

Figure 6.6 contains separate plots for males and females in the private and public sectors of the proportional differences from 1973 in mean tenure

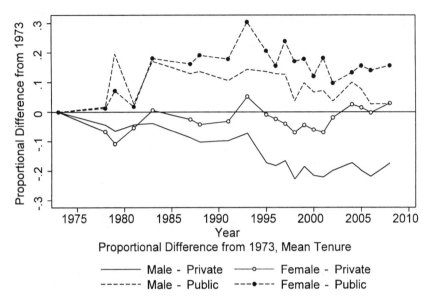

Fig. 6.6   Proportional difference from 1973, mean tenure, controlling for age, education, race, and Hispanic ethnicity

based on equation three. The time series patterns controlling for age, education, race, and ethnicity are similar to those controlling for age alone. The additional controls account for about 20 percent of the decline evident in figure 6.4.

There remains a sharp decline of about 20 percent in age-specific mean tenure for male private-sector workers between 1973 and 2008, and there is still no systematic change over time in age-specific mean tenure for female private-sector workers. The public sector continues to show an increase in age-specific mean tenure both for men and for women over the sample period. Tenure for males in the public sector increased by about 18 percent between 1973 and 1983 before declining somewhat by 2008 to approximately the 1973 level. Age-specific mean tenure for females in the public sector was 30 percent higher in the early 1990s than in 1973 and remained about 15 percent higher in 2008 than it was in 1973.

It is clear from the analysis in this subsection that age-specific mean tenure has declined dramatically over time and that only about 20 percent of this decline can be accounted for by the sharp growth in immigrants in the labor market. This decline is concentrated among men in the private sector. Mean tenure increased for both men and women in the public sector.

6.3.3   Long-Term Employment

Long-term employment is common in the U.S. Labor Market. In this analysis, I consider two measures of long-term employment:

- The fraction of workers aged thirty-five to sixty-four who have been with their employer at least ten years (the ten-year rate)
- The fraction of workers aged forty-five to sixty-four who have been with their employer at least twenty years (the twenty-year rate).

Figure 6.7 contains plots of these two measures over the 1973 to 2008 period for men and women in the public and private sectors. It is clear that the incidence of long-term employment has declined dramatically for men employed in the private sector, with the ten-year rate falling from about 50 percent to about 37 percent and the twenty-year rate falling from about 35 percent to about 22 percent between 1973 and 2008. In contrast, the incidence of long-term employment for men employed in the public sector increased over the same period, with the ten-year rate increasing from 50 percent to 60 percent in 2000 before falling to 54 percent in 2008. Over the same period, the twenty-year rate for men employed in the public sector increased from 25 percent in 1973 to 40 percent in 1990 before falling off to 34 percent by 2008.

The incidence of long-term employment among women employed in the private sector remained steady between 1973 and 2008, at a ten-year rate of about 30 percent and a twenty-year rate of about 15 percent. In sharp contrast, the incidence of long-term employment among women employed in the public sector increased substantially, with the ten-year rate increasing from 30 percent in 1973 to 45 percent in 2008 and the twenty-year rate increasing from 10 percent to 25 percent over the same period.

Because these measures are sensitive to the age distribution and other observable characteristics, I estimate age-specific year effects using the same approach I used for mean tenure. I estimate linear probability models using the same specification of explanatory variables (year, age, education, race, Hispanic ethnicity and the interaction of race, and Hispanic ethnicity) in equation (3), and I report the estimated year effects (differences from 1973) from this analysis in figure 6.8.

Figure 6.8 contains separate plots for males and females by sector of employment of the year effects (1973 = 0) for the ten-year rate (top panel) and the twenty-year rate (bottom panel). The age-specific probability that a male worker in the private sector has been with his employer for at least ten years decreased steadily by about 10 percentage points. A decline of the same magnitude is also found for the twenty-year rate for private-sector male workers. These 10 percentage points declines are substantial given the 1973 base ten-year rate of 50 percent and the base twenty-year rate of 35 percent (figure 6.7). The rates of long-term employment for females employed in the private sector show no change between 1973 and 2008.

As with the simple means in figure 6.7, the long-term employment rates for both men and women employed in the public sector have increased since 1973. The increase has been particularly sharp for women, with both the ten-

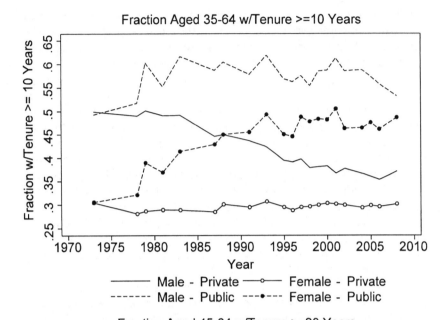

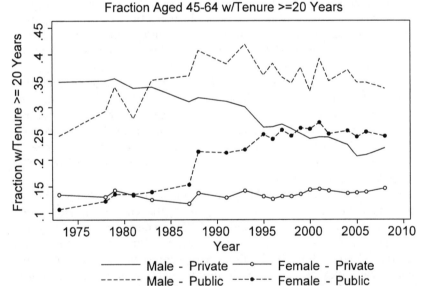

Fig. 6.7   Fraction of workers in long-term jobs, by year

and twenty-year rates increasing by more than 10 percentage points (from a 1973 base of 30 percent and 10 percent, respectively).

Taken together, the analysis of the changes in average tenure (figure 6.6) and in the likelihood of long-term employment (figure 6.8) over time shows clearly that average tenure has declined and long-term employment

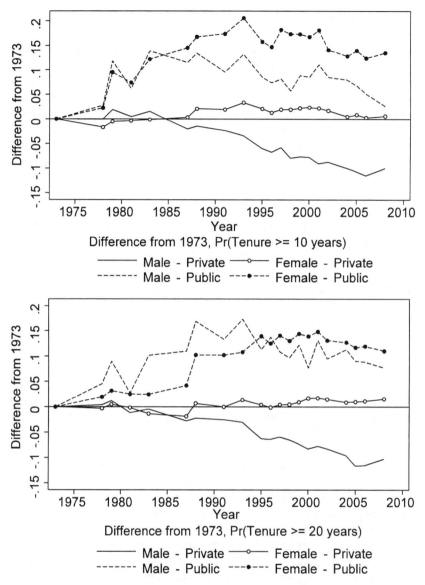

Fig. 6.8 **Proportional difference from 1973, Pr ($T \geq 10$) and Pr ($T \geq 20$), control-ling for age, education, race, and Hispanic ethnicity**

has become much less common for males in the private sector. Among females in the private sector, average tenure and the incidence of long-term employment have remained steady. Workers in the public sector, on the other hand, have seen an increase in both average tenure and the incidence of long-term employment.

The difference in patterns between males and females in the private sector likely reflects the common factors reducing tenure for all workers offset for females by their dramatically increased attachment to the labor force over the past half century. This increase in attachment is also reflected in the larger increase in tenure and long-term employment among women relative to men in the public sector.

A key conclusion is that the structure of employment in the private sector in the United States has become less oriented toward long-term jobs. Because public-sector employment as a fraction of total employment has remained steady at about 18 to 20 percent and seems unlikely to increase, it appears that young workers today will be less likely than their parents to have a lifetime job.

6.3.4   Churning: Are There More Very Short Jobs?

The opposite but related pole of the job tenure distribution is short-term jobs. In Farber (1994, 1999b), I present evidence that half of all new jobs (worker-employer matches) end within the first year. As I show in the following, a substantial fraction (around 20 percent) of all jobs have current tenure less than one year ("new jobs"). Not surprisingly, younger workers are more likely than older workers to be in new jobs. High rates of job change among young workers are a natural result of search for a good job or a good match.[13]

Table 6.2 contains the new-job rate by ten-year age group for males and females by sector of employment. This illustrates the sharp decline in the new-job rate as workers age through their twenties, especially, and into their thirties. This decline is sharper for males, and the new-job rate is slightly higher for females in all age groups. This reflects the fact that females are more likely to leave and reenter the labor force in midcareer.

In order to investigate how the new-job rate has changed over time, figure 6.9 contains plots of the new-job rate by year for each of the four sex or sector groups. In the private sector, the new-job rate decreased fairly steadily for females and decreased for males since the late 1990s. In the public sector, the new-job rate decreased quite sharply for females and generally has been steady for males.

In order to account for differences by age and other characteristics, I estimate age-specific year effects using the same approach I used for means and for the probability of long-term employment. I estimate linear probability models of the probability of being in a new job using the same specification of explanatory variables (year, age, education, race, Hispanic ethnicity) in equation (3). Figure 6.10 contains separate plots by sector for males and females of the difference by year in the new-job rate relative to 1973.

There is substantial variation over time in all four series, and it is difficult

---

13. Burdett (1978) presents a model of job search with this implication. Jovanovic (1979) presents model of matching in the labor market with the same implication.

Table 6.2   New job rate, by sex and sector of employment, 1973–2008

	Private		Public		
Age	Male	Female	Male	Female	All
20–29	0.339	0.371	0.281	0.314	0.347
30–39	0.174	0.216	0.089	0.147	0.180
40–49	0.122	0.154	0.056	0.084	0.123
50–59	0.093	0.112	0.043	0.053	0.089
60–64	0.080	0.089	0.052	0.041	0.076
All	0.188	0.221	0.100	0.133	0.188

Notes: The new job rate is the fraction of workers reporting less than one year of tenure with their current employer. Based on data for not self-employed workers twenty–sixty-four years of age from nineteen Current Population Surveys (CPS) covering the period from 1973 to 2008. Weighted by CPS final sample weights. $N = 924{,}423$.

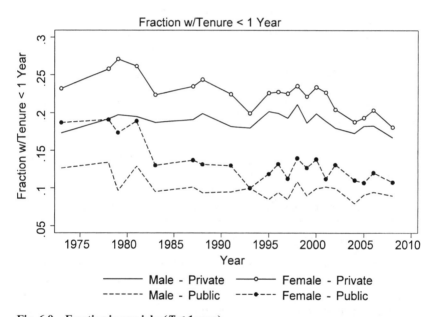

Fig. 6.9   **Fraction in new jobs ($T < 1$ year)**

to pick out clear patterns. The new-job rate for private-sector males is generally higher than in 1973 but has declined in recent rates to almost the 1973 level. The new-job rate for private-sector females is about 2 percentage points lower today than in 1973. The new-job rates in the public sector are generally lower than in 1973 for both males and females. The male rate fell particularly sharply in the 1980s and 1990s before recovering almost to the 1973 level.

The inverse relationship between the new-job rate and age evident in table

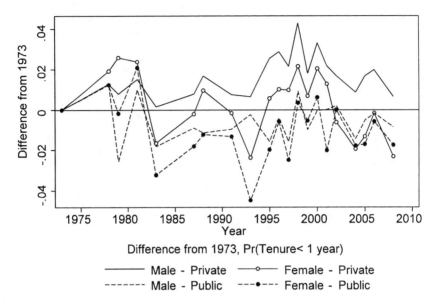

Fig. 6.10   **Year effects on Pr ($T < 1$)**

6.2 raises two interesting questions regarding the decline in mean tenure and long-term employment and how this decline is related to the rate of "churning" in the labor market:

1. Are young workers taking longer to find good (long-lasting) matches or jobs? This would imply an increase in the new-job rate among younger workers.

2. Are older workers having more difficulty finding good matches when they lose jobs that may formerly have been lifetime jobs? This would imply an increase in the new-job rate among older workers.

An implicit constraint in the model I use to estimate the changes (based on equation [3]) presented in figure 6.10 is that the changes over time are constant across age groups. Given the role that job change plays in matching and job search early in careers, I estimate separate year effects for different age groups. The top panel of figure 6.11 contains differences by year in the new-job rate relative to the 1973 estimated using a sample of workers aged twenty to twenty-nine. These estimates, which vary quite a bit year to year, show no secular pattern but a strong cyclical pattern. The regression-adjusted private-sector new-job rate for both sexes is higher in stronger economic times as employers increase hiring and lower in weaker times as workers are less likely to quit to take new jobs. The public sector adjusted new-job rate fluctuates dramatically over time.

The bottom panel of figure 6.11 contains differences by year in the new-job rate relative to 1973 estimated using a sample of workers aged thirty

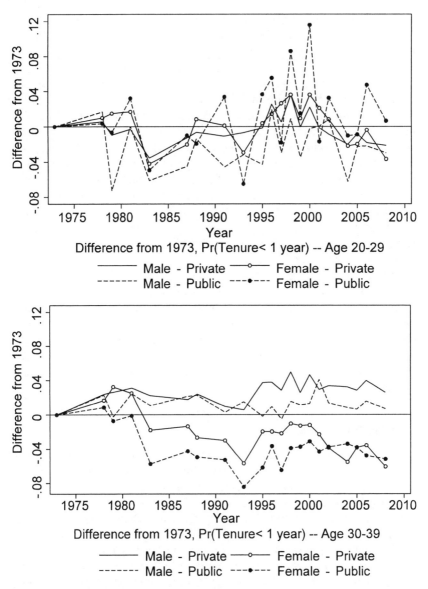

Fig. 6.11   Year effects on Pr ($T < 1$), (aged 20–29 and 30–39)

to thirty-nine. These estimated year effects differ substantially from those for workers in their twenties. There is an increase of about 4 percent in the new job rate for males in their thirties in the private sector and a decrease of about 4 percent for females in their thirties in both sectors between 1973 and 2008. The pattern for males is consistent with the hypothesis that men are job shopping in their twenties and have become less likely to settle into longer-term jobs in their thirties. The pattern for females, which is stronger in the public sector, likely reflects an increase in attachment to the labor force by women as they enter their thirties.

Given that older workers are less likely to be in new jobs, I next investigate how the new-job rate has changed for workers aged forty and older. The top panel of figure 6.12 contains differences by year in the new-job rate relative to 1973 estimated using a sample of workers aged forty to forty-nine. The bottom panel of this figure contains differences by year in the new-job rate relative to 1973 using a sample of workers aged fifty to sixty-four. Both plots show an increase in the probability of being on a new job for males employed in the private sector, although this effect is diminished in 2008 among men fifty to sixty-four. The magnitude of the increase (about 2 percentage points) is substantial when compared to the overall mean new-job rates for older men in table 6.2. The new-job rate for women in their forties in the public sector decreased substantially, but the change is not reflected in the experience of women fifty and older.

The overall time series pattern of the age-specific new-job rate is a general increase over time for men aged thirty and older. Part of this reflects an extension of the period of job shopping early in careers, and part reflects increased probabilities of jobs ending later in careers. There is not much change over time in the age-specific new-job rate for women in either the public or private sectors aside from a substantial decline for women in their thirties, likely reflecting a reduced likelihood of withdrawing from and subsequently reentering the labor force.

6.4   The Rate of Job Loss

The decline in job tenure in the private sector documented here could be the result of increased rates of increased job loss or increased voluntary job change. While there is not a large-scale comprehensive series on voluntary mobility, the DWS does measure job loss. The DWS, administered every two years since 1984 as a supplement to the CPS, is perhaps the most comprehensive source of information on the incidence and costs of job loss in the United States. In this section, I analyze data on 985,508 individuals between the ages of twenty and sixty-four from the DWSs conducted as part of the January CPSs in 1984, 1986, 1988, 1990, 1992, 2002, 2004, 2006, and 2008 and the February CPSs in 1994, 1996, 1998, and 2000.

There are three important issues of measurement and interpretation that arise when comparing job loss rates calculated using the DWS over time.

1. The DWS asks only about a single involuntary job loss. The survey does not capture multiple job losses by the same worker. Neither does it capture worker terminations "for cause." The survey is meant to capture worker terminations as the result of business decisions of the employer unre-

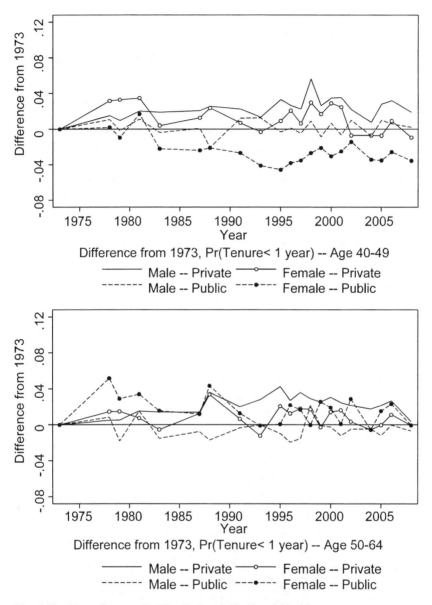

Fig. 6.12   Year effects on Pr ($T < 1$), (aged 40–49 and 50–64)

lated to the performance of the particular employee (e.g., a plant closing, a layoff, the abolition of a job). Thus, the measure of the job loss rate that I calculate is the fraction of workers who lost at least one job not "for cause" in the relevant period rather than the rate of destruction of worker-employer matches.

2. The DWS from 1984 to 1992 asked about job separations in the previous five years, while the later DWS asked about job separation in the previous three years. The measure of job loss that I use is adjusted to account for this change in the recall period so that all rates are reported on a three-year basis. This adjustment is detailed in Farber (1997).

3. The basic wording of key questions changed since the inception of the DWS in 1984. This may have affected whether survey respondents would report a job separation in a particular circumstance as an involuntary separation in one survey but would not report a separation in the same circumstance as involuntary in another year. In Farber (1998b) and Farber (2004), I use additional data from debriefing questions asked of a fraction of DWS respondents in 1996, 1998, and 2000 to investigate how changes in the wording of the key question may have affected the likelihood that a worker reported a particular separation as an involuntary job change. I use the results of that analysis to calculate reweighted job loss rates that I present in this study.[14]

In these surveys, I count as job losers workers who reported a job loss in the three calendar years prior to the survey. Based on these data, I calculate the rate of job loss as the ratio of the number of reported job losers divided by the number of workers who were either employed at the survey date or reported a job loss but were not employed at the survey date. I then adjust these job loss rates as described in Farber (2004) to account for the change in the recall period from five years to three years in 1994 and changes in the wording of the key job loss question.

Figure 6.13 contains plots of adjusted three-year job loss rates for the private and public sectors computed from each of the thirteen DWSs from 1984 to 2008, along with the average civilian unemployment rate for each three-year period.[15] Two facts are clear from this figure.

1. Job loss is cyclical, with job loss rates clearly positively correlated with the unemployment rate. Both unemployment and job loss rates were relatively high in the 1981 to 1983 period, and they both fell sharply during the expansion of the mid-1980s. However, the private-sector job loss rate rose much more sharply from the 1987 to 1989 to the 1989 to 1991 period than did the unemployment rate. The job loss rate rose by fully 3.1 percentage points (from 6.7 percent to 9.6 percent), while the average unemployment rate rose by only 0.2 percent (from 5.7 percent to 5.9 percent) over

14. Job losers are asked to report the reason for their job loss. One allowable response is "other." The adjustment for changes in the wording of the key job loss question discounts job loss rates for "other" reasons by 37.4 percent for the 1984 to 1992 DWS and by 74.8 percent for the 1994 and later DWSs. See Farber (1998b) for details.

15. Information on rates of job loss is presented most accessibly in graphical form, and the discussion here is organized around a series of figures. All counts are weighted using the CPS sampling weights.

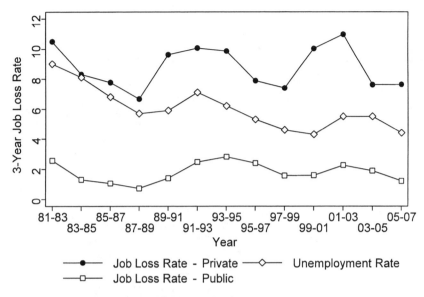

Fig. 6.13   Unemployment and job loss rates, by year
Source: Displaced Workers Survey, 1984–2008.

this period. Between 1993 and 1999, both the private-sector job loss and unemployment rates fell sharply, but the gap between them remained larger than in the strong labor market of the late 1980s. The unemployment rate continued to fall in the 1999 to 2001 period before rising somewhat in the 2001 to 2003 period. The private-sector job loss rate rose sharply after the 1997 to 1999 trough through the 2001 to 2003 period before falling off in the 2003 to 2005 period.[16]

2. The rate of job loss in the public sector is approximately one-fourth of the private-sector rate, and it exhibits less cyclical sensitivity. To the extent that private-sector jobs have become less secure, it may be the case that public-sector jobs have become relatively more attractive. The resulting lower quit rates from public-sector jobs would serve to reinforce the already high level of job security evident in the public sector.

Figure 6.14 contains three-year rates of job loss by year for each of four education categories separately for the private and public sectors. The top panel of the figure presents the job loss rates for the private sector. Private-sector job loss rates were dramatically higher for less-educated workers in the 1980s, but there has been steady convergence in rates of

16. The use of three-year averages here hides the facts that the job loss rate was steady in 1999 and 2000 before increasing sharply in 2001, while the unemployment rate declined slightly in 1999 and 2000 before increasing slightly in 2001.

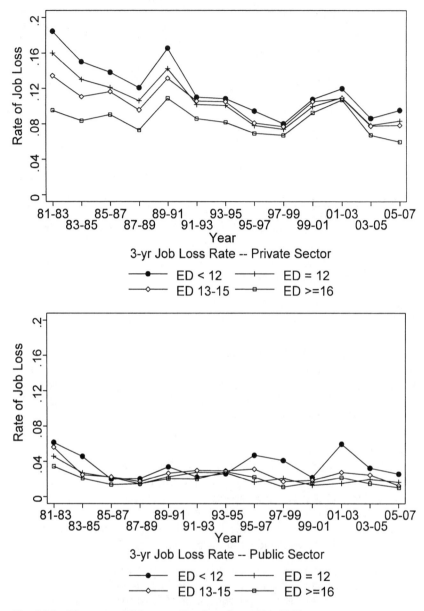

Fig. 6.14   **Three-year job loss rate by education, 1981–2007**

job loss since that time. In 1981 to 1983, the private-sector three-year job
loss rate was 16 percent for high school graduates and 9.4 percent for college graduates. By 2001 to 2003 (also a period of weak labor markets), the
gap had fallen to virtually zero, with a private-sector three-year job loss
rate of 10.7 percent for high school graduates and 11 percent for college

graduates. Interestingly, the education gap in job loss rates increased in the 2005 to 2007 period with 8.3 and 10.0 percent job loss rates for high school and college graduates, respectively. There is a clear cyclical pattern in job loss rates for all groups of workers in the private sector, and it appears that rates of job loss for the less educated have declined in the private sector.

The lower panel of figure 6.14 presents the job loss rates for the public sector. As expected, they are much lower than in the private sector. Interestingly, there is only a small difference between job loss rates by education level, even in the earlier years. And, aside from a mild cyclical pattern and some increase in rate of job loss for the least-educated workers, there is no change in rates of job loss in the public sector.

Figure 6.15 contains three-year job loss rates by year for four age groups covering the range from twenty to sixty-four years. In the private sector (top panel), rates of job loss generally show the standard cyclical pattern for each age group. Early in the period, job loss rates are highest for the youngest workers (twenty to thirty-nine years of age), but these differences by age disappear in the late 1980s. The general pattern is similar in the public sector with generally lower levels of job loss and an attenuated cyclical pattern. It does appear the job loss rates of the youngest workers (aged twenty to twenty-nine) remain above that of older workers. There is no evidence of a secular increase in job loss rates among older workers in either the private or public sectors. In fact, job loss rates have declined, particularly for younger workers.

6.5   Reconciling the Trends in Job Tenure and Job Loss

The sharp decline in job tenure in the private sector combined with the lack of any trend in rates of job loss presents a puzzle. In this section, I explore the possibility that this apparent contradiction is due to a relative increase in job loss rates among high-tenure workers.

Unfortunately, the available data do not allow direct calculation job loss rates by tenure. Tenure is not observed in the DWS for workers who do not report that they have been displaced. I use Bayes law to recover the probability of job loss by tenure category using the tenure data from the CPS as well as the DWS. The appropriate relationship defining the probability that worker i in tenure category j is displaced in period t is

$$(4) \qquad \Pr(D_{it} = 1 | T_{it} = j) = \frac{\Pr(T_{it} = j | D_{it} = 1)\,\Pr(D_{it} = 1)}{\Pr(T_{it} = j)},$$

where $D_{it} = 1$ if worker i in period t suffers a job loss, and $T_{it} = j$ if worker i is in tenure category j in period t. The only piece of equation (4) that is not available directly from the DWS is $\Pr(T_{it} = j)$, the unconditional tenure distribution. However, data from the CPS on job tenure are available for all workers in at least one of the two years immediately prior to each DWS other

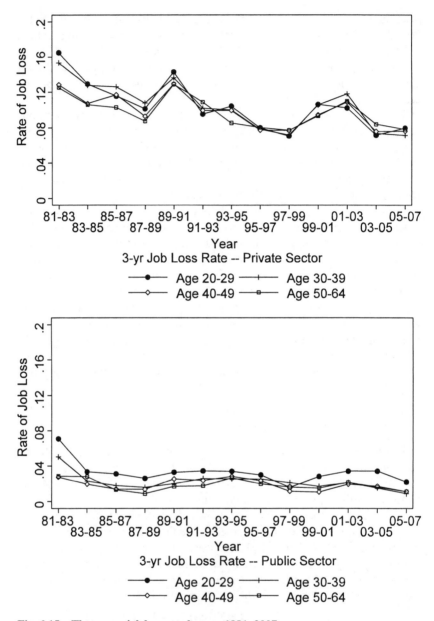

Fig. 6.15   Three-year job loss rate by age, 1981–2007

than the 1986 DWS. I use this information to compute unconditional tenure distributions appropriate to each DWS (other than 1986).[17]

Tenure-specific job loss rates calculated based on equation (4) are plotted in figure 6.16 separately for the private and public sectors. The top panel, for the private sector, shows the unsurprising result that the probability of job loss is strongly monotonically declining in tenure. The likelihood of job loss (averaged across years) falls from 14.7 percent for workers in their first year on the job to 5.6 percent for workers with more than twenty years on the job. The results are more remarkable for what is not found. There seems to be no secular trend in the tenure-specific probabilities of job loss in the private sector. The plots in the bottom panel of figure 6.16 show the typically much lower rates of job loss in the public sector, with a smaller (in absolute value) decline in the rate of job loss with tenure. Again, there is no secular trend in rates of job loss in the public sector.

Covariation between sex, age, education, and tenure in determining the rate of job loss suggests that a multivariate analysis of job loss would be useful. Without longitudinal data on all variables, a microlevel analysis is not feasible, but I can compute cell-mean level rates of job loss using the Bayes law approach. I compute job loss rates for groups defined by sector of employment, education category, tenure category, age category, sex, and time period. There are 4,224 cells, defined by these five variables, for which I have computed job loss rates using information on individual characteristics and job displacement from the CPS mobility data and the DWS. Unfortunately, cell sizes are too small to expand the breakdown to include other variables.

The job loss rates for each category are computed using Bayes law applied to the conditional probabilities associated with job loss, tenure, sex, and education. It is straightforward to show that, within each sector,

$$
(5) \qquad \Pr(D_{it} = 1 | T_{it} = j, X_{ikrmt} = 1)
$$

$$
= \frac{\Pr(T_{it} = j | D_{it} = 1, X_{ikrmt} = 1) \Pr(D_{it} = 1, X_{ikrmt} = 1)}{\Pr(T_{it} = j, X_{ikrmt} = 1)},
$$

where $X_{ikrmt} = 1$ if individual i in year t is of sex k in age category r with education level m. This particular representation of the conditional probability of job loss is used because it allows computation of the probability of displacement conditional on tenure and the other controls without direct information on the joint distribution of displacement and tenure.

---

17. Since 1994, the DWS collects information on tenure on the lost job only for the subset of displaced workers who report a reason for job loss of (a) slack work, (b) position or shift abolished, or (c) plant closing. This information is not collected for displaced workers who report a reason for job loss of (a) temporary job ended, (b) seasonal job ended, or (c) other. For this reason, the succeeding analysis measures rates of job loss only for the "big three" reasons. See Farber (2005) for more details.

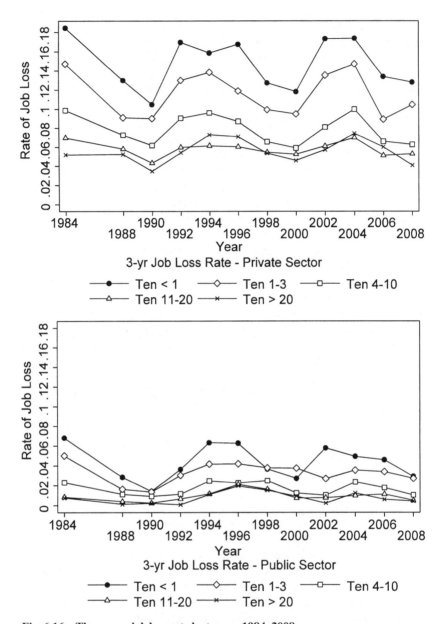

Fig. 6.16   Three-year job loss rate by tenure, 1984–2008

Table 6.3 contains estimates of weighted least squares (WLS) regressions of the log of the probability of job loss in a cell on the characteristics defining the cell. The weights used for each cell are estimates of the variance of the log probability of job loss for that cell.[18]

Specification (1) in table 6.3 contains estimates of a model pooling all years of the log probability of job loss with main effects for sex, age category, education level, tenure category, sector of employment, and DWS survey year.[19] These results demonstrate several strong patterns:

- There is a strong negative relationship between the probability of job loss and tenure. Workers with more than twenty years of tenure have a probability of job loss that is 35 percent of the rate of job loss of workers in their first year on the job.
- Females have lower rates of job loss than men (about 22 percent lower).
- Rates of job loss are inversely related to education. The rate of job loss for college graduates is 77 percent of the rate of job loss of otherwise-equivalent high school graduates (the base group).
- Controlling for tenure, there is a positive relationship between age and the rate of job loss. Workers aged fifty-five to sixty-four have a rate of job loss that is about 30 percent higher than workers aged twenty-five to thirty-four.
- Job loss rates are substantially (51 percent) lower in the public sector than in the private sector.

Of course, the key question is whether these relationships have changed over time. In order to investigate this, I reestimated the model separately for three subperiods: 1984 to 1990, 1992 to 2000, and 2000 to 2008.[20] These results are interesting both for the changes revealed in some dimensions and the lack of change in others.

18. The log of the probability of job loss in equation (5) is a linear combination of the logs of its component probabilities. Specifically,

$$\ln[\Pr(D_{it} = 1 | T_{it} = j, X_{ikrmt} = 1)] = \ln[\Pr(T_{it} = j | D_{it} = 1, X_{ikrmt} = 1)]$$

$$+ \ln[\Pr(D_{it} = 1, X_{ikrmt} = 1)]$$

$$- \ln[\Pr(T_{it} = j, X_{ikrmt} = 1)].$$

The variance of each component probability is $p(1 - p)/n$, where p is the relevant probability, and n is the sample size that the estimate of the probability is based on. The variance of the log of each probability is computed using the delta method as $(1 - p)/pn$, and the variance of $\ln(Pr[D_{it} = 1 | T_{it} = j, X_{ikrmt} = 1])$ is computed as the sum of the variances of the log of the three component probabilities.

19. The log specification of the rate of job loss neatly allows the pooling of the public- and private-sector job loss rates despite the large disparity in the levels of these job loss rates. The log specification implies a constant proportional effect of the included variables on the job loss rate, and this reflects the lower level and smaller absolute variation in the public-sector job loss rate.

20. These years refer to the DWS survey years. The 1984 to 1990 sample covers job loss from 1981 to 1989, the 1992 to 2000 sample covers job loss from 1989 to 1999, and the 2000 to 2008 sample covers job loss from 1999 to 2007.

Table 6.3   **Weighted least squares estimates of log-probability of job loss, 1984–2008, by sex, education, tenure, age, sector, and year cells**

Variable	1984–2008 (1)	1984–1990 (2)	1992–2000 (3)	2002–2008 (4)
Ten 1–3	−0.204	−0.203	−0.203	−0.207
	(0.019)	(0.035)	(0.029)	(0.033)
Ten 4–10	−0.664	−0.632	−0.646	−0.714
	(0.019)	(0.035)	(0.029)	(0.033)
Ten 4–10	−1.008	−0.986	−1.005	−1.035
	(0.026)	(0.049)	(0.039)	(0.045)
Ten 11–20	−1.068	−1.096	−1.032	−1.095
	(0.034)	(0.068)	(0.052)	(0.058)
Female	−0.245	−0.334	−0.233	−0.192
	(0.014)	(0.026)	(0.021)	(0.024)
ED < 12	0.321	0.220	0.328	0.452
	(0.024)	(0.038)	(0.039)	(0.051)
ED 13–15	−0.037	−0.110	−0.002	−0.001
	(0.017)	(0.033)	(0.026)	(0.030)
ED ≥ 16	−0.257	−0.456	−0.211	−0.173
	(0.018)	(0.036)	(0.028)	(0.031)
Age 25–34	0.204	0.183	0.176	0.274
	(0.026)	(0.043)	(0.041)	(0.050)
Age 35–44	0.255	0.200	0.283	0.300
	(0.027)	(0.046)	(0.042)	(0.050)
Age 45–54	0.326	0.175	0.352	0.425
	(0.028)	(0.052)	(0.044)	(0.050)
Age 55–64	0.470	0.350	0.509	0.553
	(0.031)	(0.057)	(0.050)	(0.055)
Public sector	−0.721	−0.836	−0.668	−0.679
	(0.022)	(0.041)	(0.034)	(0.039)
Year FEs	Yes	Yes	Yes	Yes
N	3,916	986	1,628	1,302
R^2	0.580	0.669	0.550	0.569

Notes: Based on calculated conditional cell probabilities from equation (5) using data from the 1984 to 2008 Displaced Workers Survey (DWS) and tenure data from various Current Population Surveys from 1983 to 2008. The estimates are weighted by the inverse sampling variance of the log probability of job loss in each cell. See note 18 for details.

- Conditional on age, there is no systematic change over time in the relationship of the displacement rate with job tenure. This suggests that we cannot reconcile the decline in age-specific job tenure in the United States and the lack of increase in rates of job loss with changes in the tenure distribution of job loss.
- The female-male differential in job loss has narrowed, falling from 28 percent lower for females in the 1980s to 17 percent lower in the 2000s.
- The strong advantage of education in reducing job loss rates has diminished substantially. The college or high school differential in job loss

rates fell from 37 percent lower in the 1980s to 16 percent lower in the 2000s.

- Conditional on tenure, older workers have become substantially more susceptible to job loss. Workers aged forty-five to fifty-four had job loss rates 19 percent higher than workers aged twenty to twenty-four in the 1980s. By the 2000s, these workers' job loss rates were 53 percent higher than those of workers twenty to twenty-four.
- The private-public-sector gap in job loss rates fell somewhat over time. The public-sector job loss rate was 57 percent lower than the private-sector rate in the 1980s. This gap fell to 49 percent in the 2000s.

The strong positive relationship between age and tenure may be masking a change in relationship between the probability of job loss and tenure. To this end, I reestimate the model presented in table 6.3 without controlling for age.[21] The results of this analysis are presented in table 6.4, and they are quite similar to those controlling for age. There is no evidence that the strong negative relationship between tenure and rates of job loss has weakened.

Thus, the puzzle of declining job tenure over time with no increase in measured rates of job loss in the DWS remains. One real possibility is that the DWS does not measure rates of job loss very well, perhaps because of ambiguity among workers who leave jobs in why they, in fact, left. For example, workers who accept buyouts to leave their jobs may perceive this as a voluntary job change and not report this as a job loss. To the extent that this is an important phenomenon, rates of job change, whether classified as voluntary or involuntary, have increased.

6.6   Final Remarks

The analysis shows clearly that job tenure and the incidence of long-term employment have declined sharply in the U.S. private sector between the 1970s and 2008. In contrast, job tenure and the incidence of long-term employment have increased in public sector over the same period.

My examination of rates of job loss, as measured by the DSW, showed that, while job loss rates are lower in the public sector than in the private sector and move with the business cycle in the private sector, there has been no secular increase in private-sector job loss rates that could account for the decline in private-sector job tenure. I ruled out one potential solution to this apparent inconsistency. While overall rates of job loss did not increase, it is not the case that rates of job loss for high-tenure workers increased relative to those for lower-tenure workers.

A more likely explanation is that there has been an increase in rates of job change that is not captured in the limited questions on job change asked in the DWS. Some of this seemingly voluntary job change (e.g., the taking

---

21. In other words, I estimate the model over cells that do not condition on age.

Table 6.4   Weighted least squares estimates of log-probability of job loss, 1984–2008, by sex, education, tenure, and year cells

Variable	1984–2008 (1)	1984–1990 (2)	1992–2000 (3)	2002–2008 (4)
Ten 1–3	–0.228	–0.224	–0.224	–0.235
	(0.020)	(0.036)	(0.030)	(0.034)
Ten 3–10	–0.629	–0.607	–0.608	–0.678
	(0.020)	(0.037)	(0.030)	(0.034)
Ten 11–20	–0.952	–0.967	–0.945	–0.969
	(0.028)	(0.052)	(0.042)	(0.049)
Ten > 20	–0.979	–1.186	–0.904	–0.955
	(0.038)	(0.077)	(0.057)	(0.064)
ED < 12	0.202	0.199	0.193	0.171
	(0.026)	(0.040)	(0.041)	(0.055)
ED 13–15	–0.075	–0.167	–0.041	–0.038
	(0.019)	(0.036)	(0.028)	(0.032)
ED ≥ 16	–0.272	–0.517	–0.229	–0.176
	(0.020)	(0.040)	(0.030)	(0.033)
Female	–0.246	–0.349	–0.231	–0.191
	(0.015)	(0.028)	(0.023)	(0.026)
Public sector	–1.132	–1.223	–1.060	–1.146
	(0.031)	(0.059)	(0.045)	(0.055)
Age	No	No	No	No
Year FEs	Yes	Yes	Yes	Yes
N	955	240	400	315
R^2	0.836	0.888	0.832	0.826

Notes: Based on calculated conditional cell probabilities from equation (5) using data from the 1984 to 2008 Displaced Workers Survey (DWS) and tenure data from various Current Population Surveys from 1983 to 2008. The estimates are weighted by the inverse sampling variance of the log probability of job loss in each cell. See note 18 for details.

of an offered buyout) may reflect the kind of worker displacement that the DWS was meant to capture but is not reported as such by workers. A more comprehensive survey of job changes and the underlying circumstances is needed in order to understand the decline in long-term employment more fully.

Appendix
The CPS Data on Employer Tenure

At irregular intervals, the Census Bureau has appended mobility supplements to the January or February CPSs. The years in which they did so include 1951, 1963, 1966, 1968, 1973, 1978, 1981, 1983, 1987, 1991, and in even years from 1996 to 2008. These supplements contain information on how long workers have been continuously employcd by their current employer, and they are asked of all eight CPS rotation groups. However, only the supplements since 1973 are available in machine-readable form. Information on job durations is also available in pension and benefit supplements to the CPS in May of 1979, 1981, 1983, and 1988, and in April 1993. These supplements contain information on how long workers have been working for their current employer, and they are asked of four of the eight CPS rotation groups. Finally, information on job durations is available in the continuous and alternative employment arrangement supplements (CAEAS) to the CPS in February of 1995, 1997, 1999, 2001, and 2005. In total there are twenty-two CPS supplements with information on employer tenure available in machine-readable form over the period from 1973 to 2008, and my analysis relies on these data.

A question of comparability of the data over time that must be kept in mind when interpreting the results arises because of a significant change in the wording of the central question about job duration. The early mobility supplements (1951 to 1981) asked workers what year they started working for their current employer. In later mobility supplements (1983 to 2008), in all of the pension and benefit supplements (1979 to 1993), and in all of the CAEAS supplements (1995 to 2005), workers were asked how many years they worked for their current employer. If the respondents were perfectly literal and accurate in their responses (a strong and unreasonable assumption), then these two questions would yield identical information (up to the error due to the fact that calendar years may not be perfectly aligned with the count of years since the worker started with his or her current employer). But responses are not completely accurate, and this is best illustrated by the heaping of responses at round numbers. The empirical distribution function has spikes at five-year intervals, and there are even larger spikes at ten-year intervals. In the early question, the spikes occur at round calendar years (1960, 1965, etc.). Later, the spikes occur at round counts of years (five, ten, fifteen, etc.).

There are also subtle but potentially important changes in wording of the key questions even within these surveys. All of the mobility supplements since 1983 ask individuals how long they have worked *continuously* (italics added) for their current employer. However, neither the pension and benefit supplements nor the CAEAS include the word "continuously." The May 1979 and 1983 pension and benefit supplements ask individuals how long they have worked for their current employer and specify that if there was an interruption greater than one year to count only the time since the interruption. The May 1988 and April 1993 supplements and the CAEAS ask individuals how long they have worked for their current employer without any reference to interruptions or continuity. Thus, it might be the case that the mobility supplements would yield shorter tenures than the pension and benefit supplements and the CAEAS due to the requirement of continuity in the former. And it might be the case that the early two pension and benefit supplements would yield shorter durations than the later two pension and benefit supplements due to the consideration of long interruptions given in the early supplements. I make no explicit allowance for these differences in my analysis, but they should be kept in mind when interpreting the results.

With the exception of jobs of less than one year, all of the supplements before the February 1996 mobility supplement collect data on job duration in integer form reporting the number of years employed. For jobs of less than one year, the mobility supplements report the number of months employed while the pension and benefit supplements report only the fact that the job was less than one year old. The February 1996 and later mobility supplement ask workers how long they have worked continuously for their current employer and accepts a numerical response where the worker specifies the time units. The 1995 to 2005 CAEAS ask workers how long they have worked for their current employer and accepts a numerical response where the worker specifies the time units. Virtually all workers in jobs five years old and all workers in jobs ten years old or longer report job durations in years.

One reasonable interpretation of the integer report of the number of years is that workers round to the nearest integer when they report jobs of duration of at least one year.[22] For example, a response of ten years would imply tenure greater than or equal to 9.5 years and less than 10.5 years. In order to create a smooth tenure variable, I assume that the distribution of job tenure is uniform in these one-year intervals. Given a reported tenure of T years, I replace T by $T - 0.5 + u$, where u is a random variable distributed uniformly on the unit interval.[23]

My sample consists of 924,423 not self-employed workers aged twenty to sixty-four from the twenty-two CPS supplements covering the period from 1973 to 2008. The self-employed are not included because the concept of employer tenure is less clear for the self-employed, and, in any case, the CPS supplements do not contain consistent information on tenure for the self-employed.

References

Abraham, Katharine G., and James L. Medoff. 1984. Length of service and layoffs in union and nonunion work groups. *Industrial and Labor Relations Review* 38 (October): 87–97.

22. This ignores the heaping of the tenure distribution at multiples of five and ten years.
23. Where reported tenure is zero years, I assume that tenure is uniformly distributed between zero and one and define tenure as u. Given that jobs are more likely to end earlier in the first year than later in the first year, this is not completely accurate (Farber 1994). However, the measures used in my analysis will not be affected by this representation. Where reported tenure is exactly one year, I assume that true tenure is uniformly distributed between 1 and 1.5 and define tenure as $1 + u/2$.

Burdett, Kenneth. 1978. Employee search and quits. *American Economic Review* 68:212–20.

Diebold, Francis X., David Neumark, and Daniel Polsky. 1996. Comment of Kenneth A. Swinnerton and Howard Wial, "Is Job Stability Declining in the U.S. Economy?" *Industrial and Labor Relations Review* 49:348–52.

———. 1997. Job stability in the United States. *Journal of Labor Economics* 15(2): 206–33

Farber, Henry S. 1993. The incidence and costs of job loss: 1982–91. *Brookings Papers on Economic Activity: Microeconomics:* 73–119.

———. 1994. The analysis of inter-firm worker mobility. *Journal of Labor Economics* 12 (October): 554–93.

———. 1997. The changing face of job loss in the United States, 1981–1995. *Brookings Papers on Economic Activity: Microeconomics:* 55–128.

———. 1998a. Are lifetime jobs disappearing: Job duration in the United States, 1973–93. In *Labor statistics measurement issues,* ed. John Haltiwanger, Marilyn Manser, and Robert Topel, 157–203. Chicago: University of Chicago Press.

———. 1998b. Has the rate of job loss increased in the nineties? *Proceedings of the Fiftieth Annual Winter Meeting of the Industrial Relations Research Association* 1:88–97.

———. 1999a. Alternative and part-time employment arrangements as a response to job loss. *Journal of Labor Economics* 17:S142–S169.

———. 1999b. Mobility and stability: The dynamics of job change in labor markets. In *The handbook of labor economics.* Vol. 3B, ed. Orley Ashenfelter and David Card, 2439–84. Amsterdam: North-Holland.

———. 2000. Trends in long-term employment in the United States: 1979–1996. In *Global competition and the American employment landscape as we enter the 21st century: Proceedings of New York University 52d conference on labor*, ed. Samuel Estreicher, 63–98. Leiden: Kluwer Law International.

———. 2004. Job loss in the United States, 1981–2001. *Research in Labor Economics* 23:69–117.

———. 2005. What do we know about job loss in the United States? Evidence from the Displaced Workers Survey, 1981–2004. *Journal of Economic Perspectives* 29 (2): 13–28.

———. 2007. Is the company man an anachronism? Trends in long-term employment in the U.S., 1973–2006. In *The price of independence: The economics of early adulthood,* ed. Sheldon H. Danziger and Cecilia E. Rouse, 56–83. New York: Russell Sage.

Gardner, Jennifer M. 1995. Worker displacement: A decade of change. *Monthly Labor Review* 118:45–57.

Gottschalk, Peter, and Robert Moffitt. 1999. Changes in job instability and insecurity using monthly survey data. Has job stability declined yet? New evidence for the 1990s. *Journal of Labor Economics* 17 (4): S91–S126.

Hall, Robert E. 1982. The importance of lifetime jobs in the U.S. economy. *American Economic Review* 72:716–24.

Hipple, Steven. 1999. Worker displacement in the mid-1990's. *Monthly Labor Review* 122:15–32.

Jaeger, David A., and Ann Huff Stevens. 1999. Is job stability in the United States falling? Reconciling trends in the Current Population Survey and Panel Study of Income Dynamics. *Journal of Labor Economics* 17 (4): S1–S28.

Jovanovic, Boyan. 1979. Job matching and the theory of turnover. *Journal of Political Economy* 87:972–90.

Kletzer, Lori G. 1989. Returns to seniority after permanent job loss. *American Economic Review* 79:536–43.

Neal, Derek. 1995. Industry-specific capital: Evidence from displaced workers. *Journal of Labor Economics* 13:653–77.

Neumark, David, ed. 2000. *On the job: Is long-term employment a thing of the past?* New York: Russell Sage.

Neumark, David, Daniel Polsky, and Daniel Hansen. 1999. Has job stability declined yet? New evidence for the 1990s. *Journal of Labor Economics* 17 (4): S29–S64.

Parent, Daniel. 2000. Industry-specific capital and the wage profile: Evidence from the National Longitudinal Survey of Youth and the Panel Study of Income Dynamics. *Journal of Labor Economics* 18(2): 306–23.

Podgursky, Michael, and Paul Swaim. 1987. Job displacement earnings loss: Evidence from the Displaced Worker Survey. *Industrial and Labor Relations Review* 41:17–29.

Rose, Stephen J. 1995. Declining job security and the professionalization of opportunity. National Commission for Employment Policy, Research Report no. 95-04.

Stevens, Ann Huff. 2008. Not so fast: Long-term employment in the U.S., 1969–2004. In *Laid Off, Laid Low: The social and political impact of job instability*, ed. Katherine S. Newman, 38–55. New York: Columbia University Press.

Stewart, Jay. 2002. Recent trends in job stability and job security: Evidence from the March CPS. BLS Working Paper no. 356. Washington, DC: Bureau of Labor Statistics.

Swinnerton, Kenneth, and Howard Wial. 1995. Is job stability declining in the U.S. economy? *Industrial and Labor Relations Review* 48:293–304.

———. 1996. Is job stability declining in the U.S. economy? Reply to Diebold, Neumark, and Polsky. *Industrial and Labor Relations Review* 49:352–55.

Topel, Robert. 1990. Specific capital and unemployment: Measuring the costs and consequences of job loss. *Carnegie Rochester conference series on public policy* 33:181–214.

Ureta, Manuelita. 1992. The importance of lifetime jobs in the U.S. economy, revisited. *American Economic Review* 82:322–35.

Valletta, Robert. 1999. Declining job security. *Journal of Labor Economics* 17 (4): S170–S197.

Comment   Ann Huff Stevens

This study by Henry Farber uses a wealth of available data from a large number of Current Population Survey (CPS) supplements and the Displaced Workers Survey (DWS) to illustrate the evolution of age-adjusted job tenure in the United States over the past three decades. The data show a substantial decline in job tenure among employed males in the United States during this period and no change, or small increases, among employed women. The decline in tenure among men accelerates during the 1990s. Perhaps surprisingly given the decline in tenure among men and the widespread suspicion that job security in the United States has substantially weakened, Farber finds no evidence that rates of job loss in the DWS increased between 1984

Ann Huff Stevens is professor of economics at the University of California, Davis, and a faculty research fellow of the National Bureau of Economic Research.

and 2006. Further, he shows that it is not the case that rates of job loss have increased disproportionately for high-tenure workers, so that cannot explain the shift in the tenure distribution.

Farber's simultaneous presentation of age-adjusted job tenure measures and rates of job loss helps to establish current, key facts in an area of empirical research that is often contentious. I have only minor concerns about the details of his CPS-based tenure tabulations and the broad patterns from the CPS appear to be supported in at least two other data sets. Two specific features of Farber's findings on job tenure merit highlighting here because they help both with understanding differences from previous tenure tabulations and with verifying these findings in other sources. First, the decline in job tenure among men jumps out from Farber's graphs, largely as the result of his careful, and appropriate, adjustments for age. As the labor force has aged over the past several decades, unadjusted job tenure has naturally risen. Only when researchers control for age in a fairly complete way does the decline in age-adjusted tenure become apparent. Second, Farber's study, along with his discussion of his earlier work, helps to highlight that much of this decline began, or at least accelerated, during the 1990s.

The timing of the decline in age-adjusted tenure among employed men is likely to be important as we attempt to understand what explains such changes. Being precise about the timing of the change also helps to verify this trend in other data sets. Farber's figure 6.1 shows a clear disconnect between the age-tenure profiles in the 1970s and 1980s, versus those for 1990 and later. This timing, with a focus on the early part of the 1990s, is also consistent with the time series of Farber's own earlier work. He notes that his 1998 study, using CPS job tenure data from 1973 through 1993 "found that the prevalence of long-term employment has not declined." In contrast, using CPS data going through 1996 Farber finds that "the prevalence of long-term employment relationships among men declined by 1996 to its lowest level since 1979." The current study extends this time series still further and shows a steep decline in male tenure (see, for example, his figure 6.5) from approximately 1994 to 2000.

Detailed knowledge of the timing of this change facilitates use of a greater range of alternative data sets to verify changes in tenure among men. For example, tenure questions in the Panel Study of Income Dynamics are quite consistent from 1987 through 1996 and can be tabulated for comparison with Farber's results. Such tabulations confirm a decline in job tenure of employed men over this period, with larger reductions (in terms of years) among older employed men. Similarly, the Health and Retirement Study (HRS) can be used to tabulate changes in the tenure distribution among older males starting in 1992. Using a sample of all males in waves 1 through 7 of the HRS between the ages of forty-five and sixty-four, I have estimated regressions that mimic Farber's specification summarized by equation (3). This exercise with the HRS suggests a decline in tenure of approximately

9 percent between 1992 and 2004, slightly smaller than, but generally consistent with, the decline found by Farber.

While Farber's findings on male job tenure seem robust to analysis with other data sets, there are some potential concerns with the use of these CPS supplements over time. First, it is unfortunate that the early 1990s are both the time in which the decline in tenure becomes apparent and the time in which the CPS underwent a major redesign. Given this, it would be helpful to have at least a brief discussion of the CPS redesign and its potential impact on these tenure tabulations. Because the redesign likely resulted in capturing more workers with marginal attachment to the labor force (in the main CPS surveys), it is conceivable that this could increase the number of low-tenure workers appearing in the tenure-related supplements. My reading of studies of the redesign, however, suggests that it would have had a limited effect on the male tenure distributions, and most of that effect would be limited to workers over age sixty-five, who are not included in Farber's tabulations.[1] There have also been minor changes in question wording on some of the tenure supplements over time, as Farber notes in his appendix. The magnitude of the observed changes in tenure and the similarity of results based on other data sets suggest that such question changes are probably not the driving factor here.

The next section of Farber's chapter establishes, with equal care, the absence of any increase in job loss rates as measured by the DWS, which begs the question of what is driving the decline in male tenure? Here, Farber focuses surprisingly on the possibility that the DWS is missing job separations that should be identified as displacements. The other obvious possibility is that truly voluntary job separations have increased. This second possibility is not one that should be ignored. Admittedly, the idea that voluntary job changes are behind these dramatic reductions in job tenure does not square well with media coverage of job stability, which tends to emphasize the more disastrous view that such declines signal the end of lifetime employment. Unfortunately, this is a frustrating issue for empirical work to confront because no long-term, consistent data series exist on voluntary job turnover. Farber's resulting call for "a more comprehensive survey of job changes and the underlying circumstances" is entirely appropriate here.

In the absence of such survey data, we should consider whether there is any current evidence, either direct or circumstantial, that voluntary turnover might be increasing. Recent work by Jay Stewart (2007) uses matched March CPS data to consider the time series of employment transitions. Stewart does find some evidence that employment to employment transitions without an intervening spell of unemployment trended upward from 1975 to 2001. Stewart interprets this as evidence of an increase in voluntary job changing.

1. See, for example, Polivka (1996) or Polivka and Miller (1998) for a discussion of the impact of the CPS redesign on employment-related measures.

Thinking more broadly, there are several factors that are at least consistent with an increase in voluntary job change in recent years, particularly among more senior workers. First, there has been a substantial change in the nature of pension coverage among older workers since the early 1990s. Fewer workers now have employer-sponsored defined benefit (DB) pension plans, and more have the more portable defined contribution (DC) plans. The key difference for questions of job mobility is that DB pensions typically have incentives that encourage workers to remain with the firm up to some age (or years of service) but then encourage them to leave. If earlier cohorts of workers in their forties and fifties were more likely to be bound to their current firms through DB pensions than are more recent cohorts, it would not be surprising if rates of voluntary job change have increased. My own tabulations from several waves of the HRS show the magnitude of the reduction in DB pension coverage among recent cohorts. Among employed men ages forty-eight to fifty-two, 41 percent reported having a DB pension on their current job in 1992, but only 24 percent reported such a pension by 2004. Such tabulations are only suggestive, of course, because the decline of DB pensions could be either a cause or an effect of the waning importance of implicit contracts between employers and employees. The bottom line is that, in a world in which workers in their forties and fifties are more likely to have pensions that are portable across employers (or even no pensions), we should not rule out the possibility of increased voluntary turnover.

Another change that could play a role in men's diminished tenure post-1990 is the changing level of women's labor force attachment over time. As Farber notes throughout his study, an increase in women's labor force attachment has coincided with the decline in male tenure. It is at least worth considering whether these two patterns are related. As women have become more attached to the labor force, more men have spouses with substantial earnings and benefits. If voluntary job changes are sometimes limited by the need for stability in benefits (as suggested by the literature on job-lock), women's increasing attachment to the labor force could allow men to engage in more voluntary employment transitions. It is not obvious that the timing of women's increasing labor force attachment fits the timing of the changes in men's tenure, but it could be relevant if the transition to thinking of employer benefits in a family context occurred with a lag behind the actual rise in women's labor force participation.

Farber's study will be a useful reference for those in and out of academia who are concerned with issues of both job tenure and job security. While I am not convinced from this work that the DWS is increasingly missing truly involuntary job changes, these different patterns in job tenure and job loss rates do point to the need for better measurement of job turnover in the United States. This work should help to focus attention on the necessity of developing accurate, ongoing measures of employment transitions of all kinds.

References

Polivka, Anne E. 1996. Data watch: The redesigned Current Population Survey. *Journal of Economic Perspectives* 10 (3): 169–80.

Polivka, Anne E., and Steven Miller. 1998. The CPS after the redesign: Refocusing the economic lens. In *Labor statistics measurement issues,* ed. John Haltiwanger, Marilyn Manser, and Robert Topel, 249–89. Chicago: University of Chicago Press.

Stewart, Jay. 2007. Using March CPS data to analyze labor market transitions. Bureau of Labor Statistics. Unpublished Manuscript.

7

What Do We Know about Contracting Out in the United States?
Evidence from Household and Establishment Surveys

Matthew Dey, Susan Houseman, and Anne Polivka

Companies choose the degree of vertical integration in the production of goods and services. In other words, they must decide what tasks to perform with in-house employees and what goods and services inputs to purchase from other entities. That mix often changes. Companies may contract out work previously done by in-house employees, or, conversely, insource work previously contracted out. While much attention has been given to the apparent growth of imported goods and services inputs—so-called offshoring or offshore outsourcing—our chapter focuses on contracting out that occurs within the United States—what we term domestic contracting out or outsourcing.

A variety of evidence has pointed to significant growth in domestic contracting out over the last two decades (Abraham 1990; Abraham and Taylor 1996; Segal 1996; Segal and Sullivan 1997; Theodore and Peck 2002). When organizations outsource tasks to a contract company, the employer of record for workers performing the tasks changes, and frequently so too does the industry in which the workers are employed. Thus, large shifts in the patterns of domestic outsourcing may affect the industry structure of employment in the economy.

Accurately measuring growth in outsourcing and the industries engaging in it, we argue, is important for understanding the changing industrial

Matthew Dey is a research economist in Employment Research and Program Development at the Bureau of Labor Statistics. Susan Houseman is a senior economist at the W. E. Upjohn Institute for Employment Research. Anne Polivka is a supervisory economist of Employment Research and Program Development at the Bureau of Labor Statistics.

This paper was prepared for the *CRIW Conference on Labor in the New Economy,* Bethesda, Maryland, November 16–17, 2007. The views expressed in this chapter do not necessarily reflect the policies of the Bureau of Labor Statistics or the views of other BLS staff members.

structure of employment in the U.S. economy, constructing and interpreting sectoral productivity statistics, assessing the role outsourcing plays in adjustment mechanisms, and understanding its implications for workers and a variety of labor market policies. Yet, the phenomenon is not well documented. In this chapter, we pull together a variety of evidence on the extent of and trends in domestic outsourcing, the occupations in which it has grown, and the industries engaging in outsourcing to the employment services sector, which has been a particularly important area of domestic outsourcing. In addition, we examine evidence of the contracting out of selected occupations to other sectors. We point to many gaps in our knowledge on trends in domestic outsourcing and its implications for employment patterns and to inconsistencies across data sets in the information that is available.

An innovation of this chapter is the development of data on occupation by industry, which we use to examine trends in certain types of domestic outsourcing and their effect on employment patterns. When a manufacturer, for example, utilizes a staffing agency to fill clerical and production jobs, outsources information technology (IT) work to a firm providing computer services, and outsources transportation work to a trucking company, the number and occupational distribution of workers classified in the manufacturing sector change, even if the number and occupational distribution of workers performing the tasks do not. Exploiting the fact that changes in the industry distribution of occupational employment often accompany outsourcing, we construct occupation-by-industry panel data from the Occupation Employment Statistics program (OES), which we then use to shed light on the recent growth in various types of domestic outsourcing, including, but not limited to, contracting out to the employment services sector.

The large growth of the employment services sector since the 1980s has been among the most visible examples of domestic contracting out, and thus the first part of our chapter focuses on this case. Two industries, temporary help services and professional employer organizations (PEO), account for almost all employment in this sector, and in each industry virtually all employees are assigned to other sectors as contract workers. We compare evidence from several household and establishment surveys—the Current Population Survey (CPS), the Contingent Worker Supplement to the CPS (CWS), the Occupational Employment Statistics program (OES), the Current Employment Statistics program (CES), and the Economic Census—on levels of and trends in the employment, in the occupational distribution of employment, and in the industries to which these workers are assigned for the employment services sector as a whole and for the temporary help and PEO industries separately.

Although data on contracting out to the employment services sector is rich relative to other types of contracting out, the information from these data is often inconsistent. We note discrepancies among household and establishment surveys on levels and trends in employment, trends in occupations, and industries to which workers in this sector are assigned, and we discuss possible reasons for these differences. Particularly problematic is the PEO industry, which was broken out as a separate industry with the introduction of the new industry classification system, North American Industrial Classification System (NAICS), in the late 1990s and early 2000s. Differences in state laws governing the classification of PEO employment and large discrepancies between PEO employment figures from the CES and the Economic Census render it difficult to assess even basic employment levels and trends for this emerging industry.

New evidence that we present from the OES suggests greater growth in the outsourcing of certain occupations than has been apparent from household data. In particular, the OES shows much stronger growth in the employment of blue-collar occupations within the employment services sector than has been evident in either the CPS or the CWS data. We also use OES data to detect evidence of outsourcing of other occupations to other industrial sectors. As a starting point, we examine trends in the industry distribution of the most prevalent occupations among individuals identified as working for a contract company in the five waves of the CWS. In results that parallel our findings for employment services, we report evidence of growth in contracting out for several occupations in the OES data, although the CWS shows little evidence of an increase in contract workers.

7.1   Importance of Documenting Domestic Outsourcing

Interest in documenting domestic outsourcing is motivated by several factors. One is the apparently large role that contract companies, especially temporary help agencies, play in the adjustment to business cycles. Temporary help employment is considerably more variable than other forms of employment (Golden 1996; Segal and Sullivan 1995, 1997; Theodore and Peck 2002), and, it has been hypothesized, firms increasingly use contract workers to accommodate uncertainty and flux in input and product markets (Abraham 1988; Abraham and Taylor 1996; Davis-Blake and Uzzi 1993; Golden and Appelbaum 1992; Houseman 2001). Reasons for this greater reliance on contracting out include reduction in hiring and recruiting costs and the elimination or reduction of layoffs by client companies, which, in turn, may reduce companies' unemployment insurance costs or their exposure to unjust dismissal lawsuits (Autor 2003; Dertouzos and Karoly 1992; Hachen 2004; Lee 1996; Masters and Miles 2002; Mehta and Theodore 2001; Polivka 1996a).

Adjustment of contract workers also may be used in lieu of adjusting workers' hours and inventories in response to changes in demand (Abraham and Taylor 1996). Firms adjust workers' hours and inventories in response to fluctuations in product demand, and thus changes in workers' hours and inventories are followed closely as indicators of the health of the economy (Hamermesh 1993; Hart 1984; Topel 1982). To the extent that the use of contract workers supplements or replaces these other adjustment mechanisms, accurate measurement and analysis of domestic contracting out will provide a more complete understanding of business cycle dynamics.

Economists, policymakers, and analysts who study changes in the industrial structure of output and employment also need to be aware of the effect of contracting out on their measures. If organizations outsource tasks to a contract company, the employer and, typically, the industry of record for the workers performing the tasks change. Consequently, rapid growth and widespread use of contract workers can distort measurement of changes in the U.S. industrial structure and employment trends in specific industries (Dey, Houseman, and Polivka 2008; Estavaõ and Lach 1999a, 1999b; Segal and Sullivan 1997). Furthermore, statistics that depend on the complete enumeration of employees working in an industry, such as sectoral labor productivity measures, can be biased if appropriate account of contract company workers is not taken (Dey, Houseman, and Polivka 2008; Estavão and Lach 1999a).

In addition, contracting out has potentially important implications for workers and labor market policy. Contracting out could serve to increase the probability of workers obtaining employment, but it also could reduce long-run job security. With respect to the first consideration, contract companies, particularly temporary help agencies, may facilitate the matching of workers and employers. Efficiencies may arise if contract companies are better able to recruit workers with specialized skills or guarantee continuous employment to workers in occupations or sectors of the economy subject to widely fluctuating demands for workers (Erickcek, Houseman, and Kalleberg 2003; Houseman 2001; Krueger 1993; Segal and Sullivan 1997; Theodore and Peck 2002). In addition, efficiencies may arise if employers are better able to screen workers from contract companies prior to placing them on the payroll as part of their permanent staff, and if contract companies provide some form of training and testing, such as instruction in and testing of knowledge about standardized computer programs that might be otherwise unknown to potential employers or more costly for them to provide (Abraham 1990; Autor 2001; Autor, Levy, and Murnane 1999; Houseman 2001; Kalleberg, Reynolds, and Marsden 2003; Lenz 1996; Segal and Sullivan 1997). At the same time, by reducing the costs of job matching, contract companies may also lower the costs of termination, resulting in less job security. Some evidence suggests that contract employment is associated with lower job security, as manifested through decreased job tenure and reduced opportunities for advancement (Houseman and Polivka 2000; Segal and Sullivan 1997).

Use of contract workers also may reduce wage pressures in tight labor markets (Houseman, Kalleberg, and Erickcek 2003). If workers face costs for switching employers, then market forces primarily will affect the wages of new hires. In turn, if internal labor market rules influence the wages of both new hires and those with greater tenure, or if internal labor markets reduce wage differentials across skill levels within establishments, then contract companies may be able to pay new hires or workers in noncore services a lower wage rate than establishments would pay if they hired these workers directly. Alternatively, in particularly tight labor markets, contract companies may permit establishments to pay workers who have been newly hired or who have specialized skills a higher wage than incumbent workers. Thus, they would provide a mechanism for establishments to exert greater restraint on wage increases for incumbent workers. Both more efficient matching of workers and lower wage rates may serve to increase the demand for workers and thereby reduce unemployment rates. Indeed, Katz and Krueger (1999) present evidence that states with a greater supply of temporary-help employment in the late 1980s experienced lower wage growth in the 1990s. They also estimate that the lower wage growth associated with this increase in the supply of temporary-help employment may have accounted for up to a 0.39 percentage-point reduction in the NAIRU (the nonaccelerating-inflation rate of unemployment, or the rate of unemployment consistent with stable inflation) throughout the 1990s.

Moreover, although much of domestic outsourcing may be motivated by firms' desire to tap into the expertise of a contract company, organizations may outsource as a mechanism to avoid unions or workplace safety regulations, to reduce health insurance and pension costs, to economize on compensation and benefit costs by differentially offering compensation packages, and to lower unemployment insurance costs (Abraham and Taylor 1996; Davis-Blake and Uzzi 1993; Erickcek, Houseman, and Kalleberg 2003; Government Accountability Office [GAO] 2006; Hachen 2004; Houseman 1998, 2001; Lautsch 2002; Mehta and Theodore 2001; Mehta et al. 2003; Segal and Sullivan 1997). Indeed, in response to some of these concerns, fourteen states changed the legal status of workers employed through professional employer organizations to preclude companies from circumventing unemployment insurance and workers' compensation costs through this form of outsourcing.

Each of these reasons underscores the importance of better understanding domestic outsourcing. Establishing the basic magnitude of and trends in contracting out is the first step in developing this understanding.

7.2   Data Sources and the Construction of
Industry-occupation Data from the OES

Although developments in contracting out have potentially important implications for macroeconomic, industry, and labor market analysis and policy formation, information on contracting out is scant. We draw upon data from several government, establishment, and household surveys to shed more light on trends in various types of contracting out in the United States and to examine the consistency of evidence on contracting out among data sets. We use data from the Current Employment Statistics (CES) program to examine industry employment trends, to compare trends in CES data with those observed in the Economic Census, and to benchmark employment estimates in the construction of an industry-occupation data set, described later. The CES is a monthly establishment survey conducted by state employment security agencies in cooperation with the Bureau of Labor Statistics. Each month the CES program surveys approximately 150,000 businesses and government agencies, representing approximately 390,000 individual work sites, in order to provide detailed industry data on employment, hours, and earnings of workers on nonfarm payrolls. While the CES is a monthly survey of a nationally representative sample of establishments, the Economic Census, conducted every five years by the U.S. Census Bureau, is a comprehensive survey of establishments in most industries.[1] We report Economic Census data collected from professional employer organizations on the industries to which they assign workers, and we compare Economic Census estimates on PEO employment to those of the CES.

We also draw upon data from the Current Population Survey (CPS), a nationally representative, monthly survey of approximately 60,000 households collected by the U.S. Census Bureau under the auspices of the Bureau of Labor Statistics. Every month the CPS collects labor market, demographic, and job-related information on approximately 110,000 individuals aged sixteen and older. We use the CPS to examine trends in employment and in employment by occupation within the employment services sector.

In addition to the basic CPS, we use data from the Contingent Worker Supplements (CWS) to the CPS to examine employment levels and occupational patterns of workers in temporary help services and in other types of contract companies. The CWS was designed to obtain an estimate of the number of workers in contingent or alternative work arrangements. In that supplement, a contingent arrangement is defined as any job in which an individual does not have an explicit or implicit contract for long-term employment (and thus for economic reasons the arrangement is not expected to be long-term), and an alternative work arrangement is defined as employment that is arranged through an employment intermediary or a work arrangement whose place, time, and quantity of work are potentially unpredictable. The CWS measures workers in four such alternative work arrangements, including workers paid by temporary help firms and those whose employment is arranged by a contract company. The CWS was conducted five times between February 1995 and February 2005. All employed individuals except unpaid family workers were included in the supplement. Consequently, the CWS collected

---

1. Government, agriculture, forestry and fisheries, scheduled commercial airlines, railroads, schools and colleges, political and religious organizations, private household employees, and establishments with no paid employees are excluded from the survey.

information on approximately 69,000 individuals each February or 344,000 individuals when all five years are combined. For individuals who held more than one job during the survey reference week, the questions referred to the characteristics of the job in which they worked the most hours.

7.3   Industry-occupation Data Set Construction

A principal innovation of our chapter is the construction of longitudinal data on occupation by industry from the Occupational Employment Statistics (OES) program, which we use to examine changes in the industry structure of employment within occupations and to shed light on trends in selected areas of contracting out. The OES program, operated by the Bureau of Labor Statistics (BLS), generates employment and wage estimates by detailed occupations. In its current form, the OES program surveys approximately 200,000 establishments semiannually (in May and November) and collects wage and employment information for each occupation employed by the establishment. By collecting payroll information for a relatively large number of establishments, the OES program allows precise estimation of industry-occupation employment levels at the national level.

Although the OES program has operated since 1988, thereby allowing a rather extensive time series analysis, the program has undergone numerous changes in the data collection procedure and the coding of industries and occupations that complicate the construction of a consistent industry-occupation employment time series.[2] A necessary result is that some of the industry and occupation detail that is a great strength of the cross-sectional data must be suppressed in the time series data. With this fact in mind, we estimate employment levels for eighteen broad and an additional six narrow occupation groups and for sixteen sectors from 1989 to 2003.[3]

7.3.1   Data Before 1996

Prior to 1996, the OES program collected occupational employment data for selected industries in one year of a three-year survey cycle. For example, manufacturing establishments were surveyed in 1989, 1992, and 1995, while establishments in the service sector, including employment services, were surveyed in 1990 and 1993. These data were designed to yield accurate, periodic estimates of staffing patterns within industries but were not specifically designed to yield comparisons of the occupational structure across industries. To examine changes in occupational structure over time in the pre-1996 period, we combine three years of OES data and assume that the occupational distribution of employment within an industry remains constant over a three-year period. For example, we combine OES data from

2. The predecessor program on which OES was based started in the early 1970s. The early program, however, did not cover all industries and only aggregate state estimates were generated.
3. Abraham and Spletzer (2007) also construct an occupation-by-industry time series data set from the OES using a methodology similar to the one that we developed.

1988 to 1990 to estimate the occupational distribution of employment for each industry in 1989, we combine OES data from 1989 to 1991 to estimate the occupational distribution of employment for each industry in 1990, and so forth. For any particular year, the estimates of the occupational distribution of employment within an industry will be based on an OES survey of the industry that was conducted in that year, in the previous year, or in the following year. Because we use these early OES data primarily to examine trends in the occupational distribution of employment across industries over long (ten-to-fifteen year) time horizons, the assumption inherent in our data construction for these early years should not unduly affect our results.

To construct estimates of industry-occupation employment in any given year from 1989 to 1995, we benchmark the OES data to each sector's employment levels as measured in the CES in the specified year. During this period, the OES was conducted once a year, primarily in May.[4] To generate estimates of the number of employees in a specific occupation within an industry in a particular year, we multiply the industry total employment in that year (as measured by the CES) by the share of employment in that occupation (as measured in the OES).[5] More formally, we estimate employment in occupation group i and sector j in year t (where t runs from 1989 to 1995), $\hat{E}_{ijt}$, according to the equation

$$(1) \qquad \hat{E}_{ijt} = E_{jt}^c \times \left(\frac{E_{ijs}^o}{E_{js}^o} \right),$$

where $s \in \{t-1, t, t+1\}$; E_{jt}^c is CES employment in sector j and year t; E_{ijs}^o is the employment level in occupation group i and sector j in year s reported by the OES program; and $E_{js}^o = \Sigma_i E_{ijs}^o$ represents OES employment in sector j in year s. Therefore, (E_{ijs}^o / E_{js}^o) is the share of employment in occupation i in sector j in year s as measured in the OES data, which we assume not to vary significantly in the short run. In this way, we generate estimates of employment by occupation for each sector in each year for the purpose of examining shifts in the pattern of occupational employment across industries over relatively long time horizons.

7.3.2   Data from 1996 Forward

Beginning in 1996, the OES program adopted a three-year sampling scheme that allows the estimation of employment and wage levels for

---

4. Benchmarking to the CES helps minimize sampling error, which is inherent in the random component of the OES sample design. In addition, such benchmarking is necessary for the years from 1989 to 1995 because the OES data were not collected for each industry in each year.

5. The reference month for OES data prior to 1996 is May, while the reference month from 1996 to 2002 is November. Beginning in 2003, the OES collects data in both May and November. In order to have a consistent time series we choose to benchmark to November CES data for all years. An examination of recent OES data shows that there are no systematic seasonal (May versus November) differences in the occupation distribution of the employment services sector so our estimates should not be particularly sensitive to our decision to benchmark to November CES employment totals.

narrowly defined geographic regions, industries, and occupations. Over a three-year period, the OES samples and contacts approximately 1.2 million establishments (about 400,000 establishments per year), with each industry surveyed in every year. Although the OES has been designed to produce estimates using the full three years of the sample, we only produce national estimates at a fairly aggregated occupation and industry level, and thus, for our purposes, we can use a single year of data from the OES. The OES generates official estimates using three years of data combined; however, when generating employment estimates at the national level for fairly aggregated industry and occupational categories, as we do, use of data from a single year has some advantages over combining data from three years. The annual sample sizes are sufficient to generate fairly precise estimates within broad industry and occupation categories, and for cyclically sensitive and dynamic industries, like employment services, the occupational distributions can significantly change over a three-year period.

Specifically, for the years 1996 to 2004 we estimate employment by occupation by sector according to the following formula:

$$(2) \qquad \hat{E}_{ijt} = E^c_{jt} \times \left(\frac{E^o_{ijt}}{E^o_{jt}} \right).$$

As for the years prior to 1996, we benchmark all sector employment numbers to the not-seasonally-adjusted November employment figures in the CES.[6] The only conceptual difference between our industry-by-occupation employment estimates beginning in 1996 and estimates constructed for the pre-1996 period is that starting with 1996 the occupational share of employment within each sector always comes from OES data collected for the same year.

7.3.3 Occupation Classification

From 1988 to 1998, the OES characterizes occupations by its own system of codes. Beginning in 1999, the OES characterizes occupations by a modified version of the Standard Occupational Classification (SOC) system. Therefore, we need to define a system that links OES occupation codes to SOC codes. While many OES occupations have a unique counterpart in the SOC system, a number of occupations (including those in the "All Other" category) do not have a unique match. Since our goal is to construct a time series of industry-occupation employment, we choose to aggregate occupations into rather broad categories, thereby minimizing the effect of the break

6. In 2003 the OES shifted from an annual survey of approximately 400,000 establishments conducted in November to a semiannual survey of approximately 200,000 establishments conducted in May and November. We combine May and November OES samples to compute occupation shares within sectors, and, for comparability to the earlier years, we continue to benchmark sector employment totals to the not-seasonally-adjusted November CES figures. The occupation shares of industry employment calculated from OES data use OES sample weights related to the establishment's probability of selection.

in the classification system after 1998. We also constructed time series data for six occupations that we identified as commonly outsourced. Appendix table 7A.1 presents our eighteen broad occupation groups.

7.3.4   Industry Classification

From 1988 to 2001, the OES characterized industries by the Standard Industrial Classification (SIC) system. Beginning in 2002, the OES characterizes industries according to the North American Industrial Classification System (NAICS). Therefore, we need to define a system that links SIC codes to NAICS codes. Although a comprehensive linkage system has been developed, various problems complicate this task. First, from 1988 to 1995, we do not have establishment-level data, but only have access to employment-by-occupation and three-digit SIC code. This is problematic since the SIC-NAICS crosswalk has been developed at the four-digit SIC level, and the aggregation into three-digit industries does not necessarily lead to a unique NAICS match. In addition, even with the most detailed level of SIC and NAICS codes, there are many cases for which the link is not one-to-one. For these reasons, we chose to substantially aggregate industries (roughly into sectors) with the exception of the employment services industry. While this aggregation is not perfectly clean (there are three-digit SIC codes that map into multiple sectors), it eliminates a large majority of the problems and allows a relatively consistent definition of industries over time. In addition, because we are weighting the underlying OES data in a manner to match CES employment estimates, our industry definitions allow the more or less direct use of the published estimates and are therefore consistent with the time series properties of the CES data. Appendix table 7A.2 presents our sixteen industries.

7.4   Employment Services

The growth of the employment services sector over the last two decades represents one of the most visible cases of domestic outsourcing. Under the NAICS classification, the employment services sector is composed of three industries: employment placement agencies, temporary help services, and professional employer organizations (PEOs).[7] According to CES estimates, temporary help services accounts for the bulk of employment in the employment services sector, representing 72 percent of employment in 2006. Professional employer organizations, with 19 percent of sec-

---

7. Under the 2007 NAICS, executive search services was moved out of the Human Resources consulting services industry into the employment services industry and the five-digit NAICS industry's name was changed to Employment placement agencies and executive search services. The placement of executive search services into this five-digit NAICS industry had a minimal impact on the number of employees in the five-digit industry and no discernable effect on the distributions discussed in the text.

tor employment in 2006, account for most of the remaining employment in the sector.[8]

Employment placement agencies, which according to CES data accounted for just 8 percent of the sector's employment in 2006, help place individuals into permanent jobs. Those they assist do not appear on the payroll of the employment placement agency. In contrast, while temporary help agencies and PEOs also place workers into jobs with client organizations, workers are paid by the temporary placement agency or PEO, and they generally appear in the employment statistics as workers in that industry, not in the client industry, where they perform tasks. Temporary help services place individuals into jobs at the work site of client organizations on a temporary basis, though the duration of such temporary placements varies considerably. Companies use temporary help agencies to staff positions for a variety of reasons, including the need to handle seasonal work or a temporary increase in product demand, to fill in for temporary absences of permanent staff, or to screen workers for permanent jobs (Abraham 1988; Autor 2001, 2003; Autor, Levy, and Murnane 1999; Houseman 2001; Kalleberg, Reynolds, and Marsden 2003; Ono and Sullivan 2006; Segal and Sullivan 1997).

Owing to their growth, PEOs, which had been grouped with temporary employment services in help-supply services in the SIC industry codes, were broken out as a separate industry category in the NAICS. Professional employer organizations specialize in human resource (HR) management, and they offer companies a wide variety of services. Many companies use PEOs for routine HR activities such as payroll processing, design and administration of employee benefit programs, payroll tax withholding and filing, record keeping, payment of unemployment insurance taxes, administration of disability and workers' compensation programs, and development and administration of employment policies in accordance with state and federal workplace regulations (Katz 1999). However, many companies also use PEOs for "human capital enhancing services" such as recruiting, the development and implementation of employee training programs, and the management of employees' evaluation and companies' performance reward programs (Klass et al. 2005).

Professional employer organizations and temporary help agencies often have the status of co-employers with the client company. The client company typically maintains primary responsibility for managing employees' onsite tasks and the provision of materials, supplies, and equipment to employees.

---

8. As will be discussed later, the QCEW on which the CES is based has some PEO workers reassigned to the PEO clients' industries. This reassignment could distort the proportion of employment services in the three subindustries. The Economic Census does not reassign PEO workers out of the employment services sector. In the 2002 Economic Census, temporary help services accounted for 57 percent, PEOs for 40 percent, and placement agencies for 3 percent of employment in employment services. Consequently, even based on Economic Census estimates, temporary help services and PEOs account for more than 90 percent of employment in the employment services sector.

The PEOs and temporary help agencies typically assume many of the legal responsibilities for the employees who work at their clients' locations, including the responsibility to comply with various government regulations. The Internal Revenue Service (IRS) considers the PEO and the temporary help agency to be the employer of record, and as such these staffing agencies are liable to pay trust fund income and unemployment taxes (Houseman 1998; Katz 1999).

In the temporary help services and PEO industries, which account for over 90 percent of employment in the sector, workers are assigned to client organizations and do not perform work in the employment services sector. Permanent staff of temporary help agencies represent only an estimated 3 percent of employment in that industry, while administrative staff of PEOs account for only about 1 percent of employment in that industry.[9] Thus, in two of the three industries in employment services, which represent the overwhelming majority of workers in the sector, almost all are assigned to client organizations. In this sense, the temporary help services and PEO industries are contract sectors, and the growth of employment in these industries is a good measure of a certain type of outsourcing. Drawing in part on new data developed from the OES, we examine for the employment services sector and its component industries estimates of employment levels and trends, the occupational distribution of employment, and the industries to which these workers are assigned. In several cases we note significant discrepancies in the evidence among surveys.

7.5   Overall Employment Levels in Employment Services and its Component Industries

The CES is the source typically cited for estimates of employment in employment services. However, information on monthly employment in employment services also may be derived from the Current Population Survey, which collects data on industry for employed individuals' primary and secondary jobs.[10] Estimates of employment in the temporary help industry are available from the five Contingent Worker Supplements. In addition, estimates of employment in employment services and each of its component industries are available from the Economic Censuses, which are conducted every five years. Comparisons across these various sources reveal large discrepancies in the employment levels in employment services and its component industries—discrepancies that, for the most part, cannot

---

9. Estimates of the fraction of total industry employment that is administrative staff come from the U.S. Bureau of Labor Statistics (1988) for the temporary help agencies and from Economic Census estimates for the PEO industry.

10. Data on multiple jobholders' second job are only collected in the CPS for a subset of individuals surveyed in any given month (primarily those individuals residing in a household being interviewed for the fourth or eighth time).

be explained by differences in the samples or in the construction of the statistics.

We begin by comparing employment estimates for all of employment services and for the temporary help industry from the CES with those from the CPS or the Contingent Worker Supplement of the CPS. To make estimates from the CPS as comparable as possible to those from the CES, we exclude the self-employed, unpaid family workers, and farm workers from our sample of CWS and CPS workers. Figure 7.1 shows the percentage of the employed who report being paid by a temporary help agency in each of the five waves of the CWS, along with the percentage of paid, nonfarm workers in the corresponding February CPS who work in employment services, and the not-seasonally-adjusted percentage of nonfarm payroll employment in employment services and temporary help services in the same months from the CES. Comparing employment services figures in the CES and the basic CPS, it is apparent that not only is the share of employment in employment services as measured in the CPS less than half that in the CES, but the strong upward trend apparent in the CES is almost entirely absent in the CPS.

The Contingent Worker Supplements were intended to correct what was believed to be substantial underreporting of temporary help employment in the basic CPS, which occurs in part because respondents often report the client for whom they are assigned to work as their employers. In the CWS, respondents were specifically asked whether they were paid by a temporary help agency, and this question seems to have helped identify additional temporary help workers. Although all of those who reported being paid by a temporary help agency in the CWS should also have been coded as employment services workers in the basic CPS of that survey, slightly under half, in fact, were coded in the broader industry. This finding supports the belief that workers in employment services are underreported in the basic CPS.[11]

In addition to examining the percentage of those identified as paid by temporary help agencies in the CWS who are classified in employment services, we compute the overlap in the reverse direction: the percentage of those classified in the employment services sector of the basic CPS who subsequently identify themselves as being paid by temporary help agencies in the CWS. This exercise provides further evidence of the difficulty in the basic CPS of classifying workers as being in the employment service sector based on respondents' description of their employers.[12] Because workers

11. In general across the time period we observed, the CES measured a larger number of wage and salary workers in the nonagricultural sector than did the CPS. However, the difference in these aggregate employment measures were relatively slight (approximately 1.1 percent) in comparison to the difference observed for Employment Services between the CES and the CWS.

12. In the basic CPS an individual's industry of employment is determined through the provision of the name of the employer for which an individual works and an inquiry about the industry of this employer. The inquiry about the industry in the basic CPS includes the following question, which interviewers are instructed to read if necessary for clarifying the nature of the work: "What do they make or do where you work?" This instruction could prompt some

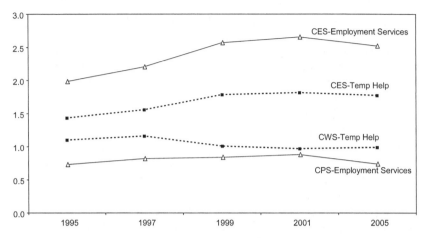

Fig. 7.1   Employment services and temporary help services employment, CES vs. CPS and CWS measures (percent of nonfarm payroll employment, February)

Source: Authors' calculations based on February CPS, CWS, and CES (not seasonally adjusted) data. Self-employed and farm workers were excluded from calculations in the CPS and CWS samples to make them as comparable as possible to the CES sample.

who were coded in employment services in the basic CPS could have been employed with a PEO or in an employment placement agency, not all would be expected to answer that they were paid by a temporary help agency in the CWS. Nevertheless, the fact that across all five waves only about half of those classified in employment services in the basic CPS were coded as temporary agency workers in the accompanying CWS is surprising given that, according to CES figures, temporary help workers accounted for over 70 percent of employment services employment throughout the period.

Estimates of the percentage employed in temporary help agencies from the Contingent Worker Supplements to the CPS and from the CES are more similar than estimates of the percent employed in all employment services in the CPS and the CES, but the CES estimates for the share in temporary help employment still are considerably larger than those derived from the CWS and display a different trend. Whereas the share of employment in temporary help rises through the 1990s in the CES, it falls in the late 1990s in the CWS and, as a result, the gap between the CES and CWS estimates widens over the period.[13]

---

respondents employed by temporary help agencies to describe the activities at the places where they are assigned to work and thus lead to a misclassification of their industries in the basic CPS. In addition, some individuals employed by temporary help agencies may be unclear about which name to provide as their employer.

13. The CPS and CWS figures represent the fraction of workers whose primary job is in the industry, whereas the CES statistics are computed as a fraction of all jobs (Cohany 1996; Polivka 1996b). Our examination of second jobs in the basic CPS shows that this difference probably accounts for little of the difference between the basic CPS and CES estimates of the

Whereas the CES suggests a considerably larger number of workers are employed in employment services than does the CPS, data from the Economic Census yield even higher estimates of employment in employment services and in the major component industries, temporary help, and PEOs, as can be seen from the estimates presented in table 7.1. The 1992, 1997, and 2002 Economic Census figures for the employment services sector have consistently been about a third higher than CES figures for the same industry and time period. Although employment estimates in the small employment placement agency industry have been higher in the CES than in the Census figures, the opposite has been the case in the other two industries and the differences have been substantial, particularly in the PEO industry. In 1992 and 2002 the employment estimates for PEOs in the Economic Census were more than double those in the CES. While both the Economic Census and the CES estimates show PEO employment increasing almost fivefold between 1992 and 2002, PEO workers constituted 1.5 percent of all wage and salary nonagricultural employment in 2002 in the Economic Census estimates but only 0.7 percent in the CES estimates.

As we will discuss later, although differences in the treatment of PEO workers in the two surveys potentially could explain these discrepancies, we find that they account for little of the difference between the CES and the Economic Census estimates in the time period we are considering. The Economic Census is collected through a mail survey that is sent to employers once every five years. The Economic Census' definition of a paid employee is the same as that used by the Internal Revenue Service on Form 941. The CES draws its sample from the Quarterly Census of Employment and Wages (QCEW), based on the industry and employment characteristics reported to the QCEW. In addition, the CES industry estimates are benchmarked to the QCEW once a year, with the discrepancy between the CES and the QCEW being distributed throughout the year. The QCEW employment figures are derived from employers' quarterly reports to the State Employment Security agencies. In these reports, employers that are covered by state Unemployment Insurance (UI) filing rules provide their total UI-covered employment in each month of the quarter and the total quarterly wages for all covered employees.[14]

Under their Unemployment Insurance filing rules, several states require PEOs to report their clients' employment and wages in separate unemployment insurance accounts and to assign the industry of the client to these

---

share of employment-services employment reported in figure 7.1. No data on second jobs is collected in the CWS, and thus we are unable to assess its importance in those data. Discrepancies in the reporting of temporary help employment between the CWS and the basic CPS of the same survey, discussed earlier, suggest that some of the difference between measures derived from the CPS and those from the CES results from problems with the accuracy of information provided by household respondents.

14. The CES estimates for March and the QCEW estimates for the third month of the first quarter were quite similar for the years we compared to the Economic Census.

Table 7.1   Comparison of Economic Census and BLS estimates of employment in employment services

	1992			1997			2002		
	Economic census	CES	Percent difference[a]	Economic census	CES	Percent difference[a]	Economic census	CES	Percent difference[a]
Employment services	1,975	1,464	35	3,622	2,738	32	4,166	3,125	33
Placement agencies	133	183	–27	114	268	–57	109	268	–59
Temporary help supply	1,500	1,124	33	2,613	1,932	35	2,389	2,096	12
Leased employees	342	157	118	895	537	67	1,668	761	119
Total private sector, nonagricultural employment	89,055	88,333	0.8	101,370	101,015	0.35	108,990	107,836	1.1

Notes: Employment estimates are in thousands. The CES figures are not-seasonally-adjusted estimates for March (as taken from the BLS website). The industry codes are 2002 NAICS. The Economic Census figures refer to the number of employees on the payroll on March 12. The industry codes for the 1997 and 2002 estimates are 1997 NAICS. The 1992 estimates were collected using SIC codes.

[a]The percentage differences were calculated as (Economic Census Estimate–CES Estimate)/CES Estimate.

accounts. This requirement should remove the client's employment from the estimates of PEO employment. Several other states require PEOs to file multiple work site reports. Under this requirement, PEOs are requested to file a separate work site report for each of their customers, providing the customers' employment, wages, and industry. If a multiple work site report is filed by a PEO, the QCEW staff assigns the PEO's employment and the industry of that employment based on this report. This again would reduce the amount of employment in the PEO industry.

In 2002, fourteen states required PEOs to report employment using an Unemployment Insurance account for the client, and another twenty states required PEOs to file a separate work site report for each of their customers.[15] Thus, QCEW PEO employment, and correspondingly CES PEO employment, should be less than Economic Census PEO employment in states with these regulations. Furthermore, if the reassignment of PEO employment in the QCEW to a client's industry were complete, the QCEW's measurement of PEO employment should be approximately 1 to 2 percent of the Economic Census figures, based on 1997 Economic Census estimates that 1.3 percent of PEO employees were involved in the management of the PEO and hence were not assigned to a client firm. Table 7.2 presents the average ratio of QCEW PEO employment to Economic Census PEO employment in 2002 for forty-five states and the District of Columbia combined;[16] it also presents the average ratio among states within each reporting requirement category. The three categories include the following: (a) states requiring PEOs to report their clients' employment using a separate unemployment insurance account, (b) states mandating a multiple work site report, and (c) states with no such reporting requirement. Figure 7.2 presents similar information for each state separately, with the ratio of the QCEW employment to Economic Census employment on the y-axis and the natural logarithm of Economic Census employment on the x-axis.[17] This graph provides a picture of the variability of the ratio among states with the same reporting requirements and across states with different reporting requirements.

The ratios reported in table 7.2 and figure 7.2 indicate that state UI reporting requirements for PEOs can account for only some of the difference in the QCEW and Economic Census estimates of PEO employment. The average

15. The fourteen states requiring PEOs to report employment using the clients' Unemployment Insurance accounts were Alaska, Connecticut, Delaware, Iowa, Kentucky, Maine, Massachusetts, Minnesota, Mississippi, Nebraska, Rhode Island, South Carolina, South Dakota, Tennessee, and Vermont. The states requiring PEOs to file a separate work site report for each client were Alabama, California, Colorado, Florida, Georgia, Kansas, Louisiana, Montana, Nevada, New Hampshire, New Jersey, New York, North Carolina, North Dakota, Ohio, Oklahoma, Oregon, Utah, Virginia, and West Virginia.

16. Four states were not included in the analysis because the Census Bureau did not release the information to the public owing to confidentiality constraints. In addition, Montana was excluded from the analysis because the ratio of the QCEW's measure of PEO employment to the Economic Census measure of PEO employment was over seven and thus the inclusion of Montana in the analysis unduly influenced some of the averages.

17. The natural log was used for the x-axis solely to improve the appearance of the graph.

Table 7.2   **2002 comparison of the ratio of QCEW PEO employment to Economic Census PEO employment (%)**

	All states	Required to file under client's unemployment insurance	Multiple work site report mandated	No state requirements
Ratio	0.43	0.20[a]	0.43	0.61
Percent with ratio less than 0.05 (QCEW employment less than 5% of EC)	13.3	25.0	11.1	6.7
Percent with ratio greater than 1 (QCEW employment more than 100% of EC)	6.7	0.0	5.6	13.3

[a]In a regression using the ratio as the dependent variable and dummy variables indicating whether a state required filing under a client's UI or a state-mandated multiple work site report as control variables, the coefficient on the control variable indicating that a state required filing under a client's UI was statistically significant at the 1 percent level. The mandatory work site control variable was not statistically significant at standard levels.

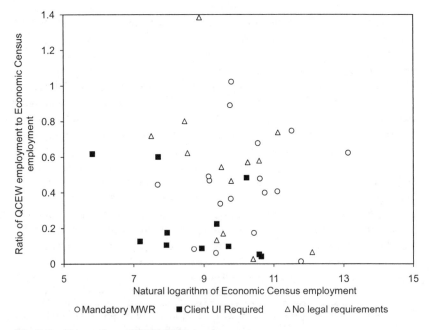

Fig. 7.2   Comparison of 2002 PEO employment

ratio of QCEW to Economic Census estimates of PEO employment was 0.20 in states requiring PEOs to report under clients' UI accounts, compared to a ratio of 0.61 in states that did not have any legal requirements, and this difference was statistically significant at the 0.01 level. The ratio for states with mandatory work site reports for PEOs also was lower than for states with no legal requirements (0.43 vs. 0.61), but this difference was not statistically significant. Given that the expected ratio in states requiring PEOs to report under the client's UI account number is close to zero, the fact that it is 0.20 implies that the reassignment by PEOs to their clients' accounts is far from complete. Only 25 percent of the states that required separate UI accounts for PEO clients had a ratio of less than 0.05 in 2002. If only the permanent staff of PEOs were reported, this ratio would be around 0.03, which further indicates that reassignment to the clients' industry in these states is incomplete. Moreover, given that PEO employment figures in the QCEW and Economic Census should be the same in states with no legal requirement to use either a separate UI account or a multiple work site report, the fact that the ratio is 0.61 implies large discrepancies that cannot be explained by differences in reporting requirements still existing between these surveys.[18] These discrepancies and the inconsistent treatment of PEO employees across states in the QCEW render it difficult to determine the amount of contracting out that is done through PEOs, as well as changes in PEO employment over time.

7.6   Occupational Distribution in Employment Services

Segal and Sullivan (1997) first noted a large shift in the distribution of employment within employment services toward manual occupations beginning in the 1990s. Paralleling our discussion of overall employment levels, we compare the levels of and trends in the occupational distribution of employment in employment services and its component industries as measured in the basic CPS, the Contingent Worker Supplements to the CPS, and the OES.[19]

We begin by comparing the occupational distribution of employment in all of employment services as measured in the outgoing rotation group samples of the basic CPS and in the OES.[20] In figure 7.3 we present the

18. In combination with the state mandates, BLS has undertaken efforts to have PEOs report workers assigned to clients in the clients' industry. These efforts may have resulted in more of the data being assigned back to clients in recent years. However, there was no evidence of a decline in PEO employment prior to 2005 in the BLS state data that we examined (and on which we base the discussion in this chapter), and estimates of the current proportion of PEO employment assigned back to PEO customers in BLS data are not available.

19. None of the other surveys provides occupational information.

20. We also have compared the occupational distribution in the OES with that for the November CPS to be consistent with the timing of the OES survey. The comparison is not sensitive to seasonality, thus we report the CPS ORG because of its larger sample.

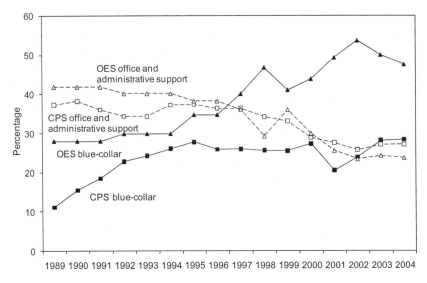

Fig. 7.3   Occupational distribution of employment, CPS vs. OES

employment shares for two broad occupational categories: office and administrative support occupations and blue-collar occupations. We define the latter as including six occupational categories, the largest of which are production occupations and helpers, laborers, and hand material movers.[21] Both the CPS and the OES show a decline in the relative importance of clerical occupations in employment services, though the decline is more pronounced in the OES. Both the CPS and the OES record large growth in the relative importance of blue-collar occupations, but the timing is different. In the CPS the growth in the relative importance of blue-collar occupations occurs in the first half of the 1990s, whereas in the OES it is concentrated in the latter half of the 1990s and the 2000s. In addition, the share of employment in blue-collar occupations as measured in the OES is substantially higher than in the CPS in all years. We also have examined differences in the two series in the levels and trends within more narrowly defined occupations. The most pronounced differences in the two series are apparent for the lowest-skilled manual occupations—helpers, laborers, and hand material movers (figure 7.4).

One might expect that the occupational distributions in the CWS and in the basic CPS would differ because, as discussed previously, reporting biases are more serious in the basic CPS and because individuals in the

21. We define blue-collar to include the following: supervisors of production occupations; repair and maintenance; construction and extraction; production; transportation and material moving; and helpers, laborers, and hand material movers.

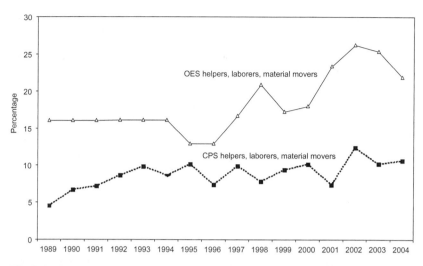

Fig. 7.4   Share of helpers, laborers, and hand material movers in employment services

CWS should only be employed by temporary help agencies, not by PEOs or employment placement agencies, which employ relatively fewer workers in blue-collar occupations.[22] Yet discrepancies between the occupational distribution of employment found in the CWS and OES, displayed in figures 7.5 and 7.6, are similar to those between the basic CPS and the OES shown in figures 7.3 and 7.4. Figure 7.5 displays the employment shares in clerical and in blue-collar occupations among those identifying themselves as being paid by temporary help agencies in each of the five waves of the CWS. Also displayed are the percentages in these two broad occupation categories from the temporary help and PEO industries combined, using data from the OES from 1996 to 2004. Because establishments in the OES were classified into a broader industry category that included temporary help and PEOs prior to the introduction of NAICS in 2002, we report figures for the combined industry category. As is the case of the comparison with occupational distributions computed from the Current Population Survey Outgoing Rotation Group (CPS ORG), the dramatic increase in the relative importance of manual occupations apparent in the OES data from the 2000s is absent in the CWS data. Differences in levels and trends among the lowest-skilled workers are particularly striking in the two series (figure 7.6).

22. We are able to compare the occupational distributions of employment for PEO and temporary help establishments in the OES data beginning in 2002, and this comparison shows a considerably smaller percentage in production and other manual occupations in PEO establishments.

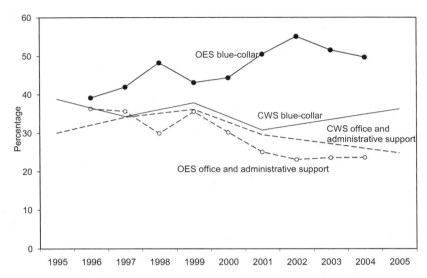

Fig. 7.5   Comparison of occupation distribution in OES (temp help and PEO) and CWS (temp help)

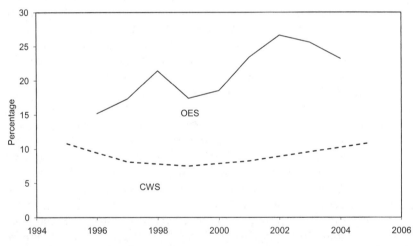

Fig. 7.6   Share of employment in helpers, laborers, and hand material movers occupations, OES (temp help and PEOs) and CWS (temp help)

Note: OES shows share of helpers, laborers, and hand material movers in temporary help and PEOs. CWS shows the share in that occupation category in temporary help.

7.7 Industry of Assignment

Information on the occupational distribution of employment in employment services and on changes in that distribution may be suggestive of which industries are outsourcing to employment services. For example, the growth of production and other manual occupations in employment services has been taken as an indicator of the growth in manufacturers' use of outsourcing to employment services (Segal and Sullivan 1997). Direct information on industry use is needed to get precise estimates of how the growth of this contracting sector affects the industry distribution of employment, however, and such direct information is quite limited.

Estimates of the industry distribution of clients using temporary help agencies are available from the Contingent Worker Supplement (CWS). In each of the five waves of the CWS, information on the industry to which individuals were assigned was collected from workers identifying themselves as being on the payroll of a temporary help agency. Table 7.3 displays the distribution of industry of assignment in each of the five waves.[23] In four of the waves, around 40 percent of temporary agency workers identified themselves in the CWS report as being assigned to manufacturing employers. In 2001, that figure abruptly dropped by about 10 percentage points. That decline mirrors a sharp decline in production workers in the temporary services industry in 2001 as recorded in the OES, which in turn likely reflects the recession and a tendency by manufacturers to reduce production employment first by cutting the temporary workforce.

Estimates of the distribution of industry of assignment for PEO workers are available from the Economic Census for 1992 and 1997. In both of those years, PEO establishments were asked to report the number of "leased employees by industry category of the client." According to those estimates, service industries were the largest users of PEOs, followed by transportation, communications, and utilities. Manufacturers accounted for an estimated 13 percent and 12 percent of PEO use in 1992 and 1997, respectively (table 7.4).

---

23. To identify industry of assignment, individuals in the CWS were first asked if the employer that they reported in the basic CPS was the temporary help agency or the employer to which they were assigned. Only if they indicated that it was the temporary help agency were they asked for the information about the employer to which they were assigned in the CWS. Apparently reflecting respondent confusion over the initial screening question, many who listed the temporary help agency in the basic CPS also indicated that this was the employer to which they were assigned, including a large number of production workers and workers in other manual occupations. As a result, about 20 percent were coded as being assigned back to the temporary help agency. Yet permanent agency staff only accounts for about 3 percent of payroll employment in temporary help agencies and temporary agencies would be expected to employ few if any workers in manual occupations as a part of their permanent administrative staff. For this reason, we deleted observations in which the employment services industry was coded as the industry of assignment in computing the industry of assignment distribution.

Table 7.3   Distribution of industry of assignment, temporary help workers, CWS

Industry	1995	1997	1999	2001	2005
Agriculture	0.4	0.0	0.6	1.3	0.0
Mining	0.3	0.9	0.2	1.2	0.6
Trade, transportation, and utilities	15.0	14.3	13.6	14.6	13.9
Construction	3.6	3.2	3.3	4.1	3.8
Manufacturing	40.0	37.9	37.6	28.5	38.7
Information	5.1	6.8	6.5	5.9	1.5
Financial activities	9.5	11.2	10.0	9.2	0.0
Professional and business services	8.8	11.3	11.1	12.5	18.4
Education services	2.6	2.2	1.2	2.9	1.8
Health care and social assistance	7.0	6.7	9.5	11.4	11.9
Arts, entertainment, and recreation	0.4	0.2	0.6	1.4	0.0
Accommodation and food services	0.8	0.8	0.4	0.0	2.5
Other services	5.0	4.5	4.0	3.5	3.2
Public administration	1.6	0.0	1.6	3.7	3.9

Notes: Calculations based on industry of assignment reported by those in CWS who indicate that they are paid by a temporary help agency. Individuals who report being assigned back to the employment services sector are excluded from the sample. All observations were weighted by CWS weights.

Table 7.4   Industry distribution of PEO clients, Economic Census

Industry	1992	1997
Agriculture, forestry and fishing	0.9	1.3
Mining	0.4	0.1
Construction	8.2	11.6
Manufacturing	13.2	11.8
Transportation, communication and utilities	18.3	16.9
Wholesale trade	3.3	3.4
Retail trade	9.5	6.5
Finance, insurance and real estate	3.9	3.6
Services	30.9	34.4
Other	8.5	10.5

In these two Economic Census years PEOs reported that only 1.3 percent of PEO employees were part of the PEO administrative structure.[24]

Using data from the OES and the CWS, we generate alternative estimates of the distribution of industry of assignment for PEO workers. To do so we assume that within occupations, the fraction assigned to an industry is the same for PEO workers as it is for temporary agency workers, where

24. In 2002 the Economic Census collected information on PEO use from client organizations, not from the PEOs. These 2002 estimates were not made public owing to concerns about data quality, and the Economic Census returned to its original format—asking for information about client industries from the PEOs—in 2007.

industry of assignment is measured in the CWS. For example, we assume that production workers in the PEO industry have the same probability of being assigned to manufacturing as production workers employed in temporary help agencies. We also assume that within occupations the CWS provides an unbiased estimate of the industry to which temporary agency workers are assigned, even if overall there is an undercount of temporary agency workers in the CWS. For instance, while temporary agency helpers and laborers appear to be underrepresented in the CWS even relative to other occupations, we assume that the temporary agency helpers and laborers who are identified in the CWS are neither more nor less likely to be assigned to manufacturing clients than is the case in the general population of temporary agency helpers and laborers.[25] Based on these assumptions and using the occupational distribution of employment in PEO establishments, we estimate that between 23 and 29 percent of PEO workers were assigned to manufacturing from 2002 to 2004.[26]

Estimates of the fraction of the employment services commodity used as an input in industries also are generated as part of the Bureau of Economic Analysis (BEA) input-output (I-O) benchmark tables. If the average price of an employment services worker does not vary across industries utilizing these workers, the BEA I-O figures represent an estimate of the fraction of employment services workers assigned to various industries. In the absence of data on industry of assignment for temporary help workers prior to the 1995 CWS, some researchers have used the BEA I-O figures to estimate the number of temporary help workers assigned to manufacturing and the growth of temporary workers in the manufacturing sector prior to the mid-1990s (Estavão and Lach 1999a, 1999b).

However, the BEA I-O estimates are based on expenditure data pertaining to a broad set of contract workers and are collected from a subset of industries. In the 1997 benchmark I-O tables, estimates were derived from data collected in the Business Expenses Survey (BES), which is administered to companies in the wholesale, retail, and services sectors. Companies completing the survey were asked to report their expenditures on contract labor, defined as "persons who are not on your payroll but are supplied through a contract with another company to perform specific jobs (e.g., temporary help, leased employees)." It was assumed that companies answering this

25. We provide a more extensive discussion of our methodology for imputing employment services workers to client industries in Dey, Houseman, and Polivka (2008).

26. While these estimates of the fraction assigned to manufacturing are roughly double those in the Economic Census, it is notable that the estimate of PEO workers in the Economic Census is comparably higher in these years, so that the total number of workers imputed to manufacturing is similar. Also, PEO employment almost doubled between 1997 and 2002 in the Economic Census, and it is unclear whether this growth was equally distributed across industries. If use of PEOs disproportionately grew in the manufacturing sector, the fraction of PEO workers assigned to manufacturing might be more comparable between the Economic Census and the imputation based on the 2002 to 2004 OES data.

question reported expenditures on six types of contract services: (a) temporary help services, (b) employee leasing services, (c) security guards and patrol services, (d) office administrative services, (e) facility support services, and (f) nonresidential building cleaning services—and thus these services were treated as a bundled commodity. Data on industry output in each of these contract labor services industries came from the Economic Census and were aggregated to match the level of commodity aggregation assumed in the BES. The residual of the contract labor services not accounted for by industries surveyed in the BES was imputed to industries not surveyed in the BES based on their output shares. To generate I-O estimates at a more disaggregated commodity level, it was assumed that industries utilized all contract labor services in the same proportion. For instance, if an industry was estimated to use 10 percent of all contract labor services, it was assumed to use 10 percent of each of the component contract services.

The estimates from the BEA I-O tables on the industry distribution of the employment services commodity are markedly different from the estimates of the industry assignment distributions of temporary help and PEO workers from the CWS and from the Economic Census. Estimates based on the BEA I-O tables also seem inconsistent with the high proportion of blue-collar workers in the temporary help sector in the OES data (as documented previously), and the proportion of temporary help workers in the OES who were in production occupations specifically (Dey, Houseman, and Polivka 2008). For example, in the 1997 and 2002 benchmarks, the fraction of the employment services commodity assigned to manufacturing was under 5 percent. Although the input-output estimates, which are based on expenditure data, are not necessarily inconsistent with those from the Economic Census and the CWS, which are based on employment data, the size of the differences raises concerns about the accuracy of the Economic Census figures and at a minimum implies that the input-output figures are a poor indicator of the number of employment services workers outsourced to various industries.

7.8   Evidence from the OES on Other Types of Domestic Outsourcing

Although discrepancies in the data pertaining to employment services and its component industries are sometimes large across data sets, information about contracting out to this sector is rich relative to other types of domestic contracting out. Historically, firms have commonly outsourced many tasks, such as legal and construction services, to other entities. In this chapter, outside of employment services, our focus is not on the level of contracting out that occurs in the economy but rather on measuring how the patterns of domestic contracting out may have changed in recent years.

In the past, researchers have used data from a variety of sources to shed light on trends in other types of contracting out. Some have used growth of the business services sector as an indicator of growth in contracting out (Abraham 1988; Clinton 1997). One shortcoming of this approach is that, while one might expect that much of the growth in domestic outsourcing would accrue to establishments classified in the business services sector, contracting out is not limited to organizations classified in business services, and thus a study focused on business services may miss other important areas of outsourcing. Several nongovernment surveys have questioned private-sector businesses on trends in contracting out, and these surveys, conducted in the 1980s and 1990s, uniformly found strong indicators that businesses were increasing their domestic contracting out (Abraham 1988; Houseman 2001; Kalleberg, Reynolds, and Marsden 2003). These surveys, however, provide limited evidence on what functions businesses have outsourced.

Several studies have used evidence from various government surveys on the contracting out of selected services in selected industries. Abraham and Taylor (1996) relied on information in the 1986 to 1987 Industry Wage Surveys of thirteen manufacturing industries on firms' use of five business services—(a) janitorial services, (b) machine maintenance services, (c) engineering and drafting services, (d) accounting services, and (e) computer services—at the time of the survey (1986–1987), and retrospectively in 1983 and 1979. Using this information, Abraham and Taylor constructed an estimate of a change over time in the proportion of manufacturing firms that contracted out for the provision of the service. Bartel, Lach, and Sicherman (2005) used the Census of Manufactures to obtain an estimate of an increase in the amount of contracting out by manufacturers of eight selected services.[27] They estimated that the manufacturing sector's spending on these outsourced services more than doubled between 1992 and 1997, increasing from 4.25 percent of total value added in 1992 to 10.68 percent in 1997. Using expenditure data from the 1987, 1992, and 1997 Truck Inventory and Use Surveys conducted by the Census Bureau as part of the Census of Transportation, Baker and Hubbard (2002) examined trends in the contracting out of trucking services. They found a decrease in the share of for-hire trucking between 1987 and 1992 but an increase in the use of for-hire trucking between 1992 and 1997.

The Contingent Worker Supplements to the CPS were designed to fill many of the information gaps on contracting out. In the survey, individuals were identified as contract workers according to their answers to the question, "Some companies provide employees or their services to others under contract. A few examples of services that can be contracted out include security, landscaping, or computer programming. Did you work for a company

27. The Census of Manufactures collects information on the dollar amount of purchased services that manufacturing firms spend on eight items: (a) repair of buildings and other structures, (b) repair of machinery, (c) communication services, (d) legal services, (e) accounting and bookkeeping services, (f) advertising, (g) software and data processing services, and (h) refuse removal.

that contracted out you or your services last week?" The share of workers identifying themselves as contract workers was relatively small, about 1.5 percent, and displayed no trend increase over the five CWS waves conducted from 1995 to 2005.[28] One reason may be that employees of one company that contracts out their services to another organization may not be called contract workers and may not know for whom their work is being done, particularly if they are performing tasks for a variety of client companies off-site. For example, advertising agencies typically provide services to many clients under contract, but their employees may not consider themselves employees of a contract company.[29]

We use the longitudinal data that we constructed from the OES on occupation by industry to shed additional light on trends in domestic outsourcing in selected occupations. The strength of the OES lies in the detailed information collected on the occupational structure within industries. Thus, with some prior information about which occupations are being contracted out and the industry or sector to which the jobs are being outsourced, we can build longitudinal data at the level of detail needed to observe whether the trend in the industry structure of employment is consistent with a growth in contracting out of that occupation. Because of the change from SIC to NAICS industry classification, which was implemented in 2002 in the OES, we only report data for the years 1989 through 2001 in this part of our analysis.

To identify occupations that were contracted out, we selected the most common occupations held by those who identified themselves as working for a company that contracted out their services in the five waves of the CWS. Although individuals likely underreport contracting out in the CWS, the CWS should be a useful tool for identifying occupations that are frequently outsourced and the contract industries in which they are employed. We supplemented this list in one instance with case-study evidence of outsourcing.[30]

Using this process, we examine trends in the industry structure of employment for six occupations: (a) school bus drivers, (b) truck drivers, (c) janitors, (d) security guards, (e) computer occupations, and (f) accountants. Figure 7.7 displays total employment in the indicated occupation, employment of the occupation in what we identify as the contract sector, and the share of the occupation's employment in the contract sector, all from 1989 to 2001.

The case of school bus drivers offers a simple example of how the OES can be helpful in identifying the growth of contracting out in a particular

28. The share of workers identifying themselves as contract workers who were assigned primarily to one client's work site was about a half percentage point.
29. Indeed, the questions on the CWS pertaining to contract workers were primarily designed to capture workers performing tasks at a single client company's work site. Follow-up questions in the CWS asked individuals who initially identified themselves as contract workers whether they worked at the customer work site and whether they worked at more than one work site. Thus, the CWS is not ideally suited for examining broader trends in domestic outsourcing.
30. We include school bus drivers on the basis of case-study evidence in Erickcek, Houseman, and Kalleberg (2003).

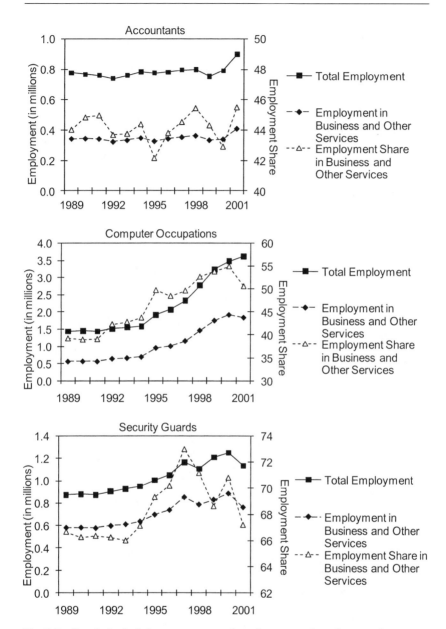

Fig. 7.7   Trends in the industry structure of employment, selected occupations

occupation. School bus drivers are, for all intents and purposes, employed by school systems (public or private), or by a contract bus service industry within the trade and transportation sector when the service is outsourced by schools. Case-study evidence that school systems have increasingly contracted out bus services (Erickcek, Houseman, and Kalleberg 2003) is borne

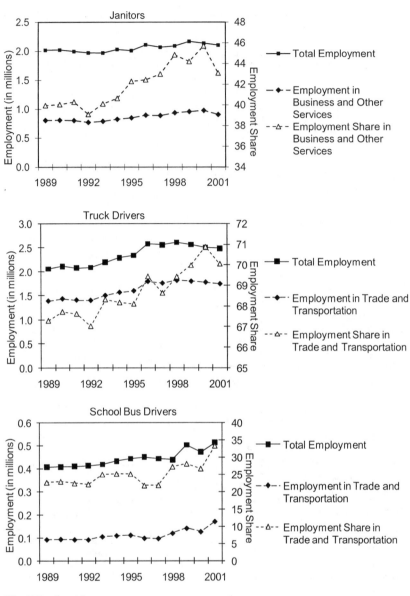

Fig. 7.7   (cont.)

out in the OES data. The share of school bus drivers employed in the trade and transportation sector grew from 23 percent in 1989 to 33 percent in 2001, according to OES data.

We also examine trends in the contracting out of truck driver services. The CWS identified this occupation as one that is commonly contracted out, and the OES data indicate that the share of truck drivers in the trade and transportation sector grew by a modest 3 percentage points from 1989 to 2001. This finding is consistent with evidence of a growth in contracting out of trucking services from 1992 to 1997, reported in Baker and Hubbard (2002).

In the other four occupations—janitors, security guards, computer occupations, and accountants—we look for growth in the share of workers in business services as an indicator of growth in contracting out in that occupation, and we find evidence of growth in contracting out in two. According to OES data, the share of workers in computer occupations employed in business services increased dramatically, from 39 percent in 1990 to over 50 percent a decade later.[31] Growth in the share of janitors employed in business services increased 3 to 6 percentage points over the same period.

Our examination of OES data overall shows considerable evidence of growth in contracting out in the occupations identified as the most commonly outsourced occupations in the CWS, in spite of the fact that there was no apparent trend increase of contract workers in the CWS. We hypothesize that small samples in the CWS for these workers and confusion among respondents over whether their work is contracted out explains why growth in contracting out is not apparent in the household survey, even when it is in establishment data.

Use of the OES to detect trends in outsourcing has some limitations that should be noted. First, except in rather clear-cut cases (such as school bus drivers) in which the industry engaging in the outsourcing can be easily identified, increases in the share of an occupation employed in a sector associated with contracting out should be interpreted with some caution. An increase in the share of workers in a particular occupation in the contract sector may reflect an increase in the propensity of firms to contract out that occupation. Alternatively, it could reflect a general change in the industrial mix in the economy, with a decline in the share of industries that historically have performed the task in-house and a growth in the share of industries that historically have outsourced the task. For example, the growth in the share of truck drivers in the transportation sector could reflect an increase in contracting out of trucking services by manufacturers and companies in other sectors; alternatively, it could reflect the decline of manufacturing, which employs relatively more truck drivers than other sectors of the economy that are expanding. In addition, the OES data is useful for detecting growth in contracting out only in cases in which an industry that employs the contract workers is distinct from the industry engaging in the contracting out. Much outsourcing may occur within an industry, and such intra-industry contracting out would be difficult to detect in the OES data. Nevertheless, in view of

---

31. The drop in the share of computer operators employed in business services between 2000 and 2001 could reflect the recession in 2001 or reduced demand for contract computer workers after the start of the new millennium.

the absence of comprehensive data on contracting out, the OES provides a useful tool in many circumstances for better understanding changes in patterns of domestic outsourcing and their consequences for the industry distribution of employment.

7.9   Conclusions

Data limitations greatly restrict the ability of researchers to track changing patterns of contracting out and study their implications for the structure of employment in the economy. Fairly extensive data do exist for employment services, a sector in which almost all of the employment represents contracting out. However, employment services only provides a partial picture of contracting out in the United States, and the information provided by various sources of data on the employment services sector is often inconsistent. The Contingent Worker Supplements include a question that allows individuals to identify themselves as working for an employer that contracts out their services, but questions in the CWS pertaining to contract workers are designed primarily to capture situations in which contract workers work at one client's work site. This focus, coupled with likely respondent confusion over what is meant by contract services, limits the usefulness of the CWS in picking up broader trends in domestic outsourcing. The Bureau of Economic Analysis draws upon a wide range of government and industry data sources to construct a comprehensive input-output structure for the economy. These estimates, however, are only as good as the underlying data, and, particularly in emerging areas of outsourcing, data may be thin. In addition, input-output estimates are typically based on expenditure data, which may not adequately measure the extent to which industries utilize workers from the contract sector. As was illustrated in the case of employment services, information from input-output tables may be a poor indicator of the extent to which various industries contract out jobs to the sector of interest.

As a first step toward improving our understanding of domestic contracting out, it would be very helpful if the statistical agencies—BLS, BEA, and the Census Bureau—provided better documentation of selected statistics and thereby allowed users to assess the quality of the data and their suitability for measuring domestic outsourcing. Specifically, the QCEW program at BLS could better document its treatment of PEOs, including, for current and past estimates, the proportion of PEO employment in each state that was assigned back to client industries and the methodology that was used to make this assignment. Moreover, to enhance our understanding of PEOs, the QCEW could publish two sets of industry employment estimates: one that includes all PEO employment in the PEO industry (without any of it being assigned back to clients), and a second in which PEO employees have been reassigned to client industries.

In addition, the Census Bureau could provide data quality measures for specific questions about PEOs and their clients, including response rates and information about imputation methodologies for missing data. It also would be useful to data users if the Census Bureau provided more complete documentation of the instructions and methodologies used for PEOs in the manufacturing and service components of the Economic Censuses. A comparison of BLS's establishment list and the Census Bureau's establishment list specifically for PEOs also could help illuminate whether the difference between the QCEW and Economic Census estimates of the number of employment sector workers results from differences in industry classification of the PEOs, variation in PEO employment over time, or different treatment of PEO employment by the two surveys.

With regard to the BEA, its input-output tables, and its annual benchmark tables, there would be great value in the BEA documenting the sources, age, and quality of the underlying data and the methodologies used to generate the estimates. This documentation could include the number of observations on which an estimate is based and its standard error, so that data users can assess the quality of the data directly. Alternatively, if releasing this information is not possible for confidentiality reasons, the BEA could provide to the public its own assessment of the quality of the data, indicating in particular when an estimate is based on good data sources with an adequate number of observations and when an estimate is based on poorer quality or thinner underlying data.

In order to use BEA input-output tables or the BEA's annual benchmark tables to study domestic outsourcing or offshore outsourcing as has been suggested by some authors (Kurz and Lengermann 2008; Yuskavage, Strassner, and Medeiros 2008), the underlying data need to be reliable, or at least a measure of their reliability needs to be known. Furthermore, the quality of the input-output estimates and the underlying data will influence other economic measures, such as multifactor productivity estimates, that assume employers' contracting out expenditures are adequately measured.

In addition to providing better documentation with sufficient resources, the BLS and Census ideally would collect more complete and better quality information about the extent of and reasons behind companies' outsourcing practices. Collecting such information at the company rather than at the establishment level, we believe, would be preferable because it would avoid counting domestic, intracompany exchanges as outsourcing. The information collected at the company level might include expenditure data on additional specific contract services and on the total of all contracting, the organizations' reasons for outsourcing, and the names of companies from which contracted services were obtained. Information on why companies contract out work would help to answer questions about whether and where contract work can be expected to expand, how contract work may vary over the business cycle, and the implications of domestic outsourcing for workers.[32] Some information on contract workers and the industries to which they are assigned might be best obtained from the contract companies.

As a starting point for the collection of information on organizations' use of contract workers, information about the clients of staffing agencies could be collected from the staffing agencies. Alternatively, organizations' use of workers from staffing services could be obtained from the organizations. The BLS did developmental work for a supplement to the CES that would have asked establishments about their use of temporary help workers, PEOs, and independent contractors. However, because of a lack of funding, this supplement was never administered during actual data collection.

Finally, resources permitting, a matched employer-employee survey could be conducted to shed light on the discrepancies between the CPS and CES estimates of temporary help and PEO workers. Matched employer-employee data also would provide more information about the effects of companies contracting out practices on specific types of workers and differences in employees' and employers' perceptions of workplace practices and expectations about the security of employment. Matching data collected in the Contingent Worker Supplement to establishment data via the Longitudinal Employer-Household Dynamics (LEHD) program could help to provide insights into the discrepancies observed through 2005, although the sample sizes may be small for some types of workers and to examine discrepancies in temporary help employment measures in the future, the CWS would have to be repeated. Furthermore, a new matched employer-employee survey would be needed to obtain information about contracting out more broadly.

Although, given resource constraints, a comprehensive documentation of changing patterns of domestic outsourcing and its employment effects probably is not feasible in the near term, existing data could be used to flag major shifts in outsourcing patterns. We suggest that OES data can be a useful, complementary tool to detect such shifts. In simple cases like that of school bus drivers, the shift of workers in a particular occupation from one industry to another in the OES represents a direct measure of outsourcing. In other cases, shifts in the industry composition of occupational employment may be valuable indicators of changing outsourcing patterns that could be followed up with targeted surveys where deemed desirable. The sector of employment services offers a sobering example, however, of how difficult it can be to obtain information on the extent of outsourcing and the industries engaging in the outsourcing, even when considerable resources are expended on collecting this information.

32. Currently, as part of the Mass Layoff Statistics (MLS) program sponsored by the BLS, establishments that have an extended mass layoff (defined as a layoff of fifty or more people during a five-week period that lasts thirty days or longer) are asked whether this layoff results from the establishment moving work to another establishment domestically or internationally. Using this information, it is possible to construct a measure of the number of individuals involved in an extended mass layoff that stems from domestic contracting out. However, this measure is restricted to contracting out that results in substantial job losses; it does not capture outsourcing that results in no or only limited job losses.

Appendix

Table 7A.1   **Occupation titles**

Management, business, and financial operations occupations
Architecture and engineering occupations
Life, physical, and social science occupations
Computer and mathematical occupations
Healthcare practitioners and technical occupations
All other professional, paraprofessional, and technical occupations
Sales and related occupations
Office and administrative support occupations
Protective service occupations
Food and beverage preparation and service occupations
Cleaning and building service occupations
All other service and agricultural, forestry, fishing, and related occupations
First-line supervisors of production, construction, maintenance, and related workers
Installation, maintenance, and repair occupations
Construction and extraction occupations
Production occupations
Transportation and material moving occupations
Helpers of production workers and laborers and hand material movers

Table 7A.2   **Industry titles**

Mining
Trade, transportation, and utilities
Construction
Manufacturing
Information
Financial activities
Professional and business services
Education services
Health care and social assistance
Arts, entertainment, and recreation
Accommodation and food services
Employment services
Other services
Federal government
State government
Local government

References

Abraham, K. G. 1988. Flexible staffing arrangements and employers' short-term adjustment strategies. In *Employment, unemployment, and labor utilization,* ed. R. A. Hart, 288–311. Boston: Unwin Hyman.
———. 1990. Restructuring the employment relationship: The growth of market-

mediated work arrangements. In *New developments in the labor market: Toward a new institutional paradigm,* ed. K. G. Abraham and R. B. McKersie, 85–119. Cambridge, MA: MIT Press.

Abraham, K. G., and J. Spletzer. 2007. Are the new jobs good jobs? Paper presented at NBER CRIW conference on Labor in the New Economy. Bethesda, MD, November 16–17.

Abraham, K. G., and S. K. Taylor. 1996. Firms' use of outside contractors: Theory and evidence. *Journal of Labor Economics* 14 (3): 394–424.

Autor, D. H. 2001. Why do temporary help firms provide free general skills training? *Quarterly Journal of Economics* 116 (4): 1409–48.

———. 2003. Outsourcing at will: The contribution of unjust dismissal doctrine to the growth of employment outsourcing. *Journal of Labor Economics* 21 (1): 1–42.

Autor, D. H., F. Levy, and R. J. Murnane. 1999. *Skills training in the temporary help sector: Employer motivations and worker impacts.* Final report. Washington, DC: U.S. Department of Labor, Employment and Training Administration.

Baker, G. P., and T. N. Hubbard. 2002. Make versus buy in trucking: Asset ownership, job design and information. NBER Working Paper no. W8727. Cambridge, MA: National Bureau of Economic Research, January.

Bartel, A., S. Lach, and N. Sicherman. 2005. Outsourcing and technological change. NBER Working Paper no. 11158. Cambridge, MA: National Bureau of Economic Research, February.

Clinton, A. 1997. Flexible labor: Restructuring the american work force. *Monthly Labor Review* 120 (8): 3–27.

Cohany, S. R. 1996. Workers in alternative employment arrangements. *Monthly Labor Review* 119 (10): 31–45.

Davis-Blake, A., and B. Uzzi. 1993. Determinants of employment externalization: A study of temporary workers and independent contractors. *Administrative Science Quarterly* 38 (2): 195–223.

Dertouzos, J. N., and L. A. Karoly. 1992. *Labor market responses to employer liability.* RAND Corporation Document R-3989-ICJ. Santa Monica, CA: RAND Institute for Civil Justice.

Dey, M., S. Houseman, and A. Polivka. 2008. Manufacturers' outsourcing to employment services. Upjohn Institute for Employment Research Working Paper no. WP07-132. Available at: http://www.upjohninstitute.org/publications/wp/07-132.pdf.

Erickcek, G., S. Houseman, and A. Kalleberg. 2003. The effects of temporary services and contracting out on low-skilled workers: Evidence from auto suppliers, hospitals, and public schools. In *Low-wage American: How employers are reshaping opportunity in the workplace,* ed. E. Appelbaum, A. Bernhardt, and R. J. Murnane, 368–406. New York: Russell Sage Foundation.

Estavão, M., and S. Lach. 1999a. Measuring temporary labor outsourcing in U.S. manufacturing. NBER Working Paper no. 7421. Cambridge, MA: National Bureau of Economic Research, November.

———. 1999b. The evolution of the demand for temporary help labor supply in the United States. NBER Working Paper no. 7427. Cambridge, MA: National Bureau of Economic Research, December.

Golden, L. 1996. The expansion of temporary help employment in the U.S., 1982–1992: A test of alternative economic explanations. *Applied Economics* 28 (9): 1127–41.

Golden, L., and E. Appelbaum. 1992. What was driving the 1982–1988 boom in temporary employment—preference of workers or decisions and power of employers? *American Journal of Economics and Sociology* 51 (4): 473–93.

Government Accountability Office (GAO). 2006. *Employment arrangements: Improved outreach could help ensure proper worker classification.* GAO-06-656. Washington, DC: GAO.

Hachen, D. S., Jr. 2004. Contracting out work in the 1990s. South Bend, IN: University of Notre Dame, Department of Sociology. Working Paper.

Hamermesh, D. 1993. *Labor demand.* Princeton, NJ: Princeton University Press.

Hart, R. A. 1984. *The economics of non-wage labour costs.* London: George Allen and Unwin.

Houseman, S. 1998. Labor standards in alternative work arrangements. *Labor Law Journal* 49 (7): 1135–41.

———. 2001. Why employers use flexible staffing arrangements: Evidence from an employer survey. *Industrial and Labor Relations Review* 55 (1): 149–70.

Houseman, S., A. Kalleberg, and G. Erickcek. 2003. The role of temporary help employment in tight labor markets. *Industrial and Labor Relations Review* 57 (1): 105–27.

Houseman, S., and A. Polivka. 2000. The implications of flexible staffing arrangements for job security. In *On the job: Is long-term employment a thing of the past?* ed. D. Neumark, 427–62. New York: Russell Sage Foundation.

Kalleberg, A. L., J. Reynolds, and P. V. Marsden. 2003. Externalizing employment: Flexible staffing arrangements in U.S. organizations. *Social Science Research* 32 (4): 525–52.

Katz, B. 1999. What a PEO can do for you. *Journal of Accountancy* 188 (1): 57–61.

Katz, L. F., and A. B. Krueger. 1999. The high-pressure U.S. labor market of the 1990s. *Brookings Papers on Economic Activity,* 1999 (1): 1–87.

Klass, B. S., T. W. Gainey, J. A. McClendon, and H. Yang. 2005. Professional employer organizations and their impact on client satisfaction with human resource outcomes: A field study of human resource outsourcing in small and medium enterprises. *Journal of Management* 31 (2): 234–54.

Krueger, A. B. 1993. How computers have changed the wage structure: Evidence from microdata, 1984–1989. *Quarterly Journal of Economics* 108 (1): 33–60.

Kurz, C., and P. Lengermann. 2008. Outsourcing and U.S. economic growth: The role of imported intermediated inputs. Paper presented at the 2008 World Congress on National Accounts and Economic Performance Measures for the Nations. Arlington, VA, May 12-17.

Lautsch, B. A. 2002. Uncovering and explaining variance in the features and outcomes of contingent work. *Industrial and Labor Relations Review* 56 (1): 23–43.

Lee, D. R. 1996. Why is flexible employment increasing? *Journal of Labor Research* 17 (4): 543–53.

Lenz, E. A. 1996. Flexible employment: Positive work strategies for the 21st century. *Journal of Labor Research* 17 (4): 663–81.

Masters, J. K., and G. Miles. 2002. Predicting the use of external labor arrangements: A test of the transaction costs perspective. *Academy of Management Journal* 45 (2): 431–42.

Mehta, C., and N. Theodore. 2001. *The temporary staffing industry and U.S. labor markets: Implications for the unemployment insurance system.* Center for Urban Economic Development, University of Illinois at Chicago.

Mehta, C., S. Braum, N. Theodore, and L. Bush. 2003. Workplace safety in Atlanta's construction industry: Institutional failure in temporary staffing arrangements. Paper presented at America's Workforce Network Research Conference. Washington, DC, June 25-26.

Ono, Y., and D. Sullivan. 2006. *Manufacturing plants' use of temporary workers: An analysis using Census micro data.* WP 2006-24. Chicago: Federal Reserve Bank of Chicago.

Polivka, A. E. 1996a. *Are temporary help agency workers substitutes for direct hire temps? Searching for an alternative explanation for the growth of the temporary help industry.* Washington, DC: U.S. Department of Labor, Bureau of Labor Statistics.

———. 1996b. Contingent and alternative work arrangements, defined. *Monthly Labor Review* 119 (10): 3–9.

Segal, L. 1996. Flexible employment: Composition, and trends. *Journal of Labor Research* 17 (4): 527–42.

Segal, L. M., and D. G. Sullivan. 1995. The temporary work force. *Economic Perspectives, A Review from the Federal Reserve Bank of Chicago* 19 (2): 2–19.

———. 1997. The growth of temporary service work. *Journal of Economic Perspectives* 11 (2): 117–36.

Theodore, N., and J. Peck. 2002. The temporary staffing industry: Growth imperatives and limits to contingency. *Economic Geography* 78 (4): 463–93.

Topel, R. H. 1982. Inventories, layoffs, and the short-run demand for labor. *American Economic Review* 72 (4): 769–87.

U.S. Bureau of Labor Statistics (BLS). 1988. *Industry wage survey: Temporary help supply 1987.* Bulletin 2313. Washington, DC: BLS.

Yuskavage, R. E., E. H. Strassner, and G. W. Medeiros. 2008. Outsourcing and imported inputs in the U.S. economy: Insights from integrated economic accounts. Paper presented at the 2008 World Congress on National Accounts and Economic Performance Measures for the Nations. Arlington, VA, May 12-17.

Comment   Daniel G. Sullivan

Dey, Houseman, and Polivka have brought together in one place virtually all that is known about the overall extent of and trend in contracting out work in the United States. They did this in admirable fashion by carefully combining and comparing numerous data sources. However, despite their careful and creative work, we are left with rather incomplete knowledge of this important phenomenon. Currently available data collection programs simply are not well designed for studying the general phenomenon of contracting out. Moreover, even when significant data collection efforts have been devoted to studying portions of the contracting out phenomenon, as with employment by temporary help agencies, alternative data sources yield very different results. Clearly, the statistical agencies have a great deal more work to do if we are to adequately understand the collection of employment practices known as contracting out.

There are two categories of reasons to be interested in the work presented by the authors. The first category relates to its implications for the function-

Daniel G. Sullivan is executive vice president and director of research at the Federal Reserve Bank of Chicago.

ing of labor markets and public policy. When a firm decides to contract out tasks it might have done in-house, the relationship between worker and firm often changes in ways that are worth understanding. In some cases, such as with the use of temporary help services employment, greater reliance on contracting out likely increases labor market flexibility, as these intermediary firms appear able to efficiently match unemployed or underemployed workers to firms that have at least a short-term need for additional help. Such increased flexibility might even allow lower equilibrium levels of unemployment, though perhaps at the cost of a general reduction in the level of job security. The increased prevalence of contracting out in general and temporary work specifically may also have public policy implications in the area of unemployment insurance, health insurance, and pensions, where institutions have evolved in ways that often assume a standard, long-term employment relationship. Finally, it is of interest to know whether contracting out is driven primarily by firms' desire to minimize inherent transaction costs, as might be expected on the basis of the work of Coase, Williamson, and others on vertical integration, or is instead a strategy to avoid taxes or regulation. As an example of the latter motivation, note that in order to obtain the tax benefits of paying workers in the form of benefits rather than cash wages, firms need to make benefit plans available to all their workers. If the optimal mix of wages and benefits differs across categories of workers, firms have incentives to create artificial divisions between those workers, perhaps by using contract help to fill roles for which the firm would not want to pay generous benefits. In order to evaluate such policy questions, we need good data on the extent and variation in contracting out.

The second class of reasons to be interested in the authors' work relates to its implications for the study of the industrial breakdown of employment and productivity. If, for example, we want to know how productivity levels and trends differ between manufacturing and other sectors, we need to match the output of each industry to the hours of work that were used to produce it. Firms' contracting out can make this more difficult. In particular, if contracting out reduces the recorded number of hours worked in an industry, but not the level of measured output, a false increase in productivity will be recorded for that industry. To properly adjust the labor input in the calculation of productivity, one needs good data on the extent of contracting out. Alternatively, one could rely on value-added measures of output, but this requires an accurate input-output table to convert nominal value added into real quantities. Either way, good information on the extent of contracting out is needed to properly measure sector-level productivity.

The authors contribute to our understanding of contracting out in several ways. They start by constructing data series on occupation by industry employment over the period from 1989 to 2004. The primary source for these new data series is the underutilized data from the Occupational Employment Statistics (OES) program, which the authors use to estimate the share of workers in eighteen broad occupations for each of sixteen industry groups. The occupational employment counts are controlled to industry employment totals derived from the Current Employment Statistics (CES) program, which are in turn benchmarked to population estimates from the Quarterly Census of Employment and Wages (QCEW). As the authors are careful to note, annual estimates of the occupational shares are based on data pooled across multiple years, so fine, year-to-year changes need to be treated with some caution. However, this new data source should be quite useful for assessing broad changes over longer periods.

The form of contracting out best tracked in official data is that which takes place through the intermediary firms of the Employment Services industry. Indeed, the number of workers employed through such arrangements can be tracked in four different ways—through the CES, the Current Population Survey (CPS), and for some years, the Contingent Worker Survey (CWS) and the Economic Census (EC). Unfortunately, as the authors show, the estimates derived from these sources differ very significantly. The biggest discrepancies appear to relate to whether the ultimate data source is workers or firms. For instance, in 2001, slightly less than 1.0 percent of the workers in the CPS reported being employed in Employment Services, while the CES figure based on firm reports was over 2.5 percent.[1] It seems likely that many workers in the CPS answer the question about industry referring to the client firm where they do their work, as opposed to the firm that pays them. The CWS was specifically designed to address that problem by asking, for example, whether workers were employed by a temporary help firm. The more specific question does appear to raise the count of workers responding that they work for a temp firm. The CWS estimate of the share of employment in the temporary help supply component of Employment Services is about 1.0 percent, but that is still much less than the CES estimate, which is about 1.8 percent. Moreover, over the 1995 to 2005 period, the worker-based CWS estimates fell slightly, while those from the firm-based CES rose by 0.4 percentage points. To add yet more uncertainty, the firm-based estimates from the Economic Census turn out to be even higher than those from the CES. For instance, in 2002 EC estimates for temporary help supply were 12 percent higher than CES estimates. Given the difficulty workers are likely to have answering the industry question, it seems very likely that the firm-based estimates are closer to the truth than the worker-based estimates, but it is hard to know how to judge the relative accuracy of the CES and EC data.

The authors also provide a good deal of new information on the Professional Employer Organization (PEO) industry. One might argue that this industry is of less inherent interest than the temporary help industry because in many cases PEO firms play little role in the recruitment of workers. Instead, they often simply take over an existing payroll and act essentially like a pay-

1. Such a discrepancy was noted in Segal and Sullivan (1995).

roll processing firm. However, the existence of PEO firms can still have a nontrivial effect on measured industry employment distributions, an effect that needs to be understood in order for one to properly evaluate trends in sectoral employment. As the authors show, this is currently not possible. First, as the authors clarify, practice varies across states as to whether PEO employees are counted in the totals of Employment Services or the client firm's industry. Moreover, comparing state-level CES and EC data, even states that claim to reassign workers to client-firm industries appear to do so incompletely. Second, we have only sketchy information about the actual industrial work setting of workers whose employer of record is a PEO.

Another significant contribution of the chapter is simply explaining how the Bureau of Economic Analysis (BEA) estimates the portion of its input-output tables covering the purchase of temporary help services, information that is not easy to find in the BEA's standard documentation. As the authors note, input-output information is potentially valuable in gauging the growth of contracting out. However, as they also explain, given the BEA's actual estimation methods, such data should be treated with extreme caution. The relevant portions of the input-output tables are estimated from only a subset of purchasing industries, several dissimilar categories of contract work are pooled together, and the published estimates rely on strong assumptions about the constancy of certain ratios.

In the final portion of their chapter, the authors use their newly constructed occupation by industry time series to study contracting out for six select occupations identified in the CWS as frequently contracted out. Their method relies on being able to identify an industry for which almost all of the employment in the occupation being studied is likely to have been contracted out from another industry. For example, employment of school bus drivers in the trade and transportation sector almost certainly reflects contracting out by school districts. This is essentially an occupation-specific version of examining trends in temporary help, for which almost all workers of all occupations are actually doing their work for client firms in other industries. As the authors note, it is possible that this methodology could conflate changes in industrial mix with actual changes in the prevalence of contracting out. However, it seems quite likely that their findings of trends toward increased employment shares of bus drivers, truck drivers, computer occupations, and janitors in the relevant industries reflect actual increases in contracting out. This is significant because these trends are not reflected in standard tabulations of the CWS.

Given the obvious shortcomings of current data collection on contracting out, it is not hard for the authors to identify possible improvements. In some cases, simply documenting current methodologies would be a significant step forward. In addition, reassigning all PEO workers to their client-firm industries in the CES and QCEW would significantly clarify the industrial distribution of employment. Improving the data underlying the relevant portions of the input-output data by surveying all using industries and examining a finer breakdown of supplying industries would also be a big improvement that would make the data of much greater use to the study of contracting out. However, I think the authors are correct in arguing that to make really substantial progress in understanding contracting out, the statistical agencies would need to field some special surveys of firms' practices. It would be highly valuable to survey firms on their practices in contracting out specific kinds of work and, in addition, to survey firms in industries such as Employment Services on the nature of their client firms. Combining the data from such surveys would allow us to develop a more complete understanding of the contracting out phenomenon.

References

Segal, L. M., and D. G. Sullivan. 1995. The temporary work force. *Economic Perspectives, A Review from the Federal Reserve Bank of Chicago* 19 (2): 2–19.

8

Measuring Tradable Services and the Task Content of Offshorable Services Jobs

J. Bradford Jensen and Lori G. Kletzer

8.1 Introduction

The services offshoring debate reached headline status several years ago, fueled in large part by the 2004 presidential campaign and the slow recovery of the labor market from the 2001 downturn. Services offshoring refers to the (potential) migration of jobs (but not the people performing them) across national borders, mostly from rich countries to poor ones, with imported products and activities flowing back to the United States. The literature on services offshoring remains in its infancy, although the number of contributions is expanding rapidly. A nonexhaustive list of recent contributions includes: Amiti and Wei (2004); Arora and Gambardella (2004); Bardhan and Kroll (2003); Bhagwati, Panagariya, and Srinivasan (2004); Blinder (2006, 2007); Brainard and Litan (2004); Bronfenbrenner and Luce (2004); Jensen and Kletzer (2006); Kirkegaard (2004); Mankiw and Swagel (2006); Samuelson (2004); and Schultze (2004). Despite the attention, relatively little is known about how many jobs may be at risk of relocation or how much job loss is associated with these business decisions.

J. Bradford Jensen is associate professor of international business and economics at the McDonough School of Business at Georgetown University, a senior fellow at the Peterson Institute for International Economics, and a research associate of the National Bureau of Economic Research. Lori G. Kletzer is professor of economics at the University of California, Santa Cruz, and a nonresident senior fellow of the Peterson Institute for International Economics.

Lauren Malone provided excellent research assistance. Financial support was provided by the Labor and Employment Research Fund in the University of California Office of the President, the Alfred P. Sloan Foundation, the John D. and Katherine T. MacArthur Foundation, the National Science Foundation, and the Committee on Research, Academic Senate, UC Santa Cruz. We appreciate comments provided by Susan Collins, Katharine Abraham, James Spletzer, and Mike Harper. Detailed tables are available from the corresponding author, Kletzer, at lkletzer@ucsc.edu.

There are a few prominent projections. An early estimate of the likely scale of future job losses due to movement of jobs offshore is Forrester Research's "3.3 Million U.S. Services Jobs To Go Offshore" (McCarthy 2002).[1] Other estimates include: Deloitte Research estimates that by 2008 the world's largest financial service companies will have relocated up to two million jobs to low-cost offshore countries; Gartner Research predicts that by the end of 2004 10 percent of information technology (IT) jobs at U.S. IT companies and 5 percent of IT jobs at non-IT companies will have moved offshore; another Gartner Research survey revealed that three hundred of the Fortune 500 companies today do business with Indian IT services companies. Goldman Sachs estimates 300,000 to 400,000 services jobs have moved offshore in the past three years, and anticipates a monthly rate of 15,000 to 30,000 jobs, in manufacturing and services combined, to be subject to offshoring in the future. Bardhan and Kroll (2003) put out an estimate of fourteen million jobs potentially at risk.

In an earlier paper (Jensen and Kletzer 2006), we advanced a new empirical approach to identify, at a detailed level, service activities that are potentially exposed to international trade. The approach uses the geographic concentration of service activities within the United States to identify which service activities are traded domestically, and then classifies activities that are traded domestically as *potentially* tradable internationally. With the tradability classification, we developed estimates of the number of workers who are in tradable activities for all sectors of the economy. The paper offered comparisons of the demographic characteristics of workers in tradable and nontradable activities and employment growth in traded and nontraded service activities. The tradability designation also allowed an examination of the risk of job loss and other employment outcomes for workers in tradable activities.

While we believe we made an important contribution to identifying tradable activities using the notion of geographic concentration, we recognize the measure is not perfect. We note here several potential problems with the geographic concentration methodology. The first potential problem is that if something is tradable but not in an increasing returns activity, it might not be geographically concentrated. A second potential issue is that an activity might be geographically concentrated and occur predominantly in large cities, due to the specialization that is possible in a large (thick) market. These activities, such as acupuncturists and manicurists, are concentrated, but not tradable. A third issue arises for a set of activities that are often associated with hospitality industries, such as gaming supervisors, bellhops, and limousine drivers, where the activity is concentrated, location in a city that serves markets beyond the locality, and is tradable in the sense of foreigners accounting for a share of demand. Yet in this case these activities are not likely to be offshored because the nature

---

1. The Forrester projection was updated in 2004 to 3.4 million.

of the activity (say, legalized gambling in Atlantic City) is defined by the location itself.

This chapter offers an alternative method of understanding tradability, based on an analysis of the task and activity content of jobs. The literature on offshoring notes that movable jobs are those with little face-to-face customer contact, high information content, and the work process is Internet enabled and/or telecommutable (see Bardhan and Kroll 2003; Dossani and Kenney 2003; Blinder 2006). More informally, it is commonly believed that if "it can be sent down a wire (or wireless)," it is offshorable. Empirically, this investigation tries to bring these basic principles of the characteristics of potentially offshorable jobs to detailed microdata on occupations. The task content investigation offers us a second and independent measure of potential tradability, to be used to refine the understanding obtained from our geographical concentration measure. More specifically, we can ask if the jobs identified as potentially internationally tradable, using geographic concentration, involve task or job activities and characteristics that fit current notions of offshorability.

This chapter begins with a summary of the methodology and findings in Jensen and Kletzer (2006). The next step involves an operational assessment of how the basic principles of offshorability (high information content, remote from customer, Internet enabled) match up to the characteristics of "real" jobs. Detailed information on the content and context of jobs (occupations) is available from the Occupational Information Network (O*Net), a U.S. Department of Labor database of 450 occupations.[2] For each of hundreds of occupations, O*Net contains detailed qualitative information on job tasks, work activities (interacting with computers, processing information), and work context (face-to-face discussions, work with others, work outdoors). We develop an index to assess occupations based on important characteristics associated with offshorability, using the information available from the publicly available and downloadable O*Net production data set (version 11).

Briefly summarizing the results, based on job task content the occupational groups with large shares of employment in the highest potentially tradable group include: Business and Financial Operations (74.7 percent of employment); Computer and Mathematical Occupations (93.4 percent); Architecture and Engineering (80.8 percent); Life, Physical, and Social Sciences (75.9 percent); and Office/administrative support (64.3 percent). The notable nontradable occupational groups, with large shares of employment identified as least potentially tradable include: Education and Library (43.7 percent); Healthcare Practitioners (78 percent); Healthcare Support (94.4 percent); and Food Preparation (100 percent). Overall for the service occupations, 27.4 percent of May 2005 employment was in the most potentially tradable group, while 43.8 percent of employment was in occupations

---

2. The O*Net is the successor to the well-known Dictionary of Occupational Titles.

rated as least potentially tradable. There is a considerable overlap between the job task content measure of potential tradable and our geographic concentration measure. We also find a positive correlation between skill (measured as educational attainment) and potential tradability—occupations with a greater share of workers with a college degree are more highly ranked as offshorable/tradable. Similarly, the more highly ranked occupations, in regard to tradability, have higher average annual earnings than do the lowest-ranked occupations.

8.2   Geographical Concentration and Tradability: Empirical Approach

To develop a measure of tradable services, our earlier empirical approach relied on the basic economic intuition that nontraded services will not exhibit geographic concentration in production. Goods that are traded tend to be geographically concentrated (to capitalize on increasing returns to scale, access to inputs like natural resources, etc.), while goods that are not traded tend to be more ubiquitously distributed. We applied this same intuition to service production. With the identification of industries and occupations that appear to be traded within the United States, the inference is that service activities that can be traded within the United States are also potentially traded internationally.

The intuition is described in Krugman (1991, 65), where he notes:

> In the late twentieth century the great bulk of our labor force makes services rather than goods. Many of these services are nontradable and simply follow the geographical distribution of the goods-producing population—fast-food outlets, day-care providers, divorce lawyers surely have locational Ginis pretty close to zero. Some services, however, especially in the financial sector, can be traded. Hartford is an insurance city; Chicago the center of futures trading; Los Angeles the entertainment capital; and so on . . . The most spectacular examples of localization in today's world are, in fact, services rather than manufacturing. . . . Transportation of goods has not gotten much cheaper in the past eighty years . . . But the ability to transmit *information* has grown spectacularly, with telecommunications, computers, fiber optics, etc.

The idea is that when something is traded, the production of the activity is concentrated in a particular region to take advantage of some economies in production. As a result, not all regions will support local production of the good and some regions will devote a disproportionate share of productive activity to a good and then trade it.

8.2.1   Measuring Geographical Concentration

Measures of geographic concentration are a way to implement the intuition described by Krugman. Most measures of concentration use the region's share of employment in an industry relative to the region's share of total employment. One issue with measures of concentration for our purposes is that they do not differentiate between the reasons activity is concentrated. In general, the reason for the concentration does not matter to us except for one instance. If a service is nontradable and demand for the service is concentrated (industries that use the nontraded service are geographically concentrated), the service industry will be geographically concentrated and we will infer that the service is tradable. To incorporate this case, we extend the intuition from the framework. If a nontradable industry provides intermediate inputs to a downstream industry, we would expect the geographical distribution of the nontraded intermediate industry to follow the distribution of the downstream industry. Instead of being distributed with income, the nontraded good is distributed in proportion to the demand for that industry.[3]

We focus here on a modified Gini coefficient of geographic concentration.[4] To build intuition, we start with industry:

$$G = |1 - \sum_i (\sigma Y_{i-1} + \sigma Y_i) * (\sigma IDS_{i-1} - \sigma IDS_i)|,$$

where i is an index for regions (sorted by the region's share of industry employment), σY_i is the cumulative share of industry or occupation employment in region i, σY_{i-1} is the cumulative share of industry or occupation employment in the region $(i - 1)$ with the next lowest share of industry employment, and IDS_i is the region's share of demand for industry i.

8.2.2 Implementation

These measures were implemented using employment information from the 2000 Decennial Census of Population Public Use Micro Sample (PUMS) files. The geographic entity is the Consolidated Metropolitan Statistical Area or the Metropolitan Statistical Area where an individual reports working.[5] The use of worker-level data to investigate economic concentration is somewhat unusual. One advantage of this strategy is that it allows consideration of both industrial concentration and *occupational* concentration. The ability to identify both industries and occupations that are tradable is an important feature of the empirical strategy because many of the service activities that are reportedly being globally sourced

3. To address this issue, we modify the general measures of geographic concentration by developing an industry-region specific measure of the concentration of demand for an industry. We construct a downstream industry-weighted average demand for each industry-region using the input-output tables. More details on the construction of the weights are provided in Jensen and Kletzer (2006). The adjustment takes account of the concentration of downstream industry concentration and adjusts the "denominator" in the concentration measures accordingly.

4. Readers interested in the full discussion are directed to our 2006 paper.

5. For regions, we use the Place of Work Consolidated Metropolitan Area (POWCMA5) field on the Decennial PUMS. When POWCMA is coded as a nonmetropolitan area or a mixed metro/nonmetro area, we concatenate the Place of Work state code with the POWCMA5 code. For more information on the 5 percent sample PUMS, see: http://www.census.gov/Press-Release/www/2003/PUMS5.html.

are tasks within the service "production" process (for example, the banking relationship is not relocated offshore; rather, the customer service/call center component is moved); thus, occupations correspond more closely to these types of activities than do industries. In addition, occupations have job task content and activities, while industries (often similar to products) do not.

8.3   Classifying Industries and Occupations as Tradable vs. Nontradable

8.3.1   Industries

In our 2006 paper we discussed extensively how to determine a tradable versus nontradable distinction for industries and occupations. Given the large number of detailed industries and occupations, some grouping is in order, to make sense of the estimates. Starting with industry, where intuition tends to be stronger, we initially placed industries into three roughly equal groups: Gini class 1 (least geographically concentrated) when the industry Gini was less than .1; Gini class 2 when the industry Gini was between .1 and .3; Gini class 3 (most geographically concentrated) when the Gini coefficient was greater than or equal to .3. Approximately 36 percent of industries are in Gini class 1, about 37 percent are in Gini class 2, and 27 percent are in Gini class 3.

Figure 8.1 plots the Gini coefficients for all industries by two-digit North American Industry Classification System (NAICS) code. The pattern is generally consistent with our priors that tradable industries will be geographically concentrated. For example, industries in the goods-producing sectors of Agriculture, Mining, and Manufacturing are typically in the top two Gini classes. Only five of the ninety-two industries in these sectors are in Gini class 1: Cement and Concrete, Machine Shops, Miscellaneous Manufacturing n.e.c. (not elsewhere classified), Structural Metals and Tanks, and Printing and Related Activities. All of these industries seem to be either nontraded because of a high weight to value ratio (e.g., Cement and Concrete), or they are categories that include a range of potentially dissimilar activities (Miscellaneous manufacturing n.e.c.) that make them appear to be broadly geographically distributed. Most agriculture, mining, and manufacturing products are considered tradable; so as a first-order approximation, classifying the lowest geographical concentration category (Gini class 1) as nontradable seems appropriate for these sectors.[6] Using a Gini coefficient of .1 as the threshold for tradable seems to make sense in other sectors as well. Industries in the retail trade sector are primarily classified as nontradable. Industries in the Transportation sector are mostly classified as tradable. For Public Administration, most activities are nontradable

---

6. There is a positive correlation between Gini class and mean trade share.

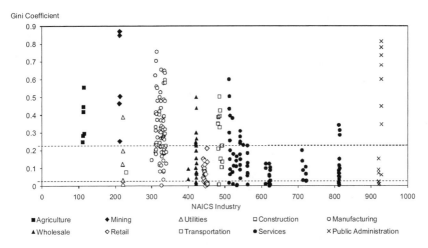

Fig. 8.1   Geographic concentration of industries

except for Public Finance and the military. For the Service sector, industries are balanced between nontradable and tradable. Table 8.1 provides a complete list of service industries by two-digit NAICS sector and the industry's Gini class.

8.3.2   Occupation Results

We constructed a similar demand-weighted Gini coefficient for each occupation, using the same Gini = .1 threshold for the nontradable/tradable categorization. Table 8.2 shows the share of employment by Major Standard Occupational Classification group by Gini class. The groupings largely are consistent with our priors. The occupational groups with large shares of employment classified as tradable include: Business and Financial Operations (68 percent); Computer and Mathematical Occupations (100 percent); Architecture and Engineering (63 percent); Legal (96 percent); and Life, Physical, and Social Sciences (83 percent). The notable nontradable occupational groups include: Education and Library (99 percent nontradable); Healthcare Practitioners (86 percent); Healthcare Support (97 percent); and Food Preparation (96 percent). On the goods production side, 90 percent of employment in Installation, Maintenance, and Repair is classified as nontradable, as is 80 percent of Production[7] and 89 percent of Transportation and Material Moving.[8]

---

7. The geographic concentration results are at first counterintuitive for production occupations given the manufacturing industry results. Production occupations are typically not industry-specific but instead functional activities and are thus distributed more broadly.

8. The inclusion of military-specific occupations (and industries) as geographically concentrated is not likely to be associated with offshorability (although perhaps tradability). The national security components of these occupations likely weigh against offshorability.

Table 8.1　　　　**Service industries, Gini coefficient class**

2-digit NAICS	Industry description	Gini coefficient class
	Information	
51	Newspaper publishers	1
51	Radio and television broadcasting and cable	1
51	Libraries and archives	1
51	Wired telecommunications carriers	2
51	Data processing services	2
51	Other telecommunication services	2
51	Publishing except newspapers and software	2
51	Other information services	3
51	Motion pictures and video industries	3
51	Sound recording industries	3
51	Software publishing	3
	Finance and insurance	
52	Savings institutions, including credit unions	1
52	Banking and related activities	1
52	Insurance carriers and related activities	2
52	Nondepository credit and related activities	2
52	Securities, commodities, funds, trusts, and other financial investments	3
	Real estate and rental	
53	Video tape and disk rental	1
53	Other consumer goods rental	1
53	Commercial, industrial, and other intangible assets rental and leasing	2
53	Real estate	2
53	Automotive equipment rental and leasing	2
	Professional, scientific, and technical services	
54	Veterinary services	1
54	Accounting, tax preparation, bookkeeping, and payroll services	1
54	Architectural, engineering, and related services	2
54	Other professional, scientific and technical services	2
54	Legal services	2
54	Specialized design services	2
54	Computer systems design and related services	2
54	Advertising and related services	2
54	Management, scientific and technical consulting services	2
54	Scientific research and development services	3
	Management	
55	Management of companies and enterprises	2
	Administrative support	
56	Waste management and remediation services	1
56	Business support services	1
56	Services to buildings and dwellings	1
56	Landscaping services	1
56	Employment services	2
56	Other administrative and other support services	2
56	Investigation and security services	2
56	Travel arrangement and reservation services	2

Table 8.1　　　　(continued)

2-digit NAICS	Industry description	Gini coefficient class
	Education	
61	Elementary and secondary schools	1
61	Colleges and universities, including junior colleges	1
61	Other schools, instruction, and educational services	1
61	Business, technical, and trade schools and training	2
	Health care and social services	
62	Hospitals	1
62	Nursing care facilities	1
62	Vocational rehabilitation services	1
62	Offices of physicians	1
62	Outpatient care centers	1
62	Offices of dentists	1
62	Offices of optometrists	1
62	Residential care facilities, without nursing	1
62	Child day care services	1
62	Home health care services	1
62	Other health care services	1
62	Office of chiropractors	1
62	Individual and family services	1
62	Community food and housing, and emergency services	2
62	Offices of other health practitioners	2
	Arts, entertainment, and recreation	
71	Bowling centers	1
71	Other amusement, gambling, and recreation industries	1
71	Museums, art galleries, historical sites, and similar institutions	2
71	Independent artists, performing arts, spectator sports, and related	2
	Accommodation	
72	Drinking places, alcoholic beverages	1
72	Restaurants and other food services	1
72	Recreational vehicle parks and camps, and rooming and boarding houses	1
72	Traveler accommodation	2
	Other services	
81	Beauty salons	1
81	Funeral homes, cemeteries, and crematories	1
81	Personal and household goods repair and maintenance	1
81	Automotive repair and maintenance	1
81	Barber shops	1
81	Religious organizations	1
81	Commercial and industrial machinery and equipment repair and maintenance	1
81	Drycleaning and laundry services	1
81	Car washes	1
81	Electronic and precision equipment repair and maintenance	1
81	Civic, social, advocacy organizations, and grantmaking and giving	1
81	Nail salons and other personal care services	2
81	Other personal services	2
81	Business, professional, political, and similar organizations	2

(continued)

Table 8.1   (continued)

2-digit NAICS	Industry description	Gini coefficient class
81	Labor unions	3
81	Footwear and leather goods repair	3
	Public administration	
92	Justice, public order, and safety activities	1
92	Administration of human resource programs	1
92	Other general government and support	1
92	Executive offices and legislative bodies	1
92	Military Reserves or National Guard	1
92	Administration of economic programs and space research	1
92	Administration of environmental quality and housing programs	1
92	Public finance activities	2
92	National security and international affairs	3
92	U.S. Armed Forces, branch not specified	3
92	U.S. Coast Guard	3
92	U.S. Air Force	3
92	U.S. Army	3
92	U.S. Navy	3
92	U.S. Marines	3

Geographic concentration is a notion that may be more suited to industry analysis than to occupation. From our reading of the offshoring literature, we note the informal discussion of job and task characteristics. We turn now to an implementation of these ideas.

8.4   Measuring Task Content of Potentially Tradable Services Occupations

The literature on offshoring posits that movable jobs are those with little face-to-face customer contact, high information content, and the work process is Internet enabled and/or telecommutable.[9] A great deal of attention is paid to Internet enabled, as the expansion of broadband and wireless (and the broad use of off the shelf software programs) having greatly reduced the transportation costs of information. Having developed a set of tradable services occupations, the next step is to consider the detailed characteristics of these jobs and whether the characteristics fit a description of offshorability. Based on these offshorability characteristics, van Welsum and Vickery (2005a, 2005b) perform a similar exercise for a selection of Organization for Economic Cooperation and Development (OECD) countries. Their methodology is based on subjec-

---

9. See Bardhan and Kroll (2003) for a list of attributes.

Table 8.2   **Share of occupation employment by Gini class coefficient, by major occupation category**

SOC	Description	Gini class 1	Gini class 2	Gini class 3
11	Management	34.48	61.15	4.37
13	Business/Financial Operations	31.73	65.96	2.32
15	Computer/Mathematical	0	73.07	26.93
17	Architecture/Engineering	36.04	58.31	5.65
19	Life, Physical, Social Sci.	16.32	58.61	25.08
21	Community/Social Svs.	100.00	0	0
23	Legal	3.78	96.22	0
25	Education and Library	99.54	0.46	0
27	Arts, Design, Entertain.	17.13	75.02	7.85
29	Healthcare Prac./Tech.	86.56	13.10	0.34
31	Healthcare Support	96.73	3.27	0
33	Protective Service	59.83	40.17	0
35	Food Prep./Serving	95.68	4.32	0
37	Building Maintenance	98.54	1.46	0
39	Personal Care Service	82.64	7.22	10.13
41	Sales and Related	75.41	21.82	2.77
43	Office/Admin. Support	93.14	6.66	0.20
45	Farm, Fish, Forestry	0	81.01	18.99
47	Construction/Extraction	61.37	36.18	2.45
49	Install., Maint., Repair	90.00	8.89	1.11
51	Production	80.30	17.15	2.55
53	Transport./Material Moving	89.20	5.86	4.95
55	Military Specific	0	0	100.00
	All occupations	71.66	24.86	3.47

tive judgments of the task content of jobs, not data on work activities or content.

The use here of Occupational Information Network (O*Net) is in the spirit of Autor, Levy, and Murnane (2003), who explored the spread of computerization using the Dictionary of Occupational Titles (DOT) to measure the routine versus nonroutine, and cognitive versus noncognitive aspects of occupations. The O*Net was developed by the U.S. Department of Labor as a replacement for the DOT.[10] Similar in theme to the DOT as a source of occupational information, O*Net reflects the expanded possibilities of contemporary information technology in that it is a database with information on job characteristics and worker attributes. Unlike the vast job-specific detail provided on 12,000+ occupations in the DOT, O*Net provides information on 1,100+ occupations, using language and assessment common across jobs. Unlike DOT, where professional analysts were the primary source of information, job incumbents provide the information, gathered by survey questionnaire. Occupations are organized at the

10. See Peterson and Mumford et al. (1999) for a history of the development of O*Net.

Standard Occupational Classification level. The O*Net is used in a variety of fields studying work and occupations, such as organizational behavior, applied psychology, career assessment, human resource management, and occupational psychology.[11] The O*Net is relatively foreign to research in economics. Blinder (2007) takes an approach similar in spirit to our discussion here.

The O*Net Content model identifies the most important types of information about work, jobs, and workers, and integrates the information into a structured system of six major categories:[12]

- Worker Characteristics (Abilities; Occupational Interests; Work Values; Work Styles)
- Worker Requirements (Skills and Knowledge; Education)
- Experience Requirements (Experience and Training; Skills and Entry Requirements; Licensing)
- Occupational Requirements (Generalized and Detailed Work Activities; Organizational Context; Work Context)
- Labor Market Characteristics (Labor Market Information; Occupational Outlook)
- Occupation-Specific Information (Tasks; Tools and Technology)

The first three categories (Worker Characteristics, Worker Requirements, Experience Requirements) are worker-oriented. The second three are work- (or job-) oriented categories, with Occupational Requirements as the focus of interest here. Occupational requirements are meant to identify requisite tasks, and are designed to cross occupations, at both a general and detailed level, while Occupation-Specific Information is meant to be quite detailed and literally occupation-specific.

The domain/category Occupational Requirements is designed to provide ". . . a comprehensive set of variables or detailed elements that describe what various occupations require" (National Center for O*Net Development 2006, 20). The focus is on typical activities required across occupations. Within the Generalized and Detailed Work Activities subdomain, we selected eleven measures to construct an index of offshorability/potential tradability.

On information content:

Getting information (+)
Processing information (+)
Analyzing Data or Information (+)
Documenting/Recording Information (+)

---

11. See http://online.onetcenter.org/ for information on acquiring the data.
12. The idea behind the six content areas is to provide multiple windows on the world of work. Information on the O*Net Context Model comes from the National Center for O*Net Development (2006). For a comprehensive discussion of O*Net from the practical and research perspectives, see Peterson and Mumford et al. (2001).

On Internet enabled:

Interacting with computers (+)

On face-to-face contact:

Assisting or Caring for Others (–)
Performing or Working Directly with the Public (–)
Establishing or Maintaining Interpersonal Relationships (–)

On the routine or creative nature of work:

Making Decisions and Solving Problems (–)
Thinking Creatively (–)

On the on-site nature of work:

Inspecting equipment, structures or material (–)

The sign in parentheses [(+) or (–)] denotes our prior on whether the characteristic is positively related to offshorability or negatively related.

Rating scales are used to quantify these characteristics. Multiple scales are provided, with "importance" and "level" as the predominant pair. "Importance" is the rating of answers to the question: "How important is this skill to performance on the job?" Answers vary from "not important" to "extremely important," on a scale of 1 to 5. "Level" is the rating of "What level of this skill is needed to perform this job?," ranging from low (level) to high (level), on a scale of 1 to 7.[13] An illustration might be useful, normalizing the two different scale ranges from 0 to 100. For the attribute "Performing or Working Directly with the Public," data entry keyers are assigned importance $(I) = 43$, and level $(L) = 33$ (for Security Guards, $I = 74$ and $L = 62$). Compared to data entry keyers, working with the public is more important to performance on the job for security guards, along with a higher level of the skill of working with the public. Tables 8.3, 8.4, and 8.5 provide summary information on importance, level, and the various work activities.

Table 8.3 provides summary statistics across occupations on the eleven work activities and their importance and level. The various attributes that involve working with information via computers have higher scores on importance than the attributes involving working directly with the public or assisting and caring for others. Importance of attributes appears to vary more across occupations than level.

Tables 8.4 and 8.5 describe in more detail some of the work activities for two specific occupations. In table 8.4, mathematical technicians are profiled; in table 8.5 bookkeeping, accounting, and auditing clerks are profiled. For each occupation, the tables list the work activities with the highest shares of

---

13. See Peterson and Mumford et al. (1999, 2001). Level allows a "not relevant to performance" rating, coded as 0.

Table 8.3   **Summary statistics for work activities, across occupations**

Work Activity	Mean	Standard deviation	Min	Max
Getting information				
Importance	0.815	0.097	0.366	1
Level	0.548	0.152	0.118	0.951
Inspecting equipment, structures, or material				
Importance	0.606	0.173	0.2	0.966
Level	0.391	0.158	0	0.855
Processing information				
Importance	0.651	0.156	0.2	1
Level	0.499	0.193	0.028	0.911
Analyzing data or information				
Importance	0.628	0.161	0.2	0.988
Level	0.451	0.194	0	0.951
Making decisions and solving problems				
Importance	0.729	0.144	0.24	0.996
Level	0.547	0.178	0.071	0.94
Thinking creatively				
Importance	0.603	0.183	0.2	0.992
Level	0.474	0.206	0.023	0.951
Interacting w/ computers				
Importance	0.604	0.243	0.2	1
Level	0.353	0.2	0	0.875
Documenting / recording information				
Importance	0.653	0.178	0.2	0.984
Level	0.436	0.179	0	0.8
Establishing and maintaining interpersonal relationships				
Importance	0.683	0.167	0.2	0.976
Level	0.583	0.177	0.028	0.897
Assisting and caring for others				
Importance	0.528	0.182	0.2	1
Level	0.378	0.192	0	0.961
Performing for or working directly w/ public				
Importance	0.56	0.221	0.2	0.984
Level	0.405	0.232	0	0.924

Source: Authors' calculations using O*Net data.

importance. It is notable that for both occupations, interacting with computers and various aspects of processing information are the highest (most important) work activities.

Our composite index of offshorability is the weighted sum of the eleven components, using our priors on the sign of the attribute in regard to offshoring potential. In constructing an index, it is not obvious how to weight importance and level. Starting from the observation that importance varies more than level across occupations, an index was created using a weight of three-quarters to importance and one-quarter to level. Higher values of the index indicate more offshorability potential, yielding a ranking

Table 8.4   Work activities, 15-2091.00—mathematical technicians

Importance	Work activity	Work activity description	Detailed work activity
100	Processing information	Compiling, coding, categorizing, calculating, tabulating, auditing, or verifying information or data.	Compile numerical or statistical data; develop tables depicting data
92	Analyzing data or information	Identifying the underlying principles, reasons, or facts of information by breaking down information or data into separate parts.	Analyze scientific research data or investigative findings
92	Getting information	Observing, receiving, and otherwise obtaining information from all relevant sources.	Collect scientific or technical data
88	Identifying objects, actions, and events	Identifying information by categorizing, estimating, recognizing differences or similarities, and detecting changes in circumstances or events.	
88	Interacting with computers	Using computers and computer systems (including hardware and software) to program, write software, set up functions, enter data, or process information.	Develop or maintain databases; use computers to enter, access, or retrieve data; use relational database or spreadsheet software
75	Making decisions and solving problems	Analyzing information and evaluating results to choose the best solution and solve problems.	Resolve engineering or science problems
75	Updating and using relevant knowledge	Keeping up-to-date technically and applying new knowledge to your job.	Use interpersonal communication techniques; use knowledge of investigational techniques; quantitative research methods
67	Communicating with supervisors, peers, or subordinates	Providing information to supervisors, co-workers, and subordinates by telephone, in written form, e-mail, or in person.	
67	Documenting/recording information	Entering, transcribing, recording, storing, or maintaining information in written or electronic/magnetic form.	

Source: National Center for O*Net Development.

Table 8.5   **Work activities, 43-3031.00—Bookkeeping, accounting, and auditing clerks**

Importance	Work activity	Work activity description	Detailed work activity
97	Interacting with computers	Using computers and computer systems (including hardware and software) to program, write software, set up functions, enter data, or process information.	Use accounting or bookkeeping software; use computers to access data; use word processing software
82	Getting information	Observing, receiving, and otherwise obtaining information from all relevant sources.	
80	Processing information	Compiling, coding, categorizing, calculating, tabulating, auditing, or verifying information or data.	Compile data for financial reports; compute financial data; compute taxes; detect discrepancies; maintain balance sheets; prepare bank deposits
74	Establishing and maintaining interpersonal relationships	Developing constructive and cooperative working relationships with others, and maintaining them over time.	
73	Organizing, planning, and prioritizing work	Developing specific goals and plans to prioritize, organize, and accomplish your work.	
65	Communicating with supervisors, peers, or subordinates	Providing information to supervisors, co-workers, and subordinates by telephone, in written form, e-mail, or in person.	
58	Documenting/recording information	Entering, transcribing, recording, storing, or Entering time sheet information; taking messages; maintaining information in written or electronic/magnetic form.	
57	Making decisions and solving problems	Analyzing information and evaluating results to choose the best solution and solve problems.	

Source: National Center for O*Net Development.

of all occupations for which the attributes are available. After discussing results, we take note of some robustness checks.

The usefulness of the index is ordinal, not cardinal. Occupations are judged on their offshorability relative to each other, not compared to some absolute standard. Tables 8.6 and 8.7 report the top thirty and bottom thirty occupations, as ranked for job task content.[14] How good are the results? Occupations at the top of the list seem unsurprising: credit authorizers, data entry keyers, accountants, medical transcriptionists, market research analysts, bookkeeping, and account clerks. One of the columns in the table indicates occupations identified as tradable by geographic concentration, and there is a close match both at the top of the ranking, with most tradable, and at the bottom of the ranking with the least tradable. The O*Net information corrects some obvious misfits of geographic concentration: crossing guards, massage therapists, and manicurists (see table 8.7).

Paralleling our discussion of economic concentration, we explore whether to divide potentially tradable/offshorable from "sticky" and nontradable. Index values span a range of $+1.777$ (Mathematical technicians) to -2.21 (Barbers). Dividing the set of occupations roughly in thirds, we established "Index class 1" (low tradability) as index values less than -0.7, "Index class 2" (medium tradability) as values between -0.7 and zero (0.0), and "Index class 3" (high potential tradability) as values greater than or equal to zero. Each class contains approximately 152 to 154 occupations.

Table 8.8 reports shares of employment (for May 2005), for major (Standard Occupational Classification [SOC] two-digit) occupational groups, across the three index classes. The occupational groups with large shares of employment in the highest potentially tradable group include: Business and Financial Operations (74.7 percent); Computer and Mathematical Occupations (93.4 percent); Architecture and Engineering (80.8 percent); Life, Physical, and Social Sciences (75.9 percent); and Office/administrative support (64.3 percent). The notable nontradable occupational groups, with large shares in index class 1 (least potentially tradable) include: Education and Library (43.7 percent); Healthcare Practitioners (78 percent); Healthcare Support (94.4 percent); and Food Preparation (100 percent). Overall for the service occupations, 27.4 percent of May 2005 employment was in the most potentially tradable group, while 43.8 percent of employment was in occupations rated as least potentially tradable.

With three economic concentration classes and three task content classes, there is a natural question of how well the two measures match up. Overall, where the two measures can be constructed at the same detailed level, 41 percent of occupations match completely (index class 1 matches to Gini class 1; index class 2 matches to Gini class 2, etc.). Looking just at nontradable

---

14. The full listing of 457 service occupations, ranked by job task content, takes up fourteen printed pages, and is available from the corresponding author.

Table 8.6 Most offshorable: Top thirty occupations, ranked by job task content offshorability index

Index ranking	Occupation title	Employment May 2005	Median annual earnings May 2005 (US$)	Percent w/ HS diploma or less	Percent w/ BA or higher	Tradable by geographic concentration	Index value	Index class	SOC code
1	Mathematical Technicians	1,430	36,470			1	1.777	3	152091
2	Biochemists and Biophysicists	17,690	71,000			1	1.510	3	191021
3	Statisticians	17,480	62,450	0.0	100.0	1	1.309	3	152041
4	Title Examiners, Abstractors, and Searchers	64,580	35,120	57.4	2.1		1.304	3	232093
5	Credit Authorizers, Checkers, and Clerks	65,410	29,330	44.1	34.5	0	1.030	3	434041
6	Weighers, Measurers, Checkers, and Samplers, Recordkeeping	79,050	25,310	61.0	0.0	0	1.026	3	435111
7	Data Entry Keyers	296,700	23,810	77.7	0.7	0	1.016	3	439021
8	Accountants and Auditors	1,051,220	52,210	2.0	92.2	1	1.010	3	132011
9	Medical Transcriptionists	90,380	29,080	34.3	0.4	0	0.999	3	319094
10	Actuaries	15,770	81,640	0.0	100.0	1	0.981	3	152011
11	Market Research Analysts	195,710	57,300	0.0	60.5	1	0.928	3	193021
12	Astronomers	970	104,670	0.0	100.0	1	0.923	3	192011
13	Bookkeeping, Accounting, and Auditing Clerks	1,815,340	29,490	21.5	18.0	1	0.915	3	433031

14	Mechanical Drafters	74,650	43,350	0.0	0.0	0	0.909	3	173013
15	Economists	12,470	73,690	0.0	100.0	1	0.905	3	193011
16	Mathematicians	2,930	80,920	0.0	100.0	1	0.905	3	152021
17	Sociologists	3,500	52,760	0.0	100.0	1	0.905	3	193041
18	Operations Research Analysts	52,530	62,180	0.0	100.0	1	0.886	3	152031
19	Survey Researchers	21,650	31,140				0.883	3	193022
20	Credit Analysts	61,500	50,370	29.3	56.8	1	0.881	3	132041
21	Payroll and Timekeeping Clerks	205,600	31,360	42.3	8.4	0	0.873	3	433051
22	Cartographers and Photogrammetrists	11,260	48,250	14.9	29.5	0	0.840	3	171021
23	Statistical Assistants	18,700	28,950	2.2	62.0	0	0.828	3	439111
24	Paralegals and Legal Assistants	217,700	41,170	10.9	29.1	1	0.809	3	232011
25	Geographers	810	63,550	0.0	100.0	1	0.802	3	193092
26	Computer Systems Analysts	492,120	68,300	1.1	64.1	1	0.773	3	151051
27	Financial Examiners	22,160	63,090	2.2	94.9	1	0.755	3	132061
28	Petroleum Engineers	14,860	93,000	0.0	100.0	1	0.753	3	172171
29	Budget Analysts	53,510	58,910	0.0	96.4	1	0.742	3	132031
30	Court Reporters	17,130	41,640	0.8	4.1	1	0.734	3	232091

Table 8.7 Least offshorable: Bottom 30 occupations, ranked by job task content offshorability index

Index ranking	Occupation title	Employment May 2005	Median annual earnings May 2005 (US$)	Percent w/ HS diploma or less	Percent w/ BA or higher	Tradable by geographic concentration	Index value	Index class	SOC code
428	First-Line Supervisors/Managers of Fire Fighting and Prevention Workers	53,490	60,840	55.5	4.7	0	−1.390	1	331021
429	First-Line Supervisors/Managers of Retail Sales Workers	1,083,890	32,840	93.1	2.7	0	−1.412	1	411011
430	Amusement and Recreation Attendants	232,030	15,920	97.8	1.9	0	−1.421	1	393091
431	Cooks, Short Order	203,350	17,230	99.9	0.0	0	−1.449	1	352015
432	Wholesale and Retail Buyers, except farm products	132,900	42,870	63.0	15.4	1	−1.475	1	131022
433	Coaches and Scouts	145,440	25,990	0.7	91.1	0	−1.479	1	272022
434	Respiratory Therapy Technicians	22,060	38,200			0	−1.493	1	292054
435	Musicians and Singers	50,410		26.3	41.4	1	−1.500	1	272042
436	Chefs and Head Cooks	115,850	32,330	58.5	4.7	1	−1.502	1	351011
437	Transportation Attendants, except Flight Attendants and Baggage Porters	24,810	19,290			0	−1.506	1	396032
438	Bartenders	480,010	15,850	74.6	0.4	0	−1.508	1	353011
439	Craft Artists	4,300	22,430	51.5	18.2	1	−1.528	1	271012

440	Lifeguards, Ski Patrol, and other recreational protective service workers	107,620	16,910	94.1	0.6	0	-1.544	1	339092
441	Dancers	16,240		81.5	15.5	1	-1.578	1	272031
442	Choreographers	16,150	32,950	40.0	40.0	1	-1.585	1	272032
443	Animal Trainers	8,320	24,800	65.1	5.3	0	-1.585	1	392011
444	Self-Enrichment Education Teachers	141,650	32,360	31.7	38.4	0	-1.607	1	253021
445	Child Care Workers	557,680	17,050	62.9	15.0	0	-1.617	1	399011
446	Models	1,430	22,700			1	-1.620	1	419012
447	Preschool Teachers, except Special Education	348,690	21,990	43.1	16.9	0	-1.626	1	252011
448	Fitness Trainers and Aerobics Instructors	189,220	25,840	59.1	22.6	1	-1.646	1	399031
449	Surgical Technologists	83,680	34,830	15.3	9.0	0	-1.681	1	292055
450	Crossing Guards	69,390	20,050	96.4	0.0	0	-1.709	1	339091
451	Massage Therapists	37,670	32,890	10.2	24.7	0	-1.719	1	319011
452	Gaming Dealers	82,320	14,260	87.5	0.0	1	-1.753	1	393011
453	Actors	59,590		60.2	11.9	0	-1.890	1	272011
454	Manicurists and Pedicurists	42,960	18,280	57.1	0.0	0	-1.962	1	395092
455	Hairdressers, Hairstylists, and Cosmetologists	338,910	20,610	6.0	0.0	1	-1.981	1	395012
456	Flight Attendants	99,590	46,680	48.2	16.8	0	-2.065	1	396031
457	Barbers	13,630	21,760	27.1	0.0	0	-2.210	1	395011

Table 8.8   **Share of occupational employment by offshoring index, by major occupation group, May 2005 employment totals**

SOC two-digit code	Description	Index class 1	Index class 2	Index class 3
11	Management	11.4	73.6	15.1
13	Business/financial operations	8.6	16.7	74.7
15	Computer/mathematical	0.0	6.6	93.4
17	Architecture/Engineering	0.9	18.2	80.8
19	Life, physical, social sciences	9.1	14.9	75.9
21	Community/social services	55.1	44.9	0.0
23	Legal	0.0	60.9	39.1
25	Education and library	43.7	52.4	3.9
27	Arts, design, entertainment	37.6	48.2	14.2
29	Health care practitioners/technicians	78.0	18.5	3.5
31	Health care support	94.4	2.8	2.8
33	Protective service	93.2	5.3	1.5
35	Food preparation/serving	100.0	0.0	0.0
37	Building maintenance	94.0	6.0	0.0
39	Personal care service	99.4	0.6	0.0
41	Sales and related	46.3	48.4	5.2
43	Office/administrative support	1.6	34.1	64.3
	All occupations	43.8	28.9	27.4

Source: O*Net.

occupations, 48 percent of the occupations classified as nontradable using the economic concentration measure are also classified as nontradable using the job task content measure. Similarly, 55 percent of the most tradable occupations, by Gini, are most tradable by job task content.

An alternative measure of fit simply counts the number of geographically concentrated tradable occupations within each task content class. In the highest task content class (most tradable/offshorable by task content), 51.6 percent of those occupations are tradable by geographic concentration. In the middle task content class, 35.6 percent of occupations are tradable by the first of our measures, and in the lowest (least offshorable/tradable) task content class, 21.2 percent of occupations were previously denoted tradable by geographic concentration.

Potential offshorability and skill is of interest. The O*Net data offer information on educational attainment, based on Bureau of Labor Statistics (BLS) data on fractions of jobholders with varying levels of education. Tables 8.6 and 8.7 offer two categories: percent with a high school diploma or less and percent with a Bachelor of Arts (BA) degree or more. Using the BA category, the rank correlation between educational attainment and relative offshorability, calculated from the full ranking of occupations, is +0.306—occupations with a greater share of BA holders are more highly ranked as offshorable. The top quartile of jobs in the ranking has a mean percentage of BA+ degree holders of 61 percent; the second quartile, 53.7 percent; the third quartile, 47.3 percent; and the bottom quartile, 29.1 percent. The least offshorable jobs are the least formally educated and have lower median annual earnings.

We have located just two other analyses that order occupations by an assessment of offshorability. Consistent with its organizational interest in occupational growth projections, the Bureau of Labor Statistics has developed a list of forty detailed occupations deemed "susceptible to a significant risk of offshoring" (United States Department of Labor 2006, 12). Of these forty occupations, thirty-nine are services occupations (the exception is aircraft mechanics and service technicians). With varying degree of "fit," thirty-eight of these thirty-nine occupations are noted for their offshorability by our index. Graphic designers and switchboard operators are included in the BLS list, with our index ranking these two occupations close to the middle of the 457. All the rest of the BLS occupations are fairly highly ranked by our index. The BLS list is not ranked; it is simply offered as a list of susceptible occupations, presumably with some more susceptible than others.[15]

Blinder (2007) explores a subjective index based on two characteristics: (a) can the work be delivered to a remote location, and (b) must the job be performed at a specific (U.S.) location? In his subjective measure, Blinder concentrates on one characteristic of the delivery of services, the separation of customer and supplier that he labels "impersonally-delivered services." Basically, impersonally-delivered services can be delivered electronically, incorporating the vast improvement in Information and Communication Technologies (ICT). His measure does not incorporate any attributes related to the kind of work sent down the wire, such as information content or Internet enabled. Most importantly, in terms of the area of traditional U.S. comparative advantage, Blinder does not consider the creativity or routineness of work.[16] In an area that needs more exploration, there are many high-skill and high-value (creative) services, that while transmittable electronically, pose opportunities for American workers and firms to penetrate foreign markets.

Using both production and nonproduction occupations, Blinder estimates that thirty to forty million workers are currently in potentially tradable jobs, based on May 2005 employment levels. Objective measures may well be preferred, given the number of occupations (> 450) and desire for replication.

15. The BLS methodology is similar in spirit to ours, considering characteristics of digital transmission, repetitive tasks, and little face-to-face interaction. Occupational analysts provided judgments on these characteristics. Further refinements included excluding occupations where technology or automation could account for a dampening of employment growth. See U.S. Department of Labor (2006).

16. The routineness of work, or the codification of tasks, is a characteristic emphasized by Autor, Levy, and Murnane (2003).

Drawing a line in our full ranking of services occupations, between offshorable and not offshorable, is admittedly arbitrary. One starting point, entirely subjective, draws a line around the offshore rank of 236 (Real estate brokers) and suggests 38 million potentially offshorable jobs; 55 million not (below the line).[17]

Our focus here is on services occupations. One natural question is where the other major occupational groups lie within this ranking. The average Production occupation, with an index value of –0.310, lies at rank 214, just below Sales Engineers. The average Farming, Forestry, and Fishing occupation, with an index value of –0.441, lies at rank 238, just below Hotel, Motel, and Resort Desk Clerks. Similarly, the average Transportation and Material Moving Occupation, with index value –0.456, lies at rank 247, just below Psychiatric Technicians. Finally, Installation, Maintenance, and Repair Occupations, with an average index value of –0.568, lies at rank 269, just below Nursing Instructors.

8.4.1   Robustness and Limitations of Our Methodology

We conducted two robustness checks of our weighting scheme. In the first, we dropped the two routine/creativity measures. These two measures may be noisy proxies for the task characteristics of "highly codified" and "nonroutine." Dropping the two measures produced a ranking that was highly correlated with our preferred index, with both the rankings and the value of the indices correlated at a level of 0.92.

In a second set of robustness checks, we tried different weights on importance and level. We use two alternatives: a more neutral weighting scheme of 50–50, and another where the weights were .75 on level and .25 on importance (the reverse of our preferred index). Our results are quite robust to weights. The value of the indices is correlated at a level of .98 and the rankings produced are virtually similar, where occupations are within 1 to 3 places of each other across indices (if different).

Our index is objective in the sense of producing a ranking that we simply report; we make no additional judgments, of a subjective nature, about any individual occupation. We do not use any additional information to change the ranking from that generated by our weighting of the individual components. Clearly, our choice of job task characteristics to include in the index is subjective, as it is based on our reading of the general discussion of offshoring. Our goal is to produce a ranking that can be reproduced or challenged in future research by considering a broader range of factors.

17. In May 2005, employment in the major occupational groups of interest here, SOC 11–43, summed to 98.3 million. Due to some data limitations, our analysis sample of services occupations sums to an employment level of 93 million. Total nonfarm employment was 130.3 million in May 2005.

8.5   Conclusions

In previous work we developed a measure of tradability based on the geographic concentration of production. In this chapter we offer a second measure of tradability, built from common notions of job characteristics related to offshorability. We find a selection of tradable occupations do indeed have characteristics of offshorability (Internet enabled, high information content, no face-to-face customer contact). The calculated index of offshorability offers strong potential for understanding jobs (tasks) at risk. The two measures of tradability and offshorability offer a combined potential to do the same. These two measures have their weaknesses, and it makes good sense to proceed in this area with a portfolio of indicators, for which we now have two items, rather than any one measure alone.

There is an important question of timing of potential offshoring, which is largely an unknown. It is clear that advancing technology will continue to increase the feasibility of providing services from remote locations. For now and perhaps the foreseeable future, however, most high-value work will require creative interaction among employees, interaction that is facilitated by physical proximity and personal contact. Moreover, in many fields, closeness to customers and knowledge of local conditions are also of great importance. The "how soon" question is very important for understanding the potential costs of adjustment. A process that takes twenty years to establish itself on a real scale allows for more adjustment than offshoring over a five-year period.

In our earlier paper, we provided evidence that service activities employ workers with higher education and more skill than nontradable (service) activities and manufacturing. Our results here are consistent, with higher average levels of educational attainment for the most highly-ranked occupations. This seems to suggest that tradable services are consistent with U.S. comparative advantage in high skill production. Unlike Blinder's view that only personally delivered services are likely to stay in the United States, we consider it important to understand how tradable services can be consistent with U.S. comparative advantage. With the expectation that as technology and policy allow for more trade in these activities, the United States should gain world market share in these activities, not lose it.[18] In this spirit, we note that the components of our index are not intended to convey strong priors about the direction of trade; that is, whether services are likely to be offshored or inshored. The occupations at the top of our list, with some of the highest levels of educational attainment, may well be those where tradability leads to inshoring and export potential.

18. Though over the longer-term, if the United States ceases to make investments in education and training, it is possible that it would cease to have comparative advantage in high-skill activities.

References

Amiti, M., and S. Wei. 2004. Fear of service outsourcing: Is it justified? IMF Working Paper no. WP/04/186. Washington, DC: International Monetary Fund, October.

Arora, A., and A. Gambardella. 2004. The globalization of the software industry: Perspectives and opportunities for developed and developing countries. NBER Working Paper no. 10538. Cambridge, MA: National Bureau of Economic Research, June.

Autor, D., F. Levy, and R. J. Murnane. 2003. The skill content of recent technological change: An empirical exploration. *Quarterly Journal of Economics* 118 (4): 1279–1334.

Bardhan, A. D., and C. A. Kroll. 2003. *The new wave of outsourcing.* Fisher Center for Real Estate and Urban Economics, Report Series no. 1103, University of California, Berkeley, Fall.

Bhagwati, J., A. Panagariya, and T. N. Srinivasan. The muddles over outsourcing. *Journal of Economic Perspectives* 18 (4): 93–114.

Blinder, A. S. 2006. Offshoring: The next industrial revolution? *Foreign Affairs* 85 (2): 113–128.

———. 2007. How many U.S. jobs might be offshorable? CEPS Working Paper no. 142, Princeton University, March.

Brainard, L., and R. E. Litan. 2004. Offshoring service jobs: Bane or boon—and what to do? Brookings Institution Policy Brief no. 132, April.

Bronfenbrenner, K., and S. Luce. 2004. The changing nature of corporate global restructuring: The impact of production shifts on jobs in the U.S., China, and around the globe. U.S.-China Economic and Security Review Commission, October.

Dossani, R., and M. Kenney. 2003. Went for cost, stayed for quality?: Moving the back office to India. Asia-Pacific Research Center, Stanford University, November.

Jensen, J. B., and L. G. Kletzer. 2006. Tradable services: Understanding the scope and impact of services offshoring. In *Brookings Trade Forum 2005, offshoring white-collar work,* ed. S. M. Collins and L. Brainard, 75–134. Washington, DC: Brookings Institution.

Kirkegaard, J. F. 2004. Outsourcing—stains on the white collar? Institute for International Economics. Unpublished Manuscript, February.

Krugman, P. R. 1991. *Geography and trade.* Cambridge, MA: MIT Press.

Mankiw, N. G., and P. Swagel. 2006. The politics and economics of offshore outsourcing. *Journal of Monetary Economics* 53:1027–56.

McCarthy, J. C. 2002. 3.3 million U.S. services jobs to go offshore. TechStrategyΠ Research, Forrester Research, November.

National Center for O*Net Development. 2006. The O*Net content model. Available at: http://www.onetcenter.org/content.html.

Peterson, N. G., M. D. Mumford, W. C. Borman, P. R. Jeanneret, and E. A. Fleishman. 1999. *An occupational information system for the 21st century: The development of O*Net.* Washington, DC: American Psychological Association.

Peterson, N. G., M. D. Mumford, W. C. Borman, P. R. Jeanneret, E. A. Fleishman, K. Y. Levin, M. A. Campion, et al. 2001. Understanding work using the occupational information network (O*Net): Implications for practice and research. *Personnel Psychology* 54:451–92.

Samuelson, P. A. 2004. Where Ricardo and Mill rebut and confirm arguments of mainstream economists against globalization. *Journal of Economic Perspectives* 18 (Summer): 135–46.

Schultze, C. L. 2004. Offshoring, import competition, and the jobless recovery. Brookings Institution Policy Brief no. 136, August.

U.S. Department of Labor, Bureau of Labor Statistics. 2006. *Occupational projections and training data, 2006–07 Edition.* Bulletin 2602, February. Washington, DC: GPO.

van Welsum, D., and G. Vickery. 2005a. New perspectives on ICT skills and employment. DSTI Information Economy Working Paper, DSTI/ICCP/IE(2004)10/FINAL, OECD, Paris.

———. 2005b. Potential offshoring of ICT-intensive using occupations. DSTI Information Economy Working Paper, DSTI/ICCP/IE(2004)19/FINAL, OECD, Paris.

World Trade Organization. The general agreement on trade in services (GATS): Objectives, coverage and disciplines. Available at: http://www.wto.org/english/tratop_e/serv_e/gatsqa_e.htm#3, undated.

Comment   Susan M. Collins

I enjoyed reading this installment in Brad Jensen and Lori Kletzer's research to understand implications of offshoring service activities for U.S. labor markets. This chapter builds on their earlier work that introduced a creative new approach for measuring tradability in services. They use domestic geographic concentration by industry and occupation to identify which service activities are traded domestically, inferring that these activities also have the potential to be traded internationally—that is, to be vulnerable to offshoring. In this chapter, they take a sensible step toward addressing some of the criticisms of their initial indicators by combining the geographic concentration metrics with indicators about the task content of service activities. Although still subject to shortcomings, some of which I will discuss later, this innovative and informative research makes a valuable contribution to the services offshoring literature. In my comments, I will briefly describe the broader context so as to highlight their contribution, discuss some concerns with the methodology, and outline some additional issues I hope the authors will consider in future work.

A few years ago there was a surge of fear about service jobs moving abroad. Widely publicized stories suggested that a substantial share of the American workers in services, who had not previously considered their jobs to be tradable, may be swimming in the same sea of competition as their counterparts in manufacturing, with low-wage foreign workers. While these fears abated somewhat as unemployment rates declined, the recent deterioration in U.S. economic performance has brought them back to center stage.

Susan M. Collins is the Joan and Sanford Weill Dean of Public Policy at the Gerald R. Ford School of Public Policy and professor of public policy and economics at the University of Michigan, and a research associate of the National Bureau of Economic Research.

Certainly it is true that services are increasingly traded. But how important is this phenomenon, what are its characteristics, and what are the likely implications for American workers? The relevant magnitudes are difficult to establish for a number of reasons. First, there are many challenges associated with constructing accurate measures of services trade. Unlike goods trade, it is not grounded in the movement of something physical across a border. Services are also often bundled together or with goods. Significant differences in data definitions used by different countries limit the information content from cross-checking U.S. services exports (and imports) with trade-partner imports (exports).[1] Furthermore, constructing an estimate of the offshorability of services jobs calls for forecasts of what future services trade might be, not simply indicators of the historical trade flows. Finally, there is no simple link between U.S. services trade and U.S. jobs. While factor-content ratios provide useful information, applying them in this context requires questionable assumptions about the extent to which available ratios are relevant for hypothetical scenarios involving a future with extensive services offshoring. There is rarely much discussion of the appropriate counterfactual, which may not be an historical status quo, but instead involve domestic production with very different factor content ratios.

Jensen and Kletzer, like other recent authors discussed in their chapter, do not try to link their estimates directly to actual trade in services. They focus instead on classifying service activities based on characteristics assumed related to tradability. While avoiding the significant challenges associated with directly measuring trade in services, these approaches raise other concerns—in particular, that the classifications are subjective. Jensen and Kletzer's geographical concentration index fares well in this context. It is objective, comprehensive, and applicable to industries as well as occupations. While it is easy to quibble with how particular occupations or industries are classified, the results are promising. However, it remains unclear to me why, in the initial paper as well as this chapter, the authors divide activities into three tradability classes, which then become the focus for most of their analysis, instead of using the more nuanced information in the continuous geographic concentration index.

As Jensen and Kletzer recognize, some activities are unlikely to be tradable even though their production is geographically concentrated,[2] some activities are likely to be tradable even though they are not geographically concentrated, and some activities that are traded domestically may be unlikely to be traded internationally. To address these concerns, they draw from the somewhat more subjective approaches postulating a priori charac-

1. Robert E. Lipsey (2006) describes many of the problems associated with measuring trade in services internationally.

2. Their modified Gini coefficient methodology is intended to adjust for production concentration to reflect concentration in domestic demand that may not be indicative of tradability.

teristics of activities that make them tradable. Specifically, they use O*Net data from surveying job incumbents about the task requirements for 457 service occupations. Jensen and Kletzer have chosen to focus on eleven of the myriad available measures. Five of these are assumed to be positively associated with tradability (related to information content and whether the task is Internet enabled) while the other six are assumed to be negatively associated with tradability (requiring face-to-face contact, on-site work, and routine or creative work content). These are then aggregated to form a single index, and the activities are (again) divided into three general classes to reflect high, medium, and low degrees of tradability. Using the O*Net data enables them to be relatively systematic and comprehensive, and I see this as a sensible and promising next step. I hope they will continue addressing the remaining shortcomings, as discussed later.

Much of the chapter then focuses on comparing the geographic concentration and the task-content indicators of tradability, and the results are quite interesting. As the authors note, there is considerable overlap between the two. Further, combining them does seem to provide a means for omitting some "misfits" such as manicurists (concentrated because they tend to be in urban areas) that the geography indicator by itself classified as tradable. I fully agree with them that it will be useful to develop a portfolio of measures of the complex offshoring phenomenon, and that they have contributed two assets to this portfolio.

Let me turn next to my concerns—many of which I hope will be addressed in future installments. First, for both indicators, as noted before, I believe it would be more informative to work directly with the continuous indices, instead of using arbitrary thresholds to construct three classes for each of the tradability indicators. The charts the authors provide do not suggest that either of these indicators naturally clusters into three groups, but instead that there are many activities at or near the selected thresholds.

Second, there is much more the authors could do to explore and exploit the relevant information in the O*Net data and I found their current usage of these data only somewhat convincing. For instance, their a priori classification of which characteristics are positively (negatively) associated with tradability would benefit from additional justification. In particular, it is not obvious to me what "getting information" means. Tasks that require seeking information that can be gathered on-line are arguably more tradable, but those requiring an employee to get certain other types of information would require direct contact. While the authors do some robustness checks, they would need independent information about services trade to explore how well their weighting scheme does in identifying the task characteristics that are associated with offshoring (or inshoring). In my view, relating these O*Net indicators to existing services trade data (as imperfect as they may be) will provide a very important perspective for drawing implications. Indeed,

I would encourage the authors to consider multifactor analysis, instead of trying to add univariate indicators.

Third, I will be very interested in further exploration of the implications and interpretation of domestic concentration for international tradability. Transportation and transaction costs may be quite different domestically versus internationally. For some activities, domestic concentration reflects U.S.-specific regulations, such as state-specific insurance provisions. State bar exams and medical licensing rules have all influenced U.S. services concentration but with very different implications globally. When is concentration in domestic production indicative of vulnerability to offshoring, and when is it indicative of relative strength? Domestic concentration in some activities may reflect agglomeration externalities that would facilitate the United States becoming an export powerhouse with growing domestic employment opportunities. If there are strong increasing returns, concentration may reflect agglomeration strength, such that the activity is less (not more) likely to move abroad. The authors are well aware that tradability may imply inshoring as well as offshoring. Trade implies potential flows in either (or both) directions. However, much (though not all) of the discussion in the chapter implicitly seems to treat services tradability as synonymous with vulnerability to U.S. jobs being relocated abroad.

A related point is that it is not clear whether scale economies are as relevant for production of services as for production of goods. We also know little about whether service activity becomes more concentrated as economies develop and become more open to trade. What determines the (clearly endogenous over time) location of service activity in a global economy? There is much interesting work to be done here. Theory is likely to provide valuable insights and help steer empirical analyses. Case studies could enrich our understanding in many dimensions.

The authors raise the important issue of timing and time-frame in their conclusion. If they are correct in identifying the service activities that are (or could become) tradable, it certainly does matter whether any changes occur over the next few years or gradually over decades. In this context, it is worth highlighting that the data they present represent snapshots, with no information about trends. The geographic concentration index uses 2000 Census data, while the O*Net index uses surveys published in 2006. It will be interesting to know whether these snapshots show pictures that have been relatively constant over time, or which have changed considerably as global trade has surged in the past decade.

Finally, trade data distinguishes four different types (or modes) of services trade: Mode 1 (cross-border trade) involves flows between countries, such as when a customer in China purchases U.S. architectural services over the Internet. Mode 2 (consumption abroad) involves movement of the consumer, such as when a Chinese student travels to enroll in a U.S. university. Mode 3 (commercial presence) involves transactions with multinational corporations (MNCs) or their affiliates, such as services provided by an international hotel chain. Mode 4 (presence of natural persons) involves movement of the supplier, such as when a U.S. physician practices medicine in China. Geographic concentration and task-related constraints are very different when the consumer or producer can move to trade the service, than when trade requires arms-length transactions with the consumer and producer of the services physically separated. I am glad to see that Jensen and Kletzer now acknowledge that their indicators are most applicable to Mode 1 services trade. They state in a footnote that this type of services trade is the most important for assessing the labor market impact of potential services tradability. However, other modes are of growing importance, and ignoring them may be quite misleading. A full understanding of trade in services and its potential implications for domestic labor markets will require an analytic toolkit that includes tools aimed at understanding all four modes.

In sum, this chapter documents an interesting next step in an innovative and valuable line of research. By using information about task requirements for service activities from O*Net data, Jensen and Kletzer have added to the portfolio of indicators for the tradability of service activities. I look forward to reading the next installments.

Reference

Lipsey, R. E. 2006. Measuring international trade in services. NBER Working Paper no. 12271. Cambridge, MA: National Bureau of Economic Research, June.

III

Hours of Work

Why Do BLS Hours Series Tell Different Stories about Trends in Hours Worked?

Harley Frazis and Jay Stewart

9.1 Introduction

The number of hours that people work for pay is an important economic measure. In its own right, it measures labor utilization. But it is also the denominator of other key economic indicators such as productivity and hourly earnings. Thus, differences in measured hours between surveys can lead to substantial differences in measured productivity and wages. For example, Abraham, Spletzer, and Stewart (1998) show that the different trends in hours measures account for nearly all of the divergence between hourly wages from the National Income and Product Accounts (NIPA), which use hours derived from the establishment-based Current Employment Statistics program (CES), and estimates from the household-based Current Population Survey (CPS). The average hourly wage from the NIPAs grew by 7 percent between 1973 and 1993, while the average hourly wage from the CPS remained roughly constant over that same period. Abraham, Spletzer, and Stewart noted that someone looking at the NIPA data would "have a very different picture of recent real wage trends than someone who looked at the CPS data . . ." (295).

Systematic over- or underreporting of hours can affect measured inequality. Frazis and Stewart (2004) found that, compared to time-diary reports, hours of work for women and college graduates tend to be overreported in the CPS. Thus, using weekly hours computed from the American Time Use

Harley Frazis is a research economist in Employment Research and Program Development at the U.S. Bureau of Labor Statistics. Jay Stewart is the Division Chief of the Division of Productivity Research and Program Development at the Bureau of Labor Statistics.

We thank Charlie Brown, Younghwan Song, and the editors of this volume for their helpful comments. Any views expressed here are ours and do not necessarily reflect those of the BLS.

Survey (ATUS) instead of usual hours from the CPS increases the college-high school hourly earnings ratio by 4.1 percentage points and the female-male hourly earnings ratio by 5.4 percentage points.[1]

The divergence in trends in CPS and CES hours discussed in Abraham, Spletzer, and Stewart (1998) has continued since their paper was published. As the CPS and CES are the two principal sources of data on the subject, both the amount and the trend in how many hours Americans work for pay are in dispute. Figure 9.1 shows trends in average weekly hours of private nonagricultural workers from the CPS and the CES. (We show data from both the March CPS and the CPS Outgoing Rotation Group [ORG] files. The ORG data are more representative, but the March data have a longer time series.) The CPS data indicate that average weekly hours worked declined in the 1960s and early 1970s, increased for most of the 1980s, and leveled off beginning in the late 1980s. The net effect of these changes is that there has been very little change between 1964 and 2007. In contrast, the CES hours series declined between 1964 and the late 1980s, leveled off until the late 1990s, then declined between the late 1990s and 2007.

The main goal of this study is to reconcile the differences between the CPS and CES hours series. Our strategy, which is similar to that used by Abraham, Spletzer, and Stewart (1998, 1999), is to simulate the CES sample using CPS data to show how differences in the two surveys contribute to the divergence in average weekly hours. Specifically, we consider differences in the workers covered, differences in the treatment of multiple jobholders, and differences in the hours concept (hours worked in the CPS versus hours paid in the CES). We also examine whether hours are overreported in the CPS, as has been claimed by some researchers. Finally, we examine whether features of the CES (in particular, changes in the reference period over time), could explain the divergence. We were able to account for most of the difference in levels between the two hours series, but could not explain much of the difference in the trends.

9.2   Why Might the CES and CPS Hours Series Tell Different Stories?

There are several reasons why one might expect estimates of hours worked from the two series to differ. First, the CPS data cover all workers, although all comparisons shown here are restricted to private nonagricultural workers. The CES data cover only production (in goods-producing industries) and nonsupervisory workers (in services-providing industries) within the private nonagricultural sector. Nonproduction and supervisory workers are more likely to work full time and generally work longer hours, so that the CPS's inclusion of these workers leads us to expect weekly hours to be higher

---

1. For a discussion of the importance of hours data for measuring productivity see Eldridge, Manser, and Otto (2004).

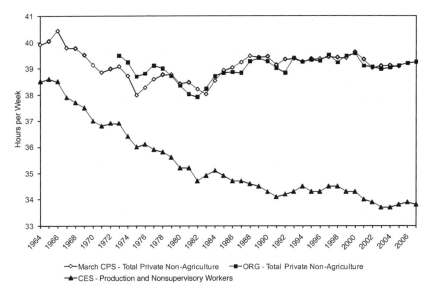

-◇-March CPS - Total Private Non-Agriculture   -■-ORG - Total Private Non-Agriculture
-▲-CES - Production and Nonsupervisory Workers

Fig. 9.1   Average weekly hours from CPS and CES data

in the CPS than in the CES. Second, the CES hours series is a job-based measure, whereas the CPS is a person-based measure. Although both series measure total hours worked at all jobs, a person working at two jobs would be counted twice in the CES, but only once in the CPS. Third, the CPS measures hours worked, while the CES measures hours paid. Off-the-clock work would cause the CPS weekly hours series to be higher than the CES series. Fourth, hours may be overreported in the CPS. Some studies (Robinson and Bostrom 1994; Sundstrom 1999) have shown that respondents in household surveys such as the CPS tend to overreport their work hours and that the extent of this overreporting has increased over time. If the CES correctly measures average weekly hours, this story is consistent with the observed relationship between CPS and CES hours. Finally, for reasons we discuss later, the lengthening of pay periods over time could have caused a decline in CES estimates of average weekly hours apart from any real changes in hours. In what follows, we examine each of these possible explanations.

9.2.1   Differences in Workers Covered

Differences in workers covered can have a potentially large effect on measured hours if the group that is not covered, nonproduction and supervisory workers, work different hours than the covered group or if the trend in their hours is different. As noted previously, the workers that are excluded from the CES sample work longer hours, which suggests that differences in sample coverage can explain at least some of the difference in levels. It remains to be seen if this difference can explain the difference in trends.

To examine the effect of differences in coverage, it is necessary to make the two samples comparable. Because the CES has not typically collected hours information on nonproduction and supervisory workers, it is impossible to adjust the CES series to be comparable to the CPS series. So we use the same strategy as Abraham, Spletzer, and Stewart (1998, 1999) and simulate the CES sample using CPS ORG data for 1979 to 2007 and May Supplement data for 1973 to 1978.[2]

We restricted the sample to individuals age fifteen and older who worked during the CPS reference week and were identified as being either production (in goods-producing industries) or nonsupervisory (in services-providing industries) workers using the CPS industry and occupation codes. The distinction between production and nonsupervisory workers is important. Occupations that are classified as nonsupervisory are not necessarily classified as production workers. For example, accountants and attorneys are nonsupervisory workers in service-providing industries, but they are not production workers in goods-producing industries.

It is fairly straightforward to distinguish between goods-producing and services-providing industries in most cases.[3] The classification of workers as production and nonsupervisory workers in their respective sectors was somewhat problematic. The instructions to respondents on the CES forms are fairly detailed regarding which types of workers should be counted as production and nonsupervisory workers. Because the definition of covered workers depends on the industry, we used both industry and occupation codes to classify workers as being covered by CES. Unfortunately, the detailed (three-digit) Census occupation codes used in the CPS do not exactly coincide with the CES instructions, and there were two major changes in the Census occupation codes during the 1973-to-2007 period covered by our simulations (between 1982 and 1983 and between 2002 and 2003).

Figure 9.2 shows the simulated CES average weekly hours series, along with the actual CES hours and CPS ORG private nonagricultural worker (PNAW) series. The first thing to note is that the simulated CES hours series is closer in level to the actual CES series than the CPS PNAW series. Hours per week are between 1.3 and 1.7 hours less in the simulated CES series compared to the CPS PNAW series. However, the simulated CES series exhibits the same roughly flat trend as the CPS PNAW series and does not replicate the downward trend in the actual CES series.

One possible explanation for the lack of a downward trend in the simu-

---

2. We did not simulate the CES hours series using the March data, because it does not have any information on second jobs or hourly/salaried status. Following Abraham, Spletzer, and Stewart (1998, 1999), we assume that the May Supplements are comparable to the ORG data.

3. There was a break in series between 2002 and 2003 when the new Census industry codes were introduced. This change likely resulted in a more accurate coding of workers, but workers who were previously coded as being in manufacturing are now classified as being in business services.

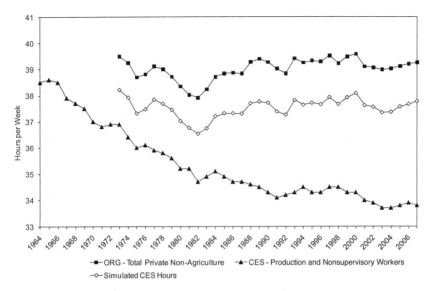

Fig. 9.2   Comparison of CES weekly hours to CPS replications of CES weekly hours not adjusted for multiple jobholding

lated CES series is that employers may not always classify workers according to the instructions on the form. This can occur for a number of reasons. First, respondents may not read the instructions on the form and instead use their own definitions, which may not correspond to the Bureau of Labor Statistics' (BLS). Second, respondents' recordkeeping systems may not allow workers to be classified using the BLS definitions. For example, the distinction between supervisory and nonsupervisory workers (in services) may not be meaningful. A more meaningful distinction may be whether workers are covered by minimum wage/overtime laws. Findings from the BLS's internal Records Analysis Survey (RAS) studies indicate that a large number of establishments reported for workers who are not exempt from minimum wage laws. However, it does appear that the production/nonproduction worker distinction (in goods-producing industries) is meaningful and that respondents are for the most part reporting for the correct group of workers.

To examine whether employers in service-providing industries could be using the exempt/nonexempt distinction, we constructed an alternative "hybrid" simulated CES series. For production workers the hybrid series uses the CES definition, while for nonsupervisory workers we attempted to identify workers who, based on their occupation and whether they were paid hourly, were likely to be nonexempt from wage/hour laws.[4] This hybrid series

---

4. The CPS does not contain information on whether a worker is exempt or not, so we used information on the worker's detailed occupation and whether he or she was paid hourly. We

was similar to the one we report, except that the 1982 to 1983 change in occupation codes caused a break in series that resulted in a onetime downward shift in the simulated hours series. Because this break in series strengthens our results by narrowing the difference between the two surveys, we took the conservative approach and used the CES definitions for both industries.

9.2.2   Accounting for Multiple Jobholding

As noted earlier, the CES measure is job-based whereas the CPS measure is person-based. The two measures would be the same if each person held only one job, but about 5 to 6 percent of the population has more than one job at any one time. To account for multiple jobholding, we reran the simulations, counting each job separately.[5] Since 1994, information on multiple jobholding has been collected every month, while prior to 1994, this information was collected only in the May supplements to the CPS from 1973 to 1978, 1985, and 1991. We combine these May supplement data with the ORG data for 1994 to 2007, but acknowledge that there may be some seasonal variation in the multiple jobholding rate.

Figure 9.3 shows the multiple-jobholding-adjusted (MJA) simulated CES hours series. In the years when no information on multiple jobholding is available (1979 to 1984, 1986 to 1990, and 1992 to 1993), hours for the MJA series are set equal to simulated CES hours (from figure 9.2) divided by interpolated values of the implied multiple jobholding rate.[6] As expected, the multiple jobholding adjustment reduces estimated hours worked compared to the unadjusted simulated CES series (also shown in figure 9.3). The MJA series is about 1.6 hours per week lower than the simulated CES series, although the difference varies between 1.1 and 2.0 hours per week with no discernable trend. The MJA series further narrows the difference in levels between CES and CPS hours, but still does not replicate the downward trend in actual CES hours.

There is virtually no difference between the MJA series and the actual CES

---

assumed that all hourly paid workers were nonexempt. The remaining workers were classified as exempt if they were supervisors or if their jobs allowed them considerable autonomy as outlined in the minimum wage law. This classification is rather crude. Determining whether a worker is exempt from minimum wage laws is complicated by the fact that exempt status depends on a number of variables that are not available in the CPS. For example, workers in "mom-and-pop" businesses are generally exempt. Another complicating factor is that the law has changed over time. We could not account for these changes in the CPS data, but the reader should keep this in mind.

5. A small fraction, about 5 percent, of multiple jobholders hold more than two jobs. We experimented with making a further adjustment, similar to our initial multiple-jobholding adjustment, to account for these third jobs, but it made virtually no difference.

6. In the years for which we have data, we computed the implied multiple jobholding rate by dividing the simulated CES hours series by the MJA series. The implied multiple jobholding rate ranged from 3.1 percent to 5.6 percent. This differs from the published multiple jobholding rate, because some people with CES-covered main jobs have second jobs that are not covered, and vice versa. The between-supplement values of the implied multiple jobholding rate were linearly interpolated using values from the adjacent supplement years.

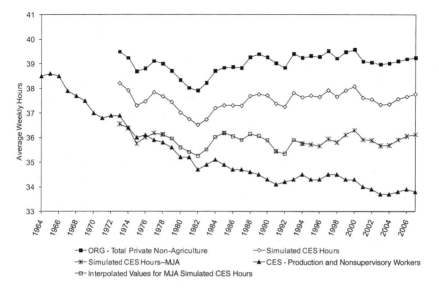

Fig. 9.3   Comparison of CES weekly hours to CPS replications of CES weekly hours adjusted for multiple jobholding

series between 1973 and the early 1980s. Over this period, both series exhibit a downward trend and turn up immediately after the 1982 recession. The fall in hours between 1982 and 1983 is larger in the actual CES series compared to the MJA series, which could be at least partially due to the change in CPS industry and occupation codes between these years.

After 1983, the MJA series behaved very differently from the actual CES series. The increase in hours between 1983 and 1984 was larger than the increase in the actual CES. And from 1984 through the rest of the 1980s it remained approximately flat, while the actual CES series declined. Beginning in 1990, apart from the higher level, the MJA series tracks the actual CES series fairly well until the late-1990s, when the CES and CPS replications diverge further. Between 1998 and 2007, the difference increased from 1.3 hours per week to 2.3 hours per week. This coincides with the conversion of the CES to a probability sample and the introduction of North American Industry Classification System (NAICS) codes. It seems unlikely that the introduction of NAICS codes could have affected the trend in hours. But the conversion to a probability sample presumably changed the sample composition, which could have led to a decline in hours.

9.2.3   Hours Paid versus Hours Worked

As noted earlier, the two series differ in the hours concept being measured. The CPS measures hours worked, while the CES measures hours paid. The usual way to account for the difference between these two concepts is to adjust the CES hours data for paid vacations.[7] Because this adjustment does not account for off-the-clock work, we opted for a different approach and instead adjusted the CPS data.

We began by assuming that hourly paid workers are paid for all of the hours that they work—so that no adjustment was necessary—and that salaried workers are paid for a standard workweek. The CPS does not have any information on hourly/salaried status for second jobs, so we assumed that multiple jobholders are paid hourly on their second jobs. Given that second jobs are almost always part-time, this seems like a reasonable assumption and should not affect the results. For individuals who are salaried on their main job, we assumed that they are paid for a forty hour workweek. Thus, we set hours paid at forty if they worked more than forty hours on their main job, or if they worked less than thirty-five hours but indicated that they usually work full time. To account for paid time off, we included individuals who were employed and did not work during the CPS reference week if they were paid for that time off. We assumed that they were paid for their usual hours on their main job (topcoded at forty if salaried).

It was necessary to impute hourly/salaried status for some observations. In the 1973 to 1978 and 1994 to 2007 data, hourly/salaried status is missing due to nonresponse for about 2 percent of the sample. In the 1985 and 1991 May Supplements, hourly/salaried status was collected only of individuals in (months-in-sample) MIS 4 and 8, and was therefore missing for three-fourths of the sample. To fill in the missing values, we used a logit equation to estimate the probability that an individual was paid hourly based on demographic and job characteristics, and then assigned individuals their predicted probabilities when hourly/salaried status was missing. For observations with imputed hourly/salaried status, the hours-paid adjustment was proportional to the probability that the individual was paid hourly. For example, an individual who worked forty-eight hours and had a 0.25 predicted probability of being paid hourly would be assigned a workweek of forty-two hours.

Figure 9.4 shows the effect of this adjustment. The multiple-jobholding and hours-paid adjusted (MJ & HPA) series is lower in level compared to the MJA series, but their trends are identical. Note also that the MJ & HPA series lies below the actual CES series prior to 1984. Other authors (Kuhn and Lozano 2008) have documented the increase in long workweeks. But it appears that any increase in off-the-clock work has not had a large impact on trends in average hours worked.

9.2.4   Possible Overreporting of Hours Worked in the CPS

The conventional wisdom among researchers who analyze time-use data is that respondents in household surveys such as the CPS tend to overreport

---

7. The BLS used to conduct a special survey, the Survey of Hours Worked, to determine what fraction of paid hours is actually worked. The fraction is about 0.93 and shows very little year-to-year variation. The survey was discontinued in 2003 and these data are now collected through the National Compensation Survey. Sundstrom (1999) makes this adjustment.

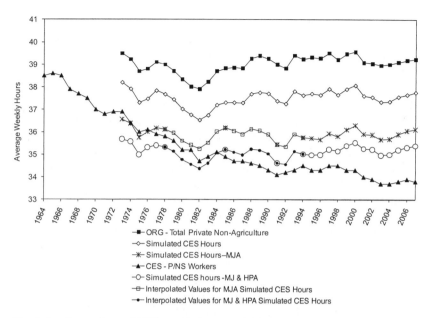

Fig. 9.4   Comparison of CES weekly hours to CPS replications of CES weekly hours adjusted for multiple jobholding and paid time off

their work hours. If this is the case and if the extent of overreporting has increased over time, as some researchers have found, this could explain the divergence of CPS and CES hours.

Research on this issue has taken one of two approaches: comparing reports from household surveys to reports for the same individuals from their employers (Mellow and Sider 1983; Rodgers, Brown, and Duncan 1993); or comparing household survey responses to time-diary data (Robinson 1985; Robinson and Bostrom 1994; Sundstrom 1999; Williams 2004; Frazis and Stewart 2004, 2007). Mellow and Sider found that workers overreported hours compared to their employers' records, and that salaried workers overreported the most.[8] In contrast, Rodgers, Brown, and Duncan found no evidence of overreporting, but their sample was restricted to hourly paid workers at a large unionized firm. The earlier studies that used time-diary data (Robinson 1984; Robinson and Bostrom 1994; Sundstrom 1999) found evidence of overreporting in household surveys. The Robinson and Bostrom study found that the extent of overreporting increased from about one hour per week in 1965 to about six hours per week in 1985. Their findings, if correct, could explain the divergent trends in CES and CPS hours as well as the difference in levels. However, more recent studies (Williams 2004; Frazis

---

8. Regarding the latter point, it is worth noting that employers likely reported hours paid while employees reported hours worked. These differing reports are consistent with employees "working off the clock."

and Stewart 2004, 2007) found evidence that household surveys correctly reported, or even underreported, hours. All of these studies found that some groups overreport hours, while others underreport.

There are several reasons why time-diary data might be preferable to data from household surveys that ask respondents to report about hours worked in the previous week. The recall task is generally easier in a time-use survey. The reference period is the previous day so that respondents need not try to recall over longer periods, and because they are reporting individual episodes of work they do not have to add the lengths of different episodes. Paid work that occurs at home or other locations, which respondents may not report when responding to retrospective questions, is counted in time-diary estimates. Time diaries also have an adding-up constraint that forces the sum of time spent in all activities to equal twenty-four hours.

In this section we use data from the American Time Use Survey (ATUS) to examine the accuracy of CPS hours reporting on CES jobs. Our main purpose is to see if differences in the reporting of hours over time can account for the divergence between the CPS and CES series. Sample sizes for previous time-use surveys are too small to allow us to do this directly (not to mention issues with comparability). However, we can use demographic and job characteristics associated with under- or overreporting of hours in CPS relative to the 2003 to 2006 ATUS and estimate the trend in reporting implied by changes in the characteristics of the employed.

The ATUS sample is a stratified random sample that is drawn from households that have completed their eighth and final month-in-sample in the CPS[9] (hereafter MIS 8) and is designed to be representative of the U.S. civilian population. Interviews were conducted by telephone every day during the year except for a few major holidays.[10] Thus, the data cover the entire year, except for the days before these holidays.[11]

As in other time-use surveys, respondents are asked to sequentially report their activities on the previous day. The diary day starts at 4:00 a.m. and goes through 4:00 a.m. of the following day (the interview day), so that each interview covers a twenty-four-hour period. After the core time diary has been completed, the ATUS asks respondents whether any activities that were not identified as paid work were done as part of their job or business. This question improves identification of paid work activities for self-employed respondents who work at home and others who do not "go to work" in the traditional sense.

9. Households are in the CPS sample for four months, out for eight, and then in for another four.

10. Reference days before major holidays are missed, as the telephone centers are closed. The remaining days in the month that fall on the same day of the week as the missing day have their weights inflated to make up for the missing day, in effect making the assumption (which we make in the absence of other information) that the activities on the missing day are similar to those on other days with the same day of the week.

11. For details about the ATUS, see Frazis and Stewart (2007) and Hamermesh, Frazis, and Stewart (2005).

We can also identify breaks, which allows us to determine how sensitive our results are to alternative definitions of paid work.[12] Given these advantages, we will proceed under the assumption that the time-diary estimates are correct.

The ATUS also contains labor force information about the respondent that was collected using a slightly modified version of the monthly CPS questionnaire. These questions allow us to determine whether the respondent is employed, unemployed, or not in the labor force (NILF). One notable difference between ATUS and CPS employment questions is that the ATUS reference period is the seven days prior to the interview—the last day being the diary day—instead of the previous calendar week as in the CPS. For respondents who are employed, the ATUS asks about usual hours worked, but does not collect actual hours worked during the previous week.[13]

For this study, we pooled data from 2003 through 2006. We restricted our sample to respondents fifteen years and older who worked at a job during the seven days prior to their ATUS interview. The combined sample size from 2003 to 2006 was 37,035.[14] Our previous work used only 2003 data.

One drawback of using time-diary data is that the reference period is only one day. Previous researchers (e.g., Robinson and Bostrom 1994) constructed synthetic workweeks by generating estimates for each day of the week and adding up the estimates. Our approach is equivalent.[15] Thus, we can compare means for specific demographic groups, but we cannot compare the distributions of hours worked between the two surveys.

As noted previously, the detailed information in the ATUS allows us to consider alternative definitions of paid work. We calculate three different measures of hours worked, each of which corresponds to a different concept. Going from the most restrictive measure to the least restrictive, these are:

12. Hamermesh (1990) is one attempt we have seen to examine the effect of paid breaks on wages. Interviewers prompt respondents by asking, "Did you take any breaks of fifteen minutes or longer?" whenever a work episode is reported. Beginning in 2004, this prompt was incorporated into the instrument. The prompt automatically pops up whenever work episodes of four hours or longer are reported.

13. Even if it were available, there is a potential problem with using estimates of actual hours worked for the previous week, because the procedure used for contacting respondents in ATUS could impart bias into estimates of actual hours for the previous seven days. Each designated person is assigned an initial calling day. If he or she is not contacted on that day, the interviewer makes the next call one week later, thus preserving the assigned day of the week. Individuals who are unusually busy during a particular week (perhaps because they worked long hours) are less likely to be contacted during that week, making it more likely that they are contacted the following week (and asked to report hours for the busy week). Hence, long work weeks would tend to be oversampled, resulting in a correlation between hours worked during the previous week and the probability that that week is sampled.

14. The response rate for the ATUS varies from about 55 percent to 58 percent. It is also worth noting that interviews with fewer than five episodes or more than three hours of uncodeable activities are not included in the ATUS public-use file.

15. For basic comparisons, we reweight observations so that all days of the week receive equal weight. When computing regressions, we generate separate estimates for weekdays and weekends and take a weighted average of the two estimates.

1. Time spent in activities coded as "Working at job."
2. Definition (1) plus activities identified as breaks and time spent in work-related travel (not commuting).[16]
3. Definition (2) plus activities that were coded as being done for the respondent's job (for example, taking a client out to dinner).

We believe that definition (2) is the most appropriate for comparison, because it is likely that individuals include paid breaks and work-related travel when reporting hours. Including these activities adds about 0.4 hours per week. The ATUS does not determine whether work-related activities were done for the main job or for second jobs, so we assumed that all work-related activities were done for the main job. Thus definitions (2) and (3) are the same for second jobs. These activities may or may not be included in CPS hours reports, but in practice, there is very little difference between definitions (3) and (2) for the main job (0.1 hour per week).

Because CES is job-based, we examine differences in hours per job between CPS and ATUS. (This differs from the person-based analysis in Frazis and Stewart [2004, 2007]). As previously stated, we simulate the CES sample in ATUS as we did in the CPS. For main jobs, this is straightforward, as the information available is identical to CPS. For second jobs, ATUS does not contain information on class of worker, industry, or occupation. We assign CES status to second jobs in ATUS as follows. If the ATUS respondent had a second job in both their last month in CPS and in ATUS, we use their second-job CES status in CPS. If the ATUS respondent had a second job in ATUS but not in CPS, we weight that job by the predicted probability of its being a CES job. The predicted probabilities come from a logit regression of CES status for CPS second jobs in their last month in CPS.[17] Because these multiple jobholders did not have second jobs approximately three months prior to their ATUS interview, we restricted the sample for this regression to CPS respondents who did not have a second job three months earlier.[18]

Table 9.1 compares estimates of hours worked from the ATUS (in the first three columns) to estimates from the CPS (in the fourth column) for the 2003 to 2006 period. The top six rows show average weekly hours averaged over all jobs, for main jobs, and for second jobs; and the difference between ATUS and CPS estimates.[19] Averaging over all jobs, the difference between CPS and ATUS estimates of hours worked varies between –2.4 and –2.9 hours per week, depending on the ATUS definition of work, with negative values

---

16. The inclusion of breaks is justified on the grounds that breaks can be productive (see Hamermesh 1990). Work-related travel is defined as travel between same-job work sites, and we identified travel spells as work-related by looking at the surrounding activities.

17. The covariates are female, age and age squared, CES status of the first job, usual hours on first and second jobs, and dummies for "usual hours vary" on first and second jobs.

18. That is, the sample is individuals who were multiple jobholders in MIS 8, but held only one job in MIS 5.

19. We performed a similar analysis on a per-person basis. The results are similar, and virtually identical to those in Frazis and Stewart (2007), which used only 2003 data.

Table 9.1 Hours of paid work per job in ATUS and CPS, simulated CES sample

Time period	Jan. 2003–Dec. 2006				Oct. 2002–Sept. 2006	
Survey: Hours response from . . .	ATUS			CPS	CPS	CPS
Sample: Respondents participated in . . .					ATUS	CPS MIS 8
Hours measure	Definition 1	Definition 2	Definition 3	Actual CPS	Actual CPS	Actual CPS
Average weekly hours						
All jobs	33.2	33.7	33.8	36.1	35.0	36.2
1st job	35.4	35.9	36.0	37.1	36.2	37.2
2nd job	9.1	9.2	9.2	14.4	13.5	14.5
Difference from CPS actual hours						
All jobs	−2.9	−2.4	−2.4			
1st job	−1.7	−1.3	−1.2			
2nd job	−5.2	−5.2	−5.2			
Adjusted difference from CPS actual hours						
All jobs	−1.7	−1.3	−1.2			
1st job	−0.7	−0.3	−0.2			
2nd job	−4.2	−4.1	−4.1			
Average weekly hours in CPS reference weeks						
All jobs	34.4	34.9	34.9	36.1	35.1	36.2
1st job	36.8	37.3	37.4	37.1	36.2	37.2
2nd job	8.2	8.2	8.2	14.4	14.8	14.5
Difference from CPS actual hours						
All jobs	−1.7	−1.3	−1.2			
1st job	−0.3	0.2	0.3			
2nd job	−6.2	−6.1	−6.1			
Adjusted difference from CPS actual hours						
All jobs	−0.6	−0.2	−0.1			
1st job	0.7	1.2	1.2			
2nd job	−6.5	−6.4	−6.4			

Note: Reported differences between ATUS and CPS may not match differences between the ATUS and CPS estimates because of rounding.

indicating *overreporting* in CPS. The difference between CPS and ATUS is −5.2 hours per week for second jobs, which is considerably larger than the range of −1.2 to −1.7 hours for main jobs.

Because our interest is in whether CPS responders overreport hours, it is necessary to minimize the effect of any differences in sample composition between the ATUS and the CPS. By using sample weights, we control for any observed differences in sample composition between the two surveys. However, the ATUS response rate is sufficiently low—an average of 57 percent over the 2003 to 2006 period—that there may be unobserved differences between ATUS responders and the broader population of CPS responders that are correlated with hours worked. As we noted earlier, households that have completed their final (MIS 8) CPS interview are used as the sampling frame for the ATUS. This means that we can use CPS data to compare the subset who responded to the ATUS to the entire CPS sample. Specifically, we compare reports of actual hours worked from the CPS MIS 8 interview for ATUS sample members to reports for all individuals in the CPS MIS 8 sample. Because the ATUS interview occurs about three months after the CPS MIS 8 interview, we made this comparison for the period covering October 2002 through September 2006.[20] These estimates are shown in the last two columns of table 9.1. We use the difference between these two sets of estimates to adjust our earlier estimates. Thus, the sample-selection-adjusted difference between CPS and ATUS hours reports is given by:

$$(1) \qquad D = E(H_{i,t}^{ATUS}) - E(H_{i,t}^{CPS})$$

$$- [E(H_{i,t-3,MIS8}^{CPS} \mid i \text{ in ATUS}) - E(H_{i,t-3,MIS8}^{CPS})],$$

where i denotes individual, the second subscript denotes the time period in months, and the third subscript (when present) denotes month-in-sample. Note that because the adjustments are based on reported hours in CPS, they are independent of the ATUS definition of hours.

The sample-composition effects are 1.2 hours per week when averaged over all jobs and 1.0 hour per week for both main and second jobs. This yields adjusted differences of between −1.7 and −1.2 hours per week for all jobs, between −0.7 and −0.2 for main jobs, and between −4.2 and −4.1 for second jobs. Thus, accounting for differences in sample composition reduces our estimates of overreporting in CPS.

As noted in Frazis and Stewart (2004, 2007), the reference periods in the CPS and ATUS cover different portions of the calendar. The reference periods for the ATUS include almost every day in the calendar, while the CPS reference week is virtually always the week of the 12th.[21] This week was

---

20. The ATUS interview usually occurs between two and four months after the CPS MIS 8 interview.

21. For some Decembers, reference week is the week of the 5th to avoid conflicts of the fielding period with Christmas.

chosen to avoid holidays, so there might be a systematic difference between reference and nonreference weeks. We now control for differences in reference periods by restricting the ATUS sample to CPS reference weeks. The results are shown in the lower panel of table 9.1. The difference between ATUS and CPS hours estimates changes dramatically, with gross differences over all jobs falling by about 1.2 hours per week for each of the three ATUS measures. After adjusting for sample composition, the differences fall by another 1.1 hours per week. These adjusted differences range between –0.6 and –0.1 hours per week and are neither economically nor statistically significant.[22] Thus, as in our earlier work, we find that the original difference of over two hours is completely explained by sample composition and the difference between reference and nonreference weeks in CPS.

This close correspondence between ATUS and CPS estimates of average hours per job is the sum of three effects, one of which works in the opposite direction from the other two. First, hours on main jobs are underreported for reference weeks by 0.7 to 1.2 hours, significant at the 5 percent level for definitions (2) and (3). Second, hours on second jobs are overreported for reference weeks by 6.5 to 6.4 hours, significant at the 1 percent level. And third, the proportion of second jobs is higher in ATUS by 3.3 percentage points after adjusting for sample composition. This high proportion of second jobs reported in ATUS relative to that reported in CPS by ATUS sample members reduces relative ATUS hours per job by a full hour.

It is important to emphasize that our result—that CPS respondents underreport hours on main jobs—applies only to the simulated CES sample. When we also include non-CES jobs, the estimated difference in hours on the main job during CPS reference week adjusted for sample composition is only –0.3 to 0.2 hours and is not statistically significant. Differences between CPS and ATUS in second-job-hours reporting and the proportion of second jobs are similar between the simulated CES sample and the larger sample. Thus, over both CES and non-CES jobs the implied difference between CPS and ATUS is –1.7 to –1.2 hours per job, which is mostly due to the higher proportion of second jobs in ATUS.

How do these differences vary across subpopulations? Table 9.2 shows a number of comparisons for the simulated CES sample for hours worked during CPS reference weeks. Underreporting appears to decrease with education, although only college graduates show a statistically significant degree of overreporting. This result matches Frazis and Stewart (2004), who used a sample of individuals who were employed at the time of both their CPS and ATUS interviews and whose reported usual hours had not changed much. Unlike Frazis and Stewart (2004), table 9.2 shows no evidence that women's

---

22. The ATUS standard errors are computed using replicate weights that account for survey design effects (BLS 2009). In computing the standard error of CPS–ATUS differences, the variance in CPS statistics is ignored.

Table 9.2 Difference in hours of paid work for simulated CES jobs, CPS reference week, ATUS minus CPS 2003–2006 (adjusted for ATUS sample composition)

	Job 1			Job 2			All jobs		
	Definition 1	Definition 2	Definition 3	Definition 1	Definition 2	Definition 3[b]	Definition 1	Definition 2	Definition 3
All	0.67	1.16**	1.23**	-6.48***	-6.44***	-6.44***	-0.64	-0.19	-0.13
	(0.54)	(0.55)	(0.55)	(1.18)	(1.18)	(1.18)	(0.52)	(0.52)	(0.52)
Men	1.24	1.78**	1.86**	-7.47***	-7.41***	-7.41***	-0.19	0.31	0.38
	(0.79)	(0.80)	(0.80)	(1.78)	(1.79)	(1.79)	(0.74)	(0.75)	(0.75)
Women	-0.02	0.41	0.47	-5.76***	-5.74***	-5.74***	-1.20*	-0.81	-0.76
	(0.65)	(0.65)	(0.65)	(1.40)	(1.41)	(1.41)	(0.63)	(0.63)	(0.64)
High school dropouts	2.33	2.96	3.06	-5.79	-5.61	-5.61	1.86	2.47	2.57
	(1.98)	(2.02)	(2.01)	(4.73)	(4.85)	(4.85)	(2.14)	(2.18)	(2.17)
High school grads	1.42	2.01*	2.04*	-5.74***	-5.70**	-5.70**	0.69	1.24	1.28
	(1.17)	(1.18)	(1.18)	(2.21)	(2.22)	(2.22)	(1.27)	(1.28)	(1.28)
Some college	0.73	1.28	1.34	-7.50***	-7.46***	-7.46***	-0.92	-0.42	-0.37
	(1.18)	(1.21)	(1.21)	(2.67)	(2.70)	(2.70)	(1.25)	(1.28)	(1.28)
College grad	-1.49	-1.18	-1.03	-4.83***	-4.78***	-4.78***	-3.04***	-2.76***	-2.63***
	(1.03)	(1.04)	(1.04)	(1.79)	(1.82)	(1.82)	(0.94)	(0.95)	(0.95)
Parents	-0.08	0.41	0.50	-4.64***	-4.58***	-4.58***	-1.21*	-0.75	-0.67
	(0.71)	(0.73)	(0.73)	(1.37)	(1.38)	(1.38)	(0.68)	(0.69)	(0.69)
Nonparents	0.88	1.37*	1.43**	-7.42***	-7.38***	-7.38***	-0.51	-0.06	-0.01
	(0.70)	(0.71)	(0.71)	(1.67)	(1.68)	(1.68)	(0.69)	(0.69)	(0.69)

Hourly[a]	-0.23	0.36	0.41	-4.40***	-4.35***	-4.35***	-1.14	-0.59	-0.54
	(0.80)	(0.81)	(0.81)	(1.65)	(1.66)	(1.66)	(0.77)	(0.78)	(0.78)
Nonhourly[a]	2.14*	2.43**	2.51**	-6.76***	-6.74***	-6.74***	0.52	0.78	0.85
	(1.09)	(1.10)	(1.10)	(2.39)	(2.41)	(2.41)	(1.05)	(1.06)	(1.06)
Hourly missing[a]	5.67**	5.83**	6.17**	-6.77**	-6.70**	-6.70**	-0.25	-0.11	0.15
	(2.51)	(2.53)	(2.55)	(2.84)	(2.86)	(2.86)	(2.15)	(2.16)	(2.18)
Manager/Professional[a]	0.19	0.51	0.61	-4.85***	-4.85***	-4.85***	-1.86**	-1.58**	-1.49*
	(0.84)	(0.85)	(0.86)	(1.37)	(1.37)	(1.37)	(0.75)	(0.76)	(0.76)
Other Occupations[a]	0.77	1.32**	1.37**	-7.13***	-7.06***	-7.06***	-0.28	0.23	0.28
	(0.67)	(0.67)	(0.67)	(1.66)	(1.68)	(1.68)	(0.64)	(0.65)	(0.65)
Goods producing[a]	1.94	2.84**	2.88**	-9.56***	-9.53***	-9.53***	-0.01	0.83	0.87
	(1.26)	(1.26)	(1.27)	(2.91)	(2.92)	(2.92)	(1.24)	(1.25)	(1.25)
Nongoods producing[a]	0.00	0.42	0.50	-6.23***	-6.19***	-6.19***	-1.07*	-0.67	-0.60
	(0.60)	(0.60)	(0.60)	(1.54)	(1.56)	(1.56)	(0.58)	(0.58)	(0.58)
Retail trade, leisure, and hospitality[a]	1.11	1.54	1.61	-4.31	-4.28	-4.28	0.47	0.87	0.93
	(1.26)	(1.27)	(1.27)	(2.70)	(2.70)	(2.70)	(1.25)	(1.26)	(1.26)
Age 16–24	1.55	2.02	2.04	-11.06***	-11.06***	-11.06***	0.04	0.48	0.50
	(1.70)	(1.70)	(1.70)	(3.96)	(3.96)	(3.96)	(1.59)	(1.59)	(1.59)
Age 25–54	1.19	1.67**	1.77**	-5.58***	-5.52***	-5.52***	-0.17	0.28	0.37
	(0.76)	(0.77)	(0.76)	(1.41)	(1.42)	(1.42)	(0.75)	(0.76)	(0.76)
Age 55+	0.06	0.57	0.61	-5.08***	-5.04***	-5.04***	-1.08	-0.60	-0.57
	(0.83)	(0.85)	(0.85)	(1.54)	(1.54)	(1.54)	(0.80)	(0.81)	(0.81)

[a]Job characteristics are for the main job, because this information is not available for second jobs in the ATUS.

[b]As noted in the text, definitions 2 and 3 are the same for job 2.

***Significant at the 1 percent level.

**Significant at the 5 percent level.

*Significant at the 10 percent level.

hours are overreported. Other comparisons in table 9.2—by age, parental status, hourly pay, occupation, and industry—are new. Most fail to show significant differences between ATUS and CPS samples.

It is important to note that the differences in table 9.2 are simple averages and do not account for possible correlations between the variables. We can control for these correlations by conditioning the terms in equation (1) on a vector of covariates. Rewriting equation (1) so that each term is replaced by the predicted value from the appropriately defined regression and arranging terms, one can estimate:

$$
(2) \quad D(X) = (X\beta^{ATUS} - X\beta^{CPS}) - (X\beta^{CPS}_{t-3,MIS8,ATUS} - X\beta^{CPS}_{t-3,MIS8})
$$
$$
= X[\beta^{ATUS} - \beta^{CPS} - (\beta^{CPS}_{t-3,MIS8,ATUS} - \beta^{CPS}_{t-3,MIS8})],
$$

where the βs are vectors of regression coefficients corresponding to the samples denoted in the sub- and superscripts. Because the samples corresponding to each β differ, we ran separate regressions for each component and generate predicted values for differences between ATUS and CPS using equation (2). This allows us to see if some of the results in table 9.2 are due to correlations with other variables. It also allows us to "backcast" differences between ATUS and CPS in different years, using regression coefficients to obtain average predicted values of the difference in reported hours.

We restricted the ATUS sample to CPS reference weeks, and estimated equation (2) for all three definitions of work. The coefficients are reported in table 9.3. Looking at the reference week results, some differ from table 9.2. There is now stronger evidence that women overreport hours relative to men and parents relative to nonparents. Age has a significant effect, with hours reported in CPS relative to ATUS peaking at age thirty-eight in our quadratic specification. To examine whether reporting could have changed over time, we backcast reporting error using data from the 1984 to 2007 CPS and the coefficients from table 9.3 for all jobs using ATUS definition (2). We generated predicted values for each individual in the simulated CES sample and computed the weighted mean for each year. The backcasts in figure 9.5 show the amount by which average weekly hours are over- or underreported for workers whose main jobs are in the CES sample. Changes in over- or underreporting come about through compositional changes among people in CES-covered jobs. As before, negative values indicate overreporting.

Figure 9.5 indicates that CPS reporting has not changed much over time. The backcast shows that, consistent with our findings in table 9.2, on average CPS respondents reported hours correctly between 2003 and 2006, and that underreporting was greater going back in time. In 1984, CPS respondents underreported hours by about 0.4 of an hour per week, so that there has been a trend toward decreased underreporting. This trend works to increase the CES-CPS divergence. Thus, it works in the same direction as Robinson and

Table 9.3   **Estimated effects of covariates on sample-adjusted difference in CPS and ATUS hours worked per job, simulated CES sample**

	Definition 1		Definition 2		Definition 3	
	Coefficient	Standard error	Coefficient	Standard error	Coefficient	Standard error
Parent	−1.61*	0.92	−1.63*	0.93	−1.59*	0.94
Female	−1.91*	1.09	−2.00*	1.11	−2.01*	1.11
HS Grad	−0.70	1.62	−0.63	1.67	−0.66	1.67
Some college	−1.54	2.20	−1.54	2.26	−1.54	2.26
College Grad	−4.84*	2.54	−4.89*	2.59	−4.83*	2.58
Age	0.31*	0.19	0.34*	0.19	0.33*	0.19
Age Sq.	−0.0041*	0.0022	−0.0044**	0.0022	−0.0043*	0.0022
Mgr/Prof.[a]	0.95	1.34	0.86	1.35	0.85	1.34
Goods producing[a]	−1.17	1.43	−0.90	1.45	−0.92	1.45
Hourly[a]	−0.24	1.22	−0.01	1.24	0.00	1.24
Hourly missing[a]	−1.83	2.75	−1.97	2.77	−1.77	2.79
Constant	−2.02	3.86	−2.22	3.92	−2.12	3.94

[a]Job characteristics are for the main job, because this information is not available for second jobs in the ATUS.
***Significant at the 1 percent level.
**Significant at the 5 percent level.
*Significant at the 10 percent level.

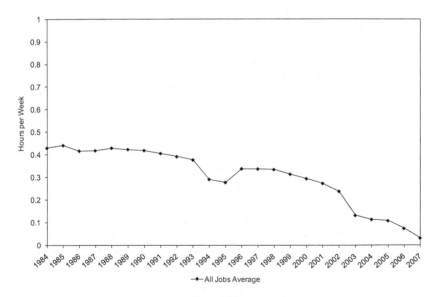

Fig. 9.5   Backcasting of misreporting in CPS

Bostrom's (1994) finding of increased overreporting. But the 0.4 hour per week change between 1984 and 2007 is small. Thus, misreporting of hours in CPS does not seem to explain much of the CES-CPS divergence.

9.2.5   The CES Reference Period

The CES reference period differs from the CPS reference period. As noted earlier, the CPS reference period is the week that includes the 12th of the month, whereas the CES reference period is the pay period that includes the 12th of the month. Thus, the CES reference period can vary from one week to one month depending on the establishment's length of pay period (LP). Length of pay period matters for two reasons. The first has to do with the distribution of hours worked over the month. A weekly pay period coincides with the CPS reference week, while a biweekly payroll will include the CPS reference week plus either the week before or the week after.[23] Given that workers work less in non-CPS-reference weeks, estimated average weekly hours will be lower in establishments with biweekly payrolls compared to those with weekly payrolls even if actual hours worked are exactly the same in both establishments.

The second reason has to do with how employees are counted. All employees who worked at the establishment at any time during the pay period are included in the employee count, regardless of how many hours they worked. If total hours are reported correctly,[24] then reported employment will be too large. To illustrate, suppose a full-time employee quits in the middle of a biweekly pay period and is immediately replaced. Ideally, both employees would be counted as having worked for one-half of the pay period. But both are counted as having worked the entire pay period and average hours for these two employees is twenty per week instead of forty. The longer the pay period and the greater the turnover, the more the employment count will be overstated (and hours understated).[25]

These biases clearly can affect levels, but will have no effect on trends unless there have been changes in the difference in hours worked between CPS reference and nonreference weeks, the fraction of jobs that turnover each month, or the average length of pay period.

There is no direct evidence on how the difference between CPS reference and nonreference week hours has evolved over time. We tabulated ATUS data and found that this difference depends on the industry group (the difference is larger in services-providing industries) and whether workers are paid hourly (the difference is larger for hourly paid workers). This suggests

---

23. It is also possible that pay periods start in the middle of the week, but this seems to be rare.

24. Establishments are required to keep records of hours worked for hourly paid workers, and it is not unreasonable to suppose that establishments report the standard workweek for salaried positions.

25. See Nardone et al. (2003) for a discussion of how turnover affects the comparison of CES and CPS employment counts.

that the reference week–nonreference difference may have changed over time through the shift of employment from goods-producing to services-providing industries and changes in the fraction paid hourly.[26]

Information on long-term trends in turnover is also rather scant, and many of the data sources that are available have breaks in series that affect comparability over time. However, there is evidence to suggest that turnover has increased since the mid-1970s. Stewart (2007), using data from the March CPS, found that there has been a slight increase in the fraction of workers experiencing a job-to-job transition during the year.

There is very little evidence on how length of pay period in the CES sample has changed since the early 1970s. Microdata are available (though not readily) from 1999 to the present. But the original registry files that contained the LP information were not kept prior to 1999. The only data we have for the pre-1999 period come from a 1981 Records Analysis Survey (RAS) (U.S. Department of Labor 1983). The top panel of table 9.4 shows the establishment-weighted distribution and mean LP for selected years. These distributions are not strictly comparable, but they are the only data that we have available to us. The 1981 data are from the 1981 RAS of respondents in four states (Florida, Massachusetts, Texas, and Utah). The 2002 and 2007 data were tabulated by CES staff on a sample of Touchtone Data Entry (TDE) respondents. It is worth noting that the fraction of respondents reporting by TDE fell between 2002 and 2007 with the increase in Internet reporting. Ideally, we would have employee-weighted distributions, but only establishment-weighted data are available to us.

Table 9.4 indicates that there was virtually no change in mean LP between 1981 and 2002. But between 2002 and 2007, there appears to have been a significant lengthening of pay periods, due mostly to a shift from weekly to biweekly and semimonthly pay periods. The lower portion of table 9.4 shows how LP changed between 2002 and 2007 for individual industry groups. Note that most of the changes are smaller than the aggregate change and that LP has become shorter in some industry groups. Thus, it appears that most of the aggregate change in LP is due to compositional changes rather than within-industry changes.

To determine whether changes in pay-period length (directly and through changes in industry composition), turnover, and the difference in hours worked between reference and nonreference weeks (through changes in industry composition and the fraction paid hourly) could have contributed to the divergence between CES and CPS hours, we simulated their effect on measured CES hours. Our basic strategy was to hold within-group work hours constant, and allow these other factors to change.

---

26. The fraction paid hourly has increased in both goods-producing and services-providing industries. However, the shift in employment toward services-providing industries (where a smaller fraction of workers are paid hourly) has offset the within-industry changes.

Table 9.4   Changes in the distribution of length of pay period

	Weekly	Biweekly	Semimonthly	Monthly	Mean LP
Total private					
1981[a]	53	23	20	4	1.59
2002	48	34	12	5	1.63
2007	32	46	19	3	1.78
2002—Major industry group					
Natural resources and mining	53	30	11	6	1.62
Construction	78	14	4	4	1.32
Manufacturing	64	25	7	3	1.42
Wholesale trade	37	39	13	11	1.90
Retail trade	61	27	9	4	1.51
Transportation and warehousing	61	24	10	5	1.52
Utilities	27	53	7	13	2.04
Information	16	61	12	11	2.11
Financial activities	46	27	21	5	1.66
Professional and business services	40	35	16	8	1.78
Private education and health	17	57	17	9	2.06
Leisure and hospitality	39	47	10	3	1.67
Other services	37	41	15	7	1.81
2007—Major industry group					
Natural resources and mining	56	27	15	2	1.51
Construction	79	14	4	3	1.28
Manufacturing	64	25	9	2	1.42
Wholesale trade	30	45	18	7	1.88
Retail trade	34	52	13	1	1.70
Transportation and warehousing	49	33	15	3	1.60
Utilities	27	62	10	1	1.77
Information	12	75	11	2	1.94
Financial activities	4	54	40	2	2.06
Professional and business services	37	36	21	6	1.80
Private education and health	13	65	19	3	1.97
Leisure and hospitality	27	55	16	2	1.80
Other services	42	35	17	5	1.70

[a]These distributions are establishment weighted. Also, the data in this table are not strictly comparable over time. The 1981 data are from U.S. Department of Labor (1983), and are for Florida, Massachusetts, Texas, and Utah. The data for 2002 and 2007 were compiled by CES staff on Touchtone Data Entry (TDE) respondents. Note that the fraction of respondents that reported via TDE declined over this period with the advent of Internet reporting.

To perform this exercise, we used data from a number of different sources to construct a second simulated average weekly hours measure. For both goods-producing and services-providing industries, we have the following information: the share of employment (from CES), the fraction paid hourly (from CPS), the LP distribution (from table 9.4), hours worked per week by hourly and salaried workers during CPS reference and nonreference weeks (from ATUS). We also use turnover rates from March CPS data, although they are not available by industry group. Equation (3) shows how the simulated hours data were constructed from these variables (we omitted time subscripts to reduce notational clutter).

$$
(3) \qquad \text{AWH}^i = \frac{(F_H^i \times F_W^i \times H_{H,R}^i)}{(1 + T)}
$$

$$
+ \frac{(F_S^i \times F_W^i \times H_{S,R}^i)}{(1 + T)}
$$

$$
+ \frac{(F_H^i \times F_B^i \times [H_{H,R}^i + H_{H,NR}^i]/2)}{(1 + 2T)}
$$

$$
+ \frac{(F_S^i \times F_B^i \times [H_{S,R}^i + H_{S,NR}^i]/2)}{(1 + 2T)}
$$

$$
+ \frac{(F_{SM}^i \times [H_{S,R}^i + 2H_{S,NR}^i]/3)}{(1 + 3T)}.
$$

In equation (3), F_H^i and F_S^i are the fractions of workers paid hourly and salaried in industry i ($F_H^i + F_S^i = 1$); F_W^i, F_B^i, and F_{SM}^i are the fractions of workers paid weekly, biweekly, and semimonthly or monthly ($F_W^i + F_B^i + F_{SM}^i = 1$);[27] $H_{H,R}^i$, $H_{H,NR}^i$, $H_{S,R}^i$, $H_{S,NR}^i$ are hours worked per week by hourly/salaried (H,S) workers during CPS reference/nonreference (R, NR) weeks; and T is the weekly turnover rate. We use actual values for each year for T and the Fs, while holding the Hs constant. Overall simulated average weekly hours in year t are equal to: $H_t^{SIM} = F_t^g \times H_t^g + F_t^s \times H_t^s$, where the superscripts refer to goods-producing (g) and services-providing (s) industries. The adjustment to actual CES hours is equal to the cumulative decline in hours of this simulated hours series. Thus, adjusted CES hours in year t equal: $\tilde{H}_t^{CES} = H_t^{CES} - (H_t^{SIM} - H_{1973}^{SIM})$, where H_t^{CES} is actual CES hours in year t. This series shows what actual CES hours would have been were it not for the interaction of changes in turnover, industry composition, and the fraction paid hourly with changes in the CES reference period.

Before turning to the results, we provide a more complete description of the data we used and how we constructed the variables. The fractions of workers who are paid weekly, biweekly, or semimonthly and monthly were generated using the LP distributions by industry in table 9.4 weighted by the share of CES employment in those industries. Given the small change in the LP distribution between 1981 and 2002, we assumed that the LP distribution was constant between 1973 and 2002 and that the fraction in each LP category changed linearly between 2002 and 2007.

Data on the fraction of workers who are hourly/salaried comes from the

---

27. We grouped semimonthly and monthly payrolls together and assumed that all of these workers are salaried. This is a reasonable assumption, because semimonthly and monthly payrolls make it more difficult to compute overtime pay for hourly paid workers. Thus, it seems likely that establishments employing hourly workers would opt for weekly or biweekly payrolls.

1979 to 2007 CPS ORG files and the 1973 to 1979 May CPS files. When hourly/salaried status was missing, it was imputed as described earlier.

Data on hours worked during CPS reference and nonreference weeks are available from the ATUS. But to prevent shifts in employment from high-hour goods-producing industries to low-hour services-providing industries from driving our results, we assumed that hours worked during the CPS reference week were the same in both goods-producing and services-providing industries. We further assumed that salaried workers were paid for the same number of hours in CPS reference and nonreference weeks. Specifically, we assigned: $H^g_{H,R} = H^s_{H,R} = H^g_{S,R} = H^s_{S,R} = H^s_{S,NR} = H^g_{S,NR} = 37$, $H^g_{H,NR} = 36.1$, $H^s_{H,NR} = 34.3$. Thus, the shift in employment from goods-producing to services-providing industries affects the overall average weekly hour measure through the lengthening of pay periods and the larger differential between CPS reference and nonreference weeks in services-providing industries.

For the turnover rates, we would ideally like to have had monthly data by industry. Unfortunately, these data are not available in the CPS before 1994. Instead, we use job-to-job transition rates from Stewart (2007) that were generated using March CPS data. The rates are computed on an annual basis and measure the fraction of people who experienced a job-to-job transition during the year. The annual rates tend to lead to an overstatement of turnover, while using persons rather than jobs in calculating turnover works in the opposite direction. We adjusted the annual number so that the monthly number is about the same as in Fallick and Fleischman (2004).[28] Thus, the transition rates from the March CPS contribute trend and cyclical variation, but not the level. Unfortunately, it is not possible to generate separate transition rates for goods-producing and services-providing industries. Turnover rates are available from the March CPS from 1975 to 2002 (see Stewart 2007). For 1973 to 1974, we assumed that turnover rates were about the same as for 1975 (8 percent), and that turnover rates started increasing in 2003 (from 10.5 percent in 2002 to 11 percent in 2003, and to 12 percent in 2004 to 2007).

Figure 9.6 shows the actual CES and the adjusted CES hours series. The adjusted series lies above the actual series indicating that measured hours would have been higher were it not for the increase in the length of the average CES reference period and its interaction with other changes that occurred between 1973 and 2007. The effect is small, about 0.5 hours per week in 2007, but not trivial. Turnover seems to have a relatively large effect on the difference between the adjusted and actual CES series. The difference is larger in expansion years, when there are more job-to-job transitions, and the increasing difference after 1982 coincides with an increase in the job-to-job transition rate.

Given that we do not know how the LP distribution has changed over time, we computed an upper bound on the effect by assuming that all estab-

---

28. Specifically, we divided the annual rate by two.

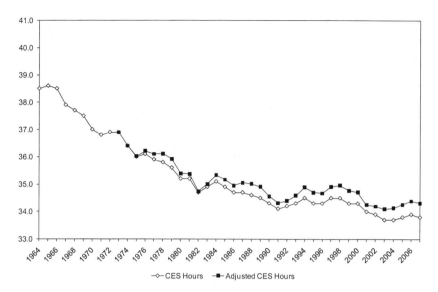

Fig. 9.6   Length-of-pay-period simulation

lishments paid their workers weekly in 1973, and allowed the fraction paying workers biweekly, semimonthly, and monthly to increase gradually to the levels observed in 2002. Between 2002 and 2007, we made the same assumptions about the LP distribution as before. The upper bound is about 0.9 hour per week in 2007, which, given our extreme assumptions, is still rather small.

Thus, the variable reference period in CES combined with other changes appears to have imparted a small downward trend to the CES hours series. However, the effect is small and does not appear to be a major contributor to the divergence of CES and CPS hours. Still, it is worth keeping in mind that this steeper downward trend in CES hours is the result of the interaction of changes in the real economy, with a seemingly innocuous feature of how the CES collects employment and hours data.

9.3   Discussion

The goal of our study was to reconcile the large differences, both in level and trend, between the two main sources of hours data published by the BLS—the CES and the CPS. We made some progress. Simulating the CES hours series using CPS data, we found that much of the difference in levels between the two series can be explained by differences in the workers covered (all private nonagricultural workers versus production and nonsupervisory workers), differences in the way average weekly hours are computed in the two surveys (person-based in the CPS and job-based in the CES), and differences in the hours concept (hours worked in CPS versus hours paid in

CES). But the simulated CES series did not replicate the downward trend in the actual CES data. All of the adjustments to the CPS data resulted in parallel shifts in the series, with virtually no effect on trend. In 2007, the last year of our data, the difference between the actual and simulated CES series in figure 9.4 was 1.6 hours after making the hours worked/hours paid adjustment. It is worth noting that this last adjustment creates a divergence prior to the early 1980s.

We also considered whether features of the CES data collection could have contributed to the divergence. In particular, we examined the interaction of the increasing average pay period length with other changes such as changes in industry composition and the turnover rate. We found that these factors explained only part of the divergence—0.5 hours per week of the 1.6 hour difference in 2007.

The hypothesis that errors in reporting hours in CPS account for the discrepancy is not supported, as a comparison with the time-diary data from ATUS shows no major differences in hours worked between the surveys for CES jobs. Using the ATUS to generate predicted changes in reporting based on demographic and job characteristics has only a small effect on reconciling trends in the CPS and CES, similar to the changes in reference period.

The end result of our analyses is that we were only partially able to reconcile the differences between the CES and CPS weekly hours series. Differences in coverage and concepts explain the differences in levels, but do not explain the differences in trends. We would like to point future researchers of this topic to avenues that we were unable to fully pursue, but that might bear fruit.

The CES recently started collecting and publishing payroll and hours data for all employees. As of this writing, these are available from March 2006 through November 2007. For this time period, we computed simulated all-employee CES hours using CPS data, making adjustments for multiple jobholding and the difference in concept (hours worked versus hours paid) as described before, and compared them to actual CES all-employee hours. The difference between the two series is 1.8 hours, which is larger than the 1.5 hour difference between the actual CES production/nonsupervisory worker and the MJ & HPA hours series. Thus, using all-employee hours data does not appear to narrow the difference between CES and CPS hours. Moreover, it also suggests that the residual differences, after all adjustments have been made, between the actual CES and the MJ & HPA series are real and not an artifact of how we simulated the CES production/nonsupervisory sample in the CPS. In any case, further analysis is warranted as more all-employee hours data become available from the CES.

Another avenue worth exploring is the role of individual industries. Kirkland (2000) argues that much of the decline in CES hours is due to retail trade and services. These are low-hour industries that saw a decline in weekly hours and a large increase in employment. Of course, what matters for our

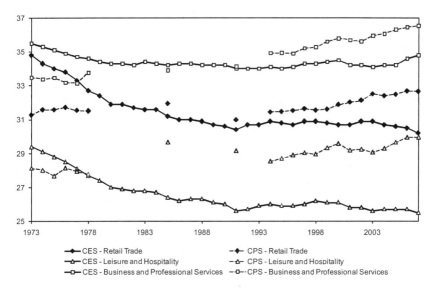

Fig. 9.7   CES and CPS average weekly hours in retail trade, business and professional services, and leisure and hospitality

question is whether these two trends were differentially picked up in the CES and the CPS.

We made an industry-by-industry comparison of CES and CPS hours, and found that three industries—Retail Trade, Leisure and Hospitality, and Business and Professional Services—accounted for most of the difference between the two series. Figure 9.7 shows that there are large differences between the actual CES and the MJ & HPA simulated CES hours for these three industries. Between 1973 and the early 1980s there were large declines in actual CES hours in Retail Trade and Leisure and Hospitality, and, to a lesser extent, Business and Professional Services. At the same time, their MJ & HPA counterparts remained approximately constant. In later years, the three actual CES series declined or remained fairly constant, while the three MJ & HPA series increased.

To investigate how the trends in these three industries affected the overall CES–CPS comparison, we performed a counterfactual experiment. Figure 9.8 shows actual CES hours and MJ & HPA hours. These were computed as a weighted mean of hours in each industry, where the weights are industry employment shares. Our CF1 counterfactual series uses CES employment shares with CPS hours, while CF2 uses CPS employment shares with CES hours. Comparing the two counterfactual hours series to the two original series shows that it is differences in hours, not employment shares, that is driving the divergence of CPS and CES hours series.[29] In figure 9.9, we modified

29. The 2002 to 2003 divergence of the counterfactual series from the actual series is likely due to the change in industry codes that occurred at that time.

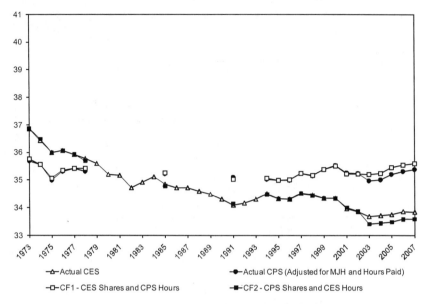

Fig. 9.8   Actual and counterfactual estimates of hours worked per week

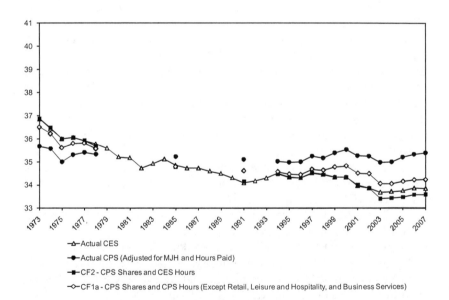

Fig. 9.9   Actual and modified counterfactual estimates of hours worked per week

CF1 so that CES hours are used for Retail Trade, Leisure and Hospitality, and Business and Professional Services; and CPS hours are used for all other industries. The CF1a series comes much closer, compared to the CF1 series, to replicating the actual CES series in both level and trend. Averaging over all years for which we have data, these three industries explain about two-thirds of the overall difference between the actual CES and MJ & HPA hours series. In 2007 the difference between the CF1a series and the actual CES is only 0.4 of an hour per week, compared to the 1.5 hour difference between the actual CES and MJ & HPA hours series. Thus, it appears that it is these industries that contributed the most to the downward trend in actual CES hours. We do not know why these three industries contributed so much to the CES–CPS divergence, but it seems that any further investigation should start there.

References

Abraham, K. G., J. R. Spletzer, and J. C. Stewart. 1998. Divergent trends in alternative wage series. In *Labor statistics measurement issues,* NBER Studies in Income and Wealth, vol. 60, ed. J. Haltiwanger, M. E. Manser, and R. Topel, 293–324. Chicago: University of Chicago Press.
———. 1999. Why do different wage series tell different stories? *American Economic Review Papers and Proceedings* 89 (2): 34–9.
Bureau of Labor Statistics 2009. *American Time Use Survey User's Guide.* Available at: http://www.bls.gov/tus/atususerguide.pdf.
Eldridge, L. P., M. E. Manser, and P. F. Otto. 2004. Hours data and their impact on measures of productivity change. *Monthly Labor Review* 127 (4): 9–28.
Fallick, B. C., and C. A. Fleischman. 2004. Employer-to-employer flows in the U.S. labor market: The complete picture of gross worker flows. Federal Reserve Board Economics and Finance Discussion Series 2004-34.
Frazis, H., and J. Stewart. 2004. What can time-use data tell us about hours of work? *Monthly Labor Review* 127 (12): 3–9.
———. 2007. Where does the time go? Concepts and measurement in the American Time Use Survey. In *Hard to measure goods and services: Essays in memory of Zvi Griliches,* ed. E. Berndt and C. Hulten, 73–97. NBER Studies in Income and Wealth, vol. 67. Chicago: University of Chicago Press.
Hamermesh, D. 1990. Shirking or productive schmoozing: Wages and the allocation of time at work. *Industrial and Labor Relations Review* 43 (3): 121S–33S.
Hamermesh, D. S., H. Frazis, and J. Stewart. 2005. Data watch—the American Time Use Survey. *Journal of Economic Perspectives* 19 (1): 221–32.
Kirkland, K. 2000. On the decline in average weekly hours worked. *Monthly Labor Review* 123 (7): 26–31.
Kuhn, P., and F. Lozano. 2008. The expanding workweek? Understanding trends in long work hours among U.S. men, 1979–2006. *Journal of Labor Economics* 26 (2): 311–43.
Mellow, W., and H. Sider. 1983. Accuracy of response in labor market surveys: Evidence and implications. *Journal of Labor Economics* 1 (4): 331–44.
Nardone, T., M. Bowler, J. Kropf, K. Kirkland, and S. Wetrogan. 2003. Examining

the discrepancy in employment growth between the CPS and the CES. Paper presented at the meeting of the Federal Economic Statistics Advisory Committee. October.

Robinson, J. and A. Bostrom. 1994. The overestimated workweek? What time diary measures suggest. *Monthly Labor Review* 117 (1): 11–23.

Rodgers, W. L., C. Brown, and G. J. Duncan. 1993. Errors in survey reports of earnings, hours worked, and hourly wages. *Journal of the American Statistical Association* 22 (424): 1208–18.

Stewart, J. 2007. Using March CPS data to analyze labor market transitions. *Journal of Economic and Social Measurement* 32 (2-3): 177–97.

Sundstrom, W. 1999. The overworked American or the overestimated workweek? Trends and biases in recent estimates of weekly work hours in the United States. Santa Clara University. Unpublished Manuscript.

U.S. Department of Labor, Bureau of Labor Statistics. 1983. *Employer Records Analysis Survey of 1981.* Final Report.

Williams, R. D. 2004. Investigating hours worked measures. *Labour Market Trends* 112 (2): 71–79.

Comment   Charles Brown

Harley Frazis and Jay Stewart have written a very careful chapter on an important topic. Trends in hours worked are a direct object of interest (how much of the improvement in living standards generated by productivity growth is being taken as leisure?) and are an essential component in computing trends in hourly wages and productivity growth. Two major data series track hours worked over time—the household-based Current Population Survey (CPS) and the employer-reported Current Employment Statistics (CES) survey. The CPS workweeks are higher, and show little of the trend decline that one sees in the CES. This substantial difference is cause for concern. In the decade since Abraham, Spletzer, and Stewart first explored the question, the simple addition of ten more years of data has done nothing to resolve it. Frazis and Stewart's contribution is an admirable blend of imagination, care, and their intimate knowledge of (and access to) a wide range of data. They make some progress, particularly with respect to differences in average hours worked over the period studied. They are less successful in accounting for divergent time patterns. Their clear-eyed assessment of what they have and have not done will make this chapter the obvious starting point as others bring further ideas to the discussion.

In reading the chapter, I found it helpful to divide it into three sections. First, CPS and CES differ in the unit for which the hours measure is being

Charles Brown is a research professor in the Survey Research Center and professor of economics at the University of Michigan, and a research associate of the National Bureau of Economic Research.

constructed: CPS includes all workers, while CES (until very recently) focused only on production or nonsupervisory workers; CPS treats two jobs held by one worker as two contributions to one worker's workweek, while CES treats them as two separate jobs. These adjustments more or less eliminate the difference between the two measures of hours worked in the early 1970s (when they start to diverge), but does not account for the divergent trends.

Frazis and Stewart then explore several other possibilities. The CPS measures hours worked, while CES measures hours paid; in addition to different treatment of paid time off, these will differ if workers misreport their hours, or if they work off the clock (leading "hours paid" to misstate actual work hours). Second, CPS measures hours worked during the reference week, while CES measures hours during the pay period, which includes the reference week. The longer reference period, interacted with worker turnover, will lead the two series to diverge and could potentially account for different trends. These two possibilities are more creative. Before looking at any data, I would not have had even a confident hunch as to whether they would resolve or deepen the puzzle of the diverging trends.

Accounting for paid time off gets the levels of the two series still closer, but once again the adjusted CPS series does not mirror the decline one sees in CES. The adjustments for hours reporting and reference periods are both small. But the available data are, here, very limited: we do not have a consistent time series of time-use data, nor of turnover at the frequency that the reference period calculations require, and the sharp change in reference period between 2002 and 2007 (reversing a striking lack of trend over nearly thirty years) may well be distorted by the comparability problems that the authors are quick to admit.

The third contribution of the chapter is a simple decomposition: the CPS-CES divergence has been concentrated in a subset of trade and service industries. Unlike the earlier analysis, where diagnosis and cure are intimately related, here we have a very interesting "fact" but no suggested interpretation. Nevertheless, this strikes me as a very intriguing clue.

The preceding comments have been strikingly short of examples where I wish the authors had made different choices in analyzing the available data. My short list of suggestions for further work on the topic thus focuses on broadening the analysis, rather than hoping that small tweaks in an already careful study will yield further insight.

The authors have focused on hours of work, and not paid much attention to either the employment counts or the payroll data that come from the CPS and CES. I believe that broadening the focus would help us better understand the consequences of the observed CPS-CES disagreement, and *might* suggest candidate explanations. For example, if differences in hours are mirrored by opposite differences in employment counts, so that aggregate hours worked are very similar, the consequences for productivity measurement are quite different than if employment counts line up perfectly and total hours differ by as much as the hours per week calculations that Frazis and Stewart have analyzed. If we have correctly mimicked the CES production/nonsupervisory worker definitions in the CPS, correctly adjusted for multiple jobholding, and made appropriate corrections for the different reference period, then adjusted employment counts (both aggregate and by industry) should be the same. If they are not, we know we have more work to do on one of these adjustments.

Finally, if we really want to understand differences between CPS and CES, we need to push harder on getting data from workers and their employers on the same employment transaction. Many of the corrections that Frazis and Stewart employ are based on reasonable hypotheses about how workers and employers report a reference week's employment experience. It would be most helpful if they were armed with actual data that mirrored this thought experiment.

IV

The Effects of Changing Demographics

The Effect of Population Aging on the Aggregate Labor Market

Bruce Fallick, Charles Fleischman, and Jonathan Pingle

10.1 Introduction

Economists have long noted the role that population growth plays in economic growth and other economic outcomes (e.g., Hagen 1959; Kuznets 1956, 1958; Becker, Glaeser, and Murphy 1999). Prior to World War II, the dominant question was how economies would grapple with declining population growth (Hansen 1939; Keynes 1937), as fertility had been declining and immigration had slowed. However, that all changed as the end of World War II ushered in an unprecedented jump in fertility rates, which Easterlin (1961) described as an "abrupt break with historical experience." In 1946 the U.S. fertility rate leapt by an astounding 19 percent, and then jumped by another 11 percent in 1947, finally peaking in 1957 at 40 percent above the World War II levels. This rapid surge in births created an extraordinary population bulge now known as the baby boom. That the baby boom

Bruce Fallick is a senior economist at the Board of Governors of the Federal Reserve System. Charles Fleischman is a senior economist at the Board of Governors of the Federal Reserve System. Jonathan Pingle is an economist at Brevan Howard Asset Management.

The views expressed in this chapter are those of the authors and do not represent the view of the Federal Reserve System or its staff. The authors wish to thank Stephanie Aaronson, Andrew Figura, and William Wascher, who coauthored a related paper on the decline in labor force participation. Special thanks also go to Karen Smith at the Social Security Administration for providing detailed data that underlies the agency's labor force projections, and Mitra Toossi, who provided data and answered questions on the Bureau of Labor Statistics' long-run projections for labor supply. John Schmitt of CEPR answered questions and offered STATA code for imputing topcoded wages. In addition, we received useful input for this line of research from Daniel Aaronson, Gary Burtless, Julie Hotchkiss, Chinhui Juhn, Joseph Lupton, Lisa Lynch, Mark Schweitzer, Daniel Sullivan, Joyce Zickler, and seminar participants at the Bureau of Labor Statistics. Leslie Carroll and Andrew Strauss provided expert assistance.

was followed by a fertility trough only reinforced the former's uniqueness.[1] Indeed, fertility rates began to decline in 1958, and demographers typically date the end of the baby boom in 1964. Over the next several years, fertility rates fell more sharply. By 1973 they were well below not only the World War II rates, but well below any fertility rate since 1909, when the National Center for Health Statistics' published series begins.[2]

In addition to their large numbers, the baby boomers are expected to live longer than the cohorts that preceded them. For example, in 1949, an American aged fifty-five could expect to live another twenty-one years, on average; by 2002, a fifty-five-year-old could expect to live another twenty-six years.

In this chapter, we examine the direct implications of the shifting population age distribution for several labor market measures: the unemployment rate, the participation rate, gross labor force flows, and wage rates. We find that the largest effects on the aggregate labor force participation rate are yet to come, while the effects on the unemployment rate have mostly run their course. In addition, the movement of the baby boomers into the high-earnings age groups has pushed up mean wages and changed the average flows though labor market states only modestly.

Because the cohorts both preceding and following the baby boom were relatively small, the aging of the baby boomers has had a pronounced influence on the population distribution. Figure 10.1 shows the shares of selected age groups in the age sixteen and over Civilian Noninstitutional Population (CNIP) taken from the Current Population Survey (CPS), along with how those population shares are expected to evolve in the years ahead, based on Census Bureau projections. The share of older Americans has already begun to rise, and this increase is projected to continue until around 2030.

Labor market behavior varies substantially over the life cycle. As a result, the aging of the U.S. population has affected headline measures of labor market activity, sometimes even obscuring more structural changes in the economy. Perry (1971) was among the first to realize that the increase in the number of baby boom teenagers in the labor force was confounding interesting economic measurement. He was interested in inflation, and the role the unemployment rate played as a proxy for labor market tightness. Increases in the share of teens in the labor force had increased the share

---

1. See also Montgomery and Trussell (1986), who provide more detail of the demographic changes, not only the fertility increase of the baby boom, but also changes in age at first marriage, marital status, and other contributing factors that underlay this pattern.

2. Fertility data is available from the National Center for Health Statistics website at http://www.cdc.gov/nchs/data/statab/natfinal2002.annvol1_01.pdf. Life expectancy tables can be found at http://www.cdc.gov/nchs/products/pubs/pubd/lftbls/life/1966.htm, for example. In 1945 in the United States there were 85.9 births per 1,000 women aged fifteen to forty-four. In 1946 there were 101.9 and in 1947 there were 113.3. In 1957 there were 122.7 births per 1,000 women aged fifteen to forty-four, but by 1973, the fertility rate had fallen to 68.8.

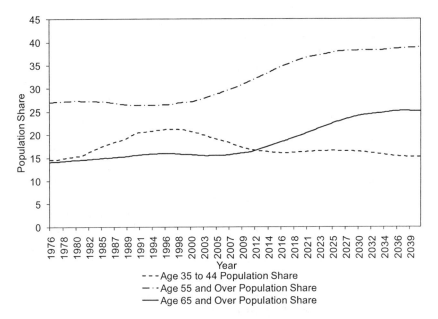

Fig. 10.1   Population shares (history and projection)

of a demographic group with relatively high unemployment rates. This demographic shift alone put upward pressure on the unemployment rate during the 1970s, and made using the level of the unemployment rate as a proxy for labor market tightness inconsistent over time. Perry constructed a demographically adjusted unemployment rate to abstract from this change, holding constant fixed labor force shares to remove the fluctuations in the relative share of boomers.[3] More recently, Shimer (1998), Abraham and Shimer (2001), and Valletta and Hodges (2005) have noted that the declines in the shares of teenagers and young adults in the labor force have put measurable downward pressure on unemployment rates beginning in the late 1980s.

Even more striking are the implications for the labor force participation rate. Participation rates rise sharply with age through the early-to-mid-twenties, and continue to rise through the thirties and forties. Although we fondly think of forefathers who worked diligently until death, participation has declined sharply with age for most of the nation's history, and retirement has been a feature of life cycle labor supply since at least 1870 (Ransom and Sutch 1988).[4] Indeed, it has long been recognized that participation rates level off from the mid-forties through about age fifty or fifty-five, and then

---

3. See also Summers (1986) and Flaim (1990).
4. See also Tuma and Sandefur (1988).

decline precipitously. As a result, Aaronson et al. (2006) showed that the pronounced shift in the population toward older age groups recently began to put noticeable downward pressure on the aggregate participation rate. This marked the start of what is likely to be a sharp decline in participation that will last another half-century. As a result, in contrast to labor supply growth of 2 percent a year for much of the 1960s, 1970s, and 1980s, the Social Security Administration (SSA) projects labor supply growth will slow to 0.5 percent by 2015, and 0.3 percent by 2025.[5]

If the levels of unemployment and the labor force are sensitive to the age distribution, it is natural to ask how the flows across labor force statuses are affected. Blanchard and Diamond (1990), for example, note that the rates of labor force transitions vary by age. Younger individuals are more likely to move from out of the labor force into employment, while prime-age males are quite likely to enter unemployment after job loss instead of going back to school. However, little research has addressed how the changing age distribution has altered aggregate flows over time, and Blanchard and Diamond's sample ends in 1986. We update their observation, and describe how the shifting age distribution has changed the evolution of labor market flows over time, and how they are likely to evolve going forward as the baby boomers age.

Wage rates also vary substantially over the life cycle. Moreover, relative cohort size may influence earnings. In particular, as the baby boomers entered the labor force as lower-skilled young workers, evidence suggests that their sheer numbers depressed their wages, perhaps by as much as 10 percent (Murphy, Plant, and Welch 1988). We show later that the mere shifting of the baby boomers in and out of high wage age groups has measurably altered aggregate mean wages, pushing them up in recent decades.

In addition, a large literature on the implications of aging on the economy has focused primarily on the influence of population aging on old age programs like social security and the related estimates of the dependency ratio (e.g., Weil 1997; Borsch-Supan 2003), rather than emphasizing the effects of aging on macroeconomic quantities that concern us here. Our contribution is to focus more specifically on quantifying or updating estimates of the direct effects of the shifting age distribution on some of the major aggregate measures of labor market activity, and to project how these measures are likely to be influenced in the years ahead.

The rest of this chapter proceeds as follows. In section 10.2 we describe the CPS data that we use. In sections 10.3 through 10.6 we consider the influence that aging has had on each measure of labor market activity and how the continued aging of the population will likely affect it going forward. Section 10.7 concludes.

---

5. See also Toossi (2006).

10.2   Data

The official statistics on the labor force published by the Bureau of Labor Statistics (BLS) come from the Current Population Survey (CPS), a survey of roughly 60,000 households conducted monthly by the U.S. Census Bureau. We use these published data along with the underlying CPS microdata to analyze labor force participation, unemployment, labor market flows, and levels of earnings.

The labor force questions are asked of all civilians age sixteen and over. Individuals are in the sample for four months, get an eight-month break, and are then interviewed for another four months. At the fourth and eighth interview months workers are asked about earnings and hours of work (these are the "outgoing rotation groups"), which form the basis of the wage measures used later. The survey includes data on the labor force status of each individual as well as basic demographic information. We have adjusted the data for the effects of survey redesigns, revisions to population weights, and other inconsistencies that would influence the interpretation of time series constructed from the microdata.

The individual observations in the CPS are weighted according to estimates of the population provided by the U.S. Census Bureau. These estimates are real-time assessments of the size and makeup of the U.S. population. The Census Bureau, of course, conducts the decennial census. In between the decennial censuses, which serve as benchmarks, the agency produces estimates that update how many people are living in the United States based on a variety of sources ranging from the National Center for Health Statistics to the Department of Defense and incorporating estimates from surveys such as the American Community Survey. The Census Bureau updates its estimates as new data become available, and at any given time represent the nation's best estimates of the population over history.

Both the Census Bureau and the Social Security Administration (SSA) produce population projections broken down by age and gender groups. The Census Bureau projections are based on the sizes of birth cohorts, assumptions about fertility rates, estimated death rates, and assumptions for net international migration, and currently extend out to 2050.[6] The SSA

---

6. The Census population estimates are updated annually while the Census projections are updated about twice a decade. Therefore, the Census projections for population levels may not be consistent with the Census' best current estimate of the historical population. This highlights where some projection risks may lie. For example, the age distribution in the population estimates reflected in the 2005 CPS population shares imply more downward pressure from aging on aggregate labor force participation than does the age distribution in the projections that the estimates have superseded. Similarly, revisions to population estimates in January of 2006 prompted revisions to the weights in the Current Population Survey, from which participation is officially measured. The resulting new population estimates, taken alone, caused the labor force participation rate to revise down by two basis points.

produces its own projections that differ primarily in the assumptions for net international migration, including undocumented immigration. Both agencies project that the population's age distribution will continue to shift markedly toward older age groups. Our analysis following relies on Census Bureau projections, but qualitatively there would be little difference if we had used SSA projections.[7]

10.3   The Labor Force Participation Rate

Of all the major labor market indicators, the labor force participation rate is likely to be influenced the most profoundly by the aging of the population. Figure 10.2 shows the aggregate participation rate since 1948. Broadly speaking, the participation rate over the second half of the twentieth century has had three regimes: a period of relative stability until the mid-1960s, a period of steady increase between the mid-1960s and the late 1980s, and another recent period of relative stability. This experience was dominated by movements in women's labor force participation, which rose sharply over the twenty-five years following 1965, and leveled off after about 1990. As noted previously, the aging of the population appears already to be making itself felt in the decline in participation since about the year 2000, which likely marks the beginning of a fourth regime: a period of falling participation.

10.3.1   The Aging of the Population

The reason that the aging of the population has the potential to drastically slow labor supply growth is that labor force participation rates decline precipitously after age fifty. Thus, as the baby boomers move into their sixties and as life expectancies continue to lengthen, the rising proportion of older Americans has the potential to lower the share of Americans who are working or looking for work. For example, by 2035 the share of the sixteen and over population who are aged eighty or above is expected to double to approximately 15 percent, and 97 percent of this age group currently do not participate in the labor force. The current downward pressure of the age distribution on participation is primarily because two forces—the aging of the baby boomers and longer life expectancies—are now pushing in the same direction, after many years in which the upward pressure of baby boomers moving into high participation rate ages offset the downward pressure from longer life expectancies.

Figure 10.3 shows the age profiles of labor force participation rates for men and women using 2005 annual averages for fourteen age categories, and the aggregate participation rate for reference. Among women, the

---

7. For more details on the sensitivity of projected labor force estimates to varying assumptions concerning undocumented immigration see Fallick and Pingle (2007b).

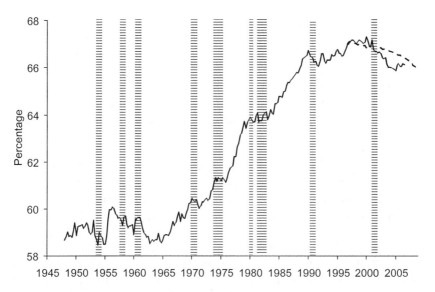

—Aggregate Labor Force Participation Rate

- - Simulation holding within-age participation rates at 1996:Q4 levels

Fig. 10.2   Aggregate labor force participation rate, 1948:Q1–2006:Q3
Source: Bureau of Labor Statistics.
Note: Shaded area is NBER dated recessions.

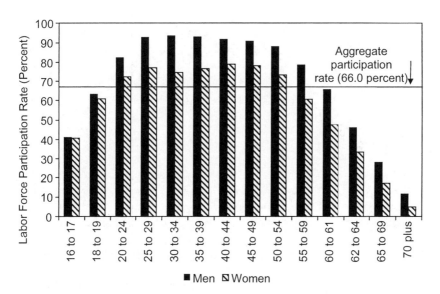

Fig. 10.3   Labor force participation rates by age and gender (2005)

groups over fifty-five years of age have below-average labor force participation rates. Among men, the age groups over age sixty have below average labor force participation rates. In both cases, participation rates begin to fall after about age fifty. Whether this is due to failing health, disability, retirement income, or wealth, it is a feature of life cycle labor supply unlikely to change fundamentally in the next few decades. While the slope of the age-participation function may change, it is quite likely to remain strongly negative.

The implication for labor force participation is striking. Figure 10.4 shows the history of the labor force participation rate through 2006, along with a projection that uses the 2005 labor force participation rate for each age group and allows the population shares to evolve as projected by the Census projections. Although other starting years can produce mildly different patterns, the implications are essentially the same: absent other changes, projected population aging will lower the aggregate labor force participation rate by 6 full percentage points over the next thirty-five years. This pace of decline dwarfs the 0.4 percentage point that shifting population shares have lowered the aggregate rate over the past four years. In sum, the projected aging of the labor force is likely to have a sizeable influence on participation, with the potential to completely unwind the increases in participation attributable to the earlier entry of more women in the workforce.

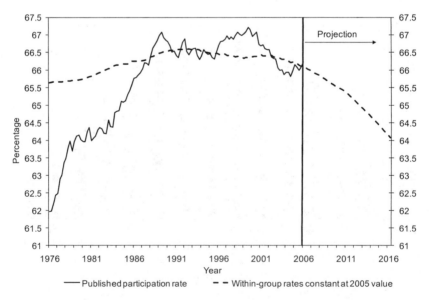

Fig. 10.4   An accounting of effect of aging on the labor force participation rate
Note: Within-group participation rates refer to fourteen age groups for men and women.

10.3.2   The Aging of Particular Cohorts

There is another aspect of aging that has implications for the aggregate labor force participation rate—not changes in the age distribution, but the movement of particular cohorts through the age distribution.

Most of the low-frequency change in the labor force participation rate in the second half of the twentieth century came from changes in participation rates within age groups rather than changes in the age distribution of the population. For women, much of this increase in participation appears to have resulted from the entry into the working-age population of birth cohorts with higher average participation rates than those who preceded them, and the progress of these higher-participation cohorts through the age distribution. As these cohorts have aged, and earlier cohorts have left the scene, the population of women has come to be dominated by cohorts who have proved to have generally higher participation rates throughout their lives. A similar effect seems to have been at work among men, but in the opposite direction, as successive cohorts of men have had generally lower participation rates than their predecessors.

This evolution of participation rates by cohort likely reflects numerous factors—such as evolving tastes, reproductive technology, wealth, education, social attitudes, retirement, welfare, and financial systems—some of which were internalized into the behavior of new generations more easily than into the behavior of mature cohorts who had already made "sticky" choices, an idea that goes back at least as far as Durand (1948).

The phenomenon is illustrated in figure 10.5, which shows the labor force participation rates for three age groups of women: age thirty-five to forty-four, age forty-five to fifty-four, and age fifty-five to sixty-four. Each line shows the participation rate of an age group over time. However, the horizontal axis shows the birth year for the middle age of the group, rather than the year of observation. In this way, the lines are shifted so that each birth cohort is vertically aligned with itself at different ages. The participation rate of the forty-five- to fifty-four-year-old group (the dashed line) appears to exhibit three rough inflections, in the vicinity of years 1960, 1975, and 1997. These correspond to the cohorts born around 1910, 1925, and 1947. The first two of these inflections line up well with the fifty-five- to sixty-four-year-old group (the dotted line), meaning that the inflection points in both age groups seem to occur when the cohorts born in 1910 and 1925 passed through those age groups. The cohort associated with the third inflection (those born around 1947) are not quite old enough to exhibit that inflection in the older group, but it can be seen when that cohort was thirty-five to forty-four years old (the solid line). Similarly (not shown), beginning in the mid-1960s and ending in the late 1970s, successive cohorts of sixteen- to twenty-four-year-old women had higher participation rates than their predecessors. Participation rates of successive cohorts twenty-five to thirty-four years old stopped

Fig. 10.5   Participation of women by birth cohort (actual data–not a projection)

rising about ten years later, in the late 1980s, suggesting that the participation rate in each of these age groups at a given time is at least partly related to which birth cohort is passing through that age at that time.

Of course, not all inflection points in all age groups line up so well by birth year; clearly, there have been developments in participation that are not well-represented by the aging of birth cohorts. However, the coincidences that do exist are sufficient to indicate that birth cohort has played a significant role in describing participation rates. Consequently, the aging of particular birth cohorts has played an important role in the evolution of the aggregate participation rate. In particular, the long increase in the aggregate participation rate from the early 1970s through the late 1980s can be attributed largely to the successively higher participation rates of cohorts born up through the beginning of the baby boom. And the end of that long period of increase can be attributed to the baby boom cohorts, who have roughly similar average participation rates, coming to dominate the population as they moved through the age distribution. Looking ahead, the same phenomenon of the aging of particular cohorts can be expected to put downward pressure on the aggregate participation rate, as successive cohorts of men and women appear to have generally lower propensities to participate.

These ideas are developed more fully in Fallick and Pingle (2007a), which develops a model of aggregate labor force participation that incorporates both changes in the age distribution of the population and the movement of cohorts through the age distribution, as well as exploring other measurable factors that appear to influence participation rates. The model relies on cohort effects in order to predict the future path of participation for individual birth years—essentially using the observed information shown in figure 10.5 to form a baseline of relative labor force attachment going forward. The authors' model contains cyclical controls, variables representing education, fertility, and socioeconomic trends, as well as the features of public programs. While we will not explicate that model here, figure 10.6 shows its implications for the future of the participation rate under one reasonable set of assumptions. The combination of the aging of population in general, the aging of cohorts in particular, and other factors imply a steeply falling participation rate over the next decade or so. In addition, although the model appears to fit closely the annual averages in 2006 and 2007, model estimation was stopped in 2005, so the subsequent years are an out-of-sample projection, and thus not necessarily end-point bias.

Most relevant to the discussion of aging, however, is that the declines projected incorporate the expectation that the baby boomers will have much more labor force attachment than prior cohorts (despite not often exhibiting this during their prime working years). As shown in figure 10.7, the participation rate of men age sixty-five and over is expected to increase as the baby boomers enter the age sixty-five and older age group, although the pace of increases is estimated to slow near 2015. In the Fallick/Pingle model the increases are attributable to a combination of longer life expectan-

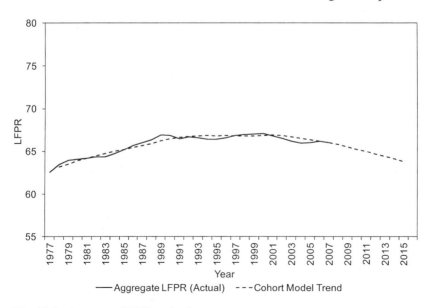

Fig. 10.6   Aggregate LFPR projections

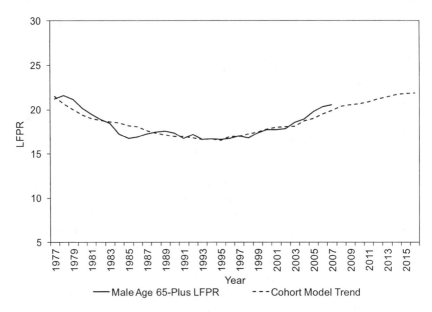

Fig. 10.7   Male age 65-plus projections

cies, higher education among the cohorts reaching these ages, and favorable social security incentives (the rising retirement age and the increases in the delayed retirement credit).

For women aged sixty-five and over, the forecast is for quite robust increases in participation as the baby boom cohorts exhibit greater attachment than the average of the preceding cohorts already over age sixty-five (figure 10.8). The cohort model trend estimates for older women are slightly steeper than forecasts produced by government agencies such as BLS and SSA, but a little less steep for the forecasts of older men. For the older men, the difference is likely attributable to the fact that baby boomer males, during their prime working ages, tended to work less than men of earlier cohorts, and our model perhaps carries forward more of these "unobserved preferences" than the BLS or SSA projections.[8] In a similar vein, for the older women, the model may carry more of the high degree of attachment of the cohorts who raised prime-age female labor supply from 1970 to 1990 into this older age category. If we look at the rough estimates, the projections expect gains of nearly 1/2 percentage point per year in this group's participation rate. The share of age sixty-five-and-over women is expected to increase from 9 percent to 10 percent of the population over this period. Roughly speaking, this implies this demographic group alone would add nearly 5

8. For BLS estimates see Toossi (2006). For a more detailed and thorough discussion and decomposition of the differences in long-run forecasts see Fallick and Pingle (2007a, 2007b).

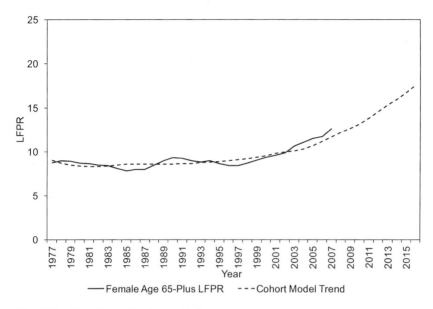

Fig. 10.8   Female age 65-plus projections

basis points to the aggregate participation rate per year. The pace of decline due to population aging shown in figure 10.5 is roughly 2 percentage points per year, on average, between 2005 and 2040. Thus, the projected increase in participation among older women would offset roughly 1/4 of that decline. In the end, the shifts in the population age distribution are a relatively powerful force for even significant behavioral changes to overcome.[9]

10.4   Unemployment Rate

Looking back over the past forty years, figure 10.9 shows that the movements in the aggregate unemployment rate can be divided into two phases: from the mid-1960s through the early 1980s, the unemployment rate moved higher; since then the unemployment rate has shown a pronounced down-

9. The sensitivity of these projections are evaluated in Fallick and Pingle (2007a and 2007b). In particular, alternative assumptions for population growth and immigration are evaluated. Under even large margins of error in these assumptions, the downward pressure on the participation rate from population aging (big boomer cohort followed by smaller cohort behind) dominates the other influences. In fact, as shown by the revised participation rate estimates published by the BLS in the January 2008 employment situation report, population growth was shown to have been overestimated thus far this decade by a substantial amount, and the aging of the population underestimated, altogether revising down the labor force participation rate by 0.1 percentage point. Although the next decennial census in 2010 will be more revealing, the downward pressure of population aging seems likely to be the dominant driver of trend labor force participation for the next few decades.

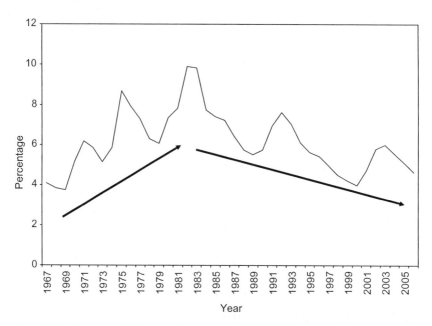

Fig. 10.9   Aggregate U.S. unemployment rate, 1967–2006

trend. These movements reflect more than business cycle fluctuations. The lowest unemployment rate achieved at the cyclical peaks and the highest unemployment rate hit at the cyclical troughs both ratcheted up from the 1960s through the early 1980s. Subsequently, both cyclical high and low unemployment rates have declined consistently, with the unemployment rate bottoming out in 2000 at its lowest level since 1969.

The apparent trends in the unemployment rate have not been associated with changes in inflationary pressures. On the contrary, core price inflation moved higher through the 1970s, and has trended downward since. This suggests that at least some of the low frequency movements in the aggregate unemployment rate have reflected changes in the structural or natural rate of unemployment. In this section, we examine several factors that help explain these low frequency movements. To preview, we show that shifting labor force shares related to the age distribution of the population can explain a good deal of both the earlier rise and subsequent decline in the aggregate unemployment rate. However, even after accounting for the effects of changing labor force shares, significant movements in the aggregate unemployment rate remain unexplained by these "between" group factors.

10.4.1   The Age Distribution of the Population

The most obvious way in which the aging of the population affects the aggregate unemployment rate is simply that some age groups tend to have higher unemployment rates than others. Figure 10.10 shows the average

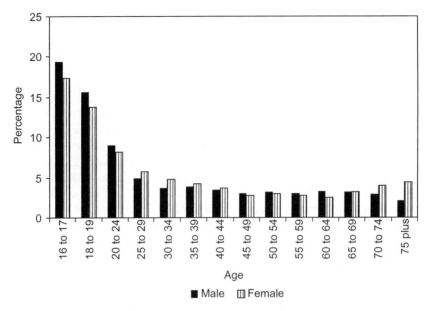

Fig. 10.10   Unemployment rates by age and sex (1997)

unemployment rates in 1997 for men and women in various age groups. The variation in unemployment rates across age is substantial but is concentrated among the younger age groups. In particular, unemployment rates fall from the sixteen to seventeen group to the twenty-five to twenty-nine group, then are pretty stable from age thirty on. Thus, as population shares change, the aggregate unemployment rate can be expected to change.

For many years it has been a common practice to adjust the unemployment rate for such changes in the age/sex composition of the labor force. The usual method is to recalculate the unemployment rate by weighting the unemployment rates of the various demographic groups by their labor force shares in some base year (Perry 1971) rather than allowing those shares to change over time.

Here we follow this practice with a couple of variations. First, most demographic adjustments to the unemployment rate are performed using fairly broad age groups, which may miss some subtleties in the evolution of the unemployment rate; we use fourteen age groups. Second, we are interested in decomposing changes in the demographic shares of the labor force into the two components of changes in population shares and changes in relative participation rates. Therefore, to compute the contribution to changes in the unemployment rate of the aging of the population alone, we hold group-specific labor force participation rates and group-specific unemployment rates constant at their 1997 average levels, and apply those rates to changing population shares to yield a counterfactual aggregate unemployment rate. The difference between this counterfactual unemployment rate and the actual unemployment rate in 1997 provides one measure of the direct influence of changes in the age distribution of the population on the aggregate unemployment rate. This difference is shown in figure 10.11.

Because the differences in unemployment rates across age groups are concentrated at younger ages (under thirty), the changing age distribution of the population had its most notable accounting influence on the aggregate unemployment rate from the 1960s through the 1980s, when the baby boomers were moving through these younger ages. In contrast, the influence of shifts in the age distribution on the unemployment rate over the past decade has been small, as the baby boom moved through ages with fairly similar unemployment rates. From 1967 to 1976, the aging of the population pushed the unemployment rate up through this channel by 0.2 percentage point; since 1976, this channel has reduced the unemployment rate by 0.6 percentage point, but only 0.2 percentage point of this decline has come since 1991. As the population continues to age in coming years, we can expect this downward pressure on the unemployment rate to increase somewhat, but not to the degree that we saw in the 1980s.

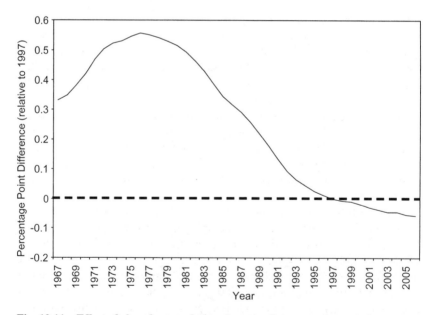

Fig. 10.11   Effect of changing population shares on the aggregate unemployment rate (relative to 1997 actual unemployment rate)

Note: Difference between reweighted 1997 age-sex specific unemployment rates (weights are age-sex specific population shares times the 1997 labor force participation rates) and the 1997 aggregate unemployment rate.

10.4.2   The Age Distribution of the Labor Force

There is, however, another way in which the aging of the population can be thought of as influencing the unemployment rate. Beyond changing the age distribution of the population, over time different cohorts of people come to dominate the labor market. As previously noted, and in previous work, we argued that as newer cohorts came to replace older cohorts in particular age groups, the labor force participation rates of those age groups changed. This is not the only source of changes in age-specific participation rates, but it has been an important one. These changes in age-specific participation rates have meant that the age distribution of the labor force has often changed more than has the age distribution of the population. In particular, as the cohorts of women with higher participation rates moved into the younger age groups and then into older groups, the share of these high-unemployment-rate age groups in the labor force rose and then fell in excess of what population shares alone would dictate. This is illustrated in figure 10.12, which shows the share of sixteen- to twenty-four-year-olds in the population and in the labor force.

The implications for the aggregate unemployment rate have been substantial. The dashed line in figure 10.13 reproduces the measure of the direct influence of changing population shares on the unemployment rate, while the solid line shows the influence of labor force shares, which comprises both changing population shares and changing participation rates. We construct

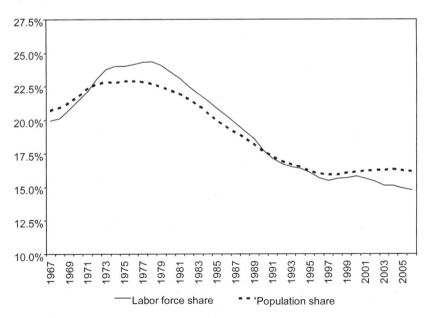

Fig. 10.12   Population and labor force shares ages 16–24

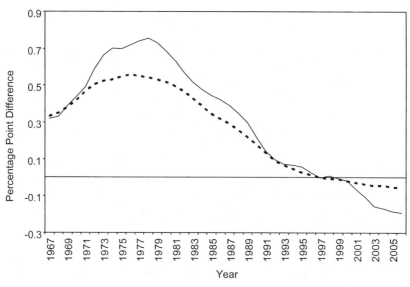

Fig. 10.13   Effect of changing population and labor-force shares on the aggregate unemployment rate (relative to 1997 actual unemployment rate)

Note: Solid line is the difference between reweighted 1997 age-sex specific unemployment rates (weights are the age-sex specific labor force shares) and the aggregate unemployment in 1997. Dashed line is the difference between reweighted age-sex specific unemployment rates (weights are age-sex specific population shares times the 1997 labor force participation rates) and the 1997 aggregate unemployment rate.

the latter by holding within-group unemployment rates constant at their 1997 levels, but allowing both the population shares and participation rates to change, and subtracting this counterfactual unemployment rate from the 1997 unemployment rate. The difference between the two lines is a measure of the influence of the changing participation rates. In total, changes in labor force shares raised the unemployment rate by 0.4 percentage point from 1967 to 1977—about twice as much as the change due only to changing population shares. Since 1977, shifts in the labor force shares have lowered the aggregate unemployment rate by 0.9 percentage point, 0.3 percentage point of which has come since 1991. Once again, the decline is bigger than can be accounted for by changing population shares alone, owing largely to the declining participation rates for young men and women.

10.4.3   Within-Age Unemployment Rates

A third element in the evolution of the aggregate unemployment rate has been changes in within-age unemployment rates. Figure 10.14 shows how unemployment rates within age group have moved over time. As one can see, a major development in the demographics of the labor market over the

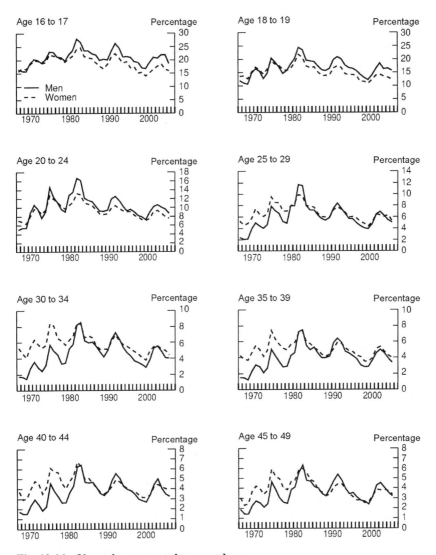

Fig. 10.14   Unemployment rate by age and sex

past several decades has been the convergence of female and male unemployment rates.

For our current purposes, we would like to know whether this convergence in unemployment rates reflects one aspect of the aging of the population—not changes in the age distribution, but the movement of particular cohorts through the age distribution. As we noted previously, the rise in female labor force participation occurred as cohorts of women with participation rates more similar to men's entered the population and replaced cohorts of

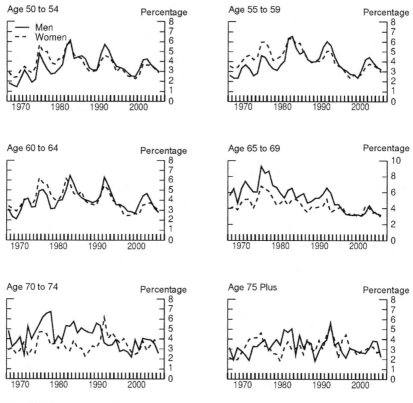

Fig. 10.14   (cont.)

women with less similar participation rates. By our estimates, the cohorts of the baby boom marked the end of decades of steadily rising cohort-specific participation rates for women. As these cohorts moved through the age distribution, they raised the aggregate participation rate. A natural question is whether the convergence of female and male unemployment rates can be described the same way. That is, did female unemployment rates converge toward male unemployment rates because cohorts of women with unemployment rates more similar to men's entered the working-age population and replaced cohorts of women with unemployment rates less similar to men's?

In order to begin to answer this question, we estimated a model similar to the basic model in Fallick and Pingle (2007a). In this setup, within each gender, the unemployment rate of an age group in a particular year is a function of an age-specific constant and the identity of the birth cohorts passing though those ages in that year, as well as cyclical controls. That is,

$$(1) \qquad \log UR_{g,t} = \alpha_g + \lambda_g X_t + \frac{1}{n_g} \sum_{b=1907}^{1989} C_{g,b,t} \beta_b + \varepsilon_{g,t} \qquad g = 1 \text{ to } 14,$$

where g indexes the age groups, t indexes the calendar year, and b indexes birth years. The $C_{g,b,t}$ are indicator variables that equal one if the corresponding cohort b appears in that age group g at time t, and n_g is the number of ages in age group g. Variable X_t is a vector of cyclical control variables, the α are age group fixed effects, and the β are birth year or cohort fixed effects. The degree of cyclical sensitivity (λ) varies by age group, while the cohort effects do not—that is, the cohort effects are constrained to be the same across all equations in which the cohort appears. The age effects (α) are constant.

In this setup, the shape of the age-unemployment-rate profile is common to all persons of the same gender, but each birth cohort has a particular "propensity" to be unemployed that shifts the age profile up or down.

An alternative formulation assumes that, within each gender, the unemployment rate of an age group in a particular year is a function of an age-specific constant and a common effect of calendar time.

(2) $$\log UR_{g,t} = \alpha_g + \lambda_g X_t + \beta_t + \varepsilon_{g,t} \qquad g = 1 \text{ to } 14.$$

In this alternative, the shape of the age-unemployment profile is likewise common to all persons of the same gender, but this age profile is shifted by conditions that change over time but affect the unemployment rates of all ages proportionately.

Comparing the fit of these two specifications provides an indication of whether the aging of specific cohorts can explain the evolution of the unemployment rate. In the case of women, the evidence in favor of a cohort effect in explaining the increase in labor force participation was so strong that we expected the evidence to favor a cohort explanation of the evolution of unemployment rates as well. In fact, as shown in figure 10.15, the estimated trend from the basic cohort specification does a reasonably good job of capturing the low frequency movements in women's unemployment rates, at least since the mid-1970s, suggesting that the decline in women's unemployment rates over that span can be usefully described in terms of lower-unemployment cohorts replacing higher-unemployment cohorts. However, the specification that substitutes time effects—modeled as a cubic time trend—for cohort effects, does a somewhat better job of capturing the initial increase in female unemployment rates through the mid-1970s.

Table 10.1 reports measures of model fit. For women, the adjusted R-squared (column [3]) for these two specifications are the same, when the model is estimated over the period 1967 to 2006. However, the adjusted R-squared for the full panel regression (fourteen age groups times forty time periods) measures the model's ability to explain both the "between"-group differences in average unemployment rates as well as the "within"-group variation that is of more interest here. As a result, the adjusted R-squared overstates how well the model fits the data for any one age group.

Columns (5) and (7) report the average R-squared (not adjusted for degrees of freedom) for the youngest eleven age groups—from age sixteen

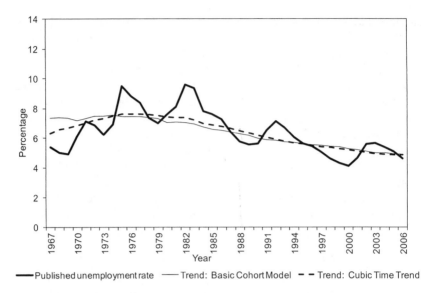

Fig. 10.15   Estimates of trend unemployment rates: Women

Table 10.1   Measures of model fit: Unemployment rate model

Model specification	Adjusted R^2		Average R^2 (11 age groups, ages 16–64)[a]		Average R^2 (All age groups)	
	Men	Women	Men	Women	Men	Women
Long sample (1967–2006)						
Cohort dummies	0.934	0.954	0.77	0.82	0.73	0.74
Cubic time trend	0.936	0.954	0.81	0.85	0.68	0.71
Cohort dummies and cubic time trend	0.961	0.959	0.86	0.85	0.80	0.76
Short sample (1977–2006)						
Cohort dummies	0.944	0.959	0.75	0.85	0.75	0.76
Cubic time trend	0.949	0.953	0.81	0.83	0.70	0.69
Cohort dummies and Cubic time trend	0.961	0.959	0.86	0.86	0.82	0.76

[a]To construct R-squared for individual age groups, we calculated the variances of the group-specific unemployment rates and the group-specific residuals from the regressions using all fourteen age groups. We did not correct for differences in degrees of freedom across specification.

to sixty-four—(column [5]) and for the full complement of groups (column [7]). We omit the oldest age groups from these columns because the specification with cohort dummies can "overfit" the unemployment rate for these groups. This is because most of the cohorts included in the sixty-five and older age groups are not well-represented in younger age groups in our data. Moreover, as shown in the last three panels of figure 10.14, the unemployment rates for the two oldest age groups are more idiosyncratic and less cyclical than those for those ages sixteen to sixty-four. The average R-squared for the groups between ages sixteen and sixty-four is a little higher for the model with the cubic time trend, even though this model has many fewer explanatory variables.

As shown on the third line, adding the cohort dummies to the specification with the cubic time trend does not improve the model's ability to explain female unemployment rates for women ages sixteen to sixty-four. Thus, we find little evidence for a substantial role for birth-year cohort effects on women's unemployment rates, in contrast to the earlier results for labor force participation.

For men, the results suggest a somewhat more nuanced interpretation. As shown in figure 10.16, the model with only cohort effects does a poor job of capturing either the increase in male unemployment rates through the early 1980s or their subsequent decline.[10] In contrast, the specification with the cubic time trend rises and falls more closely with the actual unemployment rate. These visual impressions are borne out by the measures of model fit. As shown in column (4) of table 10.1, the average R-squared for the eleven age groups aged sixteen to sixty-four improves more notably when cohort effects are replaced by a cubic time trend.

But, unlike the results for women, the model fit is notably improved when we include both cohort effects and time effects. Thus, it seems that the movements of relative unemployment rates for the different age groups are more important for men than for women, which may in turn reflect that age plays a more significant role in how men have responded to aggregate labor market developments.

Clearly there is much more work to be done in modeling the trends in unemployment rates, and a discussion of the economic factors at work is beyond the scope of the current chapter. Nevertheless, we are confident that the aging of the population per se plays only a relatively minor role in the evolution of the aggregate unemployment rate at present.

10.5   Labor Market Flows

10.5.1   The Age Profile of Unemployment Rates

The modest size of the effects of population aging on the unemployment rate in recent years stems from the fact that although unemployment rates fall rapidly with age from the teenage years through the early thirties, unemployment rates are fairly stable across ages from the early thirties into the seventies. Some of this, no doubt, reflects selection biases, as those types

---

10. The rise and subsequent decline in the trend unemployment rate from the cohort model primarily reflects the changing demographics of the labor force that we discussed previously. Holding labor force shares fixed at their 1997 values, estimated trend from the cohort model is nearly flat from 1967 to 2006.

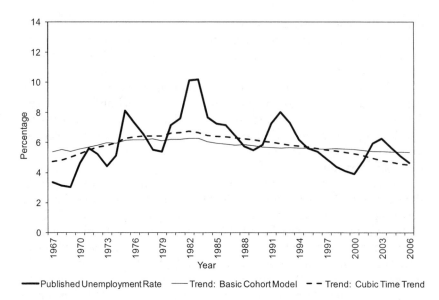

Fig. 10.16   Estimates of trend unemployment rates: Men

of persons who would tend to have higher unemployment rates leave the population or the labor force at different rates than those who tend to have lower unemployment rates. But the stability is nevertheless surprising given the profundity of the changes in labor force attachment over the life cycle. Indeed, the stability of the unemployment rates masks large but offsetting changes in labor force behaviors that, taken individually, might be expected to significantly affect unemployment rates.

The most obvious of these is retirement behavior and associated withdrawal from the labor force. Figures 10.17 and 10.18 show the average monthly hazard rates, by age, out of the labor force from employment and from unemployment, for the period 1996 to 2006, calculated from matched CPS data. Both rates rise rapidly beginning at ages in the fifties, increases that we would associate with retirements. At least qualitatively, the changes in these flows as persons age offset each other in terms of their implications for the unemployment rate.

However, other labor force flows vary over the entire range of ages over which unemployment rates are stable. Job finding rates—the hazard rates from unemployment to employment and from not in the labor force into employment—both fall over the entire range from about age thirty on (figures 10.19 and 10.20). One would expect that because of this unemployment rates would rise with age, but over the same age range the rate at which new entrants and reentrants move from out of the labor force into unemployment falls (figure 10.21). Meanwhile, the flow that one might associate most directly with the unemployment rate, the hazard rate from employment to

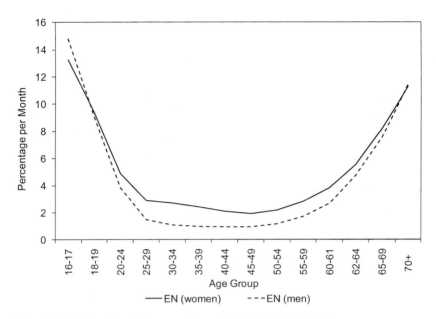

Fig. 10.17   Hazard rates from employment to NLF (1996–2006)

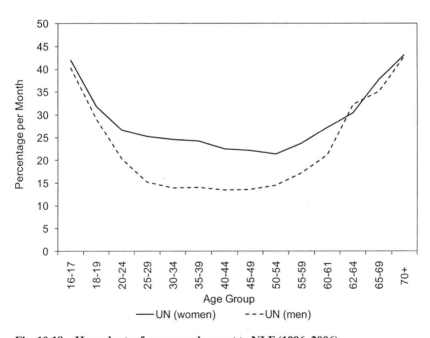

Fig. 10.18   Hazard rates from unemployment to NLF (1996–2006)

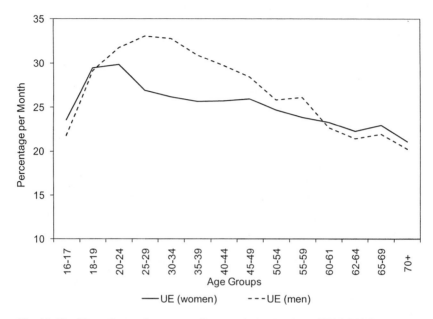

Fig. 10.19   Hazard rates from unemployment to employment (1996–2006)

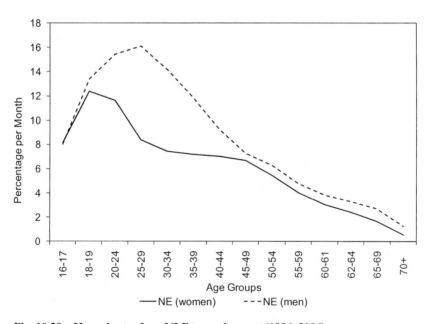

Fig. 10.20   Hazard rates from NLF to employment (1996–2006)

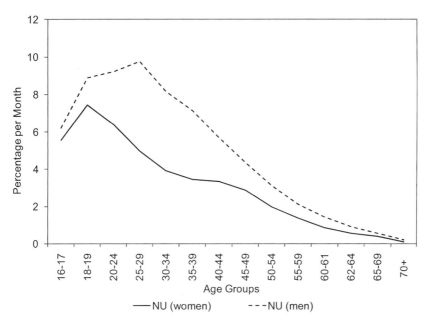

Fig. 10.21   Hazard rates from NLF to unemployment (1996–2006)

unemployment, remains fairly stable throughout life once past the turbulent younger ages (figure 10.22).[11]

10.5.2   Employment to Unemployment

Although the age profiles of labor force flows have relatively small implications for the aggregate unemployment rate, some of the particular flows are interesting in their own right. Among these is the rate of movement from employment to unemployment (the EU flow). Changes in this rate induced by demographic shifts may have implications for trends in prominent indicators of labor market conditions, such as claims for unemployment insurance, as well as for the relative importance of job separations in explaining movements in the unemployment rate, a topic that has attracted considerable attention of late (e.g., Shimer 2007; Fujita and Ramey 2009).

11. An aging population might be expected to affect the duration of unemployment in contradictory ways. As the population ages away from the high turnover young years to the more attached prime years, durations might lengthen, while as the population ages from the more attached prime years to the less attached older years, durations would shorten. We have taken a quick look at this question by approximating the expected duration of unemployment within each age group by the reciprocal of the mean hazard rate for leaving unemployment (to any destination). By this measure, aging has little influence on the expected durations, especially on the duration of unemployment. For E and N, we are looking at top differences of 1/2 and 1 – 1/2 months on levels of thirty-two and forty-eight months, respectively—for unemployment, a top difference of less than a day on levels of sixty days. However, for a more detailed analysis of the influence of the baby boomers on unemployment durations, see Abraham and Shimer (2001).

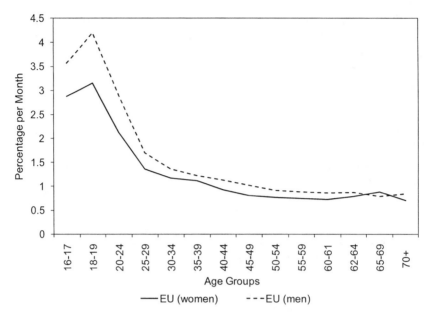

Fig. 10.22   Hazard rates from employment to unemployment

As noted previously, however, the hazard rate for EU transitions is relatively stable after age thirty, despite falling rapidly from the teenage years. Therefore, as with the unemployment rate, the direct effect of aging on the EU rate is modest. Figure 10.23 shows the effect of shifts in the age distribution of the population on the EU hazard rate, relative to the rate in 1996, by holding constant both the within-age EU hazard rates and the within-age employment-to-population (e/p) ratios while letting population shares evolve. The mean aggregate EU hazard rate over this period is about 1.4 percent, and the aging of the population changes the rate by only hundredths of a percentage point, even out as far as 2015.

Figure 10.24 puts this in terms of numbers of workers rather than rates. If we hold the level of payroll employment constant at its 2006 level, the difference in the EU flow from the change in the aggregate EU hazard between 1996 and 2006 is on the order of 30,000 workers per month; between 1996 and 2015, it is 50,000 workers per month. The largest effects of aging on the EU flow come not from the induced changes to the hazard rate, but from the changes to the base of employment to which these rates can be applied. Mainly because the aggregate participation rate falls as the population ages, this base of employment falls. Holding the aggregate population and age-specific e/p ratios constant at their 2006 levels, but allowing the age distribution to evolve, yields a decrease in the level of the aggregate EU flow of close to 45,000 workers per month between 1996 and 2006, and about 125,000 per month between 1996 and 2015. Whether

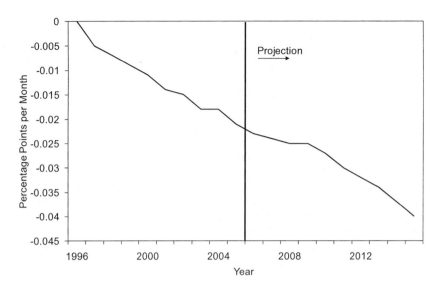

Fig. 10.23   Effect of aging on the EU hazard rate (relative to 1996)

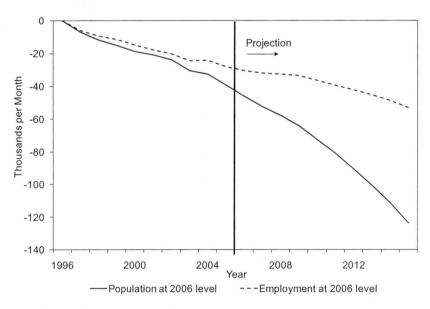

Fig. 10.24   Effect of aging on EU flow

this number is small or large depends upon the context. In terms of the importance of EU flows for the unemployment rate, 125,000 is still only a small percentage of the overall EU flow. However, it implies a substantial reduction in the number of weekly claims for unemployment insurance that one would expect to associate with a healthy rate of economic growth.

10.5.3   Unemployment vs. Nonparticipation

A related issue is the degree to which nonparticipation replaces unemployment as the alternative to employment as the population ages. Not only in the sense of retirement, but also as the state in which potential workers reside between stints of employment. Put another way, to what extent are movements into and out of employment mediated by a period of unemployment? Much of the literature that models or investigates labor market flows recognizes the importance of movements between employment and nonparticipation, and the importance of these flows rises as the population ages.

Figure 10.25 shows the percentage of transitions into employment for which nonparticipation, rather than unemployment, is the state of origin; that is, new entrants and reentrants who move into employment without a period of unemployment as measured by the CPS. The figure also shows the percentage of transitions out of employment for which nonparticipation, rather than unemployment, is the destination state. These

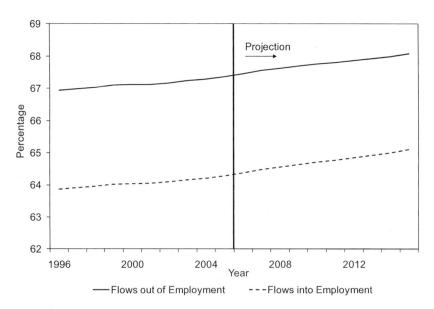

Fig. 10.25   Percent of flows involving employment that involve NLF

transitions may include retirements, discouraged workers, persons going back to school, leaving work to raise families, and a number of other categories.

As the population ages, the percentage of transitions that involve nonparticipation rises, but not by much. Between 1996 and 2015, we can expect the shifting age distribution of the population to increase the percentage of transitions that involve nonparticipation by about 1 point.

10.5.4   Aggregate Turnover

One typically thinks of older persons as being more stable in their jobs, but the relationship is not monotonic. Figure 10.26 shows average separation rates by age. These include both transitions out of employment, and transitions from one main employer to another, which can be measured using matched CPS data since the redesign of that survey in 1994. (See Fallick and Fleischman 2004.) Overall separation rates fall sharply with age into the late twenties, decline further gradually through the late forties, then rise into and through retirement ages.

As a result, the direct effect of the shifting age distribution on the aggregate separation rate, graphed in figure 10.27, is also not monotonic. Aging has mostly driven the aggregate separation rate down since 1996, as the youngest of the baby boomers entered the low-separation ages and the oldest of the baby boomers had not left those ages. Beginning a few years ago,

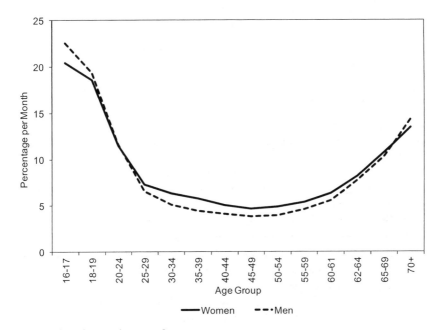

Fig. 10.26   Separation rates by age

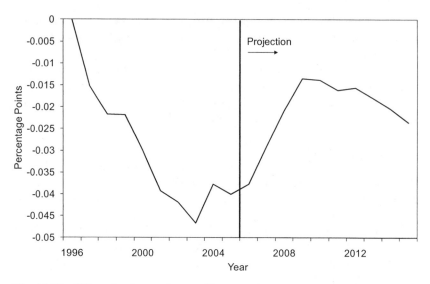

Fig. 10.27   Effect of aging on the monthly separation rate (relative to 1996)

however, the oldest of the baby boomers began to enter the upward-sloping part of the separation rate profile, and this began to push up the aggregate separation rate.

Again, however, the implications for the separation rate are relatively small, in the hundredths of a percentage point on a level of 6.8 percent per month. And again, the larger effects come from the implications of aging for the level of employment, which reduces the level of aggregate turnover (figure 10.28).

10.6   Hourly Wages

Upward sloping age-earnings profiles have long been recognized as a feature of the labor market and an influence on life cycle labor supply. Human capital theory provided an explanation for why young workers would work for low wages, and as skills and experience increase so too does marginal productivity and thus wages, as noted by Mincer (1958) and detailed by Willis (1986). Kotlikoff (1988) further argued that productivity rose over the life cycle, but not by as much as wages. Workers were paid low wages at the start of their career and high wages at the end as part of contracts with employers that provided other benefits to both parties like retention and income security. Hourly wages generally rise with age, and then decline slightly in older age groups above sixty.

To evaluate the influence of the shifting age distribution on wages, we use the reported earnings from the outgoing rotation groups in the CPS, pro-

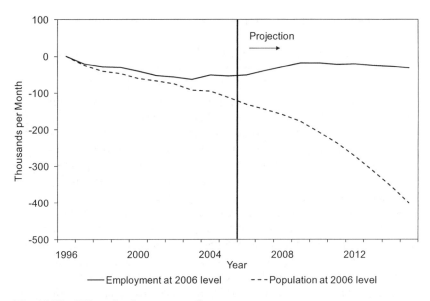

Fig. 10.28   Effect of aging on separations

vided by the National Bureau of Economic Research (NBER) CPS extraction file. Earnings were converted to an hourly wage, aggregated to an annual frequency, and deflated by the Consumer Price Index. In cleaning the data, special consideration was given to trimming and removing outliers. For example, Lemieux (chapter 1 in this volume) removes hourly wages under $1 an hour and over $100 an hour. A common adjustment, this reduces substantially the volatility in the mean and variance of wages over time, and is useful for evaluations of wage inequality. However, because the variance of wages rises with age, such trimming will bias downwards any estimate of the effect of aging on mean wages or the variance—there are a lot more fifty-year-old men making $100 an hour than eighteen-year-old men. For our purposes, avoiding this bias was judged a better trade-off than a smoother variance series over time. Instead, because most hourly earnings outliers in the CPS are due to combinations of unusually low hours combined with unusual high wages and vice versa, we dropped hourly workers who reported fewer than five hours of work a week but whose weekly earnings were over $1,000, which essentially eliminated most outliers. After that, workers reporting earnings less than a dollar an hour (in 2005 dollars) were also eliminated, which largely eliminated clumps of observations around zero, but otherwise had essentially no effect on the results. For evaluation of such trimming, using exactly the same data as shown here, see Schmitt (2003), who notes little effect on the path of mean wages once the extreme outliers are removed. Thus we feel comfortable with our data cleaning, despite the fact that our estimates of wage variance are more volatile than those in other studies.[12]

Figure 10.29 plots the age-wage profile of men in three different years: 1979, the earliest data for the reported wage measures in the NBER data; 1990; and 2005, the most recent data. The profiles follow roughly the same pattern in each year. Although, as the authors noted earlier have suggested, the sheer size of the baby boomers' cohort may have depressed their wages all else equal, the opposite pattern is observed in these profiles. Teen wages have declined since the baby boomers left those age groups and earnings of older workers have risen as the boomers have entered those age groups. No doubt the higher levels of education of the boomers are swamping other microeconomic effects.

Not only does the mean wage vary substantially over the life cycle, but the variance of wages does as well. Figure 10.30 shows the age-variance profile for men in 1979, 1990, and 2005. As has been well-established in the literature on wage inequality, the variance of wages has risen at almost every age group for men over the few decades, with a noticeable increase across age groups between 1979 and 1990. There has been an especially noticeable widening of the wage distribution among older workers, no doubt due to the rising return to skills and experience for some members of the oldest age groups. If this trend continues, as shares of the workforce begin to shift toward older age groups, this has the potential to put additional upward pressure on aggregate wage variance as the higher variance among older age groups interacts with the population shifts into those age groups.

Wages are determined in equilibrium as a function of supply and demand, and labor is a derived demand. In addition, wages are cyclical. These forces confound, decomposing the "pure" effects of population aging on the mean and the variance of wages. However, as with the other measures noted earlier, we attempt to estimate a first-order effect by using fixed weight alternatives to observe how the shifting population shares have influenced the path of wages over time. That is, we fix wages and the employment-to-population ratios to a base year (we choose 2005 in the graphs), and allow the population shares to evolve as they have in the past and are projected to do in the future. Other base years yield similar conclusions.

Figure 10.31 shows the mean real hourly wage from the CPS plotted

---

12. As noted before, implausibly high earnings were often the result of low reported hours combined with high weekly earnings, and thus hourly workers reporting fewer than five hours of work a week combined with weekly earnings over $1,000 were dropped. Workers with implausibly low hourly earnings were also dropped. Earnings above the CPS topcodes were imputed, within each age-sex category, using a lognormal distribution. Pareto distributions proved too unstable for imputation within narrowly defined demographic categories. For discussion of the sensitivity of the imputation and trimming procedures see Schmitt (2003), who convincingly argues in favor of using a lognormal distribution instead of a pareto distribution. Schmitt was also nice enough to provide STATA code for imputations, as well as comparable wage series over time for comparison. The details are described in his paper.

Fig. 10.29   Age-wage profiles for men

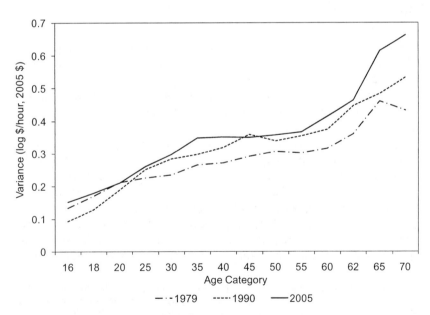

Fig. 10.30   Age-variance profile for men

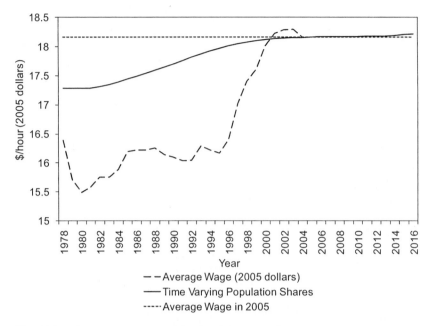

Fig. 10.31   Mean real wages and fixed-weight comparison

against a fixed-weight alternative where the employment-to-population ratios and mean wage rates within each wage-sex group were held at their 2005 averages. The actual real wage has risen from $16.39 an hour (in 2005 dollars) in 1979 to $18.17 an hour in 2005. For much of the 1980s the real wage hovered around $16 an hour, before rising in the late 1990s, and then leveling off in recent years.[13]

The fixed-weight alternative, where the increases in the series are due only to shifting population shares, rises significantly as well. At face value, the fixed-weight alternative rose by $0.89 between 1979 and 2005 while actual real wages rose by $1.78. Thus, half the increase in real wages over the period is accounted for simply by the baby boomers moving into their high wage years. Note that with the sharp drop in actual real wages in 1979, the exact contribution will depend on one's starting point. However, the shift in the age distribution of the population clearly contributed a substantial portion

13. Average hourly earnings reported by the payroll survey of establishments was $16.13 in 2005, compared to our CPS-based series of $18.17 an hour. The payroll survey excludes non-production and supervisory workers in addition to the self-employed, among other conceptual differences. The payroll survey series has a similar path as the series shown here, except for one difference: the payroll survey's average hourly earnings shows more decline in real wages between 1979 and the early 1990s than the series we derive from the CPS. Although it reflects the wages of only production and nonsupervisory workers and is based on 1982 dollars, the published BLS real earnings series available at http://www.bls.gov/ces has essentially the same contour for mean wages over the years as the data we present here.

of the measured real wage gains in the last two decades. Looking ahead, as the projections in the figure show, this upward pressure on mean real wages from aging has pretty much ended, as the baby boomers have completed their transition into high wage age groups.

Similarly, the mere shifting of the population shares has put upward pressure on wage variance. However, the amount of pressure has been small. The actual variance of log wages since 1979, deflated using the CPI, is shown as the solid line in figure 10.32. The variance, although volatile, shows the steep upward trend since 1979 that one would expect to see given the long literature on wage inequality (see similar series in Schmitt [2003]). The long dashed line shows the change in variance due to shifting population shares, holding within-group variances constant at their 2005 values and allowing the employment-to-population ratios to vary.

As is readily apparent, although shifting population shares have put upward pressure on wage variance, the effect is small relative to the secular trend since the end of the 1970s. The effect is small partly because under the surface there have been two offsetting effects at work. This is shown in figure 10.33. As one would expect, as the population has aged it has shifted toward older age groups, which have higher within-group variances. This increase in within-group variance has worked to push the overall variance up. However, at the same time the aging of the population has reduced the between-age-group variance, which has largely offset the increase in average

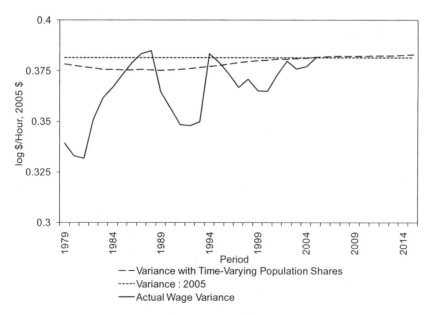

Fig. 10.32 Effect of changing age distribution on wage variance (variance log real wage; within-age/gender group variance set at 2005 values)

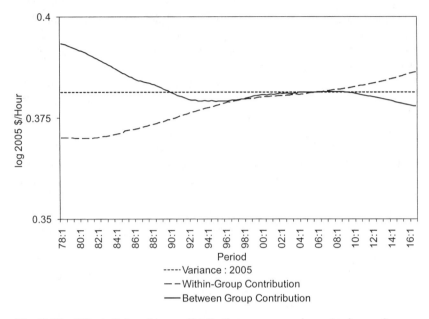

Fig. 10.33   Effect of changing age distribution on wage variance (variance of log(wage); within-age/gender group variance set at 2005 values)

within-group variance. In any case, even such upward pressure as there has been has pretty much run its course, and we can expect little further pressure in the years ahead.

10.7   Conclusion

Although changes in behavior within age groups may offset some of the influence of the shifting age shares, the aging of the baby boomers, increased longevity, and other forces influencing the age distribution have been and are likely to remain important determinants of labor market statistics. In the years ahead, the aggregate measure of the labor market likely to be affected in the most pronounced way is the labor force participation rate, as the share of labor market participants continues to shrink in the years ahead at even a faster pace than over the last several years. Offsetting some of the downward pressure, baby boomers are expected to remain in the labor force longer than prior cohorts. However, labor supply declines severely with age and, even among the baby boomers, it is unlikely that a someone born in 1950 will be as likely to work at age sixty-five as they were at age forty-five. Given this feature of labor supply over the life cycle, the shifting age distribution of the population is likely to put substantial downward pressure on the aggregate participation rate for the next thirty years.

Economists have long noted the influence of labor force composition on unemployment rates. In order to assess labor market slack, wage pressure, or the health of the labor market over time, movements in the unemployment rate must be decomposed into cyclical movements and more structural changes like an aging population. However, in contrast to the participation rate, for which large aging-induced changes lie ahead, the influence of the aging of the baby boomers on the unemployment rate has largely run its course. More important to the aggregate unemployment rate of late are other factors, such as the decline in teenage participation that continues to shrink the share of a high unemployment rate age group in the labor force.

The aging population has also changed how individuals flow through the labor market states, their persistence in a given state, and the likelihood they drop out of the labor force entirely. Although the projected changes are small, we anticipate the transitions through nonparticipation will continue to rise in the years ahead. In addition, the corresponding influence on the separation rate, which fell over time and has begun to rise again, has been relatively modest. However small these effects might be, the influence aging has on interpreting labor market statistics remains important. As we noted earlier, the analysis implies a substantial reduction in the number of weekly claims for unemployment insurance (one of the most watched high-frequency economic indicators) that one would expect to associate with a healthy rate of economic growth.

Finally, mean earnings derived from the CPS have also been influenced by population aging. The baby boomers moving into their high earnings years has put upward pressure on mean wages. Although this is a partial equilibrium accounting that does not account for such offsetting influences as how the relative supply or skill supply might have offset the influence of population aging, the effect is still dramatic. The upward pressure that the baby boom has had on mean wages has largely run its course. Without that influence the gains in mean real wages in the 1990s likely would not have been as great. Going forward, the shifting age distribution is no longer going to put upward pressure on mean wages. Thus, this contribution to related measures like the aggregate wage bill will diminish in the years ahead.

None of the projections for population are set in stone. That said, the baby boom exists and baby boomers are aging. Projections of shifts in the age distribution of the population have wide confidence intervals, but carrying forward the baby boomers from age group to age group as they pass through each year is not as uncertain as, say, projecting undocumented immigration. Life expectancy will lengthen, perhaps faster than projected (which would cause the aggregate labor force participation to decline even more quickly than projected). All in all, the population is shifting toward older age groups and, short of a substantial shift in policy not currently on the horizon, nothing will change that feature of population growth in the United States. As economists continue to study economic time series, accounting for these shifts will remain at least as important in the future as it has in the past, if not more so. Accounting for such changes will also shed clearer light on pressing economic issues and problems, analysis of which might otherwise be confounded by the influence of population aging on economic measures.

References

Aaronson, S., B. Fallick, A. Figura, J. Pingle, and W. Wascher. 2006. The recent decline in the labor force participation rate and its implications for potential labor supply. *Brookings Papers on Economic Activity,* Issue no. 1:69–134.

Abraham, K. G., and R. Shimer. 2001. Changes in unemployment duration and labor-force attachment. In *The roaring nineties: Can full employment be sustained?* ed. A. B. Krueger and R. Solow, 367–420. New York: Russell Sage Foundation and Century Foundation Press.

Becker, G. S., E. L. Glaeser, and K. M. Murphy. 1999. Population and economic growth. *American Economic Review Papers and Proceedings of the One Hundred Eleventh Annual Meeting of the American Economic Association* 89 (2): 145–49.

Blanchard, O. J., and P. Diamond. 1990. The cyclical behavior of the gross flows of U.S. workers. *Brookings Papers on Economic Activity,* Issue no. 2:85–155.

Borsch-Supan, A. H. 2003. Labor market effects of population aging. *Labour* 17 (August): 5–44.

Durand, J. D. 1948. *The labor force in the United States 1890–1960.* New York: Social Science Research Council.

Easterlin, R. 1961. The American baby boom in historical perspective. *American Economic Review* 51 (5): 869–911.

Fallick, B., and C. Fleischman. 2004. Employer-to-employer flows in the U.S. labor market: The complete picture of gross worker flows. Finance and Economics Discussion Series, no. 2007-9. Federal Reserve Board, Washington, DC.

Fallick, B., and J. Pingle. 2007a. A cohort-based model of labor force participation. Finance and Economics Discussion Series, no. 2007-9. Federal Reserve Board, Washington, DC.

———. 2007b. The effect of population aging on aggregate labor supply in the U.S. *Labor supply in the new century,* Federal Reserve Bank of Boston, forthcoming.

Flaim, P. O. 1990. Population changes, the baby boom, and the unemployment rate. *Monthly Labor Review* 113:3–10.

Fujita, S., and G. Ramey. 2009. The cyclicality of separation and job finding rates. *International Economic Review* 50 (2): 415–30.

Hagen, E. E. 1959. Population and economic growth. *The American Economic Review* 49 (3): 310–27.

Hansen, A. H. 1939. Economic progress and declining population growth. *The American Economic Review* 29 (1): 1–15.

Keynes, J. M. 1937. Some economic consequences of a declining population. *Eugenics Review* 39 (April): 13–17.

Kotlikoff, L. J. 1988. Estimating the age-productivity profile using lifetime earnings. NBER Working Paper no. 2788. Cambridge, MA: National Bureau of Economic Research, December.

Kuznets, S. 1956. Quantitative aspects of the economic growth of nations. I. Levels and variability of rates of growth. *Economic Development and Cultural Change* 5 (October): 1–94.

———. 1958. Long swings in the growth of population and in related economic variables. *Proceedings of the American Philosophical Society* 102 (1): 25–52.

Mincer, J. 1958. Investment in human capital and personal income distribution. *Journal of Political Economy* 66:281–302.

Montgomery, M., and J. Trussell. 1986. Models of marital status and childbearing. In *Handbook of labor economics*, vol. 1, ed. O. Ashenfelter and R. Layard, 205–71. Amsterdam: Elsevier Science B.V.

Murphy, K. M., M. Plant, and F. R. Welch. 1988. Cohort size and earnings in the USA. In *Economics of changing age distributions in developed countries*, International Studies in Demography series, ed. R. D. Lee, W. B. Arthur, and G. Rodgers, 39–58. New York: Oxford University Press, Clarendon Press.

Perry, G. 1971. Labor force structure, potential output, and productivity. *Brookings Papers on Economic Activity*, Issue no. 3:533–65.

Ransom, R. L., and R. Sutch. 1988. The decline of retirement in the years before social security: U.S. retirement pattern, 1870–1940. *Issues in contemporary retirement*, ed. R. Ricardo-Campbell and E. P. Lazear, 3–26. Stanford, CA: Hoover Institution Press.

Schmitt, J. 2003. *Creating a consistent hourly wage series from the current population survey's outgoing rotation group, 1979–2002.* Washington, DC: Center for Economic and Policy Research.

Shimer, R. 1998. Why is the U.S. unemployment rate so much lower? *NBER macroeconomics annual 1998*, ed. B. S. Bernanke and J. Rotemberg, 11–61. Cambridge, MA: MIT Press.

———. 2007. Reassessing the ins and outs of unemployment. NBER Working Paper no. 13421. Cambridge, MA: National Bureau of Economic Research, September.

Summers, L. 1986. Why is the unemployment rate so very high near full employment? *Brookings Papers on Economic Activity*, Issue no. 2:339–83.

Toossi, M. 2006. A new look at long-term labor force projections to 2050. *Monthly Labor Review* 129 (11): 19–39.

Tuma, N. B., and G. D. Sandefur. 1988. Trends in the labor force activity of the elderly in the united states, 1940–1980. *Issues in contemporary retirement*, ed. R. Ricardo-Campbell and E. P. Lazear, 38–75. Stanford, CA: Hoover Institution Press.

Valletta, R., and J. Hodges. 2005. Age and education effects on the unemployment rate. *FRBSF Economic Letter*, no. 2005-15, July 15.

Weil, D. N. 1997. The economics of population aging. In *Handbook of population and family economics*, ed. M. R. Rosenzweig and O. Stark, 967–1014. Amsterdam: Elsevier Science B.V.

Willis, R. J. 1986. Wage determinants: A survey and reinterpretation of human capital earnings functions. *Handbook of labor economics*, volume 1, ed. O. Ashenfelter and R. Layard, 525–602. Amsterdam: Elsevier Science B.V.

Comment   Gary Burtless

This chapter traces out the effects of population aging on a few key labor market variables: the labor force participation rate; the unemployment rate;

Gary Burtless is a senior fellow in economic studies and the John C. and Nancy D. Whitehead Chair at the Brookings Institution.

flows into and out of employment, unemployment, and the labor force; and trends in average wages and the variance of wages. The authors offer a clear survey of some of the main issues that link the population age structure to these variables. A couple of outcomes examined by the authors are mainly interesting to specialists. Others are interesting to a much wider audience, one that includes both policymakers and the economists who advise them. Labor force participation and the unemployment rate are particularly important, both to analysts who are interested in predicting the next quarter's or next year's gross domestic product (GDP) and to policymakers who want to know how closely the current path of GDP is tracking the potential growth path.

A number of economists have investigated some of the key impacts of population aging considered here. Both the labor force participation rate and the unemployment rate have been the focus of considerable research. The paper by Thomas Lemieux at this conference considers in detail the past effects of population age structure on the distribution of wages (Lemieux, chapter 1 in this volume). In a 1999 paper, Lawrence Katz and Alan Krueger examined alternative explanations for the sharp decline in the U.S. unemployment rate during the 1990s. Like the authors of this chapter, they estimated the effects of the population age structure. Reassuringly, Katz and Krueger found almost the same effect of age structure on the unemployment rate as is reported in this chapter. Katz and Krueger concluded that most of the aging effect occurred in the ten-year period after 1979. The effect of changing age structure on the unemployment rate after the mid-1990s was much less important (Katz and Krueger 1999).

The Social Security Administration (SSA) has been in the business of making participation and unemployment rate forecasts for several decades. It does not use the same methods developed by these authors, but the methods are broadly similar. Analysts in the Office of the Chief Actuary develop forecasts of the U.S. population, the labor force, and the employed population. In addition, they predict the labor force and unemployed population within subpopulations defined by age, gender, marital status, and the presence or absence of child dependents.

In making their short- and long-term forecasts, the SSA analysts do not assume future participation and unemployment rates within age-gender groups will remain stable. According to an analysis published a few years ago, their projections ". . . also include a 'lagged-cohort effect' that applies changes in participation rates for a cohort at a specific age (relative to earlier cohorts at the same age) to participation rates for that cohort at older ages (Motsiopoulos and Tucker 2005, 4)." In other words, like Fallick, Fleischman, and Pingle, the SSA analysts believe that birth cohort plays a sizeable role in explaining the trend in participation rates.

The authors of this chapter emphasize that cohort-specific effects seem to drive many of the long-term trends in overall participation and unemployment. Women who entered the labor force in 1973 were systematically different from those who entered in 1963 or in 1983, and the cohort differences have persisted in succeeding decades. More recent birth cohorts have generally had participation rates and unemployment experiences that are more similar to those of male counterparts who are the same age. Not surprisingly, however, birth cohort models have little ability to predict a cohort's early-career participation and unemployment experiences. I also wonder whether cohort models are very successful in accounting for trends in labor status among people who are past the traditional retirement age.

Women's participation at older ages is rising in line with each cohort's lagged participation rate at younger ages. This goes a long way toward explaining the elevated participation rates of women who are now between sixty and seventy-five years old. The cohort models do not provide a full explanation for rising participation rates among women past age sixty, however. Part of the recent rise is explained by other phenomena, a fact the authors recognize. In addition, cohort models cannot account for any of the rise in labor force participation among men past the age of sixty-five. Over the past three decades participation rates of fifty-five to fifty-nine-year-old men have drifted downward in an erratic pattern. In contrast, the long-term decline in participation rates of men sixty-five and older came to an end in the mid-1980s. Since the early 1990s participation rates of men past sixty-five have been rising. Figure 10C.1 shows the trend in labor force participation rates of successive overlapping birth cohorts of men born between 1922 and 1944. The top line shows the participation rate of a given cohort when it was between fifty-five and fifty-nine years old; the middle line, the rate when it was between sixty and sixty-four; and the bottom line, the rate when it was sixty-five to sixty-nine-years-old. The youngest birth cohort, born between 1940 and 1944, had a labor force participation rate at age fifty-five to fifty-nine that was 2.8 percentage points below the comparable rate of the oldest cohort, born between 1922 and 1926. On the other hand, the youngest cohort had a participation rate between ages sixty-five to sixty-nine that was 11.2 percentage points *above* the comparable rate of the oldest cohort shown. Obviously, cohort models cannot easily account for the diverging trends of men younger than sixty and older than sixty-five.

Economists are interested in these trends for purposes of explaining the trend in the average and median retirement age; that is, the typical age at which full-career workers withdraw from the labor force. My reading of the evidence is that the age of labor force withdrawal has become more variable with successive birth cohorts. In the 1960s, 1970s, and 1980s there was more clustering of retirement ages among workers in a given birth cohort. Full-career workers were more likely to retire within a few years of the modal retirement age, say, age sixty-two or sixty-five. In contrast, workers are now more likely to withdraw at ages well before sixty and well past sixty-five.

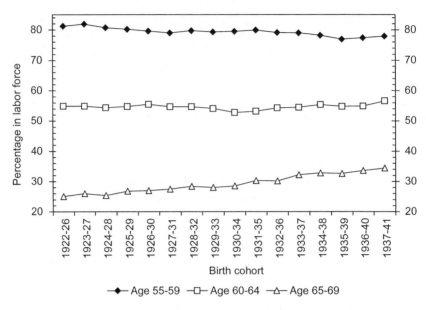

Fig. 10C.1   Labor force participation rate of successive male birth cohorts at selected ages, 1976–2009

Source: Author's estimates using source data from the Bureau of Labor Statistics.

Economists, including these authors, have offered plausible suggestions to account for trends in labor force withdrawal within successive birth cohorts (Burtless and Quinn 2001; Aaronson et al. 2006). One reason for increasing labor force participation at older ages is that both the public and private retirement systems now provide smaller incentives for early labor force withdrawal. From 1950 through the early 1980s, the net value of social security pensions tended to rise relative to after-tax wages for successive cohorts of retirees. Amendments to the Social Security Act passed in 1977 and 1983 brought this liberalization to an end. The after-tax value of social security pensions has gradually declined compared with the after-tax value of wages for workers who have retired since the 1980s. Equally important, the penalty on earning wages while collecting a social security check has been substantially reduced, and this change has encouraged some pensioners to find part-time or bridge jobs after they leave their career jobs. For a minority of workers these benefit trends have delayed the age of full exit from the labor force.

The private pension system has also shifted in a direction that encourages work later in life. Between 1980 and 2004 the fraction of workers who were exclusively covered by a defined-benefit (DB) plan fell from 60 percent to just 11 percent of all pension-covered workers. In the same period workers exclusively covered by a defined-contribution (DC) plan rose from 17 percent to

61 percent of all pension-covered workers (Munnell and Perun 2006). The two kinds of pension produce very different retirement incentives. Defined-benefit pensions penalize many workers who delay retirement past the plan's early or normal pension-claiming age. In many DB plans, it is financially advantageous for workers to quit their jobs and accept a pension as soon as they reach the initial benefit-claiming age. Defined-contribution pension plans are much more age-neutral in their retirement incentives. So long as a worker remains employed in a DC-covered job, the employer, the worker, or both can continue to make contributions to the plan, and the contribution remains the same percentage of the worker's wage. Because DC pensions provide little incentive to retire at one age rather than another, farsighted workers might choose to remain in their career jobs longer in order to build up their retirement wealth.

The changes just mentioned help account for the fact that some workers now withdraw from the labor force later than was the case among their counterparts in the 1980s and 1990s. Another explanation is needed to account for earlier labor force withdrawal among a minority of workers. One explanation for earlier labor force exit is the rise in lifetime wealth. Increasing wages and wealth have made many workers better off compared with their parents and grandparents. Some workers use part of their increased wealth to leave the workforce before reaching the social security retirement age. This behavior is economically rational if career workers find their jobs less attractive than the activities they can pursue when they retire. A second explanation for earlier labor force exit is the increased availability and generosity of disability benefits. In recent years workers have found it easier to collect benefits for some disabling conditions. Other workers have seen disability benefits grow faster than their potential wages, increasing the potential payoff to filing a disability claim (Autor and Duggan 2003).

Since 2000 there have been two major surprises in labor force trends. The first involves men and women past age sixty-two. Their participation and employment rates are currently higher than many forecasting models predicted in the late 1990s. The trend toward later retirement has accelerated among a minority of older workers. The second and bigger surprise has been the changed behavior of the young. They are less likely to be labor force participants than young adults in the late 1990s. Figure 10C.2 displays a social security forecast of labor force participation generated for the 2000 *OASDI Trustees' Report.* The report was published in April 2000, and the forecast itself was developed in the second half of 1999. Figure 10C.2 shows the SSA forecast of labor force participation among sixteen- to twenty-four-year-olds. The solid, dark line shows the actual labor force participation rate of sixteen- to twenty-four-year-olds as published by the BLS. The lighter line shows SSA's intermediate forecast of that participation rate developed for the *2000 OASDI Trustees' Report.* Starting in 2001 the actual participation rate of young adults fell sharply, declining 8.9 percentage points in nine

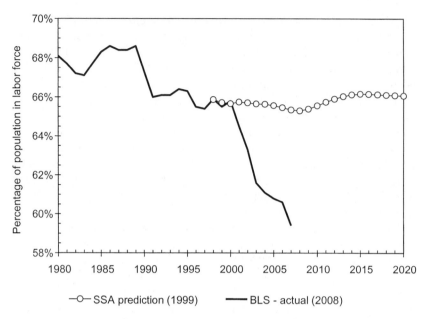

Fig. 10C.2   Actual and predicted participation rates of 16–24-year-old adults, 1980–2020

Source: Bureau of Labor Statistics and unpublished data from Office of the Chief Actuary, U.S. Social Security Administration.

years. The SSA forecast predicted a much smaller decline in young adult participation.

The error resulted in a considerable overstatement of the number of sixteen- to twenty-four-year-old labor force participants. By 2009 the over-statement of the youthful labor force amounted to 3.7 million young adults. It seems doubtful whether any economist before 1999 had a model that accurately predicted this decline. It is also doubtful whether, even after the participation decline became known, we had a model that could account for the magnitude and suddenness of the drop. In the previous recession, which began in 1990, young adults' labor force participation fell less than a third as much as it did after 2000.

In an extension of the research reported here it would be useful to show estimates of the impact of population aging on aggregate labor supply, when aggregate supply is adjusted to reflect the expected productivity of the work hours supplied. In figures 10.4 and 10.6 the authors give us projections of aggregate labor supply as measured by the labor force participation rate of the population sixteen and older. In figure 10.31 they give projections of the impact of the changing age structure on average wages. A straightforward extension is to develop estimates of the impact of the age structure on aggre-gate hours of work and on work hours weighted by expected productivity per hour. The results in figure 10.31 weight each observed wage by the number of workers who earn or who are expected to earn that hourly wage rate. An alternative adjustment is to weight each observed wage by the number of hours that is paid that wage. This weighting scheme takes into account not only the age profile of labor force participation but also of expected hours worked in a given week. When labor force growth is caused by an influx of teenagers and young adults (groups with relatively low wages), the growth in productivity-weighted labor supply is slower than the growth in either labor force participation or aggregate work hours. The estimates in figure 10.31 imply, however, that the expected hourly wage of U.S. workers has risen as a result of population aging. The average wage will continue to rise, although very slowly, over the projection period. Thus, some of the expected future slowdown in labor force growth will be offset by the rising average wage of an older workforce. For purposes of predicting the future trend growth in national income, it would be useful to know the approximate size of this offset.

References

Aaronson, S., B. Fallick, A. Figura, J. Pringle, and W. Wascher. 2006. The recent decline in the labor force participation rate and its implications for potential labor supply. *Brookings Papers on Economic Activity,* 1:69–134.
Autor, D. H., and M. G. Duggan. 2003. The rise in the disability rolls and the decline in unemployment. *Quarterly Journal of Economics* 118 (1): 157–205.
Burtless, G., and J. F. Quinn. 2001. Retirement trends and policies to encourage work among older Americans. In *Ensuring health and income security for an aging workforce,* ed. P. P. Budetti, R. Burkhauser, J. Gregory, and A. Hunt, 375–415. Kalamazoo, MI: W. E. Upjohn Institute for Employment Research.
Katz, L. F., and A. B. Krueger. 1999. The high-pressure U.S. labor market of the 1990s. *Brookings Papers on Economic Activity,* 1:1–87.
Motsiopoulos, C., and R. B. Tucker. 2005. *Short-range actuarial projections of the old-age survivors, and disability insurance program, 2005.* Actuarial Study no. 119, Office of the Chief Actuary, August. Washington, DC: U.S. Social Security Administration.
Munnell, A., and P. Perun. 2006. *An update on private pensions.* Issues in Brief no. 50, Center for Retirement Research. Chestnut Hill, MA: Boston College.

Emerging Labor Market Trends and Workplace Safety and Health

Nicole Nestoriak and John Ruser

11.1 Introduction

Emerging labor market trends will impact occupational safety and health (OSH). Certain labor market trends, such as the decline in goods-producing industries, affect safety and health outcomes in known ways, and their impact can be predicted. Other trends, such as the use of contract workers and new workplace practices, have the potential to affect not only rates of injury and illness but also OSH monitoring. This chapter addresses the impact of labor market trends on OSH outcomes and surveillance.

The aging of the workforce will affect the types and severity of injuries and illnesses received. The growth in service-producing industries and the decline in traditional goods-producing industries also have implications for the composition and overall number of OSH cases. While the shift to service industries has been accompanied by a decline in the aggregate occupational injury and illness rate, some service industries have seen rate increases. The shift has also been accompanied by greater exposure to risk by some groups of workers, such as women, who have tended to work in safer jobs.

Beyond these basic worker characteristics, there are a host of other labor market trends that are likely to have an impact on workplace injuries, illnesses, and fatalities that are not easily measurable. The Employment Services industry, which includes Temporary Help Services and Professional Employer Organizations, is predicted to be a large source of employment

Nicole Nestoriak is a research economist in Compensation Research and Program Development at the Bureau of Labor Statistics. John Ruser is Assistant Commissioner for Safety and Health Statistics at the Bureau of Labor Statistics.

The views expressed are those of the authors and do not necessarily reflect the views or policies of the BLS or any other agency of the U.S. Department of Labor.

growth over the next decade. For workers in these industries and for contract workers more generally, the separation of where an employee works from who he or she is employed by can lead to confusion both in workplace practices intended to improve safety and health and also in OSH reporting. Similarly, employers with workers who work at home are not liable for maintaining the safety and health of those home work sites. Finally, new workplace practices such as Total Quality Management have been introduced to improve quality but may also have unintended negative consequences for worker safety and health.

In the numerical analysis, this chapter focuses on the impact on workplace safety of future changes in the age, gender, industrial, and occupational composition of employment over the next decade. The chapter also speculates about the impact of other labor market trends on future occupational injuries and illnesses. It is important to observe that there are factors outside of these labor market trends that have contributed to a large decline in injury and illness rates in the United States since the early 1990s. Specifically, between 1992 and 2006 nonfatal rates dropped from 8.9 to 4.4 injuries and illnesses per 100 workers, while the number of occupational fatalities due to injury declined from 6,217 to 5,703. These declines are largely not the result of compositional changes, as they are evident even within many industries, occupations, age, and gender categories. The declines are also mirrored in the data from other countries such as Canada, Finland, France, and others (Ussif 2004).

Research has been largely unable to explain these drops. Some commentators suggest that the declines might have resulted in part from technology (Ussif 2004), stronger economic incentives for safety, and legislative initiatives both brought about by higher workers' compensation costs (Conway and Svenson 1998; Boden and Ruser 2003), the deregulation of workers' compensation insurance (Barkume and Ruser 2001), and changes in Occupational Safety and Health Administration (OSHA) recordkeeping rules (Welch et al. 2007). Declines, particularly in nonfatal injury and illness rates, have continued up to 2006, suggesting that the trend will persist in the future. We acknowledge that our empirical analysis is focused solely on the impact of workforce composition changes and does not account for other largely unmeasurable factors that have contributed to workplace injury and illness declines. In a later section we do discuss some factors other than compositional changes that could affect workplace safety and health, such as the growth of contract and alternative forms of work, flexible work schedules and workplaces, and new workplace practices.

This chapter is organized as follows. The following section discusses the OSH data at the Bureau of Labor Statistics (BLS) in detail, followed by a brief discussion of other data utilized in the analysis. The next section provides a univariate analysis of injury and illness rates by industry, occupation, age, and gender. The following section builds upon this analysis by using a multivariate framework to examine the injury and illness data and then uses BLS projections data to predict future changes. Finally, a discussion of remaining issues and their impact on OSH outcomes and measurement is provided.

11.2   Data

The Bureau of Labor Statistics (BLS) conducts two data programs to track injuries, illnesses, and fatalities that occur in U.S. workplaces: the Survey of Occupational Injuries and Illnesses (SOII) and the Census of Fatal Occupational Injuries (CFOI). The SOII produces estimates of nonfatal injuries and illnesses that employers record on the Occupational Safety and Health Administration's (OSHA) "Log of Work-Related Injuries and Illnesses." The SOII annually collects employers' reports from about 176,000 private industry establishments and from state and local government establishments in some states. The survey excludes all work-related fatalities as well as nonfatal workplace injuries and illnesses to the self-employed; to workers on farms with ten or fewer employees; to private household workers; and, nationally, to federal, state, and local government workers.

Injuries and illnesses logged by employers conform to definitions and recordkeeping guidelines set by OSHA. Nonfatal cases are recordable if they are occupational illnesses or if they are occupational injuries that involve lost worktime, medical treatment other than first aid, restriction of work or motion, loss of consciousness, or transfer to another job. Employers keep counts of injuries separate from illnesses and also identify for each whether a case involved any days away from work or days of job transfer or restricted work, or both, beyond the day of injury or onset of illness.

Summary information on the number of injuries and illnesses is copied by these employers directly from their recordkeeping logs to the survey questionnaire. The questionnaire also asks for the number of employee hours worked (needed in the calculation of incidence rates) as well as average employment (needed to verify the unit's employment-size class).

Besides injury and illness counts, survey respondents are asked to provide additional information for a subset of the most serious nonfatal cases logged, namely, those that involved at least one day away from work, beyond the day of injury or onset of illness. Employers answer several questions about these cases, including the demographics of the worker disabled, the nature of the disabling condition, and the event and source producing that condition. Most employers use information from supplementary record-keeping forms and state workers' compensation claims to fill out the SOII's case form; some, however, attach those forms when their narratives answer questions on the case form. Also, to minimize the burden of larger employers, sampled establishments projected to have large numbers of cases involving days away from work receive instructions on how to provide information only for a sample of those cases.

The Census of Fatal Occupational Injuries (CFOI) compiles a count of all fatal work injuries occurring in the United States in each calendar year. The program uses diverse state and federal data sources to identify, verify, and profile fatal work injuries. Information about each workplace fatality (industry, occupation, and worker characteristics; equipment being used; and circumstances of the event) is obtained by cross-referencing source documents, such as death certificates, workers' compensation records, and reports to federal and state agencies. This method assures counts are as complete and accurate as possible. For the 2005 data, over 20,000 unique source documents were reviewed as part of the data collection process. The scope of CFOI is broader than SOII, in that CFOI includes public sector workers and the self-employed.

Both the SOII and CFOI contain information about characteristics of the injury, illness, or fatality. This includes the nature of the case, which describes its physical characteristics, such as a sprain or a fracture. The event or exposure, which describes the manner in which the injury or illness was inflicted, is also captured. An event might be a fall or contact with equipment, for example. Also captured are the body part affected and the source of the injury or illness. All four of these characteristics are coded according to the BLS Occupational Injury and Illness Classification System (OIICS).

The SOII and CFOI provide estimates of the numbers of injuries, illnesses, and fatalities incurred by workers with various attributes, such as occupation, age, and gender. To better understand how the risk of workplace injury and illness varies among worker groups, it is helpful to control in some way for differences in the sizes of these groups. This is done in two ways in this chapter: by calculating injury, illness, and fatality rates and by including both injured and noninjured workers in logistic regressions. The injury and illness rates are simply the numbers of cases per standard unit of full-time-equivalent worker years (10,000 or 100,000 FTE in this chapter).

Neither the SOII nor the CFOI collects data on the number of workers or hours worked according to worker characteristics, such as occupation, age, or gender.[1] As a result, it is not possible with these data alone to calculate injury and illness rates or to control for different-sized groups of workers. For this chapter, we rely on employment and hours worked estimates generated from the Current Population Survey (CPS). The CPS is a monthly survey of 60,000 households conducted by the Bureau of Census for the Bureau of Labor Statistics. It provides a comprehensive body of data on the labor force, employment, unemployment, and persons not in the labor force. The survey obtains information on the labor force status of each indi-

---

1. The SOII does collect hours worked for all workers in each sampled establishment. With this data element, it is possible to calculate injury and illness rates by state, industry, and establishment size.

vidual age fifteen or older, including whether that person was employed in the preceding week, the class of the job (i.e., private wage and salary, self-employed), the industry and occupation of the worker's job, and the actual hours worked. For one-fourth of the sample, actual hours worked is also obtained for a second job held by a worker.

In addition, the Annual Social and Economic (ASEC) Supplement to the Current Population Survey (CPS) is used for the multivariate analysis. The ASEC is a survey of 99,000 households conducted by the Bureau of Census for the Bureau of Labor Statistics. In addition to providing the usual CPS data, the ASEC provides additional information on work experience, income, noncash benefits, and migration.

Finally, BLS employment projections data are used to measure changes in labor force characteristics that are relevant to injury and fatality rates. The projections data cover the period 2004 to 2014 and provide employment numbers for gender by age categories, and detailed occupation and industry. The data are estimated by first projecting an aggregate level of labor supply and demand, and then determining industry and occupation distributions. Details of the methodology can be found in chapter 13 of the *BLS Handbook of Methods* (BLS 2009).

These projections are used to estimate how changing mixes of worker characteristics will affect future injury rates. The predicted change in employment numbers by gender/age, occupation, and industry at the level of detail used in the logistic regressions can be seen in figures 11.1, 11.2, and 11.3. The occupation and industry projections have been adjusted to match the universe of the SOII data as closely as possible. Public sector and agriculture employees were dropped from both the industry and occupation projections. In the industry projections, railroad workers were also excluded.[2]

11.3   Univariate Description of Projections and Injury Data

11.3.1   Industry and Occupation Trends

The BLS projections indicate that industry and occupation employment growth from 2004 to 2014 will tend to be in jobs that have lower risk of workplace injury and illness than the average job, so that the aggregate rate of workplace injuries and illnesses should tend to decline. However, there are some instances of high growth in high injury and illness sectors, most notably health care.

From 2004 to 2014, employment growth will tend to be focused in the service-providing sector, including education, health care and social assistance, and professional and business services. Employment is projected to

---

2. Although the projections data also has a separate category for wage and salary workers that would enable one to exclude the self-employed, there is not enough information available to exclude agriculture and the self-employed.

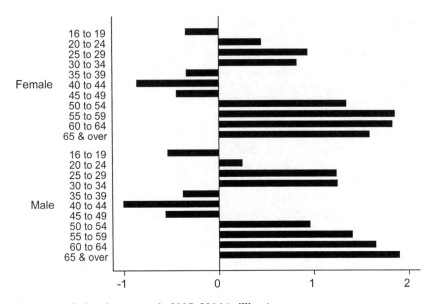

Fig. 11.1   Labor force growth, 2005–2014 (millions)

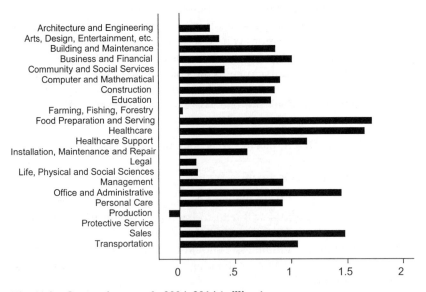

Fig. 11.2   Occupation growth, 2004–2014 (millions)

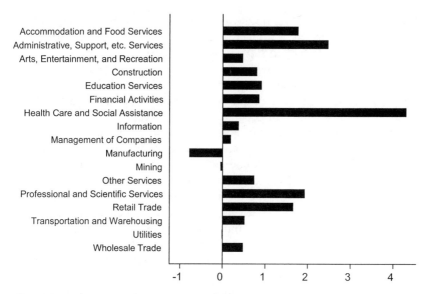

Fig. 11.3   Industry growth, 2004–2014 (millions)

grow 17 percent over the decade in the service-providing sector, while declining by a tenth of a percent in the goods-producing sector. This trend in general implies overall safer working conditions, as workplace injury and illness rates tend to be lower in the service-providing sector. In 2005, the rate of workplace injuries and illness in the private industry goods-producing sector was 6.2 per 100 full-time equivalent workers, while it was 4.1 in the service-providing sector.

Drilling down deeper, some of the fastest growing North American Industrial Classification System (NAICS) sectors also have relatively low workplace injury and illness rates, while some of the declining sectors have relatively high injury and illness rates. Educational services employment is projected to grow the fastest of any NAICS sector, at nearly 33 percent over the period from 2004 to 2014. This sector's private industry workplace injury and illness rate of 2.4 is about half the overall private sector rate of 4.6. In contrast, manufacturing, which accounts for 20 percent of workplace injuries and illnesses in private industry and an overall injury and illness rate of 6.3 (37 percent higher than the overall private industry rate), is projected to decline by over 5 percent from 2004 to 2014.

However, there are some significant instances where relatively high-risk industries are also projected to have fast employment growth. This is particularly the case for the health care and social assistance sector, whose employment is projected to grow 30 percent over the decade, the second fastest of any sector. This sector's private sector injury and illness rate was 5.9 per 100 full-time equivalent workers, 28 percent higher than the overall private industry rate. Also noteworthy about this sector is that it tends to employ a large fraction of women, who sustain many of the industry's injuries and illnesses. In fact, in 2005, women sustained 80 percent of all injury and illness cases with days away from work in the private sector health care and social assistance sector, in comparison to 34 percent for all of private industry. The strong growth of this sector will imply that a growing fraction of women will be injured or become ill at the workplace.

The BLS's projections for occupational growth tend to have the same implications for safety and health as the industry projections. Many of the fast growing occupations will be relatively safe white-collar jobs, such as those in professional and related occupations, a large occupational group (20 percent of total employment) projected to grow 21 percent over the decade. However, growth will also be strong among service occupations, including building and grounds cleaning and maintenance and health care support occupations, some of which have higher injury and illness rates than the average job. In 2006, health care support occupations had the second highest rate of cases with days away from work among all occupational groups, at 279 per 10,000 workers or 2.2 times the rate for all workers. Building and grounds cleaning and maintenance occupations had the fourth highest rate of all occupational groups, at 244. Further, among occupations with at least 0.1 percent of employment, nursing aides, orderlies, and attendants had the highest rate of cases with days away from work, at 526 per 100,000 workers, or over four times the rate for all workers.

11.3.2   Age/Gender

Because the characteristics of workplace injuries, illnesses, and fatalities vary for workers of different age, the aging of the workforce has implications for the future composition of these workplace outcomes. The SOII and CFOI data, coupled with CPS hours worked estimates, show some clear differences by age.

Figure 11.4 shows that nonfatal injury and illness rates tend to decline with age for men, but that they remain relatively constant for women starting from the forty-five to fifty-four-year-old age category. Nonfatal rates drop about 8 percent for men between the forty-five- to fifty-four-year-old and fifty-five- to sixty-four-year-old age groups, and about 6 percent between the fifty-five to sixty-four and sixty-four+ age groups. While some of this difference probably reflects differences in the jobs performed by older and prime-aged men, it is also likely that this finding persists after controlling for job mix. In contrast to men, the injury and illness rate profiles are relatively flat for women forty-five and older.

Results are strikingly different for fatalities. Figure 11.5 shows fatality rates for all workers by age category. This chart does not break out women separately, because women comprise only about 8 percent of all workplace fatalities and sustain few fatalities in the older age groups. The fatality rate

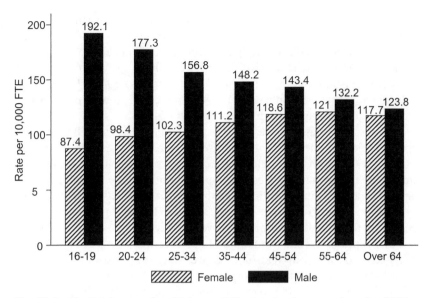

Fig. 11.4   Nonfatal occupational injury and illness rates, by age and gender, 2005

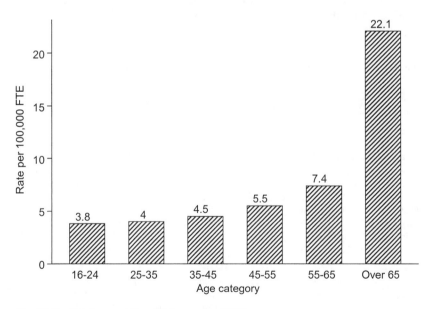

Fig. 11.5   Fatal occupational injury rates, 2005

rises with age, from 4.5 fatalities per 100,000 workers for thirty-five- to forty-four-year-olds, to 5.5 for forty-five- to fifty-four-year-olds, and 22.1 for workers over sixty-four. This may reflect the fact that older (mainly male) workers are less likely to survive a severe workplace injury. Holding everything else constant, the sharp increase in fatality rates with age found in the data suggests that we would expect to see an increase in workplace deaths with the aging of the workforce.

Aging is also related to the types of nonfatal injuries and illnesses that occur. Table 11.1 shows how the natures of nonfatal cases with days away from work vary with age for men and women. For both genders, sprains and strains are by far the most frequent type of nonfatal case, overall about 41 percent of all cases in 2005. However, the percentage of cases accounted for by sprains shows an inverted U-shape with age for both men and women, peaking at the thirty-five- to forty-four-year-old age category for both groups. For men, sprains decline from about 43 percent to 30 percent between the thirty-five- to forty-four-year-old and over sixty-four-year-old age groups, while the decline is even more notable for women, from 48 to 32 percent.

The decline in sprains for older workers is in part made up by an increase in fractures. The percent of cases with days away from work accounted for by fractures tends to increase with age for both men and women, with a more noticeable increase for women. Whereas only about 4 percent of cases with days away from work are fractures for women age twenty-five to

Table 11.1   Distribution of occupational injuries and illnesses by nature, gender, and age, 2005

	All ages (%)	16 to 19 (%)	20 to 24 (%)	25 to 34 (%)	35 to 44 (%)	45 to 54 (%)	55 to 64 (%)	Over 64 (%)
				Men				
Total	814,250	29,550	93,610	203,510	207,320	175,250	81,170	16,180
Total	100.0	100.0	100.0	100.0	100.0	100.0	100.0	100.0
Sprains	39.3	24.5	33.4	40.4	42.7	41.0	39.4	30.3
Bruises	7.9	12.5	8.7	8.1	7.1	7.3	7.5	11.6
Cuts	10.0	20.9	16.1	11.2	8.2	6.9	7.7	8.8
Fractures	8.4	6.4	7.2	8.1	7.8	9.0	10.6	12.5
Pain	7.6	5.3	6.8	6.9	8.2	8.2	8.8	7.2
All other	26.7	30.5	27.8	25.3	26.1	27.6	26.0	29.7
				Women				
Total	415,880	11,970	39,990	86,200	103,540	105,800	53,410	10,860
Total	100.0	100.0	100.0	100.0	100.0	100.0	100.0	100.0
Sprains	43.5	44.0	41.4	45.0	47.8	43.5	37.0	31.8
Bruises	10.3	13.3	10.7	9.8	9.1	10.8	11.1	12.4
Cuts	4.8	9.5	7.4	5.0	4.1	4.3	3.9	5.6
Fractures	6.6	4.0	4.1	3.8	4.8	6.9	14.2	18.8
Pain	9.3	7.9	9.4	10.7	9.2	8.7	9.0	1.7
All other	25.5	21.2	27.0	25.7	25.0	25.9	24.7	29.7

thirty-four, that percentage rises to 14 percent for women workers age fifty-five to sixty-four and over 18 percent for women over age sixty-four. This result is consistent with the increasing incidence of osteoporosis in older women. However, the increase is also apparent for men. Fractures account for 8 percent of all cases with days away from work for men aged thirty-five to forty-four. That percentage increases to nearly 11 percent among males aged forty-five to fifty-four and 13 percent for men over sixty-four. In sum, the cross-sectional evidence for sprains and fractures suggests that, everything else equal, we expect that the aging workforce will lead to a decline in sprains and a growth in fractures as a percent of all cases with days away from work.

The SOII data provide information about the event that resulted in a nonfatal injury or illness. Table 11.2 shows that the most frequent event category overall is bodily reaction and exertion, which includes those events that lead to sprains and strains. Consistent with the declining importance of sprains and strains for older workers, bodily reaction and exertion becomes less important as an event leading to injury and illness for older workers. Instead, consistent with the age profiles for fractures, there is striking evidence of the growing importance of falls for older workers. For women age forty-five to fifty-four, 28 percent of injuries and illnesses resulted from falls. That percentage increases to 41.3 percent for women age fifty-five to sixty-four and 51.0 percent for women over sixty-four. Similarly, while falls account for 19.3 percent of events for men age forty-five to fifty-four, that percentage rises to 35.5 for men over sixty-four. These data suggest that the aging of the workforce will be accompanied by a growing frequency of fall-related workplace injuries and illnesses.

The data on nonfatal injuries and illnesses display another age-related pattern. The median days away from work increases almost monotonically with age from only three days for the youngest group of workers to twelve for workers sixty-five years or older (figure 11.6). While the high median for older workers in part reflects a mix of injuries and illnesses weighted more heavily toward more severe categories, such as fractures, it is also the case that older workers remain out of work for longer periods of time for any given nature of injury or illness. For example, the median days away from work for a fracture for workers age twenty-five to thirty-four is twenty-one, while it increases to twenty-eight for workers fifty-five to sixty-four. Similarly, the median days away from work for a sprain is eleven for workers fifty-five to sixty-four, up from seven days for workers in the twenty-five to thirty-four age category. What is apparent is that either older workers suffer more severe injuries and illnesses or that they take longer to recover for an equivalent condition. This finding is consistent with the higher fatality rate for older workers.

In sum, the aging of the workforce is likely to be accompanied by an increase in the fraction of longer duration and more severe injury and illness

Table 11.2 Distribution of occupational injuries and illnesses by event, gender, and age, 2005

	All ages (%)	16 to 19 (%)	20 to 24 (%)	25 to 34 (%)	35 to 44 (%)	45 to 54 (%)	55 to 64 (%)	Over 64 (%)
			Men					
Total number	814,250	29,550	93,610	203,510	207,320	175,250	81,170	16,180
Total	100.0	100.0	100.0	100.0	100.0	100.0	100.0	100.0
Contact with objects and equipment	31.8	49.9	43.3	34.5	28.0	27.6	26.2	22.9
Falls	17.8	12.5	14.0	15.1	17.9	19.3	23.7	35.5
Bodily reaction and exertion	38.4	21.3	29.8	38.5	41.8	42.6	39.4	28.0
Exposure to harmful substances or environments	4.0	7.5	5.3	4.3	3.7	3.6	2.7	3.1
Transportation accidents	5.4	3.8	5.1	5.1	6.3	4.6	5.8	8.9
All other	2.5	5.0	2.4	2.6	2.3	2.3	2.2	1.3
			Women					
Total number	415,880	11,970	39,990	86,200	103,540	105,800	53,410	10,860
Total	100.0	100.0	100.0	100.0	100.0	100.0	100.0	100.0
Contact with objects and equipment	18.8	29.5	24.4	20.7	17.5	17.6	14.7	17.5
Falls	26.5	23.1	21.3	20.7	22.2	28.0	41.3	51.0
Bodily reaction and exertion	42.3	34.5	38.1	42.7	48.0	44.5	34.3	25.8
Exposure to harmful substances or environments	4.5	8.7	6.8	5.9	4.0	3.7	2.6	2.1
Transportation accidents	4.1	1.6	4.7	5.5	4.5	3.1	3.4	2.7
All other	3.8	2.5	4.8	4.5	3.7	3.2	3.6	0.9

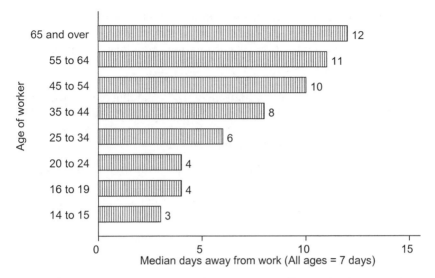

Fig. 11.6 **Median days away from work due to nonfatal occupational injury or illness by age of worker, all United States, private industry, 2005**

cases and by an increase in the rate of workplace death. These prognostications, of course, are based on cross-sectional comparisons that do not control for the different jobs that workers hold at different ages. A more rigorous multivariate analysis is pursued in the following section.

11.4 Multivariate Analysis and Implications of Projections

11.4.1 Creation of Data Set for Analysis

The multivariate analysis combines data from the SOII or CFOI with data from the CPS. By stacking these data sets, a universe of both injured and noninjured workers is obtained that contains information on age, gender, industry, and occupation of all workers combined with detailed information on worker injuries and illnesses or fatalities from the SOII and CFOI, respectively. The universe for the multivariate analysis for workplace injury and illness and for fatality projections was largely determined by the SOII data, namely no self-employed, private household workers, federal, state, nor local government workers. While the SOII does have information on employees of farms with greater than ten employees, all agriculture was excluded from the analysis as this restriction based on the number of employees at a farm could not be applied to the CPS data. Additionally, all employees of railroads were dropped from the analysis as information on gender is not available for this industry in the SOII data. From the CPS, all people over the age of sixteen who worked in the previous year for a private firm were included. To maintain comparability between the nonfatal and fatal analyses, the scope of the CFOI was restricted to be the same as that of SOII.

In order to create a data set incorporating the injury and illness data while maintaining the representativeness of the CPS, the weights need to be adjusted in the stacked data. There are many potential ways to adjust the stacked data to restore representativeness. The weighting scheme used here sums both the CPS and SOII weights for occupation by sex by age cells.[3] The CPS observations are then down-weighted by the SOII total for a given cell. The following equations detail the methodology.

$$W_{O,S}^{SOII} = \sum_O \sum_S w_{O,S}^{SOII}$$ Total of SOII weights for occupation O and sex/age S

$$W_{O,S}^{CPS} = \sum_O \sum_S w_{O,S}^{CPS}$$ Total of CPS weights for occupation O and sex/age S

$$w_{O,S}^{new} = w_{O,S}^{CPS}\left(1 - \frac{W_{O,S}^{SOII}}{W_{O,S}^{CPS}}\right)$$ New weight is down-weighted by SOII total for that cell.

The occupation by sex by age cells are defined in the same way that they are for the regressions as described later.

Because the CFOI is a census, there are no weights. In the stacked CFOI/CPS data set, the CFOI observations are given a weight of 1 and the CPS observations are given their supplement weight. While in the stacked SOII/CPS data it was necessary to adjust the CPS weights to reflect the possibility that some CPS workers were injured, there is no overlap between the CPS and the fatalities data.

11.4.2   Modeling

In order to determine the impact that changes in the labor force have on injury, illness, and fatality numbers, a series of regressions were run on a set of employee characteristics common to the CPS, SOII, CFOI, and employment projections data. The characteristics of employees used to measure labor force changes are gender by age, occupation, and industry. There are twenty-two gender by age categories, twenty-two two-digit occupations, and sixteen major industries.[4] The advantage to this multivariate approach is that

3. An earlier version of this chapter used an alternative weighting scheme in which workers in the CPS who received workers' compensation were dropped and weights on the SOII observations were adjusted so that they maintained their proportional value but summed to the value of the dropped CPS observations. The results using this weighting scheme are qualitatively very similar to the results shown later.

4. The gender by age categories are males sixteen to nineteen, twenty to twenty-four, twenty-five to twenty-nine, thirty to thirty-four, thirty-five to thirty-nine, forty to forty-four, forty-five to forty-nine, fifty to fifty-four, fifty-five to fifty-nine, sixty to sixty-four, and sixty-five and over, and the same for females. The occupation and industry categories roughly follow two-digit Standard Occupational Classification (SOC) and NAICS codes, respectively. The NAICS 55 was not included in the analysis as it is underrepresented when the Census Industry codes on the CPS are converted to NAICS codes.

one can separately examine the impact of age, for example, while holding the industry and occupation mix constant. The multivariate approach would be impossible outside of the regression framework, as the gender by age by occupation by industry cells required in a tabular analysis would quickly become too thin for any meaningful analysis. As is shown following, results projecting the impact of age on the injury and illness numbers are much lower when controlling for industry and occupation than those that do not control for them.

The primary dependent variable of interest, worker injury, or illness, is a zero/one variable, therefore the regressions are estimated as logits. Beyond these top level equations, logistic regressions were also estimated by the most common natures and events causing injury or illness. These results highlight the fact that changing age, occupation, and industry mixes have different impacts on different types of work-related conditions. In order to get a sense of the impact of changing labor force characteristics on the severity of cases, the number of days away from work was also used as a dependent variable in an ordinary least squares regression. Finally, a logistic regression was estimated for fatalities.

Following the initial estimation, the marginal effect of each independent variable was calculated for each equation. The marginal effect was then multiplied by the change in the share of employees represented by that category measured using the projections data. These results are then multiplied by the total level of employment in 2004 and represent the estimated change in the number of injuries and illnesses given a change in the distribution of employment holding the total labor force fixed. While the labor force is expected to grow by 17 million over the time period in question, the results abstract away from overall growth in order to focus on distributional changes.

11.4.3   Projections of Injury, Illness, and Fatality Changes

Table 11.3 displays the marginal effects for a subset of the logistic regression results for nonfatal injuries and illnesses regressed on gender and age in the first column and gender, age, occupation, and industry in the second column. These results highlight the importance of controlling for the full set of covariates when examining the impact of gender and age on injury and illness statistics. In the first column, men appear more likely to receive workplace injuries or illness than women in all age categories. In the second column, the difference in the coefficients between men and women are much smaller. In fact, older women are more likely to receive workplace injuries and illnesses than older men. The difference between the two columns is likely due to the different occupations and industries in which men and women work. Men are more likely to receive workplace injuries and illnesses because they work in occupations and industries with higher injury and illness rates.

Using the marginal effects from the regression in column (2) and multiplying

Table 11.3	Logistic regression of injury on worker characteristics	
	(1)	(2)
Male		
16–19	0	0
20–24	0.0041	0.0022
	(0.0008)***	(0.0000)***
25–29	0.0038	0.0028
	(0.0007)***	(0.0000)***
30–34	0.0052	0.0039
	(0.0008)***	(0.0000)***
35–39	0.0042	0.0032
	(0.0007)***	(0.0000)***
40–44	0.0048	0.0034
	(0.0008)***	(0.0000)***
45–49	0.0043	0.0034
	(0.0008)***	(0.0000)***
50–54	0.0033	0.0028
	(0.0007)***	(0.0000)***
55–59	0.0022	0.0022
	(0.0007)***	(0.0000)***
60–64	0.001	0.0019
	(0.0007)	(0.0000)***
65+	0.0012	0.0011
	(0.0008)	(0.0000)**
Female		
16–19	–0.0059	–0.0024
	(0.0003)***	(0.0000)***
20–24	–0.0031	0.0002
	(0.0004)***	(0.0000)***
25–29	–0.0022	0.0017
	(0.0005)***	(0.0000)***
30–34	–0.0018	0.0023
	(0.0005)***	(0.0000)***
35–39	–0.0008	0.0033
	(0.0005)	(0.0000)***
40–44	–0.0007	0.0031
	(0.0005)	(0.0000)***
45–49	–0.0006	0.0033
	(0.0006)	(0.0000)***
50–54	0.0001	0.0042
	(0.0006)	(0.0000)***
55–59	–0.0012	0.0026
	(0.0005)**	(0.0000)***
60–64	–0.0013	0.0021
	(0.0007)	(0.0000)***
65+	–0.0012	0.0026
	(0.0007)	(0.0008)***
Occupation		Yes
Industry		Yes
Observations	260,121	260,121

Note: Robust standard errors in parentheses. "Yes" in the table indicates that industry and occupation dummies were included in the regression.

***Significant at the 1 percent level.

**Significant at the 5 percent level.

by the change in the share of workers in each of the gender, age, occupation, and industry categories given from the employment projections data, we find that changes in the gender and age composition of the labor force lead to an estimated drop in the number of injuries and illnesses by about 2000, holding the total labor force constant at the 2004 level. The estimated change due to occupation is a drop of 30,000 and the change due to industry is an increase of just over 100. The net total change is therefore a decrease of 32,000. This represents a small fraction of total employment but a larger fraction of injuries and illnesses, which numbered 1.2 million for this sample in 2005. Compared with the earlier univariate results, it is still true that older men are less likely to receive injuries and illnesses than their younger counterparts after age thirty. The multivariate results, however, show an increase in the probability of injury or illness for men between the ages of sixteen and thirty, whether or not one controls for occupation and industry. Differences between the univariate and regression results for younger workers are likely due to the lack of adjustment for hours in the regression analysis. An hours adjustment is not possible in the regression analysis due to the lack of information on the hours for injured or ill workers in the SOII.

While gender and age are important in predicting the probability of injury and illnesses, there are competing forces that cancel each other out leading to a small net change. Partially, this is due to an increase in both younger and older workers in the labor force. In addition, as is shown later, gender and age changes have different effects on different types of injuries and illnesses. The drop due to changes in occupations is due to a drop in the share of workers in production occupations—who have a high injury and illness rate—partially offset by a modest increase in the number of injuries and illnesses to health care support workers. Industry is not a powerful predictor of injury or illness. However, underlying the nearly zero net change is a modest increase in injuries and illnesses in the Health Care and Social Assistance industry, offset by small decreases in Manufacturing, Wholesale, and Retail trade.

The affect of the changing labor force varies when looking at different injury and illness types separately. Figure 11.7 shows the top seven nature of injury and illness categories plus an additional "all other" category to capture the remaining conditions. As can be seen in the figure, one category—sprains, strains, and tears—accounts for over 40 percent of all cases, followed by bruises, cuts, fractures, pain including back pain, illness, multiple injuries, and other. A logistic regression was run separately for each nature of injury or illness, the marginal effects calculated, and then the projections applied in order to compute the results shown in figure 11.8.

The changing gender and age makeup of the labor force has limited impact on the different natures except in sprains, where there is a large decrease, and fractures and multiple injuries, where there are large increases. The increase in fractures and multiple injuries is due to the predicted increase in the age of the labor force and particularly the increased share of the labor force rep-

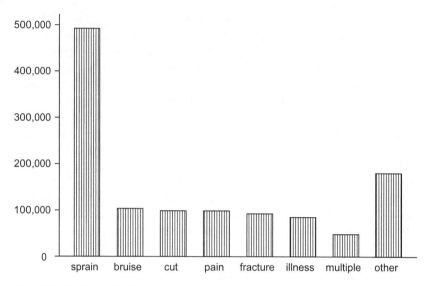

Fig. 11.7   Number of injuries by nature, 2005

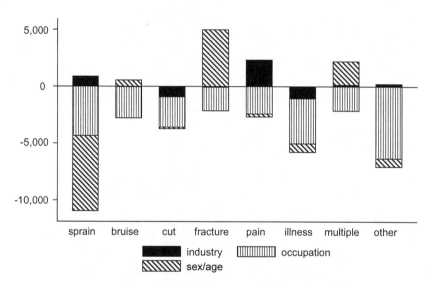

Fig. 11.8   Projected change in number of injuries, 2004–2014

resented by older women. Changes in the occupation distribution uniformly lead to lower numbers of injuries and illnesses regardless of the nature. The impact of the changes in industry is limited with an exception of the increase in the number of pain injuries, which is due to an increased share in the Health Care and Social Assistance industry.

Age, gender, industry, and occupation changes also affect injury and illness rates differently depending on the event that caused the condition. Figure 11.9 shows the five most common events leading to injury and illness with an additional "all other" category capturing the remaining injuries. The distribution of events is less skewed than the nature of injury or illness distribution shown previously. Bodily reaction and exertion is the most common event, followed by contact with objects and equipment, falls, transportation accidents, and exposure to harmful substances or environments.

The results of applying the projections to the marginal effects estimated from a logistic regression on each of the event categories is displayed in figure 11.10. The decrease in cases resulting from bodily reaction and exertion is due to an almost equal drop in cases correlated with occupation and gender and age differences. The projected decrease in the share of production occupations explains the occupation component, while a fall in the share of middle-aged workers explains the drop in the sex and age component. Similarly, the fall in contact-related cases is also due to the drop in production occupations. The increase in cases resulting from falls is due primarily to the increase in the share of older women in the labor force, but also due to aging more generally. Age, gender, industry, and occupation are not strong predictors of cases due to exposure, transportation accidents, or other events.

While the previous calculations focus on determining the impact of the changing labor force on workplace injuries and illnesses by projecting changes in the number of cases, an alternative is to determine the impact on the number of days away from work. As mentioned earlier, older workers are associated with longer injury and illness durations. However, in the projec-

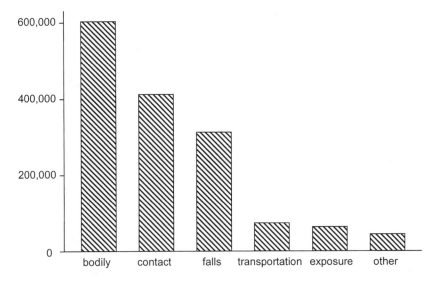

Fig. 11.9   Number of injuries, 2005

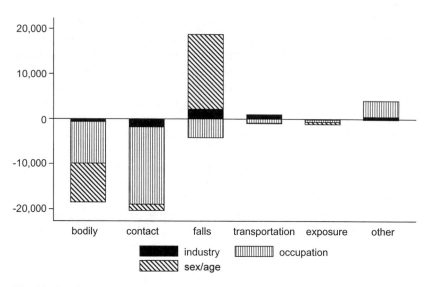

Fig. 11.10   Change in number of injuries by event, 2004–2014

tions data, while the share of older workers increases, the share of middle-aged workers decreases. Both of these groups have higher than average durations, so the net increase in the number of days away from work due to gender and age changes is small at 0.3 days. While this projected change might seem small in light of the earlier figure 10.6 showing the median duration by age, these results additionally control for occupation and industry, further minimizing the role of age and gender. Occupation changes have little effect on the projected days away from work, with a decrease of .01 days. However, industry has more explanatory power, with a projected decrease in days away from work of 0.2 days.

A separate regression was run to determine the impact of changes in the labor force on workplace fatalities. As mentioned before, fatalities occur predominately among men, and more so among older workers. Due to the limited number of workplace fatalities among women, the age categories were not separated by gender. Table 11.4 reports the marginal effects from the logistic regression of fatalities on age in column (1) and fatalities on age, occupation, and industry in column (2). Including occupation and industry dummies mitigates the impact of age on fatalities, but only by a small amount.

After calculating the marginal effects and multiplying by the change in the share for each characteristic as given by the projections data, the net effect of labor force changes on workplace fatalities is a drop of seven fatalities on a base of 3,700 fatalities in the restricted scope 2005 data. Changes in the gender and age makeup of the labor force lead to a predicted increase of

Table 11.4   Logistic regression of fatalities on worker characteristics

	(1)	(2)
16–19	0	0
20–24	0.0000101	0.0000005
	(.00000)**	(.00000)
25–29	0.0000186	0.0000028
	(.00001)***	(.00000)
30–34	0.0000222	0.0000039
	(.00001)***	(.00000)**
35–39	0.0000201	0.0000031
	(.00001)***	(.00000)
40–44	0.0000277	0.0000057
	(.00001)***	(.00000)***
45–49	0.0000327	0.0000080
	(.00001)***	(.00000)***
50–54	0.0000316	0.0000082
	(.00001)***	(.00000)***
55–59	0.0000399	0.0000115
	(.00001)***	(.00000)***
60–64	0.0000414	0.0000143
	(.00001)***	(.00000)***
65+	0.0000556	0.0000175
	(.00001)***	(.00000)***
Industry		Yes
Occupation		Yes
Observations	84,492	84,492

Note: Robust z statistics in parentheses "Yes" in the table indicates that industry and occupation dummies were included in the regression.
***Significant at the 1 percent level.
**Significant at the 5 percent level.

sixty-two fatalities, while occupation changes lead to a decrease of seventy-four fatalities and industry changes lead to an increase of five fatalities.

The fatality projections based on gender and age merit some comment. While fatality rates do rise steeply with age, the modest predicted increase of sixty-two fatalities with the aging of the workforce stems from an offset. There is an increase in the share of workers older than fifty, but there is also a decline in the share of workers age thirty-five to fifty. This latter decline leads to a drop in fatalities that offsets the increase in fatalities from the growth of the share of workers age fifty plus.

11.5   Other Issues

The preceding sections of this chapter have focused on the impact that changes in the age, gender, occupational, and industrial mix of the labor force may have on injury and illness statistics. The focus on these attributes of workers is in part due to the known relationships between these characteristics and the probability of injury and illness, but also because they are easily measurable in the SOII, CFOI, and complementary data sets that enable calculation of incidence rates. Beyond these basic worker characteristics, there are a host of other labor market trends that are likely to have an impact on workplace injuries, illnesses, and fatalities that are not easily measurable. A sampling of these trends, their likely impact on injury, illness, and fatality data, and the measurement issues involved are discussed later.

11.5.1   The Growth of Contract and Alternative Forms of Work

The Bureau of Labor Statistics projects that several industries providing contract workers will be among the fastest growing from 2004 to 2014. During that time period, BLS projects that the Employment Services industry will be the second largest source of employment growth in the economy, adding nearly 1.6 million jobs and rising to 5.1 million employees by 2014 (Berman 2005). This industry includes the Temporary Help Services and Professional Employer Organizations industries.[5] The BLS also projects that the Facilities Support Services industry will be the sixth fastest growing industry, though the number of jobs added is only 54,000.

These industries and others provide a wide variety of employees to the host businesses. Many of these employees are in relatively safe white-collar occupations. However, other workers provided from these industries perform hazardous work and their numbers are projected to grow. For instance, material-moving workers comprise over one-fifth of the Employment Services industry and that occupation is projected to add 236,000 jobs between 2004 and 2014. Labor and freight, stock, and material movers have a high rate of workplace injuries and illnesses at 3.6 times the rate for all private industry workers (USDL Release 07-1741, BLS 2007). Other contract workers work in hazard jobs such as cleaning the insides of petroleum containers.

Critics of the use of temporary and contract workers contend that they are being used in order for the host to circumvent the high costs (especially workers' compensation insurance) associated with certain forms of risky work. Further, they contend that temporary and contract workers may be at increased risk as they are less likely to recognize hazards or to be familiar with the temporary workplace (NIOSH 2002). Conversely, some contract workers may be particularly knowledgeable about the job risks that they face, as they perform specialized tasks frequently.

The growing use of contract and other forms of alternative labor creates

---

5. Establishments in the temporary help services industry supply workers to host businesses for limited periods of time. The temporary help workers remain employees of the temporary help establishments, though these establishments do not provide direct supervision. Employee leasing establishments, part of the professional employer organization industry, acquire and lease back employees of their clients and serve as the employer of the leased employees.

problems both for workplace safety and health outcomes and surveillance owing to uncertainties about supervisory roles. Safety and health may be compromised to the extent that contract workers are supervised by the supplying company, whose supervisors are not familiar with the risks of a temporary work site. Job safety may be compromised even when workers are supervised by an employee of the host, as that supervisor may not be familiar with the skills of the temporary and contract workers under his or her supervision. However, as a report from the National Institute for Occupational Safety and Health notes (NIOSH 2002), empirical studies of the impact of contract and other forms of alternative work are scarce, so the impact of these new forms of work is not clear.

What is clearer is that the growth of contract work renders more difficult the task of measuring workplace safety and health. The two workplace safety and health programs of the Bureau of Labor Statistics treat contract workers somewhat differently. In either case, however, it is difficult to relate contract workers to the work sites where they work and, hence, to get a clear picture of the safety and health of these work sites.

The Survey of Occupational Injuries and Illnesses (SOII), which tracks nonfatal cases, obtains its information from logs and supplementary records that employers maintain according to regulations of the Occupational Safety and Health Administration (OSHA). The OSHA rules state that records for contract employees are to be maintained by the employer who supervises the employee, in many cases the contracting company. Specifically, regulations require a host employer to record an OSHA-recordable injury or illness of contract workers who are supervised on a day-to-day basis, even when such employees are not carried on the employer's payroll. The regulations spell out that day-to-day supervision occurs when "in addition to specifying the output, product, or result to be accomplished by the person's work, the employer supervises the details, means, methods and processes by which the work is to be accomplished" (29 CFR 1904.31 [Code of Federal Regulations (CFR)]).

In many cases, the host employer does not provide the supervision described in the regulations. Instead, that supervision is provided by the contracting company. In that case, data on contract employees do not provide information about the safety records of particular job sites. Instead, contracting industry data provide information about the safety records of all job sites and host industries at which the contractors work. In addition, contracting industry data provide information not only about contractors, but also about other employees of the contracting industry who are not contractors.

The issue of supervision may create some ambiguity about who has the recordkeeping role. While we have no empirical evidence, it is conceivable that some contractor injuries may go unrecorded on OSHA logs due to this ambiguity.

The Survey of Occupational Injuries and Illnesses has another limitation when it comes to contract workers. The scope of SOII is limited to private industry and state and local government in some states. Among other groups, SOII excludes the self-employed. Many of these workers are contractors and thus, their safety experience is not captured in SOII.

The Census of Fatal Occupational Injuries (CFOI) approaches the collection of workplace fatality data in a different manner than SOII and also treats contractors differently. CFOI obtains information about workplace injury fatalities from multiple source documents, including death certificates, workers' compensation reports, OSHA fatality investigations, police reports, and even the press. The CFOI data compilers collate the information to rule out duplication and to identify unique fatalities that are work-related and due to traumatic occupational injury.

In CFOI, contract workers are reported as being in the industry that employs them. Typically, that means the industry of the company that actually pays that employee; that is, the contracting company. Therefore, it would be rare for a contract employee to be identified in the industry of the host company. Consequently, like the SOII, CFOI does not provide data about specific work sites or about the industry of the work sites where contract workers work. Instead, CFOI data for the contracting industries provide estimates of the job risk at all the work sites and industries where contractors in a particular contracting industry work.

The practice of assigning contracting employees to the employing industry has received attention from time to time. For example, the 2005 CFOI includes the fatalities from the British Petroleum (BP) refinery plant explosion in Texas City. The CFOI does not show these fatalities in the refining industry, but rather in the construction, engineering, and wholesale electrical equipment industries.

The practice of assigning decedents to the contracting industry does have the shortcoming of not providing site-specific fatality data. However, it does have the benefit of allowing the fatality counts to be aligned with employment data, which is based on employing industry. In this way, it is possible to calculate fatality rates.

It is important to note that, at the present time, CFOI does not identify whether or not a particular decedent was a contract worker. In some cases, it may be able to determine this from the source documents. For example, OSHA fatality investigation reports will identify contractors. However, many workplace fatalities are not identified from OSHA fatality reports and the other source documents may not provide the needed information to determine whether a particular worker is a contract worker. It may be that the best way to study the issue of contract worker fatalities is by means of a specific follow-back of fatality cases that focuses on whether or not the worker was a contract worker.

Unlike SOII, the scope of CFOI does include the self-employed. Thus,

CFOI will include the deaths of those self-employed workers who are contractors.

11.5.2   Alternative Workplaces and Flexiplace

Access to technology complementary to telework has increased dramatically since the 1990s, while at the same time the costs of both the equipment and communications have fallen. These factors have enabled a greater number of workers to telework due to both the increased communications access and the number of jobs suitable for telework. The BLS data show that the number of workers who usually did some work from home as part of their primary job increased through the 1990s, from 19.9 million in 1991 to 21.4 million in 1997. However, this number has since leveled off, with 20.7 million workers doing work from home in 2004, the most recent data available. While the overall numbers of telecommuters may not yet reflect these changes in the underlying economy, the number of potential telecommuters has undoubtedly increased.

Like alternative employment relationships, teleworking and alternative workplaces weaken employer monitoring of the OSH environment, potentially increasing injuries and illnesses. Alternative workplaces may also increase the challenge of properly measuring both injuries and illnesses and worker exposure to risk. According to OSHA rules (Directive number OSHA Instruction CPL 2-0.125, Home-Based Worksites). OSHA will not conduct inspections of employees' home offices nor will they hold employers liable for employees' home offices. However, employers who are required to keep OSHA logs are required to keep records of injuries and illnesses that occur in a home office.

11.5.3   Alternative Work Schedules, Long and
Intermittent Shifts, Flexitime

Alternative work schedules, including shift work and compressed work schedules, result in work at irregular times, more intermittency of work, and longer periods of work. All of these may affect work rhythms and fatigue, increasing injuries. Night work may be associated with riskier working environments, due to poor lighting and crime. Research on the impact of work hours on the probability of injury consistently find that the hour of work matters. Pergamit (2005) uses the National Longitudinal Survey of Youth (NLSY) to run logistic regressions of injury on a series of dummies describing a worker's schedule, including the shift and hours worked. He finds that workers who work nonday shifts have a 22 to 27 percent higher likelihood of injury.[6] Forston (2004), using Texas Worker's Compensation and a different approach, finds that inherent features of night work that

6. Nonday shifts include evening shifts, night shifts, rotating and split shifts, and irregular work schedules.

cannot be explained by age, occupation, industry, or fatigue lead to higher injury rates.

The percentage of workers with flexible worker hours has been increasing from the mid-1980s, while the percentage of workers working nonday shifts has been decreasing.[7] Both of these changes are likely closely related to changes in the mix of occupations and industries prevalent in the labor market. Professional services are more likely to offer flexible schedules and have become a larger part of the labor market. Conversely, the mining and manufacturing industries are more likely to have night shifts and are shrinking industries. However, there are also labor market trends working in the opposite direction. Health care workers are more likely to have alternative shifts than other workers and are a growing part of the labor market. While shifts in industry and occupation shares may explain the changes in the proportion of the labor force working different work schedules, research has shown that the higher rate of injury in nonday shifts cannot be explained by industry and occupation alone. That is, there are factors inherent in nonday shifts that increase workplace injury and illness risk.

Further research on the impact of different shifts may be possible, as the BLS Survey of Occupational Injuries and Illnesses now captures information about the day and time of injury or illness and the hours on the shift before onset. These data may be combined with information from the American Time Use Survey.

11.5.4   New Workplace Practices

The past two decades have witnessed the adoption of a variety of new workplace practices that involve quality and process management initiatives. These initiatives have been given a variety of names, such as high performance and high involvement work systems, flexible workplaces, total quality management, and lean production. They involve a number of practices, including shifting decision making downward to teams of workers, job rotation, process simplification to eliminate wasted time and motion, just-in-time methods, and a continuing emphasis on quality (NIOSH 2002).

In principle, involving workers in decision making and focusing on process should have beneficial effects on worker safety and health. Workers can identify sources of job risk and work to reduce or eliminate these. Further, job rotation can be used to change the tasks of workers suffering from repeated trauma disorders. Critics, however, contend that quality and process initiatives reduce worker autonomy and control and that the productivity gains obtained through the initiatives come from a speedup and intensification of work. These critics also contend that job rotation moves workers to new tasks for which they are not well trained. The result is worsened worker safety and health, particularly in the form of increased

---

7. See "Workers on Flexible and Shift Schedules in 2004," *BLS Economic News Summary.*

incidence of cumulative trauma disorders and stress (Brenner, Fairris, and Ruser 2004).

Initial research on this topic was in the form of case studies largely in the automotive industry. Among the limited cross-industry empirical work, Fairris and Brenner (2001) match industry-level measures of cumulative trauma disorders (CTDs) from SOII to a separate survey of workplace practices conducted by Osterman. They find the use of quality circles (but no other workplace practice) was positively associated with CTDs.

Research by Brenner, Fairris, and Ruser (2004) extends the work of Fairris and Brenner using establishment-level data on workplace transformations (e.g., quality circles, work teams, and just-in-time production) matched to measures of cumulative trauma disorders (CTDs) at the same establishments. The data on workplace transformations was obtained from the 1993 Survey of Employer Provided Training, while the data on CTDS came from the 1993 Survey of Occupational Injuries and Illnesses. The research found that just-in-time approaches to production and quality circles are both positively and statistically significantly associated with rates of cumulative trauma disorders across establishments. Further, the quantitative impact on CTDs of these two workplace practices was sizeable, ranging from 20 to 65 percent of the mean CTD rate, depending on sample and estimating specification.

Finally, related interesting work by Askenazy and Caroli (2006) uses data for French workers. They find that the use of quality norms and job rotation is associated with greater mental strain and more occupational injuries; though, while the probability of a "benign" injury is 25 to 40 percent higher for workers involved in these two practices, the effect on serious injuries is never statistically significant. Further, the impact of "regular collective discussion on work organization" seems to be associated with higher occupational risks. Askenazy and Caroli hypothesize that this positive relationship may stem from endogeneity—discussions are more likely when there are more safety problems. They do note, however, that their results suggest that these discussions do not result in a safer workplace.

The evidence presented previously suggests that new workplace practices may result in more occupational injuries, CTDs, and job stress. However, it must be noted that the body of literature on this topic is not extensive. Indeed, the National Institute for Occupation Safety and Health (NIOSH) states that additional research is needed to determine whether these workplace practices have a beneficial or detrimental impact of worker safety and health. The NIOSH further notes that since "these work systems are seldom implemented in a standardized fashion, their effects on worker safety and health may depend on their specific characteristics and the implementation process" (NIOSH 2002, 10). Further study will also require better measurement of the incidence of these workplace practices, as the United States has only an ad hoc series of surveys that lack common definitions (Handel and Levine 2006), and these surveys are now somewhat dated.

11.6   Conclusions

Using existing workplace safety and health data and BLS projections, we are able to assess the impact of certain labor market trends on workplace safety and health. Specifically, we are able to assess the impact of changes from 2004 to 2014 in the labor force distributions by age, gender, industry, and occupation.

The analysis suggests that labor force shifts between 2004 and 2014 will have perceptible impacts on the frequency and distribution of workplace injuries and illnesses. Aging of the workforce (and gender shifts) will result in an increase in more severe injuries, such as fractures and fatalities, while falls will become a more frequent event associated with workplace injury. The median duration of an injury or illness will also rise slightly. Decreases in the number of production workers will likely lead to decreases in the number of injured and ill. However, the growing number of jobs in health care will work to increase the number of injured and ill, particularly among women.

The data generally do not permit us to estimate the impact of other important labor force trends, such as the growth in contract labor, alternative forms of work, alternative workplaces and hours, and new workplaces. However, the literature provides hypothetical effects and sometimes empirical evidence that we have summarized in the chapter. In general, the effect of these various trends on workplace safety and health is ambiguous, though the cited literature seems to suggest that new workplace practices (such as just-in-time inventories, quality circles, and possibly job rotation) are associated with more job stress, cumulative trauma disorders, and occupational injuries.

Beyond impacting workplace safety and health outcomes, emerging labor market trends also affect the ability to monitor workplace safety and health. One important area is the growing use of contract labor. The current BLS occupational safety and health surveillance systems for nonfatal workplace injuries and illnesses and for fatal workplace injuries do not permit the estimation of injury, illness, and fatality rates according to the location of work performed. Thus, with these surveillance systems, we are not able to measure the job risks at the work sites of employers hosting contract workers. Monitoring and measuring safety and health also becomes more difficult as more work is performed at alternative work sites, such as at home.

References

Askenazy, P., and E. Caroli. 2006. Innovative work practices, information technologies and working conditions: Evidence for France. IZA Discussion Paper no. 2321, September.

Barkume, A., and J. Ruser. 2001. Deregulating property-casualty insurance pricing: The case of workers' compensation. *Journal of Law and Economics* 44 (1): 37–63.

Berman, J. M. 2005. Industry output and employment projections to 2014. *Monthly Labor Review* 128 (November): 45–69.

Boden, L. I., and J. W. Ruser. 2003. Workers' compensation "reforms," choice of medical care provider, and reported workplace injuries. *Review of Economics and Statistics* 85 (4): 923–29.

Brenner, M. D., D. Fairris, and J. Ruser. 2004. Flexible work practices and occupational safety and health: Exploring the relationship between cumulative trauma disorders and workplace transformation. *Industrial Relations* 43 (1): 242–66.

Conway, H., and J. Svenson. 1998. Occupational injury and illness rates, 1992–96: Why they fell. *Monthly Labor Review* 121 (11): 36–58.

Fairris, D., and M. Brenner. 2001. Workplace transformation and the rise in cumulative trauma disorders: Is there a connection? *Journal of Labor Research* 22 (January): 15–28.

Fortson, K. 2004. The diurnal pattern of on-the-job injuries. *Monthly Labor Review* 127:18–25.

Handel, M. J., and D. I. Levine. 2006. The effects of new work practices on workers. UC Berkeley: Institute for Research on Labor and Employment. Working Paper no. 131-06.

National Institute for Occupational Safety and Health (NIOSH). 2002. *The changing organization of work and the safety and health of working people.* NIOSH document no. 2002-116, April.

Pergamit, M. R. 2002. Work schedules and work injuries. Paper presented at the Joint Meeting of the Society of Labor Economists and European Association of Labour Economists. June, San Francisco.

U.S. Bureau of Labor Statistics. 2007. *Nonfatal occupational injuries and illnesses requiring days away from work, 2006.* News Release USDL 07-1741, November 8.

———. 2009. *Handbook of methods.* Washington, DC: United States Department of Labor.

Ussif, A. 2004. An international analysis of workplace injuries. *Monthly Labor Review* 127 (3): 41–51.

Welch, L. S., X. Dong, F. Carre, and K. Ringen. 2007. Is the apparent decrease in injury and illness rates in construction the result of changes in reporting? *International Journal of Occupational and Environmental Health* 13 (1): 39–45.

Comment   Jeff E. Biddle

Nestoriak and Ruser have written a useful chapter. There are changes coming in the nature of the labor force and its activities about which we can be fairly certain, and it is worth thinking about how those changes will influence the number and types of workplace injuries that will occur. For example, we know the workforce will be aging; Nestoriak and Ruser alert us to the fact that as a result of this we should be prepared for fewer injuries due to

Jeff E. Biddle is professor of economics at Michigan State University.

overexertion, but more falls; more fractures but fewer strains and sprains. And with older workers, the probability that a serious injury will result in a long-term disability or even death will increase. This is not idle knowledge. My experience suggests that when information like this is disseminated, the occupational health and safety community—from the people at NIOSH to the risk managers and safety directors at individual firms—talk about it and react to it. News like, "you're going to be employing more old people, and old people fall more often" really does, these days, lead to changes in workplace layouts and work practices.

I have little to say about the technical aspects of the chapter. One could discuss the issue of the proper weights to use when combining workers from the injury survey with workers from the CPS. The weights used by the authors are sensible, although they could be refined. Indeed, in an earlier draft of the chapter they used a CPS question on the receipt of workers' compensation benefits to adjust for the chance that a worker could appear in both data sets. This approach had problems of its own, however, and I am not surprised by the author's report that the simpler weighting procedure they eventually settled on produces essentially the same results as the more complicated approach employed earlier, since the injured workers represent such a small percentage of all workers in the CPS.

The major issue with attempts to forecast the number and nature of future work-related injuries is the problem that faces anyone who makes predictions about the future based on the past: in so many ways, the future will not be like the past (that, at least, is one thing we can be certain of). We are in the midst of a revolution in workplace safety. Occupational injury and fatality rates have been declining since 1992. Between 1995 and 2000, the rate of OSHA recordables fell by 20 percent. From 2003 to 2006, it fell by another 8 percent, and injuries with days away from work fell by 13 percent. In their prediction exercise, the authors focus on standard measurable factors—changing demographics, changing occupation, and industry mix—to predict the future, but existing research, including studies cited by the authors, show that little of the dramatic decline in injury and fatality rates of the past fifteen years can be explained by those standard measurable factors.

I think that it would have been interesting for the authors to apply their methodology to see how well it would have predicted the change in the occupational injury picture over some or all of the last fifteen years. For example, suppose one took occupation, industry, and demographic projections from 1995, loaded up the March CPS and the Survey of Occupational Injuries, and projected the number and mix of injuries one would expect over the following ten years? How much would these predictions diverge from what really happened?

My feeling is that much of the improvement in the occupational safety picture over the last fifteen years has to do with changes in the way that work is done within particular industries and firms. The authors speculate about the future impact on occupational health and safety of three ongoing changes in the nature of work: telecommuting, an increase in the use of leased employees, and the introduction of certain new production techniques and work practices, including just-in-time manufacturing, job rotation, and total quality management. I think the latter two are by far the more important. Unfortunately, as the authors also note, empirical research on the impact of these trends on health and safety is scarce, and is relatively hard to do. The authors provide a very useful discussion of the data problems that face any attempt to research issues of health and safety in the employer services and temporary worker industries, and, not surprisingly, little such research has been done. New work practices like quality circles or job rotation are also very challenging to study, because in different industries and different establishments they have the potential to look very different and lead to very different changes in the physical demands they make on workers. I recently saw a well-designed proposal for studying the impact of the introduction of job rotation in a large manufacturing firm. The job rotation plan was going to be introduced earlier in some locations than in others, and the firm was cooperating with the researchers, giving them input into how the plan was implemented and access to before and after data. Even in this almost ideal setting, however, the researchers had difficulties reducing the myriad possible job rotation patterns in the plan into well-defined categories for the purposes of empirical analysis, and because the plan was tailored to a very specific setting, the prospects for generalizing the results of the study beyond one particular industry were not encouraging. Still, we cannot let the best be an enemy of the good, and I hope that research onto the impact of new workplace practices will continue.

The workplace practices discussed by the authors are all of the sort that affect occupational health and safety unintentionally. However, much of the qualitative literature discussing the recent declines in occupational injuries and days away from work focuses on things that employers are doing intentionally: better safety programs, engineering safety into the workplace, managing serious work-related injury cases with nurse case managers, and return-to-work programs. Certainly the members of the employer community believe programs like these to be the most important drivers of improvements in occupational health. But if we accept this line of argument, we have to ask why these largely voluntary changes in employer health and safety practices have occurred? The extent of their growth is far beyond anything that could be attributed to incentives introduced into a few states' workers' compensation laws or changes in OSHA enforcement. As economists, we would be uncomfortable with an explanation running in terms of widespread and increasing solicitousness of employers toward the health of their workers. Fortunately, one can tell a story that is more appealing to economists. As Conway and Svenson (1998) noted in their early analysis of the decline in injury rates, increasing costs of medical care in the late 1980s led to higher workers' comp premiums in the 1990s, and gave employers increased incentives to avoid accidents and manage injury cases more closely. After a brief hiatus, medical costs have continued to rise, driving up the cost to the employer of the typical workplace injury, and increasing further the incentives to improve safety programs, return-to-work programs, and so on.

This is of course not a new hypothesis I am advancing, although it is still an underresearched one. I mention it only to make a final point about the future of occupational safety and health in the United States that has not, I think, been discussed enough. If and when the health care insurance system in this country is overhauled, the designers are going to have to decide what to do with work-related injuries. Will they still be handled separately by workers' compensation programs, or will they be lumped in for insurance purposes with all other health problems, leaving the workers' comp system to handle only wage loss payments? If the employer's experience rated workers' comp premiums no longer reflect the medical costs generated by injuries to his employees, what happens to his incentives for safety? If the hypothesis about improved workplace safety and health being driven by rising workers' comp costs is true, then discussions of reforms to the health insurance system should include consideration of the effects of those reforms on occupational safety and health.

Reference

Conway, H., and J. Svenson. 1998. Occupational injury and illness rates 1992–1996: Why they fell. *Monthly Labor Review* 121:36–58.

Measuring Labor Composition
A Comparison of Alternate Methodologies

Cindy Zoghi

12.1 Introduction

Productivity estimates require a measure of labor input, which is a combination of workers, number of hours they work, and effectiveness of those hours. A measure that only counts number of workers or hours ignores that some work hours produce more than others. For example, the work hour put forth by a brand new employee is not likely to produce as much output as the work hour put forth by someone who has been on the job many years. In this case, the effectiveness of the latter work hour is greater than that of the former.

A labor composition index[1] adjusts the total hours worked for the demographic composition of those hours, which requires identification of separate, heterogeneous groups of labor input whose work hours are likely to have varying effectiveness. This is particularly important when we consider changes over time in the labor input. For example, between 1984 and 2004, the share of workers with more schooling than a high school diploma increased from just over 40 percent to over 55 percent. Even given the same number of hours of work performed by the typical worker in each year, the 2004 hours, being more skilled and presumably more efficient, will result

Cindy Zoghi is a research economist in the Division of Productivity Research and Program Development at the U.S. Bureau of Labor Statistics.

Views and results expressed here are those of the author and have not been endorsed by the Bureau of Labor Statistics or the U.S. Department of Labor. The author thanks Stephanie Aaronson, Katharine Abraham, Joe Altonji, Bronwyn Hall, Mike Harper, Dale Jorgenson, Larry Rosenblum, Jim Spletzer, Arianna Zoghi, and participants of the NBER CRIW Labor in the New Economy Conference and preconference, the 2007 NBER CRIW Summer institute, and the December, 2007, Federal Economic Statistics Advisory Committee Meeting.

1. This is sometimes called a labor quality index.

in greater input, and productivity would increase. Yet, technically, it is not greater output with the same labor input. This distinction is one that we often wish to preserve in our statistics, separating the effect of increasing output with the exact same input versus increasing output with a different type of input.

There is an interesting distinction to be made here between inherent characteristics of the worker that vary the effectiveness of his or her work hour and characteristics of the job itself that alter the effectiveness. For example, when a year passes and a worker gains an additional year of experience, this changes the input. Similarly, if the worker is replaced by another with more education, this also changes the input. On the other hand, if the worker switches jobs with another worker, resulting in improved matching, the input remains unchanged, and productivity increases. In another example, the establishment might adopt teams, which would use the same inputs but increase productivity.

In this chapter, I first introduce past analysis of how to measure the labor input and discuss several suggested methods for obtaining the best input measure. I then look at the background evidence for whether particular demographic wage differentials are productivity differentials or are due to other factors. Additionally, I examine whether the composition of labor input changes over time across these dimensions. If there are productivity differentials across types of workers but the ratio of hours among them does not change over time, the hours can be aggregated without weighting. If the distribution of hours changes with respect to this categorization, and the consensus of the literature is that the wage differentials reflect differing marginal productivity, the category should be used to disaggregate the labor input, assuming it is empirically feasible. Finally, I compare various measures of the labor composition index. The current Bureau of Labor Statistics (BLS) methodology uses imputed wages to weight the types of labor, while other studies have used actual mean wages. I compare the two methodologies to determine whether estimation of wages is an improvement. I then compare how labor composition affects productivity under various categorizations of workers.

12.2   Literature Review

Beginning with the earliest discussions of the productivity "residual," researchers have recognized that a measure of labor input that merely sums all hours worked in the economy will not capture changes in the effectiveness of a work hour over time. Schmookler (1952) explained that to compare the magnitudes of an input between a pair of years and create a continuous, constant-price index requires that the input be homogeneous over time. He cited the example of the large wage differential between agricultural and nonagricultural workers and the shift in man-hours away from agriculture between 1869 and 1938 to show an important source of heterogeneity in the labor market. Similarly, Abramovitz (1956) noted that the period between 1870 and 1950 is characterized by a decrease in the labor force participation of teenagers and older men, with a compensating shift toward the employment of prime-age workers, who generally have a higher output per hour. He explained that this is likely to understate the growth of labor input and overstate productivity growth. Solow (1957, 317) summarized the issue thus: "a lot of what appears as shifts in the production function must represent improvement in the quality of the labor input, and therefore a result of real capital formation of an important kind."

As part of the exercise of national accounting, it is important to correctly measure the labor input in constant real-price terms. As explained by Jorgenson and Griliches (1967, 250), "the alteration in patterns of productive activity must be separated into the part which is 'costless,' representing a shift in the production function, and the part which represents the employment of scarce resources with alternative uses, representing movements along the production function." From the beginning of the discussion of this measurement issue, it has been acknowledged that the solution lies in a properly weighted index of disaggregated labor inputs. In fact, the ideal extreme case allows each worker to function as a unique input, by virtue of his unique set of relevant characteristics (Jorgenson, Ho, and Stiroh 2005).

Data limitations generally restricted early measures to adjusting the labor input for only one factor of worker heterogeneity. Schmookler (1952) divided the labor input into an agricultural and nonagricultural component and then took a sum of the two sectors, weighted by their respective wage rates. Denison (1962), Jorgenson and Griliches (1967) and Griliches (1970) adjusted the labor input measure for income differentials by years of education among workers, and for the income differentials between men and women. In most of these papers, the authors lamented the desirability and also the difficulty of constructing a proper index that would account for other sources of heterogeneity, such as age, occupation, industry, literacy, on-the-job training, nationality, and other such variables.

However, with the greatly improved access to the decennial Censuses, the monthly Current Population Survey, and other new data sources, more detailed categorizations of workers became possible. Denison (1974) classified workers by age groups, gender, years of schooling, average hours, and employment class, using data on worker demographics from the Current Population Survey (CPS) and the 1960 Census. Control totals were obtained from establishment-based data on hours. Gollop and Jorgenson (1980), Jorgenson, Gollop, and Fraumeni (1987), and Jorgenson, Ho, and Stiroh (2005) further disaggregated by broad occupation and industry groups using the decennial Censuses, reconciled to marginal totals from the Current Population Survey, and further controlled to establishment survey totals. The BLS (1993) divided workers by years of experience, years of education, and gender. Their unique measure of experience was derived from actual recorded experience in social security records in 1973.

Most contemporary adjustments to labor input involve replacing a simple sum of workers or worker hours with a weighted sum of the separate groups of workers or worker hours. The calculation of weights varies from study to study, however. Denison's (1974) education weights measured relative earnings of men at each education level, adjusted for differences in the composition of workers within an education group with respect to age, race, farm attachment, and geographic region. The weights were developed for 1959 and subsequently used in each period of the study, in part because he was unable to develop similar weights for other years that would be comparable. Gollop and Jorgenson (1980), Jorgenson, Gollop, and Fraumeni (1987), and Jorgenson, Ho, and Stiroh (2005) used average factor shares for each category of worker in the value of total sector compensation, using compensation rates obtained from Census wages reconciled with CPS marginal subtotals, and imputations of nonwage compensation from the National Income and Product Accounts. The BLS (1993) used estimated wage rates by type of worker from CPS wage regressions. Aaronson and Sullivan (2001) used a slightly simpler approach, estimating the growth in labor effectiveness with the growth in average predicted wages, where the wages were predicted using CPS wage regressions. Importantly, they found that differences in methodology across studies do not dramatically change the estimates of labor effectiveness.

12.3   The Labor Composition Model

The labor composition model uses a generalized production function that allows various types of labor to contribute to producing output. It can be written as:

$$(1) \qquad Q = f(k_1, \ldots, k_n, h_1, \ldots, h_m, A_t)$$

where output Q is produced by n different types of capital, $k_1, \ldots, k_n$, by m different types of labor hours, $h_1, \ldots, h_m$, and by the technology available at time t, A_t.

By taking the natural logarithm of both sides, differentiating with respect to time, and rearranging terms, equation (1) can be expressed as a relationship between multifactor productivity and growth rates of output and inputs:

$$(2) \qquad \frac{\dot{A}}{A} = \frac{\dot{Q}}{Q} - \left(s_{k_1}\frac{\dot{k}_1}{k_1} + \ldots + s_{k_n}\frac{\dot{k}_n}{k_n} + s_{l_1}\frac{\dot{h}_1}{h_1} + \ldots + s_{l_m}\frac{\dot{h}_m}{h_m} \right)$$

where the dot notation indicates the growth rate of that variable. The partial derivatives, s_{ki} and s_{li}, represent output elasticities, or the percent change in output resulting from a 1 percent increase in the respective input. In practice, these marginal products are unobservable. Under the assumptions of constant returns to scale and perfect competition in product and input markets, each elasticity is equal to the share of total costs paid to that input. In the case of labor, that is calculated as the product of labor's share of total costs and each type of labor's share of the total wage bill.

Assuming that the labor input is separable from capital, an aggregate labor input equation can be derived:

$$(3) \qquad \frac{\dot{L}}{L} = s_{h_1}\frac{\dot{h}_1}{h_1} + \ldots + s_{h_m}\frac{\dot{h}_m}{h_m}$$

where s_{hi} is the share of the total wage bill that is spent on each particular type of labor. Under a translog production function, Diewert (1976) showed that changes in input are exactly measured by changes in Tornqvist indexes. Thus, although $\dot{L}/L$ is the instantaneous rate of change in composition-adjusted labor input, it can be replaced by annual rates of change, measured with a Tornqvist index as the difference in the natural logarithm of successive observations, with the weights equal to the mean of the factor shares in the corresponding pair of years:

$$(4) \qquad \Delta \ln L = \sum_j \frac{1}{2}[s_{h_j}(t) + s_{h_j}(t-1)]\Delta \ln h_j.$$

Groups that make up a very small portion of the total wage bill will not have much impact on the labor input measure.

Changes in the index of labor composition, LC, are defined as the difference between the change in composition-adjusted labor input given in equation (4), and the change in the sum of unweighted hours:

$$(5) \qquad \Delta \ln LC = \Delta \ln L - \Delta \ln H = \Delta \ln \frac{L}{H}.$$

In practice, estimation of the labor composition index requires a count of the number of hours worked by each type of worker, as well as cost share weights for each type of worker. Cost share weights may be calculated using either actual mean observed wages, as in Denison (1974); Gollop and Jorgenson (1980); Jorgenson, Gollop, and Fraumeni (1987); and Jorgenson, Ho, and Stiroh (2005); or, as BLS (1993) does, replacing actual wages with imputed wages, where the imputations are obtained from a standard Mincer wage regression (see BLS 1993, Appendix E).

The key components for identifying distinct categories of workers are evident from equation (4). The group must have a different output elasticity from other workers in theory, which should be evidenced in the data by a wage differential for that group. Additionally, it should experience changing hours relative to other groups. In the next section, we discuss several potential groups in the context of wage differentials and hours change.

12.4 Wage Differentials

The basic neoclassical model assumes perfect competition, profit maximizing firms, and homogeneous workers. This results in equal wages across all workers. The human capital model relaxes the assumption of homogeneous workers, recognizing that workers can vary in their innate abilities, as well as in their human capital investments. As a result, wages will not be equal across heterogeneous worker types. Rather, wage differentials will reflect differences in the marginal productivity of workers. This suggests that a logical categorization is one that separates types of workers that obtain different wages. The literature on wage differentials is vast, and suggests some interesting categories of workers along the dimension of education, experience, gender, race, unionization, geographic location, establishment size, and other characteristics of both the worker and the workplace.

It is not necessarily the case, however, that all wage differentials represent productivity differentials. In particular, even within the competitive model,[2] there are other explanations for persistent wage differentials between groups of homogeneous workers. The theory of equalizing differences (Rosen 1986; Brown 1980) hypothesizes that wages are adjusted down (up) to account for the amenity (disamenity) of working at a particular job, which equalizes the total monetary and nonmonetary benefits across jobs, keeping the workers indifferent between them. This would result in workers of equal marginal productivity being offered different wages, depending on their job.

Another well-discussed explanation for wage differentials is the efficiency wage theory, in which managers have an incentive to pay workers above the market-clearing wage rate in order to improve the efficiency of the workers or of the organization as a whole. There are several examples of this. If managers pay workers a high wage, the workers face greater potential loss if they become unemployed. This gives the worker an extra incentive to work hard so she will not lose her high-paying job. Note carefully here, that the worker paid in excess is not intrinsically any different from another worker with the same abilities and human capital investments who earns the equilibrium wage rate—it is the same input, but she is induced to work more efficiently. Thus, it is not a different input, but a productivity enhancement. Other reasons for paying in excess of the market-clearing wage rate include reducing turnover and attracting a higher quality pool of workers from which to fill vacancies. In both cases, the labor input is constant, but the wage differentials would be related to increased productivity for the establishment.

2. In addition, there are several noncompetitive models that generate wage differentials. Since the theoretical model relies on perfect competition in the labor market to generate the result that elasticities can be empirically estimated by cost shares, these are not considered here.

12.4.1   Age/Experience

Traditional human capital models (i.e., Mincer 1974) predict that as workers age, they gain experience and skills that make them more productive, and wages rise accordingly. Productivity may decrease again later in life as health concerns begin to affect performance in many jobs. Figure 12.1 shows the average wages and annual hours worked by workers in age groups under twenty-five, twenty-five to thirty-four, thirty-five to forty-four, forty-five to fifty-four, and fifty-five and up, and figure 12.2 repeats for experience groups under five, five to fourteen, fifteen to twenty-four, and twenty-five and up, calculated from the 1984, 1994, and 2004 March CPS. Experience is imputed from experience regression coefficients obtained from the Survey of Income and Program Participation (SIPP) as described in Zoghi (2006). The pattern of increasing wages early in life/career followed by a slowdown later in life/career is confirmed in the data. The effect has gotten stronger over the twenty-year period shown here.

Lazear (1979), however, argued that the age-wage differential may not be an accurate measure of the productivity differentials between age groups, because firms may make implicit long-term incentive contracts with workers to pay wages below the value of marginal product when workers are young and above it when workers are older. Similarly, Loewenstein and Sicherman (1991) considered that workers might prefer such wage profiles in order to force their savings for consumption later in life. Again, this would imply that the age-wage differentials do not accurately measure productivity differentials. However, Hellerstein, Neumark, and Troske (1999) compared wage differentials to productivity differentials using matched employee establishment data and found that the size of the age-wage differentials is consistent with the size of the productive differences by age.

The composition of labor hours by age and experience groups has changed dramatically from 1984 to 2004. In the 1984 sample, nearly half the hours of work in the United States were performed by those ages thirty-four and under (those with less than fifteen years of experience). By 2004, as the baby boom generation aged, this number had dropped to around 35 percent (30 percent). Thus, if we believe that age/experience wage differentials reflect productivity differences, there has been a marked shift toward a more productive labor input.

12.4.2   Education

Human capital theory implies that workers with more education gain skills that should make them more productive. Figure 12.3 shows a pattern of rising wages with increased education consistent with this theory. Those with the lowest levels of education earn less than half the hourly wage of those with the most advanced degrees.

Some counter that it may not be the education itself that enhances the

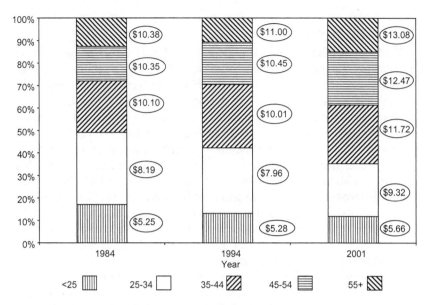

Fig. 12.1   Distribution of hours worked, by age group

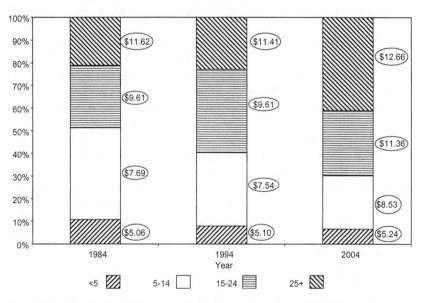

Fig. 12.2   Distribution of hours worked, by years experience (SIPP)

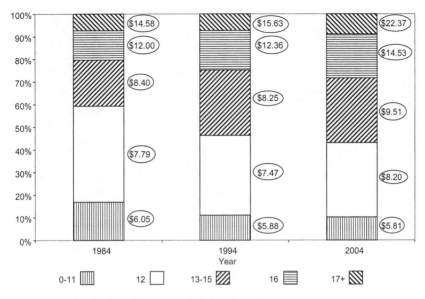

Fig. 12.3 **Distribution of hours worked, by education**

skills of the worker, but rather that workers with a certain skill level obtain an education in order to signal their skill to employers (Spence 1973). In either case, however, educational differentials are likely to be correlated with productivity differentials. This fits in closely with the idea that there are "sheepskin effects," or disproportionate effects to obtaining a particular degree, above and beyond the effect of the number of years of education that it takes to obtain such a degree (Hungerford and Solon 1987; Belman and Heywood 1991).

As with the case of age, there have been large shifts in the education composition of the workforce. As figure 12.3 shows, in 1984, 60 percent of labor hours were performed by workers with twelve years of education or less. By 2004, however, that number had fallen to approximately 45 percent. This is another example of a shift in the composition of workers away from low-wage—and potentially low-marginal productivity—workers.

12.4.3   Gender

According to Blau and Kahn (2006), women's wages, which had been 60 percent of men's wages for much of the 1950s and 1960s, increased relative to men's in the 1980s (to 69 percent of men's), and that increase continued, albeit much more slowly, in the 1990s (to 72 percent by 1999). Figure 12.4 confirms that women earn less than men, and that the gap has narrowed between 1984 and 2004, from 68 percent to 74 percent. Hellerstein, Neumark, and Troske (1999) found that although women do, in fact, have lower

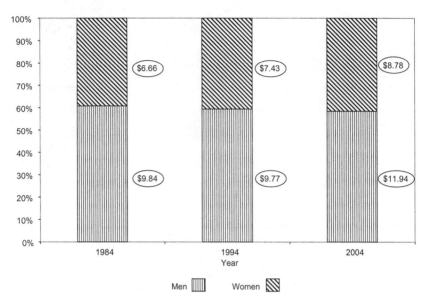

Fig. 12.4   Distribution of hours worked, by gender

productivity than men, the wage gap is much larger than would be suggested by these productivity differentials. Thus, a large part of the wage differential measures discrimination.

Another motivation used for segregating workers by gender is that the returns to other characteristics may vary across gender. For example, women's returns to age or potential experience are likely to be lower than men's, since women are more likely to have been out of the labor market for some of that time. Additionally, women's returns to education may be different, if the types of jobs they hold are more or less likely to value education than the types of jobs men hold.

In figure 12.4, the composition of hours has changed slightly toward an increasing percent of hours being worked by women. In 1984, 39.2 percent of total hours were performed by women. By 2004, that number had increased to 41.6 percent. This is an interesting case for labor composition measurement. There is a shift in composition toward a lower-paid type of worker; however, since only part of the wage differential is believed to be productivity-related, a labor composition measure that includes women as a category of worker may overstate the effect of the shift, while one that does not include women may understate it.

12.4.4   Industry

Figure 12.5 compares the wages for workers in each industry, measured by the Census 1990 code for major (one-digit) industry. In 1984, wages were

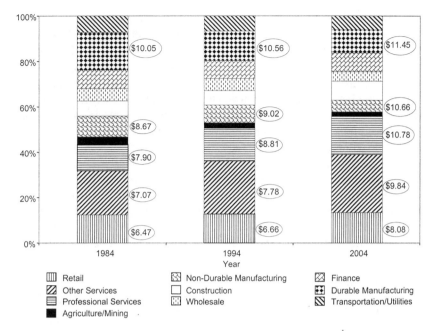

Fig. 12.5   Distribution of hours worked, by industry

highest in mining, transportation and utilities, and durable manufacturing, with the lowest wages found in personal and entertainment services. By 2004, finance and business services moved to the top of the list, along with mining.

There is a long history of debate on whether interindustry wage differentials represent differences in amounts of unmeasured skills, nonpecuniary benefits, employee or employer bargaining power, or the use of efficiency wages. Industry wage differentials are remarkably persistent over time and across countries. Krueger and Summers (1988) matched CPS workers across months to look at the industry differentials for job changers, using first-differencing to remove the effect of unobserved worker characteristics. They found that the differentials persist, and inferred from this that interindustry wage differentials are not, therefore, related to productivity differentials caused by unmeasured ability. Murphy and Topel (1987, 1990) used a similar methodology but found much lower differentials in their first-differenced estimates. Keane (1993), using a longer longitudinal data set, found that 84 percent of the wage differential is attributed to unobserved worker characteristics. One problem with these studies, however, is that they assume that the worker's skills are equally valuable after he or she changes industry, which is not likely to be the case.

Alternative explanations for the interindustry wage differentials have not been met with much empirical success. Brown (1980), Smith (1979), Brown and Medoff (1989), and others have been unable to find evidence that wage differentials are due to differences across industries in on-the-job hazards or other job attributes. Testing a model by Dickens (1986) of the relationship between unionization threat and wage differentials, Krueger and Summers (1988) and Dickens and Katz (1986) found that the patterns of interindustry wage structure are similar in geographic areas where union avoidance is high relative to other areas of the country. They also found that neither time series patterns of unionization nor differences in unionization across industries provide support for this explanation of wage differentials.

The distribution of hours of work across industry has changed enormously over the last twenty years, as figure 12.5 indicates. Employment has fallen in manufacturing and transportation and utilities, and has risen in the service industries. Unlike the patterns we see for experience and education, this suggests a shift away from higher-wage jobs—if these wage differentials reflect productivity differences across workers in different industries, not including industry in a labor composition measure will understate productivity.

12.4.5   Occupation

Occupation codes are intended to classify different skill sets (or amounts of human capital types) needed to perform different jobs. Thus, occupations are in some sense the most natural unit of segregation of workers. In addition, employers do not hire five workers with BAs and three workers with high school degrees—rather, they hire three secretaries, four production workers, and one manager. However, occupation codes have rather serious measurement issues. Levenson and Zoghi (2006) showed that there is considerable variation in skills even within occupation codes, and that the extent of variation is not uniform across occupation. White-collar occupations are much more varied than pink-collar and blue-collar ones.

Figure 12.6 shows that the wages of managers and professionals is significantly higher than that of other occupations, and administrative workers earn the least of all occupations. The relative differences in wages has changed only slightly over time, with technical workers earning slightly more relative to other groups in 2004 than they did in 1984, and handlers earning less in relative terms in 2004 than in 1984. The share of work hours performed by managers and professionals has also increased over the time period. The share of work done by the lowest skill group—handlers and other laborers, has fallen. This indicates a shift toward high-wage workers, which may indicate increasing efficiency per man-hour.

12.4.6   Union

Union workers earn approximately 20 percent higher wages than comparable nonunion workers, according to studies by Hirsch and Macpherson (2002) and Pierce (1999). This is confirmed in figure 12.7, which shows that union members earn 28 percent more than nonunion members in 1984. By

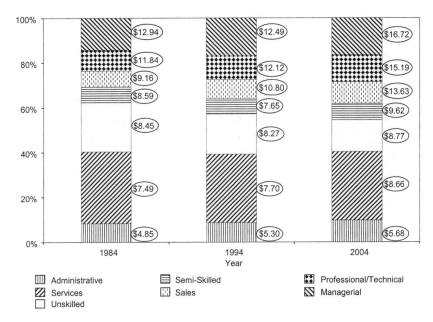

Fig. 12.6   Distribution of hours worked, by occupation

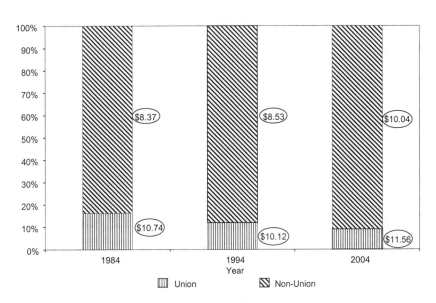

Fig. 12.7   Distribution of hours worked, by unionization

2004, however, nonunion members have narrowed the wage gap quite a bit, to around 15 percent.

While one may infer from the wage differential that unions prevent markets from operating freely, and use the bargaining power to raise wages in excess of marginal productivity, early work by Freeman and Medoff (1982, 1984) found that unions in fact also increase productivity by over 20 percent. They attributed this to the increased union voice making workers more satisfied with their jobs and less likely to be absent or quit. Meta-analysis of other studies (Doucouliagos and Laroche 2003) suggests that taking all studies into account there is a near zero relationship between unions and productivity, although there are positive and significant productivity differentials of 10 percent on average in manufacturing.

The share of work hours performed by union members has decreased over the past twenty years, as figure 12.7 shows. In 1984, union members accounted for 16 percent of work hours; by 2004 the number had dropped to around 10 percent. If higher wages of union workers indicate their higher marginal productivity, such a shift away from unionized work hours would indicate a labor composition shift that decreased productivity.

12.4.7   Establishment Size

There is much evidence that wages are higher at larger plants as well as larger firms, with the differentials being as large as that between men and women (Mellow 1982; Brown and Medoff 1989; Doms, Dunne, and Troske 1997; Oi and Idson 1999). The pattern is confirmed in figure 12.8, where workers in the smallest establishments earn 77 percent of the amount that

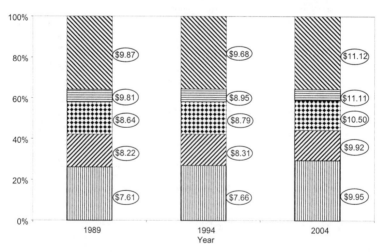

Fig. 12.8   Distribution of hours at work, by establishment size

workers in the largest establishments earn in 1984. The differential is some-what lessened by 2004, however, to 89 percent.

Evidence shows that large employers demand more productive workers, as measured by observable worker characteristics (see, for example, Personick and Barsky 1982). Thus it is possible that workers with high unobserved ability select into large establishments as well, which would indicate that the establishment-size wage differential represents productivity differentials. Adjustments for selection bias (Brown and Medoff 1989; Abowd and Kramarz 2000; Evans and Leighton 1989; Idson and Feaster 1990) are unable to eliminate the wage differentials, suggesting that the wage differential does not represent differences in unobserved worker characteristics.

Some alternative theories for the establishment-size wage differential focus on compensating differentials for the increased risk of unemployment when employed at small establishments, differences in monitoring costs between small and large establishments, and whether efficiency wages might be paid in large establishments to reduce shirking. Additionally, however, the job performed in a large firm may be different from the same job performed in a small firm, since larger firms may use capital more intensively, may use newer technologies, may have a more constant stream of customers, may organize its workers differently (as in teams), or may be more likely to train workers. It seems likely from the bulk of the evidence that workers in large firms earn higher wages because they are more productive, although whether that is a characteristic of the worker or the job that worker is in is less clear.

Figure 12.8 indicates that the distribution of hours across different-sized establishments has changed slightly over time. There has been a small increase in the work hours performed in the smallest establishments—those with twenty-five or fewer employees—from 26 percent to 29 percent between 1984 and 2004. The hours have shifted to these small establishments mainly from the middle-sized establishments—those with between 25 and 999 employees. If the marginal productivity of workers is lower in small establishments, as wage differentials signify, omitting this category from labor composition leads to understating productivity growth.

12.4.8   Regional/Urban

There are well-known and well-documented wage differentials between geographic areas of the United States, most notably the North-South differential and the intermetropolitan wage differential. According to figure 12.9, workers in the South earn 91 percent of the wages of those in the Northeast, with the gap increasing to 86 percent by 2004. Figure 12.10 shows that workers in a Standard Metropolitan Statistical Area (SMSA) but outside of the central city earn the highest wages. Those outside the SMSA earn 83 percent as much, while those in the central city earn 91 percent as much in 1984. These gaps increase to 76 percent outside the SMSA and 88 percent in the central city by 2004. Angel and Mitchell (1991) also find

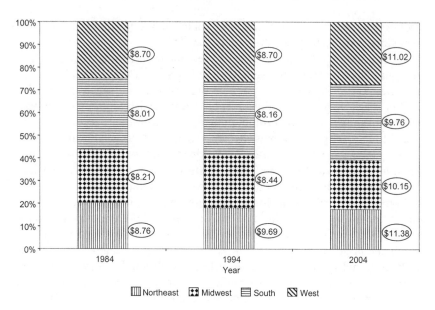

Fig. 12.9   Distribution of hours worked, by region

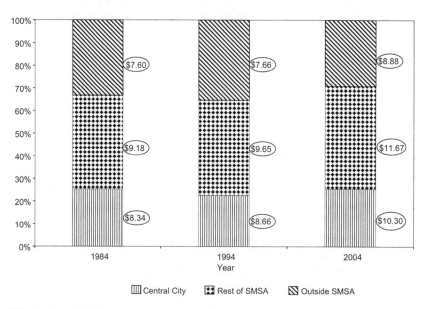

Fig. 12.10   Distribution of hours, by urbanicity

increasing variation in wages across cities within geographic regions. One possible explanation is that nonpecuniary amenities may vary across regions and across cities, so that the wage does not reflect the full compensation to workers.

Figures 12.9 and 12.10 show that the distribution of hours has shifted away from the Midwest and the Northeast somewhat, with the West increasing its hours worked. Employment has increased in the SMSA outside the central city, and has decreased outside the SMSA. A comparison of these shifts with the patterns of wage differentials does not clearly indicate which way productivity might be affected by including geographic variables in the labor categorization. The shift away from the rural areas might be interpreted as a shift away from low productivity workers, while the shift away from the Northeast might be considered a shift away from higher productivity workers according to the wage differentials.

Many of the aforementioned wage differentials are interesting potential sources of productivity differentials, and there are many others as well. In this chapter, I will restrict attention to those that are most closely linked to likely productivity differentials, and that have the most dramatic changes over time. Further, the variable must be measured consistently over time. Thus, I begin with education and age or experience as the most important baseline categories, and then consider the addition of gender, occupation, or industry independently. I leave further explorations of the effects of other categorizations to future research.

12.5   Calculating Labor Composition Index— Mincer Wages or Actual Wages

The first step in calculating the labor composition index is to collect hours worked and weights by categories of workers for each year, using data from the March Current Population Survey (CPS). The BLS (1993) currently uses a Mincer wage equation to estimate wages. One reason for this is that when hours are divided into the many distinct categories of workers, the cell sizes are often quite small. Under the current BLS categorization, more than one-fourth of the cells contain fewer than five worker observations and more than one-third of the cells contain fewer than ten. Another reason for using estimated wages is to restrict differentials to that part attributable to productivity-related human capital variables.

The wage model includes controls for imputed experience and its square; six indicators for years of schooling completed (zero to four, five to eight, twelve, thirteen to fifteen, sixteen, seventeen or more, with nine to eleven omitted to avoid multicollinearity); an indicator for part-time status, for veteran status, a set of seven indicators for region (Northeast, Mid-Atlantic, East North Central, South Atlantic, East South Central, West South Central, and Mountain, with Pacific omitted); and indicators for whether in the central city or in the rest of the SMSA. The models are estimated separately for men and women, to allow the coefficients to vary by gender.

Once hours and wages are collected and/or estimated, the growth in the composition-adjusted labor input is:

$$\Delta L = \sum_{j=1}^{J} \left\{ \frac{1}{2} \left[\frac{\hat{w}_{jt} * h_{jt}}{\sum_{j=1}^{J} \hat{w}_{jt} * h_{jt}} + \frac{\hat{w}_{jt+1} h_{jt+1}}{\sum_{j=1}^{J} \hat{w}_{jt+1} h_{jt+1}} \right] * \ln\left(\frac{h_{jt+1}}{h_{jt}} \right) \right\}.$$

The first term inside the summation sign is the average cost share for a particular category of worker, given the imputed wage rate.[3] Thus, rather than a simple sum of hours growth rates, this is a weighted sum, where the weights are the average labor cost shares. Labor composition growth makes up the difference between this composition-adjusted labor input growth and the unadjusted input growth, which is measured as:

$$\Delta H = \ln \frac{\sum_{j=1}^{J} h_{jt+1}}{\sum_{j=1}^{J} h_{jt}}.$$

Table 12.1 compares specifications of the labor composition index that are closest to the current BLS methodology. The first column is the current BLS calculation, where categories are jointly defined by years of experience, seven education indicators, and gender. The second column shows the methodology proposed in Zoghi (2006), which replaces an experience imputation derived from a onetime Social Security Administration-Current Population Survey (SSA-CPS) match with an experience imputation derived from a repeated SIPP experience regression. Alternative versions are shown in column (3), which uses age groups in place of any imputed experience, and columns (4) and (5), which repeat columns (2) and (3), substituting actual median wage rates for each type of worker for imputed wages in the cost shares.[4]

The five specifications have a similar pattern over time. Labor composition growth is nearly always positive in each year over the time period, reflecting the shifts toward workers who are older, more experienced, and who have more education. Since these are the groups that experience high wages, it is natural that a labor composition index that only categorizes workers by these factors will increase. There is some indication that the rate of growth falls slightly over time, although it is difficult to tell whether this is driven by one or two outliers.

There are three important comparisons to consider in table 12.1. The first is the difference between the SSA-CPS experience measure and the recently proposed (Zoghi 2006) SIPP experience measure. The former, in column (1),

---

3. The equation $\hat{w}_{jt} = \hat{\alpha}_t + \hat{\beta}_1 \, Experience_{jt} + \hat{\beta}_2 \, Yrs.school_{jt}$ is estimated separately for each gender. The effects of all other wage equation variables are collapsed into the intercept term, α_t.

4. These numbers look fairly similar when using mean wage rates, as in other studies; however, the volatility of the wage rates is greatly reduced.

Table 12.1   **Labor composition index under different specifications: Imputed vs. actual (median) wages and imputed experience vs. age groups**

	(1)	(2)	(3)	(4)	(5)
1984–2004	9.5%	11.8%	9.5%	11.3%	10.4%
1984	.926	.907	.928	.911	.919
1985	.929	.912	.931	.912	.923
1986	.929	.925	.930	.922	.923
1987	.937	.924	.937	.922	.929
1988	.942	.924	.943	.923	.939
1989	.947	.920	.948	.918	.945
1990	.958	.932	.958	.933	.958
1991	.969	.945	.971	.948	.970
1992	.973	.951	.974	.952	.974
1993	.979	.962	.978	.964	.979
1994	.984	.973	.983	.974	.983
1995	.986	.982	.985	.983	.986
1996	.989	.986	.989	.986	.989
1997	.993	.991	.992	.992	.993
1998	.999	.998	.999	.998	.999
1999	1.000	1.000	1.000	1.000	1.000
2000	1.008	1.011	1.009	1.012	1.010
2001	1.016	1.019	1.017	1.019	1.017
2002	1.019	1.022	1.020	1.022	1.021
2003	1.020	1.026	1.021	1.022	1.022
2004	1.022	1.025	1.023	1.024	1.023
Wage	imputed	imputed	imputed	actual	actual
Experience	SSA impute	SIPP impute	no	SIPP impute	no
Age	no	no	yes	no	yes
Education	yes	yes	yes	yes	yes
Gender	yes	yes	yes	yes	yes

shows slower labor composition growth than the latter, in column (2). Since experience grows faster under the SIPP measure, this is an expected result. It seems likely that the two measures form an upper and lower bound for the actual experience of workers in today's labor market.[5] Figure 12.11 shows the effect on multifactor productivity (MFP) growth between 1987 and 2005 when using the current methodology and the SIPP measure.[6] The productivity growth using the SIPP labor composition measure is somewhat higher in the first half of the period, and slightly lower toward the end than under the current methodology, but overall matches the current methodology.

The second comparison is between the experience measures of columns

5. A calculation of worker's experience using the Canadian Workplace and Employee Survey yields age-experience profiles somewhat lower than those from the SIPP, and higher than those of the SSA-CPS, suggesting that the former is an overestimate of true experience and the latter is an underestimate.

6. These figures are calculated from the published BLS MFP index and labor composition index numbers.

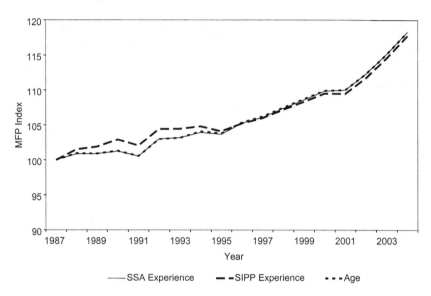

Fig. 12.11   MFP index with experience imputations/age in labor composition

(1) and (2), and a labor composition index calculated without using experience at all, but rather replacing it with age groups, as in column (3). This eliminates the measurement error that is inherent in both experience measures, and to a certain extent, any experience measure. Calculating the index in this way yields a growth rate that is quite similar to the SSA-CPS experience measure. It is impossible to be certain from this result whether important information about worker effectiveness has been lost in the replacement of experience with age, or whether the measurement error in the SIPP experience measure biased upwards the composition effects. It seems likely, however, that both are affecting the growth rate, and that a growth rate calculated with perfectly measured experience would lie somewhere between these two estimates. The MFP growth under the current methodology is nearly identical to that obtained using age groups instead of any experience measure, as indicated in figure 12.11.

The third comparison is between the use of imputed wages from Mincer wage equations and the use of actual within-group median wages. Table 12.1 shows two such comparisons, the first between columns (2) and (4) and the second between columns (3) and (5). In the first instance, which uses the experience imputation, the growth rate is slightly slower when weights are derived from actual median wages than when they are derived from imputed wages. The case for the two models that use age groups has the opposite effect. The growth rate is nearly 1 percent higher when using actual wages when workers are disaggregated by age group rather than years of imputed experience. Once again, actual wages measure something somewhat different from imputed wages. The former include all sources of wage differentials, and the latter only include those due to experience and education; both are subject to some form of measurement error. In other words, this does not imply that either approach is correct or incorrect, but merely signifies that the simpler method of calculating weights from median wage rates can be used without a dramatic change in the labor composition index. Figure 12.12 shows that there is not a tremendous effect on MFP of using the labor composition index of column (3) versus that of column (5). The MFP index is slightly lower, using actual median wages rather than imputed ones.

To compare other possible worker characteristics that might be included in the categorization of worker hours, I reestimate the labor composition index under a variety of other sets of variables. Table 12.2 shows the results of these calculations. Each estimation includes the five-year age groups and education groups from the last column of table 12.1. The first column shows the labor composition index if only age and education are taken into account as sources of worker heterogeneity. The second column repeats the measure of table 12.1, column (5) with labor disaggregated by gender, age, and education. In the third column, broad (one-digit Census) occupation categories are added in place of gender; in the fourth, broad (one-digit Census) industry categories are included instead. The fifth and sixth columns use more disaggregated (two-digit Census) occupation and industry categories, respectively. In each case, the calculations use actual median wage rates rather than the imputed ones.

Age and education are clearly the demographic features of workers that have increased the growing effectiveness of hours the most over the 1980s

Fig. 12.12   MFP index with actual/imputed wages in labor composition index

Table 12.2   **Labor composition index under different categorizations: Age, education and gender, occupation or industry (weights are median wage rates)**

	(1)	(2)	(3)	(4)	(5)	(6)
1984–2004	11.4%	10.4%	11.2%	8.4%	10.4%	6.6%
1984	.910	.919	.909	.934	.918	.954
1985	.916	.923	.917	.936	.922	.956
1986	.918	.923	.921	.938	.924	.951
1987	.929	.929	.932	.947	.933	.961
1988	.933	.939	.936	.952	.937	.964
1989	.940	.945	.940	.957	.940	.967
1990	.954	.958	.953	.962	.943	.972
1991	.967	.970	.966	.973	.955	.977
1992	.972	.974	.968	.974	.961	.978
1993	.976	.979	.975	.980	.967	.980
1994	.980	.983	.982	.986	.972	.981
1995	.985	.986	.983	.991	.981	.986
1996	.989	.989	.989	.996	.991	.994
1997	.992	.993	.992	.995	.994	.995
1998	.999	.999	.997	1.001	1.000	1.004
1999	1.000	1.000	1.000	1.000	1.000	1.000
2000	1.011	1.010	1.012	1.010	1.008	1.006
2001	1.018	1.017	1.011	1.012	1.007	1.014
2002	1.023	1.021	1.016	1.016	1.012	1.020
2003	1.023	1.022	1.018	1.017	1.017	1.015
2004	1.024	1.023	1.021	1.018	1.022	1.020
Age	yes	yes	yes	yes	yes	yes
Education	yes	yes	yes	yes	yes	yes
Gender	no	yes	no	no	no	no
1 Dig. occ.	no	no	yes	no	no	no
1 Dig. ind.	no	no	no	yes	no	no
2 Dig. occ.	no	no	no	no	yes	no
2 Dig. ind.	no	no	no	no	no	yes

and 1990s. Distributional changes by either occupation or industry have worked against the increasing effectiveness of labor, although much more so for industry than for occupation. Figure 12.13 shows that a measure of labor composition that treats occupational differences as productivity differences yields a higher estimate of MFP growth over 1989 to 1997 and 2001 forward. Recall that figure 12.5 showed that industry compositional changes have favored lower-wage workers over the past twenty years. This indicates that, assuming industry wage differentials reflect productivity differentials, omitting industry from the labor composition calculation might have resulted in an understatement of productivity growth in the 1980s and 1990s. Figure 12.14 confirms this prediction, showing that MFP growth is significantly higher under a labor composition index that segregates workers by industry.

While it is especially interesting that a categorization of workers by indus-

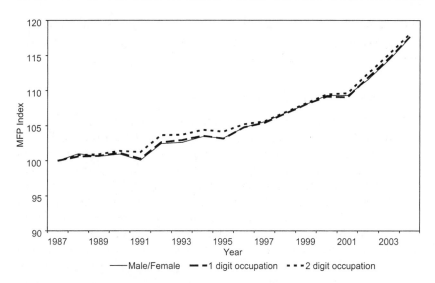

Fig. 12.13   MFP index under different labor composition worker groups

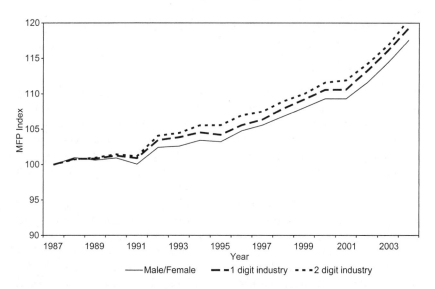

Fig. 12.14   MFP index under different labor composition groups

try or occupation would yield a lower labor composition index and more unexplained residual productivity, it is not at all clear that a worker who maintains his same characteristics and human capital becomes a different input when he moves to a new job in a different industry. Although his movement may, in fact, shift the aggregate production function, we may or may not want to include this effect with more traditional changes in the quantity and effectiveness of labor input. A natural compromise is that followed by Jorgenson, Gollop, and Fraumeni (1987), of considering separately the industry effects as a "reallocation of labor input."

12.6 Conclusion and Recommendations

This chapter explores various possible ways to estimate a labor composition index. One methodological choice is whether to measure the weights for each worker group using actual median wages within the group or using imputed wages, where the imputation is derived from Mincer wage equations. Labor composition growth is not dramatically different using the actual median wage rates. While wage equations introduce an additional source of potential error, median wage rates may differ between groups for more reasons than just differences in the defined characteristics. As a result, there is an inherent trade-off between the efficiency of the wage measures and the clarity of the conceptual basis for the wage differentials. It is not possible to determine ex post which measure is "right;" however, it seems preferable to use the simpler median wage rates, given the narrow difference between the two measures.

The second methodological choice is which set of variables to use to identify distinct worker groups, each of which has a different expected marginal productivity. Again, while we can examine ex post the effects of including different sets of variables, the set of variables must be determined ex ante, using our economic reasoning to assess whether marginal productivity differences are likely to exist between the groups under the set of assumptions of the labor composition model. A brief survey of the economic literature on this subject unfortunately suggests that there remains uncertainty as to which wage differentials represent productivity differentials. As a result, it becomes an empirical question whether the variable adds to or distorts our understanding of labor composition change. While the assumption that labor markets are competitive should be our guiding principle, it might prove better to leave an uncertain and poorly measured portion of the labor composition change in the multifactor productivity residual.

Using experience and education yields a mainly positive labor composition index, since experience and education increase the wages—and, hopefully productivity—of the worker. The two experience measures considered here result in fairly different estimates of labor composition, which is higher using the SIPP measure than the SSA-CPS measure. This is not surprising, since the SSA measure is likely to understate true experience and the SIPP measure may overstate it. Replacing the experience variable with five-year age groups results in lower labor composition growth. It is likely that an index derived from a perfectly measured experience variable would lie somewhere between these two outcomes. As neither experience imputation is well measured, and no other experience measure exists that can be used here, it seems reasonable to use the simpler and more transparent age group variable.

The addition of gender to age and education lowers the index slightly, as does the addition of either broad or detailed occupation groups. Disaggregating workers by industry, broad or detailed, significantly lowers the labor composition index, reflecting changes in the industry distribution of workers away from high-wage manufacturing jobs. While this is an important shift to capture, it seems inappropriate to lump this together with the effects of changes in age, gender, or education, as it is arguable whether such distributional shifts reflect changes in the magnitude or effectiveness of the labor input.

This chapter is meant to be exploratory in nature. The purpose of the empirical section is to determine how important the choice of labor composition methodology is to the calculation of multifactor productivity. If using real wages or imputed measures, or altering the set of variables that differentiate workers does not affect our productivity estimate greatly, it is desirable to select a methodology based on its clarity, simplicity, and adherence to the theoretical precepts. If, on the other hand, productivity estimates are greatly different depending on which methodology is chosen, then it is important to be cautious and understand what price we pay with our choice of methodology, and what implicit assumptions we are making.

Appendix

Table 12A.1　　**Determinants of wages**

	Men			Women		
	1984	1994	2004	1984	1994	2004
Experience	.059[1]	.054[1]	.045[1]	.040[1]	.040[1]	.039[1]
Experience^2	−.001[1]	−.001[1]	−.001[1]	−.001[1]	−.001[1]	−.001[1]
0–4 yrs. school	−.261[1]	−.249[1]	−.177[1]	−.127[1]	−.073	−.168[1]
5–8 yrs. school	−.099[1]	−.101[1]	−.124[1]	−.076[1]	−.128[1]	−.117[1]
12 yrs. school	.192[1]	.149[1]	.164[1]	.176[1]	.143[1]	.178[1]
13–15 yrs. sch.	.243[1]	.242[1]	.330[1]	.324[1]	.289[1]	.346[1]
16 yrs. school	.557[1]	.573[1]	.671[1]	.508[1]	.587[1]	.656[1]
17+ yrs. school	.599[1]	.737[1]	.954[1]	.678[1]	.816[1]	.909[1]
Part-time	−.180[1]	−.137[1]	−.210[1]	−.151[1]	−.132[1]	−.125[1]
Veteran	.007	.001	−.003	n.a.	.014	.050
Northeast	.013	.119[1]	.053[1]	.016	.090[1]	.068[1]
Mid-Atlantic	−.022[5]	.057[1]	.001	−.016	.070[1]	−.022
E. No. Central	−.019[10]	.034[1]	−.005	−.045[1]	−.017	−.035[1]
So. Atlantic	−.084[1]	−.032[5]	−.052[1]	−.062[1]	−.017	−.054[1]
E. So. Central	−.083[1]	−.016	−.039[5]	−.138[1]	−.079[1]	−.115[1]
W. So. Central	−.016	−.038[5]	−.051[1]	−.063[1]	−.077[1]	−.098[1]
Mountain	.010	−.003	−.015	−.027	−.017	−.038[1]
Central city	.025[1]	.009	.024[5]	.102[1]	.086[1]	.091[1]
Rest of SMSA	.130[1]	.123[1]	.116[1]	.112[1]	.158[1]	.150[1]
Number of Observations	30,794	28,558	40,115	27,573	26,539	37,582
R^2	.3705	.3283	.3214	.2099	.2353	.2567

Notes: Coefficients from log wage regression using March CPS data. Experience is imputed from coefficients on a SIPP experience regression as described in Zoghi (2006). n.a. = not applicable.

References

Aaronson, D., and D. Sullivan. 2001. Growth in worker quality. *Economic Perspectives* 2001:53–74. Federal Reserve Bank of Chicago.

Abowd, J. M., and F. Kramarz. 2000. Inter-industry and firm-size wage differentials: New evidence from linked employer-employee data. Cornell University. Working Paper.

Abramovitz, M. 1956. Resource and output trends in the united states since 1870. *The American Economic Review, Papers and Proceedings* 46 (2): 5–23.

Angel, D. P., and J. Mitchell. 1991. Intermetropolitan wage disparities and industrial change. *Economic Geography* 67 (2): 124–35.

Belman, D., and J. S. Heywood. 1991. Sheepskin effects in the return to education: An examination of women and minorities. *The Review of Economics and Statistics* 73 (4): 720–24.

Blau, F. D., and L. M. Kahn. 2006. The U.S. gender pay gap in the 1990s: Slowing convergence. *Industrial and Labor Relations Review* 60 (1): 45–66.

Brown, C. 1980. Equalizing differences in the labor market. *The Quarterly Journal of Economics* 94:113–34.

Brown, C., and J. Medoff. 1989. The employer size-wage effect. *Journal of Political Economy* 97 (5): 1027–59.

Bureau of Labor Statistics (BLS). 1993. Labor composition and U.S. productivity growth, 1948–1990. *Bureau of Labor Statistics Bulletin* no. 2426, Washington, DC.

Denison, E. F. 1962. *The sources of economic growth in the United States and the alternatives before us.* New York: Committee for Economic Development, Supplementary Paper no. 13.

———. 1974. *Accounting for United States economic growth, 1929–1969.* Washington, DC: The Brookings Institute.

Dickens, W. T. 1986. Wages, employment and the threat of collective action by workers. NBER Working Paper no. 1856. Cambridge, MA: National Bureau of Economic Research, March.

Dickens, W. T., and L. Katz. 1986. Inter-industry wage differences and industry characteristics. In *Unemployment and the structure of labor markets,* ed. K. Lang and J. Leonard, 48–89. London: Basil Blackwell.

Diewert, W. E. 1976. Exact and superlative index numbers. *Journal of Econometrics* 4:114–45.

Doms, M., T. Dunne, and K. R. Troske. 1997. Workers, wages and technology. *The Quarterly Journal of Economics* 112 (1): 253–90.

Doucouliagos, C., and P. Laroche. 2003. What do unions do to productivity? A meta-analysis. *Industrial Relations* 42 (4): 650–91.

Evans, D., and L. Leighton. 1989. Why do smaller firms pay less? *Journal of Human Resources* 24:299–318.

Freeman, R. B., and J. L. Medoff. 1982. The impact of collective bargaining: Illusion or reality? NBER Working Paper no. 735. Cambridge, MA: National Bureau of Economic Research, April.

———. 1984. *What do unions do?* New York: Basic Books.

Gollop, F. M., and D. W. Jorgenson. 1980. U.S. productivity growth by industry, 1947–1973. In *New developments in productivity measurement,* ed. J. W. Kendrick and B. Vaccara, 17–136. Chicago: University of Chicago Press.

Griliches, Z. 1970. Notes on the role of education in production functions and growth accounting. In *Education, income and human capital,* ed. W. L. Hansen, 71–128. New York: National Bureau of Economic Research.

Hellerstein, J. K., D. Neumark, and K. R. Troske. 1999. Wages, productivity, and worker characteristics: Evidence from plant-level production functions and wage equations. *Journal of Labor Economics* 17 (3): 409–46.

Hirsch, B. T., and D. A. Macpherson. 2002. *Union membership and earnings data book: Compilations from the Current Population Survey* (2002 ed.). Washington, DC: Bureau of National Affairs.

Hungerford, T., and G. Solon. 1987. Sheepskin effects in the returns to education. *The Review of Economics and Statistics* 69 (1): 175–77.

Idson, T. L., and D. Feaster. 1990. A selectivity model with employer size differentials. *Journal of Labor Economics* 8 (1): 99–122.

Jorgenson, D. W., F. W. Gollop, and B. Fraumeni. 1987. *Productivity and U.S. economic growth, 1979–1985.* Cambridge, MA: Harvard University Press.

Jorgenson, D. W., and Z. Griliches. 1967. The explanation of productivity change. *Review of Economic Studies* 34:249–83.

Jorgenson, D. W., M. S. Ho, and K. J. Stiroh. 2005. *Productivity volume 3: Information technology and the American growth resurgence.* Cambridge, MA: MIT Press.

Keane, M. P. 1993. Individual heterogeneity and interindustry wage differentials. *The Journal of Human Resources* 28 (1): 134–61.

Krueger, A. B., and L. H. Summers. 1988. Efficiency wages and the interindustry wage structure. *Econometrica* 56 (2): 259–93.

Lazear, E. P. 1979. Why is there mandatory retirement? *Journal of Political Economy* 87 (6): 1261–84.

Levenson, A., and C. Zoghi. 2006. The strength of occupation indicators as a proxy for skill. Bureau of Labor Statistics Working Paper no. 404.

Loewenstein, G., and N. Sicherman. 1991. Do workers prefer increasing wage profiles? *Journal of Labor Economics* 9 (1): 67–84.

Mellow, W. 1982. Employer size and wages. *The Review of Economics and Statistics* 64 (3): 495–501.

Mincer, J. 1974. *Schooling, experience and earnings.* Human Behavior and Social Institutions no. 2. New York and London: National Bureau of Economic Research.

Murphy, K. M., and R. H. Topel. 1987. Unemployment, risk, and earnings: Testing for equalizing wage differences in the labor market. In *Unemployment and the structure of labor markets,* ed. K. Lang and J. S. Leonard, 103–40. New York: Basil Blackwell.

———. 1990. Efficiency wages reconsidered: Theory and evidence. In *Advances in the theory and measurement of unemployment,* ed. Y. Weiss and G. Fishelson, 204–40. London: Macmillan.

Oi, W. Y., and T. L. Idson. 1999. Firm size and wages. In *Handbook of labor economics,* vol. 3. ed. O. Ashenfelter and D. Card, 2165–214. Amsterdam: North-Holland.

Personick, M. E., and C. B. Barsky. 1982. White-collar pay levels linked to corporate work force size. *Monthly Labor Review* 105:24–6.

Pierce, B. 1999. Using the national compensation survey to predict wage rates. *Compensation and Working Conditions* Winter: 8–16.

Rosen, S. 1986. The theory of equalizing differences. In *Handbook of labor economics, 1st ed.* ed. O. Ashenfelter and R. Layard, 641–92. Amsterdam: North-Holland.

Schmookler, J. 1952. The changing efficiency of the American economy, 1869–1938. *The Review of Economics and Statistics* 34 (3): 214–31.

Smith, R. S. 1979. Compensating wage differentials and public policy: A review. *Industrial and Labor Relations Review* 32 (3): 339–52.

Solow, R. M. 1957. Technical change and the aggregate production function. *The Review of Economics and Statistics* 39:312–20.

Spence, M. 1973. Job market signaling. *The Quarterly Journal of Economics* 87 (3): 355–74.
Zoghi, C. E. 2006. Changes to the BLS labor composition index. Unpublished Manuscript. Available at: http://www.nber.org/~confer/2006/si2006/prcr/zoghi.pdf.

Comment   Stephanie Aaronson

In "Measuring Labor Composition: A Comparison of Alternate Methodologies," Cindy Zoghi examines the sensitivity of measured labor composition growth to changes in the method of computation. This is an interesting exercise for several reasons. Most obviously, the measure of labor composition provides information on how the productive capacity of our workforce is changing over time and also provides a framework for forecasting the growth in labor composition. In addition, in a growth accounting framework such as that used by the Bureau of Labor Statistics (BLS), MFP growth is the residual, so a change in the measurement of labor composition affects the path of MFP growth.

At the outset Zoghi describes her criteria for choosing a methodology:

> If [the methodology] does not affect our productivity estimates greatly, it is desirable to select a methodology based on its clarity, simplicity, and adherence to the theoretical precepts. If, on the other hand, productivity estimates are greatly different depending on which methodology is chosen, then it is important to be cautious and understand the price we pay with our choice of methodology and the implicit assumptions we are making.

I would probably reword this a bit. I would say that the methodology should match up with theoretical precepts to the extent possible. Having taken that into account, I then agree that clarity and simplicity are desirable features of a model. In addition, since Zoghi's work appears to be aimed at providing guidance to the BLS on how they might change their calculation of labor composition, there are two other criteria that I believe should be taken into account. The first issue is timeliness. As it is, the BLS typically publishes the official multifactor productivity data for a given year with a lag of about one and one-fourth years (so for instance, the MFP data for 2006 were released at the end of March 2008). The wait can be longer if there has been a comprehensive revision to the National Income and Product Accounts (NIPAs)—an event that will become more frequent when the Bureau of Economic Analysis (BEA) institutes flexible annual revisions. In recognition of the long wait, a few years ago the BLS began to produce a preliminary

Stephanie Aaronson is a senior economist at the Board of Governors of the Federal Reserve Board.

series using a simplified procedure. These data are typically released within five months of the end of the year. Certainly, we would not want the methodology adopted by the BLS to slow down the release of the data much. The second issue is how a given methodology affects the comparability of the data over time. Users of macroeconomic data typically want as long a time series as possible. Obviously, the availability and quality of the data on both the output side and the labor market side have changed over time, and the BLS has adapted to this reality. Any changes to the methods should continue to take this into consideration. With these criteria for evaluating any proposed changes in mind, we can turn our attention to what Zoghi actually does.

I think the most useful contribution of the chapter is its examination of alternative ways to measure work experience and to describe the impact that these alternatives have on the growth in measured labor composition. Work experience makes an appearance in two different places in the BLS' calculation of labor composition growth. First, it is one of the characteristics used to identify the labor inputs into the production function that underlies their model of labor composition. More specifically, along with education and sex it defines the groups of workers j, in the Tornqvist index of labor input (Zoghi's equation [4]):

$$\Delta \ln L = \sum_j \frac{1}{2}[s_{h_j}(t) + s_{h_j}(t-1)]\Delta \ln h_j.$$

In addition, work experience is also used in the calculation of the weights used to aggregate up labor input (the s_{h_j} in the previous equation). Specifically, the weights are computed as

$$s_{h_j} = \frac{1}{2}\left(\frac{\hat{w}_{jt} * h_{jt}}{\sum_{j=1}^{J}\hat{w}_{jt} * h_{jt}} + \frac{\hat{w}_{jt+1}h_{jt+1}}{\sum_{j=1}^{J}\hat{w}_{jt+1}h_{jt+1}}\right),$$

where $\hat{w}_{jt}$ is the predicted value from a Mincerian wage equation that includes education and experience as well as a number of control variables.[1]

The data for this computation come from the Current Population Survey (CPS). However, as is well-known, the CPS does not include a variable for actual work experience. To get around this problem the BLS creates a predicted work experience variable using a 1973 file that matched individuals in the CPS with their Social Security Administration (SSA) data and data from the Internal Revenue Service. Specifically, they calculate work experience (measured as actual quarters of work) using the SSA data and then run a regression of work experience on explanatory variables in the CPS. The BLS uses the resulting coefficients to do out-of-sample predictions of actual work experience for workers in the CPS in other years. In their report

---

1. In calculating the predicted wage, the control variables are held constant at their mean values, so they have no impact on the growth in labor composition.

on labor composition in which they describe this procedure (BLS 1993), the BLS shows that their predicted actual experience measure outperforms potential experience in wage regressions.

Although the use of a measure of actual work experience variable no doubt improves the BLS' labor composition index, the benefit has certainly declined over time as the relationship between actual experience and the explanatory variables has evolved. It is true that the model still captures the changes in work experience due to change in the explanatory variables. For instance, the fact that women have fewer children now than they did in 1973 and that children are negatively correlated with work experience will cause predicted work experience to be higher in recent years. However, this method cannot capture the fact that conditional on having had a child, women are more likely to work.[2]

Recognizing that the data are out of date, Zoghi proposes two alternatives. First, she calculates an alternative measure of work experience using the Survey of Income and Program Participation (SIPP).[3] This work is described more fully in an earlier paper she wrote on the topic (Zoghi 2006). In the original paper Zoghi provides a discussion of the pros and cons of this measure, which she does not repeat in this chapter, but it is useful for evaluation purposes.[4] She notes that the questions are retrospective and that short breaks from work may not be captured. I would add that short spells of employment may also be forgotten. Another problem Zoghi raises is that the questions only register experience if a person works at least six months straight. As a result the measure may understate the experience for part-year workers, such as students and other seasonal workers. Offsetting this somewhat is the fact that a spell of work lasting at least six months is counted as a full year of work. In this chapter Zoghi asserts that the SIPP/CPS measure *overstates* experience. Her argument seems to be based on the fact that a Canadian study with administrative data shows lower experience than that reported in the SIPP. However, I am not convinced by this argument. Canada has a lower labor force participation rate than the United States and conditional on employment Canadians work fewer hours per year, so it would make sense that work experience in Canada would be less than here (Heisz and LaRochelle-Côté 2003).

Even if the quality of the SIPP data were high, it could take considerable effort for the BLS to produce a consistent series—an issue that Zoghi does not raise. First, the SIPP only starts in 1984, so the BLS would need

2. Other limitations of the matched data can be found in BLS (1993) and Zoghi (2006).

3. In her chapter, Zoghi uses the SIPP panels from 1984, 1987, 1990, 1993, 1996, 1999, and 2001.

4. The SIPP asks individuals the year in which they first worked at least six months straight at a regular job or business and whether they have worked continuously since then. If they have not worked continuously, they are asked the number of years in which they worked at least six months straight.

to come up with a method for imputing work experience in history, perhaps using some combination of the SIPP and the 1973 SSA data. Second, the future of the SIPP is uncertain. The SIPP recently survived an attempt to kill it—at least the second in its history. Although there is likely to be an alternative source of data on experience available in the future, this would require further work on the part of the BLS. So we certainly have to take into account the potential burden using the SIPP imposes. Finally, the SIPP has historically been released with a fairly long delay. The Census has said that the newly reworked SIPP will be available with a shorter delay—nine months—which may or may not hold up the processing of the MFP data.

Given her own criticism of the SIPP data, and perhaps with some of my own in mind, Zoghi also computes labor composition using age instead of work experience. Age has long been noted to be a poor proxy for experience (cf. Mincer [1974], for starters). Nonetheless, it is not clear a priori that using age is worse than the current BLS method. Using age in conjuction with education, as is the case here, yields something akin to potential experience. In the current method, the explanatory variables in the experience regression for men consist of a polynomial in potential experience, education dummies, and interactions. Since the coefficients do not change over time, and education has not changed much in recent years, I suspect that movements in the experience variable are dominated by changes in the age distribution.

So how do these alternative proxies for work experience affect measured labor composition growth? Zoghi's results are as one would expect. Labor composition growth is the same whether one uses age or the SSA-based work experience variable—9.5 percent between 1984 and 2004. In contrast, using the SIPP implies about 2 1/4 pp (percentage points) higher growth in labor composition. This is consistent with actual experience rising more quickly than would be expected simply by the aging of the baby boomers—in particular, as women's experience rose, even conditional on other explanatory variables.

These results are based on the current BLS methodology, which uses predicted wages in calculating the weights. However, Zoghi also explores the implications of using actual wages. There are several reasons to use predicted wages. First, the results are easy to interpret. According to the theory underlying the model of labor composition, the weights represent the marginal productivity of labor. As modeled by the BLS, movements in predicted wages are due solely to changes in education and experience, arguably the two most important factors affecting the marginal productivity of labor. Second, using a predicted value gets around the problem that many education/experience/sex groups have small cell sizes (according to Zoghi, 1/4 of the cells contain fewer than five observations). Of course, the BLS specification may exclude some factors that affect productivity and the results depend on the proxy for work experience.

The use of actual rather than predicted wages makes sense from a theoretical standpoint. Under the assumptions of the production function framework that underlies the BLS' growth accounting framework, wages are equal to the marginal product of labor—no special transformation is required. However, this still leaves the question of whether it is feasible to use actual wages, given the small cell sizes. Although Zoghi uses the more stable median rather than mean wages, the small cell sizes could still be a problem. When using age, Zoghi groups people into five-year intervals instead of single years, which should ameliorate the problem somewhat, albeit at the cost of losing some information about changes in the age distribution. Unfortunately, she does not address this issue very clearly.

Zoghi compares the growth in labor composition using actual versus imputed wages for two different proxies of experience. Using the SIPP-based experience measure and actual wages suggests about 1/2 pp slower growth in labor composition than when imputed wages are used. This suggests that factors other than education and experience generally held down actual wages relative to predicted wages, when predicted wages are computed using the relatively fast-growing SIPP-based experience measure. Not surprisingly, using age and actual wages increases the growth in labor composition by nearly 1 pp, relative to using predicted wages computed with age, since age understates the increase in experience, and hence the predicted wage is likely to be understated.[5]

The last question raised in the chapter is how to define the groups into which workers are divided. The advantage of the current BLS methodology, which uses education, experience, and sex, is that it is parsimonious and fits easily into a human capital framework. Having a limited number of categories makes it easy to understand past changes in labor composition and fairly easy to project it forward. However, the current groups may leave out important characteristics that contribute to labor productivity. These factors then get lumped into MFP, making it even more of a black box than it otherwise would be.

Zoghi describes in detail a number of possible characteristics that could be used to differentiate labor, including union status, firm size, and geography, before deciding to add occupation and industry to the current set of characteristics. Although her analysis of the different potential groupings is reasonable, it is not completely clear how she decides upon the existing categories plus industry and occupation. Perhaps it is because other analyses of labor composition, most notably Jorgenson, Gollop, and Fraumeni (1987), have used these characteristics.

This raises the question of whether the productivity associated with the

---

5. The revisions to measured labor composition imply offsetting revisions to MFP growth. The labor composition indices calculated using the SIPP measure of experience and the labor composition index calculated using age and actual wages suggest lower MFP growth between 1984 and 2004. These three indices also imply a larger step up in MFP growth after 1995 (on the order of 5 basis points) than does the current measure.

occupation and industry composition of jobs really represents the inherent productivity of the workers or not. There are differing opinions on this matter. In early work on the topic Denison argued that occupation was closely related to education and need not be treated separately (see Denison 1985; BLS 1993). However, Jorgenson, Gollop, and Fraumeni (1987) do include occupation in the labor composition index. With respect to industry, Jorgenson, Gollop, and Fraumeni occupy a middle ground in which shifts across industries are not attributed to labor composition but rather are viewed separately as the effect of resource allocation. Zoghi apparently feels that adding another category is an appropriate treatment for industry shifts, and in this I concur, although whether these shifts should be considered resource allocation or something else is beyond the scope of our discussion. Nonetheless, by identifying changes in productivity due to industry shifts, we unpack a bit more the black box that is MFP growth.

However, even if we agree in principle on where in the growth accounting system shifts in occupation or industry belong, the question of whether it is really feasible to perform this analysis as part of the BLS' regular multifactor productivity release is left open. It can be difficult to make the industry and especially the occupation variables consistent over time, particularly at the level of detail available in the CPS. Another problem is whether there is sufficient data. When incorporating industry and occupation, not only does Zoghi use the five-year age categories, she also drops gender as one of the groups. Using age while omitting gender seems particularly problematic given the differences in work experience for men and women at a given age. Jorgenson, Gollop, and Fraumeni use data from the decennial censuses to deal with small cell size problems, although this may be more work than the BLS wants.

One worker/job characteristic that Zoghi does not explore is class. The BLS' measure treats self-employed and unpaid family workers as if they had the same marginal product as wage and salary workers. In contrast, other estimates of labor composition growth, notably Denison (1985) and Jorgenson, Gollop and Fraumeni (1987) have identified workers by class, and Jorgenson, Gollop, and Fraumeni have a very elaborate method for dealing with the earnings of self-employed workers. Although I think that the BLS choices in this regard are reasonable, it seems strange that Zoghi does not at least raise this as an issue.

Zoghi's premise is that when different methodologies yield similar outcomes, the BLS should adopt the simplest procedures possible. Thus, she favors using the median wage in the weight rather than the predicted wage. Moreover, given what she sees as the problems with existing measures of work experience she also favors using age, despite the fact that the SIPP experience measure yields a significantly different picture of labor composition growth. As I noted, my own guidelines are similar although not exactly the same as Zoghi's. Therefore, while I agree with her that using the median wage appears to be a worthwhile trade-off, I cannot agree with using age as the proxy for experience. It is too far away from the desired concept. Zoghi dismisses the SIPP measure in part because she feels that it is not a good measure of experience, but I do not think that she has presented evidence that sufficiently discredits it. As described earlier, I recognize the problems that exist in developing a measure of experience over time. However, the BLS has overcome such problems in the construction of other variables. Given the centrality of work experience to the human capital model that underlies our thinking about labor composition growth, it seems worth the effort. I would prefer to see the BLS put effort into developing a reasonable measure of experience rather than trying to add the shifts in industry composition, which presents its own host of challenges, both theoretical and practical.

References

Bureau of Labor Statistics (BLS). 1993. Labor composition and U.S. productivity growth, 1948–1990. *Bureau of Labor Statistics Bulletin* 2426, Washington, DC.

Denison, E. 1985. *Trends in American economic growth: 1929–1982.* Washington, DC: Brookings Institution.

Heisz, A. and S. LaRochelle-Côté. 2003. Working hours in Canada and the United States. Analytical Studies Branch Research Paper Series, no. 209. Statistics Canada.

Jorgenson, D., F. Gollop, and B. Fraumeni. 1987. *Productivity and U.S. economic growth.* Cambridge, MA: Harvard University Press.

Mincer, J. 1974. *Schooling, experience, and earnings.* New York: Columbia University Press.

Zoghi, C. 2006. Changes to the BLS Labor Composition Index. Bureau of Labor Statistics. Unpublished Manuscript.

Contributors

Stephanie Aaronson
Board of Governors of the Federal
  Reserve System
20th Street and Constitution Avenue,
  NW
Washington, DC 20551

Katharine G. Abraham
Joint Program in Survey Methodology
University of Maryland
College Park, MD 20742

Jeff E. Biddle
Department of Economics
Michigan State University
East Lansing, MI 48824

Charles Brown
Department of Economics
University of Michigan
Ann Arbor, MI 48109

Gary Burtless
The Brookings Institution
1775 Massachusetts Avenue, NW
Washington, DC 20036

Susan M. Collins
Gerald R. Ford School of Public Policy
University of Michigan
Ann Arbor, MI 48109

Steven J. Davis
Graduate School of Business
The University of Chicago
Chicago, IL 60637

Matthew Dey
Bureau of Labor Statistics
2 Massachusetts Avenue, NE
Washington, DC 20212

R. Jason Faberman
Federal Reserve Bank of Philadelphia
Ten Independence Mall
Philadelphia, PA 19106

Bruce Fallick
Board of Governors of the Federal
  Reserve System
20th Street and Constitution Avenue,
  NW
Washington, DC 20551

Henry S. Farber
Industrial Relations Section
Princeton University
Princeton, NJ 08544

Charles Fleischman
Board of Governors of the Federal
   Reserve System
20th Street and Constitution Avenue,
   NW
Washington, DC 20551

Harley Frazis
Bureau of Labor Statistics
2 Massachusetts Avenue, NE
Washington, DC 20212

Erica L. Groshen
Federal Reserve Bank of New York
33 Liberty Street
New York, NY 10045

Robert E. Hall
Hoover Institution
Stanford University
Stanford, CA 94305

Kevin F. Hallock
School of Industrial and Labor
   Relations
Cornell University
Ithaca, NY 14853

John C. Haltiwanger
Department of Economics
University of Maryland
College Park, MD 20742

Daniel S. Hamermesh
Department of Economics
University of Texas
Austin, TX 78712

Michael J. Harper
Bureau of Labor Statistics
2 Massachusetts Avenue, NE
Washington, DC 20212

Susan Houseman
W. E. Upjohn Institute for
   Employment Research
300 South Westnedge Avenue
Kalamazoo, MI 49007

J. Bradford Jensen
McDonough School of Business
Georgetown University
Washington, DC 20057

Lawrence F. Katz
Department of Economics
Harvard University
Cambridge, MA 02138

Lori G. Kletzer
Department of Economics
University of California, Santa Cruz
Santa Cruz, CA 95064

Thomas Lemieux
Department of Economics
University of British Columbia
Vancouver, BC, Canada V6T 1Z1

Nicole Nestoriak
Bureau of Labor Statistics
2 Massachusetts Avenue, NE
Washington, DC 20212

Craig A. Olson
School of Labor and Employment
   Relations
University of Illinois at Urbana-
   Champaign
Champaign, IL 61821

Brooks Pierce
Bureau of Labor Statistics
2 Massachusetts Avenue, NE
Washington, DC 20212

Jonathan Pingle
Brevan Howard
1776 Eye Street, NW
Washington, DC 20007

Anne Polivka
Bureau of Labor Statistics
2 Massachusetts Avenue, NE
Washington, DC 20212

Chris Riddell
School of Policy Studies
Queen's University
Kingston, ON, Canada K7L 3N6

Ian Rucker

John Ruser
Bureau of Labor Statistics
2 Massachusetts Avenue, NE
Washington, DC 20212

James R. Spletzer
Bureau of Labor Statistics
2 Massachusetts Avenue, NE
Washington, DC 20212

Ann Huff Stevens
Department of Economics
University of California, Davis
Davis, CA 95616

Jay Stewart
Bureau of Labor Statistics
2 Massachusetts Avenue, NE
Washington, DC 20212

Daniel G. Sullivan
Federal Reserve Bank of Chicago
230 S. LaSalle Street
Chicago, IL 60604

Cindy Zoghi
Bureau of Labor Statistics
2 Massachusetts Avenue, NE
Washington, DC 20212

Author Index

Subject Index